Shadow Lovers

Shadow Lovers

The Last Affairs of H. G. Wells

ANDREA LYNN

Westview
PRESS

A Member of the Perseus Books Group

Copyright © 2001 by Westview Press, A Member of the Perseus Books Group

Westview Press books are available at special discounts for bulk purchases in the United States by corporations, institutions, and other organizations. For more information, please contact the Special Markets Department at The Perseus Books Group, 11 Cambridge Center, Cambridge MA 02142, or call (617) 252-5298.

Published in 2001 in the United States of America by Westview Press, 5500 Central Avenue, Boulder, Colorado 80301–2877, and in the United Kingdom by Westview Press, 12 Hid's Copse Road, Cumnor Hill, Oxford OX2 9JJ

Find us on the World Wide Web at www.westviewpress.com

Text design by *Brent Wilcox*

A Cataloging-in-publication data record is available at the Library of Congress.
ISBN 0-8133-3394-6

The paper used in this publication meets the requirements of the American National Standard for Permanence of Paper for Printed Library Materials Z39.48-1984.

10   9   8   7   6   5   4   3   2   1

The dead deserve the truth, the living deserve our respect.
—Voltaire

To the Helyns/Helens in my life:
Helyn Williams Kramer, my life mother, and
the late Helen Farlow, my mentor

Contents

Preface

I have a humanitarian nature & the remains of a Christian upbringing & my affections blow about in a disheveled manner & get entangled about people. . . . Thank you for lending me a clear eye about it. A cool eye. Whenever (I hope never) you are heated & worried my eye is at your feet. And I am, Yours to command. Your HG.

—H. G. Wells to Christabel McLaren,
May 12, 1932

On the brink of a messy breakup with one lover and what he hoped would be a smooth and orderly transition to the next, H. G. Wells did in May of 1932 what he often did in such circumstances. He turned to a woman, to *yet another woman*—in this case, to Christabel McLaren. HG turned to Christabel many times over the last twenty years of his life—both on paper and in person. He admired her "marvellous steadfastness" and delighted in her unbridled irreverence—even when it was at his expense. For example, Christabel once called HG's beloved French Riviera a "haunt of parasites," and those who frequented it, "plaster façades." On this occasion, however, it was Christabel's intelligence and uncommon common sense that HG was interested in tapping. He had long believed that her insights were keen, her advice wise and good. Two years earlier, for example, when he asked for her impressions of his latest heart's desire, she reported that the "Russian Lady," the Baroness Moura Budberg, was an adventuress, "which means that when life promises to be tedious she edits it." Such people, Christabel cautioned, "contrive to get most of the things they covet."[1] "Your estimate of my Russian . . . is very sound," he replied.[2] It was, indeed, a bull's-eye summary of the baroness.

Despite her frequent jabs, Christabel was a lovely person—indeed, "the loveliest person in the world," HG proclaimed.[3] And despite the heavy demands on her—two households, a husband, and five children, among other things—she was stability incarnate, an emotional anchor with a nurturing soul. Christabel was always there, through fair weather and foul, to offer HG an eye, an ear, or a shoulder to cry on. She was the compass by which he navigated the troubled waters of his love life, especially through the 1930s. "You would be surprised to know how astronomical you are to me," HG wrote to Christabel. "I sail my course by you more than you think. You are a star, (even to the twinkle) & sometimes I feel how far you are away & still get my comfort from the starlight."[4] Because of these things—and many others—HG felt great affection for Christabel. If it wasn't love, he once confessed, then it was "something very very like love."[5] Another time he conceded: "In some unreasonable & entirely holy spiritual way, I love you."[6]

Christabel seemed to understand HG's affection and to appreciate her position in his busy orbit. She undoubtedly knew that her self-chosen status as Woman-Entirely-Off-Limits-Sexually to HG guaranteed his staunch devotion to her over the years. In her memoir, Christabel claimed: "Once HG and I had settled that I never intended to sleep with him, [his] company was a delight."[7] He, too, may have come to realize that eliminating the burr of sex from their relationship was not entirely unrewarding, for he later observed in pages that would be suppressed from publication: "I have learnt this much of life that a good thing expected is better than a thing realised."[8] That short simple sentence may better explain H. G. Wells than anything else he ever wrote about himself—and he wrote a great deal.

Thus, for any number of reasons, HG was able to admit his frustrations, faults, and failings to Christabel. "I don't do it to anyone else," he once told her. "The purity of my relationship to you in view of its extreme intimacy is a scandal. I trust you to keep my shameful secret."[9] And Christabel was able to keep HG's shameful secrets and hear him through his many romantic crises. It wasn't a burden on her. Christabel, the future Lady Aberconway, was as fond of HG as he was of her.[10] *She* prized *his* friendship, flawed as it was. In her memoir, Christabel wrote that she rejoiced in HG's "use of words, in his anecdotes about people and places, and in his letters." She even credited him for teaching her many things: how to make tea, for example, and how to overcome her fear of death. In addition, his company added considerably to her own well-being. Christabel once told HG that she derived "a lot of re-conditioning" from simply being with him. They met over a meal at her home in the Mayfair district of London, or for a long weekend *en famille* at Bodnant, her getaway estate in Wales. HG invited her to lunch, tea, dinner, or soirées. Once, when she was without her cook, Christabel invited HG to a restaurant, "where I will do my best to give you the new sensation of feeling like a gigolo, being taken out to dine. Afterwards we will go to any play or film you like, or we will produce our own entertainment by talking."[11]

At the moment, Christabel was hearing HG through his plans for a separation with Odette Keun—his lover of eight years.[12] As he told Christabel in the letter excerpted above, he was going to Grasse, in the South of France, to "wind up" his situation with Odette. Cutting his losses there would be painful business. "I'm going to do some wrong & make some disagreeable memories for myself," he told Christabel. He and Odette had been having a spate of first-class quarrels, although HG had long recognized a streak of insincerity in their relationship. "Is there any love relationship without something forced & kept up in it?" he asked Christabel. "And that is why they come unstuck at last." As it happened, HG didn't cut his losses. Odette promised to behave and that appeased HG, at least temporarily. "My weakness," he later wrote to Christabel, "is to be kind & charming to people (until my temper gives way). The consequence is that Odette is sticking to me most desperate."[13]

As important as she was, Christabel wasn't HG's only emotional pit stop. He had dozens of women friends to whom he wrote hundreds of letters, although few of the letters approached the candor of those he wrote Christabel. Still, legions of women gravitated around HG. Like Christabel, they came to meals and to parties, and they reciprocated. HG, thus, saw a great many women between the mid-1930s and the last year of his life, not too surprising for a man who described himself, self-deprecatingly, to be sure, as a Don Juan of the Intelligentsia.

HG also aired his romantic frustrations in his books—the fiction as well as the nonfiction. Always ahead of his times, he did nearly seventy years ago what is becoming increasingly fashionable today: He wrote two autobiographies. However, HG published only one of his self-studies—the first one, which traced the "emotional development" of his brain. In that work, *Experiment in Autobiography: Discoveries and Conclusions of a Very Ordinary Brain (Since 1866)*, HG described his origins in lower-middle-class England, his struggles to find his calling and to make a living, his frustrations with his wives, and his attempts to create a "planned world." When Christabel received her copy of the *Experiment,* she told HG: "At last I may begin to read all about your early life and what has been going on inside that *first-class* mind of yours ever since. How will it affect my feelings for you, I wonder? Anyhow, God bless you (in spite of your feelings towards him)."

While the *Experiment* must have seemed complete enough to most readers—it was 718 pages—HG immediately began writing a second autobiography. He worked for nearly a decade on the next book, configured as a postscript to the first, then with great self-control sat on it for the rest of his life.[14] There was a good reason for that: The book explored, in HG's own words, his many "sexual events and personal intimacies." In other words, HG topped off his life story—its roots deeply planted in the Victorian age—with an exposé of his major sexual romantic adventures. In his dust-jacket endorsement, Carlos Baker described the work as "the history of HG's sexual exploits" and a *"Confessio Amantis."*[15] HG called it his intimate diary and the story of his amatory life. Don Juan had a thick diary, a long story, a rich trove, indeed, from which to cull.

Yet, despite his embarrassment of riches, HG claimed that his sexual life was nothing special. The only difference was that he probably had more *opportunity* than most men: "I have done what I pleased, so that every bit of sexual impulse in me has expressed itself," he announced.[16] As an aside, HG noted that he was never able to determine whether his interest in sex was average, above or below it, since there was "no meter" for that sort of thing. Still, it takes an acrobatic leap of logic to reconcile having a ho-hum libido with being a veritable (and Victorian) Casanova. As he must have known, and as should become clear in the following pages, there may have been many things about H. G. Wells that could be called "normal," but his sexual drive wasn't among them. With apologies to the more conservative Wells scholars, the evidence certainly suggests that the author of *The Time Machine* was something of a Sex Machine.

Be that as it may, HG instructed his heirs to release his piquant postscript at their earliest convenience *after* his death and *after* the women in it were either dead or beyond worrying about their reputations. HG got his wish—at least most of it. The heirs published the second autobiography in 1984—thirty-eight years after HG died—but before they did, they excised large chunks of the story and the names of two of HG's alleged last lovers, as well as a good deal of narrative about them. They also surgically removed other bits and pieces about other lovers. HG had been extremely candid, though not X-rated in his love memoir. The heirs, however, played it cautiously, their actions prompted by courtesy and concern over litigation. It is noteworthy that they released the book a year after Rebecca West died. HG had devoted an entire chapter to their passionate but rocky ten-year affair.[17]

In addition to the rejections, discards, and excisions from HG's manuscripts, the heirs also held back a huge cache of letters "of a personal nature" that HG had received over the decades from the many women in his life, including those from Christabel and also from his legion of lovers. Finally, in 1994, the family put the *Withheld Wells,* so to speak, up for sale. The University of Illinois Library, already the site of the world's premier H. G. Wells Collection, snapped up these items, the mother lode of long-suppressed personal material about H. G. Wells. This acquisition contained documents of all stripes, in addition to the suppressed manuscript pages and the massive collection of very personal correspondence—a "Closet Correspondence," if you will.[18]

Among other things, *Shadow Lovers* restores the missing pieces of HG's love memoir—aptly titled by his eldest son and chief editor, Gip (George Philip Wells), *HG Wells in Love: Postscript to an Experiment in Autobiography,* hereafter called the *Postscript. Shadow Lovers* also opens the hundreds of previously suppressed love and friendship letters to and from H. G. Wells. Drawing on these documents, this book attempts to tell the story HG intended to tell about the busy and complex—sometimes wonderful, often harrowing—life of his affections, a life that had a life of its own. The focus is on HG's last three love affairs as they are revealed through their correspondence—and now, from the grave. The lovers include our highly improbable Lothario—HG, aged sixty-eight when the story begins; the Russian baroness, Moura Budberg; a French countess, the American-born Constance Coolidge; and a French marquise, Martha Gellhorn, also an American.[19]

Other friends, lovers, and family members from the Closet Correspondence enter the story and speak for themselves, including Rebecca West and Margaret Sanger. Many other people play a part through other caches of recently released papers, some never before published. In this category are several lovers—previous, contemporary, or future—of our women in question, including the American writers Harry Crosby and Ernest Hemingway. The result of all of this eavesdropping, spying, and literary sleuthing is a portrait, hauled somewhat reluctantly out of the mists of time and, yes, the shadows of history, of three relationships and four lovers, needy and restless spirits all. In the background are glimpses of the era and the milieu in which these remarkable people lived—from the horrors of the Russian Revolution to the breezy glittering playgrounds of the rich and famous on the French Riviera. While I use the word portrait to describe this study, sketch may be more accurate, since these stories are incomplete. Many of the documents that would illuminate the shadows are still lost or sealed, most notably Martha Gellhorn's papers at Boston University, which include HG's letters to her. Rebecca West's letters from HG were said to have been destroyed many years ago. Intelligence files that would throw light into the dark corners of Moura Budberg's life are also unavailable, as are her personal papers—victims, some claim, of a house fire.

I have described these four people as needy and restless spirits; but, of course, they were a great deal more. I often think of them as rebel reinventors. Each of them at an early age and in a particularly repressive era broke out of some kind of bondage—gender, family, or social. Refusing to accept what they regarded as limited lives, each invented and reinvented himself and herself according to his or her personal needs and desires. They were risk-takers all; they used and abused the system to become their imagined selves. All carved out successful careers—the women, notably, in a man's world: journalism, horse racing, publishing, and espionage. While the women were carving places for themselves, HG was working hard for women's equality, including sexual liberation. He subscribed to the idea that women's liberation improved human life—it certainly improved his—and his lovers evidently subscribed to that idea as well. They also saw themselves as HG's equals. For these reasons, as well as others, I submit that in these relationships there were no victims.

To be sure, these four people were unusually lucky in their natural resources: their intelligence, imagination, and gumption, and all except HG were lucky in their looks and birth. All were keenly aware of—and skillful with—their considerable sexual and personal charms and their intellectual powers. They wished to do what they were eminently capable of doing, and that perhaps is one mark of genius, or at least one hallmark of their success. Sometimes their choices were peculiar, their behaviors inexplicable. Very often their actions were self-centered— even those of HG, the tireless promoter of Utopia on earth. These were original, ambitious, and irreverent people who were also human and richly flawed. HG, for example, carried a huge chip on his shoulder despite his extraordinary personal success. He went into battle over minor, indeed, meaningless offences; he was beset with jealousy, he held grudges, and he was petulant, willful, and irresponsible. All four were irresponsible at times, sometimes wildly so, and sometimes with the

heart of someone who loved them. That the women were femmes fa-
tales and that HG was a self-proclaimed Don Juan suggests that all of
them had rather oversized needs and desires. Did they ever! Each was
born with a huge appetite for life, for life not only at its fullest, but also
at its most intense.

Few people lived more intensely than H. G. Wells. His vitality, energy,
and drive were legendary. Indeed, HG was said to "radiate" energy: intellectual, emotional, physical, and sexual.[20] In its obituary for HG, the
New York Times wrote that the short, stocky writer with the tiny hands
and feet and an unfortunate squeaky voice had "superhuman energy."
Superhuman or simply well above average, his energy served him well.
Over his nearly eighty years, HG produced several film scripts, more
than a hundred books, and hundreds of articles, newspaper columns,
and talks. "Mr. Wells was a superman in many respects," the obit writer
for the *New York Times* claimed, unaware, undoubtedly, of HG's busy
romantic life! But all that was ages ago. What about today, 135 years after HG's birth in a ramshackle china shop to what we would today call
a dysfunctional and financially challenged family? Why should we care
about H. G. Wells in the new millennium? Why, moreover, should we
give a fig (leaf) about his love life?

★   ★   ★

At the very least, HG still holds a place in our reference books. In the
CD ROM that came with my computer is a succinct little entry about
Bromley, England's, first son.[21] The English novelist and social theorist
Herbert George Wells, it begins, was born on September 21, 1866, and
died August 13, 1946. One of the world's most important literary figures between 1895 and 1920, he, "with Jules Verne, was the inventor of
science fiction;

> in the tradition of Dickens, he was a master of the comic novel; in his
> prime he was also a self-appointed prophet and popular advisor to the
> public on virtually every acute problem that confronted the modern

world. By the time he was 30 years of age he had already embarked on his
famous series of scientific romances, notably *The Invisible Man, The Time
Machine* and *The War of the Worlds*. His *Outline of History* is perhaps the
best one-volume history of humankind ever compiled by a single author.

The entry ends with a sobering thought: "Although he was originally a
firm believer in the ability of science to create a more perfect world,
Wells later felt that the human race was likely to destroy itself through
its own barbarism."

HG's impact also continues to be felt at the box office. Several of his
stories or adaptations of them—*The Invisible Man, The Island of Dr.
Moreau,* and *Independence Day,* a modernization of his *War of the
Worlds*—captivated audiences at the end of the twentieth century.[22] A
new version of *The Time Machine* with HG's great-grandson as producer is soon coming to American theaters. In publishing, more than
three dozen H. G. Wells titles are still in print; several biographies and
works of criticism are released every year. Hardly a week goes by without a mention of HG's name in the mainstream media. A quick Internet search also turns up many elaborate Web sites for H. G. Wells, most
of them devoted to his science fiction.

Beyond his continuing presence in today's world, what can we say
about HG's contributions? For one thing, he not only anticipated at the
beginning of the twentieth century the enormous influence science
would later have but also recruited single-handedly thousands of people into science for at least twenty years—from 1910 to 1930. He had,
among other things, an uncanny way of seeing where this wobbly
world of ours was going—the shape, color, and size of things to come.
Trained in biology at the elbow of Thomas Huxley, HG was able, as biographer David Smith put it, "not only to describe his own world, but
also to offer a glimpse into worlds that might be."[23] Thus, beyond his
sci-fi imaginings, H. G. Wells predicted the two world wars and the various tools of war: tanks, airplanes, and rockets. He also had a sixth
sense for geopolitical change. At the beginning of the twentieth century,
in a book titled *Anticipations*, HG predicted the rise of China and the

demise of Russia. "The chances seem altogether against the existence of a great Slavonic power in the world at the beginning of the twenty-first century," he wrote in 1902.[24] Thirty-four years later, HG foresaw the possibility of total world destruction. In *The Anatomy of Frustration,* he drew up a blueprint for an alternative to self-annihilation: a world revolution that would produce a world community. "Either we *take hold of our destiny* or, failing that, we are driven towards our fate."[25]

This wasn't the first time he had confronted the idea of human extinction. In 1914, HG published *The World Set Free: A Story of Mankind,* a novel that still is considered a remarkable forecast of nuclear warfare and subsequent world reconstruction. After nuclear bombs wreak widespread destruction and catastrophe, the nations of the world joined together to end war—all war. His book became the rationale for producing a weapon so terrible that it would prevent Armageddon.[26] There are people who still remember HG's dire early warning. At the entrance to In Flanders Fields, a new museum in Ypres, Belgium—and the site of great human loss during World War I—is an immense tablet carved with the words: "Nothing could have been more obvious to the people of the early twentieth century than the rapidity with which war was becoming impossible. And as certainly they did not see it. They did not see it until the atomic bombs burst in their fumbling hands."[27]

In his last years, HG worked at full throttle to craft and promote his last-gasp effort to save the world from itself. That document later became the basis for the United Nation's Universal Declaration of Human Rights, which was adopted on December 10, 1948. HG also fought for the rights of women, primarily through his fiction; indeed, he was a major force in the "opening out of modern feminism."[28] Through several books, including *Ann Veronica* (1909), he not only widened society's view of love but also sanctioned women's sexual and romantic desires and displays.[29] His fiction also promoted new optimism for the lower middle class, from whence he emerged.

Before H. G. Wells dared to dream great things for humankind, he dared dream them for himself—this despite his mother's plans for him in the drapery trade. "Almost as unquestioning as her belief in Our Father and Our Saviour, was her belief in drapers," HG wrote.[30] But "Little Bertie" refused to accept his destiny. As his family watched in shock and horror, the teenager took a great flying leap over the drapery counter and landed a few years later in the world of publishing, where he rapidly became a huge success in a new genre. The draper's apprentice, the son of a maid and a gardener, would climb rapidly to the highest rungs of the social and political ladder.

Considered one of the brilliant minds of his age, HG became ubiquitous. His face, words, and ideas appeared in the world's newspapers. His voice squeaked out over radio waves all across the globe, and his short figure strutted across miles of newsreel. Audiences in the remotest corners of the globe crowded into lecture halls to hear the diminutive diviner. There was hardly a world leader who didn't make time for him. The author of *The Time Machine* became a modern man—perhaps the first modern man. He became an early and ardent proponent of women's liberation, human rights, and world peace, three causes that continue to top the free world's agenda. As suggested earlier, he was also an angry man, once described as the first Angry Young Man in English literature. Yet, through his books, articles, lectures, and films, he stirred a society's consciousness, sometimes even led it to places it had never dreamed of. For all this, this little man with a great gift to foresee was surprisingly modest. He once told a friend that prophecy was simply a matter of having a little common sense, a little scientific background, a little imagination, "and being a step or two in front of the obvious."[31]

Despite his role as sage during some of the worst decades of the last century, the prophet became a forgotten man—the Invisible Man he created on paper in 1909 and on celluloid in 1933. He became a victim, in a sense, of his own success as many of his predictions came to pass. In the United States, the fiftieth anniversary of HG's death came and went without notice. This book teases the complex and sometimes confounding HG out of the shadows. It is the least we can do for a man who in his time was considered the greatest intellectual force of the English-speaking world.[32]

*   *   *

A few words about this book, beginning with its organization. Chapter 1 sets the stage: the winter of 1934–1935 in the villas and hotels of the French Riviera, when and where HG's romantic life took yet another sudden and delightful turn. The chapter also explores his chief obsessions (work, love, and sex), and reviews several interpretations of them. Chapter 2 reviews HG's origins and early years and focuses on his parents, his awakening sexuality and conceptions of romantic love, his early romances, and the major romances that led to the last affairs. Chapters 3, 4, and 5 are devoted to Moura, Constance, and Martha respectively. Woven into each of these chapters, which function as mini-biographies, are the stories of their concurrent affairs with HG as they are revealed through their correspondence. The affairs are explored through themes, allowing the reader to trace HG's comments on given topics; for example, his private concerns about love, boredom, loneliness, disillusionment, and being forgotten, as well as his observations about the larger world—FDR, for example, America, Russia, and God. Newly released documents allow me to offer revisionist interpretations not only of HG but also of Moura and Martha, while the material on Constance is almost entirely new. Chapter 6, the Epilogue, brings the main characters back to the stage for a final bow and assessment. The chapter titles are taken from HG's novels.

This book is titled *Shadow Lovers* for many reasons, from the personal to the historical. At the personal level, the romantic liaisons discussed here were conducted in secret or hidden in the open. HG was married to Jane Wells when he began his affair with Moura Budberg, and he was intimately involved with Moura when he began his affairs with Constance Coolidge and Martha Gellhorn. As noted, their affairs continued to be shrouded in secrecy in the five decades following HG's death. Moreover, HG's affairs with Constance and Martha have been unknown except to a few members of the Wells family, and many gaps remained in HG's relationship with Moura. This book also explores other major romances these people had before, after, or during the primary affairs of this study. This second tier of lovers includes Rebecca West,

Margaret Sanger, Bertrand de Jouvenel, Harry Crosby, Bruce Lockhart, and Ernest Hemingway.[33] Considering this matrix of past and future romances allows us to see how the specters of other love affairs shadowed the affairs of HG, Moura, Constance, and Martha—as perhaps love and affairs always do. In a sense, the title of this book could have been *Shadow Lovers: The Last Affairs of HG Wells . . . and Their Affairs . . . and Their Affairs!* We are dealing here with a great many cases of what might be called the Repetitive Love Syndrome!

There is another human shadow: Christabel. She is a thread that runs through the chapters, just as her friendship with HG stretched across the years. While never a dark presence, Christabel has been until now a little-known factor in HG's emotional life. She is also a foil to HG's women, and a Greek chorus; for more than anyone else, Christabel knew the secrets of HG's heart. It was a place he did not open fully to his last three lovers, or perhaps to any other woman.

Another aspect of this study involves some dark realms indeed: those of international espionage. Chapter 3 explores many of the allegations about Moura. Was she a secret agent, as rumor had it? Did she use HG to influence—or obtain information from—Western opinion makers, movers, and shakers? Chapter 5, devoted to Martha, examines the possibility that she used her relationship with HG to help advance her career. Also, using never-published letters from Ernest Hemingway, we explore Martha's troubled relationship with Papa, which began soon after she met HG. Hemingway emerges as a kinder and gentler man: a revisionist image indeed.

To be sure, each lover lived with personal shadows in the form of compulsions and obsessions: for sex, for romance, for a former lover, for travel, for taking physical risks, for horses and betting, and career. Each manifested a complex of paradoxes: the need to be in company and to be alone; the need to be of use to someone and to be a free spirit; the need to play the field and to be monogamous; the need to be free and to advance a career. One of HG's inescapable shadows was his birth in lower-middle-class England. As we shall see, it was a berth he alternately embraced and rejected.

Which brings us to the main shadow in this study so full of secrets and shadows and shades of gray. This is the shadow that haunted H. G. Wells, that held sway over his imagination for most of his adult life. He called that presence his "Lover-Shadow." HG, the scientist, HG, the "World Brain," imagined that in this huge universe there existed a woman (or several) who was (were) his complete female counterpart, his intellectual-emotional-sexual equal, his soul mate, his Lover-Shadow. In his construction, this dream-lover was a powerful force and a most demanding mistress. One of HG's rationales in taking so many lovers—aside from the recreation and sexual release it provided, to which he freely admitted—was to find his Lover-Shadow. To be sure, there are those who argue that his perseveration with his Lover-Shadow was bunk: an elaborate excuse to justify his phenomenal sex drive and nonstop philandering. There are those who argue that instead of chasing this phantom, HG should have accepted his obsession for sex and stopped endowing it with phony transcendent significance.[34] In this work, I will examine HG's obsession for sex and the Lover-Shadow; for women, especially foreign women, who had social status, titles, money, and liberal views; for women who were beautiful, intelligent, charming, and liberated, and yet who would be totally devoted and submissive to him. Along the way I will consider HG's need for social validation through the acquisition of one trophy woman after another, and his inability to achieve intimacy—even with his intimates.

To be sure, Moura, Constance, and Martha had considerable cravings of their own. Their appetites for external stimuli were huge, indeed, and seemingly insatiable. They chased new thrills: new things, new places, new relationships. Whether it was opium or high intrigue, endless travel, or a rapid succession of lovers, life was only as good as the next new challenge, the next new adventure. Someone once described Constance as a member of the "Exotic Set." Moura and Martha also belonged to the club. Navigating through the minefields of the 1930s, these women fed their inordinate cravings and desires to have it all—a dynamic life, a grand career, excitement, lovers, and the soul mate of their dreams. To be sure, all four characters were demanding.

They shared ground-level thresholds for boredom and sky-high thresholds for excitement. They also grappled with the frustrations that arose from their huge personal appetites.

How familiar this all sounds. In looking at these lives, one is reminded that the late twentieth century didn't invent the Don Juan or the femme fatale. It didn't invent compulsions or obsessions, fascinating ambitious women, or powerful men. Nor did the late twentieth century invent the notions of personal reinvention or redemption through finding one's soul mate. No, creatures with powerful passions began shaking the earth some time ago—even left their footprints on history. They sought and found love, although often in all the wrong places, often for all the wrong reasons, and often excessively.

This book, then, is a laboratory of love, an anatomy of the love that took so many forms in the lives of our characters: It was, among other things, a dream-fantasy, hope, deception, delusion, a warm embrace, an icy restraint, a fond and disquieting memory. Love could also be, as HG observed in one of his shortest definitions of the phenomenon, "a clumsy search for an enduring dear companionship into which the primitive lust prowl has developed."[35] Let us then begin exploring HG's searches, some of them clumsy, to be sure, some of them artful, all of them imperfect, all of them evanescent.

Note: To preserve the flavor of the quoted material, much of it letters dashed off in haste, it is printed exactly as it appeared in the original sources and, therefore, may include misspellings or errors in punctuation.

Acknowledgments

After having written more than 300,000 words (several times over!), coming up with a scant hundred more words for this page should be a snap; and yet, as I sit here staring at my computer, I find the task daunting. Not so much because I'm written out, but because I'm finding it hard to convey my heartfelt thanks to the people who helped me through this long, long journey—the people who helped me find and gather ideas and facts, who helped me think about what I had, didn't have, and might have; who helped me put the words on paper and who helped me think, rethink, reorder, and refine those words. Your efforts—often selfless and sometimes Herculean—your acts of kindness, shows of support, and your commitment will never be forgotten.

Let me first thank my mentor, George Hendrick, a University of Illinois English professor, now emeritus, who stood by through thick and thin. Without your help, George, your unflagging interest and enthusiasm, there would be no book. Without several other scholars, this book would have been a poorer product. My tremendous thanks therefore to several wise and generous souls: Walter Arnstein, Ralph Fisher, David Fogelsong, Sylvia Hardy, John Long, Gail Owen, Barry Scherr, David Smith, Richard Spence, and longtime friend and editor-extraordinaire, historian Frederic Jaher. Fred, for your help I owe you gourmet dinners well into our sunset years. Thanks, too, to the Research Board of the University of Illinois three times over for its generosity and support; to Jeff Unger for kindnesses rendered in various stages of the project; and to former graduate students John Braun (University of Waterloo), Angie Dorman (University of Idaho), Jacqueline Orsagh (Michigan

State University), and Emmett Dever Powell (University of Illinois), for sharing their work. Many thanks to newer acquaintances, wonderful people I have met in the permissions phase: Scott Donaldson, Edward Germain, Michael Katakis, Jerry Kennedy, Michael Keun, Robin Lockhart, Anne and Christopher McLaren, and Sandy Matthews. Merci beaucoup to the late incomparable André Magnus for sharing his memories and his wife's diaries and photographs.

My gratitude for the enthusiasm, dedication, and even tempers of librarians and curators all over the globe is, likewise, immense. Karen Drickamer, formerly curator and archivist at the Morris Library at Southern Illinois University, Carol Leadenham at the Hoover Institution Archives, Richard Hurley at Brown University, Gene Rinkel and Madeline Gibson at the University of Illinois, Stephen Plotkin and Allan Goodrich at the JFK Library, and Richard Ormond at the Courtauld Institute of Art, I thank you. You went above and beyond. Thanks also to the Santa Barbara Historical Society and the Massachusetts Historical Society, where, in truth, this adventure began. To all of you, animate and in-, you have made this project not only do-able, but also fun and, not infrequently, exciting.

I am greatly indebted to several people—past and present—at Westview Press: editors Peter Kracht for his belief in my "strong writing skills," Rob Williams for his wisdom and good cheer, Carol Jones for her intelligence, sense of humor, and bravery in taking on an inherited project in its eleventh hour, and Jennifer Blakebrough-Raeburn, my superb copy editor. Thanks also go to Constance Hunting, my writing teacher at the University of Maine, who so long ago told me that I had a knack for writing.

I thank several old and dear friends in France, the Auger and the Roche families of Amponville and Montreuil for their hundreds of generous acts, their amazing meals, and the great times we shared. Michel Roche, I asked unreasonable things of you, and you always came through with grace, good humor, and the goods. Bernard Croza of Mons-en-Laonnois, at first a stranger, now a friend, similarly went out of his way for me; you put part of this story onto Kodachrome and put my feet on hallowed ground at Écuiry. Merci, merci Bernard! Many thanks also to Marc Johannes for that wonderful tour of Écuiry. Salut, mes amies!

To my birth family, my incredible sisters and brother, Sharron, Vicki, G. Meredith, and Gary, for their love and support; and to my mother, for her enduring interest, which has required not only deft diplomacy at times, but also great patience and endurance. I am forever, *forever* indebted. Thanks too to sister-in-law Janice for her tough-love advice over lunch on Telegraph Avenue. You were right, Jan.

With all my heart I thank our beautiful sons, Dan and Nate, and especially my historian husband, John, for listening, caring, and for helping in a thousand ways. I thank you three also for enduring endless meals from the freezer and Sam's Club. By the time you read this, John, I, perhaps, will have found my way into "The New Kitchen" you built me two years ago.

Last but not least, I thank the geniuses who developed the high-speed printer and the fax machine, e- and overnight mail. Life as we have come to know it has hinged on these miraculous amenities. HG would have loved them too.

Andrea Lynn
Champaign, Illinois
August 2001

1

Secret Places of the Heart: HG in Love and in His Postscript

What is that magic thing between persons, that is so bright & wonderful, so infinitely hopeful—hopeful Christabel—& sure. And it goes & it won't come back. And there is what you loved that was alive & divine—and it is nothing but a clay figure, just a suggestion of all that you thought was there.

—HG to Christabel, April 1935

The weather, of all things, brought H. G. Wells and Constance Coolidge together Christmas of 1934, in the winter of his life, the lingering summer of hers; but other forces equally beyond their control kept them true—in their own fashions—to each other over the next few years, then allowed them simply and swiftly to drift apart. Masters at the game of love—especially of winning and then letting go—both knew a potential romance when they saw it: They had seen the signs so many times before. They knew that for them, a fresh romance vanquished loneliness and boredom, that it fed the imagination, the heart, and the soul. In short, romance, with its bursts of suspense, surprise, and excitement, fed their cravings for a vivid life, a life at its most intense. Romance was love when they were together, a lovely sustaining dream when they were apart. That is how it always had been. That is how it always would be. That is how it was during Christmas of 1934. The luxury hotels, bistros, bars, and restaurants of the French Riviera, gaily trimmed and packed for the long Christmas–New Year's season, provided the backdrop for their latest adventure in love.

Nice, according to the *Daily Mail* on December 24, enjoyed one of the merriest and busiest Christmases it had known since World War I. On Christmas Eve, the streets and shops were "thronged with people buying last-moment gifts, and in the evening there was a veritable invasion of people at the places of entertainment," the paper's "Christmastide Gossip from the Holiday Resorts" column noted. Six days later, *Le Figaro* reported that the grand hall of the Riviera Place hotel at Cimiez was decorated with an immense Christmas tree that sparkled with a thousand lights, and that miniature replicas of that magnificent tree had been placed on each table. As guests dined, Guy Sarlin, Evelyn Gray, Baby, Teddy, and Paddy earned everyone's admiration for their graceful and daring acrobatics.

As the hours of 1934 ticked away, Nice took a breather, the *Daily Mail* reported, between the Christmas and New Year's festivities. Despite the lull in the round of galas, the city was in an animated and gay mood, and the crowds found plenty to entertain them. Verdi's *Rigoletto* was playing at Nice's opera house. The International Military Horse Show and the Lily of the Valley Fête would soon follow. Glittering and beautiful people, a mix of royalty, high society, and well-known literary figures, were showing up everywhere: Miss Paris had just arrived at the Negresco; the king of Sweden attended a "diner fleuri" at the Sporting Club; and "Mr. and Mrs. H. G. Wells"—in reality, HG and his latest mistress, the Russian Baroness Moura Budberg, recently of Petrograd and several major European cities—were now at the Hermitage, which overlooked the glittering Bay of Monaco.[1]

With the end of the year approaching, HG, age sixty-eight, and Moura, forty-two, had planned to spend the holidays in Palermo; they were hoping that a few weeks in a warm sunny place would melt the ice collecting on their young affair. That summer, HG had accidentally caught Moura in a stupendous and painful lie—ever after referred to as "the Moscow deception" and "the Moscow crisis." The holiday trip, then, would be an attempt to smooth over the trouble they had been having and to rebuild trust. The couple left London's Victoria train station on December 18 with salvation, sunshine, and Sicily on their minds; but a heavy fog and flooding at Ostia stranded them in Marseilles. With their few options dwindling, HG called on an old friend and Riviera neighbor.

As it happened, Willie, otherwise known as William Somerset Maugham, the British novelist and playwright, was in residence at his villa at Cap Ferrat for the holidays. In response to HG's SOS, Willie invited the uncommon writer of common origins and his titled Russian mistress to spend Christmas week with him at his Villa Mauresque; he suggested that they check into the Hermitage right away, since it had just reopened, then join him and his guests at the Cap the following week. Ironically, HG had his own vacation home—Lou Pidou—in the South of France, but at the moment it was strictly off-limits. He and his previous mistress, Odette Keun, were involved in "small border warfare," which included ridiculous legal maneuvers, over ownership of the property. Odette, a formidable woman with a wicked temper and ferocious jealousy, was currently winning control of the pretty *mas* and was not about to tolerate the incursion of a new mistress, whom she described as a "fool of an Esthonian," on the premises. Lou Pidou, a Provençal contraction for *Le Petit Dieu,* was a wonderful piece of real estate tucked into the lavender-covered hills near Grasse, with a main house, a guest house, a farm, and a massive *rocher* with a staircase. In 1927, the same year he built Lou Pidou, HG gave Odette a lifetime usufruct for it. Her impact as mistress of the *mas* had been enormous. An exotic creature—HG once told her that she dressed like an Armenian carpet-seller—Odette employed a flamboyant decorating style; Lou Pidou, it is said, compared favorably to a dwelling that Kubla Khan might have inhabited.

By 1933, the relationship between HG and Odette had become difficult. He was now less willing to tolerate her fits of rage and her accusations of cheating, often triggered by clues she found when nosing around in his correspondence. He was also fed up with Odette's public displays of outrageous behavior and foul language. HG moved his belongings out of Lou Pidou in May 1933, and the place fell into limbo and general decline for several years until he began the process of buying Odette out in 1936. "Your attachment to the place is purely sentimental. I want it vitally as a refuge from the winter climate here," he told her on April 21, 1936. Odette was too smart, too paranoid, not to realize that HG undoubtedly had another agenda—that he was entertaining notions of entertaining his Russian mistress there—and Odette was not going to let that happen. Proposals and counterproposals devolved into a battle royal, but Odette held her ground, literally and figuratively, and eventually, and with great reluctance, HG gave up the fight and abandoned the former love nest. In better times, HG had hired local masons to carve an inscription above the fireplace—"Two Lovers Built This House"—and around the windows, some free verse he had written about vines, olives, and undying love. "All that seemed as good as marriage-lines to Odette," HG asserted.[2] In his 1964 autobiography, Charlie Chaplin reported that the inscription suffered many mutilations over the years. Following the lovers' "first-class" arguments, the masons would be called in to remove the stony saying; after the lovers made up, the masons were called back to restore it. As the story goes, the verse had been taken off and put on so many times that the masons eventually stopped responding to the summons. Today, a plaque with the words "This house was built by two lovers, HG Wells, 1926," is attached to the wall next to Lou Pidou's front door.

Although this was neither the first time nor the last that HG would "ask himself" to Willie's, the request was hardly an imposition; Maugham thoroughly enjoyed HG's company. In addition, he was hosting a group of glitterati and must have been delighted with the serendipitous appearance of his old friend because it afforded him the opportunity to make "Mr. & Mrs. H. G. Wells" the social centerpiece for his holiday table. The *Daily Mail* later ran a small item reporting that Maugham had H. G. Wells and Miss G. B. Stern staying with him at his lovely villa at Cap Ferrat. Gladys Bronwyn Stern was a popular novelist and close friend of Maugham's; for reasons unknown, she went by the name of Peter, but HG called her "Tynx." The *Daily Mail* did not mention Moura Budberg, who, although then a somewhat unknown quantity on the Riviera social scene, would not be overlooked for long in European society items. Indeed, forty years later, in her glowing but seriously flawed *Times* obituary, the baroness would be described among other things as having been "an invaluable guest."

Handsome, intelligent, charming, charismatic, and, above all, mysterious, Moura was rapidly becoming a darling of London's literary and émigré circles. An aristocrat who managed to survive the Russian Revolution, she claimed two former husbands, two children, two previous high-profile affairs—the first with British secret agent Bruce Lockhart in 1918, the second with Russian icon and writer Maxim Gorky from 1919 to the mid-1930s—and at least three periods of imprisonment in Russian jails. Moura left Russia in 1921, temporarily rejoined her young children in Estonia, then flitted from one European city to another until she emigrated to England in the early 1930s, from whence she continued her habit of flitting. She and HG became open lovers in 1933, and they traveled around Europe together or met in various cities, but this was their first sighting on the Côte d'Azur and at Maugham's. Over the years other noteworthy guests to the luxurious Mauresque, with its beckoning swimming pool overlooking the Mediterranean, its impressive art collection, and its legendary cook, Annette, included Michael Arlen, Max Beerbohm, Winston Churchill, Noel Coward, Moss Hart, the Aga and Begum Khan, Rudyard Kipling, the Duke and Duchess of Windsor, and, often, G. B. Stern. Maugham bought the villa for himself and his new lover/chauffeur, Gerald Haxton, in 1929, after he and his wife, Syrie, had divorced; he paid £7,000 for his piece of the Cap. Maugham's neighbors included Bao Dai, the former emperor of Indo-China, Charlie Chaplin, and Jean Cocteau.

Meanwhile, up the coast in Nice at the New Year, throngs were enjoying the "gala reveillon" at the Palais de la Jetée, the newspapers claimed, and the annual steeplechase meeting on the Var racecourse had just opened. On February 1, the *Daily Mail* ran an item in its society column about the turf personalities being seen in Monte Carlo. Well-known figures in the worlds of hunting and racing had been spotted at the International Sporting Club's gala dinner. Mrs. Coolidge, the American horse owner, was the guest of Mr. H. G. Wells. The famous novelist's party also included Mr. Somerset Maugham, who had recently been promoted to Officer in the Legion of Honour, and Mr. G. Haxton.

Constance Coolidge, a sensational centerpiece for anyone's table, was installed for the holidays in a suite of rooms in Nice's fashionable Negresco Hotel. As HG would learn, the forty-two-year-old American heiress and former French countess was neither just a pretty face nor a garden-variety socialite. Like Moura, she was a foreigner, well endowed with physical beauty, intelligence, charm, courage, wit, and pedigree—an irresistible combination as far as HG was concerned, and a type he had been drawn to over and over again through the years. Unlike Moura, who just scraped by with the meager earnings from her sporadic translating and editing jobs and the generosity of HG and her refugee friends, mostly expatriate Russians living in London, Constance was flourishing. Set up since childhood on a generous trust fund that was doled out to her by her cousin, Charlie Adams, she was a long-term expat living in Paris who twenty-five years earlier had said, "If I can't be French, thank God I'm American." Constance wore couturier designs, dined at the finest restaurants, lived in the best arrondissements, and employed four household servants, including a chauffeur who shuttled her around in her fabulously expensive touring car, a Hispano-Suiza.[3] She also was a respected businesswoman—a winning horse owner and trainer well known at Auteuil, Longchamp, and other tracks around Paris. She once had been described as a "fervente des courses, qu'elle suit assidûment." Earlier in 1934, her horse, Jean-Victor, won the Prix du Président du République at Auteuil. "I try to earn enough for my daily needs," Constance once disingenuously told her friend Caresse Crosby.

Like her horses, Constance was a thoroughbred, sprung from generations of upstanding Boston Brahmins—people such as grandfather

Caspar Crowninshield, commander of the 2nd Massachusetts Cavalry during the Civil War; aunt Elizabeth Sprague Coolidge, a great patron of music; the aforementioned Cousin Charlie, who recently had served as secretary of the navy, and Ben and Freddie Bradlee, her contemporary younger cousins.[4] But at some point very early in her long life, Constance Crowninshield Coolidge, born in 1892, the same year as Rebecca West, Djuna Barnes, and Pearl Buck, threw off the bit of her Brahmin background to chase a free and independent life.[5] Along the way, she met a great many movers and shakers, political and intellectual, but she was particularly drawn to writers. Two years before she met HG on the Riviera, she had dined several times with the novelist Robert Herrick, whose intellect she greatly admired.[6] As she told her diary: "He has a very interesting mind. I so seldom see people who have, & I am drawn & afraid! It's like knowing how to swim in a bath tub, & then being suddenly thrown into the sea. My knowledge is the bath tub variety—strictly personal. I have never had much occasion to be intelligent outside!!"[7]

With her considerable charms about her—despite what she told her diary—the youthful, freckled, and upbeat Constance was in town and unattached when Maugham's high-spirited lover invited her to Christmas lunch at the Mauresque. She was, like the baroness, tall, dark, and smiling, but other qualities made her the exact opposite, "explicit where Moura was implicit, slender and fit where Moura was slack," HG wrote in his posthumously published *Postscript*.[8] As HG soon would discover, Constance Crowninshield Coolidge could have written her own *confessio amantis*. In her 1932 diary, she noted that "Lots of people have asked me to marry them, but I suppose that is so with everyone. I can remember 20 quite clearly, but there may have been others. And yet I have never had much confidence in myself or been ever really conceited or in fact thought much about myself at all."[9] By the time she met HG, she had had several dozen lovers, those twenty marriage proposals, and three husbands on as many continents—Ray Atherton, an American diplomat (they were married, after a fashion, from 1910 to 1924); Pierre Chapelle de Jumilhac, a French count (married from 1924 to 1929); and Eliot

Rogers, a California newspaper man (married and divorced in 1930). But then, Constance had got a head start on marriage when she exchanged vows with Atherton soon after her eighteenth birthday. After leaving Ray and China, the scene of his latest posting, she made a new life for herself in Paris, which is where, in 1923, she met the man who became, arguably, the great love of her life—poet-publisher and fellow Boston Brahmin Harry Crosby. Despite her romantic history—the dizzying number of beaus she collected and her reputation for being Europe's leading femme fatale—Constance Coolidge was not simply—or even always—a sexual adventuress. On November 27, 1938, at the age of forty-six, she confessed to her diary: "I'm not so fond of making love any-more. It never did mean very much to me, and yet I have had so many lovers—almost 40, in fact, I think it is 40." Thus, with great looks and a captivating personality, culture, intelligence, a demonstrated taste for risk and adventure, a reputation for being one of high society's loveliest, most fascinating, and funniest women, Constance was also a trophy guest at Maugham's table that Christmas of 1934. Accompanying her was her faithful dog. At the moment Simon was her preferred male com-panion. And so it was that HG and Constance, stars from very different constellations—and floors in society's house—met at Maugham's, shar-ing "a little pig," as Constance reminded HG in a warm and nostalgic let-ter more than a decade later. "I sat next to you. It was sunny and warm then and everyone was happy."[10] From the beginning, as HG wrote in an unpublished portion of his *Postscript*, he liked Constance's simple direct-ness and he found her naïve and experienced and entertaining.

On January 13, a few weeks after that magical meeting, the baroness suddenly left for London to attend to a family matter, she said, and on January 16, the former comtesse, seizing the moment, perhaps, invited HG to the Negresco for dinner. It may have been that Constance wished to explore HG's mind. An avid reader, she had devoured most of his books and, like many other people, considered him one of the greatest intellects of the age. In fact, two years before their first meet-ing, Constance wondered in her diary why HG had never received the Nobel Prize: "He has given more knowledge, more comprehension of the world and science to the general public than any other writer. His 'Outline of History' and now the 'Science of Life' are great and monumental achievements and should be rewarded."[11]

Like the Christmas lunch at Maugham's, the second meeting of Constance Coolidge and H. G. Wells was a great success. The world-renowned writer and the world-class reader "talked of books and immortality and love and what was to be put into life and what was to be got out of it," HG wrote in the *Postscript*, "and come to a point when I should have left the Negresco for my rooms at the Hermitage, I stood up to go and it seemed to be the most natural thing in the world to take her in my arms and kiss her and for her to kiss me back—and after that I did not go for an hour or so. Thereafter for a week we were together for as much as we could be. We just liked being together."[12] HG's 1935 date book corroborates that thought:

Jan. 16	*Dinner Constance Coolidge*
Jan. 17	*Lunch Negresco*
Jan. 19 and 20	*Mas des Roses*
Jan. 21	*Dine CC*
Jan. 22	*Lunch CC*
Jan. 23	*Dinner 8 Negresco*
Jan. 26	*St. Paul de Vence and dinner*
Jan. 28	*CC's car 12:30, lunch Maugham's*
Jan. 30	*7.45 Dine CC*

The attraction could not have been missed by anyone who saw the couple—whether they were cruising along the *corniches* in her magnificent car or dining on bouillabaisse in Nice's old town. Indeed, their affection for each other was so apparent that the Riviera "had a marriage with Constance arranged for me within a week," HG wrote in a suppressed portion of his *Postscript*, adding, "I have always had a delusion that I am an Invisible Man, but the fact is that nowadays I am easily made into news and gossip."[13] "Whatever I do is put in the papers," Constance complained to her diary.[14]

Moura returned to Nice and HG on February 2, and five days later HG shamelessly threw a dinner party at the Sporting Club in Monte Carlo for three of his lovers, Moura, Constance, and "Little e"—Elizabeth von Arnim Russell, a writer who had a *mas* in nearby Mougins. However, on the fourteenth, Moura shuttled off again, this time to Estonia, she said. Once again on their own, HG and Constance hopped into her car and rode in high style to Macon, where they spent the weekend, then drove on to Paris. Three days later, HG flew home to London. Before he left, he told Constance: "I'm in love with you, and who wouldn't be?"[15] Two months later, when Moura accused him of being in love with Constance, HG replied, "Everybody is in love with Constance."[16]

*   *   *

But then, finding himself in love was hardly a novel experience for H. G. Wells. It happened with considerable frequency, perhaps fifty times, perhaps more, and in varying degrees of centigrade over his nearly eighty years, and that isn't counting the minor *passades*—his term for the short romantic episodes or "events." Finding himself in lust was, similarly, a fairly common experience. It has been said that the mature HG averaged three or four new conquests a year.[17] Whatever the number—four or forty—it is no stretch to say that HG had a roving eye and unquenchable lust. Not to sell him short, he also was a romantic at heart, who "fell in love easily, and with great passion," and as a result, enjoyed a hectic love life.[18] Hectic, indeed! Between January 1935 and January 1936, Herbert George Wells, pushing seventy, round, balding, and diabetic, fell head over heels in love—not once, but twice. According to his own account, he managed within those twelve months to juggle at least three affairs on two continents, and, again, that doesn't count those casual *passade* meetings. By anyone's standards, HG was a phenomenon.

From time to time, friends, neighbors, and countrymen commented on HG's robust appetite for amour—both falling into it and making it.

Chief among them was Willie Maugham, who, as we know, saw a great deal of HG and his women from his roost at the Mauresque. Maugham once wrote that his neighbor had "strong sexual instincts and he said to me more than once that the need to satisfy these instincts had nothing to do with love. It was a purely physiological matter."[19] This characterization agrees with something HG later wrote in his *Postscript*:

> To make love periodically, with some grace and pride and freshness, seems to be, for most of us, a necessary condition to efficient working. It admits of no prosaic satisfactions. It is a mental . . . aesthetic quite as much as a physical need. I resent the necessity at times as much as I resent the perpetual recurrence of meal-times and sleep.[20]

Willie Maugham offered many keen observations about his friend over the years. Some of the best of them landed in his book *Mr. Maugham Himself*. In a chapter called "Some Novelists I Have Known," Maugham claimed that although he closely observed the writers he reported on—Arnold Bennett, Henry James, Elizabeth Russell, and H. G. Wells—he was not intimate with any of them. The fault for that, he conceded, was in his own character. "I am either too self-centred, or too diffident, or too reserved, or too shy to be on confidential terms with anyone I know at all well. I prefer to guess at the secrets of their hearts."[21] Maugham also said he was more inclined to be amused by people than to respect them.

For whatever reason, Maugham found in HG much that amused—and fascinated—him. "If humour, as some say, is incompatible with love, then HG was never in love, for he was keenly alive to what was rather absurd in the objects of his unstable affections and sometimes seemed almost to look upon them as creatures of farce."[22] When he delved deeper into HG's psyche, Maugham came up with something that in all likelihood would have stunned HG at least at first: Maugham claimed, and with good reason, that HG was "incapable of the idealization of the desired person which most of us experience when we fall in love."[23] As we shall see, HG felt he was ably equipped to idealize his lovers; the trouble came when those lovers fell short of his expectations. On that point, Maugham observed,

> If [HG's] companion was not intelligent, he soon grew bored with her, and if she was, her intelligence sooner or later palled on him. He did not like his cake unsweetened and if it was sweet it cloyed. He loved his liberty and when he found that a woman wished to restrict it he became exasperated and somewhat ruthlessly broke off the connection. Sometimes this was not so easily done and he had to put up with scenes and recriminations that even he found difficult to treat with levity.[24]

Another old friend, Charlie Chaplin, believed that HG's urge to mate was driven by boredom. In his autobiography, Chaplin explained that this insight came straight from the horse's mouth. "There comes a moment in the day," HG once told Chaplin, "when you have written your pages in the morning, attended to your correspondence in the afternoon, and have nothing further to do. Then comes that hour when you are bored; that's the time for sex."[25] Chaplin also noted that HG, who churned out 1,000 words a day, was one of the most productive writers he had ever met. Chaplin, a promiscuous and productive man himself, did not directly link abundant sex with productively—in himself or in his friend. Along the same lines, in his highly controversial biography of his father, Anthony West wrote about HG's "awkward hour"—the time between five and seven in the evening when he craved—and apparently often got—obliging young women to serve his pleasure, usually *chez lui*. "Platoons" of them, someone else once quipped of the obliging women.

One of the many women who served HG's pleasure, Odette Keun, also observed him—keenly, vociferously, and often in print. Despite her vitriol for having been removed from her lover's bed and heart, Odette had a knack for analyzing HG that rang true to a good many people. She argued, based on a decade of close study, that what motivated the highly energetic, tightly wound Wells, in the boudoir or in general, was a powerful need for renewal. "A novel emotional experience could change his state of mind, release cooped-up energies, give him freshness and vigour, a surge of intellectual curiosity and power, and the hope that at least, after a lot of traveling, he had reached an enchanting oasis."[26] When the oasis dried up, as it always did, HG would embark on another expedition: "There was always an abundance of women who were very eager indeed to participate in his voyage."[27]

In 1930, Odette wrote to Marjorie Craig Wells, HG's daughter-in-law, saying that she and Amber Reeves, one of HG's most passionate young lovers from earlier in the century, had been corresponding with each other because they were both helping HG on a book project. "Great sympathy expressed on both sides, & fervent hopes of meeting soon," Odette reported of the exchange.[28] She went on to say that she also had just spent an afternoon with her predecessor in love, Rebecca West. The three women—two former, one current lover of HG—were entertaining the delicious notion of collaborating "in a detailed, copious, veracious biography of our Great Experience. Poor little thing, [Pidookaki] might at last feel shy."[29] Elsewhere, Odette wisely pointed out that for HG "the game was the thing."

HG had found himself in the game with Miss Reeves twenty-two years earlier, in 1908. At that time, he was genuinely, hopelessly head over heels in love and lust with the brilliant and adventurous student under his tutelage. Beatrice Webb, a once-close Fabian Society friend, later observed that what HG was seeking in *that* particular extramarital romance—although it probably was true of all of his romances—was nothing short of a double life. Nobody's fool, Webb claimed that HG craved stability and respectability: home and hearth, children and wife; a life that gave him an outlet for what she called his "Goethe-like libertine" impulse.[30]

Amber was only one of several caprices HG had with young Fabians, more often than not the daughters of prominent socialists in the Fabian Society, of which he was a charter member. In the *Postscript,* HG conceded that the Fabian meetings had suddenly become "bright and animated gatherings of the young," and that a number of young women "assumed attitudes of discipleship towards" him. Indeed, it was inevitable, he wrote, that some of these friendships would take on a warmer tinge.[31] HG would give Beatrice Webb a great deal of ammunition over the next few years, and she would become one of his most vocal critics.

It is surprising that there were so few complaints from the many objects of HG's affection. Women accepted him, indeed, even embraced him, on his own fast-and-loose free-love terms. Trysts without ties. Passion for the simple pleasure of it, even in the early days of the new century. Even Jane Wells, wife number two, came around to accepting HG's serial dalliances. Although their marriage seemed to function fairly normally in its early years, HG began seeking sexual gratification elsewhere—and well before they celebrated their tenth anniversary—just as he had in the earliest days of his first marriage to his first cousin Isabel Wells. Jane, herself the "other woman" in HG's first marriage, seemed to accept her husband's affairs as a quid pro quo for a stable household and a good life for herself and their children. Even after it became obvious that she and HG were not emotionally or sexually suited to each other, they stayed together and they maintained a strong partnership throughout their thirty-two-year marriage. Indeed, Jane's central role in HG's life—her hold over him—was powerful, even extremely irritating to some of her husband's lovers. Rebecca West, for one, detested HG's unwavering concern for his wife. To Rebecca, Jane was a conniver who hid behind her respectability, who secretly enjoyed Rebecca's trials, and who always held a better hand because HG made no major decisions without seeking her counsel.[32]

Still, for the legions of women who did succumb to his charms, HG remained a good and gracious friend. As one of his biographers wrote:

> Whether the affair was a "passade," to use [HG's] word for brief encounters, or lasted a decade, the woman in question knew that he was her friend, her supporter, that she was his equal, and that she could rely on him for support, for aid if necessary, and for companionship once the relationship was over. Wells practised what he preached—sexual equality within the biological differences mandated by our genes.[33]

There were two notable exceptions to the rule that HG and his lovers remained close friends: Miss West and Miss Keun; but, like Odette, Rebecca left contradictory opinions about HG. At one point, she thought him insane, possessed, like Tolstoy, of an "anti-sex complex" that made him punish the female who evoked his lust.[34] She also wrote that the women who left HG "all felt enduring affection for him and were his domestic friends in his old age," even though the end of her relationship with HG was anything but affectionate.[35] The same was true of the split up between Odette and HG. The grim details follow in the next chapter.

★   ★   ★

Despite the importance—perhaps even centrality—of love, lovemaking, and sex in HG's life, most modern Wells biographers have danced around or skipped over his sexual-romantic life. Perhaps they shared a simple distaste for writing about the subject. Perhaps they were dubious about its relevance or in denial over the disturbing details. David Smith framed this question:

> Wells was perhaps the best known socialist in the world for much of the twentieth century, an advocate of equality of education for all according to their talents, and a gifted author who provided his readers glimpses and vistas into a world set free—free of the dominance of upper-class rules, free of hidebound and narrow education, and above all, free from irrational nationalism with its pride in killing, in slaughter, bullying tactics, and oppression. How could a man with this reputation go through life bedding women other than his wife, sireing children out of wedlock, living in "sin," and still justify the reputation?[36]

Still, some biographers *have* tried to explain HG's sexual drive, promiscuity, and serial love affairs, among them Norman and Jeanne MacKenzie. In the beginning, the MacKenzies, who adopted most of Odette Keun's views, gave HG the benefit of the doubt: They argued

that for him, sex was a powerful pain-reliever for despair. In their scenario, HG tended to overwork. He became depressed as a result, and ultimately broke down in rage or in tears. The release of emotion that this
process produced, these biographers contended, "passed into lovemaking," which was followed by a sound sleep. HG would arise the next
morning and resume writing with "fresh enthusiasm."[37] The MacKenzies also argued that in marriage, HG was torn between having strong
sexual instincts and being rid of them; in fact, he spent much of his adult
life trying to escape the "corruption of the physical appetite he so rapa-
ciously indulged."[38] HG believed that he could find salvation in moral
and domestic order, but his domestic claustrophobia caused him to look
outside marriage for a woman who could satisfy his emotional needs.
Once found, however, the ideal always developed feet of clay.

The revelations in the *Postscript* shocked—even scandalized—the
MacKenzies; HG would never again enjoy the benefit of the doubt from
them. In their revised edition of *Life*, they let HG have it with far worse
names than his self-deprecating self-moniker, Don Juan of the Intelligentsia. Now he was the memorable "philandering sybarite," known for
his "unremitting sexual peccadilloes" and his "innate irresponsibility."
The "streak of puritan self-righteousness in his nature"—inherited from
his mother—combined with a conviction that the survival of the species
depended on him, may have been what allowed him to shed the "less
cosmic responsibilities" in his life.[39]

One of the standard ways HG shrugged off those minor responsibilities was to claim that it was the woman who initiated the affair. For example, in the *Postscript*, HG wrote, with a splash of humor to be sure,
about Amber Reeves: "She fell in love with me with great vigour and
determination, and stirred me to a storm of responsive passion." She
also demanded that he give her a child. Even Amber's mother bore
some responsibility for the affair. She "encouraged the development of
a very intimate friendship between us."[40] Other examples:

Elizabeth von Arnim: "She had already called upon us at Sandgate when
she had been passing through Folkestone and had liked me; she heard

talk of my scandalous life, and it seemed to her that I was eminently fit-ted to correct a certain deficiency in her own."[41]

Rebecca West: Following a sudden mutual kiss, she "flamed up into open and declared passion. She demanded to be my lover and made an accusation of my kiss."[42]

Frau Hedy Verena Gatternigg: "She passed rather suddenly and skill-fully from an intelligent appreciation of my educational views to pas-sionate declarations. . . . I hate to snub an exile in distress, and she was an extremely appetizing young woman. . . . She wanted me; she plied me with love-letters and professed an unendurable passion. . . . 'This must end,' said I, 'this must end'—allowing myself to be dragged up-stairs."[43]

Odette Keun: "She had instructed the hotel people to send me up to her room, and I found myself in a dimly lit apartment with a dark slen-der young woman in a flimsy wrap and an aroma of jasmine. She flung herself upon me with protests of adoration. I was all she had to live for. She wanted to give her whole life to me. She wanted nothing but to be of service to me. 'If you feel like *that*,' said I."[44]

Constance Coolidge: "A day after [Moura left Nice], I had a note from an American widow who owned race-horses and whom I had met at lunch at Maugham's. . . . she asked me in a schoolgirl handwriting to come to dinner with her at the Negresco."[45]

According to the MacKenzies, this pattern was typical of the per-sonal irresponsibility that permeated all aspects of HG's life. All this, all these unattractive qualities, stemmed from HG's upbringing, the MacKenzies and other biographers have argued. Every member of the Wells household was frustrated and dissatisfied with life and with each other, and this "general state of domestic paranoia left enduring marks on Wells in the form of a pettish willfulness, the lack of any stable frame for his attitudes and conduct, and a carelessness for his effect on his wives, his mistresses, his publishers, political associates and friends," the MacKenzies concluded.[46] They also argued that HG probably knew that he had squandered his energies on the pursuit of women. Most of his writings, based as they were on a thinly disguised version of himself, suggest that uncontrolled sexual passion can distract a man, even ruin him.

Meanwhile, one of Maugham's biographers maintained that HG was a victim of "the paradox of the polygamist." His search for passion in a series of infidelities "led him to devalue and discard the women he possessed."[47] According to the biographer, HG once confided to Maugham that "women often mistake possessiveness for passion, and when they are left, it is not so much that their heart is broken as that their claim to property is repudiated."[48]

Many recent studies also lock onto HG's childhood as the source of his lifelong preoccupation with women, sex, and love. One writer, for example, argued that HG's womanizing was driven by gender confusion, the result of a miserable relationship with his overcontrolling mother and absentee father. Another writer, a feminist critic, theorized that HG's loveless childhood had rendered him incapable of intimacy. Noting that an imposter theme runs throughout HG's writings, this writer also argued that HG's sense of his own fraudulence—a product of his guilt for having risen so far above his parents—drove him compulsively to prove himself over and over again, and then to reject the evidence of his adequacy.[49] Sharing Beatrice Webb's position, another writer, Patricia Stubbs, argued that HG's self-described domestic claustrophobia drove him to lead a double life: one moment at home with his family, the next, across town, the country, or the continent with his mistress. In his personal life, he exploited his women, wives and mistresses alike. "It is very important to see HG's proselytizing in the cause of freer sexual relations for women in the light of these adventures."[50]

British writer Robin Lockhart was never much charmed by H. G. Wells; that is abundantly clear. The son of Bruce Lockhart, Moura Budberg's great love following the Russian Revolution, Robin claimed that

"Although Wells appealed to women, there was hardly a man who had a good word to say for him; he was thoroughly conceited, bombastic on political matters of which he knew nothing. Nor was there an English writer who had a good word to say for him either as a human being or as a writer except for one or two famous books written in the last century. There was one exception: Arnold Bennett respected him. I met [Wells] once and took an instant dislike to him."[51]

Maugham thought differently, as previously mentioned; indeed, he found much to like in his fellow writer, and the feelings were mutual. In January 1935, HG told Christabel that he was growing fonder of Willie. "He's a very human creature really." In Maugham's opinion, HG was self-centered, like most creative types, but he was devoid of conceit, and he had no illusions about himself as an author. Furthermore, HG was sharp-witted and had a lively sense of humor and, according to Maugham, could laugh at himself. Also to his credit, HG's humor was without malice. In addition to all those sterling qualities, HG was a splendid houseguest! In a long, humorous piece on houseguests, Maugham ranked HG right up at the top—far, far ahead of the guests who burned holes in the sheets, brought three weeks' worth of laundry with them to have washed at his expense, and took all they could get but gave nothing in return.

> There are also the guests who are happy just to be with you, who seek to please, who have resources of their own, who amuse you, whose conversation is delightful, whose interests are varied, who exhilarate and excite you, who in short give you far more than you can ever hope to give them and whose visits are only too brief. Such a guest was HG. He had a social sense.[52]

The one thing about HG that surprised Maugham was his sex appeal, since, to Maugham, HG was not particularly attractive. In fact, Maugham described his friend as fat and homely. So what did this fat and homely, short and stocky man with the peculiarly high-pitched voice have in the way of sex appeal? Not having a clue, Maugham once asked

Moura what had attracted her to HG. Instead of saying that it was his acute mind and his sense of fun, she said in vintage Mouresque that his body "smelt of honey."[53] Lance Sieveking, a programming director at the BBC who became a good friend of HG's, once said that it was quite easy to understand why women were attracted to him, why they loved him: His *mind* smelled of honey. One begins to think that HG *did have* an appealing natural fragrance. Rebecca West once wrote that HG's body smelled like walnuts. For historian and H. G. Wells biographer Michael Foot, it was neither honey nor walnuts that attracted the women. Foot suggested that HG's major draw was his "happy, guileless, infectious gift of high spirits" and his "radiant hopefulness." While his physical attraction wasn't obvious, "women fell in love with him easily, and even those who didn't could find themselves captivated."[54]

Many other people have offered their ideas about what made HG so appealing; they suggested everything from his joie de vivre to his honesty. J. B. Priestley, a writer known for his shrewd characterizations, belonged to the second school. He once said that HG was one of the most honest and frankest human beings who ever existed. Lady Cynthia Asquith, meanwhile, testified that she was drawn to HG's baby blues. All of his intelligence, she said, was in his eyes, which sparkled with mischief and interest, making him look like an exuberant and greedy schoolboy, for whom no day could be "long enough for all he wanted to cram into it."[55] Otherwise, HG did not have a particularly noticeable face, and his voice, she said, was like "a pencil on slate." Sieveking also said that, despite HG's short and stout physique, his sloping shoulders, large head with sparse hair, a straggling mustache and that famously squeaky voice, HG had beautiful eyes and mouth, and when he smiled, he radiated "vitality and a warmth of human kindliness that immediately infected everyone."[56]

Rebecca West once recalled that HG's rays of happiness "came and went several times a day. He'd frisk about like an animal, indeed, he had the moves of an animal—a very nice animal." She also conceded that it was hard to say why HG "with no personal advantage but a bright eye made everyone else in the room seem a dull dog. His company was like seeing Nureyev dance or Tito Gobbi sing."[57] She also effused—and Foot later repeated—that HG had "the most bubbling creative mind that the sun and moon have shone upon since the days of Leonardo da Vinci." Still, he simply wasn't adapted to having love affairs or being married, "although he made, God knows, enough tries."[58]

Regardless of what interpretation—or set of interpretations—one chooses to explain HG's animal magnetism and romantic-sexual behavior, the bottom line, as biographer David Smith points out, is that to know the complex Mr. Wells, "one must also at least attempt to know his life in the world of fiction and his life in love."[59]

★   ★   ★

Ostensibly, that was HG's intention in writing the *Postscript:* He wanted to understand—and to share, of course—his formidable life in love. The best way to do that was to analyze the pants off of it, so to speak. Ever the biologist, HG tended to use the verb "dissect" to describe his impulse to inspect and introspect his life. He even kept the laboratory metaphor running throughout his personal writings and often referred to himself as his own rabbit and his own toad. In his first autobiography, the *Experiment in Autobiography,* HG first dissected his brain to convey "some idea of the quality and defects of the grey matter of that organized mass of phosphorized fat and connective tissue."[60] He then did the same to his persona, which he described rather unsatisfactorily as the vanity that dominated his brain's imaginations.

The main theme of the *Experiment,* then, was his mental system— the expansion of the interests and activities of his brain. The second theme was his sexual system.[61] "I suspect," HG wrote, "the sexual system should be at least the second theme, when it is not the first, in every autobiography, honestly and fully told."[62] HG claimed, perhaps disingenuously, that his brain, like his libido, was nothing special. "If there were brain-shows, as there are cat and dog shows, I doubt if it would get even a third class prize. Upon quite a number of points it would be marked below the average."[63] Critics called him on his claim of having a room-temperature brain, saying that he was insincere, guilty of a reverse arrogance. They were, HG noted, inclined to over-rate his "quality." Still, it is doubtful that a mediocre brain could have dreamed up as complex a concept as the Lover-Shadow, or have used it to better effect, than did HG. And yet, he argued that this abstract fac-tor was present in every normal brain. In the Preface to this book, I de-fined Lover-Shadow simply as HG's "complete female counterpart, his intellectual-emotional-sexual equal." HG defined and redefined the concept dozens of times. The Lover-Shadow was a "subtle complex of expectation and hope," sexual in origin and then later, social. It was al-most as essential to our lives as our self consciousness. "It is *other* con-sciousness." He also wrote that when people make love, they are trying to make another human being concentrate for them as an imperson-ation or a symbol of the Lover-Shadow in their minds. When we are in love, "we have found in someone the presentation or the promise of some, at least, of the main qualities of our Lover-Shadow."[64]

In the closing pages of his *Anatomy of Frustration*, where he deposited dozens of pages originally written for the *Postscript*, but then retrofit them, HG aired his protagonist's statement about the Lover-Shadow— for all intents and purposes his own. He wanted

a Personal, Intimate, Subservient, Devoted, Private Divinity, a genius like the genius of Socrates, a confidant who will not know what I want to conceal but will know whatever I want to have known. And somehow this has got to be embodied in an attractive, variable, interesting woman who will respond to my desire. I have never wanted a pet of a woman or an exhibitionist Venus to worship. I am no sort of impresario lover. I have wanted a strong, quietly animated goddess-slave. Or a strong, qui-etly animated slave-goddess. Mother-mate not mistress. With some mis-tress thrown in. Preposterous—yes. But this is how I am made. This is what I find I want when I go down into myself.

I want love that will glow through my being from the smallest thrill of sense to the utmost mental exaltation. And I want it *with* my lover and my lovers and through my love. I do not want to pass into an abstract sublimation and leave smell and sight and touch behind. I do not want to float up into the sky; I want the two of us to grow up to the sky with our bare toes still pressing firmly and happily into sunlit soil.[65]

In HG's paradigm, the *persona* and the Lover-Shadow were the main elements of the human psyche—the hero and heroine of our private dramas. Other complex systems move across the stage and act out their small roles, he said, but they are essentially "subordinate."

HG intellectualized the Lover-Shadow ad nauseam; he also spent a great deal of time and effort over his long life trying to "concentrate" or "embody" his Lover-Shadow in a string of women. While claiming to have a normal brain, he admitted that it behaved differently where the Lover-Shadow was concerned. In a section of the *Postscript* aptly titled "Psychological and Parental," HG argued that there was no separation of psychological and physical in *his* personal make-up; all the love affairs in his life, therefore, were attempts to embody and concentrate the Lover-Shadow. Not every brain was as likely as his to concentrate the Lover-Shadow, and not everyone linked the Lover-Shadow "as closely to a sexual relationship as I have done. Since I am very much a body as well as a mind, all these love affairs have sought a physical expression."[66]

In the *Postscript,* HG described this complex original notion in original and often complex ways. Thus, the Lover-Shadow could be "a very grave and lively complex of desire," "elusive dream-stuff," or "a lovely, wise and generous person wholly devoted to me. Her embraces were to be my sure fastness, my ultimate reassurance, the culmination of my realization of myself."[67] Perhaps his Lover-Shadow could be viewed as his better half, the authentic half that made him whole. Perhaps it was a bogus construction, as suggested in the Preface, a complex concept HG created to deflect attention away from his rapacious sexual appetite.

Not surprisingly, HG's obsession with the Lover-Shadow has been understood in a great many ways. Feminist critic Nancy Steffen-Fluhr conceded that HG was grasping for "an important psychological insight," but that it was "just beyond his field of vision." She also suggested that HG was linking his desire for intimacy with another person and his more inchoate desire for intimacy with the estranged parts of his own personality.[68] In his treatment of the subject, David Smith tried to imagine the experience of finding one's Lover-Shadow:

> Together, the soul-mates would have transcended the biological imperative, the drag of time and custom, and even the pursuit of power for power's sake, to live in complete harmony. Wells did not find such a person (one is tempted to add, "of course"). . . . In any case Wells sought through much of his life for such relationships, came much closer than most to finding them, and wrote of them in his fiction about the real and the ideal in the world of human love and passion.[69]

Others have understood the Lover-Shadow as HG's ideal woman, or simply his sexual-emotional fantasy. Whether it was the more complex definition or the less can be endlessly debated. What is not debatable, though, is HG's statement in the *Postscript*, made after all of the women, all of the love affairs: "The fundamental love of my life is the Lover-Shadow, and always I have been catching a glimpse of her and losing her in these adventures."[70]

In the *Experiment*, HG seemed to dissect every conceivable aspect of his human experience, including the full story of his two marriages, with all their hopes and expectations, twists and turns, ups and downs. In the *Postscript*, HG promised to update the various activities of his Lover-Shadow. He promised to carve up the remaining love relationships, slide them under the microscope, and write up the lab reports. "I want [my children] to know all about me," he explained in the *Postscript*. As his note made clear, the *Postscript*, which was to be published after his death, expressed "not the main strand of my life but the sexual, domestic and intimate life sustaining it."[71] As he put it in some pages that were later suppressed from the *Postscript*, left out of publication in folders marked "rejected" and "deleted," HG wrote: "Let me, to make sure that no one misses my point, repeat that this *Postscript* is not full autobiography; it is autobiography strictly below the belt."[72] HG's plan was to package the *Experiment* and the *Postscript* together, along with his preface to *The Book of Catherine Wells*, the volume of his late wife's writings that he published in 1928. He was offering a literary one-stop-shopping trip into his life, his being, at least from 1866 to 1934, so all the "main masses" of his experiences would "fall into proportion." As we know, HG's heirs did not package the *Postscript* according to HG's orders.[73]

In the opening pages of his *Experiment in Autobiography*, H. G. Wells wrote that he put everything else aside and began the book because his thoughts and work were "encumbered by claims and vexations" from which he could not see any hope of escaping. At the end of the book, he reminded the reader that he had begun the autobiography to reassure himself during a period of fatigue, restlessness, and vexation, and that he believed he had achieved his goal.

> I wrote myself out of that mood of discontent and forgot myself and a mosquito swarm of bothers in writing about my sustaining ideas. My ruffled *persona* has been restored and the statement of the idea of the modern world-state has reduced my personal and passing irritations and distractions to their proper insignificance. So long as one lives as an individual, vanities, lassitudes, lapses, and inconsistencies will hover about and creep back into the picture, but I find nevertheless that this faith and service of constructive world revolution does hold together my mind and will in a prevailing unity, that it makes life continually worth living, transcends and minimizes all momentary and incidental frustrations and takes the sting out of the thought of death.[74]

Fifty years later, HG's son Gip would claim that his father did in fact achieve re-integration after writing the *Experiment*, "partly by proclaiming the service of a future world-state as the central purpose of his life and partly by falling (or throwing himself) head over heels in love with Moura Budberg, and persuading himself that she would make him a brilliant wife and give him the support he so badly needed."[75] But

Moura foiled HG's hope for a happy life ever after; she had no interest in marrying him, and the chance discovery he made about her in July 1934—the previously mentioned Moscow deception/Moscow crisis—destroyed all hope he had for realizing his Lover-Shadow in the form of Moura Budberg. Gip claimed that his father's "shock of disillusion" was followed by a deep and nearly suicidal depression. "Slowly he worked himself out of it. The self-analysis involved in the writing of the *Postscript*," Gip argued so wisely, "which he then undertook, played a major part in his recovery."[76]

Thus, although HG's stated purposes in writing the *Postscript* was to ensure that his children would know all about him, and also to make certain that he would have a safeguard against being misrepresented posthumously, "which I have had considerable reason to fear," it was also a therapeutic exercise, just as the *Experiment* had been. His "suicidal mood," he wrote, began in July 1934, after he caught Moura, the woman he yearned to marry, in a series of strange lies about her connections with Russia. She couldn't accompany him to Russia that summer, she protested, because it would be extremely dangerous, if not fatal, for her to do so.

Ever since coming out of Russia in 1921, Moura had insisted that she was a persona non grata there, and that if she ever dared return, she would risk great bodily harm, if not prison and death. Russia was a "barred country to her" due to her various but unspecified troubles with the authorities. A host of complex and contradictory stories circulated, and continue to circulate, about Moura's activities in Russia, including the claim that she was a spy for Russia. Although Moura used her checkered past as a compelling reason to refuse to accompany HG to Russia the summer of 1934 to meet Gorky and Stalin, she had in fact just been there. As HG explained in the *Postscript,* when he was in Moscow, he learned by chance that Moura had preceded him there by a week—stayed at Gorky's, in fact, but then had "skedaddled" back to Estonia. HG's Russian guide and interpreter were the inadvertent bearers of these ill tidings.[77] He also learned that Moura had been to Moscow three times within the past year, whereas she had led him to believe that she had not been back for more than ten years. This news came by way of Gorky, soon after the first bombshell. HG was stunned not only by Moura's deceit but also by her indifference to his well-being. "She could have been with me in private; she could have been beside me to discuss my impressions; she could have made love in Russia once more," he wrote in the *Postscript*.[78] Worse than that was the jealousy, the fear that Moura was rekindling her affair with Gorky, her former lover and employer. Even if the relationship was Platonic, as Moura protested it was, her relations with Gorky, HG wrote, "were of a nature so intimate and sentimental that she could not be with us together, in the same place. . . . Someone had to be sacrificed."[79] When HG confronted Moura about his discovery, she denied having been in Russia, then later admitted it but dismissed the event as an innocent, hastily arranged trip to see her homeland—and her old, ailing patron—one last time. Moura stuck to her story "stoutly," HG wrote, adding that nothing she said lessened his distrust of her after the Moscow deception. They would have, he wrote, "the canker of this trouble" between them.

On August 3, 1934, at Kallijärv, Moura's lake home in Estonia, not far from today's Tallinn, HG wrote to Christabel about his crisis. He said he had discovered something in Moscow that meant either that Moura had been "humbugging" him in a quite intolerable way or that Gorky was a liar. "It is queer how in a phase of jealousy one can believe anyone rather than the person one loves. Jealousy dear Christabel is the most malignant of fevers. In jealousy there is no rest, no peace, no human dignity. After sixty, one should be immune." In her previously suppressed letter of the same day, Christabel replied: "There's something all wrong in that picture—[Moura's] not like that. Is it not possible you have misinterpreted the situation? And, [if] there has been something, couldn't you forgive it?" Apparently he couldn't entirely, for in the *Postscript* HG wrote: "In an evening my splendid Moura was smashed to atoms." There is no doubt that the Moscow incident seriously wounded HG.

> There it lies between us. Everything about Moscow rests unexplained. Did she go thrice or once? I do not know. I begin to feel it does not mat-

ter. But the Moura who was never really there has vanished now for ever and nothing in earth or heaven can bring her back. We were lovers as the word goes, and intimate associates. We could still laugh and talk about a thousand things. But we were consciously apart from each other. We were sitting back to look at each other.[80]

The discovery and its aftermath changed the relationship between HG and Moura. It also motivated HG's liaison with Constance Coolidge five months later on the French Riviera, and with another young American woman, Martha Gellhorn, a few months after that in Washington. In typical style, HG blamed Moura for *his* unfaithfulness: "She had made it possible for me to be unfaithful to her," he wrote in the *Postscript,* and "to slip back to promiscuity."

HG put a great deal of energy into his *Postscript,* which had the potential of exorcising his jealous demons and sense of betrayal. He fussed over his personal love history, writing and rewriting it intermittently over a period of eight years—and in his tiny, often illegible handwriting, to what must have been the horror of his secretary and daughter-in-law, Marjorie Wells, who typed his manuscripts.[81] Gip and Marjorie Wells, Gip's wife and longtime personal secretary to HG, edited and titled the manuscript and published it fifty years after HG began it. The dust jacket touted the book as an "extraordinary publishing event," not only for its combustible subject matter—"the romantic and sexual affairs of a world-famous writer"—but also for its "self-revelation and astounding candor."

Soon after HG's *Confessio Amantis* was released, reviewers and biographers began cranking out a river of reviews. Their reactions to HG's candor and behavior were all over the map: He was both reviled and praised for his most recent work. Some described the *Postscript* as a deft bit of gossip that used psychological catchphrases but was devoid of self-insight or understanding; others saw it as the standard by which such works, in the future, should be judged.[82] The historian Michael Foot believed that the *Experiment* and the *Postscript* taken together "constitute the bravest autobiography of the century." The *Experiment* alone was "one of the greatest literary autobiographies ever written."[83] With it, HG lead the way to the fullest, freest discussion of sexual questions.

As previously mentioned, by the time the *Postscript* was published, a good deal of its revelation and candor had been chucked. Gip cut out portions of narrative that he thought might cause trouble if published, and he removed the names of his father's last lovers, Constance and Martha, replacing them with asterisks and pronouns. He also cut out long portions of narrative about them, although only Martha was still alive when the book was released. Thus, in the section where HG left explicit publishing instructions, Gip edited the published version to read that the memoir should go to press "when ***** and Moura and Dusa are either dead or consenting—for Odette does not matter a rap; Rebecca, bless her, is fully able to take care of herself; ***** won't mind, and nobody else has any justification for complaint."[84] In the original manuscript pages, HG actually wrote: "A few years after my death, when Constance Coolidge and Moura and Dusa are either dead or consenting—for Odette does not matter a rap, Rebecca, bless her, is fully able to take care of herself, the Hemingways won't mind, and nobody else has any justification for complaint." In another version he wrote: "When Elizabeth von Arnim, the dowager Countess Russell, is dead and Constance Coolidge and Moura and Dusa and Martha Gellhorn are either dead or consenting."[85]

As mentioned, HG too had jettisoned large pieces of narrative from the *Postscript*. These he bundled into a separate folder for omission. He later cannibalized a large part of that omitted text, most of it having to do with his conception of the Lover-Shadow, and put it into *The Anatomy of Frustration*. The leftovers were never used anywhere because either they referred to women in his *Postscript*—Constance Martha Gellhorn, and Moura—and thus didn't suit *The Anatomy,* or they referred to the *Postscript* or to the *Experiment,* and similarly didn't fit into *The Anatomy's* conceit: a discursive modern synthesis of current life, based on Robert Burton's *Anatomy of Melancholy.*[86] HG's *Anatomy,* supposedly the work of one William Burroughs Steele, "an observant watcher of the world," has been described as HG's interview with himself. It is an apt description. One can easily see how he attributed his ideas to Steele simply by putting quotation marks around them and changing the voice from the first person of the *Postscript* to the third person—"Mr. Steele"—of the *Anatomy*.

★   ★   ★

Some of HG's major liaisons have been documented over the years, and some have been explored in depth. A fair amount has been written about his unconventional marriages to his cousin Isabel Mary Wells, whom he married in 1891 and divorced in 1895 (although he left her in 1893) and to Jane (née Amy Catherine Robbins), whom he married in 1895 and who died in 1927; his passionate, scandalous extramarital affairs with his student Amber Reeves ("Dusa"), beginning in 1907, and with whom he had a daughter, Annajane, (outside of marriage) in 1909; and with Rebecca West, from 1913 to 1923, with whom he had a son, Anthony, (outside of marriage) in 1914. Also discussed *en passant* are his long-term and troubled relationships with Odette Keun (1924–1933), and Moura Budberg (from 1932 until HG's death in 1946)—"the very human," as he described her in his *Postscript*. HG's liaisons with writers Dorothy Richardson and Elizabeth von Arnim Russell ("Little e"), among others, also have been investigated, but there is nothing, owing to the suppression of love letters and text from the *Postscript* manuscript, about HG's last affairs, short, long, real, or, as Martha Gellhorn maintained, imagined.[87] In a series of heated (and suppressed) letters to Gip before publication of the *Postscript,* Martha wrote this about HG: "I was very fond of him, but the rest is rubbish. He used me to annoy Moura and maybe came to believe his version. There was nothing between us but friendship."[88] Still, Martha frequently signed her letters to HG with the name "Stooge."

During her lifetime, Odette Keun often had the last word. She'll get it here as well. Reviewing HG's just-released *Experiment,* Odette observed that when a "really objective" biography of HG was written, "instead of the enormous reel of self-justification which he is still producing, where his very cunning art of feinting, his very subtle trick of inaccuracy in confession, have again succeeded in blinding his audience to the nature of his play, it will be discovered that he has wounded and injured often beyond cure."[89]

What had happened to the Don Juan of the Western World? How had "Mr. Right" become "Mr. Wrong?" How had HG come to be both revered and reviled by those who knew him best? Whether adored, despised, tolerated, sought, ignored, or loved, he was not going gently into that good night. HG would put up a fight. But where was the peace that was to come with maturity? Where was the serenity? How did HG, approaching seventy, get to this rocky place in his emotional-romantic life?

2

The Anatomy of Frustration: HG's Birth and Rebirths[1]

Bless you. You are all wrong about my character. Never was there so natu-
rally a stable & domesticated man as me. Home life, the cat, the kettle, slip-
pers, the double bed.

—HG to Christabel, April 8, 1935

Herbert George Wells, the future visionary, historian, and social critic, was born in 1866 in a place called Atlas House. Despite its name, Atlas House was no one's source of strength or pride; it was, rather, a dark and dreary crockery shop and residence, a "shabby home," HG wrote, in the small town of Bromley in Kent. A lamp in the shop window gave the wretched establishment its ironic name. "Little Bertie," later to be called HG, was the fourth and last child delivered to Sarah and Joseph Wells. Four years younger than his nearest brother, HG spent most of his solitary boyhood playing in the brick yard, the scullery, and the underground kitchen behind and below his parents' shop at 47 High Street. The boys' bedroom was on the third floor, but, like the rest of the house, it was overrun with neglected crockery—and with bugs, which, HG reported, lived in the bed frames and between the layers of wallpaper. "Slain they avenge themselves by a peculiar penetrating dis-

33

agreeable smell. That mingles in my early recollections with the more pervasive odour of paraffin, with which my father carried on an inconclusive war against them. Almost every part of my home had its own distinctive smell."[2] These roots, downstairs and underground, humble, grim, and unnourishing, both attracted and repelled the young HG. They always would. Indeed, throughout his life, he would do battle with his ambivalence toward his inferior upbringing.

He was especially ambivalent about his parents. At the time of his wedding in 1853, Joe Wells, HG's father-to-be, was an unemployed estate gardener, last in service at Up Park, the Fetherstonhaugh family estate in Petersfield. Sarah Neal, his future bride and HG's future mother, was a lady's maid at the same estate. They may have met in the servants' hall, HG conjectured, at one of the weekly candlelight dances, which were brightenend by concertina and fiddle. Sarah, a product of Miss Riley's finishing school in Chichester, was religious, rigid, and driven by her hard hopes for respectability. HG later wrote that his mother's instinct for appearances, despite the realities, was formidable:

> She believed that it was a secret to all the world that she had no servant and did all the household drudgery herself. I was enjoined never to answer questions about that or let it out when I went abroad. Nor was I to take my coat off carelessly, because my underclothing was never quite up to the promise of my exterior garments.[3]

Like the bugs and the paraffin, Miss Riley's left a strong flavor of "early feminism" on Sarah's mind. The "stir of emancipation" connected with Victoria's successful claim to the throne also contributed to Sarah's feminist sensibilities, HG claimed; his mother followed Victoria's life with "passionate loyalty." The queen was, in fact, Sarah's "compensatory personality, her imaginative consolation for all the restrictions and hardships that her sex, her diminutive size, her motherhood and all the endless difficulties of life, imposed upon her."[4] HG acknowledged having his own gene for "imaginative consolation," and it probably came from his mother. Sarah's fixation on the royal family, which resulted in many trips to crowded street corners fed HG's hostility to things royal and wove a sturdy "thread of republicanism" into his self-described "resentful nature."[5]

Joe Wells, meanwhile, had little interest either in appearances or in royalty. His enthusiasm even for gardening began withering on the vine early in his career. HG claimed that he never understood why his father was so unsuccessful as a gardener, but he suspected that the failure was due to "a certain intractability of temper rather than incapacity." Joe didn't like to be ordered around and was impatient. As a young man and son of the head gardener at Penshurst Place in Kent, Joe Wells had hired on as gardener to an elderly gentleman, Mr. Joseph Wells—no relation—of Redleaf. Old Wells had encouraged erudition in Young Wells, and had ratcheted up Joe's hopes and ambitions. When his mentor died, Joe Wells felt he had been robbed of his rightful start in life, and this disappointment colored the rest of his life. Notions of gold mining in Australia and emigration to the United States also bedeviled Joe at this time, and again later, indeed whenever he felt most desperate. Why his parents had married each other was also a great mystery to HG, since they seemed to have nothing in common.[6] After the wedding, Joe found a job as sous-gardener, and for a time HG's parents lived together intermittently. Some months later, Joe got a position and a cottage at Shuckburgh Park in the Midlands, but he was dismissed from service fifteen months later. Joe and Sarah were now the parents of one child and another was on the way; because the couple enjoyed few resources, the ouster threw the growing family into a tailspin, the first of many.

When the opportunity to buy a cousin's china and crockery shop in Kent presented itself in October 1855, the Wellses jumped at it, throwing all their capital into the rundown business, which they saw as their route to respectability and the middle class. But within days, Sarah knew they had made a terrible mistake. Joe soon proved to be useless—both around the house and the shop. Because he had been brought up in a country home where the women saw to all the indoor work, Joe had, as his son later explained, no imagination or sympathy for women's work, a deficiency HG too would later display in his various households. Thus, Joe lived "from the shop outward," HG wrote, and had without a doubt the very best of things. This laissez-faire philosophy allowed Joe to pursue his real passion, cricket. For several years, he was good enough to play professionally and to bring in a small supplementary income from the sport. He even stocked his china shop with cricket paraphernalia, and, ironically, those items probably kept the establishment afloat, just as they drew in local chaps to gab about the sport and pass the day with Joe.

While Joe was amusing himself, Sarah Wells was holding the expanding household together. In a sense, she was the real Atlas of the house: an unhappy and overworked little woman doing battle day in, day out, to keep the dismal home clean, to keep her children clean, clothed, fed, and educated; in sum, to keep up the appearance of a functioning household. Sarah was a Low Church Christian, serious and seriously religious; but her faith and her heart broke two years before HG was born when her only daughter died from acute appendicitis. She wasn't a brilliant mother, HG later conceded. Indeed, sometimes she failed her children through ignorance and inflexibility, yet no one could deny the "grit and devotion of her mothering." HG credited his mother with teaching him the rudiments of education. It has been argued that she also helped make little Bertie a socialist.

Limping along at Atlas House, the Wells family would suffer many setbacks before they were completely knocked down and out. Disaster struck in October 1877, when, as the story goes, Joe fell and broke his leg while pruning some grapevines. Another version of the story was less charitable. Rumor had it that Joe was attending Sunday morning worship service with a neighbor lady while the rest of his family was at church. When Sarah returned home early from services, Joe tried to escape down a ladder, but fell in the process. Before the year was out it was clear that the compound fracture, however received, would leave Joe lame for life; this meant that his supplemental income from cricket would also be lost. HG noted that his father's accident resulted in "a growing tendency for potatoes to dominate the hash or stew at midday in place of meat," but malnutrition would hound HG throughout his youth and most of his young adulthood. As it happened, Joe's fall hastened the nearly inevitable dissolution of the home. HG admitted that he knew little about his father. He described Joe as an unsuccessful "stuck man" who had a cheerful disposition and who spent most of his energy running away from disagreeable realizations. "He had a kind of attractiveness for women, I think he was aware of it, but I do not know whether he ever went further along the line of unfaithfulness than a light flirtation—in Bromley at any rate."[7] Beneath Joe's easygoing exterior lurked a deep-seated anger that released itself in sudden and irrational outbursts.

In 1880, the heavens opened, HG reported, and a great light shone on his mother: She was rehired at Up Park, this time to serve as housekeeper. Had she not been taken back into service, HG's life would have turned out altogether differently: He surely would not have had the resources to escape his brothers' fate as bound apprentices in the drapery trade. To be sure, Sarah's ascendance was something of a miracle, for apart from her absolute honesty, she was a terrible housekeeper, perhaps the worst housekeeper ever, HG conceded.

Sarah returned to Up Park, suitably named for her personal aspirations, while Joe stayed behind at the shop. Her income gave the family the extra cash it had never had before. It allowed her not only to buy indentures—apprenticeships—for HG and his brothers but also to buy HG out of his indentures after he had failed miserably or refused to go on; it also allowed Sarah to sponsor HG's frequent schemes for getting into and out of various other establishments—commercial, educational, and residential.

H. G. Wells was born in 1866, but his intellectual life began in 1874, when, coincidentally enough, he broke his own leg. He described the accident as a cardinal stroke of good fortune: "Probably I am alive to-day and writing this autobiography instead of being a worn-out, dismissed and already dead shop assistant, because my leg was broken."[8] A neighbor's grown son was "the agent of good fortune." In boyish playfulness, "Young Sutton" tossed the youngest Wells boy up in the air but failed to catch him. HG's fall was broken by a tent peg, which snapped his leg. From that point, he was enthroned on the parlor sofa as

> the most important thing in the house, consuming unheard-of jellies, fruits, brawn and chicken sent with endless apologies on behalf of her son by Mrs. Sutton, and I could demand and have a fair chance of getting anything that came into my head, books, paper, pencils, and toys— and particularly books.[9]

At the time of the accident, HG had only just begun recreational reading. Now, and from the sofa, he not only had new status as the nucleus of the family but also was the happy recipient of all kinds of reading matter. His father went daily to the Literary Institute to fetch books for his invalid son, and the guilty Mrs. Sutton sent armloads of reading material. The new pastime allowed HG's imagination to wander—indeed, to run wild. From the poverty and paucity of his Bromley berth, he now was visiting earlier times, foreign lands, and exotic people: Tibet and China, Eskimos, the American Civil War, and the Wild West. Still, HG suspected that this literary immersion was a temporary state, since his parents doubted "the healthiness of reading."

As his parents feared, some of the books awakened not only his intellectual but also his sexual curiosity. Indeed, HG would claim that his first consciousness of women and first stirrings of desire were raised by the drawings of heroic divinities that appeared in the bound volumes of *Punch*. John Tenniel's renderings of Britannia, Erin, Columbia, and La France, with their revealing thighs and bare arms, necks, and bosoms "were a revelation in an age of flounces and crinolines." Those first erotic stirrings were helped along considerably by the plaster casts of Greek statuary at the Crystal Palace.[10] HG claimed that his devotion to these paper and plaster women was infantile, "fundamentally ignorant and innocent." Still, he was now conscious that women were "lovely and worshipful," soft and abundant—a sharp contrast to his tiny, thin, hard, and reserved mother. He was conscious of all this well before he discovered a great and wonderful secret called the facts of life:

But now that my interest was aroused I became acutely observant of a print or a statuette in a shop window. . . . My world was so clothed and covered up, and the rules of decency were so established in me, that any revelation of the body was an exciting thing.[11]

In his autobiography, HG specifically denied a mother fixation in his makeup. He argued that while his mother's kisses were important to him, they were expressions rather than caresses. He would ardently claim that he had found, when he was a small boy, no more sexual significance about his decent and prim mother than he did about the furniture in his parlor.

After little Bertie's education on the sofa, Mr. Morley's Commercial Academy in Bromley became his official seat of learning from 1874 to 1880. HG later wrote that the academy had a Dickens-like quality about it—"antiquated, pretentious, superficial and meagre; and yet there was something good about old Morley and something good for me."[12] Old Morley's chief objective was to turn out good clerks equipped with bookkeeping certificates, but he lavished special attention on HG, whose academic interests went well beyond the norm. Sarah Wells, as we know, was obsessed with the idea that her three sons would enter the drapery trade, and she began launching them one after another, like arrows from a bow, into apprenticeships around the countryside. It was only a matter of time before HG would be shot off.

Thus after his stint with Mr. Morley's Academy, HG was sent to the drapery firm of the Messrs. Rodgers and Denyer of Windsor for a trial period. It was the first of a string of "starts" in his life, as he called them. Young HG developed an instant aversion to the establishment and made only the slightest effort to do what was asked of him. Through his carelessness, money from his till went missing, his clothing was unacceptable, and he, too, was regarded as too unrefined for the profession. Everybody seemed to dislike him as a boring little misfit who stirred up trouble and didn't pull his weight. In 1880, HG wrote to his mother in what would become a standard manner: reporting on and complaining about his latest trial. He described a typical day in the life of an indentured slave in a drapery firm, calculated, surely, to wring a bit of sympathy out of her: sleep four to a bed; get up at 7:30 A.M., pull clothes over nightgowns, and hurry to dust the shop; hurry back to quarters to dress and wash for breakfast; work in shop until 1:00 P.M., then have dinner underground; work until tea; work until supper at 8:30 P.M.; have two hours free time. The thirteen-year-old added: "I don't like the place much, for it is not at all like home. Give love to Dad & give the Cats my best respects. Yours, H G Wells." He was let go after two months.

HG's second start was in the winter of 1880 as a pupil-teacher for a cousin of sorts who was in charge of a little national school in Wookey. He was returned to his mother in fairly short order. HG's third false start at a career was as apprentice to a pharmaceutical chemist, Mr. Cowap, in Midhurst; since the youngster knew no Latin, he had to take lessons at the local grammar school. HG decided he did not want to continue with Cowap, and his mother, having no other place for him, arranged for her son to board at the school until she could organize a fourth start. That start, much to HG's horror, was another drapery establishment, the Southsea Drapery Emporium in Kings Road, Southsea. Again, HG was, as he admitted, "an inattentive and unwilling worker."

The longer HG was away from Up Park and his mother, the more demanding and critical he became—especially about the family's decisions and its miserliness where he was concerned. Consider the following excerpt from one letter to his "dearest Mother," dated July 1883 from Southsea:

> Had you read my letter carefully you would have seen the Economy of my leaving at the latest early in August. This would be a direct and immediate saving to begin with. You chose to bargain with Mr. Hide behind my back and you have inflicted the misery on me of seeing you swindled by that little hound. You have paid another lot of money for him to board me in this vile hole until September & you are letting him profit by my labour & me fritter away my life here. You will not trust me. It would be the kindest & wisest thing you could do now to let me leave here very soon.

Just before his second year of a four-year indenture was up, HG, feeling like a hunted rabbit, told his mother that he was planning his escape. He also wrote to the headmaster at the Midhurst Grammar School, Mr. Horace Byatt, asking whether he could work for him in some capacity; miraculously, a job as a student assistant was created for HG. Midhurst became HG's fifth start and another turning point in his life—perhaps *the* turning point, for it set him on an academic path.

Because he would work as much as a teacher as a student, HG was required to read the entire physical and biological science curriculum; his salary would be based on his exam scores. After he passed his May exams, he wrote to his mother with the good news on July 17, 1884, closing with: "Hooray! Your affectionate goodfornaught, HG Wells, Now an independent Gentleman." In his autobiography, HG crowed that he had passed his May exams with such a bang that he was "blown out of Midhurst altogether." He was blown out of Midhurst because he had won a studentship to work as a teacher-in-training for a year in the biology course taught by the illustrious Professor Thomas Henry Huxley at the Normal School of Science in South Kensington (now Imperial College). "I had come to Midhurst a happy but desperate fugitive from servitude: I left it in glory," HG crowed in the *Experiment*. Indeed, the day in 1884 when H.G. Wells walked from his lodging to the Normal School, registered, and took the elevator to the laboratory was one of the greatest of his life. Whereas his science education had been second-, third- and even fourth-hand, now, by yet another conspiracy of wonderful accidents, he had been catapulted to ground zero of scientific education and training. Now he was under the wing of Huxley, "the acutest observer, the ablest generalizer, the great teacher, the most lucid and valiant of controversialists. I had been assigned to his course in Elementary Biology and afterwards I was to go on with Zoology under him."[13] HG wrote that the year he spent in Huxley's class (1884–1885) was far and away the most educational year of his life. He went on to study physics and geology, but his marks for the second and third years were far less impressive.

Long after his own reputation was made, HG reminisced about Huxley and the profound effect the professor had upon him. HG told a radio audience that Huxley had an excellent full voice and that he spoke in clear complete sentences in words so well chosen that only later did one realize how much he had said. Impressed with Huxley's more superficial qualities, indeed, with the very qualities that he lacked, HG was also overwhelmed by the magisterial simplicity with which Huxley conveyed life's most complex yet fundamental principles. HG described one of his first lessons with Huxley, who had brought to the lecture theater a freshly killed rabbit. As Huxley stroked the little body, he sketched its life cycle.

> He pointed out to us some of its chief distinctions from other kindred species and some of its main resemblances to other types. We were going to ask ourselves: what *was,* what *is,* this life? What was it [that] had held this small furry individual together, made it run, eat and play? What animated it. What animated the swarming, eating, burrowing, multitudes of its race? How was that race related to other living races, that sought the same food, or pursued it and preyed upon our rabbit? That little limp furry body was the key by which we were to make our way towards the understanding of the whole incessant network of life, breeding and dying and changing about the world. That is how I remember Huxley, as a mature and dignified man in a lecture theatre, assured of his position, under no sort of stress, asking the most penetrating questions in an even voice and telling us, with the completest honesty, whatever he thought might contribute to our answers . . . whatever knowledge and ability he possessed that would help us to form our own conclusions.[14]

In July 1887, HG, now in his sixth "start," joined the Holt Academy as a teacher, but in the fall, he had another serious accident: This time he crushed his left kidney in a football game. HG told his mother in September that he was in great pain and in a foul mood. In addition to the kidney, he had bruised his liver and intestines and "mashed up" various muscles in his midsection. "It has been a nasty time altogether & I hope you will forgive anything unpleasant I may have said while I have been fighting through it. Love to father & Frank. Believe me. Your very affectionate son." To make matters even worse, HG was diagnosed with tuberculosis later that year and suffered a second attack of it the next year. Thin and fragile, malnourished, banged up internally, and still financially insecure, he went off to begin his brilliant career as a teacher at Henley House School, a private school, in Kilburn. It was neither a stellar institution of learning nor a stellar year for HG. There, the teachers "launched" their students with or without a certificate, "as mere irresponsible adventurers into an uncharted scramble for life."[15]

While he was at Henley House, HG decided to commit to school teaching as a career, and he began pursuing a teaching diploma, then a degree, at London University. On August 7, 1889, he wrote to his mother with good news: "Dear Mammie, It is all over, your son are past that exam, & have got the second place, Honors in Zoology. There is one more exam and then your son will be a Batchelor of Science of the Imperial University of the British people." Apparently not certain his mother had the terminology straight, or the concept, he added that if she wanted to tell people about the accomplishment, she should put it like this: "Say second in honors in the Intermediate Examination in Science. At Cambridge they call the Intermediate 'Junior Tripos' or simply 'Tripos.' I have one more exam for a degree. The degree I shall have is Batchelor of Science written thus; B.Sc. (London). It is equal to an Oxford or Cambridge M.A."

A few months later, on October 14, 1889, HG wrote his mother an uncharacteristically caring and contrite letter that sounded more than a bit hollow and forced. He said he wished he could express his desire to help her with her "many trying experiences":

> I often think how I have hurt you by hastiness & of the many brutal things I have done to you, cross letters written & feelings disregarded. Really I am very sorry for these, I grieve over cross letters I have too often written you perhaps more than you think. Sometimes it seems to

me that I may have lost some of your affection by these things, & by what you may have thought unsympathetic coldness—you know I never was given to demonstrations of affection. Do let me now assure you of my respect & tenderness for your dear devoted life, & do not forget it if at any time you are in trouble. Your most loving son, Bertie.

In March the next year, HG was elected a Fellow of the Zoological Society of London. He took his last exams in October and earned his B.Sc. The next year he became a tutor at University Correspondence College in Cambridge; he graded lessons, designed courses, wrote short pieces for science journals and, ultimately, science textbooks, including the *Textbook of Biology* in 1893 and the *Textbook of Zoology* five years later—both of which were derived from his class notes. HG adopted the Huxley style of teaching and learning, typified by using types, drawing inferences, and making comparisons. Biographer Michael Foot observed that the way in which the poor, frail, and erratically educated HG was able to will himself into becoming a writer is a heroic story. How he transformed himself into a writer who "could not merely face the world but was determined to change it was hardly less heroic. And the whole combined, miraculous transformation was compressed into the short period of a single decade."[16]

⋆　　⋆　　⋆

HG's social life was similarly compressed, consisting of one relationship—a long (six-year) chaste courtship with his first cousin, Isabel Mary Wells, whom he married on October 31, 1891. Like his parents, he and Isabel were phenomenally ill-suited for each other. Even when courting Isabel, HG struggled to find in her the mate of his imaginings—his Lover-Shadow. He later wrote that they should have been brother and sister rather than man and wife. In a chapter of his autobiography appropriately titled "Dissection," HG theorized about why they were so incompatible. For one thing, he said, Isabel didn't share his interest in reading or in other intellectual pursuits. Her brain was equal or superior to his, he conceded, but there was between them an "inalterable difference in range and content." Isabel tried valiantly to hang on to HG's ideas, but the gap, he claimed, was "too wide." There was another much larger problem—one HG called "temperamental." His great hope, after waiting so long to consummate his love for his cousin, was that "flame would meet flame"; but instead of responding passionately to his passion, Isabel merely submitted. "I had waited so long for this poor climax," he wrote in his *Experiment*. While his love was still centered on his cousin, HG was soon letting his desires "wander" and making love to other women. Indeed, quite soon after his wedding, a young assistant to his wife "succeeded in dispelling all the gloomy apprehensions I was beginning to entertain, that lovemaking was nothing more than an outrage inflicted upon reluctant womankind and all its loveliness a dream."[17] HG's rationale for "wandering" was, fittingly, Darwinian.

> I wanted to compensate myself for the humiliation [Isabel] had so unwittingly put upon me. I was in a phase of aroused liveliness. That did not alter her unpremeditated and unconscious dominance of my imagination, my deep-lying desire for passionate love with her. I do not know what might have happened if at any time in the course of our estrangement she had awakened and turned upon me with a passionate appeal.[18]

Thus began HG's lifetime habit of blaming his wives and lovers for his infidelity; any failure on their part might elicit adultery on his. In his mind, their missteps *allowed* him to cheat on them. Operating on this principle, then, HG began undoing the knot of marriage with Isabel, began his escape from what he now saw as the "unsatisfying bond of habit and affection." Yet, while he wished to escape from the "pit of disappointment" he and Isabel had tumbled into, he also wanted to hold onto her in the hope that she would sooner or later "come alive" to him. Looking back at this time in his life, from a distance of forty years, what HG found most interesting about his early married life was that it was so easy and natural for him to replace his strong sexual desire for

Isabel with "enterprising promiscuity. The old love wasn't at all dead, but I meant now to get in all the minor and incidental love adventures I could." [19]

Ever the scientist, HG came up with a theory of sorts to explain the range of emotional responses one individual could have for another, from total devotion, or "fixation," to open promiscuity. He even posed the idea that humans are not monogamous or promiscuous by nature, but that some "happen to get fixed" for shorter or longer periods. On the whole, then, humans are constructed with a general desire to "concentrate," but something can suddenly interfere to upset that natural tendency, "until a new trend towards fixation appears. These are matters not within the control of will or foresight, they happen to us before willing begins."[20]

Another idea occurred to HG's dissecting mind. Perhaps there is potential flight as well as attraction in *every* love affair, a fugitive as well as an attracting impulse. HG recalled not only wanting his cousin to become his mistress before he married her but also wishing to continue living in lodgings with her *after* they were married, presumably to continue the fiction of an exciting illicit affair. He also recalled that even after he had eloped with his second wife, he was still trying to persuade his cousin to remain married to him. "Having got away from her I wanted to keep her. It is only now, in this cold and deliberate retrospect, that I admit even to myself how disingenuous, how confused and divided in purpose I was at that time." HG never conquered his impulse to run from intimacy. He freely admitted to bouts of emotional or domestic claustrophobia and to the need to bolt from relationships, but he never acknowledged a deeper psychological reason for these feelings. If he suspected that their roots were in his childhood and, more specifically, in his relationship with his emotionally frigid mother and his distant father, he never let on. If he ever realized that he couldn't achieve intimacy with a woman until he *left* her, he never let on.

At age twenty-seven, after a series of emotional and physical problems, HG decided to try another "start," to reinvent himself yet again.

This time he had a partner. Leaping into elopement and the brave new adventure with him was his student, Amy Catherine Robbins, whom he later renamed Jane. Amy, who endured such endearments as "Bits," "Miss Bits," "Snitch" and "It" (he was "Bins" or "Mr. Bins") before being dubbed Jane, had been attending one of HG's cram classes in practical biology, designed for candidates preparing for London University's bachelor of science exams. Her father had just died, and she was struggling to obtain a degree, HG wrote, so that she could become a school-teacher and earn a living for herself and her mother. At the time, life for HG and Isabel had just improved considerably, at least materially. While Isabel continued her work as a photograph retoucher, HG was finding publishing outlets for some of his light pieces, with the result that he was making more money than he ever had during his teaching days. In August 1893, Isabel found a new, more comfortable place for them in Sutton, Surrey, but after Christmas, HG left Isabel and Sutton, and Amy Catherine Robbins joined him in London at 7 Mornington Place.

In a chapter of his *Experiment* titled "Modus Vivendi," HG explained the motivation behind his and Amy Catherine's decision to have an open marriage. He argued that at the time both of them were fleeing from conditions of "intolerably narrow living." Her presence in his coed classes symbolized struggle and revolt against her timid and conventional mother. His notions of "freedom and social and intellectual enterprise," meanwhile, went to her head, he claimed, "and it was an overwhelming desire for emancipation from consuming everyday obligations for both of us rather than sexual passion, that led to our wild dash at opportunity."[21]

Still, one of the main things HG craved emancipation from at this time, he claimed, was the "torment of desire" he still felt for Isabel. He wrote that after having sifted through the evidence, he believed that his most powerful drive toward the end of the century was the desire to "relieve my imagination not of the real Isabel but of that Venus Urania, that torment of high and beautiful desire, who had failed to embody herself in Isabel and yet had become so inseparable from her."[22] With his hopes now shifted to Amy Catherine Robbins, HG seized on *her* "to make her the triumphant rival of that elusive goddess."

> On my new mistress, in her turn, I was trying to impose a role. Like so many other desperate young love affairs, ours was to be such a love affair as the world had never seen before. We were by mutual agreement two beings of an astonishing genius with an inherent right to turn accepted morality upside down. It was an explosion of moral light.[23]

HG and his second wife's alliance—originally made "for escape and self development"—held throughout their lives, he maintained, and after their "heroics" fizzled, they discovered that they liked and respected each other immensely. They became and remained, according to HG's testimony, "the best companions in the world." As the century flickered out, they "scribbled side by side," hunted for material for articles, and had a very happy time together. With a bright new lover, and in his new incarnation, HG launched his career in literary writing. Now he had mentors who encouraged his development and a woman who was disposed to and capable of helping him achieve his still unformulated dreams for success. HG claimed many years later, in his tribute to Jane (Amy), that they had launched themselves into life with less than £50 between them, and that they had pulled through, first to security and then to prosperity, without resorting to begging, borrowing, cheating, or stealing. Moreover, they did it, as he recalled, with a great deal of happiness. In 1894, HG earned nearly £600; in 1895, nearly £800. By 1896, he reported earning £1,056 7s. 9d. Even so, there would be a steady drip, drip from his resources. In 1927, after contributing to a fund for Virginia and Leonard Woolf, HG told Christabel that he had a very crowded doorstep, with "all sorts of stray cats & claimants upon it," and that he paid out more than £1,000 a year in annuities to various people.[24]

HG divorced Isabel and married Amy Catherine, whom we shall now call Jane, in 1895, the same year he published *The Time Machine.* Described as the earliest known work of science fiction to be based on the idea of time travel, the book won HG recognition as an imaginative writer.[25] Three science fantasies, as they then were called, followed: *Moreau* in 1896, *Invisible Man* in 1897, *War of the Worlds* in 1898. The historian A.J.P. Taylor once wrote about HG's technique and skill vis-à-vis writing science fiction: He pretended, and then took the pretense seriously. In other words, he postulated a simple impossible step, a food that produced giants, for example, and then he worked out what would follow. "The overwhelming feature of his scientific fantasies," Taylor said, "is that they are not fantasies. Except for the one impossible twist, they are exactly what would happen . . . if only."[26] The young marrieds produced their sons George Philip (called Gip) and Frank in 1901 and 1903. After World War I, HG and Jane also delivered *The Outline of History*. They never expected the *Outline* to become a profitable book; indeed, the project, on which they had worked feverishly and for which they had felt unequipped, far surpassed their wildest hopes.

HG claimed that Jane had never made a personal claim to that or to any of his literary projects, and that there wasn't a trace of ambition, social or otherwise, in her nature. In his considered opinion, her interest was focused on her home, family, and friends. Her greatest desire was to create a pleasant open environment where she could help her husband, raise her children, and entertain guests. Her joy was to see that everyone was cheerful and happy. *Those* were her passions. Occasionally she invested time and effort into writing, but that was a minor passion, if that, he claimed. Yet, despite the various apparent harmonies and the close working relationship, it didn't take long for Jane and HG to realize that there was a fundamental incompatibility between them. Indeed, soon after they eloped, HG discovered that Jane was a delicate creature—a fragile piece of china, he called her—and not only totally ignorant of sex, but unresponsive to his lovemaking. Given these conditions, it was inconceivable that he would be rough or urgent with her, he claimed, "and so the deep desired embraces of Venus Urania were now further off from me than ever."[27]

To be sure, they had other incompatibilities, as HG noted: They had dissimilar brains; their temperaments were different; and of course, those diametrically opposed "physical and imaginative responses."

These were, alas, the same incompatibilities between HG and Isabel. HG claimed that no one knew about his and Jane's problems for several years, for they stuck to each other stoutly, forged by the links of mutual aid, tolerance, and affection. Put another way, to fill the void of "a real passionate sexual fixation," HG and Jane contrived a "binding net" of fantasy and affection that was, he argued, as effective as intense sexual companionship.

As long as he and Jane struggled to make their way in the world, HG's eye didn't wander, he claimed, and he and his wife made do with little caresses and small intimacies. It was only with success that their "close strict partnership was relaxed." Once again, as he conceded in the *Postscript*, HG began to imagine "lovelier sensual experiences and to ask 'Why not?'"[28] Still linked by their cooperation in work and business, as well as by their sons, the couple eventually agreed to live separate lives. HG characteristically shifted the responsibility for the unconventional convention and suggested that the impetus to live apart and love freely came from his wife.

> Jane thought I had a right to my own individual disposition and that luck had treated me badly in mating me first to an unresponsive and then to a fragile companion. About that she was extraordinarily dispassionate and logical and much more clearheaded than I was. She faced the matter with the same courage, honesty and self-subordination with which she faced all the practical issues of life. She suppressed any jealous impulse and gave me whatever freedom I desired.[29]

Because their alliance never became intensely sexual, HG's fixation on his cousin remained powerful for ten years or more. However, in 1909, he was able, he said, to meet his first wife, who had so haunted his sexual imagination, "in a mood of limitless friendliness, free from all the glittering black magic of sex; and so things remained with us until the end of her life."[30] Others are not so sure; they believe that HG remained bewitched by his first wife well into the 1920s. In vintage Wellsian, HG reported that Isabel blamed herself for their separation when she gave HG the ultimatum to either stop seeing Amy (Jane) or face divorce. One thing is certain: HG idealized his wives and lovers after he left them, another manifestation of avoiding intimacy.

In his thirties and forties, HG admitted, he spent a great deal of mental energy on what he called the "general problem" of men and women. He realized that he needed to resolve the inherent tensions in himself, or at least remove the falseness. He wanted to live a life that would stand up to examination; but his thoughts and fancies were uncontrollable, he admitted, and his conduct now was "perplexingly disingenuous." The way he eliminated the disingenuousness, as he described in the *Experiment,* was to gather disciples and promote his lifestyle shamelessly. Therefore, he engaged in "candid public theorizing. I spoke out for Free Love. . . . I did my best to maintain that love-making was a thing in itself, a thing to thank the gods for, but not to be taken too seriously and carried into the larger constructive interests of life."[31] The information going around about birth control, HG further argued, seemed to justify his idea that love could be given and taken more lightly than it had been in the past. It could be regarded as refreshment and invigoration, as he explained in his *Modern Utopia* (1905).

HG wrote voluminously about his modus vivendi with Jane. He explained how he felt about it. He explained how she felt about it. But he never explained how any of the "other women" felt about it. Judging by some correspondence, Odette seemed to accept the arrangement far better than most. Early into their affair, perhaps in 1924 or 1925, after Jane had sent Odette a silk shawl, mince pies, and a plum pudding for Christmas, Odette wrote a warm and humorous thank-you letter, commenting that even HG was "moved to admiration" over the shawl. Odette also shared some unsolicited personal information, including the tidbit that HG thought she resembled "an Armenian carpet-seller" because of her clothing and her nose. "Anybody can have a small, straight correct nose. It's the easiest thing to be born with. Character,

character is what I go in for, and my nose shows my aspirations." Another letter was less humorous than shocking in its candor. Written on January 1, year not given, Odette offered Jane her unsolicited analysis of HG, warts and all, and of their relationship. But before she did, she thanked Jane for her sweet cordial letter, adding, "I am so glad that you are friendly. It is extraordinary that W. should have inspired so much devotion, but also I have never known any woman whose quality and high-mindedness are as fine as yours." Jane's kindness was almost enough to make Odette believe that HG's "Utopian type" woman was not as impossible as it seemed. Unself-consciously, presumably, Odette confided in Jane that HG brought out in her "an intensity of affection" that she never knew she had. His "gusts and moods" were largely caused by nervous tension, she observed, and there was no malice of any kind in him. Moreover,

> his loyalties are lasting and quite unshakeable. One can always count on his fairness and sense of justice, and the gradual realization of that has helped me to work out a relationship that fits in for the moment with some of his needs. But nobody and nothing in the world will ever hold this man completely.

There is, alas, no indication about how her lover's wife received this information.

For his part, HG, with his self-described excess of sexual energy and imagination, elsewhere conceded that his personal encounters with other women were, in fact, a revolt against the sexual code of the time. The French, he said, with their "absurd logicality" distinguished between the *passade,* "a stroke of mutual attraction that may happen to any couple," and a real love affair. "In theory, I was now to have *passades,*" he wrote in the *Experiment.* He and Jane would maintain a home, but they also kept separate apartments in London. It isn't hard to imagine how HG spent his free time at his Whitehall Court residence. Without the favor of citations, he explained Jane's activities in her rooms in Bloomsbury:

In this secret flat, quite away from all the life that centred upon me, she thought and dreamt and wrote and sought continually and fruitlessly for something she felt she had lost of herself or missed or never attained. She worked upon a story in that retreat, a fastidious elusive story that she never brought to any shape or ending; some of it she polished and retyped many times. It was a dream of an island of beauty and sensuous perfection in which she lived alone and was sometimes happy in her loneliness and sometimes very lonely. In her dream there was a lover who never appeared. He was a voice heard; he was a trail of footsteps in the dewy grass, or she woke and found a rosebud at her side.[32]

As mentioned in the Preface, the first section of H. G. Wells's *Postscript* is a prologue, previously published in 1928 as his introduction to *The Book of Catherine Wells*. After Jane died, HG culled her writings, of which he knew little since "her desire was to succeed independently" of his influence, and published what he considered to be the best of them in *The Book of Catherine Wells*. It was the husband's tribute to the wife and to the wife's alter ego, Catherine, the writer. "Jane was a person of much greater practical ability than Catherine," HG wrote in his introduction. He ticked off a laundry list of Jane's domestic virtues: She made all the household decisions, managed the house well and was an able shopper, helped people in difficulties, took no nonsense from the plumber, was competent in domestic emergencies (having passed a Red Cross course), kept a fine garden, and last but not least, "She transacted and invested for her unhelpful uncertain husband, and she was wise and wary in his affairs and a searchlight of honesty and clear but kindly illumination in his world."[33] His wife was two distinctly different people, and even more as time passed, he claimed.

HG believed that Jane began to write so that she could understand who she was and convey this understanding to some fictional but sympathetic reader. She didn't write for him, although she tried to make him feel that he wasn't excluded, he said. One of her most intriguing stories was the haunting tale, "The Beautiful House," about a young woman, Mary Hastings. The story begins with a description of Mary:

open manner, reserves of shyness, generous nature, rich in friends. When her youth was gone, she formed a very special relationship with someone and found "the love that finds no flaw." The relationship was with a *young girl,* Sylvia Brunton. It was "an intimacy which had its birth and ardent life, and faded and died at last like other human things," Jane wrote.[34] The chilling deduction is that Jane sought just what HG sought: love without flaw, an impossible love, and with another woman. HG considered many titles for the book; one of those he dismissed was *The Hidden Heart.*

HG reported that after the children were born, the serious Mrs. Wells lightened up and became a "gay, inventive and amusing actress," although, truth to tell, there is hardly a family snapshot that doesn't capture in her a vacant, faraway, or unhappy gaze—even during moments of leisure and entertainment. Ironically or not, parlor games became a central element in their lives—"play the fool," "Dumb crambo," shadow-shows, and charades—all leading ultimately to improvised play-acting in which "Mummy got better . . . and better," HG wrote. For weekend entertainment, the young Wellses brought many different types of people to their homestead; guests arrived on Saturday afternoon "a little aloof and distrustful of one another," and departed on Monday, "magically fused," after having danced, acted, played, and helped fix the Sunday meal. Jane didn't dominate, but she oversaw with such goodwill and "an unqualified ardour for happiness, that the coldest warmed and the stiffest relaxed."[35]

One Saturday afternoon open house held near the turn of the century produced a memorable literary moment. Jennie Randolph Churchill, Winston's mother, and her sisters had discovered what they considered the worst novel of the decade, and they arranged to meet at the Wellses' home to read parts of it aloud. One of the choice passages of the novel, *Irene Iddesleigh,* involved an argument between Sir Hugh and his wife, the heroine Irene. Sir Hugh began his tirade with, "Irene, if I may use such familiarity," and ended it with, "Speak, Wife. Woman! Do not sit in silence, and allow the blood that now boils in my veins to ooze through the cavities of unrestrained passion, and trickle down to drench me with its crimson hue!" After Sir H. discovered that his suspicions about his wife were true—that she had a lover—he locked her in a room for a year, then removed her from his will. "With the pen of persuasion dipped into the ink of revenge, he blanked the intolerable words that referred to the woman who, he was now convinced, had braved the bridge of bigamy." Jennie Churchill also recalled another event—a three-day party that Stephen Crane threw for sixty guests, including Henry James, Joseph Conrad, and H. G. Wells. Hard as it is to believe, HG apparently invented a game of racing on broomsticks across the polished floors, "and the guests reveled until dawn."[36]

The pitch and tenor of the Wells household's fun and games was also sketched in Cornelia Otis Skinner's memoir, *Our Hearts Were Young and Gay.* Skinner told the story of a rollicking. Sunday afternoon in 1920 that she, her parents, and a college friend spent at the Dunmow estate. Nearly two hours late for lunch because they got lost in the country, the quintessential Americans (although Cornelia's father was a Shakespearean actor who had met HG in the Swiss Alps a year or two before World War I) bumbled, fumbled, and stumbled through lunch and yard games, energized, eased, and charmed by the great writer, whose *Outline of History* had just become a runaway best-seller. In addition to his short, stocky physique and surprising voice, HG was "cheery and full of welcome and the Lord knows replete with teeming vitality. One was instantly aware of it; not nervous restlessness, but bursting energy inadequately harnessed and rarin' to go."[37] "Mrs. Birth Control Sanger," as Cornelia Skinner described Margaret Sanger, also was present.

Frank Swinnerton, an author, good friend, and frequent visitor, once recalled "the full blaze" of a typical Wellsian weekend. After breakfast, the entire group of guests rushed from the table to an old barn not far from the house where they launched into a ferocious game of something, apparently, like volleyball. HG chose the sides and made the rules, often on the spur of the moment. "What prodigies of leaping we all did, in particular, what prodigies of leaping Wells did. He jumped, he ran, he struck, he grunted, he sang, and if by the limitations of

reach or space he could not take the ball himself, he shouted to his partner or partners, 'Yours, yours.'"[38]

HG was still famous, even notorious, twelve years later for his social
gatherings, although he apparently still didn't appreciate the trouble
the hostess went to so that he could entertain hordes of guests. On January 15, 1932, Odette had had enough, and she threw in the hostess
towel. She wrote to Marjorie Wells, on the one hand welcoming her
and her family down to Lou Pidou for a rest, and on the other complaining about the never-ending succession of house parties. Odette
proclaimed that this would be the very last one she ever gave. In the future, only "Pidoukaki's" family or hers would be invited for an extended stay. After her monstrous mistake in telling everyone that they
had a guest house in Provence, they were "submerged by demands"
from prospective visitors, who, she complained, were inclined to treat
the house as if it were a hotel. Shades of Maugham and the Villa Mauresque. But Pidoo, another term of endearment for HG, was simply
"AWFUL" in this regard, she wrote.

> He has exorbitantly lavish ideas of hospitality & can't realize that to
> carry them out I need eight servants instead of two & a char, so that I
> had scenes with him day & night! The untidiness of this place when
> there were so many visitors playing games, dancing, gramophoning,
> smoking everywhere, drove me completely crazy. Not a book where it
> should be. Not an ash-tray clean. Not a chair in its place. Gods, the DIS-
> ORDER! I am expecting the Curies and the Grenfells on Wednesday, &
> that's the end of 'house-parties' here as long as I live!

Although the H. G. Wellses played together and traveled many of
life's highways together, metaphorically, anyway, they vacationed sepa-
rately. Jane loved the Swiss Alps and took many holidays there, with or
without the boys; HG wrote to her from the olive orchards of
Provence, where he and Odette shared their ménage. What he saw of
the vacationing Jane often was in her snapshots. Occasionally they vacationed together—enough for him to write: "She would toil through

long excursions upon foot or upon skis, never going very fast or brilliantly, but never giving up, a little indefatigable smiling figure, dusted with the snow of her not infrequent tumbles."[39]

Although HG claimed that Jane was a gentle and sweet spirit, like Christabel, she had another side; she was stability incarnate, while he was impatient, hasty, and incompetent about the business of life. He conceded that most of the "patience, courage and sacrifice" shown in the marriage came from Jane. HG also ardently claimed that they had genuine affection and respect for each other. "There again the feat was hers. It was an easy thing for me to keep my faith in her sense of fairplay and her perfect generosity. She stuck to me so sturdily that in the end I stuck to myself. I do not know what I should have been without her. She stabilized my life. She gave it a home and dignity. She preserved its continuity."[40]

This highly unusual alliance would not last. Jane had exploratory surgery in the spring of 1927 when HG was in the South of France with Odette. His younger son Frank sent the telegram announcing Jane's condition soon after HG and Odette took possession of Lou Pidou in March. HG rushed home to Easton Glebe, in Essex, to learn that his wife had inoperable cancer and perhaps only six months to live. He spent the next 150 days by her side. Soon after arriving in London, HG fired off a letter to Christabel saying that he had something to tell her before the news reached her in another way.

This little wife of mine who has been in my life for thirty five years is very ill & she is not likely to get much better. She has been so quiet & reserved a person & I have taken such liberties with life that nobody can realize just how close the links are between us. This Christmas she was scrambling up mountains in the snow & a month ago we were being feted by all sorts of nice people in Paris & she was buying dresses & going about with me. I left her & went down to Provence for a month because I had a cold & was run down & the night before I left I noted her face across a dinner table & saw that something was wrong. I made her promise to be overhauled and now she is in a nursing home after an op-

eration & I do not think there are very many months before her. I shall
be with her now all the time & the rest of life will have to adjust itself to
that. What a clumsy & cruel machine the human body can be![41]

Christabel responded the next day:

But oh HG my dear, I know with horrid clearness how much you are
going to miss her. She means something to you that no one else means,
and she was always *there* when you needed her. People who think that
"taking liberties with life" means that one doesn't care—and care deeply
and with tender love—for a husband or wife, are just unimaginative
fools. You won't in these coming months let the thought of those "liberties" worry you or allow them to become over-important, will you? It
would spoil the last months for you both; and I am certain she has always known that if you had been different in one way you would have
been different in all ways. She has loved you very much and been very
proud of you—that is what you must remember.

Before Jane's "gentle starry spirit" vanished, she and HG spent a good
deal of time in the garden she had created. They saw friends and listened
to the gramophone, and when her strength had all but slipped away,
they sat together in the dusk and watched a wood fire burn. One tender
mercy granted Jane was that, although her body weakened perceptively
day by day, her mind remained clear. Two weeks before Jane died, HG
told Christabel that Jane was "just sinking & fading out of life," and that
in a curious way, she was becoming the "fragile serious thing" she had
been at the beginning of their relationship. Jane died on October 6, 1927,
the day before their younger son's wedding day.[42] She was fifty-five.

HG wrote at some length in the *Postscript* about Jane's funeral. The
upshot of the narrative was that circumstances made the last scene of
their life together "a very beautiful one." After the organist played
César Franck's *Pièce Héroique* and T. E. Page read the speech that HG
had prepared, HG and his sons, at the suggestion of George Bernard
Shaw, followed Jane's coffin to the furnaces. She "had gone clean out of

life and left nothing to moulder and defile the world. So she would have had it. It was good to think she had gone as a spirit should go."[43] Charlotte Shaw, George Bernard's wife, described the scene in quite another way. In a letter to T. E. Lawrence, she said that the affair was "dreadful!"

> The organ began a terrible dirge. HG began to cry like a child—tried to hide it at first and then let go. . . . [The paper] was terrible beyond anything words can describe: a soul in torment—self torture. He drowned us in a sea of misery and as we were gasping began a panegyric of Jane which made her appear as a delicate, flower-like, gentle being, surrounding itself with beauty, and philanthropy and love. Now Jane was one of the strongest characters I ever met. She managed HG and her good curious sons and her circle generally according to her own very definite and very original theories—with almost unbroken success—*from the point of view of her theories.* Then there came a place where the address said "she never resented a slight; she never gave voice to a harsh judgment." At that point the audience, all more or less acquainted with many details of HG's private life, thrilled, like corn under a wet north wind—and HG—HG positively howled. You are no doubt aware that he was not a conventionally perfect husband. . . . O it was hideous—terrible and frightful. I am an old woman and there is one thing I seem, at least, to have learned. The way of transgressors is hard.[44]

The *Times's* obituary described Jane Wells as "her husband's devoted friend and assistant." She was one of the few people who could transcribe his handwriting, the piece said, and she had "an aptitude for business which helped him." An author herself of some short stories, her output was "necessarily restricted by her domestic responsibilities." She also was an admirable hostess, had a "pretty" sense of humor and made their home an "abiding center of harmony and good-will. For she was always ready to help any lame dog over a stile in the most tactful and unobtrusive manner."[45]

* * *

Jane had lived through so very much—and so very many. Amber, Elizabeth, Rebecca, the Frau Gatternigg, Margaret Sanger, and Odette Keun
were just a few of her trials; Amber was one of her toughest. In the
Postscript, HG wrote that he had had a "great storm" of intense physical sexual passion and desire with Amber Reeves. It took him twenty
pages to describe that steamy, sometimes farcical, storm. His former
friend and close Fabian ally, Beatrice Webb, wrote nearly as much about
that relationship; indeed, Beatrice devoted entire sections of her diary
to the developing scandal, which she astutely described in October 1908
as "a somewhat dangerous friendship." Still, she thought Amber and
HG were "both too soundly self-interested to do more than cause poor
Jane Wells some fearful feelings, but if Amber were my child I should
be anxious."[46] As no one could have predicted, there would be any
number of shocking details connected with the affair, not the least of
which was that HG had seduced Amber within the hallowed walls of
Newnham, Cambridge's adjunct school for women, which Amber attended. HG's second grave error was to pluck his young prey from the
so-called Fabian Nursery, which consisted of the children of his colleagues and friends—a second-generation of followers.

Beatrice and her husband, Sidney Webb, knew Amber and her family
very well; it was they who had chosen Amber's father, Pember Reeves,
to direct the London School of Economics, which they founded. Early
on, Beatrice described Amber as brilliant, "an amazingly vital person
and I suppose very clever, but a terrible little pagan—vain, egotistical,
and careless of other people's happiness."[47] People may have criticized
her for many things, but no one ever disputed Amber's credentials. She
was a standout in a field of standouts—a leading member of the nursery and an academic star, a shooting star unleashed from the more
mundane social conventions.[48] HG was powerfully attracted to Amber,
and she was absolutely smitten with him; he was *the* intellectual giant
of the era, perhaps of all times. In the face of conventional morality in
the early years of the new century, they threw themselves into a passionate love affair; but reality caught up with them when Amber became pregnant. HG's "sordid affair with poor Amber Reeves," the preg-

nancy, and the cover-up marriage with the clever and charming young Fabian, G. Rivers Blanco White, was extremely upsetting to Beatrice Webb. She could not in all conscience continue her friendship with HG. In her diary in early August 1909, she noted that "Amber and HG insist on remaining friends—a sort of *Days of the Comet* affair."[49]

Beatrice also told her diary that she and her husband felt obliged to warn others, including Sydney Olivier, the father of four good-looking daughters, about HG, to prevent further scandals from erupting within the fold. The rumor had been circulating that HG already had tried to seduce Rosamund Bland, the daughter of Fabian member Hubert Bland.[50] Beatrice believed that if the Reeveses had known of that seduction, they wouldn't have allowed Amber to stay at HG's Sandgate home for a month at a time, or baby-sit for his boys. Of the Amber-HG tryst, she told her diary: "It is a horrid affair and has cost us much. If Amber will let us, we shall stand by her as Blanco's wife and drop H. G. Wells, once and for all, as he no doubt will drop us."[51] Beatrice predicted that HG would probably drift into other circles and that the only person of his ménage who would suffer would be Jane, who, "having entered into that position illicitly herself at the cost of another woman, cannot complain."[52]

The problem went beyond the principals, of course. It went to the core of a changing society's beliefs. Beatrice observed that the shocking affair was "a striking example of the tangle into which we have got on the sex question."

And all of this arises because we none of us know what exactly is the sexual code we believe in, approving of many things on paper which we violently object to when they are practised by those we care about. Of course, the inevitable condition today of any "sexual experiments" is deceit and secrecy—it is this that makes any divergence from the conventional morality so sordid and lowering. It is hardly fair to become intimate with a young girl, fresh from college, on the assumption that you believe in monogamy, and then suddenly to propose a polygamous relationship without giving her guardians and friends any kind of notice.

That is not playing the game of sexual irregularity even according to the rules of a game full of hazards, at any rate, for the woman.[53]

Not knowing exactly what to do about this crisis in their circle, Beatrice confided to her diary that she would make every effort to "get a hold over" Amber and stop the "rot" from going any further. Still, she saw Amber as a liar who was "superlatively vain," who had little or no pity in her nature, and sustained considerable will power. Whether there was anything finer and nobler in her nature that could be appealed to remained to be seen. "If there is not, I fear her intelligence will not save her from a 'ruin' that will be apparent to the world."[54]

If she was hard on Amber, Beatrice Webb was brutal with HG. Her judgements of him spewed across the pages of her diary. Particularly fascinating was her August 1909 section on "the rise, grandeur, and decline of H. G. Wells." Beatrice wrote that when she and her husband first met HG in 1901, he was "decidedly on the up-grade, not merely in position but, I think, also in character. Now he is most distinctly on the down-grade, and unless he can pull himself up he will soon be little more than a ruined reputation."[55]

At the beginning of their friendship, according to Beatrice, HG was "a pleasant, breezy person eager to establish himself among interesting folk." He and Jane had created a refined and charming home and had trained themselves in dress and table manners so that they could associate with society's best. By anyone's standards, HG was living a respectable life, attentive to his work and family. Beatrice wasn't sure when "the tide turned," but she suspected that his introduction to certain people, including the Sassoons, which was her doing, had "whetted his social ambition and upset his growing bourgeois morality. His rise to literary fame and his growing conceit accentuated the irresponsible and wilful side to his nature."[56]

Beatrice Webb theorized that HG's revolt against the Puritanism of the leading Fabians drew him to the charm and glamour of smart society and the company of nobility, especially of countesses and duchesses. By the time he met Amber, who became his intellectual and sexual comrade, HG had decided to lead a double life. He desired "on the one hand to be the respectable family man and famous littérateur to the world at large—and on the other, to be the Goethe-like libertine in selected circles." Beatrice predicted that HG, now sunk in his own estimation and in the estimation of people who counted, would be utterly and permanently wretched. He would lose his health, she predicted, and perhaps even his talent. "It will be the tragedy of a lost soul."[57]

Beatrice was wrong. HG wasn't destroyed either by the affair or by the scandal. Although he lost status and friends, he managed to hold onto his health and his talent. He and Amber continued to thumb their noses at society and even to see each other, as members of the Fabian Society worked behind the scenes to bring their affair to an end. Beatrice noted in December 1909, just days before Amber delivered her daughter, Annajane, that HG, "after all his insolent bluster," had backed down and agreed to stay away from Amber for two or three years. Beatrice argued that HG was moved to better behavior because he had lost so many friends over the matter and because the *Spectator*'s review of his novel, *Ann Veronica,* was so damning. In Beatrice's opinion, the review was an exposé of HG's conduct "under the guise of criticism of a 'poisonous book,' written clearly with knowledge and intent."[58] HG timed the publication of *Ann Veronica* poorly. The novel appeared just when a national campaign for moral purity was reaching its peak. *Spectator* editor St. Loe Strachey jumped all over the book, writing that in it "a community of scuffling stoats and ferrets had been dredged from 'the muddy world of Mr. Wells's imaginings.'"[59] To make matters even worse, George Bernard Shaw also turned against HG. He read his new play, transparently titled *The Shewing-Up of Blanco Posnet,* to his Fabian friends in December. While it was "amazingly brilliant," Beatrice wrote,

the whole "motive" is erotic, everyone wishing to have sexual intercourse with everyone else. There is a reflection of the Amber-Wells philosophy of life—I think probably the revelations in the H.G.W. various escapades have largely suggested the play—and the leading woman is Amber, with a rather better excuse than Amber had for pursuing men, since this lady had no other outlet for her energies. Sidney and I were sorry to see G.B.S. reverting to his studies in anarchic love-making.[60]

HG and Amber continued to see each other—often secretly—after Annajane was born, but, as HG noted, their "flags were down and their pride was gone." In March 1910, Beatrice noted that Amber was settling down with her husband and that she was absorbed with her baby. It was turning out to be one of those rare cases where the punishment was worse for the man than for the woman. If Amber behaved herself, Beatrice theorized, she would be taken back by her friends; but HG and his wife would be dropped by most of his old friends. "He is too old to live it down. The scandals have revealed the moral rottenness of his life. I am sorry for Jane Wells, but she pandered to him and deceived friends like the Reeveses. I wish we had never known them."[61] Some, of course, supported HG. J. B. Priestley, for one, once observed that, in his opinion, much of the "quite unnecessary scandal" that was attached to HG was due to his frankness and honesty. If you took the lid off the average stockbroker, he suggested, you'd probably find more to be revealed than you would in the case of HG.[62]

Annajane was not told that H. G. Wells was her father for many years; in the time-honored tradition, she was led to believe that he was her uncle. By all accounts, the girl grew up sound and happy. Amber once wrote to HG about their daughter's talent for swimming, saying that she had his "buoyant" way of tackling life: "In fact I am very grateful to you for her. One cannot feel old or dejected with such a sunny generous creature about." In the same (undated) letter, Amber congratulated HG for his latest book. It was one of his best, she said, a pièce de résistance for having made readers see his fantasy "through ordinary life instead of creating a special universe to carry it. Hundreds of writers have tried—I can think of no one else who has succeeded." In another letter, thanking HG for a check, Amber mentioned that Harold Laski at the London School of Economics told her that HG was "the most generous man alive." Amber remonstrated in her letters to HG that not only did she still believe in him but the next generation did as well. Members of her family ripped HG's books out of each other's hands, she said, and young people "discuss them endlessly in their schools. This generation will be as far as I can see even more the children of your mind than we were." Amber often praised her former mentor-lover. For example, thanking HG for sending one of his books, she wrote: "Nobody can do these things as you can—nobody ever has except perhaps Voltaire. I don't know that he wrote as well as you do, but his sentences, as he built up an attack, must have delighted his audience as you do us."[63] Amber also said that an American who knew Lenin well during his Paris days once told her that the Russian leader had been influenced by HG's *A Modern Utopia*.

Many of the letters in their correspondence dealt with Amber's contributions to HG's *The Work, Wealth and Happiness of Mankind*, which was published in two volumes in 1931.[64] To help with the mammoth task of writing *Work*, HG shamelessly employed Amber and Odette as researcher-writers, and arranged for them to receive 12.5 percent of the royalties. Amber produced a chapter on women. "I do hope that what I have written will be of some use," she wrote to HG on June 1, adding that she and her husband were planning on telling Annajane that HG's latest monetary "kindness to her is the opportunity of her life for broadening her mind and far more valuable than foreign travel." Earlier that year, Amber wrote that, in the chapter on women, she wanted to stress the dual necessity of women's economic dependence and men's support for their children. "Everything gives way to that, and men being what they are, most women get turned away from wide issues or personal achievements."[65] On May 28, Amber repeated her hope that HG would be pleased with her chapter on women. Curiously, she added: "It is almost impossible to write about women without abusing them roundly. I agree with Odette that they are silly; they are also conceited." In addition to that chapter, Amber researched and wrote much of chapter 10, titled "The Rich, the Poor, and Their Traditional Antagonism." This included sections on business magnates Jay Gould and J. D. Rockefeller. She also contributed to sections on labor conditions, histories of the Congo and Putumayo, the world economic slump, and German international affairs. In addition, Amber critiqued HG's chapters.[66]

In a sense, Amber had helped HG write *Ann Veronica* thirty-five years earlier. *Ann Veronica: A Modern Love Story* (1909) was a publishing sensation, so sensational that it nearly ruined its author. The convention-bending novel, which openly explored free love and women's sexual liberation, was a thinly disguised account of the love affair between HG and Amber Reeves. HG later conceded that "A pallid reflection of some aspects of our situation—or rather of the sentiments of our situation—appeared in *Ann Veronica* and *The New Machiavelli* [1911]. This was the underlying reason for the campaign against those books."[67]

Amber was for all intents and purposes the main character, Ann Veronica Stanley, and HG bore a strong resemblance to the scientist, Capes.[68] Ann Veronica was a rebellious heroine who scandalized Victorian England by leaving her father, rebuffing the obvious choice in a husband, and pursuing Capes, a married man. It is Ann Veronica and Capes against the world. In her last soliloquy in the book, after her father had finally accepted her back into the fold, Ann Veronica told Capes, now her husband:

> Even when we are old, when we are rich as we may be, we won't forget the time when we cared nothing for anything but the joy of one another, when we risked everything for one another, when all the wrappings and coverings seemed to have fallen from life and left it light and fire. Do you remember it all? . . . Say you will never forget! That these common things and secondary things shan't overwhelm us.[69]

Not surprisingly, much of the United Kingdom became obsessed with the book. From Dundee on October 17, 1909, Winston Churchill wrote to his darling Clementine: "You must read Wells's new book, *Ann Veronica*. Massingham tells me (this is most secret) that Wells has been behaving very badly with a young Girton girl of the new emancipated school—& that [very] serious consequences have followed. The book apparently is suggested by the intrigue—These literary gents!!"[70] The next day, "Clemmy Kat" responded: "Your gossip about Wells is very exciting—I long to confide it to Hodgy Podgy but restrain myself.

Perhaps she will be called in to succor the poor Girton girl. I thought that Institution turned out only stern & masculine specimens."[71] In his memoir, Lance Sieveking recalled that when he was a boy, he was not allowed even to mention the name H. G. Wells in his mother's company or in the home of his best friend. Whenever some unfortunate guest broached the subject, a "sudden incomprehensible silence" followed. "It was not until long after my friend's death that I learned the explanation of the mystery. Wells had, it appeared, given a practical example of the emancipation of women with the co-operation of my friend's sister."[72] In its bibliography, the H. G. Wells Society described *Ann* rather blandly as "The story of a girl who escapes from the conformist world of suburbia to live her own life. Like its predecessor, *Tono-Bungay,* this semi-autobiographical novel is full of acute social comment. It is dedicated 'to A. J.'"[73]

HG offered his *Ann Veronica* manuscript to Frederick Macmillan in September 1908. Fearful that the novel would provoke a scandal, Macmillan rejected it on the grounds that the public would find the plot "exceedingly distasteful." HG then went to Unwin, which at the time was fishing for manuscripts from important authors, and it published *Ann* the following fall, a few months before Amber produced her baby on December 31. What made the novel so incendiary was its "fictional representation of rebellious young womanhood," wrote literary scholar Sylvia Hardy in her introduction to the 1993 edition *of Ann Veronica.*[74] HG's heroine flaunted her sexual liberation. She defied convention not only by taking the initiative in a romantic situation but also by proposing—to her married college teacher, no less—that she become his mistress. As HG explained in his autobiography:

> Ann Veronica was a virgin who fell in love and showed it, instead of waiting as all popular heroines had hitherto done, for someone to make love to her. It was held to be an unspeakable offence that an adolescent female should be sex-conscious before the thing was forced upon her attention. But Ann Veronica wanted a particular man who excited her and she pursued him and got him. With gusto.[75]

HG's achievement with *Ann Veronica* cannot be overstated. He helped spark a revolution in the depiction of women in literature. With *Ann,* literary scholar Patricia Stubbs has argued, "the old ideal of women as passive, dependent and, above all, chaste, was gradually but deliberately transformed. Women in fiction became sexual, sensuous beings. A complete about turn had taken place."[76] Indeed, in the novel, HG asserted for the first time in fiction not only that women had sexual desires but that those desires were "normal and acceptable."[77] Although the ending is unconvincing and implausible, the point it makes is critical: Ann Veronica "has claimed the right to love how and where she wants, and Wells allows her to do this without bringing down an awful retribution on her guilty head."[78]

In addition to the literary impact, there was also a social impact. HG gave young people license to defy conventional morality, to break out of the shackles of their restrictive lives, just as he and Amber had. According to Hardy, the book seemed to "open up hitherto undreamt of possibilities for women." *Ann* raised questions about "relationships between men and women and about social attitudes towards women that are still of considerable interest and relevance to today's readers. Wells may not always have provided satisfactory answers, but in *Ann Veronica* he does oblige us to look at the problems."[79] The acclaimed British novelist Graham Greene put it succinctly when he wrote that HG was "the best novelist on sex in the English language."[80]

Like the affair that prompted it, *Ann Veronica* caused a giant scandal, just as Macmillan had feared. Libraries shunned the book and the press attacked it. Some Wells biographers were also scandalized by *Ann;* among them were the MacKenzies, who called the book "a tract masquerading as a piece of romantic fiction." Furthermore, had the plot not been blatantly immoral by the standards of the day, the book "would have been dismissed as banal, humourless and sentimental."[81] As a consequence of all of the buzz, sales for *Ann Veronica* were brisk. Of course, H. G. Wells already had a reputation for being fiction's bad boy. Two years earlier, he had promoted free love and women's emancipation in his fantasy novel *In the Days of the Comet.* It wasn't the first time, nor would it be the last, that HG would try to legitimize his personal lifestyle through popular literature.

Although HG took a great deal of heat then and for a long time afterward for running around with a girl half his age, for getting her pregnant, for flaunting the affair, and for putting his young mistress in a situation whereby she would lose her educational advantage, the girl in question, as previously suggested, would not hold a grudge. Thirty years after the scandal, Amber wrote this to HG: "What you gave me all those years ago—a love that seemed perfect to me, the influence of your mind, and Annajane—have stood by me ever since. I have never for a moment felt that they were not worth the price."[82]

★   ★   ★

H. G. Wells showed up on the literary screen at the end of the last millennium in part because of the interest in one of his former lovers, Dame Rebecca West, née Cicily Fairfield, journalist, writer, and *femme formidable*. In his biography of Rebecca West, Carl Rollyson—also the biographer of Martha Gellhorn—described Rebecca as "a marriage of contradictions, a feminist, a mistress, and a dutiful wife." Her affairs with H. G. Wells and Lord Beaverbrook, he wrote, "are the stuff of legend," and her contribution to British literature was invaluable. Among other things, her *Black Lamb and Grey Falcon,* often described as one of the first nonfiction novels, was "one of the masterpieces of world literature."[83]

The story of the meeting of the two writers bears repeating. Rebecca West, the young literary upstart, slammed H. G. Wells, the master, in print in a September 1912 issue of *The Freewoman,* then a new militant feminist weekly. She called him "pseudo-scientific" and "the old maid among novelists; even the sex obsession that lay clotted on *Ann Veronica* and *The New Machiavelli* like cold white sauce was merely old maid's mania, the reaction toward the flesh of a mind too long absorbed in airships and colloids." Calling the world's premier advocate and practitioner of free love an old maid attracted HG's attention.[84] He quickly invited her to join him for lunch at his home in Easton Glebe.

When Rebecca West responded to HG's invitation on September 27, 1912, she was not yet twenty, more than twenty-six years HG's junior. They evidently had much to say because they talked for five hours. Between the autumn of that year and the spring of the next, they met frequently, though not intimately. Rollyson argues that while HG was attracted to Rebecca, he balked at the idea of having an affair, and she withdrew, suffering a nervous collapse. As her letters to HG attest, by June 1913 she was ranting at him for rebuffing her.

> I always knew that you would hurt me to death some day, but I hoped to choose the time and place. You've always been unconsciously hostile to me and I haven't tried to conciliate you by hacking away at my love for you, cutting it down to the little thing that was the most you wanted. I would give my whole life to feel your arms round me again. I wish you had loved me. I wish you liked me. Yours, Rebecca.[85]

The fall of 1913, HG's affair with Elizabeth von Arnim, or Little e, another woman of letters, was breaking apart, and HG was laying the groundwork for a liason with Rebecca. When they met again, after a long separation, it was at his London apartment, and, as luck would have it, their second intimacy resulted in a pregnancy. In a portion of the *Postscript* that was suppressed, HG wrote that since abortion in those days was illegal as well as difficult for people outside a limited circle, he and Rebecca "had to face up to our situation and go through with it. Moreover we had to reckon with her vindictive elder sister and her incalculable mother."[86] HG, who claimed that he immediately told Jane about the romance and the pregnancy, found Rebecca lodgings in Hunstanton, Norfolk; Anthony arrived on August 4, 1914, the day Britain declared war on Germany. As soon as he was able to, HG found a house at Braughing, in Hertfordshire, a dozen miles or so from his home in Easton Glebe, so that he could easily visit his mistress and son. HG set Rebecca up with a nurse and a housekeeper and she, HG, and Anthony lived together intermittently for several months.

HG would install and uninstall Rebecca and Anthony many times as it suited her comfort and his proximity: in 1915 to Hatch End, a suburb of London, where they would socialize like young marrieds; in 1917 to Leigh-on-Sea in Essex, from whence Rebecca "continued her peripatetic schedule—shuttling back and forth to London for teas, dinner, films, and facial massages"[87]; to Queen's Gate in South Kensington. HG traveled between his apartment in Whitehall Court and Kensington for what he called "long intimate half-days and evenings." He didn't mention in the *Postscript*, however, the level of erotic enthusiasm he and Rebecca shared. In their passion plays, she was Panther, he was her Jaguar, and theirs was very much a jungle-love (albeit with baby talk: "Panfer," for example, and "Fing" for thing). One letter, postmarked April 14, 1914, is illustrative:

> I shall lay my paw upon you this Wednesday night and snuff under your chin and bite your breast and lick your flank and proceed to other familiarities. I shall roll you over and do what I like with you. I shall make you pant and bite back. Then I shall give you a shake to quiet you and go to sleep all over you and if I snore, I snore. Your Lord. The Jaguar.[88]

Life was rarely idyllic for any of them, but the fat hit the fire when Anthony reached school age and his parentage became an issue. Sometimes the Rebecca West who visited her son was his aunt, sometimes his mother, and sometimes his adopted mother; HG was often an uncle or a godfather. In his writings, HG avoided mentioning the bitter relationship that developed almost from the start between Rebecca and Anthony, and that persisted throughout their lifetimes.

That Rebecca and Anthony had an extremely troubled relationship is now well known, but it was not always so. Part of the problem was Anthony's illegitimacy; Rebecca struggled to keep his heritage secret, except from close friends and relatives. It was not until he entered his early forties that Anthony revealed who his father was, and that is when all hell broke loose between him and his mother. Still, his parentage was just one of the many issues between them. Affection and money, or lack of both, were other considerable thorns. Anthony claimed that when he was a child, his mother was not only neglectful of him but also stingy, neurotic, and jealous of his affection for his father. To be sure, Anthony also went through phases, especially in his adolescence, when he sided with his mother and despised HG for neglecting him and being cheap with his financial support. Rebecca responded to Anthony's criticisms of her by saying that he was neurotic, that he never saw things as they really were, and that he distorted reality—especially concerning his parents and their affection. Later, Rebecca would attribute her son's increasingly public announcements and quixotic behavior to his mental and emotional problems, for which she assumed no responsibility. Rebecca's description of Anthony's mental health would become extreme in crisis years, to the point that, in letters to family members, she called him "a hopeless lunatic" and "insanely malicious."

Anthony was anguished by his unconventional upbringing and family life. As an adult, he admitted to having problems, including what he called "neurotic horrors" about "the speculations of fools" over his relationship with HG.[89] HG conceded that Anthony enjoyed a less than wholesome home environment, that it was rife with conflict and confusion over his parentage and upbringing. He wrote that he and Rebecca moved their "ménage from house to house and from place to place and Anthony was shifted from school to school," and that they "trailed a web of nervous irritation that twisted about us and strangled the development of the generous liking and affection for each other of which we were certainly capable," not specifying what that "web" did to little Anthony.[90] In 1932, Odette assessed the teenager, who was visiting his father. She told Marjorie Craig Wells that she liked Anthony very much, thought him "incredibly intelligent, precocious, charming, and lazy beyond all words," didn't think he was anything to be afraid of, and that "he loves Pidoo enormously." It seemed to her that Anthony hated his current living arrangements, so she suggested that he be sent as soon as possible to Oxford, "& then [stay], at least [part time] with his father in London. He's much too premature & yet childish at the same time."[91] Eighteen years later, after much poison had flowed under the bridge, Rebecca told Marjorie that Anthony's fantasy had always been that HG had only a temporary and evanescent affection for her, and that his real love was for Anthony. "It wasn't a very amiable fantasy, but it was what he lived by. You must realise that nobody in Anthony's life has mattered to him a fraction as much as HG."[92]

Meanwhile, the relationship between Rebecca and HG had been showing strains since 1917, and the differences in their temperaments eventually overran their passion for each other. In HG's words, they were "fundamentally incompatible." He asserted that all Rebecca wanted from him was "a richly imaginative and sensuous love affair." Still, as far of HG was concerned, they "came to like each other extremely and to be extremely exasperated with each other and antagonistic."[93] Part of the antagonism had to do with Rebecca's frustration over having to put her writing on hold when Anthony came along. In 1917, she began staging a slow comeback to the literary world; by the end of the year, she had finished half her new novel, *The Judge,* but she wouldn't complete it until the end of 1921.[94] Their romance hit the skids When HG announced that he had had a tryst with Moura Budberg in Russia in 1920, and with the feminist activist Margaret Sanger in the United States in 1921. Rebecca took that as an invitation to have her own flings, including a brief one with the writer Compton MacKenzie.

The attempt to revive their affair in 1922 in Spain was unsuccessful. HG had just finished an extremely invigorating romance with Margaret, who, along with the United States had spoiled him. "I am famous here," the fifty-six-year-old writer wrote to Rebecca. "People turn round in the street and when I went to a play . . . the other night the house stood and clapped."[95] Rollyson argues that HG was turned off by and unsympathetic to Rebecca's chronic physical problems, and that while both of them wanted to be spoiled and rejuvenated by the other, neither could play the role of nurturer. Another incompatibility, at least in HG's eyes, was how they approached their craft of writing. Even when their romantic and emotional lives together were going well, they quarreled about their writing techniques. HG was rational and followed a carefully laid out plan; Rebecca was schematic and open to serendipity.

She writes like a loom producing her broad rich fabric with hardly a thought of how it will make up into a shape, while I write to cover a frame of ideas. We did harm to each other as writers. She prowled in the thickets and I have always kept close to the trail that leads to the World-State. She splashed her colours about; . . . and I wrote with an ostentatious disregard of decoration; never used a rare phrase when a common one would serve, and was more of a journalist than ever. I find her excursions into general criticism, such as *The Strange Necessity,* pretentious and futile, and she finds the love-making of my later novels incurably theoretical and shallow. Neither of us, I suspect, is absolutely wrong about the other.[96]

When HG and Rebecca arrived in Paris in January 1923, their relationship was on life support. Rebecca was demanding marriage or a separation, and HG was holding on to her, though he later conceded that he should have let her go. "I realize I got much the best of our relationship; but there was no one to take her place with me, and she was fond of me as well as resentful and there was no one ready to take my place with her."[97] The effective break, HG reported, came from Rebecca in the fall of 1923. She went on a lecturing tour of the United States, made new friends, had adventures, and became a self-reliant woman. He went to Lisbon and "struck up an intimacy"—a stock phrase of his—with an unnamed widow. Back in London the next spring, HG and Rebecca were "acutely aware of each other's existence," HG wrote. He made love to his widow and to one or two other women, but he reported being intensely discontented, wanting Rebecca desperately, but "with a difference," just as she wanted him. "The world was full of men she couldn't talk to as she talked to me, and of women I had only a brief and simple use for."[98] They met a few more times, she and Anthony went to Austria, and HG decided to set off on a trip around the world because he "found England full of heart-ache." He later wished he had gone to Naples, where Moura was living with Maxim Gorky, and "looked at her again."

In Geneva, HG couldn't get Rebecca off his mind. He was in misery and haunted by the thought of her. She had become the symbol of his

Lover-Shadow and he "was unable to conceive of it in any other form than hers—or exist without it."[99] Rebecca responded to HG's telegram proposing that they try again, beginning with a winter vacation at Montpellier, with a refusal, also by telegram. In a suppressed portion of the *Postscript,* HG wrote:

> I do not know what happened to the Lover-Shadow of Rebecca after our primary breach in 1923. She had "affairs" in America and passed, I think, into what I have called in my *Autobiography* a "discursive" phase. I had no formal intimation of these experiences, but her knowledge that the ghosts were bound to rise between us, and her clear realisation of the jealousy they would evoke, may have influenced her in her refusal of my Montpellier suggestion.[100]

Luckily for HG, Rebecca's refusal for a reunion came almost simultaneously with Odette Keun's initial phone call. HG later wrote that he didn't know whether he loved Rebecca West, but that near the end of their liaison, he was in love with her. The day HG died, Rebecca wrote to Marjorie: "I have loved him all my life and always will, and I bitterly reproach myself for not having stayed with him."[101]

That feeling, if it was genuine, did not prevent Rebecca from waging a holy war on their son, or for that matter on anyone who spun history "wrong" after HG's death. Indeed, the discord between Rebecca and Anthony West only grew and intensified once HG was out of the picture. Gip and Marjorie Wells were also caught in the crossfire; from time to time they seemed to be baited into it. All hell broke loose in August 1949 when the *Times Literary Supplement* published an advertisement for Anthony's latest novel, *On a Dark Night.* The ad sneaked in a short sensational line about West and his next work: "A highly distinguished and exciting first novel which we shall publish on October 14. Mr. West is also engaged upon a full-length biography of his father, H. G. Wells, which we hope to publish in 1951." The *TLS* ad became the first public announcement that Anthony was the son of H. G. Wells, and although not saying it directly, it intimated juicy revelations about HG's private life.

As soon as she learned about the ad, Rebecca went into high gear on a campaign to control the damage, to stop further ads from appearing, and to do what she could to halt publication of the book, now heralded as the official biography of H. G. Wells. Her machinations could be Machiavellian. Rebecca fired off dozens of agitated and agitating letters to Marjorie and Gip, alerting them to her son's motives, actions, and plans. The family soap opera continued when Anthony refused to return four suitcases of HG's papers; Marjorie called him a blackmailer, and Anthony retracted his offer to the Wells Estate to write the official biography of HG. Anthony withdrew from his role as official biographer until 1953, but, once again, all the old and hard feelings were stirred up. Once again it was Rebecca at the spoon.

It is difficult not to conclude, after reading the entire run of letters between the Wests and the younger Wellses, that behind her stated reasons for involving Gip and Marjorie—to protect HG's reputation and estate—Rebecca had another agenda: To drive a wedge between her son and HG's family, and even to discredit Anthony. Rebecca certainly managed to discredit many other people in this correspondence—from Max Beaverbrook, her former lover (she called him "a queer and wicked little creature"), to Dorothy Richardson ("that old monster"), to HG himself (who "had sometimes very little respect for the strict letter of the truth"). Truth be told, Rebecca began discrediting and demonizing HG, who she felt *had* neglected their son in his earliest years and was cruel to her well before their final breakup in 1923. In this current crisis with Anthony, Rebecca not only played both sides against the middle, but also attempted to suppress her liaison with HG and the birth of Anthony, to clear herself of negative impressions, and even to elevate her reputation.

It is also hard not to conclude that while Rebecca proclaimed a commitment to serve the truth in all matters, she spent a great deal of time and energy trying to control information and spin events. She had already succeeded in suppressing a paragraph about her liaison with H. G. Wells and Anthony's birth in a December 1948 *Time* magazine cover story that featured her. It took nearly every weapon in her arsenal, including a threatened lawsuit for invasion of privacy. She next worked to stop *Heritage,* Anthony's fictional biography of his father, from being published in England, and at that, too, she succeeded. Rebecca may never have realized the irony of the situation: that she was keeping Anthony from doing the very thing she had taught him to do: to be intensely and publicly critical of HG. Eyre and Spottiswoode, Anthony's British publisher, agreed to "make no further reference" to Anthony's relationship to H. G. Wells in connection with *Heritage.* However, they couldn't control, Douglas Jerrold wrote to Rebecca, "what is in the biography which your son is going to write."[102] Houghton Mifflin, Anthony's American publisher, turned *Heritage* down, and it was published by Random House in 1955.

Twenty-three years after the first major crisis, Rebecca was once again—or still—festering over the question of who should write the official biography of H. G. Wells. On May 21, 1973, she wrote to Gip about the matter, arguing that the only person who could possibly write the biography was Gordon Ray. Not only had he collected a lot of material but he was also the only person to have seen some eight hundred letters from HG to Rebecca, which she had deposited at the Yale University Library.[103] Rebecca appears to have had a long-term love-hate relationship with those letters. Nearly a quarter of a century earlier, on January 31, 1950, she wrote to Marjorie to say that she had been going through her correspondence with HG and "destroying the letters I have which I thought would leave an unfavourable impression" of HG. Evidently, Rebecca did not consider her bonfire a crime against the Wells Estate, scholarship, or history. Six years later, Rebecca told Marjorie that she had destroyed two or three of HG's letters "because they were spiteful and unjust, not so much to me as to other people (I think only two, one long and one very short, I am not trying to rig our relationship in any way." Now, she claimed to have about six hundred letters from HG, all charming and affectionate, "except when they are amusingly cross, or at any rate, not discreditably so."[104]

Anthony West's 1955 fictionalized biography of his father, *Heritage,* was published by Random House. A 1984 edition, published by Simon

& Schuster, included an eleven-page introduction in which Anthony set the record straight about the grief his mother had caused him throughout the years. He also offered his analysis of the source of her lifelong malice. The highlights: Rebecca was treacherous and dishonest: Her primary passions were money, malice and meddling. She also was never able to forgive HG, Jane, or Anthony "for being involved in her debacle," and more than anything else, she was never able to forgive herself. In the end her story is one of self-hatred, and that is for me the saddest of its aspects, not least because having received it as her heritage she endeavored to pass it on to me."[105]

As it happened, Anthony's wasn't the only H. G. Wells biography in Rebecca's sights. She also waged a heavy campaign against the work of Antonina Vallentin. On August 20, 1950, Rebecca wrote this letter to Vallentin, a French writer of Polish origin:

> Leaving out the question of appropriateness, the trouble about this particular biography is that you really do not know enough about HG's personal life. The ground plan on which you worked is not valid. The situation of his personal life was quite different from the one you describe. I would not be doing my duty if I did not tell you that so far as my knowledge goes it is quite remote from reality, and when his full correspondence is released, I do not think it will confirm your version.

Rebecca wrote to Marjorie the same day, enclosing the letter she had sent "the Vallentin," as she called her, with the postscript: "I am sure the Budberg is behind this Vallentin life." At the beginning of the next year, Rebecca passed along another tidbit to Marjorie. She wrote on January 2, 1951, to say that Antonin Vallentin was an "old-standing Communist" who had collaborated heavily with the Germans during the war but denied that she had been taken back by the Communists, "with whom she may have been working all the time." Rebecca described Madame V. as "a close associate of Moura," who had read the typescript and "has surreptitiously been trying to arrange for the publication over here." Rebecca went on to tell Marjorie that Moura was linked to some trouble that had befallen one of her friends.

> The whole loathsome business goes back to Moura, who has—I suppose because she was told to do it by the people who control her—brought the most repulsive trouble on a woman who had never done her any harm and had trusted her as a friend. I never believed there was such plotting outside a Phillips Oppenheim novel. I have always thought of Moura as a nice plump placid pussy-cat, but she is utterly vile and sordid and nasty, and I realise what you must have felt like having this disgusting sneak and informer padding about the family mansion. I feel I never should have left HG to get into the hands of anything so venal and squalid.

If nothing else, this case study illustrates the passionate feelings that relationships with H. G. Wells inspired. It also demonstrates the lengths and depths to which people caught up in HG's myth, legacy, and heritage were willing to go. After her affair with HG, Rebecca went on to have short affairs with many men, including one giant, John Gunther, and two tiny men, film star Charlie Chaplin and publisher Max Beaverbrook, before settling into a conventional married life with a wealthy, and tall, British banker.

★   ★   ★

David Smith described HG's relationship with Margaret Sanger as "a very long and quite passionate long-distance friendship."[106] When they met, first at British birth control meetings in the summer of 1920, and later at the Washington, D.C., conference on disarmament in 1921, both HG and Margaret were internationally famous: he as a novelist, she as an American feminist and pioneering advocate of birth control. Margaret has been described as beautiful, with grey eyes and auburn hair, "combining a radiant feminist appeal with an impression of serenity, calm and graciousness," her personality "romantic, rebellious and assertive; she looked, talked and behaved like a Wells heroine, and he was immediately attracted."[107] Margaret divorced her husband in 1912 and moved into "the radical bohemia" of New York City, befriending John Reed and Emma Goldman, among other people, and starting her own paper, the *Woman Rebel*. In the 1920s and 1930s, she did a great deal of traveling, most of it on behalf of birth control, but some of it to meet her lovers, H. G. Wells and Havelock Ellis, the latter a psychologist, essayist, and art critic known, interestingly enough, for his pioneering studies in sexual psychology.

On June 3, 1920, responding apparently to HG's trial-balloon message, Margaret wrote from Rotherwick Road, London, N.W. 4, thanking HG for writing, then leaping into feminist politics.

> I too wish there could be done something by the women of the world to make peace possible. I may have an opportunity to propose such a discussion upon the return of the women from Geneva June twelfth. Of course I am not expecting those women to do it. Many of them still think Germany did not get enough! But your idea is good and right. It should take root.

Margaret then gave HG the dates of her comings and goings in London. On the top of her letter, he made the notation: "Jane, ask her to tea Wednesday." Evidently the tea went well, because the next two letters from Margaret to HG are thank-you notes for the invitation to tea and for a weekend at the Wellses. Another houseguest was Cornelia Otis Skinner, whom we have already met. On Tuesday, July 27, following that weekend, Margaret, writing to Jane, said she hoped they could get together for "a nice chat." Margaret closed by saying, "Again many thanks for your sweet hospitality and the pleasure & joy of being acquainted with you and yours." At the end of 1922, Margaret married Noah Slee, an oil tycoon twenty years her junior, but, like HG, she continued her romantic liaisons—in her case, throughout her twenty-one-year marriage with Slee.[108]

After a gall bladder operation on November 2, 1937, undertaken in anticipation of a trip around the world in 1940, Margaret was laid up in a New York hospital for a month. HG, who was in the United States, sent her flowers and a letter, to which she responded, probably on November 10:

> HG dear, Your flowers so springlike & starry-eyed are here beside me. Your letter—well it is so like you to give me that up pull just when it is most needed. The Dr has been ruthless about visitors, but I hope to see him tomorrow & ask if I can see you sometime soon. There will of course be nurses about & no privacy. Anyway it will be grand to get a look at you—again. I want to say lots of things long embedded in my heart but between us there never has been need of words. From the first there was understanding clear eyed & straight. You have been one of the great men, great enough to be there when your hand clasp counted. Always my love. Margaret.

Later in the month, HG came to visit his old friend and lover in the hospital. After she got home, Margaret wrote to HG on December 3: "It is needless for me to say that I loved seeing you. It gave our modest nurses a great thrill to peek at you from behind closed doors."

David Smith maintains that the last time Margaret and HG saw each other was in the fall of 1940 during his U.S. lecture tour. She would write to HG on November 8 of that year from her Tucson home, Casa de Adobe, to say that she was planning to take a group of people, including the owner of the *Arizona Star,* to his upcoming lecture in Phoenix. "Your *New World Order* book is superb," she went on to say. "I am giving it to my friends for Christmas to open & enlighten their dark minds." After the lecture, she sent HG a postmortem, dated November 14, proclaiming that the lecture was "a great success. Never have I heard anyone read a paper with such a speaking manner." She also took the occasion to note that his reply on the debt question was not his best, but "scattered applause seems to indicate support. I hope you will clarify that cloudy subject somewhere sometime." In closing, Margaret quipped: "You looked like you did ten years ago. *Congratulations!*"

In October of the next year, Margaret turned to HG for a favor. She asked him to compose a message that she could deliver for him at the twenty-fifth anniversary celebration of the opening of the first birth control clinic in America. He responded with the following: "The birth control movement has revolutionized human life. It has emancipated men & women alike from involuntary animal parentage. Women can now profess their own lives & be the willing & deliberate mother of a renascent world."[109] Margaret was apparently overjoyed with his offering. "Your message was truly too thrilling and I shall have the honor and the privilege of reading it at the end of my own speech." [110] In addition to being read in New York, his message would be broadcast by radio throughout the city, then sent to thirty-two other birth control groups holding similar anniversary observances; these groups would then broadcast the message from local stations.

HG and Margaret Sanger shared another passion on a very different front: their "Holy Crusade," as Margaret called it, against the Roman Catholic Church, the Vatican in particular. HG published his *Crux Ansata: An Indictment of the Roman Catholic Church* in 1943. The ninety-six-page polemical work attacked the Church for meddling in international politics and questioned why the Vatican had escaped being bombed.[111] HG asked Christabel to edit the short work, which she did. "You are the best proof reader in the world," he told her on March 22, 1943. When most major papers steered clear of the book by not reviewing it, and no American publisher could be found for it, HG's fire for the project was fueled. As early as March 1943, Margaret, who came from a Catholic family, had anticipated the refusal to publish. She was already on the case, suspicious of Catholic power and influence in Washington, particularly in the White House and the state department. An acquaintance of hers, Katharine Salter, had written a letter linking the Vatican and Nazis, then enlisted Margaret's help to have her letter published in England, as it had been published in the United States. Margaret, in turn, corresponded with HG about the Salter letter. This correspondence grew into Margaret and HG's conspiracy of sorts over *Crux Ansata*. In May 31, 1943, she wrote this to him:

Some outstanding people, who have no prejudices whatsoever against the Roman Catholic hierarchy, are beginning to have grave feelings as to their power and influence over FDR as well as their influence in the State Department. It is now a well-known fact that there was a hold-up and a demand that more Roman Catholics be placed in higher positions in Europe representing the USA in return for a statement by the Hierarchy that the Roman Catholics are now on the side of the Allies.

Margaret also reminded HG about a package she had sent him containing "material on the Nazi-Vatican tie-up." She noted that the author was an ex-Jesuit who had been connected with the Vatican for several years, and thus, should be in the know. She was curious, she said, to learn HG's reactions after reading the pamphlet "Behind the Dictators." "None of us want to be too pessimistic or be on the wrong track about this question," she said, "but at the same time we must be alert and not have the wool pulled over our eyes because of tolerance. I hope you keep well & keep your wits sharpened for the Peace to follow this war."

On April 16, 1944, HG wrote that he'd been "very ill indeed," but that he was on the mend. He was giving Margaret all rights to *Crux* to do what she thought best with them: "Marjorie will give you particulars." Margaret responded on May 23 that she was pleased and proud that he had honored her with the rights, and that she was planning to work up a campaign immediately for its publication and distribution.[112] To HG, she wrote:

> It will be fascinating and to me most interesting to watch the growth and spread of your book here. I intend that every member of the Senate and the House shall have a free copy with a letter from his constituents. It is a strangle hold that the hierarchy have upon the American people, especially through the press, other publications, and the radio. I think it is their last hold on the nation, and we must do all in our power to break it. And now my prayer is that you are rapidly recovering, and many thanks for your utter dearness.[113]

By June 6, 1944, 1,000 copies of *Crux* had been sold, Margaret wrote, but there was a new problem: The binders, who were Roman Catholic, now refused to bind the piece.

Woven into many of Margaret's letters was an invitation to convalesce at her home in the Arizona sunshine. HG always refused, despite the German bombs, which occasionally found their way to Hanover Terrace. After one of his latest turn-downs, Margaret quipped, "I often think of the remark of your small grandson when it was suggested that he leave England and come over here during the early bombing days in London and he replied 'What? And miss everything?' That is doubtless the way his grandfather feels. Anyway, cheerio."[114]

Surely one of the weirdest letters Margaret Sanger ever sent H. G. Wells was the following, undated, though obviously in response to his query: "HG darling, There were two [prostitutes] in those New York visits. Daisy the colored damsel who is so proud of having served you and our charming Juliet Rublee who was also colorful in a different way. Both would send you their love if they knew I was writing." In his *Postscript*, HG had described his first experience with a "brown" prostitute. After meeting with "President Roosevelt the First" in Washington, D.C., in 1906, HG had time on his hands. The cab driver took him to a "gay house," as HG requested, and after a bit of chitchat with several "brown women in exiguous costumes," HG chose a woman who turned out to be "much more intelligent than most of the women one meets at dinner-parties." He wrote that a mutual liking arose almost immediately, and that the two people who had met as strangers at three o'clock "parted like lovers at half-past six."[115]

One of the sweetest letters Margaret Sanger ever sent HG was penned on Sunday, November 19, no year given, but probably in the early 1940s: "I have carried a handkerchief of yours around the world with me & here it is again. It saved my neck from sunburn on the desert & it did a lot to keep out the Pekin dust." One of the last letters she wrote—and one of the most sentimental—was on January 5, 1946, from her Tucson home. She reminisced about HG's various visits to New York, including a wonderful evening walk across the Brooklyn Bridge.

That was tops in beauty & fun. But then all your visits were fun. I was very serious with the world's population problems on my back. You were too wise to worry over trifles (not that an unwanted baby is a trifle) but your vision & knowledge of the intrigues going on in International Affairs gave you an anxiety & desire to correct immediate problems which unless solved would ultimately set the world in flames—you were right then as before again & again. The world dear HG saddens me hourly, and what must you be thinking? Our own Nation with strikes & confusion adds to our disillusion. My dearest love to you wonderful man-friend et al. May 1946 give you your hearts desire.

The coming year did not grant H. G. Wells his heart's desire. He died in August. However, his death did not end the correspondence. Margaret's last letter to HG, written the day *after* he died and in huge uncontrolled script, communicated the tender and deep love she had for her old ally and man-friend, and entertained the possibility that further communication might be possible.

So, Darling, G.H. You have gone out to the Great Beyond—It's queer that with all your Greatness, your Mind, your Vision, you have not touched this aspect of our Hearafter—the over "their." You are such a darling & you know where you are at, but I don't—that's interesting.

Now today—you are over their—I am flying overseas to Stockholm & then to England. England means London & London means H G Wells; to me and to now millions of Americans. Oh, darling, HG you have been the dawn to me.

Your Great Mind—your humor—perhaps your wit, so akin to my Irish feeling & knowing of wit, may have drawn me to you from the first. . . .

So many many wonderful talks we had—about women, your women, your loves—my loves—our love—Always we met and picked

up all the threads of our last meeting & wove again a friendship which
has endured ever since.

And now you are over their. Beyond my horizon. I wish if you are
their—consciously their & alive in spirit, you will endeavor to explore
the possibilities of communication with me. I'd like to try to see what
you can do. I don't know one thing about it, but loads of things and laws
of life are unknown by us humans.

I'll be in London [in] a week & will see Frank & G.P. & your family if
I can—It will be too awful not to see you their. My love wherever you
are. Always, Margaret.[116]

HG left Margaret completely out of his *Postscript*. One can only assume
that he wished to preserve her professional reputation.

*   *   *

Odette Keun was HG's lover for ten years, sandwiched between Rebecca West, Margaret Sanger, and Moura Budberg. She dominates
forty-five pages of HG's *Postscript*. Even well after the high-octane affair, he was able to speak well of her, or at least to find positive things to
say. He opened his *Postscript* chapter, "The Vociferous Transit of Odette
Keun" with this:

I suppose I ought to write of Odette Keun as a Bad Woman, and in a
strain of resentment and hostility. She was, from certain points of view,
a thoroughly nasty and detestable person; vain, noisy and weakly outrageous. But I know one or two good things about her which are difficult
for other people to know—a very real thread of unhappiness and self
torment in her make-up—and that knowledge by itself qualifies my dislike. And also there was a strand of warped but very intense affection-
ateness in her. She excited me a good deal; she made me laugh and, for
all her spasmodic efforts to do so, she never really hurt me. She wanted

to do so at times extravagantly, but the claws never got into my eyes. As I spin my memories of her about, I realize that, if it were not for the compunction I feel for her pitifulness, she would be beyond all question the Greatest Lark I have ever had. If only she had had a spring of that deep laughter which fuses minds I might be living with her now. But she was protected by an invincible barrier from her own sense of humor. She was immensely vain.[117]

HG once said that Rebecca had a splendid disturbed brain, which was evident in all her work. Odette, though, was not sane, in his opinion. He never called her insane, but, rather, claimed that she was crazy with vanity; the "cruellest vindictiveness" emerged if her vanity was bruised. Periodically she was mad: certifiably mad. HG wrote that he did his best for her, "though it was a clumsy best." He believed that if anyone could save her from ending her life in abject loneliness, it was he. However, as she grew more vindictive he could endure her no more. At that point, coincidentally, he realized that he loved Moura, which made everything more difficult. Odette's problem, HG argued, was that she had to be "the great, magnificent, intricate, wonderful, potent and focal Odette Keun." She fought viciously for that, he said, until she made even her pets run away from her. Her father had been the head of the Dutch legation in Constantinople and her mother an Italian-Greek widow; they had raised Odette and her sisters in a poisonous atmosphere, full of temper tantrums, screaming, and beatings.

Twenty-two years HG's junior, Odette described herself as a French writer of Dutch origins. She began distinguishing herself as a writer early. In 1916, Odette produced a short novel, *Mesdemoiselles Daisne de Constantinople,* a transcript of her sisters' love affairs reflecting, as HG put it, "the Levantine atmosphere of base tittle-tattle and unscrupulous accusation in which they were living."[118] According to HG, the main fact of Odette's life was her conversion to Catholicism and her entry into a Dominican convent in Tours, France; *her* Lover-Shadow, he argued, was concentrated on Christ. After two years, Odette was kicked out of the nunnery. (HG described the Mother Church as a wary old bird, always on the defensive against modernity, always needing willing instruments rather than difficult souls.) Odette, he said, remained a novice until she was given the boot. After the Church let her go, she found a human lover in Lille, went with him to Algiers, and performed medical and nursing work there. Odette wrote two more books, *Une Femme Modern* and *Prince Tariel*. She was arrested, after a series of bizarre events, on the suspicion of being a British agent in the Crimea. For nearly a year she was held, he claimed, in the vice grip of the OGPU, the Unified State Political Directorate (Soviet Political Intelligence Service) "and she emerged with the material for what is perhaps her best and most amusing book, *Sous Lenine*."[119] For whatever reason, Charlie Chaplin intriguingly described Odette as a Russian.

Either HG wasn't aware of Odette's early trouble with the authorities or he purposely left it out of his writings. Odette had toured the Soviet Republic of Georgia on horseback and in the company of soldiers during the summer of 1920. Her first escort shot himself; her second escort, a Georgian prince, married her, but the Dutch government didn't recognize the marriage.[120] Odette stayed through the Red Army invasion in February 1921, and in June she visited Constantinople. Upon her arrival there, she was interrogated by the French, who now had a dossier on her, and she was arrested by the British on the day before her return to Georgia. Her espionage file described her as "A most dangerous enemy agent," a "confirmed communist"; the file contained documents showing that she was a member of the Soviet Foreign Office in Tiflis, that she worked in both Bolshevik and German interests against the British in Trans-Caucasia, and that she was "running an espionage organisation in contact with both Germans and Bolsheviks." The British Military Police confiscated her Dutch passport, letters, and travel notes and deported her to Sebastopol, where she was arrested by the local Cheka (forerunner of the KGB), who assumed she was a British spy." After a great deal of effort and with the help of G. V. Chicherin, the People's Commissar for Foreign Affairs, Odette left Moscow and arrived in Tbilisi three months after her arrest. Her nightmare adventure was still not over. In Tbilisi, the Bolsheviks threatened to arrest her if she didn't cease writing about them. After a protracted battle with the British Foreign Office, Odette was allowed to pass through Constantinople, then traveled to France. She had done a great deal of traveling and would do much more, even during her life with HG. Indeed, she crisscrossed continents in much the same way Moura had; this is not so surprising because she did, after all, characterize herself as a travel writer, and often as a socialist travel-writer. Whether any of that travel was to gather information of another type, espionage, is not yet known. And Odette's biographer, who has so meticulously traced Odette's life and travels, is moot on the point, suggesting merely that Odette's frequent and serious troubles with Soviet and other authorities were an innocent matter only—of being in the wrong place at the wrong time. It should be noted that Odette also spoke several languages, that she came from a family that worked in and had ties with various consulates, and that she herself worked in the U.S. Consulate in Constantinople beginning in 1911.

Before she had ever met HG, Odette dedicated a novel to him and apparently carried his *Outline of History* with her throughout her travels and travails in Russia. In 1923, after a series of "copious" good letters she had sent him, Odette asked HG to come to Paris and "take her before she died." Her letters subsided until the next year, when, hearing that HG and Rebecca West were breaking up, she packed a bag and headed for Geneva, where HG was vacationing. In vintage style, he said that she flung herself at him "with protests of adoration." Others report that it was HG who arranged a meeting with the strange ex-nun.[121] Although HG found Odette exciting and attractive, he reported that he did not fall in love with her, although he did take lodgings with her in the South of France. Because his life at this time was restless and incomplete, HG craved a retreat from England, a warm and sunny place where he could work in peace; but he hated the idea of being alone at his retreat. He wanted attached to it

someone to keep house for me—and I wanted a mistress to tranquillize me and companion me. She would be *there*. She would never come to

Paris or London with me or invade my English life. I would keep her and provide for her. She too would write and be free to do as she chose when I was away. I put the thing to her quite brutally, and she professed to be overjoyed at my proposal.[122]

HG got his retreat and his housekeeper-mistress-companion. He and Odette lived at Lou Bastio, near Malbosc, for nearly three years, most of them "fairly pleasant and successful." It became the "Villa Jasmin" of his novel *The World of William Clissold*. When he was at Lou Bastidon in the winter, Jane went to the Swiss Alps with their sons. In the summers, when Jane went to Scotland or again abroad, HG went to the Riviera with Odette. HG alleged that for one day every month Odette became deranged and scolded the servants, refused to speak, and conducted a war of insults with the landlady. When they were alone, she generally was careful with HG, and behaved devotedly. When guests appeared, however, she turned into a loud exhibitionist. Inevitably Odette would stage a quarrel with HG—whom she called Pidoukaki or Pidoo or Pee— or conduct a discourse "with vivid particulars, on the wonders of our sexual intimacy. I sat it out, with amazement giving place to rage."[123]

HG testified in the *Postscript* that he wasn't in the least in love with Odette, but that he went through the motions. Still, he was so satisfied with his Provençal lifestyle that he began building a bigger, better *mas*, Lou Pidou, which we met in Chapter 1. Their relationship developed into a long and volatile "offshore affair," as Anthony West described it. According to West, Keun was officially banned from Britain because of things she had written about the oil republics of the Caucasus, this being one of the reasons she and HG conducted their affair in France. Regardless of the restrictions, living across the English Channel gave HG some distance from the eyes of British society, and, too, he adored the warmth and sunshine of the South of France. Jane was well aware of the arrangement. As a housewarming gift for Lou Pidou, she—ever the galling good sport—sent Odette a fine painting by Christopher Nevinson.

Lou Pidou only made Odette more territorial and exasperating, according to HG, yet at the same time, "extremely tolerable." She often said the damndest things, sometimes quite shocking and unprintable, that touched "great fountains of laughter" in HG. Yet, while he was amused and energized by Odette, HG was becoming increasingly disenchanted with her, sometimes even mortified. Although she fared tolerably in Provence, she somehow kept HG from developing a sense of home there, he claimed. HG simply would not risk taking Odette to England. One wonders how dimly or brightly the specters of Atlas House and Up Park loomed when he wrote that the idea of taking her

> over-dressed, under-bred, feverishly aggressive, uncontrollable and un-teachable, to England was unthinkable. I would not have submitted Grout, my decent gardener, or my pleasant English maids, to her for a moment, for she was a hard exacting mistress. She would have insulted my London secretaries and tried to make them do humiliating odd jobs for her. She would have warped and bent all my friendships out of recognition.[124]

But HG *did* impose Odette on London, and it was as bad as he feared it would be. If she was disagreeable, noisy, aggressive, and overdressed in Paris, she was intolerable in London. As he wrote, if she would just leave England to him, he would give her France. But Odette wanted more from the odd arrangement. After Jane died, Odette asked HG to give up his home at Easton Glebe, set up an apartment in Paris, and become her French *mari*. He did take out a three-year lease on an apartment in Paris, wherein she served as companion and hostess to her famous mate; but despite the ties that bound them, Odette never held HG in the way that Rebecca had. He wrote that he had never promised even "the intention to be faithful to her. She offered herself to me and I took her upon [her] terms. . . . She was always trying to treat me as the conquered male—and I was never in the slightest degree conquered by her."[125]

In the spring of 1929, HG went to Germany to lecture to the Institute of International Co-operation, leaving Odette behind in France. Listening to the formidable triumvirate of H. G. Wells, Albert Einstein, and Gustav Stresemann was a figure from the Russian shadows, Moura

Budberg.[126] "From the moment we met we were lovers. I remembered what it was to be really in love. My stoical acceptance of the domestic life I had made for myself at Lou Pidou and Paris was undermined," HG wrote.[127]

At about this time, Odette developed a serious and painful inflammation of her sinuses, which produced disagreeable breath and also required two operations. According to HG, she was dramatic and emotional about her illness, and HG was typically unsympathetic, just as he had been with Rebecca.

> I could not feel a spark of distress about this bit of super-dentistry. I had seen Jane face a really painful illness and go on to certain death without flinching, and the fuss Odette made disgusted me. Jane had died, sweet and brave and tired out, holding my hand. Was I to start play-acting over a face-ache in Paris? [128]

HG was scathing in his analysis of Odette at this point in their relationship—scathing and blind to his own defects. Her attention to her sickness turned him off, yet at the same time he was increasingly preoccupied with his own health problems. He wasn't feeling well and suffered from low energy; later he learned that he had become a diabetic. He was also becoming progressively anxious about life and more aware of his mortality. In HG's absence during her convalescence, Odette struck up an affair with her doctor, and apparently not only saw similarities between her two lovers but also enjoyed articulating them. HG speculated that in Odette's "queer mind," the more the doctor resembled him, the less serious the infidelity became; evidently he forgot his own quick impulse to become unfaithful at the slightest misstep on his partner's part. Moreover, Odette's "incessant self-explanations" not only bored HG, but prompted him to begin thinking about separating from the woman he regarded as "still a possible associate, prostitute-housekeeper, to put it plainly."[129]

From Lou Pidou in June 1931, Odette wrote a letter to Marjorie telling her that the illness had left her lazy and chronically tired. Moreover, over the past seven days, they had entertained twenty-three people at various meals; but HG was pitching in—helping with both the chores and the entertaining, doing, uncharacteristically, her part as well as his own. He was in good form, she reported, nothing like he had been when he arrived from London in May. The man was, at that time, a physical wreck—"ghastly," in fact; she had never seen him so exhausted. "What the devil does he do in London, that he comes back in such a state?" she asked, perhaps innocently. With so many visitors milling around, Odette spent a lot of time in her study sleeping. Not so with Pidookaki, who "talks on and on and smiles & smiles, & remains as fresh as a flower." Charlie Chaplin and "his new little tart—a very young & pretty Austrian dancer" stayed with them four days. Odette sketched the movie star this way:

> He is even funnier off the films than on. I put them in the guest-house, where they played at being a ménage & were very happy indeed. He was recognized wherever we went, and trailed crowds & crowds behind him; he also brought a stream of photographers & journalists in his wake, whom Pidoo despatched with immense vigour & fury. Chaplin is extremely lovable, simple, uneducated, egotistical, autobiographical, indescribably charming & unexpected, but above all, entertaining. . . . Every evening, he gave us another chapter of his life. He acted his liaison with Pola Negri in Hollywood, & even Pidoo became almost hysterical with laughter. He mimics everybody & bursts into singing, acting, dancing, at any time, in front of anyone. He amused Pidoo so much that even the Great Work was given a rest while he was here.

HG was uncertain about how he should handle his personal life; as a consequence, he entered another long period of "shilly-shally"—not breaking with Odette completely and not becoming Moura's open lover until 1933. But by the spring of 1932, HG was beginning to know his heart and mind, and beginning to plan his escape from Odette. He wanted to set her up independently of him so that he could concentrate on his work from his apartment in London. And yet, he still wasn't keen on locking into a life with Moura. For the first time in his life, HG declared that he wanted to be independent of feminine companionship. As he told Christabel, being with Odette was fun, but the fun always became tiresome and exasperating. "I love the creature & I've got an extreme tendreness & sympathy for her, but God! How I would like to put her in a sack with sufficient lead . . . & drop her into the Mediterranean, at times. I might even not be very sorry afterwards, & yet I have an acute affection for her."[130] Meanwhile, Odette's disposition to act out and make "stupendous scenes at table" increased. HG described one example of shameless behavior: an occasion when his friends, Sir Wilfred Grenfell and his wife, were visiting Lou Pidou for several days. One evening at dinner, HG mentioned that Grenfell and his wife would be meeting a Mrs. Casenove the next day. Her son, HG continued, was the last surviving descendant of the great Casanova. He continued the story:

Casanova! Said Sir Wilfred. Casanova? Now let me see; what exactly did Casanova do?

I saw a strange brightness in Odette's eye but I was powerless to intervene—I knew what she was going to say.

She told him in a word.

The word, the awful word, the vulgarest and most indecent of English bad words, fell between us. A tremendous silence followed, which I broke at last.

Casanova, said I, ignoring that explicit word, wrote some celebrated *Memoirs*.

Ah yes, the *Memoirs*, said Sir Wilfred, and the thread of conversation was restored.

After a time Odette, who had startled even herself, came back into our polite conversation about memoirs. She supplied information about Madame de Sevigny.[131]

Interpreting her love for him as part intense exhibitionist possessiveness, part eager physical passion, HG was hoping to reach a modus vivendi with Odette, just as he had with Jane. He told Christabel in June 1932 that Odette was sticking to him "most desperate":

She hasn't anything in the world but me. And dear Christabel, it is true. She hasn't. And she won't get anything else. I don't think she has a bitch's chance to get any fresh sort of life started. I like her no end (& dislike her no end) & I'm sorry for her. And the only woman I really adore is out of my reach. I get glimpses of her. I've got no hold upon her. An illegitimate child is a great tie between a man & a woman but an illegitimate house is an even greater tie.

Lou Pidou had become less a love nest refuge and more "an irksome entanglement with its own baffling bothers and exactions. . . . I realized I could work there effectively no more."[132] The last straw was when Odette threw a screaming fit after opening HG's mail and accusing him of having an affair with Christabel, which he was not, though heaven knows he had wanted to, at least early in their relationship. On May 22, 1933, HG bid adieu to Odette and Pidou. He wrote movingly about his departure from his once-beloved place in the sun:

I cast Lou Pidou at last as a snake casts its skin. It needed an effort, but once more the liberating impulse was the stronger. I resolved that I would sell it, or if necessary give it away, and have done with it. I took a farewell stroll in my olive orchard up the hill, said goodbye to my new and promising orange-trees and rose-beds, gave my parental benediction to the weeping-willows and the banks of iris I had planted by my stream, sat for awhile on my terrace with a grave black cat beside me, to which I was much attached, and then went down the familiar road to Cannes station for the last time.[133]

But that wasn't HG's last visit to Lou Pidou, and it wasn't by a long shot the end of the Lou Pidou affair. The tug-of-war over the disposition of the *mas* produced reams of correspondence between Odette, HG, and their lawyers. HG had the correspondence transcribed because he planned to include parts of it in the *Postscript,* in an appendix to his section on Odette (to be titled "Correspondence of an Unloving Lover with a Lady of Dramatic Instincts & Incalculable Temper"), but the idea was scrapped. In these pages, apparently self-suppressed, HG wrote that in March 1936, when Odette was in the United States, he returned to Lou Pidou "with a view to a final settlement," and he stayed two weeks "to see how it felt without her. It felt very delightful without her," he reported. This is when he decided to buy the usufruct from Odette and to go for full possession of Lou Pidou:

> But so far Odette has refused my proposals for an outright purchase, and, as each winter slips by, I feel less and less disposed for the trouble of this reconstruction. The place, I suppose, must go, and everything I made and loved about it, and someday my heirs must do what they can with the derelict. The stream, my willow trees, the great arch I made beneath the house, the olive trees and the Judas trees I planted will still be beautiful. Lou Pidou, a little tumbledown and overgrown, may yet have a disheveled charm of its own for some appreciative occupant.[134]

On March 30, 1936, HG wrote to Odette, his "dear Titza," from Lou Pidou; this letter was the first of dozens of colorful, often passionate, letters between them concerning their formerly beloved *mas*. He implored that something had to be done about Lou Pidou: "It is really a pity to let it fall to pieces out of spite." HG made an offer to buy the furniture and to set Odette up with her Parisian furniture in a congenial pied-à-terre in Nice. "If we bring off the deal now I believe we shall be able to forget most of our old resentments. There is a lot we like and admire in each other, and I see no reason why we should not be lunching amiably together in Nice or London within the next three years. Yours ever, Pidoo." Titza replied: "I don't know, Pidoo, I don't know! My instinct is to say 'That house was built for me; it is the only thing for which I have a passionate affection.'"[135] She also admitted that she seemed to be incapable of forming new attachments and that her emotional life demanded that she hold onto the things that stirred her, even though they stirred her "to a deep pain." Her long rambling single-spaced typed letter closed with a reminder of all of the "monstrous conditions" HG had imposed on her.

Sometimes I think of all those years with their unnatural separations, when I went to pieces with neurasthenia, and I wonder how I am not in a lunatic asylum with the contention and the rebellion and the strain. The queer thing is, however, that you do not seem to have, now, the thing on which you used to insist so frenziedly and cruelly: solitary freedom.

No, Precious, you're too slack and facile in your optimism; not in two or three years, not in twenty, not till we die, will "we lunch amicable together and talk of the past." In Eternity I shall become your lover again, but on this earth I shall never be your friend. For friedship, one must have liking; I NEVER liked you—I LOVED you exclusively and inexpressibly and beyond reason. If somehow we meet on the other side, I shall do the same thing over again.

Odette ended with the handwritten postscript: "I love you dearly. I always will. If I keep my house—or my share of it—be sure I do not do that to thwart you. Try to understand, Pidookaki, and be kind to me for once."

HG wrote in suppressed pages from that appendix that by July 1936, the situation remained unchanged. He had discovered a legal advantage to force Odette to sell but he was reluctant to use it because she was suffering from some internal problem—"imagining cancer," he said—and was in the United States looking for treatments. Odette wrote HG magnanimous letters, forgiving him and everyone, yet clinging to Lou Pidou. Also in suppressed pages, he admitted that he could not find it in himself to do anything to make her more homeless and isolated. "I owe many bothers and much laughter to her and I hope when she has done having phantom cancer, she will recover strength and live many vehement years, too excitable still to be profoundly unhappy."[136]

In the spring of 1937, HG, Marjorie, and her two children went to Lou Pidou for what they hoped would be a pleasant vacation. But the idea of anyone else enjoying the former love nest was too much for Odette, HG reported. She broke their agreement and came back from America to resume possession and "renew the hopeless wrangle."[137]

According to HG, Odette had invented a story in which he proposed to resume life at Lou Pidou and install Moura in her bed. This story, which Odette held on to "with great persistence," HG wrote in suppressed pages, is "pure invention. Moura would certainly never dream of going to Lou Pidou with me, but this lie is necessary to Odette's justification and has no doubt been circulated extensively."[138] In one of her many proposals, Odette suggested that she and HG share the place: She would keep the old farm as a pied-à-terre, and he would resume ownership of the rest of the property. "But the prospect of living in my old home and entertaining guests with my former mistress within shouting distance across the courtyard does not appeal to me as much as it does to her."[139] The situation was further complicated by the intricacies of the documentation and the incompetence of the lawyers, who came up with four legal positions vis-à-vis ownership and usufruct of the various parts of estate. With each change Odette's behavior fluctuated between "effusive affection and frantic hate and insult."[140]

Odette's letters to HG about Lou Pidou were also running the gamut from warm and conciliatory to enraged, cruel, and scatological. A single letter could run the gamut. When Odette lashed out, nothing was held back, nothing and no one was spared. A sampling of her effusions:

April 15, 1936: *You have lost your sensitiveness.* Yet that was the thing that principally redeemed the many ugly traits in your nature.

April 16, 1936: You remind me very exactly of another un-self-controlled bully, Mussolini. *I* am Ethiopia.

September 12, 1936: I regret many things I lost in the past: the laughter which I have never recovered, your moments of sudden tendreness, which were so exquisite, the belief that I had found my justification for existence when you said you loved me and that I made you happy. . . . Curse & blast and shit the day on which we decided to live together, you swine. Can't that diabetes of yours carry you off at last! The time and nervous energy you make me waste! God damn you everlastingly!

June 10, 1937: Old Ass, Your pleasant little plan of removing my furniture and boarding up two houses which you dream are yours, has gone phut—you can shove it up your arse, where I hope it will constipate you for good. You, and your slatternly breed, and your Bedbug, will never set foot in Lou Pidou as long as I live. If you had let well alone, I would have remained for another year and a half in America. By your obscene declaration that you would install your mistress under *my* roof and among *my* furniture—a declaration I am spreading far and wide—you hastened my return to France. If you weren't such an imbecile you would have known that everything you do against me would turn out to be a boomerang. Well, this is your *quietus*, you stupid stale old man. You are out of this place for good and all. I send you in parting my pious hope that your neuritis, your diabetes, your sclerosed lung and your one kidney will soon combine to put a definitive stop to the diarrhetic deluge of driveling works with which you persist in swamping a long-suffering public—and so I end a mortally boring association.

Odette, still refusing to chuck the conviction that she and HG were "bound together by an indestructible intimacy," used any means she could dream up to hold onto Lou Pidou, including blackmail: specifically, threatening to sell HG's raunchy love letters to her. For some time—including the summer of 1933—she circulated a group of HG's letters to the editorial staff of *Time and Tide,* a "quirky feminist magazine funded by Lady Rhondda."[141] Though the staff enjoyed the letters, they passed on them. HG and Winifred Holtby, the director of *T&T* and a brilliant young feminist novelist, exchanged letters over the matter. In one, HG signed off with this comment: "[Odette's] behaving like a fool, but that doesn't alter the fact that she's damned miserable about the mess she has made of things. I can't help her, but you can. Yours ever, HG."[142]

HG eventually called Odette's bluff; he gave her permission to sell the letters and assured her that the only shame he felt was the shame of having sent the letters in the first place. Despite his appearance of nonchalance over the matter, HG did seem to care about the letters. He inquired about them several times in his correspondence with Odette. She once replied that she would return all the letters he had written to her, which she kept in her London bank. She even swore on Jane's memory that she had no important letters with her in France, so HG could rest assured that no collectors would get them, that his intimate life would always be his own.[143]

There was, of course, a price for the letters. In exchange, Odette wanted a letter signed by HG and his sons (who would inherit Lou Pidou), saying that the property would revert to the original contract between HG and her; namely, that she would be allowed to enjoy the whole property for as long as she lived. Where those letters are is a mystery. They may have been destroyed by either party, but it is more likely that they are in the hands of a family member or private collector, and that they will remain in the shadows for some time, if not forever.[144]

At about the same time that she was waging her letter campaign, Odette also launched a three-part series of "analytical" articles about her former lover in *Time and Tide*. While she was assigned ostensibly to review HG's just-published *Experiment in Autobiography*, Odette took the opportunity not only to savage that work but also to crucify HG in the process. Titled "H. G. Wells, the Player," the articles were Classic Keun: down and dirty with a good deal of truth. First, they hit HG where it hurt: his impoverished childhood and his unsuccessful parents. The Great White Hope, she observed, was in fact an Untouchable.

Despite his genius, despite his "uncommon energy," HG had a nasty and violent nature, she observed. He had failed to achieve greatness because of three major character flaws: self-indulgence, instability, and vanity. Not content with leaving it there, Odette argued that HG was a nut case, chewed away by bitterness. She described her former hero as "noisy, rude, selfish, sulky, ungrateful, vulgar, and entirely insuppressible." He operated from an "outraged ego." He had an "unconscious mental dishonesty" and "no real self-knowledge." And then she really let go. Odette suggested that despite all of HG's efforts, despite his having imposed his Utopian dream on the world and having gathered a huge following, H. G. Wells had in fact *failed mankind.* The Redeemer whose books constituted "the Great Promise," whose words breathed "an air of exalting hope," now offered only a labyrinth where once he had offered shelter. One begins to wonder, Odette wrote, "whether that fine brain had been quite able to bear his own genius."

The bottom line, her coup de grâce: HG was none of the things he was perceived to be—a leader, a chief, a master, a lover of mankind, or its savior. He was simply a player. "Strange as it may seem, he had no conviction of reality about either humanity or the individual. The game was the thing." Odette went on to say:

> He can no longer shape minds or inflame devotions. . . . If he has failed to save us, the fault is in him. He had the brain, he had the vision, he had the ability. He had, at one time, the heart and faith of multitudes with him. But that thing which makes the common man endure for an end; which makes the nobler man die for an end; that thing which is integrity of doctrine and selflessness of idealism; that ultimate genuineness which in the last analysis alone makes for permanent force and influence in life—in no form and in no measure has he ever had it at all. It was only a game. He was only a player.[145]

HG's response? He called the articles "very silly."

On a roll and unstoppable, Odette next used her pen to attack HG in a book. Her *I Discover the English,* also published in 1934, humorously lashed out at many aspects of British culture, from the "idiosyncrasies of London" to the idiosyncrasies of its people: their virtues and failings, sex habits, and morals. Although Odette did not call him by name, the generalized Englishman is no doubt H. G. Wells. He is roasted for his "lazy, rather obstinate, cautious, incurious and slow mind, attached to tradition and opposed to quick decisions," and praised for his courtesy and good temper. She composed a list of items constituting the major failings of the English, meaning the major failings of H. G. Wells: compromise, snobbism, juvenility, and insularity. Then on she went to discuss emotivity, sex, and morals. A few selections:

- *My real objection to [the Englishman] as a male is that he will not give enough time, trouble or attention to the sexual act, and thereby makes it as flat, stale and deadly as a slab of one of his own cold suet puddings. In brief: in bed, he's boring.*
- *Most of the English I have met abroad seemed to me as promiscuous as dogs. [Moreover] husbands, wives, lovers, mistresses, rubbed shoulders, mixed, dined, played and expatiated on their relations publicly. The jumble was that of a troop of monkeys mating in a cage.*
- *In the urban and industrial centres, there is an enormous amount of slipping around the corner, and the habit of the passade comes to the Englishman without what I would call an unduly arduous spiritual struggle, although he will drop like a hot coal any relationship that might threaten to seriously disturb his home-life.*[146]

In the deleted appendix pages, HG wrote that he had tried to describe the end of his relationship with Odette as objectively as he could, "I am not sorry I embarked upon the adventure. She was, as you must recognize, a very vexatious person."[147] HG woke up one night in late 1937 and thought over the whole miserable business "and laughed, and the laugh became *Apropos of Delores,* in which whatever anger remained in me was sublimated in fun. It is, I think, one of the most cheerful pieces of writing I ever did."[148] The work has been described as the most personal of HG's novels. The dustcover explains that the book is "the story of the perplexed, evasive husband of an absurd, passionate, vain and vindictive woman and of his efforts to adjust his mind and himself to her and to some tolerable conception of living. It is a novel of humor and philosophy, full of stimulus and entertainment, and availing itself of many of the liberties of Rabelais and Sterne in whose footsteps it follows." In his prefatory note, HG maintained that every character and event in the novel was fictitious, and that any coincidence with the name, behavior, or circumstance of any living person was unintentional. This was a story, he went on to say, about happiness and loneliness of spirit, told in good faith. "Nothing in this book has happened to anyone; much in this book has happened to many people."

In the last analysis, HG had little resentment toward his lover of ten years, and "not a scrap of affection," as he wrote in the *Postscript*.

> She gave me some intensely disagreeable moments, but she never did me any injury worth lamenting, and at her best she was fantastically lively and entertaining. . . . I think if I had loved her more or had a greater, more enveloping mind, I might have done better for her and by her. But I am not that much a divinity. There is something repulsive in her egotistical vanity that forbids any enduring closeness. There is no "getting on" with Odette, none at all. There is no helping her except upon her own impossible terms. Even when she is sane she is blindly egotistical, a torrent of assertion, pretension and aggression and sooner or later the malignant nerve-storm breaks upon her loyalest ally. R.I.P.[149]

HG was once again ready to jettison the old and embrace the new. Who was his next heart's desire? Would their love illuminate the heavens? Had he at long last found his true Lover-Shadow?

3

The Undying Fire: HG and Moura Budberg, 1920, 1932–1946

Maria Ignatievna Zakrevskaia (Zavresky), Marie Benckendorff, Baroness Budberg

The only woman I really adore is out of my reach. I get glimpses of her. I've got no hold upon her.

—**HG to Christabel, June 11, 1932**

All your advice is wise & good. I shall marry her next year (D. V. or even if he doesn't). I think we shall make a charming couple & [be] very popular. I can't imagine anyone not liking us.

—**HG to Christabel, August 2, 1933**

Moura insists on being my devoted mistress & won't think of marrying me. She is appalled I [put] value by the idea of settling down, furniture, servants & respectability.

—**HG to Christabel, February 3, 1934**

As a mistress, as an adventure, she's been glorious. But I can't make her over to be what I want & I'll be damned if I marry White (&Pink) Russia.

—**HG to Christabel, May 20, 1934**

The political climate in Russia, rather than the weather, brought H. G. Wells and Moura Budberg together for the first time. HG, ever the scientist, was curious about the Marxist experiment being conducted in Russia in 1920, and those in power were only too happy to indulge the influential socialist writer and his curiosity. Ergo HG's invitation from the Russian Trade Delegation to visit Lenin and Maxim Gorky, the popular writer and his old arch-friend. Many people had urged HG to go to Russia at this time, including Gorky, several Russian trade ministers, and Max Beaverbrook, the editor of the *Sunday Express*. "Wandering observantly often in different directions," HG and his teenage son Gip saw a great deal in fifteen days, as HG wrote in *Russia in the Shadows*, his illustrated report in seven chapters of a country in collapse. Their main impression was that Russia was in a state of "vast irreparable breakdown. Never in all history has there been so great a debacle before. Ruin—that is the primary Russian fact at the present time."[1] The vision of a country in ruin was offset considerably, however, by the sight of the guide assigned to him. In the *Postscript*, HG described the moment he met Moura at Maxim Gorky's colony of artists and writers in September 1920. The twenty-seven-year-old Russian was "wearing an old khaki British army waterproof and a shabby black dress . . . and yet she had magnificence. And she presented herself to my eyes as gallant, unbroken and adorable."[2]

During the visit, HG, just turning fifty-four, toured widely, both off and on the beaten path, off and on the official itinerary: schools, operas, the House of Science, the House of Literature and Art. His meetings with Lenin and Gorky were long and disappointing, as he would admit in *Russia*. Although HG had been sympathetic to the country's experiment, he conceded that just one more year of civil war would make "the final sinking of Russia out of civilisation inevitable. We have to make what we can, therefore, of the Bolshevik Government, whether we like it or not."[3]

In Petrograd, HG stayed in Gorky's twelve-room apartment rather than at the Hotel International, where most foreign visitors were put up.[4] Inevitably, he and Moura got together one evening and shared "a flash of intense passion," as HG would write some fifteen years later. "I fell in love with her, made love to her, and one night at my entreaty she flitted noiselessly through the crowded apartments in Gorky's flat to my embraces. I believed she loved me and I believed every word she said to me. No other woman has ever had that much effectiveness for me."[5]

From that first flash, Moura became a presence in HG's imagination, sometimes nearer, sometimes farther from the surface, but always a distinct possibility as a future lover. After HG and Gip left Russia, Moura resumed her life as Gorky's clerk and translating secretary. She had moved into his communal apartment-literary studio at 23 Kronversky Prospekt the year before, the latest of a dozen or so literary and artistic types, friends, miscellaneous family members, and "people previously unknown to [Gorky] who were temporarily homeless or avoiding the attentions of the police."[6] Moura once described the place as a refuge for intellectuals and stray dogs. Her limited professional skills were concentrated on Gorky's World Literature project, an ambitious venture to publish the Russian translations of 3,000 foreign literary classics, and, in the process, to provide work for many of Russia's starving literary figures.[7] Partly because of her daunting native intelligence, Moura's duties and importance quickly grew in that stimulating environment; for the next eleven years, she would serve as Gorky's assistant, caretaker, and lover all over Europe: in Moscow, Heringsdorf, Saarow, Günterstahl, and Sorrento. Although Moura was widely regarded as Gorky's common-law wife, she ardently denied having a sexual relationship with him and ardently maintained that he had become impotent. HG had his doubts on both counts, once noting snidely that Gorky kept a cast of Moura's hand on his desk.

H. G. Wells and Moura Budberg, both otherwise occupied during the 1920s, wouldn't meet again for nine years. He later cursed himself for not pursuing her sooner, especially after his affair with Rebecca. As mentioned in Chapter 2, their paths crossed in Berlin in 1929, thanks to Antonina Vallentin, who invited HG to speak to an international society in Berlin. Focusing on "The Common Sense of World Peace," he warned the packed hall, which included Professor Albert Einstein, that the world was racing toward war. "His words did not even send a ripple over the audience, a movement of fear or indignation," Vallentin later wrote.[8] She went on to say that the great British visionary

> may have already known, only too well, the sensation of speaking to deaf ears; or he may have been suddenly wearied and disheartened by the mingling of attentive interest and profound indifference that he sensed in his present audience. In any case he ended on a note whose solemnity found no echo even in the most sagacious of those around him: "But I must admit that the chances are against us . . . that they all seem to tend toward a conflagration that will destroy the future of our race."[9]

Still, all was not lost. HG's personal future was looking up. Just before the event, and out of the blue, Moura sent a note in her infamous scrawl to HG's hotel saying that she would attend the lecture if he could get her a ticket. Over the years, HG and Moura had corresponded, writing "occasional vague guarded letters to each other. . . . We doubted whether there was anything more to happen between us and yet we could not leave each other alone altogether."[10] At some point in the mid-1920s, Moura moved to Berlin, ostensibly to serve as Gorky's literary agent. Gorky, meanwhile, was taking periodic trips back to his homeland; both his wife, Catherine Pavlovna Peshkova, and Stalin beckoned him back. Being not far from Sorrento and Reval, Berlin was a good location for Moura, as her daughter noted, and it became Moura's hub for years. It isn't known whether Vallentin and Moura conspired to lure HG to Berlin, but he did obtain a ticket for Moura and she did attend the lecture. The next evening—not surprisingly—ended in her shabby apartment.

From the moment we met we were lovers, as though there had never been any separation between us. She has always had that unquestionable attraction for me, and unless she is the greatest actress in the world I have something of the same un-analysable magic for her. We made no vows; we made no arrangements for the future; we just took all the time we could liberate in Berlin to be together while my visit there lasted.[11]

HG hosted Moura at Easton Glebe, his home in Essex, in 1929 and 1930. He later wrote that she had been barred from entering England because of "some passport difficulty" before 1929. In 1930, the barrier, whatever it was, was lifted. HG suspected that it was "a personal objection to her on the part of Joynson Hicks, the Home Secretary, on account of some version of the Lockhart story."[12] At the time, HG was still managing his fizzling love affair with Odette Keun, although he had become terminally bored with her. It is still unclear when Moura, after several years of shuttling between London, Berlin, and Sorrento, settled permanently in Great Britain, but she was in continual motion between 1928 and 1933. Her children emigrated to England in waves in the early 1930s, and Moura emotionally and physically split from Gorky in 1931. It wasn't until 1932 that Moura became a fixture in HG's London life and went out openly with him. In the spring of 1933, Moura joined HG at a PEN Club meeting in Dubrovnik; then they went on vacation to Austria. Legend has it that during that vacation, Moura slipped out of HG's arms and scrambled to Istanbul to bid adieu to Gorky and his family, then en route to repatriation by way of Odessa.

Despite their now open and affectionate relationship, Moura routinely rebuffed HG's offers of marriage, and at least one of the rebuffs hurt and humiliated him royally. In November 1933, HG arranged a gala dinner party at the Quo Vadis restaurant in London and invited many friends to witness the announcement of his engagement to Moura. Several versions of the story exist, but the bottom line is the same: In front of their closest friends and England's major leaders of opinion, Moura refused HG's proposal. The dinner went on somehow, but the wound never really healed. Nevertheless, HG continued to pursue the moving target of his heart's desire. He even continued to hold out hope for Moura's hand, and he drove himself crazy over the matter. Christabel, as always, was his sounding board. Her advice in February 1935: "The best way of catching wild things like Moura is not to seem too keen. Drop the subject for a while." Even Christabel could be wrong. The wild thing would neither be caught nor tamed, and the chase would frustrate, bore, and hurt the hunter.

In addition to his pain and humiliation, and unbeknownst to HG, Moura was still seeing Gorky at least once a year during the 1930s until his death in 1936. As previously noted, HG was under the impression that Moura couldn't enter Russia for fear of imprisonment or bodily harm, since, as she had said, she was still on the Russian secret police's hit list. He also wanted to believe her when she said there was no affair with Gorky. HG's discovery, in August 1934 during a trip to Russia, that Moura had deceived him, that she had regularly met Gorky in Russia, that she had betrayed, possibly even cuckolded, him, was deeply disturbing.

> I never slept for the rest of my time in Russia. I was wounded excessively in my pride and hope. I was wounded as I had never been wounded by any human being before. It was unbelievable. I lay in bed and wept like a disappointed child. Or I prowled about in my sitting-room and planned what I should do with the rest of my life, that I had hoped so surely to spend with her. I realised to the utmost that I had become a companionless man.[13]

Clearly, Moura's betrayal stripped HG of his dream of a Lover-Shadow. She would not be the "dear presence" meeting him in his "garden of desires." He conceded that in a single evening his "splendid Moura was smashed to atoms."

Although Moura refused to live with HG, she always kept a set of "latchkeys" to his homes jangling around in her cavernous black satchel so that she could drop in and out of his life at her pleasure. And, despite their impasse over matrimony, the short British writer and the tall Russian literary and social figure maintained an intimate association for nearly fifteen years, right up to HG's death. She was "charming, close and dear," his undying fire, his latest Lover-Shadow. Even through his humiliation and tears, HG would admit: "I still 'belong' so much to her that I cannot really get away from her. I love her still."[14] Who *was* this bewitching and mysterious dark lady who often broke HG's heart, who flitted in and out of his world, who welcomed his seductions but always faded to black?

⋆　　⋆　　⋆

On October 1, 1939, a few days after England declared war on Germany, Winston Churchill went before a radio audience to talk about the future. He said that he couldn't predict Russia's actions in the days ahead because the country was "a riddle wrapped in a mystery inside an enigma." The subject was Russia, but Churchill might have been describing Moura Budberg. First impressions showed how intelligent she was, how strong, how charming and charismatic, but just below the surface lurked other things about her that soon emerged as peculiar, puzzling, and paradoxical. She was, for example, from a pro-Czarist family, part of the ruling elite; but after the Russian Revolution, having miraculously escaped the panoply of penalties for belonging to that class, she moved into Gorky's anti-Establishment literary colony. Two years later, while still part of his colony, she married a Baltic noble, a total stranger. They were fixed up, a match made neither in heaven nor in hell, but in Estonia by a lawyer and under extremely curious conditions, which we soon will explore. Even more curious, she never lived with nor loved that noble, Baron Budberg, but she would use his name and title for the rest of her life. In the foreword to her biography of Moura, *Histoire de la Baronne Boudberg*, historian-journalist Nina Berberova described Moura as a fascinating and elusive woman, part Mata Hari, part Salome. The title of the Russian edition of Berberova's biography, *Zheleznaia Zhen-*

shchina, translates to *Woman of Iron*—Gorky's name for Moura.[15] This irresistible woman of iron who translated the great works of her times, Berberova argued, changed the destinies of the three powerful men she loved: the diplomat and British agent Bruce Lockhart, the beloved Russian writer Maxim Gorky, and the renowned British author, historian, and futurist H. G. Wells. Perhaps she even rerouted world history in several ways. Still, although she was a social fixture on several continents, a celebrated and endearing presence in literary, film, and political circles, Moura was never what she seemed to be, her biographer and friend wrote. "We all have been deceived by her."[16]

To get some idea of Moura's puzzling ways, one might start with her accent. Nearly everyone who ever wrote about Moura commented on it. According to Berberova, Moura's spoken English was striking: "extremely pronounced," and hardly the product of a single year of study in England, one of her standard explanations of her facility with the language. More probably that accent was artificially cultivated, Berberova suggested, without explaining further. In a *Vogue* magazine article, Peter Ustinov, the actor and a friend of Moura's, said that the more English Moura spoke, the more Russian she became.[17] In his letters to Moura, HG often signed with the moniker "Aigee," mimicking Moura's pronunciation of "HG." She was also famous for pronouncing HG's home at Hanover Terrace as "Hangover Terrace."

Odder yet was Moura's spoken Russian, which Berberova said was "insufficient." Not only was Moura unfamiliar with Russian idiomatic phrases, but she paraded her ignorance of them, just as she paraded her affected pronunciation of various Russian words. Another one of her habits was to translate English or French idioms into literal Russian with unintended and sometimes comic consequences. Thus, Moura once said, "I sat down on my great horses" and "I cut myself in four." One can only wonder what she was trying to say. Moreover, over her long career as a literary translator, Moura primarily translated works into English and French, not into Russian. It isn't clear *what* she translated while ostensibly working for Gorky's enterprise to reproduce all the world's great works into Russian.

Moura had other distinctive traits. For example, she never responded directly to a question without taking a detour; this according to Berberova, who lived near or under the same roof as Moura for three years. Moura also dodged difficult or delicate questions with a little smile, and then retreated into silence. She never spoke about her feelings, Berberova testified, and no one ever asked her about them. She had something, a gravitas, perhaps, that no one dared challenge.

If Moura's small personal behaviors were confusing, her loyalties and loves were even harder to understand. She had at least two husbands and two children, but as we shall see, she spent little time with any of them. Her roots, as noted, were in the old Russian gentry, but she lived with and worked for a Bolshevik, Gorky, who had friends on the highest rungs of that party. She shared an openly intimate life with H. G. Wells for many years, but refused to marry him or even to cohabit. Moura was also rumored to have had many affairs with others while she was maintaining her marriages and primary affairs. She was a contradiction in terms, a chameleon, a human Rorschach test. Berberova alleged that in Moscow, Moura was thought to be a secret agent for England; in Estonia, a Soviet spy; in France, Russian émigrés believed that she worked for Germany; and in England, she was regarded as an agent for Moscow.[18] HG put it succinctly when he said that "there was nothing in the world [Moura] loved simply, wholly and honestly."

Above all else, Moura was serene; indeed, serenity was her hallmark, her defining quality. Michael Foot, the author of a 1995 biography of Wells and widely considered a first-rate historian, wrote about Moura's "sublime serenity." HG's son Anthony West called Moura intoxicating, and argued that her "fatalism enabled her to radiate an immensely reassuring serenity."[19] Martha Gellhorn veered somewhat, describing Moura's conversation and demeanor as "blissfully vague." That airy quality also applied to Moura's physical presence. Although she was a substantial woman in her middle-age years, nearly six feet tall and stout, Moura had a way of getting from here to there that seemed to defy physics. HG liked to say of her, even when she was in her fifties and "like a Vatican cherub, three times life-size but still delightful, an ample woman," that she would "flit" from place to place, often unaccountably.[20] How a woman of her size was able to *flit* from room to room, city to city, like some Russian sprite, defies understanding, but Moura was apparently able to pull it off. She was in perpetual motion most of her adult life, and accountable, seemingly, to no one.

On those rare occasions when Moura did account for an absence, she said that it was to help someone—a dear friend or relative—who was in dire need. Most often, it was her children who needed her, or so she said. Moura used Paul and Tania as a pretext for travel with all three of her major lovers—Lockhart, Gorky, and Wells. Yet, as we shall see, her children, except during their early years, were raised by an Irish governess, household staff, and two sets of Benckendorff relatives, not by their mother, whom they rarely saw. Appropriately enough, Tania Alexander described her mother as a distant and enigmatic person. In July 1918, Moura conceded to Lockhart that she didn't have strong maternal instincts, but she still loved her children and she desperately wanted to have *his* baby.

How much of Moura's ability to confound was natural and how much was cultivated will probably never be known. Her life story was, as we shall see, "intriguingly ringed about with mysteries and tantalisingly unanswered questions," her daughter conceded in her memoir, *A Little of All These: An Estonian Childhood:*

> Those who knew Moura testify at once to her courage, her charm, and her self-confidence: even her sharpest detractors do not deny her good humor, her warmth and her affection. And yet at the same time they also acknowledge the lack of scruple, the disregard for truth, the insatiable need for admiration and attention. She was somebody supremely attuned to the power of the impression she left: she behaved always according to the image she wanted people to have of her.[21]

For all the mysteries and unanswered questions, one thing is clear: If H. G. Wells invented the future, Moura Budberg invented the past, over and over again. In truth, Moura was a compulsive liar. Throughout her long and eventful life, Maria Ignatievna Zakrevskaia, as she was named at birth, bolstered herself with fabrication, her daughter claimed. Tania Alexander wasn't the only one who thought so. Michael Foot, who generally wrote defensively of Moura, asserted that Moura suffered from a "chronic incapacity to tell the truth," or, as he also put it, she had a "reckless readiness to deceive." While conceding that she constantly "spread mystifications" about her travels in the Soviet Union and elsewhere, he suggested that sometimes there was only one way to protect oneself, one's friends and family, and that was with "audacious lies." HG learned only too well that his lover was, in his words, "swathed in disingenuousness."

Moura's prevarication came in all shapes and sizes: as big lies and little lies; as low lies, high lies, and in-between lies. Some of the more entertaining tales involved her relationships with royalty. For example, she frequently claimed that she was descended from Peter the Great. One of her standard party tricks was to plant a fake mustache under her nose to demonstrate her resemblance to the Czar. Moura told Lockhart that she was descended from Lithuanian kings, and she told many others that she had had a close relationship of another kind with Kaiser Wilhelm II. She also told whoppers about her arrests and imprisonments.

The question is this: Why did this fascinating woman who was renowned for her strength of character and her courage wrap herself in lies? It certainly wasn't because she had problems with her self-esteem. In a December 1929 letter to her former paramour, Bruce Lockhart, Moura wrote: "I have no wish to 'confound my rivals,' perhaps because I conceitedly do not admit having any." Then why the lies? Did they serve as a cocoon, a protection from pain and responsibility? Did they provide camouflage for a complex double or even triple life? Did they serve as both cocoon and camouflage, or as neither? Or were they simply a way of avoiding intimacy? Whatever their purpose or purposes, which will be explored throughout this chapter, one thing is clear: The lies were tightly woven into the record. Because of the difficulty of separating the threads of truth from the web of lies, it isn't surprising that, despite Moura's amazing life, despite her ability to dominate and intrigue and make herself the center of other people's lives, no biography was ever successfully written, "for it has never been possible to pin down the real truth behind the legends," her daughter argued.[22] Moura once told her friend Humphrey Trevelyan that he was the only person she trusted to write her biography; yet even this was not true, Alexander argued, because Moura said the same thing to at least two other people. Rache Lovat Dickson, a contemporary British publisher and writer, attempted to write a biography about Moura, but he, too, found that the deeper he looked into her story, the more elusive it became.

When exploring Moura's past, one is reminded of Lewis Carroll's *Alice's Adventures in Wonderland,* where reality distorts at every turn and things become "curiouser and curiouser." Richard Spence, a historian of espionage, observes that cultivating a reputation for unreliability, as Moura did, has distinct advantages. Among other things, such "self-deniability" lets one off the hook as a serious source. "If people think you have a tendency to exaggerate or lie, they will tend to discount anything that you say, and that can work to your advantage."[23] Throughout this chapter we will listen to the many divergent, often conflicting, reports about Moura, and in so doing, try to make sense out of one person's lifetime of dissimulation and lying.

Compounding the confusion about Moura is the absence of archives and autobiographical writings to draw from and the relatively few letters. Indeed, apart from a couple of memoirs and the extant letters Moura wrote to Lockhart and to HG, little documentation has been found about Moura's long and extraordinary odyssey through life. Alexander claims that most of Moura's papers were destroyed by the new occupants of Kallijärv, the lake house on the Benckendorff estate fifty miles from Reval, now called Tallinn, in Estonia, not in a fire in her ad hoc office in Italy just before her death, as Berberova argued. For the record, Moura maintained that she burned her papers from World War II onward, and that her earlier papers, from 1920 to 1939, were lost during the German retreat from Reval and the taking of that city by the Soviet army. To date, no cache of private papers has surfaced. In 1937, the last time Berberova saw Moura, the young writer mentioned that she was anticipating the day Moura would publish her memoirs. Momentarily shaken by the comment, Moura regained her composure and replied that she never would produce a memoir, that she had only mental souvenirs. Yet five years earlier, in March 1932, Moura sent Lockhart a letter telling him that she was holed up in her Estonian "hut" working hard on her autobiography. She fumbled with the title, calling it both *Au Milieu de* and *À côté de la Mélée (In the Middle of* and *Next to the Mélée).* In August 1932, she noted that her *Mélée* "will be, is, written in English. It will be a rather peculiar English, perhaps, but I think it is more typical of me to write it that way." A few months earlier, she told Lockhart that the autobiography was progressing, "although my worries are many." *Mélée* never appeared, alas, and one must wonder whether she ever really began it or whether this was a ploy to keep Lockhart's memoir in check—a form of literary intimidation. Moura later told Constance Coolidge that she had destroyed something of great significance; was it her autobiography?

Despite the circumstances, a few journalists and documentary makers have braved the challenges of interviewing and writing about Moura. [24] When Moura did grant a rare interview, she seldom revealed anything new about herself, but rather respun the old stories—or variations thereof. Coming clean after a lifetime of spreading mystification was not an option for Moura. Still, Moura granted an interview late in her life to her good friend Kathleen Tynan, then writing for *Vogue* magazine. Perhaps Moura saw this as her last chance to set the record crooked. The piece began with a story designed to affirm the Iron Woman's indomitable spirit and adaptability. Moura told Tynan that during her first imprisonment in a Bolshevik jail in 1918 she befriended a rat who *sang* for the few crumbs she was able to feed it. "I don't say it sang like a soprano," she was quoted as saying, "but it squeaked quite melodiously, and I used to wait for that rat as one would wait for a lover."[25]

Truth be told, Moura had always been freewheeling with the facts surrounding her arrests and incarcerations. In most of her scenarios, she claimed to have spent a considerable amount of time behind bars,

although very little of it was in the company of companionable rats.
Moura told Tynan that she was arrested and jailed a day or so after
Lockhart's arrest, following the attempted assassination of Lenin, the
"discovery" of the Allied plot to overthrow the Bolsheviks, and the
roundup of diplomatic staffs in the fall of 1918. She said that she was
put in a cell with fifty-two other female political prisoners and that she
was later moved to solitary confinement, where she befriended that
musical rat. In the same interview, Moura said, "If there is anything extraordinary about me, it is the fact that I took prison as I did. I learned
what people were like, and I learned what life was about, which before
had simply been unreality."

Moura also claimed that she had been imprisoned on two other occasions: an undated two-month incarceration for black marketeering, and
a four-month stay for having attempted to leave Russia without permission, presumably in 1919. Moura told Tynan that she was in prison
when her husband was killed; however, the day her husband was murdered, Moura wrote a letter to Lockhart telling him that she was stuck
in a terrible little pension in Terrijoki, Finland, waiting for the border
into Russia to open.[26] She had been able to see her husband in Estonia,
she reported to Lockhart, and had put "a full stop" to her obligations of
the past. Moura's letters to Bruce Lockhart detailed the plans she had
been orchestrating for months: She would to go to Kallijärv via Helsingfors, now Helsinki, to get her husband's signature for starting the divorce; then she would go on to Stockholm, where she would elope
with him. "Oh Baby you cannot think how desperately I am longing for
you," she wrote on her birthday, March 6, 1919. But Moura stood Lockhart up. On the second leg of the journey, she aborted the plan, because, she said, her English visa to proceed was not ready. Moura also
told Lockhart that she'd had a very exciting three weeks out of Russia.
"I think I am probably the only Russian who has done lately this trip
there and back and you know, you can't imagine the difficulties in front
of me," she wrote on April 18.

Lockhart, meanwhile, claimed that Moura was arrested on September 1 or 2, 1918, a day or two after his own arrest; as soon as he was re-

leased, he said, he scrambled to obtain Moura's release, visiting, among others, Jacob Peters, the deputy chief of the Cheka.[27] The Cheka, headquartered in Moscow's Lubianka Prison, was the Bolshevik's intelligence and terrorist organization, essentially the political police.[28] Lockhart claimed that by September 10, after he was re-arrested, Moura was released and began visiting him in his "cell," bringing him books, clothing, food, and other amenities, a privilege he never questioned as unusual. For his entire life, Lockhart believed that Moura had been arrested and that it was primarily through his efforts that she was released. If it ever crossed his mind that Moura was working with or for the Cheka, or that her imprisonment had been a sham, part of a scheme to convince him that she was on his side, he never let on. In *Retreat from Glory*, Lockhart also reported on Moura's second imprisonment and attempted escape.[29]

Berberova claimed that Moura was arrested five times. The first time was in early September 1918, along with Lockhart and their household staff; she was kept only a few days, perhaps in the basement of the Lubianka Prison. The second arrest was in early 1919, in Petrograd, after she was stopped on the Troitsky Bridge with two counterfeit food ration cards in her possession, which she supposedly had exchanged for her sable muff. Moura spent a month in the Cheka prison on Gorokhovaia Street, and was freed after getting word through to Peters, who sprung her, as the story goes. Moura's third arrest came in December 1920, as she tried to leave Russia to join her children in Estonia; she was one of a party of five crossing the Narova River, when a Soviet border guard spotted them. They were taken to the Cheka prison, but after a series of phone calls that Gorky and his wife, Catherine, made to Felix Dzerzhinsky, Moura was released. One can only speculate why Catherine carried so much weight with the head of the Cheka.

According to Berberova, the details behind Moura's "permanent" departure from Petrograd aren't known, but when Moura got off the train in Reval at the end of January 1921 to reunite with her children after three years' separation, she was arrested yet again, this time by two uniformed Estonians. Moura was accused of working for and living with Peters, of living with the Bolshevik Gorky, and of being a Soviet spy. After learning that she would be put before the Supreme Estonian Tribunal, Moura hired a lawyer, who obtained her release.[30] Moura's fifth arrest, according to Berberova, came at the border between Italy and Austria at the end of 1925, when Moura was en route to Estonia. Berberova did not document any of the arrests—not a detail. Which of the stories originated with Moura is not known.

Along came Alexander, who shot holes in the stories about Moura's arrests and imprisonments. Alexander conceded that although her mother was arrested at about the same time as Lockhart—in September 1918—Moura was released a few days later. Her two-month incarceration for black marketeering in 1919 was impossible to verify, Alexander wrote. Moura was arrested in 1920 as she was trying to cross the ice to Estonia; she did manage to contact Gorky, and she was quickly released and returned to him. Regarding the four-month incarceration after her attempt to leave Russia in 1921, Alexander said that Moura spent only a few days in prison. Her account of Moura's return to Estonia in 1921 is quite different from Berberova's: Berberova argued that Moura and the children reunited in Kallijärv in January 1921; Alexander wrote that Moura became "a real person" for her when she turned up in Kallijärv in May of that year.

HG's weigh-in on the subject was just as confounding. He reported that in 1919, Moura had tried to escape "to get to her children at Tallinn, spent six months in prison and was sentenced to be shot. Then she was paroled."[31] That was quite a scaled-down version of the account he gave in *Russia in the Shadows*. There, he claimed that his girl guide already had been imprisoned five times by the "Bolshevist Government." Moura undoubtedly was the source of that tale. It isn't known how long HG believed it.

For the record, there is no record—not yet—and perhaps there never will be. There isn't even any proof that Moura was imprisoned in 1918. It *appeared* that she had been, but it is conceivable that her incarceration at the Lubianka was all show, something that she and Jacob Peters had choreographed to convince Lockhart of her loyalty to him. In 1919, if we believe her, Moura did manage to get out of Russia, travel as far as the family estate in Estonia and Helsingfors, and then back again, all apparently without incident. Once again, no record exists except Moura's story. The 1920 incident, when she crossed the ice at Kronstadt, is universally told and appears to be true, although Moura was imprisoned only a day or two. And when Tania Alexander wrote about her mother's grueling ordeal with the Estonian tribunal, she never mentioned that Moura was *arrested* by the Estonians, although Alexander may have had political reasons for letting that one go. The only fact that holds up under scrutiny is that Moura had multiple stories going about her arrests and imprisonments, which helps explain the many versions of her experience: undoubtedly just the way she wanted it.

Tynan also wrote about Moura's immense sacrifices in life, including the first personal treasure she was forced to sell as a result of the Russian Revolution. As the story goes, local peasants came knocking at the door of her Estonian estate, Yendel, and in exchange for her plum-colored velvet court train, which was embroidered with gold thread, the peasants gave Moura two sacks of flour. Tynan also told about the string of pearls that Moura supposedly smuggled out of Estonia, in her mouth, as that tale goes, then later sold in London for $3,000. The portrait Tynan painted was adulatory, containing only two unflattering references: to Moura's great fondness for vodka and, unaccountably, for a popular television show for children, *Perky and Pinky,* about the adventures of two pigs.

In the *Vogue* piece, Tynan also discussed Moura's relationships with men, including the celebrated film producer Alexander Korda. A native Hungarian with whom HG had worked—unsuccessfully by both of their accounts in the 1930s—Korda became a central figure in Moura's life after HG died. Later in this chapter we will explore their activities—stated and unstated. Connecting herself to important men, especially men of means and with connections, was by then a well-hewn habit. "Once attached, she never let go," her daughter wrote of her, adding that Moura "had the gift of making herself welcome, and then indispensable."[32] Indeed, when one man died, Moura—ever the survivor—picked up like a Mongol nomad and moved into the next tent.

Moura's knack for gossiping also was legendary. She was, by anyone's standards, one of the best. Moura seemed to know everyone, to hear and to read everything, and to forget nothing. Her specialties were divulging the secret and often scandalous parentages of prominent literary and political figures, and relating vivid firsthand accounts about social life in Imperial Russia. One of Moura's best and most-often told stories was about the time she danced the night away at Yousoupov Palace in Moscow while Rasputin was being murdered in the room directly below her. A good story to be sure, but highly unlikely; none of the many incarnations of that widely told tale place Moura there. Still, Moura spun a good yarn, though not necessarily a true story, and not necessarily original with her. "When it came to anecdotes she was no respector of ownership—the perfect magpie."[33]

More detailed published accounts about Moura's life are rare and thin on detail; and many, in addition, are derivative, contradictory, and suspect. The major sources are Tania Alexander, Bruce Lockhart, H. G. Wells, and Nina Berberova. All these people, whether a relative, a lover, or a friend, had compelling reasons to write about Moura, but perhaps none more so than Alexander and Lockhart. Alexander presumably wanted to set the record straight, and in the process, redeem her mother's honor. After all, the major capitals of the world had been buzzing for decades with rumors about Moura's suspicious activities. Alexander also used the opportunity to take a few jabs at Moura, an absentee mother for years, later a somewhat Machiavellian parent who enjoyed putting her daughter in compromising, even demeaning, situations. "I was," Alexander wrote, "dragged into her deceptions, used as an accomplice or an alibi, forced into telling lies for her, brought face to face on numerous occasions with the unscrupulous side of her character."[34] It is noteworthy that in her memoir, Tania Alexander placed the chapter on her parents *behind* the chapter on her Irish governess, Micky Wilson, who had raised her and whom she adored.

Bruce Lockhart had other motives for writing about Moura. In addition to his many entanglements of the heart, the Scotsman was perennially in over his head financially, and thus was desperate for the income from book sales and box office receipts. He was also desperate to save his reputation. Soon after his expulsion from Russia and arrival in London in October 1918, after nearly a month in the Kremlin jail, Lockhart discovered that not everyone at the British foreign office was impressed with his work as the special agent in Moscow. He feared that future employment with the foreign office was doubtful, and even conceded in a secret memorandum to Lord Balfour and the war cabinet that he felt his mission had in many respects "not succeeded." He also apologized for the trouble and inconvenience he had caused His Majesty's Government.[35] As it turned out, he was shelved for nearly two years, regarded as a rotter by the old hands at the foreign office.[36] Still, although Lockhart had many detractors, the foreign office would become his chief employer.[37] Despite his intelligence and talent, the flaws in Lockhart's personality caused him to conduct his careers, not to mention his life, erratically. He was "easily cast down" by people, according to Kenneth Young, the editor of his diaries, and he was "no paragon of virtue." Among other things, depression and self-indulgence became Lockhart's constant companions as his marriages fell apart one by one. The author of nine books, Sir Robert Hamilton Bruce Lockhart would be best known for his first book, *Memoirs of a British Agent,* published in November 1932 in England. It was the story of his jinxed 1918 mission to Russia and his short passionate affair with a daring Russian beauty named Moura—her last name never given.

While Lockhart wrote a great deal—some 3 million words in two hundred volumes of diaries and journals, in addition to the books—he wrote sparingly indeed about Moura. *British Agent* did well with reviewers and sales, but it revealed little about his former lover beyond a few highly complimentary passages, such as the oft-repeated description of their first meeting in February 1918:

> She was then twenty-six. A Russian of the Russians, she had a lofty disregard for all the pettiness of life and a courage which was proof against all cowardice. Her vitality, due perhaps to an iron constitution, was immense and invigorated everyone with whom she came in contact.

Where she loved, there was her world, and her philosophy of life had made her mistress of all the consequences. She was an aristocrat. She could have been a Communist. She could never have been a bourgeoise.[38]

In 1934, a refictionalized version of *British Agent* was released as a motion picture. Instead of dispelling rumors about Moura, the film only fanned the flames of suspicion and rekindled the sparks of mystery, which Moura "was by no means in a hurry to dispel," her daughter wrote.[39] Although melodramatic by today's standards, the film was extremely successful. "A situation richly veined with striking dramatic values has been utilized with considerable vitality," wrote the *New York Times* movie reviewer Andre Sennwald. Leslie Howard played Stephen Locke (Lockhart) and Kay Francis played Elena (Moura). Michael Curtiz directed. Howard's performance was "played in a key of high nervous tension and desperate courage" . . . and "the dark-eyed and vibrant Miss Francis makes a handsome undercover agent for the Cheka."

Lockhart's second book, *Retreat from Glory*, which was released in October 1934, spans the ten years (1919 to 1929) the former vice-consul worked in Central Europe. In the book, he offers a sentence here, a sentence there, about his fabled romance with Moura and their meetings in 1924 and 1929. He painted this period of Moura's life as one of monumental struggle and courage. As we shall see later in this chapter, there was a very good reason why Lockhart's books were short on narrative about Moura: She was not pleased with much of what her former paramour wrote in draft, and her critiques showed this. Lockhart gave Moura free rein to edit his manuscripts; with it, she excised many sentences and demanded the revisions of many more. However, either she missed one intriguing sentence from Lockhart's *Retreat* or Lockhart overrode her veto: "The story of our unofficial romance had already been recorded in the archives of the Foreign Office."[40] To date, that story remains either buried in tons of bureaucratic paper or "weeded," in either case lost, perhaps forever.

The Diaries of Sir Robert Bruce Lockhart (in two volumes) document Moura's 1918 arrest and visits to Lockhart's "cell" at the Kremlin, their 1924 reunion in Austria, luncheons and dinners he gave for her, and various rendezvous in Berlin and elsewhere; but again they reveal little about Moura's personal or professional activities and allegiances before, during, or after the revolution.[41] Nevertheless, the diaries are a rich source of gossip, passed from Moura to Lockhart, and, as such, they attest to her awesome ability to gather news, to tell good stories, and to serve as an information pipeline to Lockhart. One example from Lockhart's diary is representative. Moura, who had just returned from visiting Gorky in Russia in 1931, reported that the Russian writer was now "ultra-Bolshevik, has returned to his own class, believes implicitly in Stalin, and justifies the terror from which formerly he shrank. He and Moura both believe in the danger of foreign intervention. Moura assures me that the recent trials in Moscow were by no means 'faked.'"[42] Moura often passed along gossip for Lockhart's ears only: "And you'll never mention to anybody what I told you, will you . . . you're the only person I could make such revelations to," she wrote in September 1932. From beginning to end, their relationship was symbiotic, but, there is evidence that Moura sometimes resented it. She once accused Lockhart of being "out for material." Robin Lockhart, Bruce's son, described the dynamic another way. Moura "occasionally gave tidbits of unimportant news to my father and to members of the Soviet hierarchy. A typical Russian, she loved to tell fancy stories—rather like the Irish."[43]

In 1958, forty years after their romance began, Lockhart wrote an essay titled "Baroness Budberg." It was a glowing tribute to the brave and courageous women of Russia, Moura being the prime example. Interestingly, he referred to her throughout the piece as Maria Ignatievna. "She was not merely fascinating; she was remarkably well-read, highly intellectual, and wise beyond her years. . . . Men adored her, especially authors, composers, painters and poets." In the typescript, which was more than lightly edited in Moura's hand, Lockhart wrote that Maria "was under constant suspicion because she had known so many members of the British Embassy."

Berberova maintained that in writing Moura's biography she neither judged her subject nor pronounced a sentence. Her sources, seventy-five years' worth of documents and other works dating from 1900, allowed her to discover "the truth regarding Moura's ancestors, the details of her personal life, the names of her friends and her enemies, the chain of events to which she was intimately or indirectly tied."[44] Although saturated with historical detail and analysis—and defenses of Russia at a tragic period in its history—the biography is often light on critical detail and is full of gaps. Berberova's narration of the Bolshevik reign draws heavily on Lockhart's published works; as noted, his works were heavily biased—not to mention edited—by Moura. In addition, Berberova's treatment of Moura's life with H. G. Wells up to her death in 1974 is sketchy at best. After all is said and done, *Histoire* contributes only modestly to our understanding of the Baroness Budberg. Many people are even more critical of the biography. Soviet scholar Mikhail Agursky, for example, described the book as an "unreliable and even misleading biography."[45] Yet, despite the shortcomings of her book, Berberova, a prolific and respected writer, journalist, and professor, had one considerable advantage in writing her biography: proximity. She and her lover, the poet Vladislav Khodasevich, lived from 1922 to 1925 near or with Moura and Gorky and the Gorky entourage in Heringsdorf, Saarow, Günterstahl, Prague, Marienbad, and Sorrento. Berberova kept a journal during this time, which included notations about Moura's comings and goings, phenomenally frequent by anyone's standards. She also routinely transcribed their conversations. Consequently, sections on these years are far more detailed than those that deal with earlier or later periods in Moura's life, and are therefore extremely helpful in plotting Moura's movements. Berberova conceded that because she was nine years younger than Moura, Moura didn't seek her company or engage her in conversations.

Others wrote about Moura, too. Meriel Buchanan, the only child of George Buchanan, the British ambassador to Russia (from 1910 to 1917), and Moura's close friend, told wonderful insider stories about life in Imperial Russia and at the British embassy in Petrograd, in which Moura played ostensibly a social role; however, like Lockhart,

Buchanan wrote only superficially about her friend. In her first book, *Petrograd: The City of Trouble,* Buchanan simply referred to Moura as her friend without mentioning her name.[46]

Like many of Moura's friends from the British embassy, Meriel often visited Yendel, the Benckendorff's estate some 150 miles west of Petrograd. Moura threw memorable parties at Yendel and often entertained weekend guests, Buchanan, Captain Francis Newton A. Cromie, and Captain Denis Garstin typically among them. Garstin, affiliated with Britain's Secret Intelligence Service (SIS), was so smitten with life at Yendel that he wrote a humorous poem about it. It begins: "At Yendel girls begin the day/in optimistic negligé /followed hot-footed, after ten/by the pyjama radiant men." And it ends:

> Oh God, and I must take a train / and go to Petrograd again / and while
> I deal out propaganda / my nicer thoughts will all meander / back, back
> to Yendel, oh to be / in Yendel for eternity. For there beneath the sum-
> mer skies / it's easy to be awfully wise. . . . And even singing such as
> mine/heard from a distance, sounds divine.[47]

Most of that wonderful time at Yendel, from the end of 1914 to the end of 1917, Djon Benckendorff, Moura's husband, was away at war. The idyllic charms of the place would soon be replaced by what Buchanan called the "pernicious evil of Bolshevism," which was oozing across Russia and into the Baltic provinces. In *Petrograd,* Buchanan described the rampant anarchy in the city and across the provinces at the end of 1917, just before her family left for England:

> My friend's place near Reval, where I had stayed several times, had been
> completely destroyed and pillaged, the horses and cows on the farm taken
> or killed, the pigs cut up alive for lard, while she herself barely escaped,
> having to hide for five hours in the gardens with her two small children.[48]

Another good story, but doubtful, since according to Tanis Alexander, Moura, Djon, and the children were safe and sound in Petrograd at the

time. In January 1918, Djon—just back from the Northern Front—
went to check on the estate. The children joined him in the spring, but
Moura stayed behind in Petrograd. Then in 1919, the household temporarily moved from Yendel to Kallijärv, the lake house, a short distance away, because of rampant pillaging by armed gangs.

In *Ambassador's Daughter*, Buchanan repeated many of her stories, but
now she revealed the identities of her friends, Moura Benckendorff and
Miriam Artsimovich, the latter an American who, as we shall see later,
worked alongside Moura under highly suspicious circumstances at the
British embassy.[49]

> How often I think of the days we spent at Yendel. . . . The unhurried
> movable hours, . . . the disregard of time, . . . the sudden impulsive
> plans, a visit to Reval, a fancy-dress dance, a picnic in the snow, the
> gypsy songs Moura sang to us, sitting on the floor with her golden eyes
> gazing into the fire.[50]

Other friends from her early married life in Berlin or her wrenching
but exciting Petrograd days might have written about Moura, but they
never had a chance; many died young—and violently. Captain Garstin,
for example, was killed in August 1918, at age twenty-seven, mowed
down attempting to capture Bolshevik machine guns in Archangel. According to Alexander, Moura and Bruce Lockhart met in March 1918 at
what would be the last birthday party for "Garstino," as Moura always
called Garstin, a fellow known for his joie de vivre, his courage, and his
sense of humor.[51]

Captain Cromie also might have written about Moura. A naval attaché in 1918, and linked to British Naval Intelligence (NID), Cromie
sailed with the Baltic Fleet and was in charge of keeping Russian sub-
marines out of the hands of Germans. He was murdered on August 31,
1918, as he valiantly defended the British embassy from Chekist intrud-
ers. His body was trampled, thrown into a cellar, and left for five days
after his death.[52] Although she maintained a close friendship with him,
Moura had curious problems with Cromie, as we shall see later in this

chapter. Her other companions in 1918 were Captain William Hicks, a member of Lockhart's mission and their Moscow roommate, and Liuba Malinina, a well-connected Russian who would become Hicks's wife on the day he and what was left of the British embassy staff shipped out of Russia. Most of Moura's friends were, then, engaged in some form of propaganda—meaning intelligence—and most were on the payroll of the British Ministry of Information.

Gorky, an internationally renowned writer and the father of literary socialist realism, spent a decade with Moura but never wrote about her, although he did dedicate a novel, *The Life of Klim Samgin,* to her. In the book, his unfinished masterpiece, Gorky attempted to portray forty years in the life of the Russian intelligentsia.[53] Generally regarded as *the* Russian writer of his age, and widely popular, Gorky was born Aleksei Maximovich Peshkov in 1868; like his heroes, he faced times that were often terrifying and brutal. Like HG, Gorky managed to pull himself up to society's highest rungs through grinding hard work and a keen intelligence. As a child, he worked as a ragpicker, a ship's cook's boy, and a shop boy to an icon-maker, among other things, but well before midlife, he was moving in the same circles as Lenin, Chekhov, and Tolstoy. The author of five novels and fifteen plays, Gorky also produced many short stories and two works of nonfiction, including a three-volume autobiography. In Stalin's camp in the 1930s, Gorky propagandized the good things being done in Soviet Russia, especially in his last works. On November 27, 1929, he wrote a letter to Stalin saying that the Soviet press must remind itself and its readers that the building up of socialism "in the Union of Soviets is being achieved not by slovens and hooligans, nor by crazy fools, but by a powerful and new historical force— the working class. One must write about this in a simple, sound, and literate manner."[54]

H. G. Wells did not mention Moura in his first autobiography, although he and Moura had been open lovers for at least a year, and acquaintances for at least fourteen. Moura did play a large role in HG's chronicle of love, begun later the same year. In the *Postscript,* HG spoke openly and candidly about his life with Moura, and to Gip's credit, very little of that narrative was excised from the manuscript before it went to press. HG painted a picture of an intriguing and charming woman—his best bet for a Lover-Shadow—but a woman who constantly frustrated him and his hopes for idyllic and eternal love. Following the major crisis of their love affair in the late summer of 1934, HG wrote that the reveries he had indulged in of a wonderful end of life "with a splendid mate beside me were lost in a swarming exaggerated realisation of her defects; her small human greeds, her flashes of scheming, her innate slovenliness, her moments of vanity and her discontinuities."[55] For HG, Moura clearly was hard to live with and hard to live without. He even titled his chapter on Moura, the last major love of his life, "Moura, The Very Human." Still, it is clear that her pluses outweighed her minuses. As HG would admit: "Her I love naturally and necessarily and—for all the faults and trouble I shall tell about—she has satisfied my craving for material intimacy more completely than any other human being."[56] For the record, HG also wrote critically of himself in that anatomy. The story of his relations with women is "a story of greed, foolishness and great expectation, and it would not be worth the telling if it were merely my particular story. But it is really a tale of a world of dislocated sexual relations and failure to adjust."[57]

There were so many others who knew Moura through the 1920s, 1930s, and 1940s, and who might have written about her but didn't. Perhaps they couldn't, given the difficulty of pinning down the *real truth,* as Alexander called it. Perhaps they lacked the desire. Or perhaps they chose to not write for other reasons. There were so many reasons.

And finally, there were the modern Wells biographers: Smith, West, the MacKenzies, and Foot. It could be argued that, focused as they were on HG, they would take a hard look at Moura; harder, anyway, than Berberova and Lockhart took. Yet each of these biographers treated Moura in a limited and positive fashion, even though she presided over HG's last fifteen years, often hurting him along the way.[58] Foot, like Berberova, had known Moura; but *he* was captivated by her, and very approving indeed. She was an "adventurous woman," he wrote, and "an embodiment of the true internationalism which HG preached."

She was, in fact, "one of the most considerable women of the century," and "something of a heroine."[59]

Anthony West, who also knew Moura, was just as charmed and nearly as approving. Aside from the Moscow deception and one or two other dirty tricks Moura had played on HG, and her possible involvement in espionage (which will be analyzed later), West was sold on Moura and spun her as a formidable woman. She had an "irrepressible wit" and a "bubbling good humor," and she was cool under pressure. West recalled his first "breath-taking sight" of Moura. A great beauty just past her prime, she was sitting in HG's garden at Easton Glebe in 1931,

> and her good humour made her a comfortable rather than a disturbing presence. . . . I believed unquestioningly in her *bona fides,* and had never a doubt but that without her warmth, affection, and calm stoicism behind him, my father would have been a gloomier and more pessimistic man in the years that lay between his seventieth birthday and his death. Whenever I saw them together I felt sure they were truly happy.[60]

The MacKenzies didn't trade in superlatives when writing about Moura. They didn't trade in adjectives, period. Moura was HG's girl guide in 1920. They kept up a correspondence throughout the 1920s. Moura was HG's interpreter on the project to produce a screenplay for *Things to Come.* Moura and HG lunched and dined. They went to the ballet. They were an intimate couple, but they never married. Moura was, perhaps, a surrogate "mother-love," the MacKenzies conceded, as Isabel and Jane had been.

Moura is a more rounded human being in Smith's book. More details of her life are sketched, including her upbringing, work, and major love affairs. She was, for example, so wired into Russia that HG and his old Fabian friends, Sidney and Beatrice Webb, used her in the 1930s "as a postbox for ideas, letters, and . . . comments," Smith wrote. Moura also was a conduit for Soviet material from Gorky, as well as HG's conduit to various women's groups. She translated HG's "Declaration of the Rights of Man" into Russian, and was present, perhaps even responsible, for HG's third period of high productivity during World War II. They lunched and they dined, of course. The bottom line: Moura played a huge role in HG's observable life, but she also played a starring role in his equally important dream world. After Jane died, Moura became HG's "seeking spirit," Smith wrote, a lovely term, though not explained.

With her hearty laugh, sometimes described as Falstaffian, that reputation for being uncommonly courageous, a penchant for drinking all comers under the table and for smoking them out of the room with a cigar, Moura Budberg was by anyone's standards larger than life: colorful, amusing, affectionate, charming, charismatic, and, of course, serene.[61] There were other qualities. Lockhart noted in his diary on August 25, 1944, that although Moura made good conversation, she was "expensive to feed or, rather, to water. Today she drank only beer with luncheon, but she had an aperitif of three double gins at eight shillings apiece and with her coffee a double brandy at twelve shillings!"[62] Those who knew her well knew that she was resourceful and manipulative: the ultimate survivor. And she was smart, the "most intelligent woman in Europe," they said, "the most intelligent woman of her time."[63] Alexander regarded her mother's intelligence as intuitive. Moura had "native cunning and the ability to pick the brains of brilliant men and women without their realising it."[64] HG analyzed it another way:

> Mentally she has no great power or originality, but her mind is very active, full and shrewdly penetrating. It is silk, not steel. She thinks like a Russian; copiously, windingly and with that flavour of philosophical pretentiousness of Russian discourse, beginning nowhere in particular and emerging at a foregone conclusion. Yet she has streaks of extraordinary wisdom. She will illuminate a question suddenly like a burst of sunshine on a wet February day.[65]

★   ★   ★

Regardless of what it ran on, whether it was native cunning or Russian wind with intermittent bursts of wisdom, Moura's brain, as we have seen, invariably chose the route of obfuscation. Given her penchant for lying, indeed, for legendizing herself, and given the agendas of those who wrote about her, one quickly realizes that even the most basic facts about the woman are arguable, including even her date of birth; indeed, Moura told conflicting stories even about that, "for there were times when this could interfere with a good story."[66] She was born into a prosperous, if dysfunctional, family on March 6, 1892 or 1893, at Beriozovaya Rudka, the family estate in Poltava, Ukraine, to Maria Boreisha and Ignatiy Platonovich Zakrevsky—these facts according to Alexander.[67] Like HG, she was the fourth and youngest child. Moura's mother, described as extremely opinionated and snobbish, chose favorites among the children, pitted them against each other, and essentially disowned her eldest child and only son, Platon, called Bobik. Moura's father, described as an intelligent, energetic, and impulsive man, was a wealthy landowner who had studied law in St. Petersburg and Berlin and at Heidelberg University, and was by anyone's standards very successful. Rapidly moving up the ranks of the judicial system, Zakrevsky became a senator and for a short time the chief prosecutor for the Russian senate, but the Dreyfus affair in France ended his brilliant career.[68]

Moura was her parents' favorite child. After her father died in 1905, when she was twelve, Moura and her mother moved back to the family estate in the Ukraine.[69] Unlike her sisters, twins Alla and Assia, who were sent to the fashionable Obolensky Institute in St. Petersburg, Moura would be raised and educated by relatives, tutors, and an estate staff, including her beloved Irish governess, Micky (Margaret) Wilson, who later became surrogate mother to Moura's own children. To the horror of the family, Father Zakrevsky, a Freemason, gave a large part of his estate to fund a Freemasonry lodge in Scotland; this action further hamstrung what was left of the intact family and ensured Moura a haphazard education.[70] In 1911, and at age nineteen, Moura married Djon (John) Alexandrovich von Benckendorff, a Russian aristocrat of Baltic heritage and a member of the diplomatic corps, whom she met at the Russian embassy in Berlin during a visit to see her sister Assia.

Djon was sent to that embassy in 1909 and was named second secretary there the following year.[71] All these historical facts derive from Alexander's memoir.

Moura apparently was less desperately in love with Djon than she was desperate to escape her smothering mother and the isolation of the Ukraine. Life at the Russian embassy in Berlin was everything a bright young lady could have wished for: both high-level diplomacy and glamorous social functions. Moura's brother was also in the diplomatic service in Berlin at the time, as was her brother-in-law, Nikolai Ionoff. Before his marriage, Djon Benckendorff, nearly a decade Moura's senior, had inherited Yendel, his father's estate in Estonia. The estate, which later became a college of agriculture and, much later, the Jäneda Museum (specializing in local history), would serve as the Benckendorff family homestead through 1918. Djon and Moura's first child, Paul, was born there in 1913. When World War I broke out in August 1914, according to Alexander, the staff of the Russian embassy in Berlin and their families, including Djon, Moura, and baby Paul, were recalled home. A few weeks later, Djon enlisted in the army and was appointed staff officer at the headquarters of the Northern Front. This essentially marked the end of the marriage, or at any rate the end of their cohabitation, which never was very steady anyway.

While Djon was away in military service, Moura, her children— Tania was born in 1915—and her mother lived in a luxurious apartment in Petrograd; this was where Moura befriended and kept in touch with those connected to the British embassy. Several biographers argue, mystifyingly, that many of Moura's friendships originated in London in 1910 or 1911. [72] One of the great legends about Moura was that she studied at Cambridge when she was a girl.[73] Inaccuracies about Moura and her family abound, especially mistaken identities; for example, her husband Djon has been confused with other members of the Benckendorff clan.[74]

Djon returned to Petrograd in December 1917, and, as mentioned, in January of the new year, went to check on his estate in Estonia, having been away from it and from his wife and children for three years. The children and their governess followed in March, but Moura stayed behind, for the purpose, she said, of caring for her ailing mother, who had her own maid and cook. Removed from mothering and other domestic responsibilities and apparently feeling no great economic distress, Moura had a lot of free time beginning in March 1918. She claimed she took first aid courses and that she worked for the Red Cross and in a military hospital, but no record of those activities exists.[75] Moura also claimed to have taken law and history courses at a local university. It was at this time, in early 1918, with the family away in Estonia, that Moura met Bruce Lockhart, the new head of Britain's special mission to establish unofficial relations with the Bolsheviks. His profession, as stated on his diplomatic passport of 1917, was "Member of British Commercial Mission to Russia." He was described as being five feet nine inches tall, having a high forehead, blue eyes, an ordinary nose, a medium mouth and chin. His hair was brown, his complexion was fair, and his face was square. No special peculiarities were noted. Lockhart presented himself and these physical characteristics to Petrograd on January 29, 1918.

Despite both their marriages, Moura's children and mother, and the chaos and danger swirling around the embassy and Russia, Bruce Lockhart and Moura Benckendorff seem to have fallen in love soon after they met.[76] Indeed, without much subterfuge or shame, they became open lovers; but some serious affairs of state, including the attempt on Lenin's life, yanked their intense affair to an abrupt and premature end. On August 31, 1918, the night after a young terrorist named Fania (Fanny) Kaplan allegedly shot Lenin, Lockhart and several other members of the British legation, as previously noted, were arrested and taken to the Lubianka 11 Prison.[77] Lockhart had ostensibly masterminded the plot to assassinate Lenin, hence history's label: "The Lockhart Plot." He was kept overnight, but rearrested on September 4 and hauled back to the jail. Four days later, Lockhart was transferred to the Kremlin and given a suite of five small rooms, a fairly cushy arrangement to be sure. Moura, as noted earlier, was allowed to visit her lover daily, and to bring him luxuries: also highly irregular. He was released on October 4; he and the remaining embassy staff were then put on a train to Sweden, from where they sailed to England, eventually reaching London on October 19. Lockhart was condemned to death in absentia and never returned to Russia.

After Lockhart's removal, Moura kept a vigil for her lover through the long, hard Russian winter of 1918–1919, indeed for the next several years, pursuing, as HG often did, the unattainable. Judging by her letters to Lockhart, Moura believed his parting words that promised their separation was only temporary, that they would meet up in the West and marry.[78] But, instead of calling for her as he promised he would after the dust had settled, Lockhart cut his ties with Moura and resumed life with his wife. Possibly Lockhart was the only man Moura ever really loved—and lost. But being a survivor, she learned several hard lessons from her heartbreak, and, "above all, she learned never to give herself away again. From now on she would take what she could, but she would be careful what she gave."[79]

The following spring, on April 18 or 19, 1919 (Alexander said it was on the eighteenth; Moura said it was the nineteenth), Djon Benckendorff was murdered on his estate. Alexander said they never knew who shot her father, but Moura told Lockhart that it was Estonians, who did it out of revenge. Paul and Tania, their cousin Kira, and the family nurse happened upon his dead body lying on a path not far from the thawing lake on their property. Moura's mother died a few weeks later, following surgery. Moura did not see her children from the spring of 1918, when she packed them off to Yendel, to the spring of 1921, and very little is known about her activities during this time. Alexander reported that on the morning of her mother's arrival in Estonia in 1921, Micky, the governess, took her to meet Moura, "as far as I was concerned for the first time."[80] Both Alexander and Berberova left five years of Moura's life blank, from 1924 to 1929. Over the next decade, Moura's children would see their mother twice a year for a short visit in the winter and a longer visit in the summer.

Berberova and Alexander both report that soon after Christmas of 1918, Moura settled into one room of a grand apartment owned by

A. A. Mosolov, a man she supposedly had known at the military hospital in 1914.[81] Moura's letters indicate that she had moved back to Petrograd sooner than that; in fact, right after Lockhart and the embassies pulled out of Moscow in early October. "I fled from Moscow as soon as I could. It was horrid to be there where everything reminded me of you and of better days," she wrote Lockhart on October 24, 1918. Moura heard that Kornei Ivanovich Chukovsky, a writer, critic, and translator, was looking for translators for a new publishing venture that Maxim Gorky was launching.[82] Late that year, Moura visited Chukovsky at his office, and Gorky sat in on the interview. As Moura wrote to Lockhart:

We talked of English authors, of which, strange to say, [Gorky] knows a good deal, even the modern ones. He asked me to give him a list of books I thought would be interesting to translate! It all amused me rather and I will go there twice a week to kill time. The whole atmosphere there is very bohemian, but rather stimulating.[83]

In a letter Moura wrote to Lockhart on February 12, 1919, she said she was at Gorky's place, translating modern French poets. Later, she told Lockhart that she wasn't sure what Gorky's part in the publishing enterprise was. "His idea is to have the world ruled by people of creative thought, he told me, without any definition of class. He thinks himself a d'Annunzio of Russia."[84] Berberova and Alexander maintained that within weeks of having met Gorky, Moura moved into his colony. Once again the cat had landed on her paws.

Moura later wrote somewhat awkwardly in the preface to her translation of Gorky's *Fragments from My Diary*, that Gorky's life could be compared to a "march to the stars," whatever that meant. "Born a poet, he became a teacher, not because he liked teaching but because he liked the future." She also observed: "The man who as he dies thinks of the future is truly immortal."[85] Gorky, who loved to use pet names for members of his family and his intimates, called Moura "Titka." The family called him "The Duke," but he called himself Gorky, meaning "the bitter [one]."

*　　*　　*

One of Moura's life-changing experiences came in 1920, when she was
assigned to be H. G. Wells's translator and "girl guide"—as she described her job—during his fact-finding trip to Russia. The meeting ultimately changed both their lives. For HG, the attraction was immediate;
it was love at first sight, or at least, at his *recollection* of first sight. Although he thought he first met Moura in 1920, Moura maintained that
their first meeting was at a dinner party in Petersburg in 1914. Maurice
Baring, a British diplomat and war correspondent who was HG's guide
for that trip, supposedly introduced them.[86] Therefore, in the first two
pages of his book *Russia in the Shadows,* HG wrote that the guide and
interpreter assigned to him and his son was a woman he had met in
Russia in 1914. She was

> the niece of a former Russian Ambassador to London. She was educated
> at Newnham, she has been imprisoned five times by the Bolshevist Gov-
> ernment, she is not allowed to leave Petersburg because of an attempt
> to cross the frontier to her children in Estonia, and she was, therefore,
> the last person likely to hoodwink me. I mention this because on every
> hand at home and in Russia I had been told that the most elaborate cam-
> ouflage of realities would go on, and that I should be kept in blinkers
> throughout my visit. As a matter of fact, the harsh and terrible realities
> of the situation in Russia cannot be camouflaged.

HG, then, either mixed up the facts about Moura or unwittingly became a source of some of the errors, lies, and legends later circulated
about her. In the worst-case scenario, Moura planted the stories with
him from the start—stories about her heritage, her education, her imprisonment, and her virtual house arrest in Russia after her attempt to
see her children; perhaps she even planted the idea that she and HG had
met in 1914. Moreover, HG's perception of reality about Russia *was*
shaped by Moura, a person he believed to have an impeccable character, "the last person likely to hoodwink" him, but who in fact was an

able prevaricator. HG, like Alexander, had been "dragged into [Moura's] deceptions" from the get-go. Lies and deception, it would appear, formed the basis of their relationship.

Michael Foot did not restrain himself when describing the relationship between H. G. Wells and Moura Budberg. He called it "one of the great love affairs of the century." They were both brilliant lovers "in the technical sensual sense," Foot wrote, without offering evidence to support that intriguing statement.[87] How in the world would *he* know? But on he went. No one, he argued, could nurse HG's genius, restore his spirits, or give him new poise as well as Moura could. What HG gave Moura in Foot's scenario is not spelled out, but as it will become clear, the liaison with HG like the liaisons with Lockhart and Gorky before him, would be Moura's entrée to the opinion leaders of the time, her ticket to the front row, her roost in the cat-bird seat.

Berberova constructed an elaborate and dramatic theatrical analogy to describe the relationship between HG and Moura. Their love, she wrote, was a game played out on the stage of an empty theater. All the fire, all the energy, all the inspiration connected with the game amused and nourished them. In addition, Moura served whatever role HG wished her to serve; she was always at his side, always tender, warm, ready to respond to the least of his whims and orders. Moura brought HG what he had searched for all his life:

> Sympathy rather than impetuous passion, and instead of protests of independence or originality, a complete submission which brought joy to one as much as to the other, to him as fighter and victor for whom the hour of repose had sounded, to her as a goddess providing to him this repose in which she found physical and moral blossoming, goddess with unlimited power for which all was divinely possible and of whom the empire had no limits.[88]

How Berberova arrived at these conclusions is mystifying. That Moura was *not* always at HG's side, *not* always ready to respond to his orders and *rarely,* if ever, completely submissive was the greatest source of friction and frustration between the couple; indeed, a source of great sadness and distress for HG. Independence was what Moura Budberg was about. Berberova got right the idea that Moura used her charm, her wiles, and her sexuality to such great effect that men fell hopelessly in love with her. Right, too, was her statement that nothing of any consequence stopped Moura's relationships: not moral considerations, not false modesty, and not common taboos. If nothing else comes through loud and clear, it is that Moura quite consciously and methodically used her considerable powers to trap her victims, HG among them. He once described Moura as "outstandingly charming. Quite an exceptional number of people love and adore her, admire her and are urgent to please and service her."[89]

To be sure, HG never described his love affair with Moura as one of the century's greatest. That wasn't his style. Nor was it even remotely true. To begin with, theirs was a mature love and relationship, with all its implications. In addition, it was flawed nearly from the start, and HG was aware of this. Nor did he comment on Moura's submissiveness—why should he, for she wasn't submissive—or her great natural passion. Instead, he wrote that Moura wasn't a "feverish lascivious woman like Odette; she has no sensuous initiative, but she loves to be made love to and she is responsive. She told me she found the thought of self-abandonment to anyone with whom she was not in love unnatural and intolerable."[90] Moura also told HG that she had had a total of six lovers, and apparently he believed that, too. In his *Postscript,* he named names: Engelhardt, Benckendorff, Lockhart, Budberg, an unnamed Italian from Sorrento, and himself.[91] Of the six romances, only two—those with Lockhart and with HG—are documented to any extent. Engelhardt is a new name and husband, HG being the only writer to mention him. In a suppressed portion of the *Postscript,* as will be explained in more detail later, HG believed that Moura married Engelhardt, no first name or date of marriage given, then divorced him after he had an affair with one of her sisters. The only former lover/husband Moura discussed in her letters to HG was the shadowy Budberg, her known second husband, and a husband of convenience with whom she lived a few weeks, if that.

Baron Nicolai Budberg entered Moura Benckendorff's life in 1921, a full year after HG had. Lai, as he was called, was an Estonian subject from a landowning German Baltic family, and he lived—according to Alexander—an aimless, wasteful, and undisciplined life. She painted him as an inveterate gambler who gamed away his family's land and his inheritance to the point that he was no longer welcome in his country. As the story goes, Moura consulted an unnamed Estonian lawyer in 1921 about acquiring an Estonian passport, since she had lost her right to one when she stayed in Russia after 1918. The lawyer told her that her options were limited: Either she marry an Estonian or she marry an Estonian; and then he found Lai. At the time, Lai quipped that everyone on the Baltic Riviera was talking about the upcoming marriage of "the Chekist (Moura) and the fainéant," or loafer. The deal was sealed: Moura, a minimum-wage clerk, would pay Lai's considerable gambling debts in return for his name, Estonian citizenship, and a passport, which in turn would give her both mobility and nobility. In several versions of the legend, Gorky bankrolled the deal.

Alexander claimed that Moura and Lai exchanged vows in a Russian Orthodox Church in Reval in November 1921, hung around for a while, and then early the next year left for Berlin. Berberova said the wedding took place in early January in a government office, and that Lai then bolted for Kurfurstendamn, while Moura stuck around in Reval before going to Berlin. Oddly, before Moura left, she wrote to Maurice Baring asking for the addresses of H. G. Wells and Bruce Lockhart, and, instead of meeting Gorky in Sankt-Blasien, Germany, as planned, she went to London for a week. Upon her return, Moura wore not only fine shoes and a fur overcoat, Berberova reported, but also a chic London coif, a pleated black silk skirt, stockings, gloves, a white angora beret, and a matching scarf: a far cry from HG's first vision of her in that shabby dress and army raincoat. Meanwhile, in the fall of 1922, Lai shipped off to Argentina, where he would eke out a living giving bridge lessons, of all things. The Budberg's divorce was granted in Berlin in December 1926; neither party was present. Responding to something HG had said in a previous letter, Moura wrote this on October 11, 1922:

And what do you mean about: "What are you really up to?"

And you talk about the Baron Budberg as though he were a clay figure of some kind—or as though I kept him concealed under lock and
key in seven towers, or something equally mysterious! In reality, the
poor boy lives in Berlin, but as he seems to beleive that earning money is
a job suitable only to those who can do nothing else—we are compelled
to lead "menage apart." That's all.

A lame explanation indeed for newlyweds living separate lives. Moreover, Lai in all likelihood was already in South America when Moura
wrote those words to HG, and yet he remained her convenient lie.
Berberova recalled an interesting incident between Christmas of 1922
and the New Year when she spotted Moura at the Berlin Zoo railway
station "in the arms of a tall blond (perhaps it was Budberg). Elegant and
gay, she was not at all dressed as she was at Saarow."[92] This is curious,
since the day before, the Gorky household had received a letter from
Moura in Reval saying that she was busy with her children and Christmas and would stay there perhaps another week. For the record, the
tall blond probably wasn't Lai, because Alexander, who met him, described him as ugly and bald. At some point, HG picked up bad vibes
about Moura's relationship with Lai Budberg; he later wrote: "I did not
care to imagine the particulars of that marriage."[93]

*   *   *

Moura wrote to HG on May 27, less than a week after she left Russia in
1921, to announce her arrival in Estonia. "My dear Mr. Wells, I am sure
you will be surprised to get my letter. Myself, I cannot yet get accustomed to the idea that I am out of Russia and I cannot say that the comparison I make between 'your' world and 'ours,' after three years absence, is to the disfavour of my country." In that first letter, Moura set
up what would be the pattern for all her correspondence, and presumably her relationship, with HG: flirtation, praise, and business—or vice
versa. "I was greatly interested to get your book, 'Russia in the Shad-

ows'—and everything in it reminded me of the pleasant times we spent together." She dropped names and gossiped a bit: "Gorky is still in Petersburg, but I hope very much that he will get out in the course of a month in order to get a good rest and pull himself together. He needs it very much. But you know how difficult it is for him to tear himself away." Pleasantries out of the way, Moura got down to business.

> The "House of Science" was tremendously grateful to get 2 large sendings of books from the British Committee for Aiding Russian Men of Science which was formed at your initiative. . . . It was very welcome—for we are in sore need of food-stuff in Petersburg and I am afraid that this state will not improve, as the crops promise to be bad all through the country. As to the rest, we remain cheerful.

Moura's letters often carried a strange word such as "sendings." She also used the words "publishment," "reducement" and "consentment." "Did I really say publishment? What a shame," she once said shamelessly. Her spelling wasn't great, either, but rather idiosyncratic and fluid. There was one word that she consistently misspelled, and that, appropriately enough, was "believe." "Beleive me," she appealed throughout her correspondence to HG. In addition to the strange words and spellings, Moura's syntax was odd, indeed. "There exists a rough translation of it into English, guaranteed for its exactitude with the Russian text," she wrote to HG, and, "We are expecting you to send it to us with the greatest impatience." HG would tease her about her spelling and syntax; she would respond, sometimes defensively: "Why can't I write letters? I think I write them very nicely, indeed."[94] These language skills, or lack of them, are surprising since by this point, Moura was thoroughly entrenched in her literary career.

If Moura stuck with a simple formula, part ego-stroking, part business, HG went with a complex one, covering the waterfront efficiently in his short, nearly illegible, but often entertaining letters. Typically, he started with the mechanicals—the mail, the weather, his movements across time and space—then went on to discuss work and personal matters, to ask a few caring questions and make a few caring comments, to sketch a few details about his trip, and to make some sweeping national or global observations: truths as he saw them, such as, "[Australians] are like what you would meet in the Midlands, Yorkshire or Kent—they have exactly the same speech & the same curious inefficiency about eating, drinking and decoration." And: "FDR will sail back for a third time." And: "Jerry has lost his war but I am afraid that cleaning him up will make an awful mess of the world."[95] When closing his letters, HG often threw in a blessing, a humorous anecdote, or one of his amusing picshuas, or cartoon drawings, the word derived from his childhood pronunciation of the word "pictures." Simply but well drawn, and resembling James Thurber's cartoons, HG's picshuas might show a single figure, or many, and they were often humorous, often self-deprecating.

Naturally, the letters between HG and Moura, which span twenty-three years, changed over time as their relationship changed. This is especially true of Moura's letters, written from 1921 to 1940. Her letters to HG can be separated into three periods: 1920 to 1929 (the post-tryst/separated period); 1929 to 1940 (the courting/affair period); and 1940 to 1946 (the "married" period, when, as war encroached and HG's health slipped away, their relationship settled into a warm and comfortable, mostly monogamous habit). Unfortunately, and significantly, there are no extant letters during the crisis years of the mid-1930s: from the Moscow deception and Moura's malaise to Gorky's death.

In the early correspondence, Moura is coy, coquettish, and provocative, but still aggressive and intent on getting what she wanted. Judging by her letters, she was successful; HG was inclined to grant Moura's every request; he sent her letters, money, books, articles, prefaces, and reviews. Still, in the early 1930s, a handful of Moura's letters dealt, uncharacteristically, not with business deals but with her own physical and emotional constraints: an abortion, a mysterious trip to a French doctor, an even more mysterious flight from London. Nevertheless, business was her main agenda and theme. In the 1940s, a mellowing Moura often kept the home fires burning while HG traveled abroad. He scheduled a nearly three-month tour of the United States, from September to December 1940, and while he was gone, Moura kept an eye on his real estate. "I spent the weekend at Tania's," she wrote on September 23, 1940. "Have been once to Hanover Terrace, where all is going on well. I might go there to-night perhaps and stay the night." In that same letter, she instructed HG to "get" Robert Sherwood to send his new play, *It Won't Be Night Again*, "or something like that," to her for produc tion in London.

HG's remaining letters to Moura span a relatively short period, from 1938 to 1944. They consist primarily of reports from the field: the trip to Australia from December 1938 to January 1939, the tour of the United States the following year, and his trials holding the fort during Germany's "robot bombing" of London during the summer of 1944, when he was also battling some personal enemies; namely, disease and weakness. During the bombing, HG boarded himself and an occasional day nurse into Hanover Terrace. He refused to leave town, and despite losing many a window to concussion shocks, and one or two near misses from "doodlebugs," as German V-1 rockets were called, he and his property just off Regent's Park got through the war relatively un-scathed. He once told a friend that "That [expletive deleted] Hitler wasn't going to get me on the run!" HG told Moura: "The robot bombs came in increased quantities but thanks to my punctilious observance of your instructions no harm has come to me (or to anyone else in this house)."[96] Moura issued her commandments from the safety of the countryside. Marjorie Wells checked in on HG several times a day.

Since HG and Moura were often apart, their plans for work and for play figured heavily into their correspondence. Even from the first, when there seemed little reason for it and little possibility that they would get together, Moura kept HG informed of her status and plans. On July 29, 1921, she told him that she might go to Finland to meet Gorky, who was coming out of Russia. The next year, she wrote that she was going to Paris in November to visit her sister. The year after that, her plans were to go to Estonia at the end of April to spend some time with her "offsprings." And so on. Following their meeting in 1929, nine years after their tryst in Petrograd under Gorky's nose and roof, Moura's tone and message changed. Sensing that she had HG in her clutches, she now sounded proprietary. From Berlin, Moura wrote on September 29, "You are in Paris now, and I have just arrived here, with a lot of work in front of me to-morrow. Write to me soon and tell me how you are and take care of yourself."

HG was a faithful correspondent and kept Moura apprised of his schedule. "I'm on my way to Melbourne. I shall come to Athens as we have arranged but I shall have to be in London before March 1st," he wrote on January 3, 1939. Two weeks later: "In ten days I shall be in the air coming home. On Feb. 11th we dine (no fuss) with Sidney Waterlow in Athens." Similarly, during that long trip through the United States, HG wrote on October 19, 1940, "I'm launched on the journey. All goes well but there is never a moment to [sit] down to write a letter."

Without a doubt, HG and Moura were world-class globe-trotters. As for long hauls, he traveled to, and throughout, the United States five times (1906, 1921, 1935 twice, and 1940), and to Russia three times (1914, 1920, 1934); he took an extended trip to Czechoslovakia in 1923. As noted, HG went to Australia in the winter of 1938–1939. He also visited the war front in 1916, and of course traveled all over Europe from the turn of the century to the period when his health deteriorated in 1944. Moura's travels are much harder to pin down; but in principle, she was in perpetual motion, moving around Europe, including Eastern Europe, from as early as 1911 to as late as 1974. In a period of about five weeks, the period this book opened with, from the end of December 1934 to the end of January 1935, Moura traveled from England to the South of France, back to England, and back to the South of France, then on to Estonia, where she stayed until early April; then she returned to London. Certainly she took annual trips to Moscow from various European cities throughout the 1930s, and two or three trips a year to Estonia, primarily from London, Berlin, and Sorrento. Moreover, French secret police and Russian Intelligence Service records place Moura in Poland in 1921, and French authorities also believed she worked in Japan for a time!

With all that travel it isn't surprising that in their letters, HG and Moura often commented on the routine things of life, including the weather and the mail. Remarks about the mail and letters—sent, received, gone astray, and hoped and begged for—rank as a leading topic of conversation. Typical is the following, which Moura wrote on September 14, 1928: "It is ages since I have written to you—or you to me—which I think unpardonable on both our parts." Curiously, Moura was keenly aware of HG's activities; and for whatever reason, not only didn't she hide her knowledge but she seemed to flaunt it. "I hear you were quite a long time in Italy, recovering from your illness. Are you all right now?" she asked from Estonia in 1921. "How was Geneva? You met Rolland, I know, as well as Hansen," she wrote in 1928 from Sorrento.[97] HG may have been charmed by her interest in his activities, but he also must have wondered how she came by such detailed information and what that said about her. Since his own business was wrapped up with the mail, so to speak, HG was often frustrated with the postal service, which by today's standards appears to have worked amazingly well. Still, on December 22, 1938, he wrote this to Moura from the Indian Ocean as he headed for Freemantle: "This incompetent British Empire isn't to be trusted with a letter."

The themes of love, of memory, and of dreams that will be so prevalent in HG's correspondence with Constance play little part in his extant correspondence with Moura. This correspondence is caught up, rather, with life's realities: work, business, books, journals, literature, and changing the world. In all her letters to HG, Moura used the word "dream" only once, and then in its negative sense. Life in wartime London, "has lost almost all aspect of reality, so that I sometimes think I'm just having a bad dream and will wake up and find you there," she wrote on October 22, 1940. In his letters to Moura, HG never philosophized about dreams and dreaming.

Work, after all, was their common denominator, their bond. Moura often wrote about her own literary work, and rarely failed to ask HG about his, to comment on it, or to tap into it. Her first letter to him was about work. She told him on May 27, 1921, how "greatly interested" she was to have received his *Russia in the Shadows,* sniffing, however, that the Russian translation had a preface "which I do not care much about." Two years later, Moura would ask HG what he was up to, and then offer, tantalizingly: "Here, my occupations are varied—extremely. I translate books for Russian writers. I dance with German officers and I flirt—with both." That same year, she told HG that her main publishing activities were in Berlin, although much of her time was taken up assisting Gorky, who, she crowed, couldn't manage without her. At Easter of 1925 she sent a postcard saying: "I like the 'Dream' so much—is it your last?"[98]

In 1928, Moura asked HG if he had been working a lot. Whether she knew the answer, and she probably did, it had been an amazingly productive year for him: three film scripts and four books, including *The Book of Catherine Wells.* Moura sent HG an Italian review of his *Outline of History* in 1930. A decade later, she wrote that she was working "in a slightly desultory way at the French periodical," *La France Libre.* "Am going to look at some shots of Kipps, which I am told is very well done. The 'Babes' are not yet out. I am very curious to see how it will be met." Moura closed that letter with the information that the publisher Frederic Warburg was satisfied with the progress of HG's *All Aboard for Ararat.*[99]

From Canberra in January 1939, HG reported that he was having a tremendously stimulating time, and that all his lectures and radio talks had gone very well. In addition to that, he was writing a weekly series for the *News Chronicle,* indeed, mailing one to be typed and cabling another in a few days. "Marjorie will probably ask you to look over the typescript," he wrote on the eighteenth. HG noted that he was also giving a public lecture and two radio talks in Sydney, making him "pretty busy." The next year, writing from Columbia University Club in New York, he bragged that he'd had "very considerable lecturing success." HG sent Moura an article on the Western desert offensive in North Africa for *La France Libre* at the end of 1941. On July 21, 1944, he was writing "in the happy absence of interruption." The next day, he reiterated that he was working and growing more self-reliant every day.

As mentioned, flirtation was the engine that drove Moura's relationships, even those maintained by mail. In a letter from Saarow in October 1922, she started her engine. Responding to something HG had
asked in a previous letter, Moura challenged: "What about [my] Secret
Ways?"; she then purred, "I'd like to know what yours are." In the next
letter, she asked HG to write to her, though admitted she'd rather have
a nice long talk with him. And so it goes with Moura:

February 10, 1923: So we missed each other again. And I would like to
see you so much. Well, let us be patient.

March 18, 1923: Gorky sends his very warmest wishes and I—lots of
other things too.

Easter, 1925: This is just an "Easter postcard." I've caught the disease
from my children who are sending them to all the world. So from this
you see that to me "all the world" is you! That's an hyperbola as good as
yours.

Two years later, Moura was still angling to see HG. "When are we
going to meet," she asked, reminding HG that it was now seven years
since his last trip to Russia, "and we have missed each other across all
Europe. For my part, I grieve about it very much. Where are you
now—and where are [you] going this summer?"[100] She would bait him
with the same question in letter after letter. In 1929, after they finally
had their rendezvous in London, Moura wrote from her hotel in Paris
to thank HG for the visit. She was shameless. "Waiting for a faithless
swain in the Meurice [Hotel], I spend the time much more pleasantly in
writing to you to tell you how charming [and] delightful you have
made my visit to London, dear. I am a very grateful little person (little
is hardly accurate!) and will never forget it. Love—as much as you want
of it. Moura."[101]

As we have seen, Moura was equally adept at using praise and thanks
to wiggle her way into HG's heart. The praise, for the most part, was
heaped on his works; the thanks for letters, books, and articles, and
consent to publish. Shortly after Moura arrived in Estonia, HG sent her

Russia in the Shadows and *The Salvaging of Civilization*. In thanking him, Moura noted that *Salvaging* was "brilliant and true and clever."[102] Several years later, she commented on a new title, probably *The World of William Clissold*, a novel that attacked contemporary education and proposed HG's theory of world revolution. "I have read your last book and—although you must have heard it praised so many times already—I do not think that any other book of these last three years has given me more enjoyment than that one."[103] From Sorrento on April 19, 1928, Moura wrote that it was "a great shame to admit" that her letter was inspired by reading for the *sixth* time HG's novel *Tono-Bungay*, published in 1909, "and thinking what a wonderful book it is." Three months later, she said of another book, probably *Open Conspiracy*: "Do you know, of all the psycho-political books you have written, I like it most. I would have liked so much to talk with you about it. You don't mind my calling it psycho-political, but there, you are not a dry politician and never will be and the idealism of your politics is something for which I like you tremendously."[104] It is intriguing that Moura's favorite book should be so titled. A few years later, she thanked HG for sending a book, probably *Work, Wealth and Happiness of Mankind:*

> I am ever so touched—and very grateful for the book and inscription, the latter somewhat contradicting the opinion shared by many that I "showed" Russia to you with all the intolerance of a proselyte. All this, of course, is piffle for you would have seen beyond anybody's "showing"—and I only did my best in showing what I could, "la plus belle femme du monde ne pourant donner que ce qu'elle a."[105] [The most beautiful woman in the world can give only what she has.]

Moura was often flirtatious and praising, but she was not afraid to be critical. Nearly from the beginning, she criticized HG—even chastised him for one thing or another, demonstrating her fearlessness in the presence of A Great Man, her tendency, as HG put it, to "brave the world" and also to "order it about," as he wrote in the *Postscript*. Here I stand, a woman, she was announcing, who will not shy away, who *will* stand her ground. For example, Moura once wrote to HG to say that by mistake his letter had gone to a relative of hers in Rome. "This is dreadful, unless you'd be kind, shake off a certain natural laziness and write the letter all over again."[106] In the same letter she commended HG on his latest book, saying that it was very good, "but lazy, too. You force your reader to put two and two together himself as he reads it, and it is not good for him. You should have done it yourself." Despite her growing library, Moura had the chutzpah to chide HG in 1925 for never sendind her any of his books. Three years later, after having tried to squeeze translations out of him over the past several letters, she suggested that *he* stop being "so entirely business-like!"

HG could take it, and he could hand it out, too, but he was kinder, and his teasing was only softly insistent. Often, he was plain funny. Writing from Government House in Canberra on January 12, 1939, just before delivering his "big discourse," HG closed his letter with this: "Be a good pure Moura—chaste, non alcoholic, reading one of my books for an hour every night before going to bed at eleven, walking 4 (four) miles every day." A week later, he signed off with the same theme: "Are you being a good Moura? And is your weight falling & falling?" At the end of 1940, writing from New York City, HG sent his last letter from America. "I've flown already 21,000 miles. When I get to London I shall have flown . . . round the Equator, 30,000 miles. (This is to teach you geography & improve your mind.)"[107] HG could also admit *his* shortcomings. In 1937, he found that he owed a large amount in back income taxes. By January 1939, he was explaining his plan to raise £18,000 by March 1; until that was accomplished, he would be anxious, he told Moura, and after it was done, he might have to "entrench or economize or do something of that sort. I really am very incompetent financially, but I guess I can pull it through with an effort. The worst of it is that I can't always produce effort as readily as I used to do. You'll have to be kind to me for a bit Moura dear," he wrote on the third. In his next letter, HG was more confident about his financial situation. "I am cabling a weekly article to *News Chronicle* on world affairs, beginning the 16th, toilsome but profitable and I hope to get round my financial corners without very severe suffering by March."[108]

Unlike Moura, HG requested very little through the mail. Once in a blue moon he asked her to deposit a check or to cash one. Much more often, he begged for a letter:

December 22, 1938: Still not a line from you since your radio.

January 3, 1939: I've had a New Years greeting from you—in Adelaide but no real letter. I'll hope to get something more than that in Melbourne.

September 26, 1940: I shall send this by airmail from NYC & there I hope to find letters from you & home generally.

October 19, 1940: Write me a perfect love letter.

Occasionally, HG needed Moura's professional help. In 1942, for example, he was working on a project sometimes called "The Sankey Declaration of Rights." He wrote to Moura saying that he needed the document translated into French and Russian as soon as possible "for propaganda purposes and I want your best advice how to distribute it."[109] The next year, the tables were turned: Moura was working on an independent film project that was to take a historical and international look at censorship and book burning, and she turned to HG. He, obviously, was not happy with the way Moura was managing the project and also seemed to have little confidence in her associates. "There must be hundreds of thousands of feet available *if your man has the knowledge and enterprise to get hold of it,*" HG snapped on February 23, 1943. After making a few cursory suggestions, he agreed to appear as a talking head, "but there must be a scenario first, showing how all this is to be arranged, and an assurance of access to the material. Otherwise there is nothing doing." And then HG cut the discussion short with this: "That is all I can do for the enterprise at present."

He had been equally ungracious ten years earlier. Not uncharacteristically, Moura had dropped the ball on a project, and HG wrote to say that either she get going on it or he would withdraw his help. It isn't known how long HG carried around the idea of organizing a women's progressive movement, but in 1932, he sent a circular letter about his vision to nineteen prominent women, including Moura. In his own words, "A special organization of intelligent women might play a very important role in organizing study circles influencing education and sustaining when necessary war resistance—having regard to the special abilities, opportunities and immunities of women." HG had just published *The Work, Wealth and Happiness of Mankind,* a comprehensive account of economic life; this work included, as previously noted, a large section on the influence of women in the Western world, and his movement was clearly an offshoot of the magnum opus. By the time he wrote to Moura, he was grumpy indeed:

> I find it quite impossible to go on with this attempt to organise a women's progressive movement. If women are to be [of] any service in putting the world into shape they must do this job for themselves. If my idea is an impracticable one the sooner it drops and dies the better. It will be inconvenient to hold a meeting here next Thursday. I enclose the three papers we discussed and the list of names of people to be consulted. If you can get together with one or two of the people who came to tea here yesterday and can call that meeting in any place you like, I shall be pleased to contribute £25 to the secretarial and other expenses involved. If not the whole thing can die now. Very sincerely yours.[110]

One wonders how his vision for a women's movement might have affected women's rights and world politics. Still, HG knew that Moura resented playing a subservient role. She "doesn't like being mistress as a sort of appendix to me," he wrote to Christabel in June 1940. Most of the time, HG was far more civil. He asked Moura to rest and take care of herself, to get well and not worry. "Now rest my dearest, rest for my sake, sleep & very soon we will be together again," he wrote in July 1944.

Moura was shameless about asking for favors—frequently artless, often transparent, and always tenacious—a human octopus! Her system was to ask for something, and then follow the request with the suggestion that the two of them get together. Moura certainly didn't waste much time after meeting HG to seize upon his considerable resources and connections, and she didn't beat around the bush. A few examples:

January 26, 1923: I wonder if you could suggest anything about the publishment of Gorki's last book in England. It would be awfully kind if you would write and tell me what you think should be done for it. Gorki is starting here a Russian Review and asks if you would care to take part in it? He would be so very, very glad if you would.

February 10, 1923: Do you think you could send us something for Gorki's review? About 20–25,000 words? We would be very grateful.

March 18, 1923: What [Gorky] is most keen about is your "Godlike Men" and we are expecting you to send it to us with the greatest impatience. Please do it as soon as possible so as not to lose time!

October 11, [1922 or 1923]: My German firm is called "Epoche Verlag." It is absolutely trustworthy. May we have your next book to publish in German? Please let me know if you will give it to us for publication in German and what your previous conditions with German publishers were, for we pay better.

In 1925, Moura moved in for the kill, though not for an article, a book, or rights to one of HG's titles but for economic and organizational assistance in restoring Estonia, of all things. She began typically disarmingly: "I know you will laugh over this letter"; then she fired,

Does Europe want to fight Bolshevism? Well, if it does, why doesn't it do it sensibly, confound it! Esthonia is in danger. It would cost almost nothing to reestablish it economically. On the other hand it would mean giving it 95 percent chance to fight Communism. Why doesn't one do it? The merest undertaking, the setting up of a water-philtre, for instance, would mean a reducement of the number of out of work, and that is, after all, the beginning and the end of revolution.[111]

There is no evidence that HG took up the cause for Estonia. Truth to tell, Moura herself was not always heavily committed to Estonia, at least personally. As earlier noted, after having been in Estonia for less than a week in May 1921, reunited with her children after three year's absence, Moura wrote HG on May 27 that she was already longing to get back to Russia "in spite of everything. But of course I am so happy to see the children, who have grown into hard little internationalists." Then she griped that Estonia wasn't Europe, "but only a very poor parody of it." Two months later, Moura wrote that she was "still stranded" in the Estonian Democratic Republic. On February 10, 1922, she chided HG for not finding her in Paris, and then confessed that she had left the city early so that she could join her children in "the depths of Esthonia" for New Year's Day. When she wrote from Saarow on October 12, 1922, where she expected to stay for a while, she conceded that she had "had enough of frontier countries—and here things are interesting." It is certain that life left something to be desired at Kallijärv—or so she made it seem.

In 1927 Moura began hitting HG up for articles for a new bilingual publication, *Europa Magazin,* which was to be a collaboration between Gorky, Romain Rolland, and HG to combine literature, art, and science. Moura conceded that HG was probably thinking her "an awful nuisance" for always asking him for articles. "I do not think it will infringe any matters of copyright if you do us the great great honor of giving us a few pages—anything, in fact, that you would choose to give. When are we going to meet?" Later, she thanked HG for agreeing to send her something for the review, and then added, "I am so sorry to hear of your wife's illness and do hope she will recover soon. And you will send me something, no matter how short? I am very very grateful." But Moura outdid even that. Six months after Jane Wells died, she sent the following: "It is ages since I wrote to you. I hope you got my last note, telling you how grieved I was to hear of your loss. Now, I just want to remind you of my existence and ask you to give me some news of yourself."[112]

Becoming more and more inventive, aggressive, and a pain in the neck, Moura pounced on HG in 1928 with a sleazy-sounding scheme, "a business proposition," she called it. She asked whether he had an arrangement with a Russian firm for the translation of his books into Russian:

I don't expect so, for Bolos being "unconventional" in more ways than one—they probably take without asking. If I am right, would you care to have to do with a Russian firm with European methods, a firm in Berlin? In that case we would have to outwit "them" and the only way to do so would be letting us have the Ms. for translation before it was published in English. Would you let me know if you agree, if not forever, why then, for your next book only and what your terms would be. . . . I have not seen you for such a long time. Are you thinking of coming over this year to this part of the world? For I could, in that case, attempt to see you once again.[113]

At the top of the letter, HG scribbled a note to Marjorie: "File. Write I said Yes, Right O." He then crossed out those instructions and wrote: "Marjorie, what shall I tell her? . . . Is not a translation into Russian published in Berlin subject to the German laws of copyright?" Whether or not Moura was trying to pull a fast one on HG is not known, but three weeks later she responded in a face-saving manner, and with her typical nerve, saying that she hated having to tell "a mere man" that he was right, but that he was—this time. Then she proposed "another way": to publish in Czechoslovakia, where Russian publications were free. She also wanted to know whether HG had "permanent arrangements" for German translations, because her editor issued them as well, she wrote, "and pays better than others do—and I would like him to get books that I think good, therefore I want yours! Please forgive me for bothering you again and do let me know this. . . . And tell me when I shall see you![114]

And so it goes; letter after letter carries another request for a "favor," as Moura liked to call them: a little preface for the Russian writer P. Muratoff, who "has little chance to be published, unless you, for instance, would be such a dear and write a little preface for him";[115] a request to subscribe to "a very important publication" from Pushkin Press; a request to reprint an article in *France Libre*; constant pecking reminders for £50 to be sent to Reval and Berlin banks. At one point, Moura even wrote to Marjorie about the money, and also asked about

HG's birthday plans. HG's instructions to Marjorie on September 14, 1931: "Say nothing about my birthday. She is a bother."

To her credit, Moura always kept her comments about Gorky professional. Never did she allude to the romantic relationship between them, much less speak of him as her lover. Her tactic was to follow a comment about Gorky with bait; for example, she would ask HG when he and she could meet, often proposing a time and place. In the beginning, Moura focused on Gorky's emigration plans. Yet even as she announced that Gorky was finally out of Russia and that she was staying "for the present" with him near Berlin, Moura flirted with HG: "Do let me hear from you soon. I am going to Paris in November, where I will visit my sister. Won't you come there?"[116] Moura tried the same strategy in 1923:

> I came here [Günterstahl] to help Gorky who has been very ill and has not been allowed to do hardly any work himself. So although my chief publication activities are centered round Berlin, I am staying here for the present. . . . It would be delightful if you really came to the Riviera, for you surely would allow me to find you in your [H]ermitage, wouldn't you? And we would talk—but why only two or three days?

Occasionally, the comments were simply friendly. "Gorky sends you his love—he was very much touched by your tribute to his 60th birthday," she wrote on May 2, 1928. That same year, Gorky, who was working on a long novel, sent HG his best wishes and his compliments on *Christina Alberta's Father*. Moura's last direct mention of Gorky came in a letter from Kallijärv in Estonia. Her hunch was that the great Russian writer would remain in Russia a long time. "He is so young and so keen to see all there is to be seen after 10 years' absence."[117] As it happened, Gorky lived only five more years.

Moura mentioned Gorky in half of her letters to HG, but HG, for strategic reasons, perhaps, never picked up on the topic, although he and Gorky often corresponded by way of Moura, to be sure, who was their translator. Once, HG allowed himself to make a little joke for himself and for Marjorie about Gorky. At the bottom of a January 26, 1923, letter Moura sent HG, Gorky wrote a one-line message to HG in Russian. Under Gorky's message, and as a response, of sorts, HG, who did not read or speak Russian, penciled in: "Exactly."

During what would be his last meeting with Gorky, in the summer of 1934, HG broached two issues of great interest to himself: birth control and freedom of expression. They met at Gorky's home, which HG described as "the beautiful and beautifully furnished house the government places at his disposal."[118] HG reported that Gorky had changed little since their first meeting on Staten Island in 1906. At their 1934 meeting, HG planned to float the idea that it was time Russia began to "decontrol literary activities . . . and form a free and independent P.E.N. Club in Moscow."[119] It was a lost cause, as HG explained:

> I unfolded my ideas about the necessity of free writing and speech and drawing in every highly organized state; the greater the political and social rigidity, I argued, the more the need for thought and comment to play about it. These were quite extraordinary ideas to all my hearers, though Gorky must have held them once. If so, he has forgotten them or put them behind him.[120]

Two things were particularly notable about the conversation, HG wrote: the idea that literature should be under political control and restraint, and the readiness "to suspect a 'capitalist' intrigue, to which all their brains, including Gorky's, had been <u>trained</u>. I did not like to find Gorky against liberty. It wounded me."[121]

Sometime in early March 1936, Gorky reported to Stalin his impressions of the French writer André Malraux. Gorky was looking for European writers who had a huge standing with Russian leaders to lead an effort at unifying the European intelligentsia against fascism. He asked informants, among them Isaak Babel, a Soviet writer (and later, a purge victim), to look into Malraux's background for this purpose. "My other informant," Gorky wrote to Stalin, "Mariia Budberg—you have met her at my place—confirms Babel's opinion. She has long frequented literary circles in Europe and knows all the attitudes and opinions that prevail there. In her view, Malraux is truly a man of exceptional value."[122] In a letter to his old friend Romain Rolland, written a few weeks later, Gorky commented on Malraux; on his own bad health—he was coughing up a lot of blood; and his work. Gorky reported that he was irritated "by the egotism and hypocrisy of the 'aristocratic race' which inhabits the islands beyond the [English] Channel—I am irritated and feel ill will towards that race. It appears that it is abandoning France to pillage and destruction by the German Fascists. That self-important cockerel Wells is wisely keeping silent, although he ought to feel somewhat ashamed of his countrymen."[123] Thus, whether HG and Gorky knew it or not, the disenchantment was mutual.

Despite the little time she spent raising her children, Moura wore her motherhood on her sleeve. Among other things, she managed to slip references to her offspring into most of her letters to HG throughout the 1920s and 1930s. With those references, she tucked in little lies. For example, a couple of months after settling into hearth and home at Kallijärv in 1921, she wrote that most of her time was spent in the country with the children, "which is very relaxing after Russia." We know from her daughter that Moura spent half of each week in Reval, fifty miles away. Still, the displays of dedication, for example, February 10, 1923: "At New Year's Eve I was making '*la bonne aventure*' with my children . . . for where should a mother's place be on the first day of the year, if it isn't there." Her children's education was the "motive" Moura gave in her application for emigrating to England, which was denied in mid-1928, or so she told HG. She said that she didn't know why her visa had been denied—"the office here said it was refused without motives and without having referred to the people I had mentioned," she wrote on July 28, 1928. It isn't known whether HG interceded for Moura and her children's visas, although it sounded as if he had. It wouldn't have been the first time he tried to help Russians emigrate to England. HG once went out on a limb for Marie Andreeva, Gorky's common-law wife from 1903 to 1919, and several of her friends. On April 28, 1921, Nikolai Klishko at the Russian Trade Delegation wrote to HG in response to HG's letter of April 23 to tell him that he had asked the British foreign office for visas for Marie Andreeva and her party. He didn't know when the visas would be granted, but he felt that it would help if HG reminded the FO about it.[124] Although Andreeva indulged in radical politics and maintained ties to the Bolsheviks, Gorky described her as "noble Marusia," his beautiful woman friend, and as a "wondrous person" whom he loved and respected with all his heart.[125] Andreeva was an actress at the Moscow Arts Theatre; during his 1920 trip to Moscow, HG had attended a performance of Othello in which Andreeva played Desdemona. They had also met socially at Gorky's. A few weeks after receiving Klishko's letter, HG received a telegram from Andreeva inquiring about their passports and asking HG to cable her. Her cable was signed "Marie and Reeva," a telegraph operator's humorous mistake. On May 15, 1921, she wrote to HG from Riga thanking him for his help, even though it was unsuccessful.

> I think it is very sad . . . it would be good for both of our countrys, should the people of both of them meet and see the conditions of ech other. You can understand better as everybody how dreadful it must be to live in such a small and blockaded circle as we did all those last years. Solovei, Mr. Rakizki, by his real name, dreamed to have some delicious cowboying dances with Gyp in any little hotel in London. Poor old Solovei, the best man I ever met. Now he is going to all the kinotheatres to admire the American films. Perhaps we should stay a long time in Germany, it would be such a great pleasure, could you come there and find us. Kindest regards to you and Gyp and love from Solovei and Kriutshkoff to you both.[126]

That HG had the desire and the clout to help Andreeva and company could not have been missed by Moura. Perhaps she even suggested that Andreeva turn to HG for assistance. Still, how disturbed HG would have been to learn that at the same time he was trying to help Andreeva, she was callously betraying her fellow Russians. More on this later in the chapter.

Moura lived for a while with Kira in Berlin in the 1920s, and she saw a good deal of Andreeva there. She lived with Tania in London in the mid-1930s. After her children had married and set up their own homes, Moura visited them, often for several days at a time, as she often reported to HG. For example, on December 11, 1930: "My child is in London and has dined with Marjorie." September 23, 1940: "I spent the weekend at Tania's." October 22, 1940: "I'm writing this having returned from Yorkshire, where I spent 4 days with Paul." Although he resented them from time to time—not because of Moura's professed devotion to them but because of her frequent flittings to and fro, allegedly on their behalf—HG was generous to Moura's children. He always remembered their birthdays with money and gifts. On Tania's twentieth, he gave her a "handsome" portable typewriter. On her twenty-first, £20, which to Tania "seemed like a fortune." With part of that fortune, she bought a long evening gown. HG also helped fund more than a few of the family's summer holidays with a timely check.

Still, he must have wondered about Moura's devotion to her children. What she told him often contradicted what others—her own daughter, for example—said about their upbringing. He must have wondered why Moura had lived apart from them for much of their youth some 150 miles away in Petrograd, and why she had rarely seen them between their preschool years and their late teens and early twenties. Tania Alexander wrote that "for the whole of our early life we were, in effect, without parents. Our father was dead and our mother, we had been told, had stayed in Petrograd with her own mother, who was ill."[127] As mentioned, Moura would stay on in a sumptuous apartment for some time both before and after her husband and her mother died, even though caring for her mother was her stock reason for living in Petrograd. When the children were reintroduced to their mother in May 1921—they were eight and ten—Moura "returned as a stranger, as one who had left her children and who had, as I later learned, been prepared to sacrifice them for ever."[128] Was this behavior simply because Moura wasn't "into" child rearing, not very maternal, as she once told Lockhart? Why then did she work furiously to demonstrate the opposite to HG?

Moura claimed to live with her children from 1921 to 1922, yet, as noted, according to her daughter, she spent half of each week that year in Reval. By Alexander's account, Moura stayed at the apartment of old family friends, Baron and Baroness Bengt Stackelberg. Alexander never said what Moura did there. Thereafter, from 1922 through the 1920s, Moura visited her children twice a year: a short visit in the winter, a longer one in the summer. Yet Berberova, who had lived near or with Moura throughout that decade, claimed that Moura took three—not two—annual trips to Estonia to visit the children: at Easter, during the summer, and at Christmas. Where Moura went every third trip, if indeed she took *three* annual trips, is not known, although Berlin and Moscow come to mind.

One even wonders how many children Moura had. Writing in the early 1930s to thank HG for a signed copy of his latest book, Moura said that she had just come to Kallijärv, where she had sixty hens and *three* children. She said she might go to England "to bring my eldest girl there in September. Will you be in London?" The girl to whom Moura referred was Kira, who was five years older than Paul, seven years older than Tania, and described throughout Alexander's memoir as "our cousin." Neither her last name nor her parentage was given.[129] Kira lived and moved with the Benckendorff clan. She was with the children when they discovered Djon Benckendorff's body in April 1919, and when they visited Gorky at Sorrento the summer of 1925. She was there to greet Moura each time she returned to Kallijärv and there to say goodbye each time she left. "My cousin, Kira," Alexander wrote, "who had grown up with us . . . was more of a sister to me than a cousin."[130] Kira was the first offspring to leave Estonia. She went to London in late 1930 or early 1931, where Moura had arranged for her to stay with a friend. Paul followed in 1933 and Tania in 1934.

Curiously, it was HG who shed some light on the subject of Kira. In the *Postscript*, as mentioned, he wrote that Moura's first husband was named Engelhardt, and that she had divorced him. Since no other biographers of HG or of Moura ever mentioned an Engelhardt, it's possible that HG mixed up names; he did that on occasion. In a suppressed passage of the *Postscript,* though, HG wrote: "One husband, Engelhardt, [Moura] had divorced because he betrayed her with her elder sister." He then noted that *the eldest child Moura raised, Kira Engelhardt, was really her sister's child by Engelhardt.*[131] HG also wrote in 1934 that Moura was Tania's age when she got divorced—which would have made her eighteen or nineteen. All this, one must assume, is information that Moura fed HG; whether it is true is another story. There is another wrinkle. In recently repatriated documents collected by France's Secret Service (Deuxième Bureau), is an intriguing note in Moura's dossier. The note says that while Moura was carrying on a love affair with H. G. Wells, she was also the mistress of her own Benckendorff brother-in-law. Presumably this would be Paul Benckendorff. In her memoir, however, Alexander didn't mention her uncle Paul.

Characteristically, Moura cast herself in a role she never played: an earth-mother yanked by powerful circumstances from the bosom of the family. Explaining to Tynan in that 1970 interview why she had refused to marry HG, Moura disingenuously said, "I'd felt very possessive with my first husband, and probably if he had not been killed and there had been no Revolution, I should now have eight children and be living in the country surrounded by animals and governesses." And yet, in July 1918, when she was planning to divorce her husband and abandon her children so that she could spend the rest of her life with Bruce Lockhart, Moura wrote to Lockhart about her children: "Losing them will be very painful to me. But it is just a matter of how to find a way to do it in the kindest and best way possible." Carrying Lockhart's child, on the other hand, became Moura's greatest desire. "I want [your baby] so much my little one—do you understand me?" she asked on December 16, 1918. After she allegedly became pregnant by Lockhart, she referred to the baby she was carrying by several names, including "little Peter" and "little Willy."

This brings us to yet another offspring. In a dramatic letter dated July 28, 1933, Moura, then forty-one, told HG that the thing they had joked about happening had happened: She was pregnant by him. On her own, and demonstrating that renowned courage, Moura made plans to have an abortion. Apologizing profusely for bothering him, she told HG:

> So better get it over, while it is so small and unimportant little matter that I almost would not have written to you at all about it, except that it will alter your plans a little—that is, of the 4 weeks you will spend in Portmerion I will be with you for only two! This is a great blow to me and I know how you hate changing plans, but don't be angry, for this time it really can't be helped.
>
> I will "disappear" the day after tomorrow and in a fortnight will be ready to do everything all over again! But please do not worry. I know it will be <u>all right</u>. I am a little sad to do what I am doing, but I suppose it is not the right moment and you would be vexed. Don't be vexed and don't be annoyed at the change of plans and don't let all this interfere with all our lovely beautiful in-love friendship. All, all my love, my HG. Your Moura.

Moura was begging off from a month-long vacation in Portmeirion on Tremadog Bay in Wales. Plans for this vacation had been in the works for some time. A few days later, HG wrote to Christabel to say that he would be "all alone" at Portmeirion for two weeks. "My Moura has to stay in Germany for reasons you would find quite sympathetic if you knew them. So I shall go tomorrow to the wonderful place alone for a week or so & then motor across to Harwich & pick her up when she comes again. Fine & funny thing life is—full of freakish turns." Later that night, HG again wrote to Christabel, this time from an inn on the A-5, to tell her that he would be "ALONE & oh so LONELY" on holiday, and wanted to take her to lunch. He said he would bring a "renewed & refreshed" Moura back to Portmeirion. Marriage was at the top of his agenda. "I think we shall make a charming couple & [be] very popular. I can't imagine anyone not liking us."

Shocking as this news is about Moura's pregnancy and decision to end it, and while we will probably never know HG's true feelings about the situation, we do know that he later regretted not having had a child with Moura. He wrote that in 1929 he told Moura he felt they must not have a child and that he would not "exact fidelity from her. All that seems amazingly pedantic and clumsy-minded to me now. I subordinated her not indeed to Odette but to my work and my pose of balanced integrity. I certainly ought to have got that child and we ought to have taken the consequences."[132] However, given Moura's track record for telling the truth, one must wonder whether she really was pregnant. It wouldn't be unlike her to fabricate the pregnancy if she needed a good excuse to break her plans, if she needed two extra weeks for some purpose or another. HG conceded in the *Postscript* that Moura "did cheat, did lie." What's more, she practically announced that it was a covert plan midway through her letter; she said she didn't want to attract any attention, she didn't want anybody else involved, so she wouldn't tell anyone where she was going. Also, HG mustn't write to her, she instructed, and he should expect a little delay. "I've told the 'family' that I'm going, perhaps to Esthonia," she said.

Unfortunately, it isn't known what Moura meant by such words as "anyone" and "anybody else involved," by "there" and by "family." Gorky and his entourage had already repatriated to Russia. Paul and Tania evidently weren't at Kallijärv. Why Moura couldn't give HG her address is intriguing, but we can speculate that she was going incognito somewhere for some reason.[133] There is another matter. Listening to this story, one hears an echo from July 1918, when Moura supposedly fled from Russia while she was carrying Bruce Lockhart's child, which she claimed to have miscarried in September. The story went that she rushed, with great physical difficulty, to hearth and husband to have relations with Djon; thus it would appear that the child she was carrying was his, even though that scenario doesn't make sense. It doesn't make sense that Moura would try to legitimize her being pregnant with Lockhart's child if she was planning to leave her husband anyway. As with the pregnancy of 1918, no one was present to corroborate the pregnancy, or the loss of the child, in 1933. It was Moura's story, and a compelling one. Why Moura concocted either story, if she did, remains to be seen. To date, there is no evidence about the 1933 pregnancy and abortion—nothing else in Moura's correspondence or in Alexander's memoir. HG never mentioned the event, except obliquely, as we have seen, to Christabel. There is another possibility: Moura may have been pregnant by some other man. But more likely, this abortion story was a cover for something else.

For HG, the end of the 1930s and the beginning of the 1940s was an unprecedented period of long transoceanic tours, the record of which can be found in his letters to Moura, among others. He was at his best—and his worst—when writing from the field, from his working trips abroad. As previously mentioned, during the period for which we have letters from HG to Moura, 1938 to 1944, HG took two major trips: a month-long trip to Australia and a ten-week trip to the United States. It is clear from these letters, and from many others, that something happened to HG when he went shipside. Perhaps it was the invigorating sea breeze. Perhaps it was the fixed social environment, which was quite beyond his control. Perhaps it was because he was out of his element, or because he traveled alone. For whatever reason, ship crossings made HG broody, critical, introspective. Christabel knew that mood better than anyone. HG often wrote to his confidante from sea in the mid-1930s. These letters sail the gamut from whimsical to adoring. They were, in his own words, "passionate confidences." Frequently he was flummoxed by something: the crossing, his shipmates, his relationship with Moura.

April 27, 1934, on board the SS Washington: On steamboats I am always moved to write to you—why? But this time I mean to keep the impulse well under control.

March 3, 1935, aboard the Bremen: Up we go up & up & up. And down we go down & down. So that I cannot collect my mind to write the usual Atlantic letter about my affections. I seem to have nothing but a precarious Equilibrium to write about. . . . Although I am moving forward & sideways & up & down & then other sideways, & then same, I still love you & my heart after every violent oscillation, turns again with

a curious obstinacy toward South Street Mayfair. I think of your pose—
of the marvellous steadfastness with which you stand on Earth. O God
is thy Servant a cocktail that he should be thus shaken? Dear Christabel.

Early April, 1935, aboard the *Bremen*: Since last summer gradually
gradually I have come unstuck from dear Moura. Nothing really healed.
I just find there isn't any adhesive quality left. . . . And suddenly except
as matters of intent and curiosity, I don't care a damn. There won't be
any sort of breach. As we've been so loosely knit, it need not be a matter
of remark that we have come unravelled. My dear, perhaps it is just as
well that you & I were never lovers.

November 14, 1935, aboard the *Majestic*: Always in the Atlantic he
writes to his Christabel always. The Majestic is a Holy Roller. The Majestic is quite the bloodiest old ship you ever saw. Christabel dear I am
becoming a bad, discursive old man—no credit to anyone. I give myself
up. Moura ought to have taken care of me and all this wouldn't have
happened. As it is I shall now become the Bad Man of Hanover Terrace—spreading ruin. Christabel I don't like this piece of life that is being left me. I want someone to smack me in the bathroom & be gay at
breakfast. I don't like flirting & having little escapades. I don't like going
about kissing wild & free. Everybody kissed in Hollywood. . . . Moura
gets up too late in the day & doesn't look after me. She neglects me
dreadfully. Christabel darling you have poise & a position but why
haven't you a twin sister who would like to nurse a lonely (lonely not
lovely) scrap of cheerfulness through his last ten or twelve years of life.
Bless you dear Christabel. Yours ever, HG.

To be sure, the ocean crossings stimulated HG but at the same time
bored him silly, his mood generally determined by his fellow passengers. "Nobody very interesting to talk to" was a common refrain. Indeed, dullness and boredom were a recurrent theme and problem.
Then again, sometimes the dull routines of the ocean liner were just
what he needed. As his ship steamed toward the United States, HG
wrote to Christabel: "It is very restful to be out of reach of Sibyl &
amusing to talk to all sorts of people where names vanish as they tell

you them."[134] When he wasn't anxious or bored, HG was energized by the novelties, human and otherwise, that he met en route and on tour. On December 22, 1938, aboard the *P & O Comorin,* he wrote to Moura about the dinner parties he had attended in Bombay and Colombo on his way to his Australian tour:

> Marvellous to meet women in Saris & pearls in their noses who talk excellent English & know books and ideas & compare it with the accents & illiteracy of the real British. I have been in a perspiration but otherwise well for the last eight or ten days. We stroll about in vests & Palm Beach pyjamas & no sox. I have seen the Southern Cross (bah!) Dear Moura, darling Moura. Don't forget you belong to me. Aigee.

Two weeks later, and writing from somewhere in Victoria, HG told Moura that he was accompanied by two very pleasant men who seemed to have been brought up entirely on his books. Australia, he observed, was "a very interesting sample of purely English people under novel circumstances (of which gum-trees, sheep, drought & vast spaces are the chief)." Nine days later and from Government House at Canberra, just hours before he was to deliver a major speech, HG reported that he was fit and sunburned, that the temperature was scorching— 114 in Melbourne, 108 in Canberra—and that the dress code at Government House was "marvellous Victoriana. White waistcoats for dinner & orders & medals." At one garden party, he saw an Ascot topper, two "real" toppers, a frock coat, and Sydney-Paris costumes. "Victorian England is not dead; it sleepeth." HG went on to see the bushfires raging across the countryside and the efforts to extinguish them. His is a vivid and chilling description of the conflagration:

> Victoria and N. S. Wales had temperatures up to 109 & the bush fires burnt over 100 people. We saw a house with its hay blazing & all its fence posts like candles. All the horses & cattle standing in the paddock & the sheep stampeded God knows where. Every advance of the fire had to be held back by beating with wet sacks. People quite cheerful.

Writing to Moura from the mid-Atlantic during his 1940 crossing, HG described a few of his new shipmates: "A religious lady in the tourist class is having a sort of religious service aft, dropping a bottle of greetings & religious consolations to the people who went down in the *City of Benares,*" while a Miss Mudie sat below him in the library "writing importantly. She is a sort of Dorothy Thompson with a motherly dullness all her own." An acquaintance named Halperin was good company, but he tended to introduce all the ship's boors to HG. "There is really no one of interest on board. There is a woman resolutely adherent to Halperin who speaks 'refined' English and says original things such as 'I think our airmen are perfectly splendid. Don't you Mr. Wells? Such heroes!'"[135]

That 1940 crossing to America started badly. The ship from the Cunard-White Star line was detained in Liverpool, ordered to stay in harbor until an armed ship could escort it. At midnight on September 22, 1940, a fuming HG wrote to Moura:

> Here I am cut off from the world & stuck. Nobody can come aboard, nobody can leave. Having got us concentrated on the ship we must now wait until some other blasted ship or ships can load up & proceed under convoy. Perhaps two or three days here! It is fantastic: the idiotic policy of stopping everything while a raid is on means that the ship lies inert. Even my bags have not reached me, so that I can get no papers and do no work. No slippers, no pajamas, even my copy of *Guilty Men* locked out of reach.[136]

Three or four days from New York, the ship went through a gale, and HG slept on a sofa in the saloon so that he wouldn't have to hear people being sick in the cabins around him.

HG often wrote about the VIPs he met on tour—in this case, everyone from the prime minister of Australia, with whom he was involved in a controversy, to Alexander Kerensky, the former Russian prime minister. The latter "wasn't worth meeting, but his wife is a 'ducky Aussie'—and very good fun," HG wrote to Moura on October 12,

1940. At the Tutwiler Hotel in Birmingham, Alabama, a week later, HG said that he had undergone "much photography" with Charlie Chaplin and Paulette Goddard during the opening of Chaplin's "very fine" new picture. HG felt that he had met just about everyone in New York, including Madame de Balsan—Consuelo Vanderbilt.[137] He had mentioned the Jacques de Balsans in a previous letter to Moura. He met the couple, whom he described as "Riviera Refugees," at the Colony Club in New York. They were under the sway, he said, of Elsa Maxwell. HG's fascination with the aristocracy was alive and well.

During his lifetime, HG was occasionally criticized for being anti-Semitic. Several attacks against him were aired in the press in the 1930s, and he responded promptly to each of them with letters to the editors. The letters were usually published, and HG usually received a published apology. As David Smith and others have said, while there was a considerable amount of heat over the question, HG maintained that he was an anti-Zionist, not an anti-Semite. Two of his letters to Moura, however, add tinder to the fire of anti-Semitism: "There are two others in Cabin 61B with me & (thank God) not Jews," HG wrote on September 22, the day after his birthday, in 1940. Four days later, he reported that there had been an improvement: The "little Italian snorer" had been kicked out of his cabin. Now they were three Englishmen, who neither snored nor showed any "disposition to panic when a depth charge is dropped (we wasted one on a porpoise yesterday) or a gun fired." And then he observed: "I think the way Germans treat Jews is scandalous but after five days on a mainly Yiddish boat, I realize there is a slight but perceptible strain of Teuton in my composition."[138]

In a passage from the *Anatomy of Frustration,* which was reprinted in the *Jewish Chronicle* on July 10, 1936, HG tried to explain his thinking on Jews and Zionism. It turned into something of a dissertation: "A man may have the fullest apprehension of the great history and exceptional quality of the Jews, he may have the utmost liking and admiration for individual Jews and for Jewish types and traits, he may want to get together with Jews in every possible way, and still regard Zionism and cultural particularism as a blunder and misfortune for them and for mankind."[139] One wonders whether this helped or hurt his case. He also stated, through his mouthpiece Steele, that Jews were not inherently different from Gentiles.

By September 29, HG was feeling better about his trip to the United States. Most of the danger was behind him, he wrote, but again, there was no one very interesting to chat with, and the ship made him "too lazy & thick-headed for descriptive writing. Dear Moura, writing to you like this is like talking to someone who is fast asleep. I just can't keep it up. Bless you my dear." From the United States, HG reported that everything was going well, and then noted that Emerald Cunard was the best-read society hostess he had ever met, and also that he would be a featured speaker at the premiere of Charlie Chaplin's film, and probably would make a few observations about the United States. "The whole country is in a state of self-preoccupation over the Presidential Election. The political fighting strikes me as pretty foul but it's customary & means much less than it says. F.D.R. will sail back for a third term. Wilkie means everything & nothing—a man without a single distinctive feature so that even the sensationalists can't individualize him."[140]

In the early 1940s, Moura also became mixed up with politics when she joined the staff of *La France Libre,* an anti-DeGaulle monthly magazine begun in London by the journalist André Labarthe. In essence, her role was to raise funds and pump her many literary friends and contacts, including HG and Maugham, for articles, which was much the same thing she had done at Gorky's enterprise. To escape the London blitz, members of the editorial staff of *La France* often joined Tania at her home near Oxford. Moura would bring HG for the weekend, or sometimes he would stay for a week without her. Meanwhile, Moura continued to hold court in her sitting room in London. During her forty-four-year tenure as hostess and intellectual begum, she used her friends and acquaintances to locate and secure jobs, mostly as a translator.[141] She used them in other ways, as we shall soon see.

But did the relationship between H. G. Wells and Moura Budberg play out in their correspondence? The answer is yes, certainly. One of

Moura's earliest letters demonstrates this. In 1929, following their re-union, Moura wrote from Berlin, setting the record straight and along the way establishing her (strangle)hold on HG's heart. She said on September 29 that she wanted to feel in a "womanly, unintellectual" way that she belonged to HG, even if they met only occasionally.

> You mean such a great deal to me, have meant ever since I met you in Russia; you must know it—don't you? I wrote you a silly letter from Paris, that you should not feel my heartache. But even if it is there—the memory of very wonderful moments and the thought that you care—is worth all the heartaches in the world. This is a little philosophy I have learnt—and it is a good little philosophy. Yes, I am strong, I suppose, strong enough not to make a fool of myself. But do not be too strong, HG, my dear, be a little "weak" as far as I am concerned—if that means thinking of me more than you ought to. Write to me soon and tell me how you are and take care of yourself. Yours, Moura.

In reading this, one can appreciate why Tania Alexander believed that at the root of Moura's behavior was her need "not to loosen her grip on anything or anybody, once she had got hold of them," and her willingness to use unscrupulous methods and feminine wiles to maintain her hold on her lovers.[142]

To be sure, few of the extant letters between HG and Moura dealt with so-called state of the relationship issues. The letters that might have done so have not yet surfaced, and may never. Most, rather, contained the little comments and questions about each other's health and well-being that imply a level of caring and concern. As early as 1921, Moura was asking HG about his health. Are you all right now? Is your cold better, you sound depressed, I hope you're well and getting a lot of sun, and so on. Much later, Moura was distressed to learn that HG had been separated from his belongings temporarily when his ship was kept in the harbor in September 1940, "and my thoughts are now following you tenderly and trying to protect you from cold and heat and all other discomforts. Be good, dearest."

HG did the same sort of thing. For example, he had heard that London was in the grips of a Russian winter and he hoped the grip hadn't affected Moura. "You'd be lovely & dear even with a snow bitten nose but I'd rather you didn't," he wrote on December 22, 1938. Two years later, he wrote tenderly from aboard ship, "Bless you dear Moura. Bless and keep you. Be a good good good Moura. Take great care of yourself and pray for your Aigee." We recall HG's teasing comments about Moura's alleged self-improvement program: leading a pure life, exercising, and reading all his books. HG also reported dutifully about his own condition. "I've had no end of fun & my health gets better & better," he wrote on December 5, 1940. And so it goes throughout the early 1940s: "Everyday I grow better & better & better & more pugnacious, as becomes a convalescent in these irritating times," he wrote on July 21, 1940.

During World War II, HG and Moura, like everyone else, were constrained by censors. After writing a string of dull mechanical comments, Moura apologized for her emasculated letter, but asked, since politics and obscenities were censurable, what else could she do? "Darling, I love you very much and miss you more than I can say, like a child striking off the days on the calendar until mid-December!" The irregularity of the mail and the difficulty of not knowing what one was allowed to write "paralyzes one," she wrote a month later, when HG was in Birmingham, Alabama.[143]

On July 18, 1944, HG wrote to Moura, then staying with Tania in the country, a simple love letter "to say nothing in particular. . . . It was jolly to see you battered but invincible & able to laugh. Now rest my dearest, rest for my sake, sleep & very soon we will be together again." Later that day, he wrote a second letter, saying that he was longing to talk to her on the telephone. "I hope you are sleeping & sleeping." HG's last letter to Moura expressed that warm and affectionate love. He promised on July 22 that when she returned to London they would take little walks together, "but just now there is no one to go with me, & everybody kicks up a fuss if I go out alone. I love you my dear & I am as ever your Aigee."

To be sure, the letters between HG and Moura were not the torrid love letters of young lovers. Moura's early letters, as we have seen, were flirty and coquettish, but mainly business-related. Her later letters, like HG's, were newsy, affectionate, and domestic. In one sense, these letters were the tip of the iceberg of their relationship. Below the surface was another world, quite dark, with another set of possibilities and realities. Below the surface was the subject HG and Moura *didn't* discuss.

★　　★　　★

There was arguably no subject more important and less discussed between HG and Moura than the question of her involvement with espionage, a question central to understanding her values, character, and allegiances, and, too, her relationship with HG and his with her. Was she involved, as legend had it, in espionage during much of her adult life? If so, for whom did she work? What was her role and what did she accomplish? Did she, as some have charged, spy on all three of her main lovers, Lockhart, Gorky, and Wells? Was the spying business just another good yarn, or was it a double bluff? Historian Richard Spence concedes the difficulty of ferreting out the facts in lives such as Moura's. "This area of research is like peeling an onion—from the inside. As each layer is revealed, the scope grows ever larger, not smaller. Every answer raises at least another question. Anything is possible and nothing is what it seems at first glance."[144]

While rumors circulated for years, it was HG's own son, Anthony West, who publicly outed Moura as a spy, although several others, including Richard Deacon, had hinted at it in their books and reviews. In *H. G. Wells: Aspects of a Life*, West blueprinted Moura's dark past. He claimed that Moura lost control of her life in 1916 when the Germans caught her spying on them on behalf of the Russian military. Sentenced to death, but obviously spared, she was from that point under the thumb of the Soviets.[145] Two years later, Moura was imprisoned for being an accomplice in the plot to overthrow the Bolsheviks, but she was quickly released on condition that she serve the Russian Secret Service as an informer. Shortly after, she was planted on Gorky, found her situation intolerable, and confessed to him. He was so impressed by her courage, as the story goes, that he instantly became her protector and "used his considerable influence with Lenin to get the heat taken off her."[146]

With regard to the 1930s, West argued that Moura had been entering Russia as often as every three months "and circulating with impunity."[147] This meant that what she had told HG about Russia's being a barred country to her, about there being apparatchiks in the NKVD who still regarded her as "unfinished business," was untrue.[148] West reasoned that there was "only one circumstance" in which anyone with her record could move between the two worlds and within Russia as openly as she did: "Her movements had to be made with the knowledge and consent of the secret police. She had to be a Russian agent in good standing."[149] West believed that Moura was planted on HG in the 1930s just as she had been planted on him in 1920 and on Gorky in 1919. Moreover, HG came to realize that she was a Soviet agent and that she had used the same tricks on him that she had used on others. According to West, HG even confronted Moura in 1934 about her deception and her past, and she admitted to everything. Yet even more astounding than all this was HG's response to the hideous truth: *He simply couldn't let Moura go.* "Spy or no, Moura was Moura, and in spite of all that he had learned about her double dealing, her physical and emotional holds upon him were strong as ever."[150] Since West didn't document his claims—most were unattributed and unsubstantiated—one can only wonder how much of his story derived from HG, Gip, or Moura, and how much came from other sources, hearsay, conjecture, and thin air.[151]

In her book three years later, Tania Alexander attacked West's case against Moura piece by piece. It was pen-fencing: Moura's daughter versus HG's son. Strangely, Alexander's case was also argued without sources and evidence, and her logic was pretty lame at times. For example, Moura couldn't have spied for the Russians near the German front in 1916 because she had two small children and lived with her mother in Petrograd. When she disappeared in July 1918, it wasn't to report to her espionage masters but rather to get to her husband in Estonia *"to give her unborn child a chance of legitimacy."*[152] Moura was assigned as HG's guide and interpreter not for intelligence purposes but simply because she was the only one around who was fluent in English. "She could not have been guilty of many of the things of which she was accused," Alexander wrote; Moura simply preferred "to let people think what they would."[153] Alexander's premise was that most of the rumors about Moura's espionage activities had originated with Moura and her "compulsive need to reinvent the past, and exist in a world of half-truth and surmise."[154] In the last analysis, the key to Moura's behavior, including deceptions and rumors and her lying to HG about Russia and Gorky, and even inventing the business about her involvement with the Russian Secret Services, was in Moura's past: She had lost everything and was in a perpetual struggle to rebuild her life. Why Moura rebuilt her life on lies and legends, Tania didn't answer.

Foot, meanwhile, dismissed all the allegations, including the "monstrous" charge that Moura had been a Soviet spy all her life, planted on Lockhart, Gorky, and Wells. "No-one who knew [Bruce Lockhart] . . . would accept that, either," he wrote.[155] The MacKenzies didn't open the can of worms. After reading this manuscript, Smith now concedes that Moura was "well known to members of the shadowy British intelligence underground of the inter-war period," and that *au fond,* she "certainly acted like a courier."[156] Berberova basically catalogued other people's beliefs about Moura, although she intimated throughout the book that she too thought Moura was a spy, perhaps even a double or triple spy.

So, where does one begin reconstructing the case and deconstructing the legend encircling Moura and entangling HG? Certainly West's argument that Moura traveled a great deal to places where travel was difficult, if not impossible for most mortals, is persuasive—a firm base on which to begin. Indeed, her frequent trips to and from the Soviet Union during the most repressive phases of the Stalinist era, in combination with her presumed influence over Lockhart, Gorky, and Wells, were the primary reasons Moura was accused of being a Soviet agent, as people have said. She also maintained many strong ties with Western intelligence, was a friend of the Soviet spy Guy Burgess, and worked for at least one Cheka enterprise, as we shall see.

Moura also had strong roots in Imperial Russia and strong Anglophile ties. Many family members, as we have seen, were involved in law and order, diplomacy and intelligence. Moura's father was a judge and prosecutor who had Czarist connections. Her brother was in diplomatic service, first at the Russian embassy in Tokyo in 1908 and then at the Berlin embassy in 1909.[157] Moura's brother-in-law, Nikolai Ionoff, also served at the Russian embassy in Berlin, as did her husband, of course. Djon came from a long line of Benckendorffs who were so aligned.[158] Cousin Constantine Benckendorff served in the Imperial Navy, was a cipher clerk at his father's embassy in London, and a naval attaché in intelligence in Moscow from 1919 to 1922. Even Moura's governess, Micky Wilson, was linked to espionage through her "stepdaughter" Maud Gonne, an Irish nationalist and William Butler Yeats's muse and lover.[159] It is quite possible that Micky had her own direct link to intelligence from her "station" at the Benckendorff estate. For this family, most brains led to intelligence, most roads to Berlin and Moscow.

To be sure, HG had his own interlude with propaganda. At about the same time that Moura was pursuing Lockhart in Petrograd, HG was being courted by Lord Northcliffe. A newspaper magnate working from the government propaganda unit at Crewe House, Northcliffe needed HG's help with his Enemy Propaganda Committee.[160] The idea for the enterprise, Northcliffe said in a February 25, 1918, letter to HG, had originated with "fighters who have begun to realize that brains are a factor in war, as well as bombs. I have no doubt that we shall be able to shorten the war if we are sufficiently ingenious and vigorous." HG worked feverishly over the spring and early summer of 1918 toward that goal.[161] In July, however, he resigned his position as "organiser and conductor" of German propaganda. Among other things, he groused in a letter written on July 17 about the "imperfect" quality of information available at Crewe House and the difficulty of the task "due very largely to the absence of any clear conception of what our work was and of any preliminary definition of the country's war aims and purposes." What really got HG's goat was the idea that Northcliffe's newspapers were conducting a campaign of "indiscriminate and irrational denunciation of all things German" that was "entirely mischievous and injurious to the interests of the Allies." Then again, HG, with his strong rebel streak, had a reputation for losing interest in committee work. Margaret Cole recalled seeing HG at the meetings of various societies intent on "planning the world properly. You always knew," she said, that by the third or fourth meeting, HG would have had enough of it and have decided that everyone had "mean little souls" and weren't worth "bothering with."

As we have seen, most of Moura's closest friends were attached to the British embassy in one way or another as propaganda and intelligence officers, including Captains Cromie, Garstin, and Hicks. Several members of the staff of the British Propaganda Office in Petrograd under Hugh Walpole and Colonel C. M. Thornhill were also her close associates. As it happened, many of her best friends began irritating her during the long year of 1918.[162] For example, Moura once reproached Lockhart for thinking that she confided in Cromie. "I only believe half he says and am more careful with him than you think. Still, he is a kind of a grammophone for all this infernal gossip in the Embassy. That's why I cultivate him."[163] She also had problems with the aforementioned Thornhill, military attaché in Petrograd and later chief of British military intelligence in Russia. In May 1918, Moura told Lockhart that she might have to go away—she gave neither the destination nor the reason—but she promised to tell him some "interesting things" about Thornhill. Later that month, she wrote that Thornhill was in Murmansk. "I am so suspicious of him in every way. If he comes here and suspects something between you and me and even without that, he will be sure to try and blame me in your eyes. Will you believe him?"[164] Later, Moura told Lockhart that she was deeply disturbed that he had to face so much "unpleasantness" because of her. She would give anything, she said, "to wipe out all the useless frivolities . . . which have made me such bitter enemies as Thornhill and led people to beleive me to be something which I am not."[165]

Rumors and suspicion became common topics in Moura's correspondence with Lockhart. Indeed, in her previously unpublished letters to him—she wrote frequently during their six-month affair and nearly every day for months following his expulsion from Moscow Moura often mentioned the rumor going around that she was a spy.[166] In early July, 1918, for example, soon after the assassination of Count Wilhelm von Mirbach-Harff, the German ambassador to Moscow, Moura wrote that there were "new facts" against her, and that she had been seen with a member of the German embassy. "I wonder who of you [Brits] has been taken for a German. It is really funny," she tried to joke. After Lockhart had left Russia, Moura wrote that she was afraid that people were warning him about her, and also conceded that the Germans, who then occupied Estonia, were making things unpleasant for her husband because of her. Moura later reported that her friend Miriam Artsimovich was once again "full of [news of] scandal" about Moura.

In response to her first letter from the exiled Lockhart at the end of October 1918, Moura fired off a long passionate letter: "Baby, my Baby, news at last. I read, reread, kissed again and again the dear letter that your hands had touched, my beloved one, my little one." In the same letter, she reported that the Swiss guide who had helped her cross the border at Narva was now under house arrest because of her, "and altogether that yarn about my being a ~~German~~ English spy has been tremendously moussé [lathered up] over there. [The guide] says he saw an enormous dossier concerning me in Reval. Isn't it too ridiculous. I only hope it won't cause any new complications." Two months later, Moura assured Lockhart that the rampant gossiping wasn't getting to her. "As long as I know that you love me, I can bear anything."[167] On January 24, 1919, she admitted that she had had enough of the Bolsheviks. "I'd go like a shot to Stockholm for a week and come back again if it wasn't that gossip clings to me like flies to tanglefoot paper—and people would surely call me a spy on either side." A few weeks later, she wrote that she had heard amusing things about herself and "the old spying story."

In the winter of 1918, as previously mentioned, Moura began hatching that curious and elaborate scheme to meet Lockhart in Stockholm the following spring. As it happened, she arrived in Reval and Helsingfors all right, but couldn't get out of Finland. Stuck for nearly a week in a dirty, bug-infested hotel, she had suffered a physical and emotional breakdown, she wrote to Lockhart on Easter Sunday. Her misery was made worse by her being suspected and watched and prevented from acting like a free human being, she said. Things got worse. In May, Moura wrote from her apartment in Petrograd that her husband had been killed on April 19 at their estate in Estonia. "I must try and get the children away from that place as soon as possible, but I am afraid that the tragically absurd opinion that I am some kind of a spy is going to make things difficult for me in Finland." The mystery here, of course, is whether she ever intended to meet Lockhart. If not, why did she bait him for so many months about their meeting in Stockholm? Was the plan really foiled because she couldn't obtain a visa? Was it all arranged to establish an alibi, a cover for some other activity? Was it pure coincidence that Moura was out of Russia, indeed, according to her own account, in Estonia, at the same time her husband was murdered there?

Long after these events, Moura continued to obfuscate and to behave defensivly. In the early 1930s, for example, Lockhart submitted his manuscripts to Moura, now romantically involved with HG, for her editing suggestions, content approval, and blessing. Her response to *British Agent* was unequivocal: She would not tolerate certain passages. "Dear Baby, Yes, I think the book is very good. I would change nothing in it. Except—and I am very sorry to have to say so—pages 69 and 104. The bit about the spying business gives it . . . a Mata-Hari touch which is quite unnecessary for the book . . . and quite impossible for me."

Her protests to the contrary, Moura's letters to Lockhart demonstrate that she was some sort of player. Certainly the letters show that she had her ears to the ground and her eyes and nose everywhere. But although much of what Moura said in her letters to Lockhart was suspicious, most of it was too vague to be conclusive. Still, she frequently instructed him to send urgent letters, photographs, films, and packets of news to various people, and she wrote about the "stupid blunders" at the embassy.[168] She said her friend Miriam needed the key for the dispatch box, that "the news" had arrived and that there were many things she'd love to tell him—but couldn't.

Some of Moura's information concerned local opinion about Lockhart. In July 1918, she traveled with an unnamed admiral to Vologda, where she picked up the news that, among other things, the French General Noulens and the people of Vologda were "rather set against" Lockhart. "Your chief mistake they say is that strong desire to be independent of them—this is from Cromie with whom I lunched and very confidential. The chief character of the things those swine spread about you is that you have lost your prestige at the F.O." Moura also relayed information from Cromie that Lockhart had enemies in Moscow, and that if she didn't want harm to come to him, she should stay away from that city.

Moura also acquired a good deal of logistical and tactical information. For example, in May 1918, she suggested that, considering the circumstances, Lockhart should flee to Vologda. In addition, when two of her friends, A. E. Lessing and Bobby Yonin, were en route to Archangel to meet a Major General Poole, who commanded the small Allied force in North Russia, Moura wrote that if Poole continued

to be in with the Jews and make himself unpleasant, there is nothing easier than to expose him. As to Thornhill, no one even out here seems to know what his mission is, unless he has come with troops. However you have Cromie and Lepage entirely on your side and I don't mind saying that Cromie is a little due to me (I hear you saying the conceited girl!)

Following Mirbach's assassination, Moura wrote that she was terribly worried about Lockhart's safety. "Don't you think it is time for you to leave. . . . There is no doubt that the murder will have great consequences and there is nothing more to be done, is there?" A few days later, Trotsky put out an order that British and French diplomatic officers would not be allowed to travel because of their counterrevolutionary tendencies; a month later, Lockhart and his staff were arrested. In that same letter, Moura wrote that the Bolsheviks would kill the emperor and his son if the Czecks lost Ekaterinberg; a few days later, Czar Nicholas II and his family, who were being held in Ekaterinburg, were murdered there. In November, Moura tantalized Lockhart with the news that someone named "Crooked Neck," whose name he would have to translate into Russian, was making big preparations in her "native place, but entirely on old principles. That is the only bit of certain information."[169] A few days later, Moura said that the Right Socialist Revolutionaries were preparing something for the next day, although Boris Savinkov was in Siberia.[170] While her motives may not be known, it is clear that Moura was deliberately gathering intelligence from around the embassy—and sharing some of it with her lover, among others, no doubt.

Given all these facts, the salient question becomes: Where did Moura stand? Did she have an official or unofficial relationship with the foreign office, the British embassy, and/or British intelligence? What was her relationship with the Soviets and the Germans? Why did she work so hard to set Thornhill and Cromie up as threats? Aside from Berberova, who didn't publish in English, and Robin Lockhart, previous scholars have ignored or overlooked Moura. On the rare occasions when she is mentioned, it is only in the context of her steamy affair with Lockhart, which perhaps is just as she wanted it. Nevertheless, two current historians—Gail Owen, an independent scholar, and Richard Spence, previously mentioned—have noticed Moura Budberg.[171] Their acquaintance with her comes by way of their research on yet another Russian rascal, Sidney Reilly.

Owen has looked at the puzzling and still largely unexplained aspects of Moura's relationships with the Soviets—her rapid release from Cheka custody in September 1918; her seemingly unrestricted access to Stalin's ultra-restrictive USSR before 1937; her trips with Gorky to Soviet labor camps in 1929 and 1933; her ties with people aiding Western intelligence; her pro-Soviet party line; and her alleged friendship after World War II with the Soviet spy Guy Burgess. [172] Owen has also explored Moura's considerable Anglophile background.[173] In addition, he has traced Moura's connection with a diabolical Soviet cash-raising program, *valiuta,* and her ties with the powerful Genrikh Yagoda, head of the Soviet secret police, and with a Lieutenant Reilly and his activities in Russia in 1917 and 1918.[174]

Born Salomon Gershovich Rosenblum—neither his date of birth nor his parentage is certain—"Sidney Reilly" would come to be known around the globe as "The Ace of Spies."[175] A double agent aligned first with Britain, later with the Soviets and probably others, he was a kingpin of sorts in the game of espionage for at least a quarter of a century and the model for Ian Fleming's fictional super spy, James Bond. Reilly carried out complex and daring assignments around the globe through at least 1925, and was, among other things, a skilled recruiter of double agents who at times seemed to run his own operations. As an agent for Great Britain, he suddenly appeared at Lockhart's mission in Moscow in May 1918.[176] Lockhart would later concede that he was overwhelmed by this brilliant, larger-than-life figure whose presence and activities were never explained to him. "The sheer audacity of the man took my breath away," Lockhart later wrote.[177] By the late summer of that year, Reilly would be heavily involved in orchestrating several anti-Bolshevik plots. Indeed, many scholars of this period of Russian history now believe that the so-called Lockhart Plot to kill Lenin and overthrow the Bolsheviks was in fact the Reilly Plot.

Owen argues that the only way to understand Moura's puzzling associations and mystifying actions is to see her as Reilly's colleague: a double agent, working first for the British Secret Service and later for the Soviets, just as Reilly had. One possible scenario is that she was originally brought into employment in early 1918 by her British intelligence friends to prevent Lockhart, a known womanizer, "from interfering with their budding anti-Soviet plans. Somewhat by way of an apprenticeship in their service, she may have been induced to act as a decoy or distraction in relation to the new arrival."[178] Lockhart, as we have seen, was sent to Russia by the British foreign office to establish a line of communication with the Bolsheviks and search for an accommodation with them. However, by the time the foreign office announced Lockhart's mission in February 1918, many members of the U.S.-Allied underground in Russia were already preparing to ouster the Bolsheviks. If Moura was used to "neutralize or at least befuddle" Lockhart in early 1918, the ploy seemed to work, because within ten weeks of meeting her, he "was plotting to topple the Bolsheviks too, having in the meantime accomplished nothing."[179] Very early into her mission, as no one could have foreseen, the befuddler seemed to have fallen in love with the befuddled—and she probably never fell out.

But it was even more complicated than that. Moura appears to have had several hoops spinning with British intelligence: one, with the MID (Hill, Garstin, and Hicks), one with the MI 1c (Reilly, Thornhill, Boyce, and Somerset Maugham), and a third with Reilly.[180] Thus, she may have had several different missions beyond the one to distract Lockhart, including assistance with the plot against Lenin's regime. To confuse matters even more, throughout this period, Reilly acted as a British agent, officially and unofficially; but he probably also served, often simultaneously, as an agent for Germany, Russia, and Japan. "He was, to say the least, a man of dubious loyalties," Spence observed. It is conceivable that Moura was doing the same. Reilly's pro-Soviet actions were probably an effective cover for clandestine work on behalf of the British, however, and the same was probably true for Moura. Thus, Reilly functioned as a Western mole inside the USSR even while he assisted the Soviets in establishing their own penetration of British intelligence.[181] Possibly Moura had yet another role: to help deflect Cheka provocateurs away from Reilly's operation. In July 1918, the month Mirbach and Nicholas II were murdered (July 6 and 16, respectively), Moura supposedly took, as we have seen, a mysterious, sudden, and daring trip to Estonia, laying over in Petrograd both coming and going. Owen theorizes that Moura did this not to legitimize a baby, as Moura and Alexander argued, but to throw off Soviet agents, who were homing in on Reilly and his plot. Petrograd was "right where and when the Soviet agents seeking Reilly were set on their false path to Lockhart, a convenient scapegoat if ever there was one."[182] When Russia succumbed to Bolshevism, Moura threw her loyalties to Britain, probably at Reilly's behest. It should be noted that in 1918, Reilly's key mission was not to overthrow the Bolsheviks wholesale but to keep the regime in line with certain British policies and to prevent the Germans, Americans, and French from gaining too much advantage.[183] Reilly essentially managed to eliminate the American and French networks but to leave the British network intact. Not only were the intelligence operations of various countries "cross-pollinated" at this time but also the various entities within a government had conflicting aims and methods and worked with each other's enemies according to Spence.

After Reilly and Lockhart got out of Russia in 1918, Moura picked up with Gorky; but, as Owen has discovered, she also spent a good deal of time working for the Soviet secret police's *valiuta* program between 1920 and 1923.[184] The Cheka enterprise cashed in movable confiscated wealth, mostly gold and jewelry, not to help feed starving Russians, alas, but to help fund Lenin's government, especially its cash-starved operations abroad.[185] Owen speculates that Moura got involved in these "low endeavors" through Marie Andreeva, Gorky's former lover and the actress HG tried to help in 1921. Moura's long association with Genrikh Yagoda, the OGPU deputy chief and later NKVD chief who was overlord of the first *valiuta,* the GULAG, and Gorky, suggests to Owen that Moura worked for the Soviet secret police and its *valiuta* program.[186]

In 1929, when Gorky decided to come out of exile and return to Moscow—the second of several visits back—Moura opted for England, H. G. Wells, and Bruce Lockhart, and it was largely through these men that she met most of the Western movers and shakers of the era. It is conceivable that Moura continued to work for British intelligence, yet most of her efforts appear to have benefited the Soviets. If she switched her allegiance back to the Soviets, it is not known when. Historian Spence observes that Moura's association with Gorky was important for the Soviets "because Gorky, a famous revolutionary writer, had been critical of the Soviet Regime, and then was brought back into the fold. Moura may have had some influence on that. H. G. Wells, similarly, was a prominent British writer, basically leftist, whose views on Soviet affairs were influenced by her." According to Owen, all the major players in Moura's life—Lockhart, Gorky, Wells, and even film tycoon Alexander Korda—were potentially of interest to Soviet intelligence as political agents, propagandists, or intelligence operatives. Before reading the manuscript for this book, Owen described Moura as an "agent of influence," a person who, while never officially on anybody's payroll, "could have been paid by favors—travel in Russia with ample disposition of visas and things like that, but she probably never actually took pay from the KGB." After reading this chapter, Owen concluded that "Moura was very likely an espionage operative."[187] Spence described Moura as "an agent of influence, a consistent advocate—a kind of roving ambassador—for the regime, and also an apologist. Right up to the latter years of her life she defended Soviet policies, which was part of her job. Here was a woman who was influential, who was invited to the right parties and rubbed elbows with important people. She was observant, collected information and passed on anything that might be of value."

Robin Lockhart, Bruce's son, also acknowledged that Moura "was exceedingly well-placed to keep Moscow informed of the 'temperature' in Britain."[188] Various pieces of secondhand evidence, which include a newsreel showing Moura standing next to Stalin at Gorky's funeral and testimonials by Russian and British intelligence officers that Moura had been a Soviet agent, led Robin Lockhart to conclude in print that Moura may have been the Soviet Union's most effective agent-of-influence to operate from London. In correspondence with this author a decade later, however, he argued that Moura was never an employed agent of any government, but rather "liked to feel important and mixed with high-ups in the U.K. and in Soviet Russia." She kept Bruce Lockhart informed of HG's "every move and mood."[189] One of the most dramatic examples of Moura's briefings came on March 18, 1932, from Estonia.

She began in her typical way by chastising Lockhart for not writing her. "Baby dear, don't you think that I am worth a few lines in your precious handwriting, or is it all for the Evening Standard?" After telling him that she had nothing to report—no stories, nothing to say—she closed her letter with a bombshell: "R. is not dead, as our friend said. All my love. Moura." R, presumably, was Reilly. That he was not dead, that she had the information, that she passed it along to Lockhart, is yet more compelling evidence that, in the boondocks in Estonia in 1932, Moura was very much in the center of intelligence. The identity of "our friend" is unclear.[190] Many authorities believe that Reilly was liquidated in 1925, though the details vary widely. Some believe that he was lured to Russia in 1925 on the pretext that he would meet the leaders of the "Trust," and then, just inside the border, he was murdered.[191]

In 2001, more than eighty years removed from these events, most of the intelligence on these players and their roles has either been destroyed or is still sealed in the archives of the relevant agencies of England, the United States, and Russia. From time to time, bits of information are released or slip through the cracks of the bureaucracies and archives, but scant few files of substance have emerged from Russia's KGB, the U.K.'s MI 5 and MI 6, and the U.S. Central Intelligence Agency.[192] The Russian Intelligence Service's press bureau has promoted two interesting and curious articles in 1997 from *Trud* (Labor), both of them purportedly based on recently released documents on Moura Budberg.[193]

Leonid Kolosov, the Russian author of the *Trud* articles, previously wrote for *Izvestia* in Italy in the 1960s. Like his headline—"From the Archive of a Spy: Moura, She Satisfied the Requirements of Members of the Secret Service and the Sexual Needs of Famous Writers"— Kolosov's articles were highly dramatic pieces. The first story ran with a police lineup photo of Moura; the second with photos of Moura, HG, Gorky, and Jacob Peters. The rambling articles make strong, often shocking allegations about Moura. The least extreme was that Moura worked for the Cheka. At the middle range were claims of her romantic liaisons with various German Baltic nobles and her covert ties with the Bolsheviks. Far and away the most extreme of all of the allegations was that Moura, in league with Yagoda, not only turned over Gorky's archive to Stalin but also helped kill Gorky.

Kolosov's source on the Gorky murder story was Michael (Misha) Alesandrovich Tseitlin, the editor of the foreign department of *Izvestia*. Tseitlin reported that Yagoda and Moura visited Gorky just minutes before his death in June 1936, at the magnificent Moscow house Stalin gave him in 1931 as a lure to return to Russia. As this story goes, Moura and Gorky talked for about forty minutes, and then Moura left with Yagoda and his guards. After twenty minutes, pandemonium broke out when a physician on duty announced that Gorky was dead. In Tseitlin's opinion, Gorky had been "calmed" by Moura, although the only "proof" was a missing glass of water that had been next to his bed. At the trial in 1938, Yagoda and two of Gorky's doctors confessed to having killed Gorky, and were executed, although it still is not known whether they were, in fact, responsible. More recently, Kolosov is one of several authors—all ex-KGB or current officers of foreign intelligence services—who were published in the book *Undercover Lies: Soviet Spies in the Cities of the World* (1998). Kolosov covered Madrid, Paris, and Rome, which corroborates, anyway, his mention in *Trud* of an assignment in Italy.

Intrigue and mystery have always surrounded Gorky's death, although outside the *Trud* articles, Moura has never been implicated. Why the Russian Intelligence Service promotes the idea is unclear, although the stories have become part of the fabric that is Moura's legend. Officially, Gorky died from influenza complicated by heart disease and inflammation of the lungs; some, however, suggest that his involvement with Stalin's enemies, and his plans to expose an upcoming show trial as a lie, could have pushed Stalin to have Gorky, already in failing health, "calmed."[194] Russian historian Barry Scherr argues that since Gorky's health had been bad for years, it is reasonable to think that a serious respiratory ailment killed him. "And yet, most people see Stalin's hand in this, and some talk about an indirect role—something as simple as having doctors withhold proper treatment. The notion that his death was at least helped along has an appeal to it."[195]

Mystery also surrounds Gorky's legacy: his archives. According to Berberova, who said she heard the story from Boris Nikolaevsky, a Russian émigré professor and author, Gorky entrusted his papers to Moura in April 1933, although he had been sending them back to Russia from as early as 1926 in preparation for his eventual return.[196] It was a massive archive: some 1,000 books and 9,000 letters from émigrés, Soviet writers and artists, political types, and, most important of all, people critical of Stalin. As Berberova's story goes, Gorky made Moura promise that she would not give his papers to anyone—not even to him should he ask for them. She traveled from Berlin to London in the spring of 1933, presumably taking the dangerous cargo with her. That summer, she had to bow out of her Welsh vacation with HG. In the summer of 1935, Catherine Peshkova, Gorky's wife, visited Moura in London to persuade her to return the archives to Moscow, but Moura refused. The next spring, an unnamed messenger appeared at Moura's door with a letter from Gorky imploring her to come see him before he died, and to bring his papers. The person who carried the letter would accompany Moura to and from Moscow, and Stalin personally guaranteed her safe passage both ways. Berberova said that Moura consulted Lockhart about the situation and that he told her she had no choice; if she didn't comply, both she and the archives might be taken by force.[197] Moura went, saw Gorky, and turned over the papers. Despite Berberova's scenario, many scholars maintain that to this day no one knows whether the transfer occurred, but "most recent Russian researchers strongly doubt that it did," Scherr said.[198] Still, Mikhail Agursky, a previously mentioned Soviet and East European scholar, claimed that if Moura did do something with these documents, "it was probably only to cooperate with the GPU in burying [Gorky's] secrets."[199]

There are no extant letters from Moura to HG or vice versa that document those trying days of 1936, but there is a most puzzling note from Moura to HG that may date from the period. Hastily scribbled across four half-sheets of paper and without any indication of the date or place it was written, the three-sentence letter demonstrates emotion, tenderness, and vulnerability, and suggests that Moura was in imminent danger:

> Darling, dearest mine, don't be alarmed at this letter—it may be all nothing but I thought I would like to tell you that if anything happens to me, I am going away with a last thought of you and of all that you have been to me. There is nothing but gratefulness and tenderness in my heart and love and if I have not always been what you wanted—it is only through clumbsiness. Be good to Kira, Tania and Paul—they'll miss me and you too, perhaps. Moura.

The letter stands alone, without predecessor, successor, cross-reference from any correspondence, or clues. Thus, one is forced to speculate on the circumstances Moura was in when she wrote this most compelling letter, and whether her emotion was genuine, although it certainly appears to be. What could have threatened Moura to this extent? There are at least three possibilities: the Soviet authorities or the intelligence agencies of Germany and Great Britain. To be sure, Moura's relationship with Gorky was potentially dangerous because Gorky's relationship with Stalin and the Soviets was so precarious in the mid-1930s. It has been argued that in the last years of his life, Gorky became increasingly disillusioned with Stalin and Stalin's methods for bringing about the revolutionary utopia. It has been argued that it was Stalin who wanted Gorky back in Russia so that he could be both silenced on some issues and harnessed for others, primarily those promoting his new cultural policies.[200] Still, Moura had come and gone to Moscow many times since her original immigration in 1921 and had never found herself in serious trouble with the Soviets.

One possible scenario is that Moura's mystery flight was a trip from London through Paris to Moscow to return Gorky's archives, just as Berberova had claimed, although Tania Alexander argued that all that was a myth Moura created. Meanwhile, the French secret police, who were watching Moura's movements in 1936, report not only that she went through Paris in May 1936, staying from May 9 to 12 at the Hotel

Continental at 3, rue Castiglione, but also that she went through Paris earlier that year, staying at the same hotel from March 17 to 19.[201] She drew little attention to herself, the police report stated, and apparently had no visitors. In March of 1936, Gorky was still at his winter home in Tesseli, on the southern shore of the Crimea. He wasn't rushed back to Moscow and into the hands of a team of doctors until May 26. It is conceivable that Moura did respond to a Soviet request, possibly from Stalin, and despite the possibility of a double-cross or trap awaiting her, traveled to Moscow to return Gorky's "suitcase" while he was away. Without a doubt, she stayed on through his death and funeral, which in any case makes her presence and his demise coincidental.

Coincidentally, HG wrote that in May 1936, "a peculiar malaise" came over Moura, accompanied by "storms of weeping"—highly unusual for her—and a strong desire to go to France.[202] He couldn't have known that beginning in March 1936 people outside Russia, including the French poet Louis Aragon, and perhaps even Moura, were receiving desperate letters from Gorky urging them to come to his aid in Russia—this according to Mikhail Agursky.[203] Agursky also noted that no one knew or knows whether she was depressed because of her devotion to Gorky and her expectation of his death, "or because of the need to betray his confidence by returning all his papers to the GPU." A few days after the newspapers announced that Gorky was mortally ill in Moscow, HG received a telegram from Moura in Russia. He later reported that he believed she had no thought of going to Russia when she went to France, but suddenly "packed off" to nurse Gorky through "his last delirium." As he wrote in the *Postscript,* HG also believed that Moura

did certain obscure things about [Gorky's] papers that she had promised to do for him long ago. I think there were documents that it was undesirable should fall into the hands of the Ogpu and that she secured them. I think there was something she knew and that she had promised to tell no one. And I believe that she kept her promise. In such matters Moura is invincibly sturdy.[204]

Although Moura told HG that she was going to visit her sister in Paris, she went straight to Gorky in Moscow, according to Alexander. Moreover, even before Moura left London, she constructed a ruse: Her daughter was to tell HG that while Moura was in Paris, she had become quite ill and had to enter a nursing home. Alexander's diary reported:

> June 10, Pestered by HG all week; how is it I don't know the name of the nursing home? Hate having to tell all these lies.
>
> June 11, dined HG (Antony & Flora R.) M. rang from Moscow middle of the night. Told her it would be much better to tell HG the truth now.
>
> June 13, Good. M. has phoned HG from Moscow telling him she's left the nursing home and flown to Moscow as Gorky was dying and has asked for her. Thank goodness no more lies required. Still have to pretend I knew nothing of all this till today. Fed up being intermediary every time. Makes me look a complete fool.
>
> June 18, Gorky died. M. staying for funeral. Sad.[205]

At 1:00 A.M. one Monday morning many weeks after she left London, "Moura, the incorrigible, unchangeable Moura, whom manifestly I love by nature and necessity," phoned HG, "as if she had never been away. . . . It was as if she had come home." To top off this twisted wreckage of stories, we learn from Lockhart's diary that a couple of days after she got back to London, Moura the incorrigible left once again, this time for Estonia.[206]

Hard evidence about Moura's clandestine past is scant, but a small and intriguing string of documents has somehow survived the redacted and sanitized British foreign office's correspondence with Russia.[207] On May 24, 1918, the foreign office received a telegram from Admiral Sir R. Hall, the director of Naval Intelligence: "May Foreign Office be informed of the following. The employment of lady clerks of foreign nationality by missions in Russia now occupied on confidential work is considered dangerous, as they deal with work of a secret nature leakage of which would prove useful to the enemy. In my opinion these women should not be used in cyphering and decyphering telegrams." These are the foreign office's internal comments on the docket sheet;

- *This evidently refers to Madame Beckendorff & Miss Artsimovich who with other ladies were employed in semi-official British organisations in Petrograd.*
- *I did not know there were other ladies besides Mme. Benckendorff. I think all our missions should be warned against employing them.*
- *There are certainly ladies employed as clerks in the British Consulate at Petrograd. But I cannot say if they were ever employed in cyphering or decyphering.*

A week later, the under secretary of state for foreign affairs in London responded, saying that the foreign office had received information from other sources of "this most irregular proceeding" and fully shared Hall's opinion on the danger of such employment. "The officials concerned have been severely reprimanded and strict injunctions have been issued prohibiting any such employment in the future." Unfortunately, the messages end here.[208] It is not known whether the "strict injunctions" were issued; nor is it known whether Moura and Miriam were let go. But in July, Moura wrote Lockhart a long chatty letter about events in Petrograd, saying, among other things, that a telegram of apology from the foreign office was on its way to her.

What makes the correspondence even more intriguing—beyond the fact that the foreign office in London knew about Moura—is that it divulges that Cromie blew the whistle on Moura.[209] In addition, two weeks before the "lady clerks" wires began flying back and forth, Cromie alerted his superiors to something else. On May 13, Naval Intelligence sent the foreign office a copy of a letter it had received on April 10 from Cromie, then at the American Legation in Christiania, now Oslo, Norway. His six-point message began, "Before leaving Petrograd I was informed by one in a position to know that the Bolsheviks were in possession of keys to all codes in use by the Allied Embassies and Legations in Petrograd."[210] There is no record of Lockhart's reaction when he learned that many, perhaps all, of his reports to Lloyd George and the foreign office had been deciphered—for the eyes of Trotsky, Lenin, and Dzerzhinsky, no doubt—before they had been sent. He had often complained about the inordinate amount of time it took for his messages to reach London. Berberova said that Lockhart kept his keys in a locked drawer in his bureau and that no outsiders entered the apartment he shared with Hicks and Moura unless one of them was present. Berberova stopped just short of saying that Moura had purloined the keys to the ciphers. Coincidentally or not, three months later, Cromie was shot to death in Petrograd. According to Spence, Moura's apparent work for the SIS in 1918 and the displeasure it provoked in the NID "is a good example of the competing factions within governments. Groups of British agents were deceiving other groups of British agents, and some Bolsheviks were doing the same on their side. Common interests among these factions impelled or necessitated their cooperation."[211]

Moura turns up in another set of documents, these from Germany. In 1940, anticipating the invasion and occupation of Britain, the Germans compiled a *Sonderfahndungsliste;* this was a list of suspects to be rounded up and arrested. Moura appears on the list in two places.[212] In the first, she is listed as "Moura Budberg, born Sakrewska, baroness, cover name Mura, a member of the British Intelligence Service." In the second, Moura is cross-referenced by her maiden name, with a note that she was presumed to have served as a British agent in Estonia. Her appearance on the list does not prove that was a British agent at this or any other time, but it does show that the Germans believed she was one. Reilly also appears on the list, rather odd for a man supposedly dead for fifteen years.

The repatriation in 1994 of seven shipments of French Secret Service/ Deuxième Bureau files back to Paris from a half-century of exile in Russia, and the recent cataloging of the files, opens up new secret service information collected by the French.[213] Among these files, most of them marked "Secret," are documents on Moura Budberg. In a dossier on "Russian personalities of emigration suspected of informing the Soviets" are some twenty-five documents dating from 1921 to 1936 and written by the Deuxième Bureau, the Ministère de la Défense Nationale et de la Guerre, and the French embassy in London. The files refer to Maria or Moura Zakrensky, Benckendorff, and Budberg as a "known woman," suspected and under surveillance since November 1921. In that year, her activities, one document claimed, revolved around anti-Bolshevik organizations and foreign missions, notably Polish and Japanese, and around obtaining information from her base in Reval on the Estonian military forces. (One recalls all the time she spent in Estonia in 1921, in that apartment in Reval. Whether she was gathering intelligence on the Estonian military force or was aiding Ernest Boyce, head of the Russian section of the SIS, is not known, and probably never will be.) The Soviet citizen now at Reval is "a redoubtable secret agent," the document read, "always busy with the Ukrainian organization Koussakov," and she is a member of Petrograd's Cheka.[214] A January 1922 document stated that the Countess Benckendorff had told friends she was affiliated with Chekists, but not with the Cheka, so that she could give information to the Germans. The documents also report that

This woman seems to be a double agent of the Soviets and the Germans. She travels constantly across all of Europe.

Considered as suspect. Reported as having obtained a number of visas for the Western countries and as being the fiancée of Baron Budberg, former secret agent of the emperor, then became the friend of Maxim Gorki and of Zinovieff and agent of the Soviets.

Of very great intelligence and of considerable education—she speaks fluently and without accent English, French, German and Italian— seems to be a very dangerous spy in the service of the Soviets. The fact alone that she accomplished four voyages in the USSR in three years constitutes an irrefutable proof of the relations of the Good Budberg with the Soviets.

In London, she slipped into the most closed circles, in particular in the entourage of the members of the Cabinet. She also tried to extort military information from diverse and well-placed people [Mr. Duff-

Cooper].[215] She works as much for the Germans as for the Russians.[216]

When she returns to the USSR, she returns to Berlin, where she receives a special entry authorization, of the kind that no trace of her trip is left on her passport.

She returns very often to France on the pretext of visiting her two sisters.

The Baroness B would work without doubt also for us if we would pay her.[217]

Like the German list, these documents do not prove that Moura was a spy. They only demonstrate that the French intelligence services believed she was. Still, this body of information stands to date as the most comprehensive official report of Moura's espionage activities. When added to the informed speculations and documents previously discussed, the case against Moura grows beyond rumor and legend. If one accepts the idea that she did manage what must have been a most complex life in espionage, working concurrently for three sides— British, German, and Soviet—then many of the puzzles, peculiarities, and paradoxes surrounding her behavior begin to make sense.

Her fluency in several languages was helpful when dealing with agents of many countries. She flitted—to borrow HG's verb—from place to place across half the globe because she was a courier, an agent of influence, or a bona fide spy. She cultivated few binding relationships for the same reason, and those she did cultivate were with men in the vortex of power, from whom she could extract information or pump with disinformation. She separated herself from other binding relationships, including her marriages to Benckendorff and to Budberg and her children, to remain free to live an unencumbered independent life; indeed, a life of intrigue. She used her children, sisters, mother, governess, even her old friend Gorky, as covers or pretexts for travel. She also used lies as a cover for her behavior and activities. And she used the double bluff brilliantly. That seemed to have been Moura's preferred method for gaining credibility and loyalty. She told Gorky that she had been planted on him and that she could no longer stomach that work; but she did continue. She told HG the same thing. State the worst-case scenario, then assure your lover that it is no longer the case, and you've won over his heart and his mind. Lockhart was not spared Moura's machinations. Over and over again she presented the accusations against her as if to prove to him that she wasn't a spy.

★   ★   ★

Moura's early letters to Lockhart speak of love and desire and loneliness, of ordinary and extraordinary events, of information and disinformation, and of schedules, plans, comings and goings. Letters from the 1930s, written after she and Lockhart reconnected, are some of the most fascinating and illuminating—especially those written between 1932 and 1934, which center around Lockhart's book manuscripts. As previously mentioned, Lockhart gave Moura carte blanche in editing *British Agent* and *Retreat from Glory;* however, he apparently wasn't prepared for what he got. On June 18, 1932, Lockhart made this entry into his diary: "This morning I had a shock—a letter from Moura in which she requests me to alter the part in my book referring to her. . . . This will be very difficult. The book, however, will have to be altered. She is the only person who has the right to demand an alteration." What that right was may never be known.

Ten of Moura's letters carry not only corrections but also reprimands and mini-lectures. In June 1932, she wrote this about his portrayal of "the spying business": "Don't you see yourself that it is all out of proportion and not typical of me? I am sure we will find a way that will not spoil the book & be acceptable for me. Once again—forgive me." In an undated letter, probably written in December 1932, she lied, saying that she had never worked as a translator before coming to England: "Hadn't the time, patience or need!" And yet, throughout 1919, Moura commented on her work. For example, on February 9, she wrote to Lockhart that "translating is a wonderful means of killing thought. That's why I do it, for things are so black, Baby." The most serious edits concerned Lockhart's characterization of Moura. "I must say that you exaggerate my qualities but you also give a horribly untrue mercenary and calculating picture of me," she wrote, probably in 1933. "Never could I have married a man in order to get some facility! I never sought Gorki because I wanted to have a friend in the regime. I don't want the trip to Russia talked about as you know. Do let me see it when you've mended it." Moura's substantial edits left Lockhart with substantial gaps to fill, and when he asked for her help in plugging them, she obliged. Most of her suggestions revolved around compliments she had received from important people. For example, Lockhart could write about her first meeting with Gorky: "In the presence of a strange, new young woman, he displayed a special eloquence . . . like a peacock spreading his beautiful feathers," she suggested in an undated letter. Or, Lockhart could say that upon meeting Moura, Alexandre Blok wrote a beautiful poem dedicated to her.

It isn't known whether Moura ever found out about a series of telegrams Lockhart received in April 1934, well before *British Agent,* the movie, was released. One of the telegrams, an alarming and unsigned message from Hollywood, said that the script was "burlesque and libelous," and that it presented Moura as Lenin's assistant and as a "fanatic member of the communist party" who betrayed Lockhart to the Soviets. In addition, the script showed Lockhart and Allied representatives as having an arsenal in their apartment and preparing an armed attack on the Soviets. The author of the telegram also said that Leslie Howard's "endeavors" claimed that the script was "unsuccessful"; Lockhart should cable Warner Brothers immediately. Another telegram cautioned Lockhart to not mention the source of the information about the script. The author of the telegram, "Kropotkin," told Lockhart that she was staying at the Beverly Wilshire Hotel in Hollywood.[218] A third telegram signed "Sasha" was more emphatic, emphasizing the importance of Lockhart's keeping source information on *British Agent* secret. Tremendous damage might be done to Howard and her if their communication got out. There is no additional information about the telegrams in Lockhart's files. On August 10, 1934, after having just viewed the film, Lockhart told his diary that he wasn't concerned about repercussions from "governmental authorities." He found his film to be "an entertaining picture, and the love scenes are done with great restraint. I think that provided Warner Bros put in that the characters are fictitious (as indeed they are) and that the historical accuracy has been sacrificed to make [the] film, there will be no objections."[219] Still, it is clear that for some, the fictionalization came too uncomfortably close to reality.[220]

It also is unclear from reading the *Postscript*—even between the lines—whether HG believed Moura was a bona fide spy. He never directly said so, although a suppressed portion of the *Postscript* alluded to the possibility. In the passage, HG discussed a chance meeting in March 1935 in the United States with the writer Rosa Graefenberg, whom he described as "an ugly, active, aggressively amorous little Jewess, who . . . announced herself as a friend of Moura's. She wasn't the sort of friend who reflects prettily upon those who know her, a vain, chattering, intriguing woman. . . . She behaved as though I must necessarily respond to her trite sexual provocations, and I had to snub her to the pitch of incivility."[221] Later in the suppressed pages, HG returned to the subject of the frau.

> [She] jumped out of the unknown during that eventful Washington week, to the great damage of Moura's background . . . [giving] just the shapes of that diplomatic running to and fro, in a world of attachés and foreign correspondents and publicists and politicians, the anecdotes and small gossip and intrigue, the Russians in exile, the mischievous tittle-tattle, the polyglot "fun," the faint aroma of espionage, of Moura's world in Berlin and Paris and Knightsbridge.
>
> "This Graefenberg," I wrote to Moura, "is a stink and she makes you stink. I won't marry you now anyhow. Send back my latchkey."[222]

The stink lingered. During that trip to the United States, HG wrote to Christabel from New York City on March 27: "I think I am really going to break up with Moura. She's lovely to me—she's adorable—but I can't stand any more of this semi-detached life. I'm tired, I'm bored by a Moura whom I can't bring to America & who rambles round corners & for all I know is a drug trafficker or a spy or any fantastic thing." The year before, he told Christabel that Moura had been a glorious mistress and adventure, but he'd "be damned" if he'd marry "White (& Pink) Russia." Moura was "an incurable émigrée & refugee," just one of many now living in England who had been "turned upside down in the War & the Revolution," who had acquired an "aimless uselessness, a shiftlessness," who had acquired a "taste for accidents & violent changes." Furthermore, HG was "not going to be trailed."[223]

And, too, in August 1935, HG noted in the *Postscript,* in pages that were later suppressed, that he had his suspicions:

> Moura, through sheer thoughtlessness, has so deranged my world that I have nothing here before me but work and more work or just jaded inaction, while she flits away to her old familiar gossips at 88 Knightsbridge, and to Berlin and Paris and Warsaw—and maybe even Moscow.[224]

These are the only known references HG made to the possibility that Moura was involved in espionage. Whether he was better off wondering or knowing that she was a spy—indeed, one possibly planted on him—will, like so much else, probably never be known.

★   ★   ★

It will also probably never be known whether HG knew the real relationship between Moura and Lockhart. HG never saw the letters between them—not just from the first fiery months of their relationship, not just from the first few years when she waited for Lockhart, but throughout the decades. For example, before Moura left for Estonia, to sleep, she said, with her husband, she wrote to Lockhart in July 1918:

> Your photo is on my night-table and I look at it with such an aching at my heart, Baby Boy. You have become the only thing in the world for me—the only reason for existence. And so it will remain . . . for some-

thing so great cannot cease being. . . . I am talking with you from my heart, from my soul, and because I want you to feel as sure of my love as I am myself, and I want you to realize the great, wonderful and everlasting power you have over me. I want it to be of some use to you, Baby-Boy. There isn't anything in me that isn't complete and infinite devotion.

A month after Lockhart left Russia, Moura wrote that her life without him was not worth living. He was everything to her, "the beginning and the end of everything, my baby. My little one, good-night. Sleep well and God watch over you. I kiss your eyes, your dear lips, my Baby."[225] At the end of 1918, or the beginning of 1919, she promised that they would start life anew, "on just and kind principles—and be happy, so happy. I will go with you my Baby to the end of the world—wherever you want me to. Nothing else matters now. . . . I love you so." Although Moura wrote to Lockhart nearly every day, he rarely wrote to her between October 1918 and February 1919, the period of the "Stockholm Plan"; and then, after she had stood him up, he apparently stopped writing to her for two years. Each day without news was slow torture for Moura, but it never quite killed her or her love and desire for Bruce Lockhart. "I know that nothing can bring us apart. Isn't it strange, Baby. Only a few months were we together, but the trace remains for life," she wrote in the early 1930s.

Although comparing Moura's letters to Lockhart and to HG isn't a fair test since Moura was at different stages in her life and in her relationships with each man at any given time, it is instructive to see how she operated at about the same time with them. As mentioned, Moura wrote to HG in May 1921 to tell him that she was out of Russia, and she wrote again in June and July. She was charming, grateful for his personal kindnesses and for his generosity toward Gorky's enterprises. Moura praised HG's work and expressed nostalgia for their time together. "I do hope this letter will reach you and that you will soon let me have news from you."[226]

Moura wrote Lockhart at about the same time. She had been resisting the urge, but succumbed after receiving his first letter in two years.

Her pain was great. What hurt her most, or so she said, was that he mentioned his young son, Robin:

> Your son? A fine boy? Do you know, as I write those words—it seems to me that I will not be able to live with that thought. I am ashamed of my tears. I thought I'd forgotten how to cry. But there was "little Peter," you know. Good-bye, Baby. Be happy if you can, but I don't think you can, quite. The rocks, for me, have not melted in the sun. And never will. Your Baby.[227]

Later, with Gorky at the sanatorium in Saarow, Moura wrote Lockhart another poignant letter. Knowing him gave her more happiness than she had ever known before and was the only thing that mattered.

> All these years in Russia, up to May 1921, I lived, waiting for you. . . . I only want you to know. Despairing at times, finding a thousand reasons for hoping at others, less acutely conscious of you at the periods when my whole being was engrossed in the miseries of my country, I still lived, feeling sure, somehow, that you were there. Then, at the eve of my leaving Russia, I got a letter, the first one, telling me all about you and Robin. Then, I had to face the future without you. It was as I suppose death is to those who suddenly lose faith in life after death.[228]

Moura explained that the only way she could face life was to "build a reason," so she married Budberg—"to be of use to someone." She told Lockhart that she would come to see him, but that he must be patient and help her find her "way out." She didn't want to suffer "so much" any more. "And oh, how shall it be when we meet, Baby Baby." Still at the sanatorium twenty days later, Moura wrote to HG, scolding him for not having written for so long. She asked him to help her work up a more cheerful view of the world "which, it seems to me is again preparing to bring to life a bastard. Isn't it? How naughty of it!"

⋆ ⋆ ⋆

Had HG's aching letters to Christabel not survived, we might never have had the insights into *his* mind and character; indeed, we might never have known his heart. The same is true of Moura's letters to Lockhart throughout the 1930s. Consider the letter she sent him from Estonia in August 1934, written during the Moscow crisis. HG had just arrived at Kallijärv, after his disastrous trip to Moscow where he learned that Moura had just been there to see Gorky. HG was mortally wounded from the discovery that Moura had been lying to him all along about her travels to Russia and her relationship with Russian authorities and with Gorky. They argued, but came to no understanding. It was an impasse unlike any they had experienced before with each other. And yet Moura wrote this to Lockhart: "Dearest Baby Mine, I had an interesting time [in Moscow]. I'm simply bubbling over with the desire to tell you about it, because there's nobody else I can speak to. HG is here now. He is disappointed in what he saw, I think. But that was to be expected. Darling, I'll be back early in September. Am I never going to have my 'percentage.'"

Several intriguing questions arise out of this letter, especially about Moura's fascinating business in Russia. It is also illuminating that of all the people in the world, Lockhart was the only one she could talk to about it—whatever "it" was. Presumably, the business was of a political nature. It is clear that Moura and Lockhart still had an intimate relationship after all those years, one that HG was shut out of, even though he was her lover. It is also interesting that Moura chose not to mention the trouble that was brewing between her and HG, and it is chilling to see that she seemed to have little feeling for HG's disappointment over Russia. In addition to all this, of course, Moura was still begging Lockhart for her piece of him—his heart, his soul, his body—or all three.

When Moura wrote the previous letter to Lockhart, HG was pouring out his guts to Christabel. The last time he had written to her was from Moscow, where he had been talking to Stalin and Gorky during the day and fretting during the night.

In the midst of it I found out something which meant either that Moura had been humbugging me in a quite intolerable way or that Gorky was a liar. It is queer how in a phase of jealousy one can believe anyone rather than the person one loves. Forgive my squeal of dismay at the prospect of having to do the rest of my life as a solo. Jealousy dear Christabel is the most malignant of fevers. In jealousy there is no rest, no peace, no human dignity. After sixty, one should be immune.[229]

Christabel responded that she was bewildered and distressed by the news because it didn't agree with what she knew about Moura. If it was as HG feared, then she hated its happening to him—"others mightn't take it so badly," she said. Christabel then tried to comfort him:

A passing infidelity wouldn't be so completely wrecking, would it? The matter is graver, more humiliating than a passing light-hearted infidelity (what one might call an accidental adultery). And it's this element of humiliation in the affair that makes me doubtful of its truth. . . . I hate to think of you being hurt and sore, and left alone and rather frightened of the future, and humiliated about the past. There's something all wrong in that picture—she's not like that. I care for her a great deal too much to believe in this situation—it's false and untrue somewhere. If I'm right in part, and yet there has been something, couldn't you forgive it? She's such a lovely person, and you and she are so happy together.[230]

HG responded a week later. Perhaps it wasn't as final and tragic as he had originally thought, but it was a great disillusionment just the same, and

the extravagant happiness I got to a few months ago won't come back. We shall have a modus vivendi & not be so inseparable & I suppose drift apart. I'll have to keep the queer story until I see you. . . . I've got to get, if not out of love, at least head & shoulders out. None of us ought to be so obsessed by another human being & so easily vulnerable as I have been by Moura during the past year. How are you? I'm longing to see you. If it weren't for you I should have been bottled up altogether about the affair. And the bottle might have burst.

Moura's letters from Maugham's villa in the South of France that Christmas also survive and give us some extraordinary insights into her relationships with HG and Lockhart. Moura wrote to her former lover from the Marseilles train station, an odd thing to do when she was just launching into a long, lazy vacation with her current lover. "Darling, All plans changed owing to overflowing 'Tiber' and my sudden reluctance of repeated geography. We are going to stay with Somerset Maugham. Will you write me c/o him. Love, my dear. Moura."[231]

Moura clearly didn't want to lose touch with Lockhart—not even for four weeks. When she got no response, she fired off another letter, this one scolding Lockhart for not writing. "Darling, you are, of course, quite impervious to the fact that if I gave you my address, it is to have some news from you! This is . . . a lovely house-party, rather like a Onida of 1934. I play tennis, bridge and all the games that don't matter. It's curious that life should have come to that. Write to me darling. All best wishes and remember your promise. Isn't 17 years almost a record?"

One can only speculate on the games that did matter to Moura, but access to men in power comes to mind. At any rate, this letter got Lockhart's attention, and he soon replied. While his letter has not surfaced, we do have Moura's quick response:

Darling, Thanks for your letter, wishes, thoughts, love. How much love, Baby? The holiday is—well—middling. I like the place and I'm learning to like Maugham very much and it is all quite funny & light & easy. But there's the other trouble all over again, it always comes when the London happily separated routine is broken—and I don't think I can stand it very much longer. It has such a dreadful sapping character about it. I'm sorry to "complain" to you about it all, but I have to, to somebody. And I feel imprisoned in a net of considerations which are the most deadly of all—compassion, pride, self-reproach. And age. Darling, take me away with you to the East. Dear, it will be dreadful if you go before I get back. What a dreary London it will be without you—your voice at the telephone and occasional lunches and "dropping" in on your way home. Write me something warm before you go. There must be something warm in you for me. All my love, Baby, and a real new Year and don't forget my "three days."[232]

The other trouble all over again . . . I don't think I can stand it very much longer . . . imprisoned . . . take me away with you. At the same time that HG was stinging from what he interpreted as a cruel double-cross, and while he and Moura were *en vacances* and hoping to mend their wounds, Moura was feeling smothered. Trapped day in, day out, around the clock and sticking with the relationship out of obligation and compassion rather than love, she felt free to unload on Lockhart. At this same time, HG wrote to Christabel about the change in plans and Christmas at Maugham's.

We have played tennis every day for a fortnight & I got better and better. And now Moura has scuttled off to London because her daughter is out of a job & her son is in trouble about his permission to stay in England. I am a lone deserted man going back to the Hermitage Hotel at Nice & then I shall have a week end with little e (who introduced me to you years ago, when I first fell in love with you) & if I can trust these film people not to ruin my film while I am away, I shall stay down in the sunshine here for two or three weeks more & Moura, after the manner of Russians, will scuttle back to me. Why do all the people I love have these compelling families? How are you? Dear Christabel.[233]

HG wasn't completely truthful with Christabel, as we know. He was not a "lone deserted man," but rather, trysting pleasantly with Constance. Christabel told HG that she was distressed to know he was not "lolling lazily" in Sicily, but rather on the Riviera. To think that he was in "that haunt of parasites"—with its "overdressed and underreputational women"—was more than she could bear, she joked, adding, "not that I am one to mind too much about reputations. All the same, I loathe the people who haunt Riviera hotels, and I hate that you should waste yourself on such plaster facades as they are." If she only knew how much he was wasting himself!

Moura's flame for Lockhart obviously burned long and strong. It may have flickered during the long dark days of 1918, 1919, and 1920, but it was never extinguished. HG mentioned the early love affair between Moura and Lockhart. "She had had that fantastic love affair with Bruce Lockhart he recounted in his *Memoirs of a British Agent* and *Retreat from Glory*."[234] But try as she might, Moura couldn't get Lockhart back in her clutches, HG reported. "She had stirred among the ashes of an old affair with him . . . and she had found not a spark left alive in them."[235] That wasn't true of course. There was enough heat on Lockhart's part to keep up the friendship—to write to Moura and to see her from time to time. One wonders how HG might have reacted to the following letter Moura wrote Lockhart, probably in 1931, after an evening together in London:

> I love you in the same all-absorbing way as I did 13 years ago. And I want you just to tell me, Baby, quite frankly, even at the risk of being cruel—I like being the only person you hurt: When you see me, do you do so just because you think you ought to, or because it gives you some pleasure, because somewhere very deep there perhaps still lives a slight, a faint subconscious little thrill. I see you too spasmodically to look into your heart. So tell me, Baby dear, what is it? A little reflection of love only or staunch friendship? I must know. You have taught me to descend the scale of my exigencies. I first wanted all, then a little and now something so infinitesimal that I do not know whether it is worth asking for. My Baby, how wonderful it is to love you.

Lockhart's response isn't known, but it is likely that he chose "staunch friendship." Perhaps this is why Moura opted for HG in the ensuing months. Gorky may have had Moura's head, HG may have had her body, but Lockhart had her heart. After he died in February 1970 at the age of eighty-two, Moura arranged a special memorial service for him at London's Russian Orthodox Church. They were alone once again; Moura didn't invite anyone else.

And as for HG, he reconciled himself to bits and pieces of a flitting, scuttling Moura. He had her company from time to time; she had his latchkeys. Even so, he admitted that when all was said and done, she was the woman he really loved.

> I love her voice, her presence, her strength and her weaknesses. I am glad whenever she comes to me. She is the thing I like best in life. In the last resort, in this sort of love, the rights and wrongs of the case are interesting but they do not alter the deep primary fact to any material degree. She is my nearest intimate.
>
> Even when I have let my vexation with her take the form of an infidelity, or when she has behaved badly to me and driven me to anger and reprisals, she has remained still the dearest thing in my affections. And so she will remain to the end. I can no more escape from her smile and her voice, her flashes of gallantry and the charm of her endearments, than I can escape from my diabetes or my emphysematous lung. My pancreas has not been all that it should be; nor has Moura. That does not alter the fact that both are parts of myself.[236]

Despite all justifications and appearances to the contrary, HG "was bothered to the end of his days" by his inability to come up with a rationale for continuing his relationship with Moura, as Gip told Anthony, and Anthony repeated in his biography. "It distressed him almost beyond measure to have to admit to himself that his reason had no voice at all in determining so vital a matter as the nature of his principal association."[237]

★   ★   ★

It isn't known where Moura was when HG died, but it wasn't, as some have suggested, by his side. With HG gone, Moura took up with Alexander Korda, whom she had known well before he and HG began making *Things to Come* in 1934. Korda hired her as a script reader and paid her a small weekly wage. He saw Moura as a kindred spirit, according to his nephew, Michael Korda. In his family biography, Michael Korda asserted that Alex essentially rescued Moura from poverty after

HG died, although most people thought that Moura's real function was to amuse and entertain the producer with the gossip du jour. She also played matchmaker—hooking Korda up with a young and questionable Canadian-Ukrainian woman, Alexa, who became his last wife. Lady Alexa Korda apparently grew tired of Moura's ubiquity and influence and weaned her from their circle. Truth be told, Moura wasn't always thrilled with her employer and benefactor. Lockhart once reported a long conversation he and Moura had that raked over the coals of literary personalities she had known. "She was subdued in spirit and drank very little. She finds her work for Korda very trying and now inclines to agree with Cyril Radcliffe's verdict: 'That Korda is an interesting man to know but impossible to work for.'"[238] Moura probably had heavier assignments from Korda than Lockhart suspected. It seems that in addition to his moviemaking, Korda was a secret agent for friend-spymaster Claude Dansey and his top-secret Z Organization, which Dansey set up in the mid-1930s. Korda's film studios in London (Denham) and his U.S. office in New York City's Empire State Building served as covers for Z operations. Moura was, once again, right in the thick of it, but what her specific duties were is still unknown. Still, she surely saw to it that HG met Korda and selected him as his producer for his 1936 film, *Things to Come.*[239]

When Korda died in 1956, Moura continued on as an historical adviser to a few films, and even had a small nonspeaking part in Carol Reed's film, *The Accident.* She translated literary works to make ends meet, although by many accounts she still hadn't become much of a translator. Alexander claimed that her mother routinely had her friends correct her copy before she sent it in. A late riser, Moura began her work at midday and continued on her own schedule, more often than not pretending she was in the office when in reality she was still in bed—this according to her daughter.

Approaching eighty-one, with her friends and patrons dying all around her, Moura retired to Italy, the scene of some of her happiest times—with Gorky. She took rooms in a country hotel in Tuscany, three miles from her son and her daughter-in-law. In less than two months, she was dead. Paul and Tania were with her that day, October 31, 1974: four years after Lockhart died, twenty-eight years after HG, thirty-eight after Gorky. The London *Times*'s headline for Moura's obituary was "Baroness Budberg, Hostess and Intellectual Leader." The glowing piece, which began with "For nearly four decades she was in the centre of London's intellectual, artistic and social life," went on to catalogue nearly every role Moura played:

> Author, translator, production adviser on plays, films and television programmes, an occasional actress herself (mostly in striking silent parts), sometimes a stage or costume designer, historical researcher and artistic codirector, publishers' reader of manuscripts in five languages and during the Second World War managing editor of *La France Libre,* a devoted matriarch to her own large family, a solid friend and ever ready mother confessor to people of the utmost variety, a grande dame but equally at her ease with the poor and humble, a generous hostess, an invaluable guest, this fantastic woman was unique.

The obituary was shot through with errors, many of which have been discussed here. It said that she spent six months at Cambridge's Newnham "polishing up her English," that she and HG met socially in 1914 in St. Petersburg, and that her romance with H. G. Wells began soon after she had settled in London in 1933. There is also the odd claim that Moura brought her French chef to Gorky's commune, and that the chef "contrived to make quite good meals out of the poorest material." But odder yet is the muddled story about Djon's death. It said that Moura got in touch with her husband, who was still in the army, and told him of her affair with Lockhart. "They agreed to meet at his estate in Estonia and both set out on foot for the reunion. She was caught, arrested and brought back to the capital while he was killed by his own peasants soon after reaching the house." If nothing else, this story demonstrates that you live by the myth and you die by the myth. The piece ended:

To those whose life she touched she will always remain an unforgettable person. But for those who knew her well and especially the small circle of really close friends, her going leaves a vacuum that nothing can fill. There is an old American saying that fits her well: "After they made that one, they broke the mould."

The funeral service for Moura, which was held at the Russian Orthodox Church at Ennismore Gardens, Kensington, was well attended by her family and friends, many of them social and literary celebrities, statesmen, titled nobility, and royalty: Sir Carol Reed, the French ambassador, Lady Diana Cooper, and Prince George Galitzine. Moura, the mythtress of all she surveyed, would have been pleased with the turnout.

4

Star Begotten: HG and Constance Coolidge, 1935–1937

Constance Atherton, Countess de Jumilhac, Constance Rogers, Constance Magnus

Moura is coming back to rescue me on Saturday & my lonely vigil on this dangerous coast is over. I've been mercifully spared by the Harpies—confining myself entirely to such little friends as Elizabeth & Maugham found for me. But I've had a long quarrel with Moura by post. I want her to be just like she is but entirely different. She persists in thwarting this simple & reasonable wish. What parasites lovers can be! What resentments spring like weeds in the rich soil of love! If this goes on much longer it will read like an eighteenth century sermon!

**—HG to Christabel, January 30, 1935,
Hermitage Hotel, Nice-Cimiez, France**

HG wasn't entirely truthful in his holiday report to Christabel—or at least not entirely forthcoming. We know, for example, that although

Moura abandoned him twice during the vacation, HG certainly didn't need to be rescued from that "dangerous coast," or from anything else, for that matter. Nor did he keep a lonely vigil. We also know that the weather put HG down in Nice, that Maugham and friends put HG and Constance together at a Christmas dinner, and that Moura's impromptu departures put in place a delightful and serendipitous romance for the English writer and the American reader. That HG considered Constance one of those "little friends" to whom he confined himself seems doubtful, but if he did, and if she was, then it was surely a most pleasant confinement indeed.

In the *Postscript,* HG wrote that Constance lived "an oddly orderly and industrious life at Nice—the funniest life by my standards." Her modus vivendi was "a residium" of the things that had happened to her. "She was as fond of the morning sunshine as Moura disliked it, and she would be out walking her 'dorg' before breakfast," he wrote, mimicking Constance's Boston accent. Constance's face was splashed with freckles, and HG thought that the "golden patches" suited her. "I cannot convey the refreshment of her explicitness."[1]

When Constance and HG met in the South of France in the last days of 1934, life was pleasant for both of them. He was producing a steady stream of books and articles and exploring new ideas and means for expressing them; namely, the feature film. He was making headlines and being profiled in the leading publications of the day. And, although some thought him passé as the world inched closer to war, HG was still revered the world around. He could still fill a hall. He was not yet his own *Invisible Man.*

In 1935, the author of *The Time Machine* crossed the Atlantic twice, first to size up his Yankee cousins for a *Collier's* series on "The New America," then to scope out the movie industry for a filmmaking scheme. In the United States, HG met with the movers and shakers: Chaplin, Cecil B. De Mille, and Franklin Delano Roosevelt. He also rubbed elbows with Frank Crowninshield, Constance's debonair cousin and the editor of the influential magazine *Vanity Fair,* and later, of *Vogue.* Back on his home turf after the new year, HG slaved over and eventually produced a film treatment, *Things to Come,* a frightening story about a twenty-five-year war that would commence in 1940. He received an honorary doctorate from his alma mater, London University, and he moved into new digs in London's Regent's Park in 1936. HG also published *The Anatomy of Frustration* and several shorter works, and he turned out another film treatment, *The Man Who Could Work Miracles,* about a draper's assistant, of all things, who was suddenly empowered to reshape the world. It had a familiar ring.

As for Constance, although her monthly trust checks were shrinking as her bills and taxes mounted, she was sitting pretty while much of the world reeled from the Great Depression and its aftermath. As HG wrote in a portion of the suppressed *Postscript,* she owned an apartment in Auteuil, a suite in the swank Negresco Hotel, a first-class racing stable, and "an impressive" Hispano-Suiza.[2] Constance also traveled widely, wore designer clothes, ate at the best restaurants, ran with the rich and famous, and employed four servants. Despite her complaints, she enjoyed the privileges her money and class brought her.

It was during their winter fling in the South of France that HG learned about Constance. He must have been intrigued by her tale because he later wrote nine pages about her in his *Postscript.* Gip came along later and suppressed three of those pages, most of them having to do with Constance's parents, husbands, and lovers. The pages that were published contained several errors. For example, HG described Constance as "an American widow who owned race-horses," noting that he couldn't imagine a less apt description. It was true that she owned a fine stable of horses, but she was never a widow; all her husbands were alive and kicking at the time of their divorces, and her last husband outlived her by twenty-eight years. HG also got Constance's great paramour's name wrong, calling him Henry and Frank, rather than Harry Crosby. He also mixed up Harry's literary nickname for Constance and called her the "Fire Princess" rather than the "Lady of the Golden Horse with the Diamond Eyes"—so-called because of the bracelet she wore. In addition, HG got the name of Constance's no-count count of a husband wrong, calling him Jumiege instead of Jumilhac. Even with all these errors, HG had a good idea of who this dazzler was. This was a woman worth knowing. This was a woman worth pursuing.

As it happened, Constance had had a relationship with H. G. Wells long before she met him, and it was all her grandmother's fault. Granny Coolidge got Connie, as she called her, hooked on H. G. Wells when she was a young diplomat's wife in China by shipping boxes of books to Pekin.[3] Despite her daunting duties as an undersecretary's wife, Constance found time to read the books and was able to stay on the high road with history, philosophy, and political science. In a sense, they were the glue that held the women together when they were so far apart. Books also kept Constance whole when her world fell apart, which was often, indeed. In the spring of 1921, she told her Granny that she was "enjoying so much Wells history, which you gave me. It is fascinating. I always did like his books, except when he tried to invent a religion." On Christmas Day, 1921, Constance and her husband, Ray Atherton, ripped opened another care package. "Your books we love darling Granny & we are going to start reading Wells aloud—which will take us some years I'm sure—but we will be extremely intelligent at the end of it, I know!" After Constance had plunged in, she told Granny that she found Wells's work "perfectly fascinating. I am reading it slowly & really trying to get something out of it. Of course it is most interesting & instructive to know instantly on meeting a person whether they are Brachycephalic or Dolichocephalic. It helps you so much in talking to them! Personally I think I am a Dolichocephalic—it sounds better (& I can't pronounce the first one anyway!). Which are you?"

Without knowing it, of course, H. G. Wells had worked his way deep into Constance's consciousness. His ideas often buzzed in her head. Apparently she so perseverated on HG and his books that when the Pekin legation put on its annual spoof, Constance and "HG" starred in one of the vignettes. The American foreign minister, played by a student interpreter, quipped: "I've had a most interesting conversation with Mrs. Atherton. She gave me a brief outline of Wells' history & then in the same breath told me the names of all the race ponies in Pekin. Most interesting personality." Some time later, Constance asked Granny how she liked HG's *Mr. Britling Sees It Through,* then observed: "Of course it's a novel & an essay all in one, but I think it's very clever—altho I don't think Mr [Direck] is at all true to life." It was one of many criticisms Constance would make of HG's writings—in her letters, diaries, and eventually to his face.

Constance was still reading H. G. Wells in 1932. Throughout the late winter and early spring she kept her diary apprized of her progress through his books, including *Science of Life.* "He does not believe in individual survival. Indeed, it is difficult to after reading his book. He says only the young hope for it. The old are only too glad to slip away into nothing. I wonder." The next night, after she had finished the book, she wrote that she was "thoroughly depressed. An amazing farce, if he is right. Consciousness a temporary thing, entirely accidental. Common sense tells one this must be so, & yet one does not want to go by common sense."[4] In a sense, Constance had been preparing all her adult life to meet H. G. Wells. A great believer in the unseen forces and spirits of the universe, she would have said that destiny brought them together.

When Constance's father, David, learned that his daughter was dating H. G. Wells, he wrote from Santa Barbara, California, on February 18, 1935: "Dearest Connie, To say that your last letter astonished me would be putting it mildly . . . [it] has certainly aroused me out of my depressed & nervous condition." His reaction might have been worse. David had survived a series of heart attacks and was staring at "a long lingering incapasitation already 2 1/2 years old." In the same letter he tucked in a clipping from a San Francisco newspaper, reporting that Constance had been seen with HG on the French Riviera. "You see you are already in the Wells limelight. Oceans of love. Pa."

The news got around. From Switzerland, Freddie Foster kidded Constance about the limelight and asked how she felt about her new-found celebrity in being HG's girl. On February 8, 1935, just as the gossip was spreading from the Riviera about HG and a dazzling American divorcée, Foster, a good friend, unloaded with: "You evidently haven't quite made up your mind whether or not to accept Celebrity. There seems to me one paramount reason against it & that is that you would be forthwith swept up into the Walhalla where the Gods live & I would see you no more. Are you sure that you would like that rarified air?" Foster, a serious bibliophile who had a penchant for drama, reminded Constance that H. G. Wells was the author not only of a history of the world but, even more ambitious, of a "History of all Human Knowledge! He is or should be a walking encyclopaedia. I should think it might be rather difficult to keep in step? You seem to be doing pretty well so far & you are certainly not one to halt on the road to adventure." Still, he cautioned, if she stayed with HG she'd have to read all his works: "from the really amusing ones—'Invisible Man,' 'The War of the Worlds,' & Whatnot—right down to the 'History of Everything that Ever Was' & all the schemes for Utopia. Have you thought of that?" Apparently he didn't know that Constance had already read most of HG's writings. On another line of questioning, Foster asked: "Do you call him Herbert? Or George? Or has he a nickname, like 'Whoops' or something? It's all faintly like 'Alice in Wonderland.'"

In her reply, Constance passed along some gossip she had heard from HG, including the news that the writer Katherine Mansfield had died of a broken heart. Foster, in turn, exchanged his critique of Bruce Lockhart's second book, *Retreat from Glory*. "I don't recommend it to you. It's very obvious & trite & very condescending to the world that languishes in the outer darkness beyond the frontiers of the British Empire." It was interesting, he said, that the "real" Mrs. Lockhart was all but missing in the book, present only to "give birth to the Pukka Sahib's son & heir," and to be dismissed a few paragraphs later. "Poor Mrs. Lockhart! The whole wide <u>world</u> now knows that fabulous continental adventuresses are far more desirable to Mr. Lockhart."

In another letter, Foster pointed out that Moura strode through the pages of Constance's letters "with a fine ruthlessness." He was relieved to know that Constance wasn't underestimating her.

> Don't leave her alone with a cup of tea or a glass of champagne that you haven't finished. If you should suddenly appear in the obituary column I shall at once present myself at the Sureté Generale or at Scotland Yard

with your letter. I haven't read detective stories for two years for nothing. I know exactly how it's done. However, since there have been no
headlines in the Paris Herald: (SOCIETY WOMAN FOUND MUR-
DERED IN HISPANO AFTER WILD TRIP FROM NICE—POPULAR
NOVELIST MISSING) I gather that [your] lunatic idea was abandoned
& that you all went your various ways in a proper & seemly manner.

Freddie gathered wrong, of course. Constance and HG did travel ensemble through the French countryside while Moura was away, and
they didn't seem to care who knew it. Who was this brazen Boston
Beauty and Brain with the huge appetite for ideas and books, adventure, romance, and men? Who was HG's latest trophy girlfriend, and
how did she get to Wellshalla?

*   *   *

The answer is that she was born there. With Adamses, Amorys,
Coolidges, Copleys, Crowninshields, and Peabodys on both sides of the
family, Constance, like her horses, was a thoroughbred. Whether at the
track, dining at Fouquet's, listening to Wagner at L'Opera, or "trying
on" at Vionnet or at Lanvin, she ran with the bluebloods: counts, earls,
duchesses, and kings; writers, journalists, artists, and playboys; the
Palmers, Doubledays, Astors, and Rothschilds, just to name a few. She
was up for the race. Her Chinese ponies, after all, were named "Why
Not" and "If Not."

Still, while Constance was often amused by her patrician relatives
and élite society, she accepted their company on her terms, meaning
when it wasn't boring and when it didn't get in the way of her first priorities: books and horses. As HG observed in his *Postscript:* Constance's
"social occasions were incidental" to horse racing. She would have
agreed. Reflecting on her keenest enjoyments in life, Constance told
her diary in 1938: "I think I would say reading, racing, traveling, people—occasionally & in small doses, lovers—even more occasionally &
for very short times, & perhaps most important of all, loneliness, that

is, to be alone. Happiness to me is never associated with people. It is a state of mind only attainable by reflection, awareness and solitude." As we shall see, that great tension between society and solitude would remain part of her life. Like HG and Martha, when Constance had one, she craved the other.

Constance Coolidge became fascinated with ponies, horses, and racing during her time in Pekin; there she learned the fundamentals of the sport and discovered that she had the talent and the passion to make it in a man's world. It was later, in Paris in the early 1920s, that she began carving a life for herself as the owner of a string of racehorses, and at that métier she was surely one of the most winsome, if not winning, attractions at Auteuil, Enghien, Longchamp, and Maisons-Laffitte. In 1954, Constance wrote somewhat disingenuously to her old friend Caresse Crosby that she tried to earn enough at racing to meet her "daily needs." More to the point, Constance lived off a sizable trust fund left by her mother, and, fortunately for her, overseen by her Cousin Charlie: Charles Francis Adams, the secretary of the navy.[5] As legal trustee of Constance's considerable funds, Cousin Charlie rode shotgun on his niece's financial affairs for a quarter of a century, including through the stock market crash. CFA, as he signed his letters, was very much a Dutch uncle, but he was wise about money and human behavior.[6] Moreover, he adored Constance; she, in turn, respected him. "I admire Cousin C more than anyone I know," she told her diary on July 3, 1938, "and it distresses me to think he is getting old, for who can I turn to then?"

Constance and CFA weren't the only relatives who made news. Aunts, uncles, and cousins often wound up in newsprint. Consider the wedding notice for Aunt Elsie and Uncle George in June 1891:

> In the 200 years that have elapsed since "Essexes have married Suffolks" . . . there has not been a more notable union among the old families which represent New England's bluest blood than that to-day of Miss Elizabeth Copley Crowninshield, daughter of Gen. Casper Crowninshield, and Mr. George Lee Peabody, youngest son of Mr. S. Endicott

Peabody of Salem. Gen. Crowninshield represents the old Salem family of that name; the bride is connected through her mother's family with the Copleys, Amorys, and other old Boston families, and the bridegroom represents the clans of Peabody, Endicott, Lee, Saltonstall, and others as well known, who have since colonial days distinguished themselves in Essex County.[7]

The couple exchanged vows in Trinity Church. The ceremony was "impressively performed" by the Rev. Dr. Phillips Brooks, assisted by the groom's brother, the Rev. Endicott Peabody. Uncle George and Aunt Elsie would play important roles in Constance's early years.

Constance's parents were also married in Boston, on November 25, 1890. While newsworthy, their union was not on the same order of magnitude as that of Aunt Elizabeth's. The newspaper notice began, "A brilliant society wedding took place on Commonwealth Avenue this afternoon. Miss Harriet Sears Crowninshield, daughter of Gen. Caspar Crowninshield, and D. H. Coolidge, Jr., were married at the Crowninshield residence at 1:30 p.m. The mansion was thronged with a distinguished company of guests." The stately blonde bride wore a beautiful "costume" of white satin and mull, her tulle veil was fastened with orange blossoms, and she carried a bouquet of lilies of the valley. The Rev. Dr. Phillips Brooks officiated. Afterwards, a wedding lunch was served, and the newlyweds left for an extended trip through the American South. They would take up residence on Marlborough Street.

As it happened, most of the Crowninshields had not only social status but also money—gobs of it. Constance's great-grandmother Harriet Sears Crowninshield wrote, signed, and sealed her will on January 24, 1872, bequeathing all her interest to her son Caspar, Constance's grandfather. At that time, great-grandmother Crowninshield's personal estate, including dozens of securities in railroads and a good many properties, was appraised at $390,000. The family managed to increase that nest egg, and a good deal of it eventually went to Constance.

David Coolidge Jr. was also from a good family; indeed, he was from a presidential family, a distant cousin of President Calvin Coolidge and the son of a prominent Boston lawyer and civic figure. One of four children, David Jr. attended the Boston Latin School, then went to Harvard, graduating in the Class of 1886. He studied at the Bussey Institute for a year, then worked as a landscape architect for five years with Frederick Law Olmsted. In 1893, David put down roots in the landscape architecture firm of Coolidge & Titus, in Boston, and later worked alone. He also served in the military, ran a pear and alfalfa ranch near Medford, Oregon, then returned to Boston. In the late 1920s, he picked up stakes and moved to Santa Barbara, where he lived the rest of his life, occasionally traveling abroad to see Constance, his only child, in the Far East and France. In Harvard's twenty-fifth anniversary report on the Class of 1886, the notation for David was "He traveled much abroad." The editor of the fifty-fifth anniversary report wrote that Coolidge maintained his debonair appearance and "jaunty air."

Thus, Constance came by her great attributes naturally: Her beauty, grace, and money derived from her mother, her charm from her father, and her intelligence was a gift from both parents. These features alone could explain what made her so attractive to legions of men. But more than anything else, and much like Moura, Constance had "an irresistible charm and aura," said her last husband, André Magnus. "When she walked into a room, everyone watched her and wanted to meet her. You could not be indifferent to Constance. She was the most fascinating woman I ever met."[8] Magnus was not the only man who felt this way about Constance. An anonymous diplomat once said that she had the charm of Cleopatra. The American writer Speed Lamkin once told Constance that she was "touched by a divine fire," she was a "great candelabra of charm." Cousin Charlie, as straightlaced as he was, once wrote, "Even a father confessor has to admit that you have 'that fatal charm' which makes companionship a joy." But Constance also had "an enormous sense of humor," Magnus said, "and a wonderful voice." Felix Doubleday, another suitor and the son of the New York publishing mogul, Frank N. Doubleday, once described Constance's voice as "vibrant, hypnotic and soul-searching." The American expatriate poet Harry Crosby called it a "Star-Voice."

No one was more aware of Constance's charms than Cousin Crownie: Edward Augustus Crowninshield. "I love you. You're every-thing that I want in a woman," he told his "Connie" over and over again in his many letters to her. "You have a power of attracting everyone." But, as he must have known, as anyone close to her must have sus-pected, and as Magnus observed, at some point in her life Constance became "a prisoner of her charm." When she began to sense that she was losing that charm, Constance confided to her diary: "I never knew before how used I was to admiration. Can I now do without it and not mind?"[9] There was another strong force working in her. According to Magnus, Constance adored adventure, including the game of romance. She made a career of betting on horses, after all. Constance also en-joyed the idea that she may have been a femme fatale. "She was not at all embarrassed by having an affair with one man and being in love with another," Magnus observed.

David Coolidge didn't always understand his daughter, but he re-mained dedicated and attentive to her throughout his life. His ability to raise her, to live with her, and to keep up with her, however, was seri-ously hampered—first by his cash flow problems and later by his health. In the suppressed pages of the *Postscript,* HG wrote that David was a "poor man" still living in Santa Barbara, but Constance's mother "had been a rich heiress and she (Constance) had inherited a very con-siderable fortune."[10] That is what it boiled down to. After David retired, in the late 1920s, he lived within his means on $7,000 a year—then a tidy sum, but a pittance compared to his daughter's income.

Constance may have been flush enough to shuttle back and forth to the United States, to travel all over the globe, and to entertain writers and royals, but the 1930s caused her serious grief, especially after FDR took the United States off the gold standard and the franc-to-dollar ex-change plummeted. She received many stern letters from Charlie Adams, full of facts, figures, and suggestions. In one letter, he cau-tioned that when the new year rolled around she would see a drastic cut in her monthly allotment. She might have to give up her house and move into a hotel, he suggested. Her father's letters echoed the same grim message, but Constance was opposed. She wrote to her father in the mid-1930s asking him how she would be able to live

> on, say F20,000 a month when I have to pay F13,700 every three months. I will have to put up my car of course & let Henri go. It will be so hard if it comes to that, after all, you have Elizabeth & George & I have Victor, Helene & Henri & I don't see how I can do without them. Oh why did Roosevelt have to go & upset the exchange like this & all for no good reason at all. I can't see that it has had the slightest effect except to make me utterly miserable. How lucky I won that race & can pay off my bills. They never never would have been paid otherwise.

FDR wasn't the only source of Constance's money troubles. Her unusual attitude toward finances was to blame, based, seemingly, on the whimsical philosophy of *Alice in Wonderland*. For example, when Constance was living in China from 1920 to 1922, she bought a share in a Mongolian gold mine. "I suppose everyone has to have at least one gold mine in their life & this seems to be mine," she told Granny. In another letter from China, Constance said that she was going to take advantage of the exchange rate and order a Russian sable coat—"very dark and very long"—from Paris. "It makes one feel so awfully rich this way, but as I always spend it before I get it, the result is always the same—that I never have a cent!" Constance also once lost Fr 30,000 when her French bank in Pekin failed. She had deposited that sum to pay for some clothes from Paris. "Moral: never save money to pay bills in <u>advance</u>. I always did think it a foolish mistake, but Ray being cautious & economical by nature advised & insisted on my doing it & now it is all gone," she confided in Granny.

Even when she was making money, she couldn't seem to hold onto it. In her first truly successful horseracing season—in China in 1922—Constance pulled in $8,000, and was offered another $5,000 for one of her horses; but she refused the offer and gave away most of her winnings. "I have not gone into it for money," she told her grandmother. And yet Constance did enjoy playing games with money, just as she enjoyed playing games with romance. She always seemed to have a scheme for making a bundle, in the same way that she—and HG, for that matter—always seemed to find a new lover before having dispensed with the old one. She co-owned stables and horses in China and France and property in the United States.

As stretching the income across an expensive lifestyle became increasingly more difficult in the 1930s, Constance tackled the problem with a sense of humor and that whimsical approach, just as she did with most challenges. For example, she told her diary on April 7, 1932, "I only lost 400 francs, which is almost like winning." Twenty years later, she told Caresse Crosby: "I owe the hotel 2 million francs, & see no way of paying. I give them 100,000 now & then, but it doesn't help. It's like the Red Queen running as fast as she can to stay in the same place." In the back of her mind she was worried: Even Daisy Fellowes had fallen on hard times; she had been forced to sell her jewelry and go to work.[11]

As HG noted, Constance had been given "an extremely informal education," most of it "in tow of her wealthy and fitful mother; the father had been taken round the world for a time and then 'parked.'"[12] Nonetheless, Constance's mother had exerted little influence on her daughter's education. It was, rather, managed by committee; the attentions of many relatives, including her Aunt Isa (Coolidge) Councilman, were focused on young Constance for decades. It was they who pulled out all the stops to get her into Dobbs, the present-day Masters School at Dobbs Ferry, New York. When Dobbs opened in 1877, its founder, Eliza Masters, proclaimed that it wouldn't be a typical "finishing school." Instead, she planned to instill in her girls "the need to live useful, orderly lives, based on truthfulness, integrity, and responsibility." Dobbs's motto was taken from the Bible: "Whatsoever thy hand findeth to do, do it with thy might." This education, including its reliance on the Bible, would have a lifelong effect on Constance. She often repeated the Bible verses she had learned as a girl and she often turned to the Bible—and the Ouija board—for guidance before a horse race.

David Coolidge wrote several letters imploring the Masters sisters to accept his daughter. One letter explained the urgency, although it is unknown how much it advanced his daughter's case. "I sincerely hope you can find a place in your school for my daughter next fall [1905], as my house will then be broken up which makes it necessary that she should go somewhere."[13] The letters from her previous school also hinted at a problem. "When she came to us," one educator wrote, "she found the school work and discipline rather difficult, as she had had most irregular training at home." Another letter said she was "socially the sort of girl you want in your school." Constance stayed with the Masters sisters for three years. Incredibly, her highest grades were in spelling, banking, and the Bible. Her lowest were in algebra, order, and control.

Constance's education was advanced by the many extraordinary things she was exposed to as a member of a prestigious Boston family. For example, during a 1905 summer vacation with her mother in Dublin, New Hampshire, a popular haven for New England's rich and famous, she met Samuel Clemens, who was summering there following his wife's death. In her 1905 diary, Constance, aged thirteen, reported her July 15 meeting with Mark Twain, as she called him: "I managed to say that I had read all his books, which was a story, & liked them all very much, which was another."[14] She also noted: "He is very deaf & you have to almost knock heads to speak to him." It was the first of a great many encounters she would have with authors across the length of her life. Tucked into her 1905 diary is the small white calling card Mark Twain autographed for Constance that day. Her chaperone, Miss Stauffer, or Miss S., as Constance called her, was not Constance's idea of good company. She was "the most uninteresting & stupid person to talk to & be in any way connected with that I have ever had the misfortune to meet with in my life," Constance told her diary. That having been said, she checked herself. "Yet, poor thing, what am I to criticize her? Have I failed many times in my arithmetic test? Yes. Have not I desended a class lower in gegoraphy and French? Yes. Then wherefore talk. First get 100 in your arithmetic test & assende classes higher in your French & gegoraphy. Then may you talk & critisize poor Miss Stauffer, & in your talking do good." These self-reproaching lectures became a standard part of Constance's behavior her entire life.

Constance had a great many advantages in her early life, to be sure, but they were offset by a great many disadvantages. Indeed, she suffered more than her share of tragedy. One of her most profound misfortunes was to be abandoned by her mother when she was a young girl, perhaps only eight years old. Details are still sketchy, but it appears that Harriet Coolidge had an extramarital love affair and a baby, which precipitated her departure and exile from her family.[15] Fortunately for Constance, the extended family rallied around her and helped her father, who never remarried, raise his daughter. Of all of the relatives, it was David's mother who won Constance's heart. Her fondness for and loyalty to her Granny is demonstrated in hundreds of long, affectionate, and documentary letters to her "dearest most beautiful love."[16]

By Christmas 1903, the eleven-year-old Constance was receiving what must have been disturbing letters from her mother, whom she now rarely saw. Living in Bryn Mawr, Pennsylvania, the wife of one Isaac Norris, and mother of a baby, Mary (Norris)—born in 1902—Harriet missed her firstborn. With every letter, she begged her daughter to remember her. There was an undercurrent of urgency in her letters. "Darling, I want you to promise me that you will love me always just as you used to and that you will never never forget me. My sweetest and my darling Constance. God bless and take care of you is the prayer of your ever loving faithful Mother." Some thirty-five years later, Constance asked her diary: "Oh why could [father] not have taken [mother] back. It was like Ray and me all over again, only Ray had less reason, as I had no child."

During her vacation in Dublin in 1905, Constance filled her days pleasantly with buggy riding, swimming, rowing, tennis, visiting, going to the library, reading, and shopping. Yet, two things gnawed at her. The first was an unspecified "feeling—a great longing and yearning for something." Throughout her long life, Constance remained attuned to those inner feelings and voices. The world of the human spirit and soul was never very far from her thoughts. The other thing gnawing at her was much more tangible. Constance's mind was often on the boys and the impression she was making on them. She had a good sense of humor about it. As she told her diary:

Sunday, July 16: (At church). You may think that I am getting very religious all of a sudden, but I am sure you must know that it is the array of boys in the front row & not the minister which attracts me. Every body in church was gasing at me & I didn't know which way to look.

July 17: (Driving the pony cart around the lake) Because I looked nice, of course, we did not meet a single solitary person. That's always the way. I have noticed it particularly when I look awfull & have an ugly dress on, why the way is swarming with people. (Later, after changing her clothes) I noticed that when I left the store [a boy] leaned way out of the door & watched me till I had almost disappeared. I declare, that skirt works wonders with me. I wish I could wear it always. I would give $5 to know who that boy is.

Very soon thereafter, the fun and games came to a halt. On August 19, 1905, while still on that rare vacation with her mother, Constance's life changed profoundly and permanently. The gentle, shy, rich, charming, and beautiful Harriet Sears Crowninshield Norris, thirty-four, suddenly died, a victim of Bright's disease, diabetes, and peritonitis. Three days later, Constance, barely a teenager, wrote in her diary:

My mother, my only complete friend, comfotor & protector, the one to whom I could always tell my secrets & sorrows & be sure of love & sympathy, my mother is dead. It has all happened so suddenly. I, who am selfish, need her now more than anything. Oh, Lord, why could I not have lived with her all the time she was alive, & now just when we are united again she is torn away to go to a place where I can never see her, or hear her sweet voice again until I too die and go to join her.

After the dust settled, Granny invited Constance to live with her and promised to try to make her happy. Nearly three decades later, the forty-three-year-old Constance entered an item into her diary that may have had its roots in her mother's early death and also served as her life-long mantra: "You must never let anything get you. Get above it and realize that you are the stronger." She later told her diary that her mind ruled her. "I consider the mind superior & master of the emotions. It must not be the other way round. That leads to chaos." Several years later, she reminded herself to keep all important things, including pain, buried in the garden, among the roses.

Constance would share her trials and joys, her adventures and observations with her surrogate mother. Indeed, Constance wrote Granny Coolidge—the former Isabella Shurtleff—more letters than she wrote anyone else, including her husbands and her father.[17] Granny was not only Constance's sounding board but also the center of her emotional universe. She alone earned Constance's complete and unconditional love. When she left for the Far East in 1917, Constance promised Granny that she would try to write every Sunday, rain or shine. She came close to keeping her promise. Whether it was a book report or a report on the servants, a catalogue of the things she had just purchased, the places she had just visited, or the people she had just met, Connie poured it out in long, loving, candid, and humorous letters. Often her letters reflected her philosophy of life. For example, when Granny was sick, Constance once wrote, "I think we ought to have the privilege of having life & using it as we do electric light—of having it at its full strength & brilliance for as long as we like, & then of turning it off ourselves." Like Moura, Constance had a keen eye, an excellent memory, and a rare ability to tell her stories. Still, she probably couldn't have dreamed where her life would take her.

On January 25, 1910, some three weeks after her eighteenth birthday, the daring ingenue with the *beauté du diable,* as people described her drop-dead good looks, exchanged vows in Paris with Ray Atherton. After graduating from Harvard in 1905, Atherton went into banking for a couple of years and then decided to study architecture at the École des Beaux-Arts in Paris, hence his nickname, "the beau of the Beaux Arts." Constance was sent abroad soon after she graduated from Dobbs; it was in Paris, where she was under the wing of her Aunt Elsie, that she met Atherton. They began seeing each other on the sly in the autumn of 1908. Nine years older than Constance, Ray was an aristocratic, charming, and handsome young man from Brookline, Massachussetts, a stone's throw from Boston. Although Constance's reason for marrying Ray is not known, it would appear, judging from things she wrote in her diary decades later, that she was genuinely in love with him, at least in the beginning. In the 1930s, she wrote, "I don't suppose I have ever loved anyone but Ray all my life" and "I will never never forget him." Atherton was absolutely smitten with Constance. During one separation very early in their marriage, he closed his letter to her with: "Take one long look in the mirror at the most beautiful & wholly adorable woman I have ever imagined & remember me." Constance's prospects for an exciting life were better in Paris than in Boston, where, like so many of her contemporaries, she felt suffocated by conventional Brahmin values and life. Cousin Charlie once told Constance that she was "not to be judged by Boston morals, but a flower to be understood." Whether she liked it or not, those hard-nosed values, along with the Bible lessons from Dobbs, were deeply imprinted on her brain.

There was genuine affection between the newlyweds, but also a basic incompatibility that would intensify over the years. In essence, Atherton was a nose-to-the-grindstone guy; Constance was a free spirit, an adventurer. There also appeared to be a sexual disconnect of some kind. Constance once told her diary that if her husband had been "normal," they might have lived happily ever after.[18] There were also early signs of trouble, though not of Ray's doing. Constance began receiving love letters from other men only two years after her wedding. One young student from the University of Chicago wrote in 1915: "Tell me that you were not playing, that along with your love for your husband you had some feeling for me, even as I have a <u>great</u> feeling for you." This pattern would continue for the next three decades.

Six years into the marriage, Atherton switched careers again, this time to diplomatic service. He had been working in Chicago when, in August 1917, he received the post of third secretary to the American embassy in Tokyo. In late November 1917, on the eve of her twenty-sixth birthday, Constance stepped aboard the *Empress of Russia* for the long trip to Tokyo, where she would join her husband in his new role with the Foreign Service. As she did wherever she went, Constance spent a good deal of time talking to the males on board—everyone from her Chinese steward to the captain. At the meals, dividing her time between the army and the navy, she "felt rather grand sitting in the center of so many uniforms." Still, Constance had little competition for attention since most of the other women on the ship were missionaries. Evidently, these women saw something in Constance that worried them, for every morning, stationed just under her window, they serenaded her with "Nearer My God to Thee." Once she had settled in, Constance wrote to her grandmother from Tokyo saying that "this life is interesting & I love it & of course the other way we were just drifting drifting & now it is a real occupation & a work & and it has made all the difference to Ray."[19]

Constance met many people in Japan and China, many during official visits, and many more who came through as tourists. "We are always entertaining perfect strangers, but I rather like it," she told Granny. The entertaining and socializing were part of Constance's duty as a secretary's wife—an enormous amount of work, sometimes tiresome and boring. The get-togethers could be stimulating, even exciting, however, and often they paid high dividends. For example, in 1920, an Admiral Gleaver invited the Athertons and Dick Crane, the new U.S. minister, to join him on his yacht for a trip through the South Seas. "Won't it be wonderful," Constance wrote to Granny. "It will take about six weeks, I suppose, & we start from Manila. I am so glad I gave him those cocktails this summer!" On another occasion, when an old friend, Nancy Field, came through Japan to avoid the notoriety of a lawsuit, Constance volunteered to be her guide. Constance, Field, and a third companion escaped on a three-day horse trip to Shoji Lake, at the foot of Mount Fuji.[20]

Constance thrived in the Far East; indeed, she blossomed. She wrote to Granny about her first spring and the huge crowds that were making pilgrimages to see the cherry blossoms:

Showers of them like handfuls of confetti flutter by the window & lie like a thin covering of snow. People come in great crowds from the country with their lunch in little bundles to spend the day under the trees—looking at them and admiring them. The view from my window is really lovely now but then, I always hated people who wrote letters describing the view from their window so I won't, except to say that it's a mass of green—all shades—everywhere, with nightingales singing in the branches all the time, especially in the early morning. It is a regular concert. I know you would love it.[21]

From this postcard setting, Constance also reported on the grim march of events around the globe, including the horrors following the revolution in Russia, which she learned from U.S. attachés who were passing through Japan. That same year, Constance was asked to translate the French minister's report on the Russian situation. "As no one speaks French as much as we do in the Embassy & as Ray was very busy, they gave it to me to do. There is nothing I do not know about Russia now." At one point, the American ambassador, Roland Morris, arranged to send Constance to Vladivostok on an official assignment to serve as matron of a hospital, of all things; but much to her disappointment, the plan fell though. "I did so want to do something before the war ended, but I suppose we cannot all be heroes."

In January 1920, when she left New York to join Atherton, who had gone on to his new post at the American legation in Pekin, Constance was wretched. "I wish I wasn't married at all," she wrote to Granny. "But you see, I am going back & that is the main thing. Perhaps when I get there I will forget a little & life there will be interesting." She was told that she wouldn't be in China for more than eight months. "I am always dreaming about trains & boats & don't know whether it's because I have been or am going to be on them," she told Granny. As it happened, Constance found life fascinating. She lived in China for nearly three years, long after Ray had gone to his next assignment. There, she would fall in love three times, establish herself as a favorite diplomatic wife, a fearless adventurer, and a horsewoman of distinction.

In suppressed pages of the *Postscript,* HG wrote: "She had gone as a very young wife to Pekin and her interest in horses began with racing

ponies there. Various men had fallen in love with her, and her husband
had fallen out of love with her, and one storming lover had pursued her
to America from Pekin and shot himself when she had refused to
marry him after her divorce."[22] Despite her initial reluctance about going to China, Constance soon became enchanted with the country and
found it even more extraordinary than Japan. In her first letter from
Pekin, she described her new surroundings to Granny:

> Everytime you go out it is an adventure for the streets are so fascinating
> with hens & camels & donkeys & thousands of coolies & rickshaws in a
> hopeless confusion. The tiles on the Emperor's Palace are all yellow &
> shine & glitter in the sun like gold. The Temple of Heaven has blue—
> deep blue—tiles & oh the articeture of it is so beautiful. There's no com-
> parison between this & Tokyo.

In another early letter from China, Constance painted a vivid picture of
a day trip she took by pony to Tongshang. The country outside the
West gate looked very much like Egypt, she wrote, with "brown plains,
mud walls, misty purple hills in the background. Strings of camels passing one slowly with their riders like bundles of old rags asleep on their
backs." Her group bathed in the marble baths at the hot springs of
Tongshang and then dined on a decidedly Western meal of Irish stew,
salad, and dessert. Another time she and Myron Hofer, an undersecretary at the Pekin consulate, rode on horseback to the home of Alexander Kirk, another secretary. Inside, great long rooms opened onto a terrace, "with the whole of Pekin stretched beneath one." Huge pots of
lotus framed the view like a painting. It was "more like a stage than a
house, but wonderfully beautiful at night in the court yard overlooking
thro rooms to the great moon & large fire flys that float like diamonds
thro the warm soft air. Granny dearest, this must bore you to death.
Forgive me."

Constance also enjoyed adventures, and all the better if they posed
risks. In June 1920, she got her wish. A "rather rough diamond" of a pilot named Captain MacKenzie invited her to take a spin in his two-

seater, which Constance thought looked like a mosquito. After repeated efforts to get rolling because the engine kept cutting out, the plane, "with a sudden crash bang & a deafening rush & roar [began] bounding over the ground & then gently, up up with the wind tearing thro your hair & your eyes blinded. Well, I must say I was rather scared. You are so absolutely in the lap of the Gods."

Sensing they were up to the challenge, MacKenzie put his plane and passenger to the test with a series of loop-the-loops. "You are literally going head first straight to the ground," she wrote Granny. "It was awful. The engine would stop dead & you'd fall about 60 miles an hour, then suddenly he would turn it on again & you'd soar up again then stop & drop like an elevator, then up again a little." The windshield broke, "so I nearly suffocated at one time with the wind. It took all the breath out of your body. I had to crouch down & cover my face in my hands." Despite the sheer horror, Constance said she wouldn't have missed it for anything. To top off that day, she and a group of twenty friends rode out to the racecourse—an hour's trip—had a picnic, and then rode back by moonlight over the plains. Although that was an exceptional day, life had become extremely busy. Consider a typical day: "Got up at 5:30, dressed & rode to the race course, saw the ponies run, rode back on horseback, had eight people to lunch, went to a YWCA meeting, played four sets of tennis, dined out, went to a club dance & stayed til half past three. It is easy to get into a rush here & it is very difficult to stop."

In another letter, Constance reported the "auspicious" fortune she was told in June 1920. "In everything without your seeking you have good fortune. You receive wealth in unexpected ways—it does not come as the result of planning or thought on your part." She was lucky indeed in her physical surroundings. Her never-ending official but unpaid duties were considerably outweighed by her standard of living. After visiting her in Pekin in 1920, David Coolidge reported back to Granny that Constance and Ray had a Chinese maid who spoke perfect French; "Boy No. 1"; two second men; two chambermen; two cooks "who produce the most wonderful food"; two chauffeurs; a seven-seater Hudson; a private rickshaw and livery; two gardeners and a "formal garden continually filled with flowering plants as the old ones fade, house full of large dahlias, oleanders and pruepanettes in large pots placed in appropriate places, cut flowers all over the house, arranged every morning"; two coolies to run errands; and "God knows how many laundry people." In the stable were five ponies, two for Ray's polo playing, one for Constance to ride, and two that were being trained to race. David, who was invited to all the consular parties during his visit, was enormously proud of his daughter. He told his mother that Constance entertained beautifully and that she was a great favorite in the diplomatic community. "One lady told me that everybody was in love with her & that she was the only woman here that never had a word said against her. If she gets into trouble she seems to get out of it all right."

In spite of her privileged life, by early 1921, Constance had become jaded. She was sick of her role as a diplomatic wife, sick of the visitors, of rushing from one event to another, of planning events, of seeing the same people all the time, and of having the same conversations. She told Granny that she wondered why she was doing it, and, then, without any qualms, admitted:

> I rather wish I loved someone very much & lived in a tiny house in the country & had a garden & read a great deal & had an old horse that took me to the village once a week to the drugstore—"the world forgetting, by the world forgot." If one could only be left alone in [the world] for a while. I have gone out to dinners almost every night for two years & met I suppose heaps of so called distinguished people & what has it given me—just a terrible longing to get away from them all—to be alone & come up for air. None of these people have given me anything very much. Some have given me love, of course, which is very beautiful, but more or less useless if you're already married.

This may have been the turning point in her life, or, perhaps, in her attitude toward duty and marriage. Constance told her Granny that she craved to go away to the Mongolian desert and ride all day and sleep under the stars and have peace and quiet with "a feeling of God somewhere, which would be alright, because you wouldn't have to talk to him, or ask him silly questions of how he liked the Orient, or if he thought Japan would really ever give up Manchuria, or if he took cream or lemon in his tea. No, I'm really getting rather fond of God in a way. He's the only person in life who never bothers one. There, I feel better now my darling Granny." Nevertheless, in March, Constance agreed to be patroness of the American Bachelors Ball.

As it happened, horseracing would snap Constance out of her blues that spring, give her a new lease on life. She had seen her stable humming by the previous October, "not that we any of us know anything about it really, but everyone takes it very seriously & it is loads of fun," she wrote Granny. She co-owned the stable, which was near the racetrack, some eight miles from the city gate, with a Mr. Bushnell; thus the name, "The A & B Stable."[23] Little did she know when she started the enterprise that she would achieve great success. With the help of two friends, Clarence Chabannes and Julian Brown, Constance whipped her ponies into shape, hired a jockey, and won number-one ranking for her stable, the prize being $585. It was the first time in fifteen years that a purely American stable had won in Pekin. "Oh it has been too wonderful. The fact that I did it all alone more or less made it more exciting & perhaps made people more enthusiastic. When I go out to dinners now people drink my health to the best trainer in China!!" When her second pony, Petrushka, won, people carried her down to the gate. "Everyone cheering & screaming, cameras clicking—oh it was too delerious."

Constance would be nearly delirious a second time that month, but not from happiness. Instead of foregoing her daily ride after some guests had stayed too long at lunch, she saddled up and started out at 5:00 P.M.—much too late in the day, especially across fields that were full of sunken wells. "There are no particular roads out here," she wrote to her grandmother. Unaccompanied, as usual, Constance set out for the distant mountains that she didn't know, arrived in the foothills just as the sun set, and found the sight beautiful, "absolutely wild, with traces of an old wall." In pitch darkness, and having no idea what direction to take to get home, she and her horse plodded on, now with the intention of riding all night if necessary to get home. After several hours and a tumble into a hole, they came to a steep embankment. Her horse wanted to go down it, so she closed her eyes and let him go. At the bottom, they found themselves on a road, then half an hour later, at 11:00 P.M., Constance heard a Chinese voice saying

> "Ly la ly la" (she's coming) & then the horse turned to the left & Granny, it was my own house. . . . Julian had just telephoned . . . to have the mounted detachment of the Marines come out. Chabannes had left with three other men with lanterns & a pistol—other mafoos had taken other ponies & gone out in all directions! Everyone was perfectly hysterical. Well, anyhow, my darling Granny, except for being altogether knocked out for two days after, nothing happened. But Julian & Chabannes will never let me ride alone again. They are going to dismiss the mafoo if he isn't always with me & it will be very dull I'm afraid.

Eleven days later, Constance took off on a seven-day riding trip to Dung Sing, the Eastern tombs of the Emperors. "It certainly will either kill or cure me," she quipped.

At this time, Constance also befriended people connected with commerce in Pekin and Tientsin. Several of them became her soul mates and lovers, among them Frank Fearon, who worked for Arnhold Brothers in Pekin. Fearon, who was thirty-nine, died a year or so after Constance met him, following surgery for cancer of the stomach. She also had a passionate love affair with Clarence (Charles Antoine) Chabannes, a relative of Jules Mazarin, a French cardinal and minister to Louis XIII and Louis XIV. By day, Chabannes worked for the Banque Industrielle de Chine in Pekin, but, as mentioned, he also helped with Constance's stable. Chabannes and Constance shared an interest in horses, to be sure, but they also shared things far more ethereal. Philosophy, love, things of the spirit and the soul dominated their conversations. "I always want to be your amie, amante spirituelle," she wrote to him in the spring of 1921. Sometime later, Chabannes wrote: "Tu es la perle de cette huitre qui est mon coeur." "I will see you soon," Constance responded, "and we will discuss the futility of life together!"

Part of Constance's problem, as she explained to Chabannes, was loneliness. Ray was never at home, and when he was, he was too tired to converse with her. Moreover, she made him nervous. Although her escapade with Chabannes soothed her loneliness for several months, Constance eventually cut him off. His response in July 1921: "I cannot admit that your soul of last winter is still in the same place. Goodbye Dear Constance. Have a splendid time and forget everything but yourself." Soon thereafter, Chabannes fell while racing a horse named Avalanche and never regained consciousness. He died in October 1921, only two months after Fearon. Constance was distraught over Chabannes's death. One of the last things she said to him was, "I care for you in some ways more than anyone I have ever known."

In March 1922, Ray received the telegram telling him that he was being transferred to the State Department in Washington. He was enormously relieved. The Far East had been grueling, the four years grinding hard work. Constance was devastated by the news. "Oh Granny, I am so glad & so sorry, & long to see you most of all, yet at the same time cannot bear to think that I am not going to live in China any more." Later, she had to do some fast talking to explain why she wasn't coming home with Ray. Granny must have had her hunches after reading Constance's letters filled with lame excuses.

Constance "remained behind" in Pekin, as a New York Times item put it, "on the plea that her horses needed her attention." She explained to her Granny: "Oh I do, I love it here. I shall never like anything so well. I would like to live here a whole year more—or even always. Ray didn't really like it like I did. The climate got him in the end. He had to go. But the climate suits me. I have never been better." The meteorological climate probably had very little to do with their separation and split. Nor did Atherton begrudge his wife's enthusiasm for racing ponies; he had several polo ponies of his own. It was more likely Constance's penchant for boyfriends that pushed Ray to sue for divorce. Although she was hurt and humiliated at the time, Constance later credited her first husband for giving her a new life. She told her diary in 1932: "If Ray had not cast me off and left me as he did, I would never have been the person I am now. He is the cause that enabled me to develop and grow and understand."

In addition to the ponies and her house, Constance also loved Eric Brenan, a young man with the British foreign office who in a sense took the place of Chabannes at her stable and in her heart. Neither of them was careful about hiding the liaison. Telegrams and letters flew between Constance and Brenan, Pekin and Tientsin, about their plans. Constance contemplated a life with Brenan in a cottage near the racecourse, or in Shanghai, where he was to be posted—not a life with Ray in Washington. If she didn't join him, Brenan said, he would be "finished. But you will have nothing to blame yourself for. You have given me already more happiness than any man has a right to expect, & if I died to-morrow, I would still have had more from life than most men."

Like other young lovers, they took many ill-advised risks, one of them nearly fatal during "the most exciting war here that you could ever imagine," as Constance wrote to her grandmother, "and I was right in the middle of it." That happened in May 1922, when the foreign office ordered Brenan to the battlefront to collect intelligence on the campaigns of two warlords, and Constance insisted on going with him. Despite all of the early warning signs near the train station at Chang tsien tien (today called Changxindianzhen)—the arrival of more than 1,000 soldiers and the shrapnel bursting in the air—Constance wanted to get closer to the action, so she and Brenan rode past the railway station and up into the hills. Minutes later, the station was bombed and several people were killed. "So strict orders have been given that no one is to go to the front," she wrote to her grandmother. "I am so glad I managed to go before this happened." A few days later—and without authorization—she returned to her house in the country, and soon realized that the war was still on; she heard volleys of gunfire and witnessed hundreds of retreating troops of both sides marching past her house. When an American marine appeared at her door with orders to bring her back, she learned that she was the only foreigner out there. "Well, darling Granny, I was thus dragged back. I had 12 invitations for the next day!"

The media heard about Constance's adventure. Ellery Sedgwick, editor of the *Atlantic Monthly*, asked Constance to write an article about it. A Chicago newspaper ran a sensational headline: "Pretty Mrs. Atherton Weeping at Gates of Pekin." From Kyoto, en route to Washington, D.C., to begin his next posting, Atherton, who thought his wife was safe within the city walls the whole time, wrote to Constance that he was "at ease" to know that she was at the legation. Atherton was told that he would be in Washington for a year or longer. He wasn't sure when Constance would join him, and in his heart of hearts he probably knew she wouldn't.

Shortly after Atherton left, and with Brenan as trainer, Constance pulled off a stunning victory for her stable at the May races. In addition to the usual duties and distractions, some of Constance's attention was now focused on new friends, Katherine and Herman Rogers, who were spending a lot of time in Pekin and at the beach in Peitaiho.[24] "I don't know who they are," Constance wrote to Granny, "but they are very good looking & attractive." The newlyweds seemed to be vaguely traveling around the world, and because they liked Pekin so much they took a house there. The friendship between the Rogerses and Constance would continue throughout the 1920s and 1930s, and through the chaos surrounding the romance and marriage of their mutual friends, Wallis Simpson and Edward "David" Windsor.[25]

In August 1922, Constance left her little beach house in Peitaiho for the last time. "I have had my last swim in [this] sea & wonder what the next sea will be that I shall swim in," she wrote to Granny. Constance stayed on in China until the end of November 1922 and told her family that she couldn't get tickets before then; meanwhile, Brenan thrashed over his career options and Constance's inability to come to a decision about him. He resigned from the foreign office in September 1922, became a cowboy in Arizona, and then took a series of backbreaking jobs while he waited for Constance to decide his fate. The following autumn he told her that he was beginning to think she was "incapable of feeling anything serious, or of realising how much you hurt others."

Steaming for home on the SS *President Cleveland* on December 12, 1922, Constance dined on lobster à la Newburg, an assortment of vegetables, and Chinese preserved Chow-Chow with café noir. She may have been going home, but she was also sailing into the unknown yet again. A decade later, after reading *Peking Picnic,* Constance reflected in her diary that the book "brought back pictures with a rush, & a memory & longing not of people but for Pekin itself." She reviewed the high and low points of her years and "the camels, the noise of the water carts, & the feeling of it, the awareness & wiseness & beauty of it all. How happy I was—& sure. But what a fool at the end."

Instead of settling down with her husband in Washington or with her beloved Granny and father in Boston, Constance moved into the Ritz-Carlton Hotel in New York, and was instantly swept up in the social scene. But after China, even Manhattan seemed colorless. Constance's letters to Granny were growing shorter and shorter, less and less doting, less and less soulful and introspective. In August 1923, Constance returned to Paris, her first love, and, among other things, hired Cousin Carl deGersdorff to represent her in the upcoming divorce proceedings. Atherton was publicly humiliated by his wife's liaisons, but he was not permanently damaged. After he and Constance were divorced, in April 1924, he married another Boston girl, had two children, and pulled off a brilliant diplomatic career, as a fortune teller had said he would.[26]

Constance was back in the City of Light in August 1923; not surprisingly, she began life anew and accumulated friends and lovers as she had done in the Far East. This time, she drew from different wells: the commercial and the American expatriate colony. Within days, she met Felix Doubleday; they began a whirlwind romance that led to a quick engagement—this while Eric Brenan was still twisting in the wind in the United States. Brenan's letters were pitiful. In the last one, dated November 24, 1923, he wrote that if it weren't for his mother, he would kill himself.

It seems impossible to make you feel anything, but in case it may make you think twice before treating some other unhappy man in the same way, I tell you that you have broken my heart & any belief I ever had in human nature. I shall try to forget you altogether, but it will be useless because I still love you.

Felix, too, was head-over-heels in love with Constance. A business-man based in London, who traveled back and forth to the continent, he was intelligent and charming and had "a divine sense of humor," Constance said. He also had a decent income, a good name, and inter-esting friends among the social and cultural elite—Princess Bibesco (Elizabeth Asquith), Elsa Maxwell, Reginald and Daisy Fellowes, and a legion of writers, economists, actors, and painters. Felix never saw the ax falling on him after what he thought were five or six rapturously happy months. Nor could he have known that he would have the sorry distinction of being dumped by Constance more times than anyone else. In July 1938, Felix asked Constance yet again if she would marry him. She told her diary, "He must have asked me 25 times at least now."

Even while she was seeing Felix—and stringing Eric along—Con-stance found another love object in the form of a Boston-Bad-Boy-turned-Paris-Bohemian, Harry Crosby. According to André Magnus, *that* was the love affair of her life, "a beautiful love." Constance held nothing back when she wrote several years later in a condolence letter to Harry's widow, Caresse, after Harry's 1929 suicide: "He gave me more beauty [in a spiritual] way than I ever had in my life or ever will have. I loved him entirely and absolutely on account of that." In 1932, Constance confided to her diary: "It is three years now since he died and always, always I need him. No one can ever take his place."

The affair between Harry and Constance started improbably at a ladies' luncheon. Caresse Crosby later wrote that if she had known it was to be a ladies' event, she might not have gone, in which case she "might not have met Constance or brought her to Harry, or helped pro-pel the chariot of chance."[27] In her autobiography, Caresse explained that Constance was the "C.C.C." in Harry's diary.[28] "Being a Crownin-shield and also a Coolidge and a Peabody she should have been 'typically Bostonian,' but no phrase could suit her less. To this day she has remained one of those rare gems of humanity—a pure, naive individual, and with more charm and humor than is usually allotted to any one darling of the gods."[29] From the moment she saw Constance, Caresse was captivated.[30] Among other things, she was just back from the Far East, still glowing from her adventures in exotic lands. It was there, after all, that she had earned the title "Queen of Pekin," Caresse wrote,

> more for her ability to dazzle than to rule. She had lived in a temple, raced Mongolian ponies, defied convention and was generally an exciting pagan. She was perfection. . . . All that season the Lady of the Golden Horse was tangled in my hair—all through the Paris years she was my most formidable antagonist, but I could not help immensely admiring her. The only weapon worthy of such mortal charm is a more wily brand of the same, and 'may the best woman win,' was my consolation, for try to annex my husband she did.[31]

Truth be told, Harry was responsible for much of the annexing—of women, girls, and an occasional boy. It was his untamed spirit, with all its quirky, ritualistic, and experimental dimensions—and its immense appetite—that drew groupies. Drugs and alcohol, gambling and philandering were Harry's main obsessions and compulsions, but he also lived on risks and tests. Constance once described him as "Light & Honour & Beauty & a little boy who never grew up." For years after he died, she kept a line of verse in her heart to remind her of Harry. As she inscribed those lines in her diary: "You are a burning lamp to me, a flame the wind cannot blow out, & I shall hold you high in my hand against whatever darkness."[32] Constance and Harry would be friends and lovers alternately for six years—almost from the day they met, in late 1923, right up to his tragic and mystifying death by his own hand at the end of 1929.

Crosby wasn't the first young American blueblood to rebel, the first Boston son to turn eccentric and embrace Bohemian Paris, but he certainly was a prime example. His transformation occurred on the battle-field. A month after graduating from St. Mark's in June 1917, Crosby sailed for France, exchanging antics for ambulance duty in the American Field Service. A month later, he was carrying his first casualty at the Somme. Crosby's miraculous safe delivery from the second battle of Verdun on November 22, 1917, after a shell vaporized the ambulance he was in, changed the direction of his life. From then on he would focus his fascination on death by twinning love and death. Thereafter he celebrated every November 22 as his "death-day."

After the war, Crosby came home, attended Harvard, tried banking, and flipped out, unable or unwilling to conform to the standards for Boston's elite. He scandalized his family, first by going on benders, and then by carrying on a love affair with a married woman who was mother of two small children. After Harry threatened to commit suicide if he couldn't marry the woman—Mrs. Polly Peabody—his mother intervened. Henrietta Grew Crosby arranged a job for Harry as a banker, of all things, in the employ of his uncle, J. P. Morgan, in Paris. Soon after Polly obtained her divorce, she and Harry married, on September 9, 1922. On the last day of 1923, he quit his poor impersonation of a banker and reinvented himself as a writer, a trade for which he had real enthusiasm and talent. Four years later, he and his wife, now calling herself Caresse, began what became the influential and avant-garde fine-book operation, Black Sun Press. From the tiny Rue Cardinale on the Left Bank, and to their credit, the Crosbys were the first to publish James Joyce. They also brought out books by Ezra Pound and Marcel Proust, and by their friends Kay Boyle, Hart Crane, D. H. Lawrence, and Archibald MacLeish.

Caresse Crosby, née Mary Phelps "Polly" Jacob, was also an unconventional Bostonian, although she claimed she wasn't a rebel until after she married Harry. In 1913, she tweaked convention by inventing a backless brassiere, fashioned out of handkerchiefs and ribbons. She and her maid produced an inventory of these daring undergarments, obtained a patent, and later sold it and their samples to Warner Brothers Corset Company. It was Harry who renamed her Caresse, but then, he was an inveterate re-namer of things, especially the women he loved.[33]

The Crosbys had been married about a year when Constance, another untamed and adventurous soul, wandered into their lives. She had been in Paris only for a few weeks when they met. At the moment engaged to Doubleday, Constance would very soon fall in love with Harry but marry a French count.

The Coolidge-Crosby love affair was complicated by a host of problems: their engagements and marriages, to be sure, but also drugs, gambling, guilt, and Crosby's unrelenting philandering. The lovers would renounce each other several times over the years, and rejoice madly in each reunion. Constance and Harry began writing to each other soon after they met, but they engaged only in innocent common interests, including horseracing. "I would rather see a good horse race than all the theatres and operas and concerts in the world," Crosby wrote. Their early letters were also literary exchanges: They compared notes on Byron, Debussy, and Swinburne. Harry once asked Constance to read Debussy's poem "La Ceinture Perdue" to him "with that incomparable voice of yours." By October 1923, she was dominating his diary entries:

> A Sunday and a beautiful lost lady. Dressed in red, with a small black hat with a black lace veil which concealed her eyes so that she looked mysterious. She wore a jade pendant and her rings were of jade. Nails hennaed and dark red lips. Chinese. And her voice (I shall never hear voices again) low, very sad, very weary. . . . Chinese. . . . Absorbed the gray melancholy of Autumn . . . I was bewildered and confused and lost in a dream.[34]

Not long after, Harry was telling Constance that he missed her "so dreadfully all the time." And later, "I must see you to-day as I shall be miserable. . . . I loved your voice last night even more than ever before. It means <u>everything</u> to me. I call it a Star-Voice. I should be so proud if you could care enough to give it to me. I should guard it as no Midas ever guarded his gold." And later still, "<u>I am so in love with you Constance. No one else means anything any more</u>."[35]

Harry and Constance had two love affairs: one over parts of 1923 and 1924, the other in 1927 and 1928. The breakups were for the sake of Caresse, who for the first time was threatened by one of Harry's lovers. In the beginning, she gave him a lot of freedom; later, she began having her own affairs. The Crosbys became known for their bathtub parties; indeed, for orgies with and without a tub. Still, Harry was miserable without Constance. During their separation, he often wrote to her begging to see her and promising to control himself.

> You have awakened everything that is beautiful in me Constance. God knows I've been an awful hound most of my life but if I ever had anything inside me that was pure and good you have inspired it. You have taught me that life is glorious. I worship you as God—you are God to me but beside this I do love you most passionately. I want to hold you in my arms and kiss your dear eyes and your adorable mouth and tell you how much I care.

Caresse eventually caved in to Harry's desire to see Constance again. "Perhaps still we could all manage to be friends," she wrote to Constance. "Things seem in an awful mess just now but as you say, you and I have both been through so much, that together we ought to be able to find an answer to this. I am so glad you are so nice." Harry was inundating Constance with poems, filling entire notebooks with them. One, titled "Sunrise," begins, "I have seen the sun rise a red ball of flame above the tents of the Monad shepherds encamped on the Grey face of the Sahara." After describing exquisite rising suns and allusions to Van Gogh, Rimbaud, and Stravinsky, he closed with:

> and I brush them aside with my thoughts / as one brushes aside with one's foot / the leaves in the woods in late Autumn / (How quickly these are forgotten) / that I fearless may turn / to look deep into the celar gold / of your eyes / where I shall see reflected / in the dark tone of your eyes / Twin Suns / That like dark flowers / Open and rise.

Meanwhile, Constance won her count. HG wrote in pages that were suppressed from the *Postscript* that she married Pierre Chapelle de Jumilhac in the United States, which wasn't true, and that she bought a chateau for him near Paris, which was partially true; Jumilhac used money from the sale of Constance's New Hampshire property to buy Écuiry, about seventy-five minutes northeast of Paris. HG went on to say that Jumilhac taught Constance "the life of the turf," that their stable was well run, and that one of their horses almost won the Grand National Steeplechase at Aintree, but fell at one of the last jumps. Jumilhac also initiated Constance to opium smoking. "She had learnt all that and none of it changed her. She was simple and young-minded," HG wrote.[36]

Constance and Pierre exchanged wedding vows in Paris on October 11, 1924. The groom was a charming cad from one of Brittany's oldest families, and one of the few horse owners who made sports' page headlines for both horseracing and jockey-whipping. Husband and wife were a prime example of opposites attracting, their temperaments and most of their interests being poles apart. Still, Constance was strongly attracted to Jumilhac's physicality and even his wildness. Early on, he was a most affectionate lover. As Constance told her diary in 1932: "Latins do know how to excite one, & with Anglo-Saxons it's you who excite them. I like the French way best." And later, in 1938: "The first years with [Pierre] were worth a whole life. I was a slave of love, & he passionately loved me. What more is there?" Jumilhac was also smitten in the early days: "Darling, I am so awfully happy to love you and so wonderfully pleased to give you all my heart without a look behind me or any 'pensée étrangère.'"

Before the marriage, Jumilhac's letters expressed love and desire for Constance, but also discussed big-ticket items: ponies and horses, fancy cars, and real estate. In this sense, they were birds of a feather, protesting poverty while spending like kings on luxuries, bending the system without breaking the law. Having just bought a Hispano-Suiza and looked at some ponies, Jumilhac wrote a letter to Constance in 1924 from the Circle Club in Cannes in which he claimed that he was now "very poor," having just paid many bills and "been undone in all kinds of ways. If we buy [Écuiry] that would make a huge hole in my small budget, and I must be extremely economical." In the end, Pierre would squander much of his wife's inheritance—a good deal of it on drugs and gambling. After he died, Constance told her diary that he was the most attractive man she had ever known. He had "the greatest charm and personality, but [was] quite ruthless, after his own desires." (October 20, 1932)

In the beginning, Constance and Pierre lived a manorial life at their Chateau Écuiry near the village of Septmonts and the bustling town of Soissons. For Constance, the exotic rhythms and interests of the past were left far behind in Pekin, Peitaiho, and Paris. Despite the general banishment of books in this life, Constance had Harry's book next to her bed and often read it. Reading, she wrote to him, "gives one something that nothing else can in life—something that one needs terribly at times. I wonder if it isn't a form of weakness. Pierre never needs anything like that." Jumilhac once told Constance that he didn't read novels because he lived them, but his disapproval was broad. He once asked Constance why she wasted time playing the piano when a good player piano would produce better music than she could "possibly attain." Even thinking, according to Pierre, was a kind of laziness. "One must <u>act</u> every second. Once you begin to think you're lost. Now I must say, I think I like thinking better than acting. Up to now I found this all quite natural, but with Pierre, who is energy personified, it does seem to be a form of laziness."[37] Gambling and horses were central activities for the count and countess. They made headlines for flying between Paris and London twice a week while their horse, Maguelonne, trained for the Grand National.

Constance once told a friend that she was grateful to have a place in Paris because Jumilhac was "easier to live with" there. It wouldn't be long, however, before he became impossible to live with anywhere. After the couple separated, Constance told another old friend, Roland Ellis, that she had been through "worse than Hell" with Pierre for more than two years. "You see he always was very cruel," she wrote, noting that he once broke her eardrum. "But I was weak in love, Roland. I wanted so much to make a success of it."

Much of Jumilhac's violence was brought on by drugs. Constance said that Pierre shot himself up so much that his leg was black with marks. He took drugs "always—and often he was quite wild," Constance told Ellis. Indeed, it was fortunate that he hadn't killed her; twice he had come close. In the beginning, as HG wrote in some suppressed pages of the *Postscript,* Constance smoked opium with Jumilhac, but while it "was nice occasionally," she didn't want to make a habit of it. When Jumilhac saw that she didn't like doing "dope cocaine and morphine," he lost interest in her, and found it in the person of Yvonne de Bray. "We no longer even shared the same room."

Constance admitted to having done "coco," but the effect was so terrible that she would rather die than take it again, as she told Harry. "It makes one's mind go so fast its terrifying." Only one drug was worth taking "& only now & then & not too much & that is in a pipe. There is nothing more delightful or more soothing than that one's thoughts become jewels & one lies without sleeping all night in a kind of glorious contemplation." Constance told Ellis that she was happy only at the racecourse. "I loved the horses more than anything in the world. Pierre never loved me really; he never loved anyone but himself. I think he was attracted [to] me in the usual way at first but that soon wore off."

Constance couldn't get out of the marriage, as she explained to Ellis, because she was penniless. She had married without a contract, had no bank account of her own, and couldn't cash a check without Jumilhac's signature, and he had all the legal rights to her income. Occasionally, he tossed her a few hundred francs. Meanwhile, he bought racehorses, gambled, and made—and lost—a great deal of money, although Constance never saw any of it. She even gave Jumilhac her jewelry—except for the beloved pearl necklace that she had worn during her sitting with John Singer Sargent in 1916—so that he could buy her a wedding ring.

When Constance and Pierre finally went to court over their marriage and belongings, he claimed that she, like her compatriots, was extravagant in her spending, and that he had suffered greatly because of that. Constance made a long and impassioned speech in French, telling the court that when she met Jumilhac, he had only a small apartment on the Avenue Montaigne, four horses, and no income, while she had a nice house on the Quai d'Orsay, a property in America, $100,000 in securities in the bank in addition to her trust income, jewels, and tapestries. "Now I live in a small apartment. I have had to sell my property in America, the $100,000 have gone, my jewels have gone. I have nothing left while [Pierre] has a chateau in the country, 30 race horses, a large property in Maisons-Laffitte. I ask for you to look & compare the situation of us both & decide who has benefited & who has suffered by this marriage." Constance's pièce de résistance: She said that she had always admired Frenchmen, but now she thanked God every day that she was an American.

Moved by her account, the judge told Constance that she must never judge Frenchmen by Pierre's behavior, and that "it was a pity to see actions so low from one who carries so good a name." Pierre had debts of Fr 3 million, and by law, Constance was responsible for half of them. As the settlement was finally arranged, she renounced all claims to the chateau, to their stable at Maisons-Laffitte, and to the horses. She was to pay Pierre Fr 200,000, and she could keep the apartment and be relieved of all debts. "So now I am saddled with debts, everything gone, a very reduced income & nothing nothing to show for it—except a profound disgust for Frenchmen & matrimony," she told Ellis. As for her feeling for Pierre? "If I heard he was dead tomorrow, I should be interested but completely indifferent. I thank God to be rid of him."

But Pierre had other dirty tricks up his sleeve. On the day before a steeplechase with a purse of Fr 1 million, he sold Constance's favorite horse, Maguelonne, winner of the Grand National the year before. "It really nearly killed me," she wrote Ellis. "I would not have sold her for 10 million dollars." As for herself: "I live here in the apartment & wait for the races to begin. Lots of people make love to me but I don't like any of them—not one. In fact, I actually dislike most of them, but I suppose that is one of the penalties of being alone."

On May 15, 1929, the day Constance received the notice that she was divorced from Pierre, she wrote to say adieu and to wish him good luck and happiness. "I am sorry that we did not make a success of things. I did try. Perhaps you did too. But in any case let us end *en beauté*. I forgive you for all the suffering you caused me & I thank you for all the happiness we once had. Au fond tu sais je n'était pas méchante et je t'aimais beaucoup." She later asked Jumilhac if she could keep his name, and, even more amazing, they considered remarrying. Cousin Charlie was livid about the idea of a reunion. "[Jumilhac] has never played the game honorably from love to cards, and he won't begin now." CFA even dusted off his Latin aphorisms. "Do you remember 'Facilis decenses averno'—It is easy to go down to Hell, but very difficult to get up again? You can never change a man who has no good in him." In February 1930, Constance decided that no matter what happened, she would never marry him again. "I hope I never do. But he has always had an influence over me—the facination one has for a brilliant crook."

Throughout this emotional hell, Harry Crosby continued to write reams of letters, poems, and stories. He told Constance over and over again in lines long and short, rhymed and not, and frequently unpunctuated, that he loved her and that she had taught him that life was glorious. He, in turn, wanted to teach her to attack life. She must pay her debts, sell her car and apartment, stop buying designer gowns, stop smoking, and harden her body.

> Attack and if you are beaten counter-attack and if you are beaten re attack And for Christs sake attack don't sit and wait to be attacked If you have to sell some of your pearls sell them And my heavens get rid of those frightful books and come with me and let us precipitate ourselves through stars I say this because I love You Harry

The writings were suffused with metaphors about sun and gold. All Harry's metaphors revolved around the sun. His adoration of the sun was an adoration of many things: nature, light, self, body, and especially sex.[38] Many of Harry's writings in the red leather notebooks were written under the influence of opium. In 1928, as his tender was pulling away to meet the *Berengaria,* which would take him to America, Harry wrote Constance: "You are Star-Goddess and I am Sun-God and everything is reduced to chaste simplicity and strength and nothing can ever hurt us the real us anymore and your Star sleeps in my inmost Sun in irrevocable foreverness. I feel so strange Dear The opium is still at work you should see my eyes—wonderful and they are looking at you." Harry, fixated on signs and symbols and marks of all kinds, especially celestial, told Constance that their private design was the star within the sun. His benediction: "Goodbye Dear I bless you with Sun for all the Beauty and all the Perfectness we are shareing and I love You and we belong to each other For a Sun-Eternity forever & Ever & Ever I Love You Your Harry."

Harry devoted another notebook to original aphorisms—"The world is made by the singer for the dreamer"—and to such proclamations of love as "Nothing exists in comparison with you." On the inside cover of this notebook, inscribed "To Constance His Queen From Harry Her Clown," is a photograph of Harry in his military uniform. Next to the photograph, Constance left a lipstick kiss. She did the same in a small red notebook on the lines, "I Love You and I could repeat these three words until there was no writing paper left in all the world," and in another small notebook of poetry, mostly in French, under Harry's last three words, "I love you."

It isn't known when Constance and Harry had their last real kiss, but their affair ended abruptly when he fatally shot Josephine Rotch Bigelow, then himself, in a borrowed studio in the Hotel des Artistes in New York on December 10, 1929, only three weeks after he, Caresse, and Constance had crossed the Atlantic to spend the holidays in the United States. Josephine, twenty-two, and Harry, thirty-one, were found on a bed, fully clothed, and holding hands. Harry and Josie, the former Miss Rotch who had only six months before become Mrs. Albert Bigelow, met in 1927 in Venice and soon became lovers. Both from Boston's Back Bay, they were wild birds of a feather who delighted in shocking people, taking risks, and testing each other. Despite Harry's stunning last act, Constance later claimed that from her tastes in art and literature to philosophy, her life had been shaped by Harry Crosby. And yet, after those lines of Harry's about belonging to each other for a sun-eternity, Constance wrote a few rather clinical lines of her own: "Harry commited suicide with a girl in [New York]. He wanted to commit suicide with me, but I refused."

Of all of Constance's lovers, HG was most fascinated by Harry Crosby. In suppressed pages of the *Postscript,* HG wrote that in Paris, Constance "had seen a good lot of the world of literary eccentrics, poets and writers, who centered around Joyce, Lawrence and the like. Among them was a queer rich American youngster of considerable poetic gifts, ~~Frank~~ Henry Crosby, who has left a volume or so of poetry and a privately printed diary behind him."[39] HG claimed that when Pierre de Jumilhac left Constance for a woman more skilled in opiates, Crosby devoted himself to her.

> He was already married, but he was as fantastically assured of the exalted righteousness of his whims as Shelley. He brought the wife and the goddess together, but Constance did not become his mistress until one night on the eve of his [1928] departure for America, when she was suffering from some unendurable, humiliating message from [Jumilhac]. She went to Crosby's rooms and took opium with him. After that he thought it would be splendid if she came on the liner with him and they committed suicide together. But when Constance demurred, he forgave her, and went off alone.[40]

After reading Harry's love-letter notebook to Constance and his diaries, HG was "half-disposed to write a book about this queer child of rich America." He confessed that he identified with Harry's demons and his quests for love and vitality: "He was drunk with the craving for an unattainable intensity of life and in love with the idea of suicide, as being, as it were, the sharpest possible point of willful living. I understand something of that. I have thought even of writing about him as a sort of embodiment of the insatiable desire for the splendid life that troubles so many of us."[41]

As soon as she learned that Harry had shot himself and Josie, Constance fired off a telegram to Caresse asking what she could do to help.

She followed that up with a letter, suggesting that Harry "must have been completely out of his mind by drink, & not understood what he was doing."[42] She also blamed Josephine Bigelow for precipitating the deaths. "She would do anything on a dare you know. She put the idea in his head & he could not back out. It was something like that. He never would back out of anything. It would be a point of honour." Harry once told Constance that the main reason he cared for Josephine was because she was so in love with him. Neither of the dead lovers left a note—at least none was made public.

Constance also blamed herself for the tragedy because she thought she could have kept Harry from meeting Josephine in New York. "He told me he wouldn't see her if I would come. I am frantic with grief too," Constance wrote Caresse. "He was everything to me too & gave me more than anyone else ever has." In that letter, Constance attempted to console Caresse with the idea that, despite all, she—Caresse—had been Harry's first love and only love, that she had made his life beautiful and had given him more than any other woman had or could have given him. And then Constance went too far. She said: "No one could or ever did understand him except you, & a little bit me."

Once Constance had gathered her wits—and her tact—she encouraged Caresse to publish Harry's diary and to continue the work that the Crosbys had begun. Constance offered to help. "I am alone & useless in the world. It will be doing a kindness to me."[43] Constance realized another thing: No one could have changed Harry's fate. "His apprenticeship here was finished. He wanted to try the glorious adventure. Can we blame him for that?" And then Constance asked Caresse to return the belt with the golden clasp that she had given Harry and which he had been wearing when he died, and also to return her letters to him. "He gave me all the beauty & spirituality I ever had in my life, & I was not worthy to receive it."

In his will, Harry left Constance $10,000 and several gold and porcelain horses. In her heart, he left a permanent scar. On the evening of December 10, 1932, she told her diary that she had been thinking about Harry all day, and that it had made her profoundly sad.

He lay beside me in this bed & read Omar Kayham. . . . He wrote . . . on the card, "You are the star in my sun for Eternity. Reculer pour mieux avancer." Yes I understand so much now, but what good does it do me? He is gone, gone from me & no one is more terribly alone than I. He led me out & away. He lighted the torch in me, but it was his <u>love</u> I need. Oh waken in me again that divine fire, come back to me again messenger of the sun—my star is dim. I know now what you were to me—pure & chaste & beautiful Love. Why did you leave me, was I so unworthy? You gave me of the Water of Life, but I knew it not. Now that I know, it is gone from me. I salute thee, Love & Life, Harry.

Despite the awkward things Constance said to Caresse, the two women remained friends until Caresse's death in 1970. Along the way, Constance, who was only three months older than Caresse, peppered her friend with advice and aphorisms, just as Harry had done to her. One of the earliest bits of advice came four months after Harry's death. Caresse worried that making love with someone new would harm Harry's memory. Constance didn't see it that way. "Of course you must have someone to love, or at least have a lover. How could you think it would hurt what you felt & feel for Harry. What you had with him, as you wrote me, is indestructible—forever—it is now, always & forever, something so big, so great that nothing can hurt or destroy it." She also, on the other hand, cautioned Caresse to be careful about whom she chose to love. Constance spoke from a great deal of firsthand experience. At the time, she was trying to extricate herself from her impromptu marriage to Eliot Rogers.

I assure you Caresse there is nothing more terrible than having to sleep with someone you aren't in love with. I don't at all mean by that someone who appealls to you physically & who you see now & then, but being as I am now with someone I <u>should</u> love, & who I *can't*, & who makes my flesh creep whenever he comes near me. I never knew anything could be worse. But you see I made the mistake of trying to get comfort for the body & spirit from one person, & oh that can never be done—or hardly ever. You must have one for the one & one for the other, & don't live with either in the same house. Rest & get well darling. The world is full of things to do, & thoughts to have, & beauty to create.

Constance also advised Caresse on how to deal with everything from her daughter, Polleen, to gall stones. Her suggestion for adversity: "I would try & get an inner independence which would be proof against any hurt I could get from outside," and "Have an armour to protect you inside. Be strong & unassailable—a fortress with a shining light in the tower." On maintaining her spirit: "Garde [ton] panache toujours."

Constance would have a steady stream of lovers throughout the 1930s—old men, young men, horsemen, newspapermen, working men, playboys, men of nobility, men of art. They included Russell Page, a landscape architect from Lincoln, England, 1928 and 1932 ("I was crazy about him for a short time & then got over it as suddenly"); Felix Doubleday, 1923–1924 and 1932–1933 ("Felix had a divine sense of humor & liked books & music, but he was a little bit clammy to touch, & had gotten fat at the end"); H. G. Wells, 1935–1937; Lord Beauchamp, 1936 ("I do not see how you can marry a man who is an outcast from society fired out of his own country & retain your own self-respect"—David Coolidge); Philippe Barrès, 1936–1937 (He "only saw me to make love to me").

One of the first men of the new year, 1930, was Eliot Rogers. In the suppressed pages of the *Postscript,* HG described him as "an extremely incidental American whom she had left after a month."[44] Sometime after midnight on Friday, February 21, 1930, the former French countess married the California newspaperman in the First Christian Church of Santa Barbara. The news made the *New York Times* five days later. "The bridegroom is a brother of Cameron Rogers, the author, and a nephew of Charles Fernald, Chicago banker, and Reginald Fernald, local newspaper publisher," the short piece read. Rogers was running the business end of his family's paper, the *Morning Press,* in Santa Barbara. They had met the previous March in Santa Barbara, a haven for the rich, the famous, the hangers-on, and the wannabes. David Coolidge pushed the idea of marriage in the belief, among other things, that the union would bring Constance to the American Riviera, as Santa Barbara was called, and keep her there. He was dead wrong. Within days of the wedding, she was on a train bound for New York, then on a ship that would take her to Paris and her horses. Constance saw Rogers as a refuge from her grief over Harry Crosby's death and her failed marriage with Jumilhac; yet almost as soon as she had married him, she knew it was a colossal mistake, as she later told Caresse. More or less clueless, Rogers wrote optimistically about the future soon after putting his wife on the train: "Constance, just think what must be in store for us. A honeymoon in Paris, Cannes and Venice . . . a house we both like and then just what I don't know but don't worry about the future as I am resolved that we will do that which will make us both happy. I promise to arrange it somehow." They parted with the understanding that he would join her in Paris that spring—as soon as he could get away from the paper. "Every nerve in my body shrieks out to hold you in my arms again my dearest Constance and I am utterly wretched. Was ever a lover in such a desperate situation? Frankly my sweet, at times I call you all kinds of names for leaving me for the raceing season and I am in thorough accord with the man who said that he was fond of shooting horses."[45]

In the early spring, Rogers sailed for Paris and his runaway bride, but after a brief reunion, he knew there was no hope for the marriage. Confused and devastated, he sent his estranged wife a string of begging letters. On May 4, 1930, from the SS *Ile de France,* just pulling away from Le Havre, he wrote these words to Constance, who was with her horses at Tremblay: "I am leaving, perhaps for ever, the one person I love more than life, and it has taken all the courage I could muster. Goodbye my darling. Keep well and happy and remember that I shall always be ready if you should ever need me. I love you love you love you. PS. I shall be strong always after this." On May 26, he told her that if he couldn't have her love, he didn't want anything. "I would rather have you happy without me than unhappy with me." Over and over again, his letters promised eternal love, a declaration that rang in Constance's ears for decades; only the voices changed. Eight years after her third wedding, she told her diary: "Eliot was a poor sweet stopgap for sorrow who I should never have married." In another entry, she wrote: "Ray was very sweet, but he had no personality. Pierre had an extraordinary facination, was ruthless, dashing, goodlooking with no moral sense. And of course Eliot was just nothing at all—a timid rabbitt." Rogers didn't die of a broken heart; he found a wife and lived happily. Toward the end of his life, he devoted much of his time to an industry he had developed from his hobby of raising cymbidium orchids.[46]

As 1931 drew to a close, Constance's "father confessor," as he called himself, again turned into her stern Dutch uncle. "You are in great financial danger," CFA wrote. "I cannot be sure there will be as much as $3,000 a month for the rest of your trust year." He told her that she had to cut down her lifestyle at once until she was living within her means. And she shouldn't even think about selling her pearls, he growled. Aunt Elsie had entrusted them to her, but at Constance's death they were "to go elsewhere. I hold them in trust for you, but for you to sell or even to part with one of them would be correctly termed theft.[47] If you believe in anything, dear Connie, go to the nearest church and on your knees pray for a new sort of wisdom, and pray for the character to live within your income and then to live as an honest lady. I love you dearly even if you have at times some rather human ways."

Constance seems to have had more than her share of watershed years—1905, 1910, 1921; 1932 was another one. Although the year began well enough, it would fill with financial woes and tragedies. Constance was in St. Moritz for the Christmas and New Year holidays, enjoying the company of friends, including Elsa Schiaparelli. From the Palace Hotel, she observed a significant birthday, her fortieth. She was, she reflected, "definitely facing now the so called descending years." On February 12, she told her diary that she had probably never loved anyone but Ray. "But Ray lacked a broad understanding. He is narrow. He could not see that I was not bad underneath, indeed, perhaps almost fine, but perhaps it needed the shock of the seperation with him to de-

Sarah Wells, HG's ever-striving mother, around 1900. UI

Isabel Wells in early 1890s, HG's cousin and a Jezebel, who later became his first wife. C/P

HG at the turn-of-the-century and his life. UI

*Jane and the boys,
Frank (l) and Gip.
UI*

*Amber Reeves and
daughter Annajane—
HG's only daughter.
UI*

Rebecca West and her baby son, Anthony. Yale

Odette Keun on a white charger. UI

Christabel Aberconway with her "personal cat," Antonia. Cecil Beaton, photographer. S

Moura in Petrograd in 1918. JM

Bruce Lockhart's well-used diplomatic passport, issued in late 1917. H/RL

Yendel, the Benckendorff Estate in Estonia, now site of the Jäneda Museum. JM

Kallijärv, the lake house on the Yendel Estate. JM

Moura en famille during HG's visit to Kallijärv in Estonia in 1934, just following his trip to Russia and the 'Moscow Crisis.' JM

Moura in the lead, en vacances in 1935 with HG in Brighton.

John Singer Sargent's original 1916 charcoal drawing of Constance, then Mrs. Ray Atherton. AM

Constance leading a winning pony in China in the early 1920s. MHS

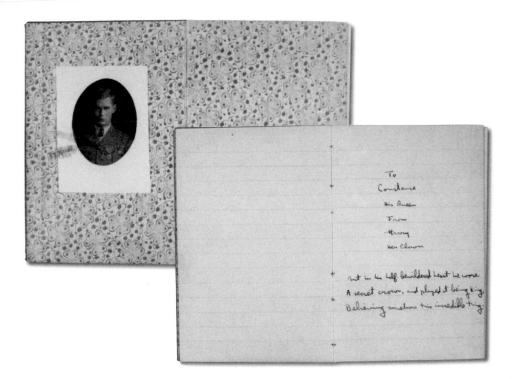

Front inside cover of Harry Crosby's notebook of writings, inspired by and dedicated to Constance. Br

Ecuiry, the Count and Countess Jumilhac's 17th/18th century country estate in France. BC

HG's picshua for Constance Coolidge, depicting 'Fate' as the culprit for keeping them apart. Constance called HG's 'Fate' a 'Horrid little Goblin.' MHS

This is Fate.
He is just juggling with C.C &
HG.

Don't forget my Portrait. y you.

Constance at the races with the Duke and Duchess of Windsor, Wallis Simpson and 'David.' AM

Martha Gellhorn, the girl, and a young suffragette in 1916. LWV

Young French Turk, Bertrand de Jouvenel, Martha's beau—perhaps even husband—in France. HJ

Two works of art: Martha and a Miro. JFK

Martha meeting the admiral. JFK

Martha and Ernest and other observers during the Spanish Civil War. JFK

because through her incurable vagrancy, there will
never be that garden, _our_ garden about _our_ house. It
is the Lover-Shadow of my Persona I want in the garden
of my desires, and that is not Moura now, I realise,
but Jane plus Moura plus fantasy - a being made up
of a dead woman, a stimulating deception and the last
dissolving vestiges of imaginative hope. There is no
right nor reason in my wanting this, but this is the
common dream of the normal active man who still has
work to do.

Nature has not bothered to produce any special consolations for her creatures, after her own vague ends
have been fulfilled by them. There is no last phase
with its distinctive happiness, in a man's life. If
we want that we must make it for ourselves. I can still
entertain imaginative hope. All my imagination did
not die at Moura's feet. But I doubt if there is any
other woman now for me in the world. ~~I have tried.~~
~~Constance and again Martha - my last~~ flounderings
~~towards the wife idea. Even as I write them down I~~
~~stubbornness.~~
~~realise their essential shallowness.~~ Friendship perhaps

Manuscript page from H. G.
Wells in Love, *showing edits
made by Gip Wells.* UI

*HG at the phone in his Hanover Terrace study. One of the phones was
his business line, the other his private line: Wellbeck 6303. Moura's
photo was close at hand, even if she wasn't.* UI

Lou Pidou, HG and Odette's love nest near Grasse in the South of France. INSET: front door of Lou Pidou showing plaque: "This house was built by two lovers, HG Wells, 1926." D-M

Early manuscript page from H. G. Wells in Love, showing the tyranny of HG's handwriting. UI

The always beguiling Moura in Petrograd in 1918. H.

British Embassy (R.) on the former Embassy Row facing the Neva River in Petrograd. Au

Kronversky Prospect, St. Petersburg, as it appears today. In the 1920s it was Gorky's commune for homeless writers and artists, and where HG and Moura had their first tryst in 1920. Au

Photo of Constance Coolidge in the 1920s, found in Harry Crosby's wallet after he committed suicide in December of 1929. SIU

Mrs. Hemingway striking a dramatic pose at the Finca. JFK.

HG's pocket date books, from 1903 to 1946. UI

velop me & make me so." A few days later, she told her diary that she was tired of "dull dull men. They are always nice so it is so hard to get rid of them. Oh really why go out & be bored to death. I had rather be alone & read. . . . I will not sacrifice myself to these dull senseless people." By the nineteenth, she was analyzing herself as HG had often analyzed himself: "I am too kind, that's the trouble. I feel sorry for them, & then suddenly I am involved in an intimate friendship, telephone calls every day, & flowers. Naturally, but I shan't do it any more. I will get out of it."

Constance continued to have money problems. Her allowance was to drop Fr 10,000 indefinitely. Several horseracing people who owed her money couldn't pay her, and one of Pierre's lawyers told her that she would have to pay a huge sum of interest on a loan Pierre had taken out. "I <u>can't</u> pay. Everything may be seized. Oh was ever anyone so persecuted as I have been all my life over money?" By April, Constance was in a funk: bored with the people she associated with, just as she had been in the Far East.

> There is not one who has a spark which lights anything in me. My books save my life & what little mind I have. If only Harry were here. He lit a torch without even knowing himself where it led. . . . It comforted me, & inspired me, & showed me a way & now I have lost it again & I am unhappy in my soul, & long to be shown that way again but all these people around me are dead, dead. There is no light from within. The stars are indeed now suffocated inside.

Constance realized that she was leading two lives—an inner private life and an outer social life—and that despite the energy she put into the latter, she preferred the former. "What I do in the daytime, that is automatic. My real world and my real life begin when I open these books, and yet I am all alone in it and I know nothing." And then she did what she had so often done: She sorted through the men in her life. She had been playing these ranking games ever since Sunday school in New Hampshire. On May 4, 1932, she told her diary: "First of all Ray, then Chabannes and Frank Fearon, Harry next to Ray, and Pierre has no place at all, or a very small one, and Eliot just none at all. 'So shines the sun on a distant field.' Ainsi soit il." Later that year, after she had hurt Crownie's feelings, she chastised herself, just as she had done in Dublin after cutting down Miss S.: "True devotion & love no matter who it comes from should be respected & reverenced. It is terrible that of the men who have given me that—Ray, Brenan, Harry, Crowny—I have pushed them all away, & mortally hurt them all. It is Harry I miss the most, for he gave me the most—of the spirit."

At the racetrack on October 18, 1932, Constance learned that Jumilhac had died earlier in the day; unbeknownst to her, he had been ill for some time. The news had a shattering effect on her. She acknowledged that her love for him had been different, "not mental—or spiritual—like the others." After seeing his lifeless body at the hospital, she wrote that he was "so thin, so terrible to see. . . . his hair unbrushed, & not shaved. Pierre who was so soigné'd. I prayed beside him, to be forgiven for not having helped him more. I bought him some roses & patted his hand, to say all was well now, & all forgiven. Pierre dear—all finished—God forgive him. Rest now in peace." Constance pasted a half dozen newspaper obituaries for her ex-husband into her diary. In one of them, Jumilhac was described as "the husband of Constance Coolidge of Boston." His other accomplishments: He was a Knight of the Legion of Honor and a recipient of the Croix de Guerre. A "turfman," he was the owner of Maguelonne, winner of the 1928 Grand Steeplechase, one of the biggest turf events on the continent. Constance told her diary that Jumilhac had loved her for a few years, and then followed his destiny. "I am glad I met him, that we loved & married. I would do it all again." At the funeral, she carried a telegram he had once sent her—"VERY LONELY HERE WITHOUT MY REASON IN LIFE." In her diary she wrote: "I am sorry it ended like that. At one time he was a Grand Seigneur, & I was proud of him."[48]

In a few months, Cousin Charlie was once again telling Constance about her financial problems: On February 4, 1933, he wrote that he was terribly sorry about her remittance, and that all hands were waiting to see whether FDR was going to stick to his gold standard. "My heart is heavy as I write this. Your troubles are acute I know but here literally millions are just ruined." Four months later, he wrote about the decreasing value of the dollar compared to the franc. In six months, perhaps, her dividends should be back to where they were five years ago. Toward the end of July CFA told Constance that he was delighted to hear that she had been able to buy a new car and hoped he could send more dividends to help finance it:

> but dear lady please don't wake up some day to find that you just can't pay enough of the bills to get along. You are still young, much of life is before you. You have all the charm and beauty that men and women crave. You have brains and are gathering the wisdom of the owl or the serpent. Just now you are happy enough and have occupations that entertain you. . . . but please permit an affectionate cousin to say that sometimes he wonders what fate lies in store for you. I can hear your reply: "Cousin Charlie, I share your doubt and your interest, but I am happy and must accept fate." Then I reply, "Yes, my dear, but your charm and your brains ought to control your fate and make a sure and happy future."

Constance was also getting an earful from her father, who begged her to liquidate her assets and move in with him. Any other arrangement would be suicide. He also worried about Constance's constancy and dedication to him and his well-being.

> If I was only a horse now instead of a horse's ass what a lovely life we might have together for I know how you love your horses. The only sensible thing for you to do during the present crisis is to get out of France for at least a year, get out of debt. It is a crime for you with the money you have & have had to have any [debt]. Take advantage of the present exchange. Sell your horses, shut up the apartment, put what things you want to keep in storage & come over here for at least a year. That would put you right on your feet again.

Constance did nothing of the sort, although she did visit her father several times in the mid-1930s. Her behavior with him was not always classy, however; she once left him with bills amounting to $95. "As you know perfectly well," he wrote, "I would be only too glad to give you anything I have, but I cannot give what I have not got." Now supporting a live-in nurse in addition to his three other household employees, he was contemplating taking funds from his principal just to get by. Constance was facing French taxes amounting to $13,000. Her father suspected that she had been evading her taxes. "Not only would you have to pay terrible fines but they might confiscate your personal property & put you in jail, like Al Capone. When you talk about pulling your horses & selling pearls that do not belong to you, these are acts of a crook. You might be fired off the race track & then where would you be?"

Crownie was one relative who rarely ragged on Constance; despite the steady flow of lovers, Constance remained more or less true to her cousin. Of all of her relatives, close, distant, removed, and otherwise, she spent more time in his company in the 1930s than she did with anyone else. He had visited her in Paris every summer for years and was part-owner of several of her horses. They wrote faithfully to each other, long, frank, and affectionate letters. Crownie had other lady friends, including a few celebrities—the tennis star Helen Wills Moody and the cosmetics queen Edna Hopper. In 1934, Mary Pickford invited him to spend a month with her in Hollywood. As for Frank Crowninshield, Crownie's high-society brother, Constance saw him only when she was in New York. She once told HG that Frank was a "sauve & social, has-tasted-life-and-spit-it-out kind of person."[49]

During his checkered lifetime, Crownie maintained a great love and affection for Connie. Perhaps it was simply the affection of a doting cousin, although Constance once described it as "an insane fondness" for her. "Every minute of the day he must know what I do." He was jealous, like a child, and got on her nerves, and yet he was "so sweet & kind I can't help being fond of him underneath, altho he bores me terribly." In a 1932 diary entry, Constance mused about the people who "last in one's life, usually the one's who expect the least. I have never had an affair with Crownie. I think [he] loves me—& yet [he] is very close in my life, while all the other grand passions have vanished into air!"

Crownie's letters dripped with desire to see Connie. From London in the 1930s he wrote: "My sweet one, Seems I am writing you very often, but the reason is that your always on my mind & I do miss you so. Please don't thank me or even have it on your mind about the very little I may have done for you, for it was my great pleasure." Crownie once told Constance that he never enjoyed himself unless she was with him. "You will never know how much I love you darling & how I depend on you for everything. Oh why can't we be together a bit more, why? I sometimes wish I could forget you just a little." Constance once asked Crownie why he liked her when she tended to treat him badly and to be selfish. His response was a masterpiece of sorts. He said that he didn't just like her, he loved her, always had and always would, and that she wasn't selfish. On the contrary, he found her generous and thoughtful; she was a woman with a "big warm heart." She meant everything in the world to him and always had. That having been said, Crownie let loose:

> Yes, you do say some awful things to me—perfectly dreadful—but I know you don't mean [it]. Of course, I am cursed with being sensitive—that I can't help, but my feelings are not hurt as they were once. You have changed in some ways lately. . . . I don't think I mean as much to you as I did. But I don't blame you dear—this is a funny world. We go on loving one & all of a sudden we wake up & wonder if it was really love. But dearest one, I do love you & probably always will, & anyway I send you all the love that I have within me now.

It may have been Crownie's exotic interests and appearance that kept Constance amused. He was an accomplished magician, dabbled in tap-dancing, horses, and the good life; he was also tattooed from head to foot. According to his great nephew, Ben Crowninshield Bradlee, the former editor of the *Washington Post*, Crownie was "quite a swordsman" and "a total fainéant. I don't think he ever had a job a day in his life."[50] In his autobiography, Bradlee recalled that "Uncle Edward" attempted the antiques business twice, but only "to dispose of the heirloom furniture he inherited from various relatives and parents. He didn't stay in the business long, because my grandmother always bought all the family heirlooms back, leaving him flush and out of business."[51] Bradlee remembered a "wonderful family story" about Crownie tap-dancing on Harold Vanderbilt's yacht, which had been docked in Newport Harbor. "He had had too much to drink and when the boat pitched, he was tossed out into the harbor; he wasn't rescued until early morning." Bradlee also recalled seeing the coiled snake tattooed around Crownie's wrist. When he "shot his cuffs," the tail of the snake seemed to strike. Crownie also displayed a four-masted schooner under full sail on his back. Bradlee caught up with "Cousin Connie" in Paris in the 1950s when he was writing for *Newsweek*. His dazzling female relative was cut from the same cloth as Crownie—"something of a rogue who had beaten the system," he said, "and she brought quite a lot of color into our family of Boston-baked-bean-wasps." Meanwhile, Freddie Bradlee, Ben's writer and actor brother, remembered his American cousin as being "immensely charming," and having a pretty smile and "a very sexy voice."[52] Patricia Morange, owner of a Beverly Hills boutique and Constance's goddaughter, described her godmother as "a character, definitely." She was "a great lady, such a great sense of humor, so much fun."[53] Morange's grandfather, Willie Head, was Constance's horse trainer in Paris for many years. Whenever Willie offered to drive Constance back into Paris after training sessions at the track, his wife, Netta, jumped into the car to act as a human shield. On May 22, 1932, Constance noted in her diary: "[Willie] drove me a little in the forest & wanted to make love—I didn't, but really, some day if the sun is shining in those lovely woods amid the flowers & grass—I might."

⋆   ⋆   ⋆

HG didn't have to ask Constance twice. Whatever it was, whatever he said, did, or had, was persuasive. Indeed, the attraction, if we believe

HG's account in the *Postscript,* was immediate. An evening led to a week and a week led to series of rendezvous. The meeting of minds and bodies also led to a frisky ten-year correspondence.

HG's letters to Constance reveal much about his head and heart during the last decade of his life, including his concerns about his dual passions—his various professional projects and his love life. For example, they expose his gut-wrenching frustrations with his films and with Moura Budberg, his bouts of loneliness and boredom and depression, and the role of work, fantasy, and humor, and of course, of romance and lovemaking, in counteracting his doubt and despair. The letters speak of the joy of remembering and of being remembered, and the fear of being forgotten. As much as anything else, the letters between HG and Constance revolve around the themes of love and lovemaking, dreams, wishes, and food: sustenance for the heart, body, mind, and soul. [54] Speaking in a candid and vulnerable voice, HG wrote about his physical attraction to Constance. "I wish I was in bed with you now," he said in February 1935, and often thereafter. But just as often he spoke of his craving for a more generalized love. "The dear close sweetness of love is my incessant need," he admitted the next month.

Love was often an issue, but so were the joys and nuisances of everyday life. In the midst of his unsettling move to Regent's Park in the summer of 1936, HG wrote: "I'm all homeless between the old flat and the new house. Everything I possess is in vans today, going from one to the other." Constance talked about life at the stables and the track and at home on Rue Maspero, around town, and with her father, whom she visited four months a year throughout the 1930s at his mountaintop hacienda, "Mi Casita," above Santa Barbara.[55] And she discussed her "work"—horse racing, reading, and many self-imposed translation projects.

In reading HG's letters to Constance, one begins to understand that the mind of the man later eulogized as "a non-stop genius" was preoccupied with a desperate and ultimately unsuccessful quest for intense perfect love, for his "personal lover," his Lover-Shadow. During his affair with Constance, HG came to terms with the idea that his Lover-

Shadow was a phantom, an ideal, ephemeral and unattainable. Constance's letters to HG demonstrate the affection of a much younger woman for a great man; indeed, he held a special place in her intellect even as he wooed her heart, body, and soul. During her affair with HG, Constance explored an old idea that still held appeal: the possibility of finding a soul and spirit mate. She also flirted with a newer idea: devoting herself to the work of an important man. She could not, she told her diary, "go on leading this useless life. It is all so empty. I must do something. If only I knew what. I wish I was married to a clever man I could help."[56]

Their letters followed certain patterns, covered certain bases. They discussed their work and everyday occupations, the people they were seeing, special occasions, problems and irritants, and miscellaneous topics such as the home front, finances, and plans. They also discussed issues of substance—love, life, loneliness, and, of course, their relationship. Constance and HG also shared a deep self-truth here and there: "I have been missing my horses terribly," Constance said in August 1935. "I almost think I like horses better than people." A few months later, when he was deep into his film projects, HG confessed, "I've never had to do with a lot of human beings before. I've just floated past my fellow creatures."[57] More than anything else, their letters communicated the notion that they were thinking about each other, that they cared about each other, that they wanted to be in each other's lives.

An early example of Constance's concern occurred shortly after their fling on the French Riviera. Within days of arriving back in Paris, she began receiving a blizzard of newspaper clippings from family and friends all over the world—gossipy little blurbs about sightings of her with HG on the Côte d'Azur. These articles seemed to ruffle Constance. She wrote to HG, who now was in the United States, saying that she was appalled by the articles and worried that the stories might trigger a scandal for him, or at least temporarily hurt him. "I simply can't believe my eyes when I read [the articles]. And what must you think?" she asked HG in mid-March. Constance speculated that it might have been Maugham or his lover, Haxton, who fanned these little tabloid fires. "It is most flattering for me but I am afraid it may annoy you, and above all, I hope Moura won't hear of it. But it is all very amusing and I don't mind at all as long as you don't. But I shall be interested to hear if they said anything to you about it in America." Perhaps it tickled Constance just a bit to have precipitated this moment, or at any rate, to have been a part of it. HG was not in the least disturbed by the gossip. "Here is your precious cutting back," he wrote on March 14, 1935, from the Mayflower Hotel in Washington, D.C. "It is nice to be in the same paragraph with you, but it will be nicer to be in the same bed with you & unless Jeans gets time & space so mussed up that nothing further will be doing ever, we'll be together like that before very long."[58]

Judging by the letters that flew between H. G. Wells and Constance Coolidge soon after their French fling, it was love at first sight: "Bless you my dear for existing," HG wrote from London in the early weeks of 1935, soon after they had parted in Paris. "You are the loveliest thing that has happened in my life for years & years. It's been a lark & it's been like spring sunshine—& we have had some wonderful meals—& laughed. Until I see you in London I shall sit about & remember things." Truth to tell, for HG, it was also lust at first sight. "When I got your letter," he wrote, "I had a great desire to kiss you"; and, "I wish I was in bed with you now." In March 1935, he was becoming aggressive about his love and desires. "I want a day or so of talk with you before you go back from London to Paris. Try and manage that. Get [Crownie] out of the way. I want to get close to you. I want that a lot." Only rarely did Constance tease HG via the mail service, as she did from her beach house in Montecito, just south of Santa Barbara: "If you were here we could lie on the sand . . . & dig holes & look at the sky & hold hands, perhaps, & talk & kiss each other good morning," she suggested on May 25, 1935. Two weeks later, the old time traveler fired back: "How gladly would I leap across space and come in from the beach through your open windows one morning and kiss you and creep into bed with you," to which she responded: "I wish you were just walking thro the glass door. I'm still in bed, too." Another time, Constance ended a letter by asking, "Did you ever notice how loudly the clock ticks when one is alone? When you are in England, it doesn't tick half as loud, & if you were right here in this room I daresay it wouldn't tick at all."

From the start, HG was more forthcoming with his love and affection, and, like Harry Crosby before him, he seemed to need more assurance. Indeed, many of his letters proclaimed love, then turned right around and asked whether it was reciprocated.

> March 9, 1935: I've got no right to ask it dear, but do you still love me?
>
> March 13: Are you beginning to forget me? Or are you still in love with me?
>
> March 16: You and I are very different creatures, but I find you lovely and I love you. We might perhaps do a lot for each other. Or am I dreaming dreams?
>
> May 25: Don't get up to mischief or go marrying someone, but stick to the memory of your own True Love H. G.
>
> July 10: You are a dear & I adore you.

Constance often sent her love at the end of each letter, and occasionally offered her affection, but generally it was in response to HG's query. "Of course, I love you HG. I will kiss you goodnight now to prove it," she wrote on March 20, 1935. "Give my love to Moura. I think you have mine already!" she said on May 25.

The correspondence behind a romantic relationship revolves to some degree around missing each other, the desire to see each other, and plans for getting together. Such was very much the case for Constance and HG. "I miss you very much. I loved all the time we were together," she said in her first letter from Paris on February 18, 1935, and throughout the correspondence. Even her last letter, on December 23, 1945, reiterated that idea: "It is two days before Christmas & always at this time, and at many others, I think of you, & miss you, & wish that I might see you." Soon after they met, Constance told HG that she wished she could go with him to the United States, but she realized that there wasn't time to make the arrangements. She said she would always remember the lunch he gave for her on the Riviera, and hoped that someday they could go back together. In March, Constance asked when they would dine together again, then said that she could hear people chatting below her window, but their conversations were boring— "just about themselves. And yet <u>how</u> interesting it would be if you & I were here together talking about ourselves." The next month, she admitted to a "sneaking hope" that HG would get off at Le Havre and visit her in Paris for a day or two. In the summer of 1935, Constance even proposed that she, HG, and Moura travel together through the American Southwest. She had been talking to an artist who told her that it was the most extraordinary and beautiful country in the world. At the end of the summer, Constance wrote that since her ship left New York later than she thought, she would have five days in the city. "If only you will be there then too. I will stop, I think, at the Savoy Plaza, so you will know where to reach me. How nice it would be if we could go back together on the Normandie. At least we can see each other in New York. I send you a kiss, HG. We will meet in NY." The meeting never came off. "This is a note to catch you in NY perhaps," HG responded on September 4. "I am not coming to America until late October. Perhaps we shall meet this side before I start." Three years later it was the same message: "I wish I could see you," she said. "I expect to come back to France in October & I will come to London if you are there."

HG's expressed wishes, needs, and desires also often revolved around seeing Constance. "I'd love to have a good look at you for a day or so more than anything else in the world. Where will you be?" he asked on August 6, 1935, a fairly standard comment and question for him. A couple of months later, HG wrote that on their next meeting, he would be shy for ten minutes "& then I'll surely want to hug you." He once said that he wished Constance's street and his were nearer, so that he could look out and see her walking her "dorg" under the trees and down the sidewalk. HG also frankly wanted some of that "dear close sweetness" he talked about: "I am all alone in this flat & I wish I could kiss you," he wrote then and throughout the correspondence. When HG talked about arranging a meeting, his meaning wasn't a bit ambiguous; indeed, he complained that they didn't "hear & see & have enough of each other."

HG was planning meetings with Constance from Day One. "Are we going to have a meeting here?" he wrote from his hotel, the Hermitage, on Sunday, February 3, 1935. His first trip to the United States in the spring of that year killed the possibility of their going together to the Grand National horse races, but HG wrote that he would be back in Europe before May, and that they must meet before she went to the United States. And on it went throughout the spring and summer of 1935.

> March 13: I shall be coming back by the Bremen leaving NY on March 30th. After that I'll try to see you in Paris—if you will still be there. I want very much to get together with you before you come to America. Can we fix up something?
>
> April 8: We will go places somewhere Constance—we will.
>
> July 10: I almost came over on a ridiculous contract to Hollywood in order to come & sleep & eat with you at Santa Barbara. When are you coming back to Europe?
>
> July 26: I may be in America in the end of October for a week. I have some urgent business in New York. Where will you be & what will you be doing?

Nostalgia also played a major role in their correspondence; their letters are filled with memories of the Riviera. "I loved all the times we were together," Constance wrote, soon after parting, and followed it up four days later: "How glad I am I went to Nice and that [Gerald Haxton] asked me to lunch Christmas day." From New York, HG reciprocated: "It's queer how vividly you come alive in my brain at times and walk about it."[59] In response, Constance admitted that she was a little jealous of all the nice people HG was meeting in the United States— "Beautiful ones with blue eyes probably! But I'm sure you won't fix their egg so nicely for them as you did mine that morning not so long ago." In June and from London, HG wrote that Constance's letter filled him with "wild nostalgia" for her. A year later and from Cap d'Antibes, hc wrote that the countryside was alive with memories of her. And much later, in her last letter, Constance wrote, "How is Moura? I think of her often, and the night we sat so late at Fouquet's talking to Bernstein and Eve Curie (who never spoke)." And she added: "I think back to that happy winter in Nice, and the talks we had, and wish with all my heart that those days might come back—or rather, like the man who wanted all the Wednesdays of his life to come back, I would like to relive them once more."

Like many lovers, HG and Constance threw compliments around, and their praise sounded sincere. Like many lovers, their praise for tangibles was entangled with flirtatious and suggestive remarks and responses. Most often, Constance and HG praised each other's minds and judgments, suggesting perhaps that intellect was the ground zero of their attraction for each other. Of HG's decision to take up *Collier's* offer to assess Roosevelt and the United States, Constance wrote in February 1935: "You are wise to go. It is the right moment. What you can say now will influence them, before the NRA has embedded itself too deeply." In the same letter, she teased HG, saying that at their next meeting she would wear her prettiest outfit, and that they would dine together. By that time, HG would be thoroughly entrenched in his movie productions, which prompted her to write: "What a wonderful life you have, darling HG. I can't imagine anyone who I [would] rather be than you. . . . You give so much of yourself to the world that the world becomes in a way you. There, very bad, I can't explain." When he was in the dumps, Constance wondered what had brought him down. She speculated the reason was that perhaps his movie wasn't going well, that too many people were bothering him, that there were too many begging letters coming in. "But you certainly won't be blue for long, for you love life so & get more out of it & put more into it than anyone I ever knew." After his first article for *Collier's* was published, Constance wrote to HG from her beach house saying that it was unnecessary to tell him how good it was. "How tawdry it made all the other articles look! It is perhaps only the *young* who can accept the new world possibilities. Oh, HG, you are young. I want to be young too. This kind of youth is not a question of <u>years</u>." On another level, Constance told HG that he was right about calling Leslie Howard a weak actor. In the same letter she told him that he was right again about France. He was right, and he was calming, and even at a distance he could work his magic. "Darling HG, I must be boring you with all this, but I needed to talk to you. I kiss you good night, and thank you for being alive."

Perhaps it was because she had read so many of his works, or perhaps it was because she believed in the unproved possibilities of the universe and of individual people, but whatever the reason, Constance believed in HG's prophetic powers. At times, she credited him with superhuman strength and ability. Explaining her father's limited routines and failing health, for instance, she burst out with: "Oh, HG, please fix it. I'm sure if it can be done, you can do it." She asked if he remembered the book *The Miracle Man*. "Perhaps you wrote it. Did you? I don't remember—I just saw the movie. Everyone became young and cured of everything, just when they approached this man, because they believed they would be. It's wrong, too, that you shouldn't be completely and always happy, but there is where individual selfishness comes in."[60] In 1945 she wrote:

Everything that you wrote about has come true, except the Time Machine, and I hope I will live to see that. I am glad I have lived so long and can remember so many things that this new generation will never know, and when I die, I shall want to hurry back here again to see what happens next, for at the moment, I just cannot imagine. I suppose you know, you always do, and if only I could see you, you would tell me. Are we going to destroy ourselves, or is the new order to come to pass, wherein all will enjoy equal rights and universal happiness—which will it be? Somehow I can't imagine either of these things happening, but the first seems more logical at the moment, and it's dreadful to think that. Even you never imagined anything more grotesque than these war criminal trials.

HG tended toward lighter fare and praised Constance for her adorableness, her loveliness, and her wisdom.

To be sure, the talk was often more pedestrian on both sides of the correspondence when it addressed the daily grind and the routines of life. Constance was especially good at reporting her activities in detail, particularly when they involved her sometimes suffocating life in Santa Barbara tending her ailing father. David became a topic in their correspondence right from the start. While they were still on the Riviera, Constance bowed out of a dinner engagement with HG because she was tired and had to write her father. "I'm rather worried about him," she admitted in her note from the Negresco. Then, only days after HG arrived back in London from his trip to the United States, Constance wrote with the news that her father was very ill and that she was being advised to go to Santa Barbara at once. Her father had suffered several more heart attacks, so she would be sailing immediately and be gone all summer.

> It is hard to leave my horses just when they are about to run, and to give up the pleasure of seeing you, but of course this situation has to be faced, & I cannot bear to think of my father alone & ill when I am so far away. I know you will agree that I am doing the only possible thing. I would have normally sailed in June, but now it seems urgent, & I must go at once. I shall not stay in New York, but go straight thro. What a trip it is—really awful. The dog will not like it.

"Tell me how you are and how your Father is & anything else you want to tell me, please," HG responded. Soon after arriving in Santa Barbara, Constance did so. She spoke about her father's health, her living arrangements, and her routines. "David, my father, has a mild form of angina & a mild form of diabetes. He was ill two months ago but now is alright again. I tried living in his house, but my room was on the roof. Nice when you got to it—one has to climb a sort of fire escape to reach it & there was no bathroom & no closet & no dressing table, so I was very uncomfortable."

The beach house Constance quickly found and rented in Montecito in early May 1935 suited her nicely; it was located some six miles from her father, who lived on a hilltop above Santa Barbara. She described her new habitat as a "divine beach cottage"; it overlooked "a quite wild beach" and "the sea all beautiful beyond." Perhaps it even reminded her of her beach house in Peiteiho in 1922. The forty-foot living room had sliding glass doors that opened onto the beach, but the bedrooms were tiny cabin-like rooms. Constance took one and gave the other one to her French maid, Helene, who frequently traveled with her. She hired a cook, who prepared the meals they took *en famille* at the cottage. David and the nurse went home around 8:00 P.M. every night. "The evenings for me are rather long, but I read and listen to the radio," Constance wrote to HG in May, noting, "I think it will work out very well. But everyone here seems old and ill and it will be long till September." She later wrote HG about her father's financial woes and his physical limitations. "Poor David. He is so sweet. He is so fond of his bird & his dog & me, & he just sits & takes a little walk in the sand & sits again & has dinner & plays backgammon. He's tired after three games & then he goes home. And the next day is the same & the next & the next, only each time he is a little more tired." "Sounds like you was awful bored," HG drawled in response to her dreary letter. Miraculously, David's health did improve, so much so that he planned to go with Constance to Maugham's villa in August 1936. "I am so thrilled & delighted for my father will love it," she wrote to HG in April.

Later, Constance told HG that she saw no one outside the household and that since she wasn't doing much, her letters couldn't be very interesting. David couldn't be on his feet for long, so sedentary activities prevailed. They went to the movies nearly every afternoon. To break the monotony, Constance took up tennis and hired a pro to coach her. It didn't take Santa Barbara society long to notice her, and she was soon being invited to lunches and dinners, a mini-celebrity by virtue of her expatriate status, horseracing career, and romantic liaison with H. G. Wells. Late in the summer of 1935, Constance made plans to return to Paris. "I shall be glad to leave," she told HG, "for altho it is charming here, one feels out of the world and isolated from everything."

In Paris, Constance's spring routine revolved around the racecourse. After the races she would dine, sometimes across the street with Hugo

Baring, Maurice's brother. When the conversation waned, she told HG, she'd turn on the radio or play checkers, "& I look secretly at the clock & wonder when I can go home. Very rarely do I go to dinners & even more seldom to teas, to sit in a chair & 'languish into hate.' Usually I just come home from the races & go to bed!" she admitted in March 1936. Indeed, even in Paris the evenings were long for Constance, and although she often filled them with reading, sometimes even that wasn't enough. "I don't know or rather <u>see</u> many people," she wrote to HG, "but those I do always seem to say the same things. You look at them, & think, 'I've heard all this before. Must I listen to it again?' That man who wrote that you must consider everyone you meet [with a] new & startling interest must have changed his mind by now." Shades of Constance in Pekin, when she found people too wearing and boring. In the *Postscript,* HG drew a pen portrait of Constance, describing her as she was on the Riviera: "She was not a talker in public, but she sat listening very brightly and understanding very quickly. In private she talked most entertainingly, very frankly and with keenly appreciated detail. She did not go out very much, and generally she dined alone in the hotel, and gave herself up to reading."[61]

For whatever reason—whether it was because he was more private and guarded about his children or family, or less connected—HG almost never wrote about them in his letters to Constance. One exception came in the spring of 1936 when he was trying to wrestle back control of Lou Pidou. "If I succeed I shall put in my old cook & her husband again & use it sometimes for myself & sometimes for my sons & daughters & their spawn. And you will slip over to see me there from your Negresco. Please." Another reference came a year later: "<u>Gone With the Wind</u> is a great book. My daughter-in-law has laid hands on it & I am instructing her to return it to you when she has finished it. And with all my love."

Their own health, mental and physical, found its way into their letters. Twice while she was on the Riviera, Constance sent HG notes saying that she wasn't feeling well. This was probably due to her severe monthly "troubles." She was generally in excellent health and in fine form. Once in Montecito, Constance reported that she hadn't been feeling well, and that she had been in bed for six days "with interior problems." Her doctor was giving her injections—piqueurs, she called them—every day, and he had scheduled her to have a battery of tests. She didn't think there was anything seriously wrong with her, although it seems, she said, that

> once you have a doctor, they attach themselves to you, & as they are all crazy on the subject of glands just now, they test every gland in your body in the hopes of finding some deficiencies. I expect it will be some time before they will have finished exploring all mine. However, as there is very little to do here, I suppose it is as good a way of passing the time as another.

One of the few times Constance was debilitated was in the early days of 1936 after a freak accident. A French doctor, injecting a painkiller after Constance had strained her back playing tennis, accidentally broke the needle in her hip. She spent two days in the hospital and another week in bed at home, in addition to the three days she stayed in bed following the original injury. HG, after learning about the accident, chose to be humorous: "My dear! Dear Needle book. Dear Pincushion. I shall never <u>dare</u> ever to put you on the back again. I feel it is all right really but what a hideous experience. Gradually—very gradually—you will find it is nothing & you will forget about it. Bless you & keep you my dear." Two months later, Constance told HG that people were still asking her about the accident, and that she was getting "rather tired" of the topic; but HG's comments helped soothe her: "I feel much better already. I can see how you would laugh at all my irritations & make them nothing. With love, Constance."

David's sickness, compounded with Crownie's bronchitis and his displeasure when he heard that Constance would be away during most of his annual visit, succeeded in bringing Constance down. "This is a letter of woe," Constance wrote to HG in April 1935, "but I am happy in my heart, for it is Spring, & you are my friend, & I feel that things will get better. If it was winter, it would be different." Still, Constance admitted that she was restless, as always, before a long journey, especially when she didn't know what she would find at the end. "If only people didn't have to suffer, and could just die always in their sleep. It was wrong not to arrange it that way." On April 17, 1935, the day before she left for America, Constance sent HG a farewell note. "It is horid all this going away feeling—a kind of goneness inside. I wish you were here. But I think of you often. I hope everything is well for you. I send you my love." In California, she told HG that she was "homesick." Later, in July, she noted that HG seemed "rather sad at the time, which made me wish I was there to make you laugh by telling you about all the funny people here. It isn't half so nice being amused by things all alone, for in the end you begin to wonder if perhaps you aren't the funniest one of them all!" The next year the tables were turned. "I am blue tonight and wish I could be there with you," she confided to HG. And so it went: back and forth, up and down. Constance would be thrilled beyond belief to see a collection of Van Gogh's paintings, then dragged through hell by her father's death in May 1938: "I feel rather as tho the world had fallen about my ears. I hope I am wrong about this, & that days of carefree happiness will come back again. Can't we all go somewhere this winter & be gay & carefree together?" And much later, in 1945, Constance asked HG about his health. "I have heard that you were ill, but I hope it is not true, & that you are now alright again."

HG reported everything from colds and "frightful coughs" to being overworked and discontented. "When I am well & vigorous I want to get hold of you & boss you rather & carry you about the world with me, & when I am down (& just now for a tangle of small reasons I am very much down) then I wish I could be Simon & lie in your bed & be taken for a walk & be taken care of & petted," he wrote in June 1935. Twelve days later, he wrote much the same thing to Christabel. "I'm jaded Christabel. I am doing good work, life is full, all too full, of intent, and how gladly would I step out of it all through a small door into a green place—with sunshine." More often, when he was in a state of exhaustion and discontent, he was moody, resentful, and angry. HG admitted that at these times the child in him had its sway: "I feel very like my little grandson in his tantrums when he says, 'No, I don't want' to everything that is prepared him. I suppose everyone has to go through these phases of unsettlement & indecision. Bless you! If I can produce a better mood than this I will write a better letter later." To shake himself out of his moods, or at least to give himself some peace, HG escaped to the Riviera for a week now and then, just as he always had. But he was in turmoil throughout the spring and summer of 1935 as he tried to find a resolution to the things that were troubling him.

In the midst of his discontent over his love life and his films in 1935 and 1936, HG began preparing to move into a new house, yet another source of unsettlement. And as 1936 rolled into 1937, he was battling a bad case of the flu. HG and Constance got together in Paris in April 1937; immediately afterwards, he went down to Maugham's for a little visit, then on to "clear everything up" at Lou Pidou. Instead of luxuriating in the calm and peace of his beloved villa, which he longed to do, HG wound up instead in physical hell. "Suddenly," he wrote to Constance, "I got neuritis in my right arm & it's frightful. It is like three toothaches. I can't sleep, I can't work. The good doctor Blés down here does things to me that seem to make me hurt more. The only comfort I get is that everybody says it will pass away. If it doesn't I shall."[62]

The weather and the elements inevitably played a part in the correspondence of two people who frequently basked in the sunshine of the South of France. After HG left Constance in Paris in early 1935, she accused him of taking the sun with him because it had been dark ever since he had left. It was a dreadful February in Paris, with torrents of rain and gusts of wind. March was even worse and began with a snowstorm and predictions of a cyclone. "I worry about you & hope there will not be a cyclone on the sea." She needn't have worried. HG wrote that the crossing was "as good as gold. I am in my usual halo of sunshine." On July 1, 1935, Constance reported that it was raining in Santa Barbara, the first time it had done so since her arrival on April 28. "It's rather nice," she said, as if it were the first time she had experienced rain. "One feels soothed and relaxed. I think continual hard sunlight can become rather irritating." HG reported more "<u>beastly</u>" weather at Cap d'Antibes. And a year later he was craving a week of sunshine in "Cannes or Nice. Solo," he wrote Constance. In December 1945, Constance was anticipating a white Christmas in Washington. It was snowing on the twenty-third, the day she wrote to HG, and it was very cold and dark, a stark contrast to the Christmas of ten years earlier when they had met in the glorious sunshine of the Riviera.

Nourishment, equally basic (food, meals, eating and drinking), was a favorite topic with HG and Constance. Their relationship was built, after all, on an orgy of good meals, good conversation, and romance. "We have had some wonderful meals—and laughed," HG acknowledged just after leaving Constance in Paris in February 1935. She responded: "The Olympian Feasts I shared with you have made it rather difficult to go back to my vegetable and fruit meals, so the chocklate cake is your influence! 'May I offer you a piece of chocklate cake sir?' But no, of course not. It would not be good for you. Shall we have snails or pâté de canard instead? I did enjoy it all so." In the *Postscript,* HG noted that Constance "lunched and dieted with great discretion," so that her mind should not be heavy and confused for her "grave" racing duties.[63] Dining well was often on HG's menu:

> March 11, 1935: Stay on some days and we will have a little dinner in my little uncomfortable flat.
>
> August 22, 1935: One day before the year is out we will dine well together in Paris.
>
> May 21, 1936: It would be lovely to eat with you up & down the Riviera once more.
>
> March 27, 1937: Can't we get together next week for a nice serious dinner?

Perhaps simply to amuse him, Constance served up a theory about the histories of countries based on the food their inhabitants eat:

America loves ice cream sodas & candy & lolipops, which proves it's young. In England you excell in pies & roasts, which shows a comfortable civilization—sits-at-home-&-purrs idea. Here in France it's all sauces & pastries, which denotes shallowness & brilliancy. But dear, I will not go on. I fear you are yawning. And then we do talk a lot about food you & I. Have you ever noticed it? But I think it's mostly I. Think of my taking up all your time like this. It's outrageous. Forgive me.

She closed her letter with a caution: "Darling H.G., take care of yourself & don't eat any canned food. I think half the trouble with America is canned food and frozen meat."[64] Ten years later, when she was fifty-three, Constance told HG that she was for the first time in her life competently cooking vegetables on a hot plate in her Washington hotel.

A devotee of the arts, Constance often wrote to HG about music, film, theater, and literature, and sometimes about lower-brow activities such as boxing matches. Her tastes were eclectic, especially in literature. Over the course of their affair, she read works by Bergson, Chekhov, Eliot, Joseph Kessel, Margaret Mitchell, Rostand, and Wilde, and usually completed a book a week. When they met, she was poring over Dunne's *Immortality* and *The Letters of Katherine Mansfield,* and several works by Spengler and Russell. HG respected Constance's intellect. "She read widely, with a wide-eyed curiosity, and her commentary was naive and shrewd and 'illiterate' as only America's commentary can be. She had none of that façade of culture an educated European woman is given as a matter of course. Passages she liked, she copied out in an unformed schoolgirl hand."[65]

Early in their relationship, Constance sent HG a volume of T. S. Eliot's poetry and asked for his opinion. Thoroughly unimpressed, HG returned it forthwith, sniffing: "I don't find the Prufrock love song good. And generally I find this book making me think that a classical dictionary must have been raped by *The New Yorker* in the extremely dirty gutter of an extremely disgusting back street in Paris." "But oh, you are a little hard on poor T.S.E.," Constance fired back the next day. She liked the poem for its rhythm and phrases. She could imagine "the poor bald-headed gentleman going up the stairs to ask his 'overwhelming question' & being awed by the footman, & upset by the teacups, & just not daring to do it, & going sadly away, realizing that the mermaids would no longer sing for him. I am probably quite wrong but I sympathized with him & rather liked him." HG later recalled the exchange, saying that they had "anatomized a volume" of Eliot's poems. "She knew and felt infinitely more than I did about modern poetry, but I don't think she had the faintest inkling that that was how things were between us."[66] Shortly after she and HG parted in February 1935, Constance began reading Chekhov. She commented on March 20, 1935, that the book was depressing, like all Russian books. Russians spend too much time wondering about "the whys" of life, she observed, but what good does that do? There is no answer. "I love you because you haven't got time to ask or even think why. It is a question which should never be asked anyway." In her last letter to HG, Constance wrote that she had been reading Aldous Huxley's *The Perennial Philosophy,* "but it is obtuse & full of too many such and suchness. It is not simple," she said, noting that in her opinion, "all great truths should be simple."

Constance often tried her hand at writing. Her archive contains dozens of drafts of original poems, many of them limericks. In 1936, she submitted a story to Ellery Sedgwick, the editor of the *Atlantic Monthly,* who, despite his stated desire to publish the piece, was compelled to reject it on the grounds that it seemed "really too dangerous to put it before the conservative Atlantic audience," he said. He passed it on to *Harper's,* which, to his amazement, also rejected it as too incendiary. Still, Sedgwick was encouraging. "Why do you not use your talent for writing? Yours is a far better narrative than is usually the case with beginners, and of course your life has been as varied as a movie. I should be more than glad to be of service to you in any way, and hate to write so lame and inconclusive a note as this." Constance did use her talent for writing, especially in her diaries. There she drew many enchanting pen sketches of the literary people, nearly always men, weaving in and out of her life, the lesser knowns and the greater: Logan Clendening, Gerald Lymington, and Speed Lamkin in the first group; Winston Churchill,

Somerset Maugham, Louis Bromfield, and Robert Herrick in the second. [67] Constance wrote that Winston Churchill had a "very interesting mind" and that Mrs. Churchill was charming. In her correspondence with H. G. Wells, Constance shared her experiences with some of these writers and her observations of them. For example, she once mentioned that she had been dining after the races with her neighbor Hugo Baring, the brother of Maurice Baring (a person, as we have seen, who figured into Moura's life). Maurice, Constance told HG, writes books, "but the most boring books. If you can imagine it, he actually managed to make Mary Queen of Scots thoroughly uninteresting, so he must be clever in a way." [68] On another occasion, after having lunched at Chantilly with the Bromfields, she noted that Louis Bromfield had two plays running in New York, and that he reported they both were "flops." In Santa Barbara in the fall of 1935, Constance was seeing a good deal of Logan Clendening, who wrote a dozen books about health and diet, including *The Human Body* and *The Care and Feeding of Adults, With Doubts About the Children*. She sketched the writer and his works.

> Clendenning is a big congested looking man with gout, who drinks too much. He has a very interesting even brilliant mind & has read everything, but now he just likes to drink & play the clown. It is rather depressing to see someone who at the end of his life turns to drink as the summit of felicity. He might be an example in your book of the frustration of success. He talks very brilliantly, and how often I have wished you were here to answer him. He is a great admirer of Huxley and used to go to his lectures and recited to me one evening the lecture he, Huxley, had once given on the parable of the swine. This lecture for some reason caused [Clendening] to no longer believe in religion as we know it. He has now a vast contented cynicism concerning religion, doctors' diets, & most accepted things, but then he is <u>fat</u>, has gout and drinks, so is not so convincing as he might be.

Maugham—Willy, as she called him and usually spelled his name— was frequently on Constance's mind, and had been ever since she first met him at his Christmas dinner at the Villa Mauresque in 1934. The next summer, when she was in Santa Barbara visiting her father, Constance quipped to HG that she couldn't imagine Maugham in that setting. He wouldn't like it at all, she said. "There's not a single duchess, only Amie MacPhearson."[69] Constance dined with "Willy and Jerry" several times, and always reported their get-togethers. Following a dinner in Paris in the spring of 1936, she said she found Maugham looking well, but thinner. He hadn't said much about his trip to the United States, other than that he liked San Francisco and was uncomfortable everywhere else. His daughter was to marry a Swedish diplomat, which seemed to please him, "altho I find it hard to tell what he really thinks about anything. He seems to guard himself continually from showing any emotion, or rather he finds it difficult to be spontaneous & frank. He absorbs everything, & gives out very little. But he is very kind & I am very fond of him."[70]

It was at that same dinner that Maugham offered Constance the use of the Villa Mauresque during August. She could move in as soon as his daughter and future son-in-law moved out; they were to spend ten days of their honeymoon there. As it turned out, there was a glitch. Liza Maugham and her groom, Vincent Paravicini, were not yet out of the Mauresque when Constance and her group arrived. The newlyweds also left the place in shambles. Maugham wrote that the only conceivable excuse for them was that they were in a daze while they were there; they could not have known what they were doing. Beyond that, Maugham was delighted to learn that HG would be spending some time at the Mauresque, since, although HG never would admit it, no one liked a party more than he did. As for himself, Maugham reported that he was feeling very well, and that he had been taking the cure and hiking. HG did not make it to the Mauresque, although at one point he offered to pay Fr 6,000 toward the rent if David Coolidge would fork out Fr 4,000. After Constance had been there a couple of days, HG wrote to "say hello." He also wanted to communicate his frustration over the matter. "I'm very divided just now. I want to come & Mauresque with you & I'm tied by all sorts of silly things. If by a gigantic effort I snap all these silly things, what is the telephone number of Villa Mauresque & will you be my own true love & nobody in the way?" The next time HG would "ask himself to Willie's" was in March the next year.

After Constance had settled into the Villa Mauresque, she received a note from Maugham asking a favor: Would she hunt through his papers for a description of a man and then send it to him? He also wrote that he couldn't imagine why there wasn't a copy of *Cosmopolitans,* his new collection of short stories, in the house, and offered to have his publisher send her a copy. At the time, Maugham was reading nothing but short stories in preparation for the anthology he was doing. He had just finished reading Hawthorne, and was sorry to report that he found it "rotten." But he thought Washington Irving's "Rip Van Winkle" a very good story indeed. Maugham blessed Constance and hoped she was having good weather and "a bit of fun."[71]

In June the next year, Maugham wrote to Constance apologizing for the delay in responding to her letter and thanking her for the things she had said about *The Summing Up.* He was happy to know she liked it, especially since he had given so much thought to it and had tried to make it as good as possible.[72] Although it wasn't specified in their correspondence, there had been a patch of trouble between Maugham and Constance, apparently revolving around some gossip. He wrote in the summer of 1937 to say that he was very sorry that Constance had been troubled over this matter. He was not in the least angry with her, he said, but "scared." In closing, he said that in his opinion, people who repeat things are as dangerous as those who said them in the first place. The only way he knew of dealing with such people, he said, was to stay out of their reach. And then Maugham asked Constance to believe that he harbored no bad feelings toward her.

In connection with these events, HG wrote to Constance on July 14, 1937, to console her. "Don't believe anything that anyone tells you about anybody. Willie adores you." Six weeks later, HG told her that she shouldn't worry about Willie, that he'd come around. "I won't write to Willie about it; that will make it too important, but when I see him I'll drop in a soothing word. Because you are a dear & everybody ought to love you as I do. HG will always love you whatever Willie does." On March 1, 1938, Constance told her diary that she had spent the afternoon and evening writing to Willie Maugham. Her comments are illuminating:

> I really don't know why he has not treated me very well—perhaps it is on account of that I wanted him to know me better so he would be sorry. His book Summing Up has impressed me by his desire to be frank, & by its rather hopeless philosophy. I never thought he was a happy man, which proves that success has nothing to do with happiness. My life from the world's point of view cannot have been succesful—with three divorces—but I have always been happy. Even when I have suffered the most underneath, I have known it was alright & something unknown, either a force inside or outside myself has comforted me.

The last time Constance wrote to HG about Willie was in 1945. She reported that she never saw him anymore except for once the previous summer, and then only for a few minutes. She had heard that he was writing a play for Ethel Barrymore, and that he lived in North Carolina in a house Nelson Doubleday had given him.

Harry Crosby was the only writer Constance discussed in any detail in her diaries; she did so only once in the extant correspondence. As mentioned, HG was fascinated by Harry. In a letter HG wrote soon after he returned to London after his tryst with Constance on the Riviera, he said he couldn't get Crosby out of his head, that his life was "curiously interesting." HG told Constance that he would like to go through Harry's letters and diaries again. She must have had Harry's papers with her on vacation that winter—a testimony to his ongoing importance in her life. "What you said about Harry Crosby delighted me," Constance wrote back on March 5. "I would love to send you his diary & letters when you get back. He really was an extraordinary personality—an unforgettable one to those who knew him." Constance relayed a story to prove that point. A "rather grand French duchess," a friend of Harry's mother, once called on the Crosbys at their Paris apartment. The woman brought her daughter, who was, according to Constance, "a typical French jeune fille about 18, but very unattractive and inane." Harry sat off in the corner, offering nothing and allowing Caresse to shoulder the social responsibilities. When the visitors got up to go, Harry told the duchess that he hoped she'd visit again, but that she needn't bring her daughter. He never wanted to see her again.

> You can imagine the scene! The duchess's departure—she had no sense of humor & just glared. Caresse's tears & my hysterical laughter & Harry, perfectly serious. 'Why the hell shouldn't I have said it? I don't want to see her again.' Combined with this extraordinary frankness, he was at the same time very shy. No one ever understood him. That was what was so tragic. Caresse, his wife, & I knew him better than anyone. But his family & his friends all misjudged him. Caresse was wonderful when he died. She sent me a telegram saying, 'Harry died yesterday, sympathy & love Caresse.' An ordinary woman could not have sent that.

Constance told HG that Eugene Jolas had published an issue of *transition* in Harry's honor. Norman Macleod wrote an article comparing Harry to Rimbaud, Cummings, and Eliot. "He was nothing like any of these men," Constance said.

In that same letter, Constance condemned Malcolm Cowley's depiction of Harry's life and death in *Exile's Return*, calling it "false and untrue." After reading Harry's letters and diary and hearing Constance's stories, HG wrote in pages that were later suppressed from the *Postscript* that Harry's long stream of (un)consciousness epistle to Constance "was not altogether madness and fantasy; it had a sort of philosophy."[73] HG also told the story about how Harry Crosby very dramatically sent some of his writings to Constance. "He entrusted his book-letter with 1,000 francs to a boy he saw standing about on the quay at Havre, and directed him to deliver it personally into her hands. The youngster did so. Crosby went abroad in a state of exaltation."[74] HG also wrote about Crosby's suicide. Having failed to persuade either his wife or Constance "of the charm of a joint suicide, he found a young woman in New York willing to face the great experience, and he shot her and himself there in 1930. From all these experiences Constance emerged with a puzzled expression, and rather anxious to discuss it all with anyone intelligent who might be able to proffer some sort of explanation of what she was about and what the world was up to."[75] Despite his fascination, HG never wrote that book about Constance's great love, Harry Crosby.

A good deal of the correspondence between HG and Constance revolved around the plays and the movies she was seeing or wanted to see. She had just seen *Miss Ba,* and raved about it, noting that "they overdid the part of the father rather, they would, but it was still an excellent play."[76] The movie stars shooting in and out of Constance's life, in France, Santa Barbara, and Hollywood, were also a popular topic. At "the club" in Santa Barbara, where "everyone gets slightly drunk and shouts a lot," Constance met many actors, including Gloria Swanson, Edmund Lowe, and Herbert Marshall. Marshall was charming, "nicer off than on the screen, rather English, but he *is* English, attractive. Everyone dislikes Marlene Detrick, and adores Kathrine Hepburn." In Paris in the spring of 1935, Constance had dinner with Dolores Del Rio and her husband. Del Rio mentioned that she had met HG in Hollywood. "I thought she was so nice. She has just gone to London to do a picture with Douglas Fairbanks Jr."

HG, on the other hand, shared little about the people in his life, only snippets about his meetings and phone conversations with FDR and assorted American friends and business partners such as Thomas Lamont and film producer Alexander Korda, the latter of which he should have been attentive to, as noted. But they both often wrote openly about Moura Budberg. Despite the odds against it, the three "got on extremely well together," HG wrote in the *Postscript.* Constance was barely back in Paris after their initial romance when she shot off a letter saying that she was wondering about Moura and hoping HG had good news from Estonia about her; perhaps it was a touch of guilt that prompted that question, perhaps grandness of spirit. A few days later, on February 22, in anticipation of HG's trip to the United States in

1935, Constance wrote, "You will be so busy and popular. Moura and I will be all forgotten over here." From the ship, and beginning to feel abandoned and characteristically edgy, HG responded on March 2, 1935: "Two women say they love me and one is in Estonia and one is in Paris and what is the good, dear, what is the good of being loved by women who are hundreds of miles away?" In April, Constance asked HG to tell Moura that she must see *Quiola,* an animal film, and *Bengal Lancers.* Later, she offered: "I hope you do love two women, particularly if I'm one of them. I understand it perfectly, for I rather love Moura too. One feels happy with her, and it is rare that one woman can feel happy with another woman, especially when they both like the same man. Yes, that is really very unusual."

Later that summer, after asking HG whether all three of them might travel together, Constance offered her unsolicited analysis of Moura's independent behavior vis-à-vis HG. If she and Moura had talked this over, Constance did not let on; if they had, it must have been a fascinating discussion. Constance tried to be subtle, but her segue was obvious. She had been talking about her father's deteriorating health, and the boring routines they were all locked into as a consequence of it.

> One gets selfish as one becomes older—you of all people have a complete right to be, but other people like to feel free & individual, too, in their own way. They don't want to be submerged in anyone or by anyone, I'm sure that's what Moura feels. You are so great a person don't you see that you would submerge them completely without knowing it! They'd come up struggling & say, "I want to be I. I want to be myself," & they would be you instead, & that would be greater of course, but they would lose that free feeling. Dearest, I guess I'm talking complete nonsense, but I've been thinking about Moura & you, & I think it must be like that with her. Oh dearest how I wish you were here.[77]

By the spring of 1936, Constance was still asking about Moura, and still suggesting a vacation ensemble, this time at Maugham's. "If only you & Moura would come and stay with me, it would be perfect. Don't you think you could? We could swim in the lovely pool, and play tennis. Do say you will." They never did vacation or travel together, apart from that first winter holiday. In her last letter to HG, in the mid-1940s, Constance once again asked about Moura. "What is she doing? I think of her often." In his letters to Constance, HG often mentioned Moura, especially his frustration with her for frequently abandoning him. He never mentioned Martha Gellhorn or Christabel Aberconway, just as he never mentioned Martha or Constance to Christabel. Among Constance's papers is a letter from S. N. Behrman, the American playwright, dated January 16, 1961. It carried a most intriguing postscript: "I am sure [Moura] was right to destroy the book." His meaning is still unknown, although it suggests that Constance was close enough to Moura to have such insider information. Whether it was true information, or disinformation, or Moura *Mélée* is yet unknown.

As they should have, major political figures worked their way into the conversations, including those that shot back and forth across the ocean. While both of them were liberal in their leanings, Constance wasn't above telling the jokes about President Roosevelt that were going around her country-club circles in Santa Barbara. And HG wasn't above scolding her for them. "I <u>like</u> Franklin & by liking I shall bless him. Will you love me just the same if I do?" he asked her on February 26, 1935, after a joke she told. That spring, Constance had her eye on the Bonus and the Senate's decision to uphold FDR's veto. She admitted that she knew nothing about Roosevelt beyond what she read in the papers and heard on the radio, but that while Cousin Charlie and all the businessmen and bankers she knew disliked FDR, she couldn't help admiring him. His speech before Congress was "excellent," and he should be praised for vetoing the bill, although it would cost him many votes in 1936. All in all, Constance wrote, "the worst thing about him is his wife. To say nothing of her looks, she seems to be an interfering busybody, just the kind of woman I most dislike. She should stay at home and have her teeth arranged," Constance sniffed.

By early August 1935, Constance was telling HG that the "whispering campaign" about the president's having lost his mind and being no longer responsible for his actions was only one of the "wild rumors" going around. At the end of the month, she said she realized that she was right for having disliked Mussolini. "If only all this vitality could be turned into other channels," she mused, theorizing that by October the Italian dictator "will have taken Abyssynia & Japan will have filtered thro China. The League of Nations will have died a slow & agonizing death, & a general throwing off of things will have started here." Much later, in Washington at the end of 1945, she scrutinized Harry Truman, calling him "our nice drugstore President," who was doing his best, but with no firm conviction. "He gives the impression of being slightly confused about everything."

Constance and HG also had strong opinions about particular cities and countries. As Constance told HG in the 1930s, her soul lived in Paris, but the West Coast was slowly growing on her. When she was planning a road trip with her father to see the giant sequoias, she wrote to HG that there were many trips to take "& the country gets really wild & beautiful, but of course the most lovely ones are over mountains, & my father can't go anywhere near a mountain." Still, her opinion fluctuated wildly. On July 1, she said she would die if she thought she'd have to live in Santa Barbara for long. At the end of the summer, Santa Barbara was comparing favorably to the French Riviera. "You would love it out here dearest. It is beautiful & it never rains, & there is a calm about it which you don't get on the Riviera. The Riviera has a nervous slightly fussy atmosphere. Here, it is calm & beautiful, secure in the sunlight." Despite her descriptions and invitations to Santa Barbara, HG never managed to get there when Constance was there. Earlier, she had been less generous about Beverly Hills: "It is just a small Main Street town like all the others. There is no glamour at all, & the movie people I have met are nice, but dull, rather just like everyone else. They only talk shop & are very conceited. Perhaps the interesting ones stay at home, like in other places." Constance had more to say about New York. At first, she was not a big fan. On May 11, 1935, she hated the city: "Dirty newspapers blew in my face & I saw a great many terribly ugly people & fat women eating candy." Late that summer, she hated the idea of New York "all agitated & hurrying. It is a wild mob of people & every inch of space so occupied. I wish I knew where all these people came from. I suppose it is the new world, taking possession." Later, however, she found New York "invigorating, inspiring & terrifying all at once." HG saw Gotham in quite another way. On March 9 of the same year, soon after arriving there, he told Constance that he had heard a woman speaking with her voice in the Colony restaurant "& I turned round all agog. And I went about New York this afternoon thinking how that it was your city & that you ought to pull up Henry at the side walk & put your head out & say 'HG! Do you want a lift?' It's queer how vividly you come alive in my brain at times & walk about it."

Constance's opinion of her homeland also fluctuated. Writing to HG who was crossing to the United States, she said: "I shall be so interested to hear what you think of America and shall read Colliers Weekly with excitement. How is America," she asked. "I long to hear what impression you have." His impression was mixed. Soon after he disembarked in New York, HG knowingly or not borrowed from Alice: "The American situation is very curious & gets curiouser. I'm glad I came. It's the live spot in the world's affairs just now." After seeing the president, he drove to Virginia to lunch with some horse breeders. HG told Constance that it seemed to him to be "a clean open life after politics in Washington. The New Deal is a confused mess & I don't like the outlook here, Constance. They drink too much, they talk too much & they think at odd times in taxicabs when the radio isn't on." Constance's response must have delighted HG:

America must be rather like Alice in the Looking Glass—everything distorted, with fantastic people & ideas about, & the people, like Alice, crying in the middle of it all, & perhaps you are the Chesshire cat sitting on the branch of a tree watching & smiling at it all. Only no, you are much too nice to be the Chesshire cat. Who could you be? But really there was no one very nice in Alice—except Alice herself. The White Knight was just foolish, & the Red Queen fussy, & the duchess just sneezed. I hated the walrous & the Carpenter & Tweedledum & Tweedlee were just Babbits. Perhaps you will brush them all off the mantlepiece, & sail away & they will lie writhing among the ashes in the fireplace.

When she learned that her father was ill, Constance told HG, just back from the United States, that she was glad he had returned even though she had to leave. She was sure that over there, "one is never at peace." Then at the end of the summer of 1935, Constance decided, along with many others, that America was in mortal danger. In her extended metaphor, her homeland was a patient who had survived a serious operation, but who was at the mercy of "the quack doctors in Washington." All it really needs is some care and rest to allow the simple laws of nature to take hold and allow a natural recovery, she said, "but with these queer new medicines the poor patient is having a relapse & may not recover without an old-fashioned purge, which now it may be too weak to live thro. The whole of Europe could fly at each other's throats tomorrow & I doubt if America would even notice it— so absorbed, so sunk is she in her own miserable troubles. Truly I have never seen such gloom anywhere." A decade later, Constance's condemnation was for her beloved France. It had become "a diminished little country now—rather like Spain," she wrote to HG. "There are so many things I am ashamed of for her that I hate to go back." But the next year she did return to France, and she stayed for the rest of her life.

Despite their personal problems and the gloomy international and financial picture, the letters on both sides were full of fun and good humor. When he was moving into his new house in the summer of 1936, HG wrote: "All my work is in arrears. I am all behind like the Queen's vache." That fall, he quipped, "Why not come over for a week and I will take you over to Madame Tussaud's where you can see . . . what I really look like." Once, when he was begging off the rendezvous at Maugham's villa on the grounds that he was too "tied up with work and complexities," HG told Constance he had tried everything, "even to asking God to stretch out August and September and put in a new month—Coolidgember—but bless you, the Old Boy won't." Intolerably lonely, as he said he was, in Washington, D.C., HG complained that he was "made to have a woman (a dark woman with an American accent I think) always about—just to kiss as one goes by—& with a dear naked body to take in my arms any time. I am evidently leading a very chaste life to write like this." Another Old Boy on HG's mind at the top of 1936 was the king of England. HG reported to Constance that he had experienced a terrible crossing on the *Majestic* and had caught a cold. To make matters worse, "my King (who always bored me) is dead & we have Edward VIII who will be I hope a much more eventful monarch. I liked his Mrs. Simpson, who said the most lovely things about you. When we have stopped pretending to mourn, London will I think do its best to spoil the young man."[78]

Constance often included amusing little flourishes in her letters. Her playfulness and sense of humor delighted HG. "If you were here we could lie on the sand and dig holes and look at the sky and hold hands, perhaps, and talk and kiss each other good morning. Instead of which I must do these things alone, except that I can't kiss myself good morning," she quipped in mid-1936. Like Moura, Constance was sometimes inadvertently funny, such as the time she wrote that her father was "in bed with a trained nurse." Once, while writing to HG, Constance noted that "the woman upstairs has turned on the radio, so now half of me will be irritated all down the rest of the page." And, later: "I've been doing accounts, hence the pen. I always use this pen [when doing the accounts], for the figures look less important and smaller." Relating humorous stories, including those that made fun of herself, was, in fact, Constance's specialty. One story involved her "performance" at a local Spanish-heritage fiesta in Santa Barbara. She and her father had attended a dinner-dance at a local restaurant; for the occasion, David wore a Spanish costume and Constance attempted a few accessories,

—only the comb was made of cardboard, & it began to wilt as the evening wore on & as I danced. The man I was sitting next to—a movie actor, [Michael] Bartlett, who sang in Grace Moore's last picture—said, "Oh dear, you looked so lovely when you first came in, but I wish you could see yourself now!" So I looked, & the cardboard comb was over one ear, & the lace [mantilla] was torn, so I took it off & realized I couldn't be Spanish after all.

On another occasion, Constance wrote about an incident that happened at the horse races in France when she sat between two feuding prima donnas: the Princess Anne Duleep Singh—"a rather large elderly woman with a bright red face and slightly disappearing features, bright-yellow hair <u>frizzled all around her face</u>"—and Madame Jean Stein—who is "also large, slightly younger, wears heaps of clothes, is always bundled up, but has a very decided manner and a rapier-like wit." The two women had been arguing about everything, especially horses and jockeys. It got so bad that they stopped talking altogether, and Constance had to mediate. "I have to sit between them while each whispers things to me about the other, hoping to be overheard. They sit like porcupines on each side of me now, and it is a war to the death."[79] On April 4, 1936, HG wrote that this was one of her loveliest letters, "and I have to refrain from telling the Princess Duleep Singh story to everyone I meet." In her last letter to HG, Constance told him about a wonderful two-month vacation she had just had in the Adirondacks at a small camp in the middle of a forest. Most of the campers played cards all day and drank. "It seemed such a funny thing to do in the forest. I never understood why they came there in the first place, to do just what they did in the places they came from. But it worked out very well because I had the whole lake & all the trees to myself."

Peppering the letters between them was a running conversation about a charcoal drawing the American artist John Singer Sargent had made of Constance in 1916, when she was Mrs. Ray Atherton. HG, like Harry Crosby before him, was smitten with the drawing, and in February 1935, just weeks after he and Constance parted company in France, he asked for a photograph of it, "either a little copy . . . or/and a little one for my pocket book." He asked several more times that spring: on March 13, "You never gave me a picture of yourself"; on April 8, "Don't forget my portrait of you." Then, thoroughly exasperated, he wrote on

April 25, "<u>You promised me your portrait and you never sent it</u>. Wicked you are. And you seemed so sweet and dear. Bless you, my dear, anyhow." On October 7, HG once again brought up the subject, now instructing Constance to not sell her Sargent portrait "to anybody in the world but me—you can find out the price & can ask me whatever you like for it. I am going into a new house and everything else shall be built around it." Ten days later, he reported that he had been asking around about Sargent's drawings: "It seems £100 is a fair price for a good one. Yours is a very good one." And then he noted, disingenuously, that he didn't have £100 to spare, but that he did have $500 in New York. "But don't send me the drawing or do anything about it until I am in my new house. Write me a separate little note to say that the drawing is mine and we will see about bringing it here later." Constance wisely kept the original drawing. It hangs in a gold frame in André Magnus's living room, Constance's wise, dark, and sparkling eyes fixed on the Eiffel Tower.

When she was living in the Far East, the Sargent drawing was stashed in a Chicago attic. During the war, the drawing traveled from cellar to cellar. Constance finally found it in the salon of a Monsieur Riou, "from whom at last I managed to get it back. It has been blurred a little by its voyages, & now the photographs are almost better than the original," she wrote to David McKibbin, the librarian of the Boston Athenaeum, in 1947. Constance went on to tell McKibbin, who wanted to exhibit some lesser-known Sargent works, that "Mr. Sargent told me he liked it better than any drawing he had done, but then perhaps he said that to everyone." Sargent wrote to Constance several times following the sitting on January 17, 1916. On the twenty-fifth, he said: "It is very good of you to let me know that the drawing looks all right," and then he asked her for a photograph of it. "Please let me know, but don't tell anybody but Mr. Atherton. I must keep this [request] dark or lots of people will wonder why I don't ask for their drawing and perhaps guess why." Sargent charged the Athertons seventy guineas for the original drawing.

Home was a common topic in HG's letters to Constance. Although during his teens, twenties, and early thirties he frequently changed addresses, and although from the early part of the century he traveled widely and often, HG's personal place (and space) was extremely important to him. Home represented not only family and stability but also achievement, refuge, and escape. As previously noted, HG entertained *chez lui,* frequently having friends for meals and soirées and overnight visits. He would spend the last forty-six years of his life primarily in four houses.[80] From New York in March 1935, HG invited Constance to join him in London and stay at his "little uncomfortable flat" at Chiltern Court. By July, he was hating the place, although for undisclosed reasons. On the tenth, he told Constance that he was buying a house in Regent's Park, "but I'm not sure whether it is what I want. I suppose everyone has to go through these phases of unsettlement and indecision." In the midst of making plans to move into the new house, he was up to his ears in negotiations to buy Odette out of Lou Pidou, "my queer little pretty quiet house to go to when I am so disposed." By the end of April 1936, he still hadn't moved into Hanover Terrace, nor had he made a deal with Odette, and Moura was planning her annual summer trip to Estonia for the harvest. These factors caused HG to fear on April 30 that he would be "just left about and homeless" that summer, which to some extent he was, having to shuffle between several places, including his brother's house in Digswell. Still, HG wrote in pages that were suppressed from the *Postscript* that he was in no hurry to move into Hanover Terrace and establish that household for his "concluding years." "I have learnt this much of life that a good thing expected is better than a thing realised. I shall keep my hopes in that house and tenant it as a relief for my imagination. I shall equip it and furnish it very slowly and carefully and comfort myself against a score of dissatisfactions by telling myself that in Hanover Terrace all will be well with me."[81]

Constance was thrilled about HG's new abode. "When are you going to move in?" she asked in August 1935. "I love moving into a new house, & you talk of it so casually as tho you were trying a new hat. I would like to know all about the walls, & the curtains & the rugs. I see I shall have to come over & look at it—if you don't tell me more than that." Christabel also offered to help decorate HG's new pad, but he turned them both down. As it happened, getting into the house in June 1936 didn't cure his sense of dislocation. Still unsettled, he apologized for sending Constance a postcard. "God knows where the letter paper is anyhow." The postcard showed the central hall of his new abode. "Calm as it looks I (& several other students) once fought the police on that staircase," he pointed out that summer. HG would invite Constance repeatedly to stay with him in the new digs, just as he would Martha, baiting her with a private room and bathroom, a good cook, and all the amenities. "Why not hop over when you are in Paris again & do theatres & movies with me for a week? I should adore it," he wrote to Constance in August 1936. On another occasion, he described his house as "very nice," and, unlike Wallis Simpson's place, his was on the "agreeable" side of the park. Auction documents describe HG's home as a "Regency Period house in charming situation." It had five bedrooms, two bathrooms, three reception rooms, a morning room, a cloakroom, and "good domestic offices." The garage had a "bed-sitting room" and bathroom, and there was a small garden behind the house.

As the summer of 1936 rolled on, Constance began feeling the pinch of renting the beach cottage while still paying taxes on her apartment in Paris. Despite the expense of running two homes, she would sign a six-year lease on her Rue Maspero apartment in the spring of 1936, not long before HG moved into Hanover Terrace. She wasn't altogether convinced that she had done the right thing when she committed herself to another six years in the same place. "I always feel I want to go exploring somewhere, and yet I never do—it's rather hard to alone. This is the only home I have so I thought I might as well keep it." Both of them worked from their homes; indeed, work was the most common topic of conversation on both sides of the correspondence, just as it had been with Moura. While he was seeing Constance in 1935, HG was working at full throttle on his movies. As he told here:

February 23: I have done no end of work since I got here. Everything is going well.

February 25: I'm very busy. I am starting the production of a *second* film.

May 25: My film is working me to death. It is two films now.

June 7: I am frightfully overworked & discontented.

July 10: I am working hard & rather discontented.

October 7: I'm working very hard indeed and it's worrying, irritating & intensely interesting.

October 17: I'm all tied up here with my film work. It's irritating and fascinating.

For this reason, perhaps, and without any apparent self-consciousness, Constance often advised HG on his projects, just as she had done ten years earlier with Harry Crosby. A few days after she left HG, Constance quipped: "But there are so many bad movies. That's because you haven't got started yet." That spring, she reported that she and her father had just been to see Mae West's latest film, *Goin' to Town*. She was not impressed. "Forced vulgarity is terrible. I think often of your movie and long to have it appear. There is a crying need for a new departure in the movies." Once she even suggested a plot for a motion picture. She had been reading the French philosopher Henri Bergson, and wrote out a paragraph for HG to consider as the main idea for a film story. He replied forthwith: "That idea of Bergson's has been done—in Kapek's *Robots* for example. All my love my dear." By August of the same year, Constance had seen so many movies with her father that she was beginning to hate them all. "I wait in fear & trembling to see yours," she joked. "Becky Sharpe in colour was a great failure. 'She' impossible & . . . the decorations were abominable—so truqué'd [fake]. Rocks made of cardboard with glazed paper over them to make them icebergs— childish. Hollywood is in a horrible rut. It needs a new influence—it needs you indeed, HG. Why don't you come?" We know that he did just that at the end of the year—to frolic with Martha in the Connecticut snow and to snow certain Hollywood producers. Constance cautioned HG to be firm about one of his film projects and not to let it drag "as so many, and in fact, all English movies do." He responded that he hoped she wouldn't find his films too slow. The same thought arose on August 22, 1935. HG told Constance that he was working hard on both of his films, "and I go in great fear of your judgment on them."

In April 1935, HG was, like many filmmakers, in money straits. Something unspecified had "gone wrong" with the financing of his film, so he would have all his work "cut out to save it from being spoilt & wrecked by economics—a vexatious battle," he told Constance. The next month, he reported that he had found a producer, the Hungarian Alexander Korda. By July 10, HG had three films going. They were entertaining when he was "fit & fresh. I like all the work," he told her, adding that he was also writing "a very profound book, The Anatomy of Frustration." That fall, HG announced that his films "go on & go on. They will both be good & bad in streaks. I hope you will like the good parts. But when we shall release them only God can tell." HG told Christabel much the same thing: It was fun to start "a new art" in one's "old age, &, if the truth must be told in spite of my modesty, I'm doing it pretty well. I have it seems a screen imagination. I'm more excited artistically than I've been for years."[82] When HG arrived back from his "raid on America," he wrote to Constance about his trip. "I stayed some days in New York, I got snowed up in Connecticut, I week-ended at the Hearst Ranch (Have you ever been there?) and with Cecil B de Mille & at Palm Springs. Mostly I was staying with Charlie Chaplin and nearly everyday I visited a studio or suchlike, & what I don't know about making films now, is hardly worth mentioning." No mention, of course, about his snow bunny, Martha Gellhorn.

In response to Constance's analysis of his film script for *Things to Come,* HG wrote, "You are a wise & subtle critic. [It] isn't right. It's confused, incoherent, hurried at the end, muddled & badly directed. I'm partly to blame but also I was considerably let down in its production. Still it [appears to be] a box office success, I've learnt a lot from it & please God (or not) I'll do better next time."[83] Writing from "Hou-Zee," Charlotte Boissevain's villa at Cap d'Antibes, HG went on to tell Constance that he was resting for a week before heading back to London where he would work on *The Man Who Could Work Miracles*—"cut it & clean it up—for most of it is shot already. I'm more than a little disillusioned about films. They could be magnificent art, but all the art has still to be learnt & the temptation to go back to writing books with nothing between you & your [work] but the printer—no producers, directors, art directors, camera men, actors & actresses, cutters & editors—is about irresistible."

Constance always asked HG about his work whether it involved making movies or meeting presidents. She often reported on her own work, translating, always with some amusing anecdote. When she was in the thick of translating Joseph Kessel's *Le Coup de Grâce*, a self-imposed project, she wrote to HG on July 1, 1935, about the frustrations she was having with her stenographer, a local Santa Barbara woman

> who is an old maid with fuzzy hair, & rather gushing, who is so efficient she changes most of [my] words. So when I get the copy back the words are very perfect, but the spirit & atmosphere of it all has gone. So I spend hours rubbing her words out & putting mine back again. At times, it's rather an improper book, & one just has to use the word "bitch"—but she shies off that like a horse. In fact the whole thing has come to a standstill almost on account of that one word. She has typed a great many people's books she says, & put me right in my place.

Kessel's book, according to Constance, told the story of the relationship between a sergeant and his captain. "The captain is evidently taken from [T. E.] Lawrence & what a pity that he is dead. Did you know him & what was he like? Don't you think in the long run that it is sincerity that one admires most in people?" Perhaps following HG's lead, Constance hoped Hollywood would be interested in her translation of *Coup.* "It appears producers are terribly short of manuscripts at the moment & are crying for new material. Of course mine will have to be all rewritten for the movies. I have done it as a book." Although she apparently never sold a translation or script, Constance, like Moura, continued to keep her hand in translating. Ten years after she wrote the letter about her Kessel manuscript, she reported to HG that she was doing a good deal of translating—"a book of Gen. Odic (very dull) & articles for magazines, written by Camus & Jean Paul Sartre—young writers of the underground, all very cynical."

Constance translated mainly for the exercise. Her real work throughout this time, of course, was running a stable and horse training and racing, and she didn't spare HG the details of her enterprise. When they were on the Riviera, Constance explained her world; but HG's interest, as it later emerged, was lukewarm. He promised that they would go together to Aintree, the site of the Grand National races, "DV or not DV"—*Deo volente,* God willing or not. A few days after arriving back in London, however, he had to beg off Aintree because *Collier's* had persuaded him to go to the United States. Nevertheless, HG wrote to Constance asking her to stay on in England a few days after the Grand National so that they could have "a little dinner" at his place. As it happened, she didn't go to the Grand National in London after all because she was "too poor" after buying a new horse, "L'Estague." "My best one's leg has gone bad, so I <u>had</u> to get another to comfort me. I hope he will be winning very soon." In early April, the new horse took a third in "quite a good race," Constance reported. Unfortunately, she would have to leave for California and thus not be able to see the horse again that season. When she got to Santa Barbara, she found her father much improved, and therefore was somewhat bitter about having to miss the races. When she was arranging her trip back to France at the end of the summer, Constance told HG she would have to sail in mid-September to see her two-year-old, "Le Saulin," run in early October. By this time, she was missing her horses "terribly," she told HG. Just days after the first anniversary of their affair, HG wrote about his winter trip to the United States. "How are you? What are you doing? Are you just as grave and sweet and absurd about your horses and your betting?" The next racing season, Constance was at the races every day. "It is ages since I have written, & it is all the fault of these miserable races, & because I bought a one-eyed horse called 'Casier'—who ran once second, & then won & I sold him to go to England to a club to run in pony races. I only made F 4,000 on the whole deal, but it was better than losing. Sometimes I wish I wasn't so occupied with races for when I take a day off I love it."

Although Constance was ostensibly on vacation when HG met her in the winter of 1934, he found her hard at work with her "racing forms." After she had her coffee, she'd sit down with her newspapers and stacks of notes and reports, and work

> industriously and competently, for three hours, upon the "form" of the current horse-racing. Her knowledge, I am assured, was wide and competent, shrewd and profound. Equipped for the fray she went out—if there was a race-meeting—to bet, or if there was not a race-meeting, then, with a system she had come to believe in, an extremely tedious and boring system (which carried her along for a number of weeks and then let her down), to the Casino.[84]

Crownie was Connie's co-conspirator in horse racing. They co-owned several horses and shared knowledge and a strong passion for the races. Every spring for a decade Crownie visited his cousin in Paris, primarily for the races, but many of their adventures occurred well beyond the tracks at Auteuil and Maisons-Laffitte. In her letters to HG, Constance often mentioned Crownie and their escapades. Crownie and HG met in New York soon after HG and Constance met in France. For whatever reason, whether it was jealousy or bias toward Crownie, HG was neither complimentary nor kind toward Constance's cousin. Indeed, he often demeaned Crownie in word and picshua. On March 11, 1935, HG wrote Constance a short letter with a picshua.

"I met this"

And he sketched a monocled, rather aesthete fellow gesturing vaguely

"at the Colony Restaurant today. It talked of you all the time & seems to love you almost as much as I do. It told me you always kiss your horses & cross them before a race—& all sorts of things about you. Bless you, HG." On the twentieth, Constance replied that "It" had just arrived in Paris. "He was terribly pleased and proud to have met you, & said you were one of the nicest & simplest people he had ever met. I did laugh at your drawing and you can imagine just how he talked. He is a child really, putting on airs rather, but kind and sweet underneath, [and] exasperating to distraction at times."

One of the most exciting adventures Constance and Crownie ever shared was during a road trip in the spring of 1936 to Auvers-sur-Oise, an artists' village three hours northwest of Paris. The purpose of their trip was to view the private art collection of Paul Gachet *fils,* the reclusive son of the late Dr. Gachet, Vincent Van Gogh's physician, friend, and mentor in the last months of Van Gogh's life. They traveled in the company of a young art critic, Alexander Watt, who was to negotiate the viewing. Gachet's house, as Constance described it to HG, was small and ordinary, much like the others in the village, except that it sat on a hill and had a wonderful view of the town and the pretty valley and river. Acquiring most of her information from Watt, she explained that Gachet lived in the house "alone with his cook who is also his wife," and also that after Gachet's father died, the cook tried to throw herself into his grave. "In a moment of sympathy, [the son] helped her out, & married her, but now he treats her badly and she just cooks." Gachet *fils* was "an extraordinary man," Constance wrote, but he "had a horror of picture dealers," which is why he kept Constance and Crownie waiting in the car for nearly an hour while Watt tried to gain their entry. Gachet, as Constance described him to HG, was about sixty years old. He had white hair, a Van Dyck beard, and "piercing blue eyes." At last he was persuaded, and he led the group into a tiny room, which had only a table and six chairs; but the wait was well worth it: The walls were covered with original paintings by Cézanne and other artists. "He talked on & on about Van Gogh. I was afraid we were never going to get any farther," Constance wrote, adding that she eventually summoned up the courage to ask Gachet whether they could move on to see the other art works in his house, since the light was slipping away. Without saying a word, he jumped up from his chair and led the party up a narrow winding staircase and threw open the door of his bedroom. Constance continued:

I will never forget the thrill I had. A tiny room with a narrow bed along the wall facing a window, a chair—no other furniture in the room—and on the wall 12 of the most marvelous Van Goghs you could imagine!! There was a self-portrait over the bed—unbelievable—with a waving blue background (done after the ear was gone). It was in the most ghastly frame all bright gold and heavily carved—by hand he told us proudly. But the portrait was amazing. There was another of the church at Auvers. One of the view from the window of Gachet's house. One of the garden of the asylum at St. Remy where [Van Gogh] was shut up. One of trees—a lithograph done in Japanese style. It took one's breath away literally! Gachet has no money—practically nothing—yet he will never sell a picture, will never let a dealer inside the house. He won't allow anyone to photograph them. Van Gogh pallets with the paint still on them are hung on the door. I like so much the idea of him having them all in his bedroom. Nothing in the room at all except the bed and those twelve paintings.

Gachet told his visitors that the pictures were his "life. I want nothing else." He said he was fifteen when Van Gogh died, and that he had been writing about him and his works ever since. Watt later told Constance that Gachet never finished anything he wrote and never showed his writings to anyone. Watt also told Constance, who repeated it to HG, that Gachet had to be "a little crazy," since "he could get 10 or 12 million francs for those pictures & yet he lives on 5 or 6 francs a day. Ekes out an existence to remain there alone with his pictures and the old woman."[85] Constance closed her letter to HG:

How I wish you had been there—you who understand people so well—for you never can see from this description how really extraordinary it all was. That's what's so wonderful about being alive—you go along thinking you know it all, and then suddenly out of a clear sky something utterly fantastic and unbelievable happens. I can't imagine anybody not being perfectly delighted to be alive, for something wonderful may happen any minute. If only you were here this evening we could talk about it all, instead of which I have probably bored you with this long letter. Good night dear HG. I am so happy because I know you and feel near to you today.

Unlike Paul Gachet, Constance played high-stakes games with her money. As mentioned, she had an unusual, almost paradoxical, attitude toward funds, and she was well aware of this. A comment she made in her 1932 diary said it all: "Whenever I have any money I want to save & save, & when I haven't any, I want to spend & spend!" Later, fully aware of the ridiculousness of her behavior, she wrote to HG about her extravagance: "I went out today & ordered lots of lovely clothes—just because I felt so poor! In May when you come back I will put on the prettiest of [them] & we will dine out somewhere." And, "I haven't been able to pay my stable bill once since I arrived here. The rent of this house & running it, besides the rent & taxes in Paris has been blighting financially for me." HG wasn't fooled by Constance's protestations of poverty, just as she probably wasn't fooled by his. "And you're back in Paris—& you're broke & selling things! My heart is broke in sympathy. When I think of you starving there in Paris I'm tempted to come flying over just for the sake of taking you out to lunch & dinner," he wrote to her on October 7, 1935.

Part of the problem was the global financial crisis. Constance told HG in February 1935 that the Depression in France was worse than ever before. "Everyone is complaining bitterly. If they would only devalue the franc half of their ills would be over—only they won't face it. I wonder if they _ever_ will." A few weeks later, she was back on the subject of the gold standard. She said that her friend Philippe Barrès agreed with HG that France will slowly but surely be forced off the gold standard, "and that when this happens there will be serious trouble. If only you were here you would explain all this for me, but as you are explaining things to Mr. Roosvelt at the moment, I will talk of something else."

Constance had been hearing about various get-rich schemes from her father, who was investing in several projects, one of them a sump-pump of a land deal called the Bruneau Experiment, headquartered in Idaho. The underwriters had a meeting in Santa Barbara, and after her father returned from it, he had another heart attack. On the strength of a rumor that he might get part of his money back, and in spite of Constance's protestations, David sold stock from his other investments to sock another $5,000 into the project. After witnessing this, Constance told HG: "I've decided that betting at the races is but a Sunday School pass time. But in this—racing—you at least get a return on your money in a few minutes, while in their schemes you have to wait years with no return at all—before you finally hear you have lost it all!"

David was not the only speculator in her midst. Constance was surrounded by legions of businessmen in Santa Barbara, but she cared little for their schemes or conversations. All the men she dined with were engaged in some money-making project: land, oil wells, or gold mines. Their passion for the subject made conversation boring but effortless, Constance told HG. "All you have to do is to find out which one of these schemes they've invested large sums of money in—the flood gates then are let loose, & you can sit back quietly & enjoy your dinner without uttering another word." However, if you wanted a little excitement, you simply mentioned someone else's scheme, whereupon the man would "get purple in the face, gesticulate, & explain to you for hours that the other man . . . has, poor fellow, been fooled from the start!"[86]

Remembering and forgetting were favorite topics for Constance and HG. The requests to remain in each other's memory, and conversely, not to be forgotten, occur often in their correspondence. "Lovely to get your letter. And my mind is packed with dear & full memories which I take out & look at and put back again," HG told Constance early on. "I do hope you will not forget me, and that you will write me from time to time. It will help so much," she wrote. "Please don't forget me." In Paris in the summer of 1937, HG told Constance that he liked American books because some of the women reminded him of her. "Not that I need reminding of you." In one letter, HG asked the question twice: "Are we forgetting each other?" "There is no such thing as forgetting between me & you," Constance observed. And then the inevitable happened. HG admitted to having forgotten Constance "a little as something close to me. You've become just a lovely adventure, something warm & dear that happened & went away." By August 3, 1936, he was back to his original position: "I shall never forget you." And in her last letter, Constance wrote that she would love to hear from HG, "if even just a line—to know how you are & that you remember me."[87]

Still, while their affection for each other appeared to be genuine, their relationship was in no way exclusive. In one letter, HG drew a humorous little sketch, as he often did in his letters. "This is Fate," he wrote under the picshua. "He is just juggling with C.C. and H.G." The drawing referred to the difficulty they had in getting together, their schedules always precluding a "meeting"—HG's euphemism of choice. Constance told him that "Fate" looked like "a horrid goblin. I wish I knew him so I could talk to him nicely and arrange several things otherwise." Later in the year, HG announced that it was God who was "really against us." To an objective observer, however, it looked more like human intervention that was keeping them apart. They both talked a good game about arranging a rendezvous, but neither went out of his or her way to make it happen, or to lament very convincingly when meetings couldn't be arranged or fell through. Moreover, they both acknowledged that a certain amount of dodging was part of the game. "It will be too silly if as soon as I get back," Constance wrote, "you come over here, as though we were playing tag across the Atlantic." HG replied, "I shall do all I can to find an excuse to come to Hollywood. If I do, I suppose you will start for Paris at once." They were, to be sure, constantly on the move. When HG didn't go to Santa Barbara as he thought he would in 1935, he gave the lame excuse that the days just "washed by" him, "& before I could turn about I was on the plane flying from Los Angeles to Dallas."[88] When he fired off a note chastising Constance for not phoning him, she responded equally lamely: "But how could I telephone you when I didn't know exactly where you were?" and "The telephone I hate too, above all instruments."[89] Even David Coolidge had trouble keeping up with Constance. "Pa" put it succinctly at the end of 1936: "I never knew you were in Egypt last winter any more than I know where you are now."

HG and Constance were, after all, managing complex schedules—not to mention multiple relationships, if not affairs. In addition to HG, she, like "Fate," was juggling Philippe Barrès, the editor of *Paris Match* and *Paris Soir,* and also the newly widowed Earl of Beaucham, who would ask for her hand in marriage not too long after his wife died in 1936. David Coolidge was relieved that his daughter had declined the offer: "I think you have acted very wisely in turning down the Earl." As it happened, Beaucham, the seventh earl, born William Lygon, died unexpectedly in New York City in 1938. HG, meanwhile, was balancing relationships with Moura, Constance, and Martha—if his account is to be believed—and perhaps sporadic rendezvous with Margaret Sanger and others in the late 1930s. Stringing Constance along week after week, HG finally wrote in July 1936: "I do most extravagantly want to come to Cap Ferrat & I don't think I can. And the more I can't the more I want. But this is to say don't count on me for it." But Constance shed no tears. Although she was disappointed, she understood the implicit terms of the relationship. They were her own terms, after all. Indeed, they were the terms of most of HG's liberated women. Soon after returning home from her trip with HG from Nice to Paris, Constance wrote, as if to demonstrate her understanding, "Write me just when you feel like it, & about anything, & I will do the same. Even if you never write I will always love you a little, as you will me, I hope."

Emerging from HG's letters, however, was the growing frustration with his life and loves, which we saw emerge in the last chapter. "I am all alone," he repeated over and over again, whether he was on land or sea. In an especially revealing letter to Constance from Washington, D.C., in March 1935, where he was meeting with FDR, HG blurted out: "I am lonely. I am afraid as a child of being lonely. I want my woman at my beck and call. I don't want to follow her about. I want her to follow me about. But that is where [we] break away from each other. [Moura] is always flitting off. I scream with rage when I am left alone, like a bad child." In May, HG reported that Moura was "about as ever & there is no doubt that I am in love with two women. But I tell you that & I don't somehow tell her. And she looks at me suspiciously & says 'HG, you were in love with Constance. I know you.' And I say, 'Everybody is in love with Constance.'" In July, the same frustrations rang out again. As HG wrote to Constance:

> I am working hard & rather discontented. I hate this flat. Moura sleeps with me & goes to parties & places & travels with me & won't marry me & take care of me. She's a vagabond. She's lovely & fond & damned selfish. I want to see Mexico City & I want to winter in the West Indies & she clings to her ramshackle Russian life and European gossip. Lovers ought to make sacrifices to each other. Meaning <u>my</u> lovers ought to make sacrifices to me—me being busy writing & creating.

Then, on August 22, he conceded, albeit with a bit of self-deprecating humor, "I and Moura are unchanged. I think perhaps it is time I finished with love & gave myself to high thinking & the solitary life." And on and on, the same immutable problem: "Moura will miss me for a time & then forget about me more & more & whether I shall find her when I get back or not I don't know."[90] HG also wrote about the frustration his relationship with Constance caused him; as he told her on April 30, 1936, "I love you for yourself & for this & that & for all sorts of things & your freckles & Macon & the Negresco & your dear body & for your letters. And now all I get is your letters. But they are lovely letters." That is what it often came to: correspondence from Constance and moments with Moura. On October 27, 1936, HG noted that "Moura flits in & out."

As for Constance, loneliness was also a constant companion that she sometimes despised, sometimes cherished. "I am lonely in the world. I have given [my friends] what I have of sincerity and beauty sometimes but they give me nothing and I am lonely. I have been lonely for years and years, married or alone," she told her diary nearly three years before she met H. G. Wells. Soon after she had met him, she said that seeing him and having his photographs made her feel a little less lonely.

Three years later, she observed in a diary entry, "I am lonely for some-one to love me in spite of everything." Later, on November 12, 1938, Constance mused in her diary that if she had only married a clever man whom she could have helped, "How different, how wonderful my life could have been."

When separations stretched across weeks and months, HG and Constance both observed that perhaps their love had been a dream. That notion emerged just weeks after their first meeting in the South of France. "I am now in such a different life from what I was in Nice," Constance wrote to HG. "Once more it seems as tho it had all been a dream." He wrote, "I'm beginning to feel that you were just a lovely dream & I want you to keep real for me"; and later, "Macon, the Chateau de Madrid, the Colomb d'Or seem like lovely things in a lovely dream." After HG had blessed Constance for existing, she replied, "In-deed, it is I who thank you for existing, & long before I ever met you. The reason for my existence is still rather problematical, but it is per-haps enough that you should have said that, to make it worth while & important to me. Goodnight, sleep well."[91]

Despite their mutual attraction and their fondness for each other, Constance Coolidge and H. G. Wells met infrequently, perhaps only eight times between 1935 and 1937. They drifted apart as easily as they had come together during that enchanting holiday in the South of France in 1934, and they found other diversions to soothe, amuse, ex-cite, and sustain them. Although they continued to correspond regu-larly throughout 1937, their letters were sporadic after that. It isn't clear why HG stopped pursuing Constance, but we can reasonably suppose that he ran out of steam, had nothing left to drive and sustain his dream for a wife. He was frustrated on his major front—with Moura. As for Constance, it may have been HG's age that put her off, or his dedica-tion to Moura, or his insecurities. In her diary entry for February 19, 1938, reflecting on HG's novel, *Brothers,* she sniffed, "He goes a little far in saying aristocracy is the syphilis of humanity. It is the one thing he has never been able to achieve in himself." Or, perhaps, up close the cel-ebrated "World Brain" was not the intellectual Constance had hoped

HG would be. Even while they were still seeing each other, she told her diary, "I have never known an intellectual and I say it with shame"—an odd thing for someone who had met so many intellectuals to say. Perhaps she realized that HG was not the reincarnated Crosby, or that the love she yearned for, the love that would make her whole, was unobtainable. Or perhaps it was something else. In June 1938, she conceded, "I think I have never known how to love. I have always been too selfish." Ultimately, one comes to the same conclusion that Constance so often arrived at: Books and horses were her first loves, and they were safer bets than men.

★ ★ ★

Even when she was seeing HG, Constance was spending a good deal of time with his social nemeses: her wealthy friends from Pekin, Katherine and Herman Rogers, and their friends, David and Wallis, the future abdicated king and his American wife. Although the week Constance spent with the Rogerses in the summer of 1936 probably solidified her place in the royal circle, she began to feel more and more estranged from the Rogerses and their friends from that time on. "They gave me nothing," she wrote to Caresse Crosby. "I didn't like them except thro habit anymore. That happens to me so often, doesn't it to you?"⁹² Still, in October 1936, Constance told her father that she had invited Wallis to stay with her in Paris—"if she wanted to get out the limelight. The whole of Europe was in an uproar when the Hearst press published the news that she was to marry the king. I don't believe it can be true. They might be married morganatically but I doubt if he would dare make her really Queen of England. It would be <u>too</u> fantastic. I hope she comes over to stay with me & then I will know more."

Constance repeatedly invited Wallis to take refuge with her in Paris that fall. On December 9, 1936, she received a typed letter dictated by Lord Brownlow from Villa Lou Viei, the home of Katherine and Herman Rogers, near Cannes, where Wallis was holed up. He told Constance that Wallis's plans were "naturally" in a state of confusion and that she was unable to make engagements. He thought it "likely," however, that she would be staying in the South of France for several weeks. Constance heard that the king had settled £30,000 on Wallis and had bought her a house in Regent's Park, "but Wells says hers is on the wrong side of the street!" Constance told her father.

When *Liberty Magazine* writer Helen Worden was looking for people to interview for an article about the rumored marriage of Wallis Simpson and the Duke of Windsor (the title given Edward VIII after his abdication), she turned to Constance, who apparently intrigued her. Worden described her source as a member of the "so-called exotic set. After three husbands she has gone back to her maiden name," Worden wrote, noting that the divorcée had invited her to "take tea" with her one rainy December (1936) afternoon soon after Worden had arrived in Paris from Cannes, "where Wallis Simpson was beginning her self-imposed exile."[93] Poised on a "low divan spread with red-fox skins," Constance told the reporter that she seriously doubted there would be a union. She said that Wallis was never in love with "David," and that it was the other way around. "From the moment they first met, he wanted her to divorce Ernest. I don't believe she will ever marry David." Worden reported that in Constance's opinion, the whole affair would "break" Wallis, whose "charm lay in her gayness." "'Do you think Wallis Simpson has ever been in love?' I asked Constance Coolidge in Paris. 'No,' she said."

Worden reported that Wallis's other American friends in Paris agreed with Constance. Without naming her source, Worden characterized Mrs. Simpson's marriage to Edward as "the greatest tragedy in the world." Worden also quoted an unnamed source as saying, "Can you imagine a more terrible fate . . . than to have to live up publicly to the legend of a love you don't feel? To have to face, morning, noon, and night, a middle-aged boy with no other purpose in life than a possessive passion for you?"[94] Little did Constance know, indeed, little did the world suspect, that on December 11, King Edward VIII would abdicate the throne, and that on the following June 3, he and the American divorcée would marry.

Despite her comments, Constance somehow remained in the Windsor's inner circle. At the end of September 1937, Wallis and David did visit Constance in Paris. Wallis was very thin and looked tired; the crowds bothered her "terribly, & really it is awful," Constance told her father. They went to Schiaparelli's, but hundreds of people gathered at the entrance. Wallis's bodyguard drove off in her car as a decoy and the two women got into Constance's car, but were charged by a mob of fans just the same. The same thing happened when they emerged from an early movie. The only peace the duchess had that day was during luncheon at Constance's quiet apartment. "She is nervous & afraid to go out. It really must be awful," Constance reported to her father. Lloyd Thomas gave a Paris dinner party for the duke and duchess; but few royals attended because the British embassy had been instructed not to allow French royalty to meet the duchess of Windsor. As Constance told her father:

> Only the Princess de Lucinge (Natty, who really has no right to call herself princess as she divorced & remarried & then divorced again & took back the title). I believe the Duke was very annoyed by the dinner, as he was not properly placed at table. He does not speak French & was put next to the French woman & not at the head of the table, as he should have been.

Constance missed several racing days during their visit and slept thirteen hours the day they left. They were to return in two weeks and would then sail for America—"a most foolish thing to do," in Constance's opinion. "They won't have a moment's peace, but the Duke is very anxious to study housing conditions of the poor on the East side." Because too many people were showing up at Constance's door or calling her on the phone that fall, she instructed Victor, her head of household, to tell most of them that she was out. "I simply cannot go out all the time & race too, & these people would just swamp me."

1938 was another royal year for Constance; she saw a great deal of Wallis and David, particularly in the spring and during the winter holidays. Their charm and sense of style fascinated her. It was also a watershed year since there were, as in 1932, so many deaths. She rang in the year with her father, who now was suffering with "a nervous pain near his heart." She was not happy to be there to hold his hand and oversee his care: "If *only* he could take a little iniative & live his own life, instead of someone else having to plan <u>everything</u>."[95] Still, she was helping him to organize his house, his servants, and his medical care, and she took pride in what she was able to do for him. As she told her diary in January: "Usually in life I have been a rather useless person—at times decorative, & possibly charming. But here & now for the first time I have done something." Constance now wanted to be alone so that she could attain happiness through solitude, reflection, and awareness. "You get awareness by inspiration from books, & individual contemplation. People destroy it utterly."[96]

Nevertheless, Constance began wallowing in self-pity and doubt. She felt like her father's prisoner "every hour of the day," but she also was ashamed for feeling that way. She was frustrated and becoming depressed by all the sickness and ill health. "Thought of Crownie & his cancer of the throat. Trajedies all around me. I have seen so many, & love is so far away from me. I was perhaps tried & found wanting. . . . God knows I need it now. My heart is turning to stone. But I ask too much." In the midst of this, Constance's beloved dog, Simon, suddenly became very sick. "Please God don't take him away from me. I have so little to love in life," she wrote in her diary. With Simon in the hands of veterinarians, Constance and Fred Cowles, a Santa Barbara friend, set off on a day trip for a short escape from the gloom surrounding Santa Barbara. They had wanted to see William Randolph Hearst's ranch in San Simeon for some time, and the trip turned out to be fascinating. As she noted in her diary on January 25, 1938:

A long drive, then the sea, & on the right something that looked like the Great Wall of China, with a palace at the top. . . . Wild animals on the way up, & gatekeepers. "Cowles & Coolidge." "Yes, pass on." We went in the back way by mistake, but looked thro a door at the most magnificent swimming pool I ever saw. Blue & gold mosaic, white statues. The chateau—Gothic, towers, carvings, marble everywhere, palms & flowers, magnificent view of green mountains & blue sea. Menials appeared. Fred whispered I was a friend of the Duchess of Windsor—we were shown right in. Mr. Hearst a Nero among his slaves dressed in pajamas. Marion Davies charming. Showed me all over the house. Such rooms, dining room like a cathederal. One hundred people stayed in the house New Years. Exquisite colors—blues, golds, reds. Priceless tapestries. Everything priceless. Breathtaking, fabulous place. A pool on the front terrace with black marble bottom so the water looked like ink. Talked a long while to Hearst. A big man loosely knit, a yellow sagging face with keen blue eyes. She calls him W.R. Great men seem to like to be called by their initials.

They declined Hearst's invitation to spend the night because Constance wanted to get back to Simon. At 11:00 P.M. that night, he died. They dug a little grave in the rose garden, where the dog would be "sleeping, dreaming of those he loved, forever happy, amen," as Constance entered into her diary the next day. Meditating on the event, Constance said that grief was in some ways like an illness. "It puts you on another plane of consciousness, where the ordinary objects of life appear different. It also anilhates time & space. Everything seems to stop. I feel I haven't the courage to go on, so utterly alone now without him. I have never been so near in love & understanding to any mortal as I have to this small dog, & my grief is greater than it could be for any human being." That was an extreme statement, of course. Two weeks later, Constance was once again full of joy. "Life is a marvelous thing. Every day I am happy just to have been born. Indeed, I could come back joyfully many times to this world I love, & when I do leave it, I believe it will be to return again. Indeed, I would live my same life all over again & face my joys & sorrows with pleasure again."

Now forty-six, Constance was conscious of the effects of time and gravity on her face and body, and she was exceedingly critical of herself. She faced some stiff competition, for many of the women she compared herself to were movie stars who passed through Santa Barbara. She had seen Marlene Dietrich, for example, several times at a local restaurant, and was quite struck by her: "extremely good looking. Very chic. She looks extremely aristocratic, but she talks a little too much of money & names." Constance's hairdresser said that Dietrich was impossible to work for. "This is probably true, but in this sloppy era I admire anyone who is soigné'd." Lying in bed in her old room on Samarkand Drive, Constance could survey the hills that stretched into the horizon. She could also see herself in a mirror on the door. "It is far enough away to hide all the defects, & I look like I did when I was young—'beauté du diable' they called it. One should always keep on being beautiful—as far as one is able. Never let go. Never give up, & talk little about it—or about anything which is very important in your life. Keep them in the garden among the roses, like my Simon. Hidden, but very real."

Back in Paris, Constance saw a good deal of Wallis and David in March and April, and she commented on the get-togethers in her diary. She wrote about Wallis's clothes, jewelry, charm, and figure: "She is very thin—eats nothing—sometimes a chop and puréed carrots," she noted on March 16. They often talked about the Versailles house, its furnishings and servants, and about David. "She said the Duke never noticed when English people were rude to him in the Riviera. 'Do you realize he has never told his side of the story? He has never said one word. Do people give him the credit for that?'" Constance gave the couple a dinner on March 22, which "was a great success."

> Wallis looked lovely in a blue sequin dress. [She] did interrupt the Duke rather but then he stayed in the dining room a long time afterwards, & talked politics very well. He said Ceckoslovakia is a ridiculous country, how could anyone go to war for that. We went to the movies after & it was very funny. He didn't laugh as much as the rest of us, but I think he had a good time, & called me Constance for the first time, which pleased me.

Constance was called back to California and her father later that month, and despite her attention and tender loving care, David died in May. In her 1938 diary, she told the gut-wrenching story of his last days, the dispersal of his household, and the long trip back east to bury his ashes in the family plot at Mt. Auburn. She had been back in Europe only a month when she received the telegram saying that her father was in very bad shape. When Constance arrived at the hospital, David was comfortable, but he soon lapsed into delirium and became more and more delusional, even off morphine. On April 27, Constance wrote in her diary that "his mind is gone"; and on May 1, "David is dying." When she learned in the early morning hours of May 2 that her father had died, she was relieved that his torture had ended. "My darling Pa, now you become mine for ever as you were, young & charming & very sweet," she wrote in her diary. After David Coolidge was cremated, Constance told her diary: "Now my night has another star. I have so many!" She had "a ghastly time" during and following her father's death, she told Freddie Foster. "With him goes forever all my youth—& no one left to remember things with. He kept my baby clothes, & every letter I ever wrote him, every post card." She told HG that David was the last of her family, "& now he has gone too. No one will ever again think of me as a child, or scold me, or remember things with me."

The *New York Herald Tribune* ran a two-paragraph story describing David Coolidge, seventy-five, as a former Boston and New York landscape architect, who, among other things, had a hand in the artistic development of Staten Island. The *New York Times* noted that he had designed many fine estates in New England and in New York City. His daughter, Mrs. Constance Coolidge of Paris, France, was with him when he died, the piece said. A few weeks later, Constance pasted into her diary three obituary clippings for her father and a photograph of Simon and wrote, "Two best friends gone in the same year." In one of their last conversations, her father told her that he often was "astonished that an old fool like me could have had a daughter who has made a name & position for herself in all the world." Constance stayed on through the summer and took care of David's affairs and household. On June 14, she had an epiphany of sorts after reading *Amitié Amoureuse* by Stendhal. The book was "exquisite," but it gave her a shock to realize how "material" she had become.

Is it too late to get back? I think I have never known how to love ever. I get around it by saying I have never seen anyone worthy to be loved. But that is certainly not so. Harry was. I could have made of him what I wanted at one time. But then, I took real love for hysteria & he was so young. . . . I am not a fine or strong enough person to be worthy of love or even to recognize it when I have it.

Five days later she thought, "Sometimes I wonder if I had not better do something constructive."

From her perch in Santa Barbara society, Constance stayed in touch with the outside world. She continued to write to HG. When one of her friends mentioned that HG had been her idol when she was young, Constance was inspired to write this diary entry in July 1938: "But people no longer listen much to him. People do not want to be taught any more. They have discovered that what they have learnt is all wrong & who can truly proficy the future now? A feather blown by the wind, & which wind will blow?" The old specter of loneliness returned. She asked herself whether it was time for her to retire to a life of reading. "I am lonely for a man, for some one to love me in spite of everything. Am I strong enough to stay alone & grow old, & know that I can no longer inspire love? I never knew before how used I was to admiration. Can I now do without it, & not mind?"

Constance would have to test her mettle again that summer. Crownie was very ill with throat cancer. Too many x-rays, forty-two treatments of fourteen minutes each, had burned him "all up. I can't talk or swallow. Well enough dear about me & how are you dearest? How I think of the past dear. Those wonderful times we had racing in Paris together. The lunches at Willie Head's, how I miss those times & besides we were so successful in racing—oh my what a wonderful dream it all seems now darling." Connie told her diary that Crownie was able to make even cancer attractive "because he has it."

Early on, Constance had suspected that Crownie was exaggerating his condition, but as his letters throughout 1937 and 1938 grew more and more pathetic, the reality set in. In early 1937, Crownie craved

Constance's presence. "You are so brave and I such a coward. You give me courage always." By August, he was fading. "You will never know what I have been through & am still going through. I can't stand the pain much longer." And then, as if liberated from all former and normal constraints, he zeroed in on another subject: their relationship and her lack of candor over the years.

> As for my being jealous—that is really foolish. Of course I haven't been in any way hurt at your having your little affairs with your men. You know I have never minded that as long as you told me everything. You sometimes did but not always. For example, you always spoke of Barrès as a friend & nothing more. Of course I believed you—in every way. Only about two months ago, for the very first time you told me he had been your lover for some years. Of course this did hurt me a very great deal, for I always believed you & it sort of made me lose confidence in you. I also was told—though could not believe it . . . that "what's his name"—seems to me it was a Rothschild—you used to go & dine at his house quite often for a time. I never thought anything about it [until] one day at the Club a friend of his & also mine came to me and told me all about it. Of course it was hard to believe because you had said there was nothing in it. Oh dear how I wish you could pick out some nice, honest, & attractive man, & <u>no Frenchman ever</u>. All my love, your heartbroken Crownie.[97]

The next month, he poured out more emotions: how he missed her and how often he thought about "those happy 12 years of our wonderful friendship—something that does not come very often. But the end, I suppose, must come sooner or later to everything & it's all very very sad. I love you darling & don't want you to leave me now. P.S. Am enclosing bill for stable." Surgery was performed just days after David's death. While technically a success, the operation left Crownie incredibly weak.

On August 26, 1938, while in Santa Barbara, Constance received the news that Crownie had died. Frank Crowninshield sent the telegram.

Part of it read, "I KNOW HOW YOU WILL GRIEVE YOU WILL NEVER REALIZE HOW HAPPY YOU MADE HIM SUZETTE AND I SEND ALL OUR LOVE AND GRATITUDE." Constance was crushed once again. That night she wrote in her diary, "Oh my Crownie, how can I bear it without you? My one understanding, kind, generous noble friend. What a year this has been. There is no one left for me to grieve over now. Everyone has gone. Now I am really alone." She wrote that she could never again have as loving and understanding a friend as Crownie. It had taken her years to appreciate him, "but I did at last, & I think he knew I did." Constance never explained, either to Crownie or to her diary, why she didn't go to be with him at any time throughout his dying months.

Her problems compounded. Constance received a letter from Cousin Charlie on December 1 saying that as there was no money for December, he would loan her $700 to get through the month. After hearing her guardian's explanation of the situation, Constance was furious. In the privacy of her diary, she vented some spleen over Charlie: "I do feel that Charlie Adams is extremely casual & careless in his management of my affairs. It seems almost as tho he enjoys having me worry. It is all most discouraging."

With her American world falling apart, Constance spent the holidays with the Rogerses at their Basque-style villa, Lou Viei, which they had just remodeled. "Now it is all white with a glass table, in other words, a small house trying to look pretentious." Worse yet, Constance's room had white walls and black cretonne curtains with giant white flowers. "How the ghost must suffer," she wrote her diary on Christmas Eve. In a letter to Freddie Foster, Constance observed that the year before she was celebrating a quiet and lovely Christmas with her father. "It is sad to know that now all these days of fete—Xmas, New Years, birthday— will forever more be spent alone or as an interloper in other people's families."

The Christmas dinner at the Windsors was amusing, Constance wrote to Foster. The house was beautiful, and there were seventeen guests, the André Mauroises having been the last to arrive. Wallis's dress was stunning; it was heavily embroidered and looked "rather like a Xmas tree, very magnificent & a beautiful diamond necklace—a Xmas present from the Duke—only she wore it as two sprays of diamonds instead of a necklace." All the guests received small presents; then, after the turkey and plum pudding, a gypsy orchestra played and sang, and Lady Brownlow danced the Lambeth Walk alone.[98] "The Duke wore his kilts as he always does in the evening except when he goes out."

Constance noted in her diary that the dinner was not very good, and the periods between courses were long. When Wallis and David entered, no one curtsied to Wallis. Constance sat next to Colin Davidson, David's friend and equerry. Wallis's Aunt Bessie wore a red satin dress with a huge red rose, and the duke "hurried about" talking to Constance, but only about racing. On the twenty-ninth, Constance and the Windsors dined with the Rogerses at Lou Viei. This time, the duke was difficult to talk to. Even at his best, he had a one-track mind: "Only one woman exists for him. All others are just bores. Yet he likes to talk to me," Constance told her diary. She also noted that the royals and their entourage spent New Year's Eve in Monte Carlo, but that the crowd was awful, "just standing around them staring." The duke wouldn't return to England until "they acknowledge his wife on the same rank as himself. He feels very strongly about this as it was promised him by his brother before he left England. It has nothing to do with [Wallis], as she does not care at all," Constance wrote to Foster.

As she entered her thoughts for December 31, 1938, Constance first reflected on the people she had lost that year. "The last day of a sad year. Pa. Crownie. Anne Gould Strotz. Dick Crane. Richard McCreery. Where are they all now? & my Simon.[99] And so this book is ended & another cover shut." At the back of her diary, Constance graded the books she had read during the year. She gave Louis Bromfield an A-plus for *The Rains Came*.[100] Eve Curie got an A-minus for *Madame Curie*. HG earned a B-minus for *The Brothers*, while Margaret Mackay scored lowest, with a C-minus for *Like Water Flowing*.

Back in Paris, Constance again wrote to Foster. She was brought down by the holidays. As she surveyed the photographs in her room, she realized that except for HG, all her nearest and dearest friends and relatives were dead.

> Moura is dining with me Tuesday. She has gone to Esthonia but comes back then. HG is in Australia & getting in very wrong I hear. No, there is a certain desperateness about having no one left. I like vaguely a lot of people. I see them all & I meet new ones, but it's the old ones I want. The ones like you, who have lived my life with me. Only those can be real friends. Only those count.[101]

While the invitations and notes passed back and forth between Constance and Wallis over the following months, their relationship began to fade. Perhaps what troubled it was Wallis's request that Constance pick up several pairs of stockings, size 9, from "Peter's," and send them to her. Still, they saw each other into the 1950s, and Constance always had a new anecdote about the duke and duchess. She relayed one to Caresse in 1954, after lunching with Wallis: "The man who wrote 'Gone with the Windsors' dropped dead in the street the other day, & Wallis said, 'At last I can believe in God!'[102] She looks wonderfully, really, & is amusing. One can forgive a lot for that."

In the midst of her frustration with friends and friendship, Constance met someone new—someone who would change her life. She was swept away by the charm, attentiveness, and good looks of André Magnus. She reported to her diary in March 1938 that he was handsome, clever, shy, not very temperamental, and "surprisingly sentimental—the first Frenchman I have ever known like that." Constance was seeing other men, notably Philippe Barrès, but Magnus was now making an impression on her. "It is nice to have someone devoted who calls up twice a day."

On April 7, Magnus put Constance on the train that would take her to the ship that would take her to her father, who was in critical condition in a Santa Barbara hospital. In front of everyone at the train station, he proclaimed that he loved her, "& he kissed me & kissed me," Constance wrote in her diary that night. "I was quite carried away. All the way to Cherbourg I thought of him & was in a glow. I couldn't even read." The next day, Constance wrote, "Really, that last week in Paris was extraordinary. Philippe who only saw me to make love to me, broke the Tuesday engagement, & never even said goodbye. He will say he didn't know I was going, & André Magnus who phoned twice a day & really was quite mad at the station. 'You won't kiss anyone on the boat will you,' he said."

After having been Platonic friends for less than two years, Constance and Magnus married—on a lark—in October 1940 in Antibes, where she was living; unlike her other spur-of-the-moment marriage, this one worked. According to Magnus, they had "a long beautiful love affair that lasted until the end." In his apartment overlooking Paris's swank 16th arrondissement, the charming and elegant Magnus, a recipient of all three levels of France's Legion of Honor (he found it amusing that he has been decorated by both De Gaulle and Mitterrand), was surrounded by dozens of photographs of his late wife, sixteen years his senior, and several fine works of art she had acquired in the Far East. Magnus's fondness for Constance is nowhere more evident than in the hundreds of letters, notes, and postcards he wrote to her over their thirty-three years of marriage. His amusing letters never failed to carry a whimsical pet name for his wife: Petit mousie, little snowball of mine, little pearl in the big ocean, My Easter Bonnet, my crystal teardrop. "I love you with love sincere," he once wrote to Constance.

In a suppressed portion of the *Postscript,* H. G. Wells wrote that he ran into Constance in New York City in December 1940. She appeared "rather less happy about life, married to a young Frenchman, her hair dyed, as though she was trying to climb back to youth instead of going on to the valiant middle age she deserves. With so many of us, sex, having served its purpose, becomes an incurable habit, and that I think is the case with her."[103] Whether his hunch about her was correct is not known; however, fourteen years later, Constance confessed to her old friend Caresse that the urge to have affairs had passed: "Even when I see lovely young men . . . I have no yen to go to bed with them at all. In fact, I sigh with relief that I'm not going to get in any agonizing situations. Will he call? Where is he now? Does he really love me? It is so peaceful & nice this way to look at them objectively, with no personal connection."[104]

The Magnuses saw World War II from the United States. At the end of 1940, they caught a ship out of Portugal bound for New York. Magnus almost immediately went to work for J. Walter Thompson, the city's leading ad agency, first assigned to a campaign to promote milk. Soon he was chosen to lead the campaign, suggested by Eleanor Roosevelt, to make New York City the fashion center of the world. "I knew nothing about fashion," Magnus said, "but I was a Frenchman—so *I knew* about fashion!" In 1941, Magnus, who had been an officer in the French air force, was inducted into the United States Army Air Force. While he trained at Sheppard Air Force Base in Texas, Constance kept the home fires burning in Washington, D.C. Among other things, she volunteered a few days a week as an aide at St. Elizabeths, a psychiatric hospital. Magnus was assigned to intelligence, never left the country, and was discharged in 1946, just after his thirty-eighth birthday. They returned to France, set up housekeeping in a string of Paris hotels, including the George V, and Magnus continued carving what was to become a brilliant career in media and public relations.[105] He and Constance traveled a great deal, trekking all over the Western world taking cures, hiking, swimming. They were fixtures at Aix, Vichy, Evian, Annecy, St. Moritz, Ischia, and Arosa. For the next thirty years, Constance lived life happily and fully, pursuing her passions: buying, training and racing horses, reading, going to the theater.

She also continued to work on her spiritual health, delving deep into Eastern religions. Among other things, she attended Hindu "healing" lectures for her arthritis. By 1960, she was thinking a good deal about the difference between the human being's physical and spiritual forms. "The spirit of man," she told Caresse, "can never be destroyed. It leaves the body & takes on another form. The physical dies, is cast off like a cloak, & the spirit is freed, & lives. There, I do believe this." Eastern religions did not quash Constance's love of shopping. "I hear Schap's collection is awful. Dior's is lovely. I wish I didn't like to try clothes, above all when I can't afford to. It is wicked really. Let's go to India & live in Kashmir. I am weak & foolish & spoiled," she wrote to Caresse. During a two-month rest in Switzerland, Constance recommenced work on her autobiography, although she admitted that "I speak & write now a mongrel language—neither French or English, & can spell in none of them!"[106] The old specter, debt, continued to haunt her, even into her sixties. "I am saving & hope to begin to pay some on my worst bills this month," she told Caresse Crosby. And, as in the earlier days, she always had a few schemes going.

In her last letter to HG, Constance described her new home in The Anchorage, an "apartment hotel" at 1900 Connecticut Avenue and Q Street in Washington, D.C. She had been there only a few months when she wrote on December 23, 1945, that she was in conflict about their next step. "It is possible that we will come back to France in the spring, although I do not look forward to it very much. It will be so different. I do not know where I want to live anymore." In 1946 and 1947, the Magnuses and Caresse Crosby made extensive plans to produce an ambitious motion picture in Technicolor about life at the Vatican, of all things, focusing on Pope Pius XII. Because of his experience with the French entertainment industry, Magnus was to be the chief adviser. "It's a million-dollar idea," he wrote to Caresse. "It should be one of the biggest pictures ever made." Caresse did most of the early legwork, found "a man in Rome," Romolo Marcellini, and corresponded with Vatican representatives and the Catholic Moving Pictures Center. The project floundered over Vatican permissions, distribution rights, percentages of box office receipts, and options.

Undaunted, Constance and Caresse planned another venture in the early 1950s: They would publish titles that were out of print or had no English translation. Caresse would find the titles, handle the editing and some production. Constance would do the translating, some of the production legwork, and some marketing. The imprimatur was to be "C.C.C.C." or "Four C's." One of the first titles was Leo Tolstoy's *The Law of Love and the Law of Violence*, a book about the moral and ethical aspects of pacifism. Constance sent Caresse chapters as she completed them. In one shipment she included a note about her work: "Working hard. Hope you like it. At times, due to [Tolstoy's] age, it is very confused. I've had to clarify it as much as I dared without losing the sense. Of course there probably [are] lots of words spelled wrong, & perhaps words to change. But how wonderful to think he wrote this so long ago, & yet it is as aplicable today as then." Another cover letter read, "Believe me, this French translation is *not* very clear—is often confused, probably mine is too. But Tolstoy . . . what long sentences. I think I've done the last part better. I got more in the swing of it, but change it as you see fit—words, etc." This project also fizzled.[107] Caresse considered other titles: *The Matador* by Marguerite Steen; *High-Minded Murder* by Christopher Sykes; Harry's *Diary* in a continental edition; and her own short stories. She thought there was a good chance that she and Constance could bring out eight titles a year, for a net profit of about $6,000. It appears that all the projects were eventually scrapped for one reason or another.

Meanwhile, Constance kept hatching schemes. At the end of 1954, she received a Christmas card from Ray Atherton; this prompted her to write to him, suggesting, as she told Caresse, "that we break the Trust I made for him in 1912, & I would give him part of the capital. However to this he never replied even. He really is pretty much of a 'petit monsieur' & always has been. Au fond, I prefer a brigand like Bert! Especially if he has a fortune & gives you half!!"[108]

★　　　★　　　★

Constance Crowninshield Coolidge Magnus died at the American Hospital on the fashionable west side of Paris on April 30, 1973. Her husband placed her ashes in a vault on the highest hill at Pere Lachaise in Paris, the cemetery to die for, being, then as now, some of the most expensive real estate in Paris. He kept three fresh pink roses in a vase attached to her white marble stone. Engraved in gleaming gold letters are two words: "My Love."

While not a celebrity of H. G. Wells's caliber, Constance Coolidge was a colorful personality of international renown who was watched for decades. She got her fair share of notice—and ink—on several continents. In death, however, Constance was overlooked. The obituary for the serial heartbreaker was little more than a perfunctory notice. The *Boston Evening Globe* ran a short Associated Press story. Filed in Paris, the piece described Constance as a native of Boston and the wife of André Magnus, a public relations and management executive in the French film and radio industry. She was "well known in Paris horse racing circles" as the owner of a string of racehorses, and she had been a distant relative of Calvin Coolidge and a niece of Charles Francis Adams, secretary of the navy under Hoover.

There wasn't a hint about the exceptional life Constance had led all over the world. Nothing about the Brahmin background she had rejected early in her life, or the wild Parisian life that replaced it. Nothing about her meetings with Mark Twain and Winston Churchill, her sittings with John Singer Sargent, her friendships with the Windsors or the literati: the Crosbys, Hart Crane, Somerset Maugham. No mention that as a young wife in China, she trained Mongolian ponies, lived in a temple, and rode cross-country on horseback to the Eastern tombs, and later, into battle. Nothing about her hosting world leaders, or about her being one of the first female airplane passengers in China. Nothing saying that although she was sometimes interested by high society, she was more often bored by it; that she considered herself a socialist, but turned to the Ouija board and the Bible for comfort and advice; or that she was a self-made intellectual who forever doubted her intelligence ("I have a vagrant mind with a smattering of knowledge of many things and a real grasp of none of them"), but preferred horses and books to people and things of the spirit to things of the body. No mention that while she met life head-on—"Indeed, I would live my same life all over again and face my joys and sorrows with pleasure"—she often chastised herself for not having accomplished more. "What a frittering away life I lead," she told her diary in 1938, just after she declined an offer to write a European column for United Press.

In Constance's obituary there wasn't a word, of course, about her love life, not the slightest suggestion about her role as an international femme fatale: four husbands, dozens of marriage proposals, and a trail of broken hearts wrapping around the globe. And certainly no mention about her liaison with H. G. Wells, ignited on the Côte d'Azur in the winter of 1934, long after she had taken the writer as her intellectual hero and a year after the writer, a self-proclaimed feminist and notorious lady-chaser, had fallen in love with someone else and had all but sworn off womanizing.

Over her long lifetime, Constance found many compromises to be sure, but she harbored few regrets, for as she once wrote to Caresse about their futures: "I think whatever happens will be alright . . . for I have loved the stars too much to ever fear the darkness."[109]

5

The Passionate Friends: HG and Martha Gellhorn, 1935

Marquise de Jouvenel, Martha Hemingway, Martha Matthews

Christabel dear, I am becoming a bad, discursive old man—no credit to any-one. I give myself up. Moura might to have taken care of me & all this wouldn't have happened. As it is I shall now become the Bad Man of Hanover Terrace—spreading ruin. I don't like flirting & having little es-capades. I don't like going about kissing wild & free.

—HG to Christabel, November 14, 1935

National and world affairs, appropriately, brought Martha Ellis Gellhorn, twenty-six, and Herbert George Wells, sixty-eight, together. The White House was their vortex in March 1935, FDR and Eleanor their surrogate parents and kindred spirits, respectively; as hosts, they were also inadver-tent matchmakers. HG was looking for a world leader to connect with. Martha was looking for someone to complain to. From that point, other forces would take over: HG's strong physical attraction to the vivacious, intelligent, good-looking, and well-born young woman in his midst, and

Martha's gravitational pull to influential people, especially men of letters. As the story goes, the aging writer and the young federal employee met over a meal at the Roosevelts' residence in the mid-1930s. That they were both guests of the first family in 1934 and 1935 is without question, and, as it happens, Martha claimed the White House as the site of their first meeting. She told this author: "I met Wells at the White House in 1934 or 35 and saw him last in London during the war [in] 1943. He was not a central feature of my life nor I of his."[1] As it will become clear, Martha left a good deal out of that chronology.

In the mid-1930s, H. G. Wells was an institution, a household name, and Martha Gellhorn was an ambitious and fearless young woman carving out a new career with the U.S. government. It wouldn't be long before the sassy blonde from St. Louis would be signing book contracts, filing stories from Spain, and marrying one of the most popular writers of the century, Ernest Hemingway. Still in the future were her many daring exploits—dodging bombs and nursing wounded soldiers—encountered as she covered the world's wars in Spain, Finland, China, England, Italy, France, Germany, Java, and Vietnam. Indeed, much lay ahead for Martha, although by 1934, she had already published her first novel, *What Mad Pursuit,* the odd story she later disavowed about the adventures of three college girls. After the book was published, Martha's father commented, "rightly, that he could not understand why anyone had published it. I have, also rightly, obliterated it ever since," Martha later wrote in her volume of collected peace-time articles, *View From the Ground.*[2] By 1934, Wells—as she always called him, never HG—had held court with the major statesmen of the era and advised prime ministers, presidents, and kings. Still ahead was his frenetic work to draft and translate into many languages of the world several versions of his *Declaration of the Rights of Man,* the document the United Nations later would adopt as its own. [3] In the future lay his work on a world encyclopedia, a low-tech forerunner to the Internet, and his unsettling novel, *You Can't Be Too Careful.*

Being careful, taking things slowly was never Martha's style. Back in May 1931, she had told a former, though still-hopeful, St. Louis beau by the name of Joseph Stanley ("Stan") Pennell, that life, as she saw it, was "an ecstatic business of drawing breath and beating the system."[4] Martha knew of what she spoke. By her twenty-first birthday, she had essentially beaten the system bloody. In the summer of 1929, for example, after dropping out of college that spring because she was restless and bored, Martha wangled her first jobs, at the Albany (N.Y.) *Times Union* and the *New Republic,* by sweet- and fast-talking the editors. Although she claimed to have started writing at fourteen, she had no training in journalism. She landed her first freelance assignment the same way—through the back door. In that case, Martha went to the editor of the *St. Louis Post-Dispatch* proposing a series of articles about the Southwest. He refused to assign her, but agreed to read her stories after they were written. Martha then went to the Santa Fe Railroad, told them she had been assigned to write the series, and asked them to arrange free transportation for her, which they did. As it turned out, the railroad company was pleased with Martha's publicity, the *Post-Dispatch* approved the articles, and the *New Republic* saw the pieces, triggering a job offer.[5] Martha was on a roll. Martha was on track. Martha had a shtick—a modus operandi and vivendi. A few months later, in February 1930, she pulled the same trick to send herself to Europe. This time, she talked the Holland America ship line into giving her free passage in return for what she later described as "a glowing article" for their trade magazine. Barely twenty-one, she had one suitcase, $75, and her sights on Paris and a brilliant career. "I intended to become a foreign correspondent . . . and Paris was the obvious place to launch my career," she later wrote in *View.* As it happened, the launch was temporarily delayed. Martha spun her gears for several years before jettisoning herself into the hard and cold world of the war correspondent.

In the autumn of 1934, and back in the United States after ambling all over Europe, Martha landed a life-changing job as a relief investigator for the Federal Emergency Relief Administration (FERA). This work was well-suited to her; she traveled all over the country to interview unemployed relief recipients about their lifestyles and then filed reports to Washington. Travel was in her blood; she was absolutely energized by it.

Years earlier, from the "Sunshine Special," Martha told Pennell that "one ought to travel more—farther. It makes one come alive."

Martha landed that government job after yet another bit of quick thinking and system-bending. She asked Marquis Childs, a friend and reporter for the *St. Louis Post-Dispatch*'s Washington bureau, to arrange an interview for her with Harry Hopkins, the head of FERA. Qualified by virtue of her obvious intelligence and spunk, her backpacking travels in Europe, her roamings across the United States, and her patchwork quilt of writing experiences, Martha leapt into the fray. For nearly a year she crisscrossed the country talking to a socioeconomic set she hadn't mixed with much during her privileged upbringing in St. Louis and her three years at the seven sisters' college, Bryn Mawr. Martha described what she saw in New England and in the South as scenes out of Dickens. Among other things, she reported on fertility among the poor in Nashua and Concord, New Hampshire; syphilis and economic hopelessness in Gastonia, North Carolina; and "poor whites" in the South. She was one of three professional writers Hopkins would tap.[6] In July 1933, he picked Lorena Hickok, the great intimate friend of Eleanor Roosevelt's, to be FERA's chief investigator. Martha also grew to love Hickok, although probably not in the same way Eleanor may have. Still, in January 1935, Martha confided to Hickok that, for her, one of the best things about returning to America and becoming "a slave in the great forward movement of progress (known otherwise as the New Deal) is to have found you in the midst of it all. I consider you a definite addition to my life and am quite childishly delighted about the whole thing."[7] Perhaps Martha had come a long way since July 1931, when, rather importantly, she had written to Pennell during an extended tour of the United States that work was "loathsome, but no work is even more so." As her letters to the unrequited lover so well demonstrate, Martha at that time was neither in love with nor even in synch with her fellow human beings. At the time she was a young snob, full of herself; she was decisive in her expressions of annoyance and disgust for the many assaults on her five senses. For example, traveling across country in 1931, she reported to Pennell:

April 16, in Los Angeles: Palm trees along the boulevards, and God boun-
tiful with greenery. But as usual humanity is a stench in the nostrils of the
knowing. If there is anything which screws my guts into spasms of hatred,
it is the nasal voice. And cow-like, superlative-slinging enthusiasm.

April 27, from Reno: Women with indiscrimate hips, clothes by Sears
Roebuck, speakeasies serving dago red [wine] called sparkling burgundy.
Christ I am fed to the gills. The beauty of this land—and it is beautiful—
comes as an insult to eyes blinded with the dismal spectacle of humanity.

May 14, Indianapolis: Why is travelling third class in Europe so en-
nobling—but simply degrading here.

Dayton, Pickwick Terminal restaurant: Disgruntled vegetables floating
in grease, strangled with extraneous long black hairs.

Martha's revulsion, thus, was not limited to St. Louis or to the Midwest; nor was it just a phase she went through as a girl. Throughout
her long life she claimed to hate her homeland, her fellow countrymen,
and, indeed, the American way of life. She once said she would never
return to California, for example, because that state was "the absolute
end of the line." For the most part, however, her disgust was politically
motivated. In 1990, she told Milton Wolff, an old friend from the Spanish Civil War (the last commander of the Abraham Lincoln Brigade,
and, at that time, a tall, dark, and handsome young man), that she
wasn't an ideologue, "but a simple soul, fixated on justice and injustice
and I mistrust all governments and some I plain hate. Like here [Wales]
and in the U.S."[8] She also said that she hated being a citizen of the
United States. That statement was prompted by a trip to Panama in
1990, when she had covered the U.S. intervention. Later that year, she
vented her spleen over the U.S. government's backing of the Khmer
Rouge. "That backing was purely spite against Vietnam but it may well
kill Cambodia a second time. It's hell to be a citizen of the last super-
power." Thirty years earlier, Martha had told Wolff that the United

States gave her "acute claustrophobia. I am happiest in small backward countries."[9]

Despite her revulsion for humanity in 1931, Martha soon became outraged by her agency's treatment of the unemployed, and that rage brought her to the White House a few months after she began the FERA job. She wanted to resign in protest over several examples of what she believed to be an ineffectual, corrupt, even heartless government program; but instead of letting her go, Hopkins suggested she take her complaints to the top—to the president of the United States. Martha was not in the least intimidated by the suggestion since, through her mother's connections, she already knew the Roosevelts—having dined with then-Governor and Mrs. R. during her Albany days. With her trademark nerve, Martha described for Eleanor the indignities the poor suffered under the government's umbrella; then she repeated herself to the president and his guests over an otherwise polite December dinner in the first family's home. The Roosevelts not only heard Martha out but also talked her into staying on the job. Moreover, what began as a huffy little visit led to a lifetime friendship with Eleanor Roosevelt. Throughout her early career, Martha would return again and again to the Roosevelts for moral support, advice, and help. Once, for example, she asked FDR to send wheat to the Spanish Republic and to come to the aid of Spanish Civil War veterans. To convince the president of the desperate situation, Martha arranged for a July 8, 1937, White House screening of Joris Ivens's documentary film, *The Spanish Earth*. Her then-lover, Ernest Hemingway, not only helped shoot the Loyalist documentary but wrote and narrated the script; he also shelled out more than $3,000, one-fourth of the cost of producing it. A half century later, Martha would tell an old friend that in her opinion there was only one other great man of politics after FDR, and that was Mikhail Gorbachev.[10] Through Eleanor, Martha once obtained letters of safe passage to various countries.

While her federal career seemed to be going extremely well once she had recovered from her initial burst of outrage, Martha was fired, albeit reluctantly, in the fall of 1935, for her part in stirring up sentiment among some Idaho farmers and ranchers who had lost their property.[11] Again, the Roosevelts came to Martha's aid. Before she had even cleaned out her desk, they invited her to come and stay with them, feeling they could be a positive influence on Martha at a critical time in her life. Eleanor suggested to Hickok that Martha needed to "learn patience & not have a critical attitude towards what others do for she must remember that to them it is just as important as her dreams are to her."[12] Martha boarded with her surrogate parents, the president and the first lady, for several weeks; then she moved to Connecticut to try to finish a book that would draw on those Dickensian lives she had witnessed for FERA.

HG also went to see the Roosevelts in 1934, not to complain but, rather, to look closely at the man he believed to be "in a key position in the world's affairs and extraordinarily right-minded and right-spirited. . . . I shall probably be writing articles and talking on the air later, and I want to feel that I am as close to the personal reality of the situation as I can be," HG told FDR in April 1934. HG had an open invitation to visit the White House; when he signaled, the Roosevelts found time for him. On May 11, a Friday, he dined at 1600 Pennsylvania Avenue. FDR, as it happened, was a big fan of HG's and had written to him the previous December:

> It is because I have read, with pleasure and profit, almost everything that you have written, that I want to send you this note to tell you that I like and appreciate your article in Liberty Magazine. You are right that "the days of one-man leadership are at an end" but I am equally confident that a growing number are beginning to appreciate what you so well call "the needs of the case."
>
> In any event, you are doing much to educate people everywhere, and for that I am grateful. If you come over here again I do hope that we shall have the pleasure of seeing you.

HG took FDR up on a second offer to visit in March 1935. Again, the president expressed eagerness to see him. In a letter written on February 13, FDR said that he had just read HG's autobiography and was impressed with it. In fact, he wanted to know how HG had managed to "retain such vivid pictures of events and such extraordinarily clear impressions and judgments." And then he turned to politics: "We are still moving forward, not only as a Government but very distinctly as a people. I believe our biggest success is making people think during these past two years. They may not think straight but they are thinking in the right direction—and your direction and mine are not so far apart; at least we both seek peaceable conveyances in our travels."

This time HG was on a three-week fact-finding trip for *Collier's* that was to result in a series on the New Deal. "I lunched with the President in Washington and talked to all sorts of people; I had a very good time, and I wrote four articles which were published later as a book, *The New America: The New World.*"[13] Privately, HG wasn't thrilled with what he found. He told Christabel that, on the whole, he was "disappointed & dismayed" by the new America. "I've never felt so sure that all that life means to us, civilization, freedom, decency is toppling over. Into nasty things." Still, it was an extremely profitable trip, indeed, a bonanza: HG not only received a huge $12,500 payment from *Collier's* but he also met the lovely and vivacious Martha Gellhorn.[14] As HG described in pages suppressed from the *Postscript*, he had a very good time with Martha during his trip to Washington:

> I found myself making love to a vivid young woman, Martha Gellhorn, who was working in one of the administrations. We like each other, mind and person, and we have corresponded ever since. For some time she had lived with Bertrand de Jouvenel as his wife but he could not marry her because his former wife refused him a divorce. She has an adventurous honesty about her that I find very fine; she has written a first novel, *What Mad Pursuit,* that has some performance and more promise. And I have never had more amusing love letters. These experiences made me more and more determined to grapple with Moura or break with her. Here again, I thought, is what I want. Here is the way out for me.[15]

When he returned once again to the United States that November, HG had, as he said in his *Postscript,* filmmaking on his mind; in pages that were suppressed from the book, however, he wrote: "I shall look up Martha Gellhorn who continues to write me the most interesting letters, and perhaps I shall fly over to Hollywood."[16] HG said he was even entertaining the notion of wintering in Tinsel Town.

HG described his second trip to the United States in 1935 as a "raid on America." In the *Postscript,* he wrote that he stayed for a few days with G. P. Brett of the Macmillan Company in New York, traveled across the country, and pitched his tent in Hollywood at the home of Charlie Chaplin for five weeks. The California sunshine and his visits to Palm Springs and the Hearst and Cecil B. de Mille ranches rejuvenated him. But in pages that were excised from his *Postscript,* HG noted that, after he left Brett in New York, he went to "an extremely modern little house in the Connecticut hills which W. F. Field, who wrote about China, had lent to Martha Gellhorn.[17]

> We two had a very happy time together for a week, making love, talking, reading over her second book. Field came to fetch me back to New York, and he and Martha and I had a lively hour digging his car out of a snowdrift into which it slipped at the start. Martha in skiing trousers with her shock of ruddy golden hair in disorder, her brown eyes alight and her face rosy with frost, is unforgettable.[18]

On December 5, HG wrote to Marjorie saying that he would send Chaplin's check for $30,000 for her to deposit in his London account. One of the reasons HG went to California was to pick up Chaplin's check for movie rights to *Mr. Polly.*[19] "I had a great time in Connecticut with the Fields and Martha which ended in digging a car out of a snowdrift," he continued. Marjorie apparently knew who her father-in-law meant by "Martha." On Christmas Day, heading back to the East Coast after his invigorating time on the West Coast, HG was delayed by ice in Dallas, so he went on by train to Washington and New York. This is where his account of the American trip ends in the published *Postscript.*[20] In his excised pages, however, HG continued with several versions of his story:

Martha, now changed into a well-dressed young lady, was staying with a Mrs. Lewishon in Park Avenue, and I put up at the Ambassador Hotel close by. We lunched, dined, went to theatres together; I gave a party for her in my sitting-room and she flitted in and out of my apartment at all hours. I found that more and more she was ousting Moura from my imagination and becoming the person at the centre of my reveries. I was quite definitely in love with her at this time and she with me. We discussed our future relationship. We discussed our future gravely and frankly. We both felt the manifest incompatibility of our ages. There was no sense in her becoming my kept-mistress and we both were divided between the desire and inclination to marry and a realisation of the impossibility of marrying. If we could stay as we were—or at least if I could stay as I was at sixty-nine, we had all that was needed for a happy and vigorous life together.

But I was not going to stay at sixty-nine; I'm vulnerable now, and a touch of infection or any such accident, might precipitate old age upon me—and her. She is too good in quality for that. She has always shown me such affection and jolly fellowship and such lively understanding of my ideas and purpose that I believe I might even impose my old age upon her. But I don't want it like that.

We parted—indeterminate. I had a queer feeling in my mind that she would marry Field. She went off to St. Louis, where her father, a well-known surgeon, was being operated upon for some internal disorder, the day before I sailed for England on the Majestic. I had the manuscript of her second book with me; I found Hamish Hamilton the publisher aboard and I had got him enthusiastic for it before we landed at Southampton.

Martha's father died in February, and I am finding Hamish Hamilton's agreement unsatisfactory. I planted *The Trouble I've Seen* with Putnam who hopes great things for it.[21]

That winter, at Field's house in Connecticut, Martha was putting the finishing touches on her *Trouble* manuscript. HG never described it as quid pro quo, but their little tryst almost immediately blossomed into Martha's book contract for *Trouble.* HG personally worked out a good deal for her with Putnam and agreed to write a preface for the book. His imprimatur virtually guaranteed its success. For his part, HG was "greatly edified" by his 1935 raid on the United States, and particularly by Hollywood, as he wrote in suppressed pages of the *Postscript.* "I was built up again, restored, put upon my feet, and made to forget that wave of real pessimism that had passed over my spirit in 1934 and 35, after my discovery about Moura in Moscow, and my progressive disillusionment about her."[22] Indeed, HG was emotionally and spiritually reborn by his passade with Martha, by his discovery that women were still attracted to him, and, just as important, by the realization after the Moscow crisis that his emotional imagination could still "draw other pictures and build other hopes" than those that centered on Moura, as he wrote in a suppressed portion of the *Postscript.*

In May 1936, as she hoped she would, Martha sailed to England and stayed several weeks with HG. In an entry added to his *Postscript* on July 17, 1936, he reported on the past couple of months and his life with Moura. He said that they had weekended here and there, gossiped, and made love like husband and wife. But in a suppressed page of his *Postscript,* HG wrote:

> Martha Gellhorn has stayed in my visitors' room for three weeks. She came over on the Bremen and resumed a violent love affair aboard with a man named Willert, so that she arrived caressing but tabu—and I didn't in the least mind. There is a frankness about Martha and a freshness of laughter that is amazingly antiseptic. Moura took her presence very calmly for three weeks. I had cheerful company to my breakfast on the sunlit loggia I have made in my garden.[23]

HG and Martha continued their friendship and lively correspondence—even after she met Ernest Hemingway, some eighteen months after meeting HG. HG and Martha also met from time to time in England. Cut from his *Postscript* was the following notation: "I add here that Martha Gellhorn, bless her, is now Mrs. Hemingway and I think now a settled and a happy woman. I dined with her and Hemingway in New York last December (1940), and took an immense liking to him."[24]

Charming as it is, there is a problem with HG's story about a brief, May–December love story: Martha Gellhorn rejected it out of hand. She adamantly denied a love affair between her and HG, even one of short duration. Indeed, a romance between the elderly English writer and the attractive young American was "imaginary" and absolutely "non-existent," she said. To be sure, Martha admitted to a friendship with HG—even an affectionate one—but nothing more. What we have here, then, is the classic "He said/She said" story. "She" told this author:

> [Wells] had a tendency to suggest things that weren't so. I can only tell you to be wary of Wells and women and boastfulness, because he was by no manner or means a heartbreaker. His tendency to boast I find peculiarly unattractive.[25]

> I was furious at the assumption that Wells and I had been lovers. This assumption came I suppose from Gip Wells including my letters with women who had been in love with Wells. [Wells] was about my father's age and no beauty.[26]

> I am outraged by Wells' lying about our relationship, in fact that lying has soured my memory of him. His son Gip, who had read my letters to Wells, persisted in thinking I was lying by denying this non-existent love affair.[27]

In her heated and suppressed correspondence with Gip Wells in the early 1980s, on the eve of the publication of the *Postscript,* Martha vented a good deal of her outrage, although the first letter in that series began nostalgically. She told Gip in April 1983 that his handwriting reminded her of his "papa's tiny neat script." Nostalgia out of the way, she went on to say, as if it were a classroom lesson:

> Now then: All women know that all men are silly and vain, but honestly this effort of Wells' [writing the Postscript] takes the cookie. Consider. I

was 26 or 27 when I met him; he was my father's age and not, you will agree, physically dazzling. I had a large constant supply of attractive young gents and have never been lured by men who were smaller than me. This must be due to having a tall father and tall brothers and also to being tall. I towered over Wells. I was very fond of him but the rest is rubbish.

Later that year in another letter to Gip, Martha suggested that there was some "strange failing" in men that forced them to believe that much younger women were in love with them. She'd seen it often, she said. "Anyway you will understand my objection to his imaginary love life with me. All the imaginary stuff connected with Hemingway is plenty to darken one life. I don't need HG too." And yet, despite these protests, Martha routinely signed her letters to HG with the intriguing name, "Stooge." In fact, she always signed her letters intriguingly: Other monikers included "your devoted henchman" and "your humble servant." In all likelihood, Martha earned the name Stooge for her role as a romantic irritant. "[HG] used me to annoy Moura and maybe came to believe his version," Martha told Gip in that April 1983 letter. When this author asked her about the name fourteen years later, she had another answer: "I signed my letters 'Stooge' because Stooge meant to me somebody who just ran around and took orders, a sort of goafer. Wells was a very bossy man."[28] In a 1942 letter to HG, Martha signed herself "ex-Stooge," then wrote, "(for the censor: Martha Gellhorn Hemingway)." She also added a postscript to that letter: "Our censorship law says that nicknames may not be used. Also letters should be brief. Tough luck about that brief business."[29] As for HG having popped the question, Martha informed Gip that his father had had a "vague crush" on her and that he had, indeed, suggested marriage.

I bet he'd have been horrified if I hadn't gently and politely pointed out that it would look pretty funny, and wasn't a good idea. I may tell you I'd have swum the Pacific rather than get involved with him beyond friendship, and not too much of that. He did bully a lot, spent his time saying I must go to a polytechnic and study science, and I'd just started to enjoy life after Bryn Mawr.

That HG was getting on in years, that he was short, "no beauty" and not "dazzling," is a theme that runs through the correspondence between Martha and Gip. So does the idea that HG had deeper problems, the boasting and the bullying being particularly offensive to her. "Wells was a very bossy man," she said over and over again, and, "He was fun unless he was bullying intellectually."[30]

As for that Connecticut "honeymoon" at the end of 1935, it was anything but fun; indeed, it was more like pure hell. As Martha explained to Gip in 1983, HG "came self-invited to Connecticut and nearly drove me mad by talking for at least 10 hours a day when I was trying to write a book. Finally I sent secretly a telegram to Charlie Chaplin, who of course I didn't know, to tell him Wells was in Conn., and would probably like to come to Hollywood; and thus he was pried out of my borrowed country retreat." As we have seen, however, HG had contemplated going to Hollywood from the start, or so he said.

And when Martha stayed at HG's London apartment in May 1936—she described it as "cadging" bed and breakfast from HG ("Cadging room from those who had it was a major occupation of the moneyless young in those days")—she found that he was nearly as much a bother as he had been in the United States.[31] This time, HG mercilessly nagged her about her writing discipline and habits, she maintained, but having just finished *Trouble,* she wanted to party—not slave over a hot typewriter. Thus, she "was not about to adopt his 9:30 A.M. to 12:30 P.M. regime. Not then or ever."[32] In a letter to Gip about that stay, Martha wrote that she went out dancing nearly every night she was there "with young gents of my acquaintance and every morning I was forced to get up at dawn because Wells insisted I have breakfast with him. Hardship."[33] Nevertheless, one sunny London morning, a story, "Justice at Night," emerged "intact, from its burial in my brain, and wrote itself as if by Ouija board," Martha later wrote in *View.* "That morning, to show [HG] I could write if I felt like it, I sat in his garden and let [the story] produce itself. Wells sent it to the *Spectator.* I had already moved on to Germany where I ceased being a pacifist and became an ardent anti-Fascist." In 1996, Martha told *Salon* writer Kevin Kerrane quite a different tale about the story: She said that while she was staying with HG that spring, he bullied her into writing an article; after she finished it, HG swiped it from her desk, submitted it to the *Spectator* without her knowledge, and pocketed the fee. "We were charmed by Gellhorn's fierce honesty and bright energy," Kerrane later wrote.[34] The kicker to this story is that although Martha wrote the piece as an eyewitness account, she later admitted, under pressure, that it was based on a story she had heard from a drunken truck driver.

★   ★   ★

Not that Martha Gellhorn couldn't or didn't collect her own firsthand accounts. Not that she didn't produce first-rate stories. She had plenty of talent, desire, and opportunity. Among other things, like Moura and Constance, she was a world-class globetrotter. At the tender age of twenty-one, she later confessed in *Travels with Myself and Another,* she "decided that it would be a good plan to see everywhere and everything and everyone and write about it." She came close to realizing her plan. By 1978, twenty years before she died, Martha Gellhorn had racked up quite an impressive "country list." In *Travels,* she claimed to have been to fifty-four countries: twenty-four of them multiple times, and the United States of America "up, down and across." As previously mentioned, for Martha Gellhorn, travel was a powerful drug, therapeutic and renewing, much as making love was for HG. In her last years, feeling trapped and limited and disgusted, Martha told her friend Victoria Glendinning that she hoped "travel, even limited as it is now, will not fail me, will still revive me, because it is change, because there is chance of newness."[35]

The same rule applied to homesteads. By 1978, Martha had established, by her own count, eleven successive and permanent residences in seven countries. (Somewhere she wrote that home was where the chores were.) Martha also roamed the earth while working. She was a war correspondent for *Collier's Weekly* in Spain from 1937 to 1938; in Finland in 1939; China from 1940 to 1941; England, Italy, France and Germany from 1943 to 1945; and Java in 1946. For the *Guardian* (London), she was a war correspondent in Vietnam in 1966, and in Israel in 1967. And she worked as a freelance journalist in Europe and Asia from 1967 to the end of her life.

Whether at home or on the move, Martha certainly seemed to have a healthy sense of herself early on, although in the 1940s, Ernest Hemingway discovered the chink in her armor. In a letter, he once described her as lacking confidence. His actual words were, "I know you never have conceit. Much oftener lacky de confidee."[36] However, when she was twenty-three, she wrote to Stan Pennell, again rather self-importantly, about her future as she envisioned it:

> I shall doubtless write and struggle and worry and try to get ahead but I know now for sure that living my favorite life I would never do any of these things and would just ripen into jelly in the sun and sleep 14 hours a night and not talk if I could help it because there is nothing I want to say and nothing I want to hear. Disgusting isn't it but Great God how close to the dream of what life might be if one weren't a moralist longing (or rather forced) to seek ultimates.[37]

Despite her exciting life with its ever-changing venues, Martha described herself at age seventy-five in a letter to Gip as "a footnote in history, a passing reference in others' books and letters."[38] Strangely enough, she had a point, for despite her part in world affairs as early as 1935, well before she was thirty years old, and despite her daily associations with many of the movers and shakers of the age, the author/journalist/war correspondent rarely saw more than a cameo appearance in the works that document the last half of the twentieth century. It is almost as if this larger-than-life personality was, indeed, a footnote, a phantom.

There are exceptions to this rule, of course. Martha figures prominently in the biographies of Hemingway; but then, she was his third wife. Hemingway's male biographers all gave Martha her due, as did Bernice Kert in her examination of *The Hemingway Women* and Denis Brian in *The True Gen*. Martha also starred, obviously, in the two Gellhorn biographies, "A Critical Biography of Martha Gellhorn," a 1977 doctoral dissertation by Jacqueline Orsagh, and *Nothing Ever Happens to the Brave: The Story of Martha Gellhorn* by Carl Rollyson, published in 1990.[39] It is amazing that there are even two biographies; after all, Martha lived a cloistered existence for much of her adult life, the final years in a large apartment on Cadogan Square in London. Still, another biography and a film are currently in the works.[40] Always a private person, she argued for years that a writer's personal life was off limits. "A writer should be read, not written about. I wish to retain my lifelong obscurity," she told Victoria Glendinning in a 1988 interview for *Vogue* magazine.[41] Until her death in 1998 at eighty-nine, Gellhorn did her best to hold onto that obscurity. In those last years, she saw "no one," she said, and gave few interviews. Rollyson never got one—but perhaps he never asked. Orsagh was either luckier or braver. She interviewed Martha during four meetings and several phone conversations. Their correspondence lasted more than six years.[42]

Even stranger is how Martha passed like an apparition through the pages she might otherwise have occupied, if not dominated, including the biography and autobiography of Bertrand de Jouvenel, her lover— perhaps even husband—in the early 1930s. Jouvenel was a charismatic young Turk and intellectual keen on politics when Martha met him in Europe in 1930, and "a playboy of no small stature, especially in the late 1930s," his biographer, John Braun, wrote in his 1,000-page dissertation on Jouvenel.[43] The son of Henry de Jouvenel des Ursins, the editor of *Le Matin* and a senator and ambassador of France, and the stepson of the popular French writer Colette, the younger Jouvenel would experiment with various political ideologies before building a respectable career in journalism and literature. Rollyson maintains that Martha and Bertrand were married in the summer of 1933 in Spain. Pearl K. Bell, in her review of Martha's *Novellas,* also claimed the two were husband and wife.[44] It was in Paris, Bell wrote, where Martha "met her first husband, Bertrand de Jouvenel." Whether or not a great arbiter of such things, the 1934 *Book Review Digest* identified Martha as the Marquise de Jouvenel.

Nevertheless, in his 1979 autobiography, *Un Voyageur dans le Siècle,* Jouvenel mentioned Martha only five times, and then simply to describe her as "une amie" and traveling companion during his tours of the United States in 1931 and 1935. He didn't mention her at all in his *Itinéraire: 1928–1976.* And, as if taking his cue from Jouvenel, Braun also downplayed Martha's role in Jouvenel's life. In his work, "Une Fidélité Difficile," Braun wrote that Jouvenel lived with Martha from 1931 to 1934, and that she later married Hemingway—*c'est tout.* Braun did discuss Jouvenel's 1931 tour of the United States, when he and Martha witnessed the "grinding poverty" of tenant farming in Mississippi, and his 1935 visit with Martha at Coeur d'Alene, Idaho, when she was working for FERA. But that is all the mention she got—probably more than she wanted—in Braun's massive examination of Jouvenel's life.

As for the biographies of H. G. Wells, Martha Gellhorn is truly the footnote she claimed to be. This is curious, since she and HG were open and affectionate friends during the last decade of his life. They visited each other when their schedules permitted, and they wrote friendly and warm letters back and forth. Indeed, their lives were entwined in many ways. There is no mention of an intimate relationship in the literature, however; only an intimation here or there. Martha either escaped the major H. G. Wells biographies altogether or merely popped in and out, as she had when she "cadged" from HG in London.

For example, Norman and Jeanne MacKenzie mentioned Martha once, and that was in connection with her response to HG's circular letter soliciting support for his *Declaration of the Rights of Man* in the summer of 1943. Anthony West didn't mention her at all in his biography of his father. And, in his comprehensive biography of H. G. Wells, David Smith cited Martha just once, in a section, appropriately, on HG's appetite for women. Smith quoted from HG's November 27, 1935, letter to Sinclair Lewis: "(N.B. [Martha] hasn't seduced me & my interest is purely friendly, although she is 27 & quite attractive.)" It should also be noted that in his index, under the category of HG's "significant relationships," Smith didn't include Martha's name, apparently buying into the claim that she and HG had nothing going beyond a casual acquaintance.

For his part, Rollyson simply borrowed the business about HG's letter to Lewis, the only time Rollyson addressed the issue of intimacy between HG and Martha. Orsagh mentioned HG once, in connection with his having written the preface to Martha's *The Trouble I've Seen:* "Having visited the United States just as Gellhorn finished her book, H.G. Wells was so enthusiastic about it that he wrote a laudatory preface to *TTIS* and took the book to London where it was immediately published."[45] It also is true that Martha's intriguing association with HG is absent from the Hemingway biographies. Whether any of these omissions stem from loyalty to Martha, professional courtesy, lack of evidence, or fear of lawsuit is not known. Martha's reputation for being a pit bull about published references to her, however, was well known.

It is far easier to understand what happened to Martha in HG's own writings. *Experiment in Autobiography* was published in 1934, a year before his friendship with her began. Shortly after he released *Experiment,* HG began working on the *Postscript* to his autobiography, the cerebral analysis of his chief love affairs. As we now know, Martha, like Constance Coolidge, was very much a part of HG's love memoir. We also now know, as previously discussed, that a funny thing happened on the way to the publication of the *Postscript:* Gip removed Constance's and Martha's names from its pages. The letters that flew between Gip and Martha clearly demonstrate that Martha demanded to be cut out; she even threatened a lawsuit if Gip didn't fully comply, which seemed like a strange reaction from an old and affectionate friend. On September 18, 1984, she upbraided Gip:

> You deceived me. You gave me to understand that you were selling the mss. of Wells' love life to a university. I warn you that if my name appears or any of my letters are published, I shall sue everyone in sight. To make doubly sure, I am putting the matter in the hands of my lawyer now. I shall hope to hear from you at once that you have excised me from the book, but if not, woe to all. Do you think this book will enhance Wells' reputation or are you in need of money?

As we now know, Gip's project to publish his father's *Confessio Amantis* had been troublesome for some time, and well before he locked horns with Martha. But in the end, except for two veiled references that Gip mischievously kept in about ***** (Martha) not minding and about HG falling in love in Connecticut, Martha won her battle. She managed to remain "a footnote" even in HG's account of their *passade*.

It is unlikely that additional papers will tumble down from heaven to shed any more light on the relationship between H. G. Wells and Martha Gellhorn. She sealed all her papers, including HG's letters to her, at Boston University for twenty-five years after her death, which will be 2023. "My certainty is that I will be totally forgotten by then and thus [will] have escaped biographers. I can't make exceptions, and I can't ask Boston University to fish out individual letters."[46] In any case, Martha maintained that she didn't have many letters from HG, "as I tend to answer letters and throw them away. I thus discovered very few letters from Wells, or Mrs. Roosevelt or B. P. Berenson or anyone else."

Since it grapples with two conflicting stories, this chapter hinges on the nature of truth, and interestingly enough, truth was a subject near and dear to both HG and Martha. Trained as a scientist, HG grew up with a self-proclaimed deep respect for veracity. Indeed, his study and teaching of biology at the elbow of Huxley, among others, provided the basis for his attempts to understand himself. To discover, admit to, and write the truth about his love life in the *Postscript,* after prolonged dissection and self-analysis, "played a major part in [HG's] recovery," as Gip wrote in his "Explanation" section of the *Postscript.* As HG once wrote, "Candour, like everything else worth while, is a thing to be achieved with infinite difficulty."[47]

For her part, Martha practically staked a claim to The Truth, even invented the words *apocryphiars* and *apocryphism* to refer to liars and their lowly acts. In a spring 1981 article in the *Paris Review* titled "On Apocryphism," Martha lashed out against apocryphy—in particular, what she called the "apocryphal stories" that poet Stephen Spender and writer Lillian Hellman had spread about her and Hemingway. "I stop reading wherever apocryphism rears its two-faced head," Martha wrote. "If what I know about is untrue, why trust the parts I cannot check? For that reason, long long ago I stopped reading anything on the Spanish Civil War or Ernest Hemingway." Spender wrote in an earlier issue of the same journal that Hemingway made a man of Martha, or at least a tough reporter, by routinely taking her to the Madrid morgue to cure her of her squeamishness during her first weeks covering the Spanish Civil War. As one of the few surviving witnesses to that war, Martha felt she had to set the record straight.

"The trouble is: it didn't happen, any of it," Martha wrote of Spender's claims, two years before she wrote Gip the same thing about her alleged affair with HG. In the first place, she said, she had cut her teeth as a reporter in the Albany, New York, morgue long before she met Ernest. In the second place, she'd "bet a diamond tiara that nothing on earth would have got Hemingway near the Madrid morgue." Martha threw more evidence at the "wild inventions," saying that it was highly unlikely that "Hemingway of all men would bare his soul only to Spender of all men and talk about cowardice, his fear of." Martha, furious that Spender claimed a close personal relationship with Hemingway, also attacked his allegation that Hemingway went to Spain not because he was motivated by the cause but because he wanted to test his courage under fire. She wrote in a rare defense of her former husband:

> There was plenty wrong with Hemingway but nothing wrong with his honest commitment to the Republic of Spain and nothing wrong with his admiration and care for men in the Brigades and in the Spanish Divisions and nothing wrong with his respect for the Spanish people. He proved it by his actions, and if they aren't well enough known, you can look them up in any of the innumerable books on Hemingway.

And then Martha went on to catalog and trash Spender's experiences in the Spanish Civil War, which in her opinion were minor, undistinguished, and, worst of all, soft.

The rest of the piece is Martha's refutation of Lillian Hellman's published anecdotes that were, among other things, "apocryphal put-downs" of Hemingway—including reports of moderately brutish acts. Martha plotted Hellman's moves during her brief assignment in Spain ("ah research, research," she wrote in parentheses) to show that Hellman had lied about her interactions with Hemingway and her involvement in war, just as Spender had lied, to enhance her own "importance" and to demonstrate her own courage and bravery. What infuriated Martha was that by greasing the truth, Spender and Hellman had inserted *themselves* into Hemingway's life—and thus into the Hemingway myth. Along the way, of course, Martha demonstrated *her* centrality to Hemingway during this period, her superior and intimate knowledge of war, and her own bravery and courage, as certified by Hemingway. She also showed off her investigative skills and no small amount of cattiness and sarcasm. Hellman's "sojourn in Spain was not sufficiently vital to the Republic to be documented in any book I can find," Martha hissed, and went on, "Her incomprehension of [the] war is near idiocy." Martha also took a punch at a comment Hellman made about Martha as a fashion-plate war correspondent. "That is a delightful put-down which I enjoy for its open bitchery. In a spirit of fun, I return it here: if Miss H's beauty had matched her brains, she would have been a more cuddly personality." Hellman was not only unlucky of appearance, Martha went on to say, but also stingy, suggesting that Martha was just the opposite. Furthermore, in her reporting, Hellman not only got her facts wrong but they were often secondhand, and, far worse, she made things up. And the ultimate slam: Hellman, whom Martha dubbed Miss H. throughout, had "the cojones of a brass monkey."

In sum, Miss H:

has written a great part for herself throughout [her book *An Unfinished Woman*], with special skill in her Spanish War scenes. She is the shining heroine who overcomes hardship, hunger, fear, danger—down stage center—in a tormented country. The long endurance of the Spanish people and the men who fought to defend the Republic was true heroism. Self-serving apocryphisms on the war in Spain are more repellent to me than any others.

In sum, Hemingway:

Became a shameful embarrassing apocryphiar about himself, which I believe damaged him as a man, but he was not like that in Spain nor in China . . . never in my hearing. He had a fair amount of hyena in him, as he admitted, but he made good jokes and was valuable cheerful company in those wars and no more boring than we all are the rest of the time. In Cuba, in World War Two, I watched with anger the birth and growth of his apocryphisms about the spy factory, the Pilar submarine patrol. As far as I could see, apocryphisms grew like Topsy until I stopped being there to see.

The Hemingway saga, probably swelling with each new book on Hemingway, is bad news. His work sinks beneath the personality cult and the work alone counts, the best work from the beginning through *A Farewell To Arms*. He was a genius, that uneasy word, not so much in what he wrote (speaking like an uncertified critic) as in how he wrote; he liberated our written language. All writers, after him, owe Hemingway a debt for their freedom whether the debt is acknowledged or not. It is sad that the man's handmade falsehoods—worthless junk, demeaning to the writer's reputation—survive him.

In sum, on apocryphism:

Nothing excuses apocryphism by anyone about anything. No good comes of it. It is cheap and cheapening. The world would be a far far better place if people—especially writers and politicians—stuck to fact or fiction. Not fiction passed off as fact. Literary apocryphiars, it seems to me, confuse and distort the record; political apocryphiars can be fatal. Alas, the chances for a far better world are as usual slim but we might train ourselves, our heirs and descendants, to be wary of all apocryphism.

The same issue of the *Paris Review* carried Spender's response. In addition to correcting some of Martha's claims—"I am sorry that Miss Gellhorn is having trouble with her memory: something that can happen at our age, with which one can only sympathize"—he took issue with her premise that he was claiming a friendship that didn't exist. Among his main points:

> As everyone knows, there was sometimes a gap between what Hemingway said he did and what he did.

> Miss Gellhorn should not judge the limitations of Hemingway's vocabulary by those of her own Hemingwayese.

> Spender had never suggested that Hemingway did not support the Spanish Republic. But Hemingway's concern with the question of his own courage—shown throughout his life in so many of his activities—was something apart.

> Finally, he did know Hemingway "very slightly better" than Martha's rendition.

The relevance of the *Paris Review* battle royal is obvious. It has a direct bearing on the relationship between Martha and Hemingway—and what others felt compelled to say about it. As the relationship fell apart for the last time, Hemingway picked up his attacks on Martha, especially in his correspondence, for many of the things she criticized others for: taking the easy way out in covering conflict and war, being cheap and lazy and allowing him to do her writing and editing for her, always making herself the "shining heroine" of her plots, and, interestingly, for apocryphism—for lying, especially about money. Others— many others—would accuse Martha of inserting herself into the Hemingway myth for professional and financial gain while all the time loudly protesting her disinterest. It is a common thing for people to criticize others for what they detest about themselves, and Martha may have seen and heard a bit too much of herself in Spender and Hellman.

The *Paris Review* article also bears on the relationship between Martha and HG, since she so hotly denied that relationship and he so lovingly detailed it. In her relationships with both men, as indeed in most relationships, "the facts" are in the eyes of the beholder, and perception overshadows what may be the most sincere attempts to tell the truth. An old man may read more into a kiss than he should, or into a comment. A young woman may read less. In the end, there are many truths. Drawing on previously suppressed passages from the *Postscript* gives one perspective on the relationship between H. G. Wells and Martha Gellhorn: HG's version. Drawing on letters between Gip and Martha and HG and Martha gives another: Martha's. This perspective is limited due to Martha's refusal to share her letters from HG. The "truth" in this narrative, therefore, is on a continuum—*He said* on one side, *She said* on the other. *We were intimates, we made love,* he said. *I asked for her hand in marriage. There was no affair, only friendship,* she said. *Everything else is rubbish—delusional on HG's part.* When a fundamental disagreement such as this one presents itself, the best one can do is to show the evidence on both sides. Let us turn to Martha's side. Who was this woman who brought so much "adventurous honesty" to HG's late life, but who called him a liar and shielded herself from what was either ugly apocryphy or the ugly truth?

*   *   *

Whether or not she told the truth as a child isn't known, but that Martha Gellhorn, the only daughter of a distinguished St. Louis physician and a well-known and highly respected civic-social activist, had spunk was never in doubt. She would summon her chutzpah and resourcefulness repeatedly to propel herself into and out of any number of challenges throughout her long life. She would report on events in Czechoslovakia both before and after the Munich Pact. She would stow away on a hospital ship during the invasion of Normandy, be evacuated out of Helsinki, advance with the Eighth Army across Italy, and witness the horrors of Dachau. Her publishing career would be equally impressive. In addition to dozens of newspaper and magazine articles, Martha Gellhorn wrote and published ten novels, two collections of short stories, three books of nonfiction—one travel memoir and two collections of news articles—and one play, a comedy. In 1992, she released a volume of previously published novellas. At some point fairly early on, the chutzpah or courage—her own special brand of nonchalance or fearlessness when facing the unknown—must have become second nature. In her writings and recollections, Martha Gellhorn never appeared to be intimidated by circumstances, never overwhelmed, never paralyzed.

Born November 8, 1908, to an old-world father—a gynecologist and obstetrician who was born and educated in Germany—and a new-world/new-woman mother, and the baby sister in a family of three older brothers, Martha grew up in a stimulating environment indeed. That stimulation was due to the high jinks of her older brothers, to be sure, but also to her mother's interests in social and political issues that ranged from women's rights, including suffrage, to pure milk for St. Louis. Edna Gellhorn made friends and influenced people, and she brought many of them home with her. Herbert Hoover, for example, once dined at the Gellhorn table during World War I when Edna was playing an important role in the War Food Administration. The Gellhorn children also carried banners and flags at their fair share of political events. In 1916, young Martha campaigned for the vote with her mother and a group of St. Louis suffragettes. Such activities had, no doubt, a profound effect on the girl. Meanwhile, George Gellhorn apparently passed his passion for travel on to his daughter. After receiving his M.D., he worked at several university clinics in Germany and Austria, then sailed the world for a few years as a ship's doctor before settling down in St. Louis in 1899.[48] Well before she got to know the world, the young Martha would get to know St. Louis, tagging along with her brothers or hopping the streetcars to destinations of her own choosing. With a father who was on call or on duty much of the time, and a mother who was both extremely permissive and out of the house a great deal, Martha was destined to become independent. The Gellhorns, who were described as cosmopolitan individualists, evidently reproduced themselves in her.[49] Martha certainly behaved like an individual when she left Bryn Mawr—her mother's alma mater—at the end of her junior year in 1929. Although her parents expressed simple disappointment with her decision, privately they were deeply disturbed. From that point on, Martha would live independently—and by her wits—accountable to no one, just as Moura had been.

Indeed, and as noted, the young Martha did nearly everything *her* way, always an original way, and often unorthodox. She wasn't even marginally prepared for her first job as a cub reporter covering women's clubs and the city morgue for the Albany *Times Union*. Martha was also less than thrilled with the work at the Hearst paper—and with her colleagues; she asserted that a certain amount of petulance and a good deal of alcohol flowed through them. They had a few names for her, too, including "the Blonde Peril" for her assertiveness.[50] Martha stuck it out a few months, wrote some unsigned book reviews for the *New Republic* and an uninspired story on Rudy Vallée ("He is young, he is handsome, and tenderly, coaxingly he sings love-songs to every romance-silly female in these U.S.A. And that is that.")[51] By the end of the summer, after "running through two jobs," she later wrote, she was itching to move on and returned to St. Louis with the notion of working for the *Post-Dispatch*. But for one of the first times in her life, the young Martha was turned down, prompting her to gumption herself out of St. Louis—a place she disparaged to her dying day—and on to the American Southwest and Paris. Once out of the house, Martha refused to take money from her parents as proof of her dedication to her chosen career, writing, but she liberally and unapologetically sponged off friends and acquaintances. She never looked back. Years later she would write: "My life began in February 1930."[52]

Martha had visited the City of Light twice before on summer vacations. This time, in February 1930, she was alone in the French capital, which later prompted her to describe herself as "a joyful confident grain of sand in a vast rising sandstorm."[53] Undaunted, Martha presented herself to the Paris bureau chief of the *New York Times* and informed him that she was prepared to start work on his staff. She was turned down, but her spunk and her in-your-face attitude landed her a job at the Paris Bureau of United Press, which she held for all of two weeks. Martha then went to work for *Vogue* magazine, pounding the pavement, to be sure, but not primarily in pursuit of stories. This time, she was hired *for* her good looks, not just because of them. *Vogue* was looking for someone to parade their fashions, including the first halter-neck backless evening gown, around town and beyond. One of the venues, the World Economic Congress in London, was odd indeed, but the dress and the model became international hits. From *Vogue*, Martha moved on to the Paris office of an American advertising firm, where she wrote advertising copy.

In Paris, Martha reveled in her own and the culture's intense interest in politics while she eked out an existence, acquiring, now characteristically, one job after another, and amassing an eclectic group of friends who were drawn from the seemingly incongruent worlds of fashion, philosophy, and fascism. Among her new friends were some radical young French intellectuals, mostly pacifists, who later began the journal *La Lutte des Jeunes* [*Young People's Battle*]. Martha kicked around France "and adjacent countries," and lived in Germany for a while. By her own account, she came home only once during her "France years," as she called them; in the spring of 1931, she took a leisurely year-long tour of her own country, observing the flora and fauna and beginning "the stumbling interminable work" on her first novel, as she explained in *View*.[54] She mailed letters to Stan Pennell from the West Coast and the East, Mexico, the northern Midwest, and again from the East. In October, a "French companion"—Jouvenel—joined her on that "long hardship journey" across the continent. He called it his trip to discover America; Martha was his guide and his lover.

She was stunning in her chic sleeveless blue linen tunic when she met Jouvenel at the *Ile de France* in New York. From October to April, they crossed Eldorado, his name for the United States, in what he described as "an immense torpedo"—an old Dodge touring car that he bought in New Jersey for $30. One of the first stops for the politically alert young couple was the cotton empire of the American South, which, like everything else, had fallen on hard times. Jouvenel based his book, *The Crisis of American Capitalism*, on his observations during this visit. In his autobiography, he included a chapter on his second visit to the United States in June 1935; this was his "tour of a revolution in twelve hours," which focused on *les miracles rooseveltienne*. Three months later, in September, he was back not only to observe the country but also to make a last-ditch effort to win back the affections of his "friend" Martha Gellhorn. He went to Washington, D.C., which was preoccupied with the Italian menace regarding Abyssinia. He and Martha met in Coeur d'A-lene, Idaho, where he was bowled over by the fortitude of the pioneers who, using only their brute force, had cleared land in the forests.

Five years Martha's senior, Jouvenel was a visionary of sorts, something like HG, but also handsome, daring, and pedigreed. Like HG, he would become the prolific writer he had once told Martha he hoped to become; indeed, Jouvenel turned out more than thirty books and hundreds of newspaper and magazine articles during his long life. In retrospect, Martha described him as "a scholar, a thinker," as she told biographer Braun, but noted that "otherwise he is the least practical man alive; he can hardly tie his shoelaces."[55] Nevertheless, Jouvenel would become—again like HG—a renowned Don Juan. Perhaps that was the main source of friction between Martha and Jouvenel. As she told Pennell quite heartlessly in May, 1931, from the Barclay Hotel in New York City:

> I have loved a man for almost a year. He didn't mean to, but he took me so completely that he left nothing for my own use. I have been colorless and undecided ever since. This is rather ghastly. I have marked time and wanted him and filled my suddenly purposeless days with activity. I love him terribly. But he is never to be attained. And [he] doesn't realize that, loving as I love, with the peculiar intensity of those [who] have too much nervous energy, he is—in effect—the Angel of Destruction. I am trying, suddenly, to get over it. To convince myself of some realities, to care about some things really. That's me—why I am and what I am. Take it or leave it.

Martha was often cruel to Stan Pennell, but never more so than when she talked about marrying Jouvenel. At some point, Pennell accused Martha of betraying him; she snapped back in August 1931 that she rejected his "implication of treachery . . . and I think if you intend to make me feel that I have judas-ed [you] in no uncertain way, you've got to have the guts to specify your accusation." As if that wasn't enough, she claimed that she hadn't been planning the nuptials behind his back, but, rather, only "learned about" the wedding a week before he did. "Whatever else I may have known about my future (or my past) you knew too. If you are angry, it is your pleasure . . . and privilege," she spat. Martha and Jouvenel may have dropped the idea of marrying because his wife refused to grant him a divorce, as HG said. Then again, perhaps he never proposed. Fifty years later, Martha wrote to her "darling chum," Milt Wolff, ranting about her unofficial biographer Carl Rollyson, calling him a "disgrace" as a scholar and a researcher. "He gave me a husband and wedding ceremony I never had."[56]

Jouvenel's "easy success" with women, his biographer argued, flowed from "the most often repeated error about his life, his identification as the Chéri of Colette's novel of that name." Although that novel was written before Bertrand and Colette met, the attachment that Bertrand developed for his father's second wife, according to Braun, "only fuelled speculation that here, as in the novel, was a love between a mature woman and a very young man."[57] Joanna Richardson, another biographer, wrote that after a woman by the name of Germaine Beaumont offered, and failed, to "educate" the virginal stepson of Colette, that Colette stepped up and did the deed herself, and more: She became Bertrand's mistress. Whatever the truth may be, Braun claimed that "this identification with Colette coloured perceptions of Jouvenel for more than two decades."[58] After *Chéri* came out, Colette gave Jouvenel a copy, in which she had inscribed: "To my son CHERI Bertrand de Jouvenel." "In a way, it was a premonition of a legend that has a long life," Jouvenel later wrote in his autobiography, *Un Voyageur dans le Siècle*.

Jouvenel married a writer, Marcelle Prat, at the end of 1925 but they split up five years later. They collaborated professionally, both before and after their marriage, co-writing several novels, including *La Prochaine* [*The Next*] in 1934. It isn't known when or where Jouvenel and

Martha met; the standard line is that they met when she was backpack-ing in Europe—and undoubtedly it was sometime in 1930 and some-where in France. One of the places they turn up together is in Roubaix-Tourcoing in early 1931 to visit striking textile workers. Before that, Martha had covered, among other things, the meetings of the League of Nations in Geneva for the *St. Louis Post-Dispatch,* profiling Mary Agnes Hamilton, a member of the British House of Commons, and Hanni Forchhammer, the first woman delegate to the league.

In her 1979 letter to John Braun, Martha said that she and Bertrand had remained "close friends to this day," and she explained the circum-stances of their early relationship. "We lived together for some years when I was a girl; he simply walked out of his home and followed me, and we had a hell of a hard time due to being a scandal (people did not behave like that in those days) and being penniless and neither used to that condition." As for their activities, they were a "bunch of young men" and one girl "passionately engrossed in saving the world from war, to say nothing of being on the side of the starving unemployed." In the end, the bunch divided into "collaborators (Drieux la Rochelle for instance) and heroes of the Resistance; life is like that, not orderly."

In the same letter, Martha claimed that Jouvenel "wandered around among parties and ideas," always gentle and decent, but she doubted anyone ever took his politics seriously. "He ended up being a Monar-chist; God knows what he is now and it hardly matters. He is a good man, the main fact. He continues to admire my books. I can't under-stand a word of his, which is unfortunate. I know he is a big shot in the academic world and much respected for his intellectual theories, whether I understand or not." Martha also attempted to clarify her ide-ology and behavior in the 1930s, especially with regard to her activities in Germany and her involvement with Nazis.

I disliked those Germans, instinctively in 1934, though they swore they were *socialists,* the national part was just words etc. In fact I loathed von Shirach who was their boss; I left his house in a rage, after lunch, when he hit his servant for spilling coffee. By 1936, I knew them for what they were—I was in Germany—and by 1937 I was in Spain. But I was never a Communist; I am not a joiner and cannot take orders on how to act or think from anyone, and besides really mistrust all politics and politicians; all of them—some are simply more revolting or deadly than others but none ever get my undivided approval.

Jouvenel, coincidentally, was an ardent devotee of H. G. Wells. Indeed, he thought HG was the most important thinker of the twentieth century, and because of that, he devoted an entire chapter of his autobiography to England's great visionary. Jouvenel said that he put HG on that pedestal because HG was preoccupied all his life with the future of the human family. "If one picks up by chance any one of his imaginative works, one only finds a fantasy. But read several of them and you will recognize an ensemble of speculations on possible futures."[59] *When the Sleeper Wakes* (1899 and 1910), for example, was "one vision of the future manifestly inspired by Marx. The sleeper wakens in order to observe the effects of the accumulation of capital and the concentration of property. *The War of the Worlds* (1898) is an anguished preview of the means of destruction that he attributes to the Martians, but anticipates on Earth. *The World of William Clissold* (1926) is his most moving work, for it is the portrait of a man who tries to marshal goodwill to separate himself from foreseeable evils."[60]

By January 10, 1930, Jouvenel was well enough connected to arrange an important meeting with HG and Henri Barbusse, the founder and director of *Monde,* a newspaper aimed at rallying leftist intellectuals against war, capitalism, and colonialism. [61] The three men met in the Alpes-Maritimes, where HG and Barbusse had homes, and Jouvenel later reported on the meeting of the minds in *Monde.* HG and Jouvenel saw each other from time to time throughout the 1930s and they also corresponded. The younger visionary inquired about translation rights to several of HG's books, and asked to see HG whenever he was in London; several times he asked to accompany HG to Elstree, where his films were being shot. Jouvenel's style was reverential bordering on worshipful. In a 1934 letter to HG he wrote:

You have such a marvellous memory that you may remember a young Frenchman you received at Lou Pidou with extreme kindness. You certainly will not remember his telling you how much The New Machiavelli and later the World of William Clissold had mattered to him. Now at the moment when a revolution is at last on its way in France (but a puzzling revolution which followed no preconceived scheme), you bring out The Shape of Things to Come and it settled many questions which had arisen in a very wide open (I flatter myself) but somewhat disorderly brain. Will you allow me to tell you that you mean more to me, to some of us, than any other writer or thinker, alive or dead? That your books are not "helpful" but an absolute necessity, that they light up the long winding road we have to travel towards the distant goal of civilization?[62]

One wonders if Jouvenel was able to sustain that level of adoration after learning that at one point he and HG were both "seeing" Martha.

★   ★   ★

Because of HG's *Postscript* account as published, we know that, by the end of 1934 and the beginning of 1935, HG had become fatally disillusioned with Moura, his great hope for a Lover-Shadow. In the *Postscript,* as we have seen, he wrote about her Moscow betrayal in the summer of 1934. He also wrote about his exasperation with her for not accompanying him to Washington, D.C., the following March. Typically, he shifted the responsibility for his subsequent unfaithfulness to someone else—in this case, to Moura:

My anger mounted at the failure of Moura to realize my desire for her companionship. It infuriated me that for my sake she would not rouse herself from that petty squalid exile life of hers; the endless gossip, the higgledy-piggledy of 88 Knightsbridge, the too much vodka, the too much brandy, the lying in bed until midday and the chatting nocturnalism. I was angry with her too because she made it possible for me to be unfaithful to her and that I was likely to slip back to promiscuity. In

Washington I was reminded at one or two parties that women could be attractive to me and seem attracted by me.[63]

In the suppressed pages, as we have seen, HG also "found himself" making love to Martha Gellhorn in Washington. In an earlier fragmentary version of that suppressed page he wrote: "In Washington I had a note one day," followed by "Madame de Jouvenel," followed by "For the second time I was realising that it was still possible for my emotional imagination to draw other pictures and build other hopes than those that centered on Moura. Slowly & steadily that one strand rope of love which held me to her was being frayed away."[64]

The intimate affair between Martha Gellhorn and H. G. Wells lasted less than a year; then it turned forever Platonic. In the published *Postscript,* HG wrote that he doubted there would be any other woman for him in the world. Well before the affair allegedly ended with Martha, HG wrote in the *Postscript* that he couldn't begin "another vital intimacy." In the suppressed pages, he followed that up with:

I love and admire Martha Gellhorn; I shall do what I can to help her in her ambitions and perplexities, but her vigorous young life is not for me. She is extremely incidental. I'll have, as people say, a time with her when next I go to America, and that will be all. We may give very much to each other but finally we shall go our several ways. . . . A passing love adventure without falsehood or vain promises is something more vital and enlarging than reading any good novel can be—but now not so excessively more.[65]

My love for Martha Gellhorn is a very real & releasing thing on my mind; but it is not a love of contemporaries; it is the Indian Summer of my imagination & desires & it remains unconcentrated, unpossessive & unjealous. Bless her.[66]

In 1987, some fifty years after HG wrote these words, Martha, for the first time in her life, broached the subject of her friendship with HG with someone outside the Wells family. She wrote her friend Victoria Glendinning to praise her for her new biography of Rebecca West. That letter, along with many others, turned up in *The New Yorker* after Martha's death. "I knew so many of the people you write about and sometime I must tell you about me and Wells. The old fool asked me to marry him in 1935 when he was older than God and I was just twenty-seven. I've never told anyone; it seemed so ludicrous. I thought he was a bore, too."[67] In a follow-up letter written a week later, Martha filled Glendinning in on some of the details, apparently at Glendinning's request. Martha said that she and Gip went around and around over the letters, but in the end, she told him—in vintage Gellhornian, to be sure—that if after reading her letters to HG he still felt they were love letters, then he didn't know his love letters. Indeed, he must never have received or written any.

> I also told Gip that his papa now had destroyed himself in my memory by claiming me as a love affair. Why the hell would I sleep with a little old man when I could have any number of tall beautiful young men? My letters, sent to me by Gip, are good, amusing. I wrote letters instead of seeing people, like now; and especially when I was married because I was loneliest then. Gip had to admit that they were not love letters. I found it disgusting that Wells needed to add my scalp, and refused to play. Before I thought he was mostly a bore, but a serious man; and I could write to him about my endless preoccupations with the history of our time. Now I find that, since almost everyone is dead, I am hard up for anyone to whom to write when the news suffocates me with anger or grief or both. Time for the 9 p.m. news.[68]

It isn't known why Martha Gellhorn kept her friendship-affair with HG a secret. Nor is it known what her rationale was in ordering her letters from HG along with everything else in her archive, to be sealed. Was this her extreme need for privacy, or was it her desire to conceal the evidence? Martha did tell Gip what she thought of HG's *Postscript*—which she described as "that ghastly book."

Writers need ego to keep them going, over the solitude and the blank page, but nobody ever needed quite as much caddish ego as is displayed in that book. If I had read it before meeting Wells, I would not have spent five minutes with him and far from enhancing his reputation, as I am sure he intended, (and God knows what you understood or intended), I think it makes one doubt his right to be the great ideologue of Utopia. For it shows him up as selfish and careless beyond belief; he impregnated two young women at a time when illegitimate children were social suicide for the woman—while he went safely back to his respectable and secure home, and his glorious career. I wonder that Rebecca didn't kill him; he deserved it; poor Amber didn't know what she was asking for—he was older, it was up to him to keep his overanxious penis in control. I find him so contemptible in this book that I cannot imagine why you didn't suppress it.

I can't imagine anything worse than to have appeared in that book, and I must say he makes Hemingway seem a gentleman by comparison and not, as one might have thought, the world's leading male chauvinist pig; that was our "world-man," HG Wells who wanted his women as slaves. I imagine your mother decided he was a brilliant impossible child and endured and forgave on that basis. Yours, Martha Gellhorn.[69]

With Martha's side of it shut, one has little to work with from that angle. As it turns out, HG left many other clues, as did some others. Martha made at least nine appearances in the suppressed pages of HG's *Postscript,* but she also appeared elsewhere, including, oddly enough, in Jouvenel's letters to HG. Spanning a period of about eleven months, Jouvenel's six letters began on July 3, 1934, and ended just before his second trip to America, in June 1935. In the first letter, which is the only dated letter of the lot, Jouvenel reminded HG that they had met at Lou Pidou, but the date of the meeting was not given. After praising HG for his work, he asked whether he might have the rights to translate and publish in French *The Shape of Things to Come.* HG replied on July 5 that he believed other arrangements had been made. The fourth and fifth letters in the series are more relevant.[70] Jouvenel opened his fourth letter with high praise for HG: "If ever a man fired a girl's imagination, you are the man and my Marty is the girl. I got two long memoirs full of footnotes about the evening you spent with her, and I gathered that I was almost outdone in admiration. (I'm not sure that is decent English, but what I mean is, we both feel the world would be a better one if it were William Clissold's.)"[71] Jouvenel was evidently referring to Martha and HG's meeting at the White House in March 1935. In the fifth letter, Jouvenel thanked HG for asking him to lunch in London, and told him that the few minutes they had together would make him optimistic for at least a month. He went on: "Also, I was anxious to know your impression of my wife, not my eighth, but the real one, the unlawful one, the blonde one, I mean." There can be no confusion about whom he meant, although the reference to "eighth" is confounding. Having told HG how impressed Martha was with him, Jouvenel couldn't resist asking HG his impression of Martha. Little did he know how impressed HG was.

Meanwhile, Martha told this author that she met Odette Keun in the South of France, but never HG. "I knew one of [Wells's] mistresses whose name I have forgotten. He kept her in his house in France. I met her there once, in Wells' absence when I was ambling around the South of France with a knapsack. She was a strange creature, quite ugly and generally inexplicable. As far as I know Wells never produced her in England."[72] Martha never explained what she was doing at HG's doorstep in the South of France in the early 1930s.

In addition to the suppressed pages of the *Postscript* and the letters, including Jouvenel's, are HG's date books, which pinpoint meetings and offer additional bits of information. In most cases, the entries and notations taken from HG's date books correspond to and corroborate his *Postscript;* he probably used his date books when writing it. But the dates and notations can also be challenging because they pose their own problems, HG's handwriting being one of them. Also, cancelled appointments were not always scratched out, and cryptic notations are confounding and can be misconstrued. Confusion surrounds many entries, including some ostensibly referring to Martha. In fact, it would appear that HG first met

Martha much earlier than March 1935. For example, the first possible entry for her appears on Monday, March 14, 1932, when HG noted in his date book, "12:30, Madame de Jouvenel." He must have been at Lou Pidou with Odette Keun, because an entry for March 29 says, "Cannes, 6:12," presumably reminding HG to meet a train. Cannes is just down the mountain from Grasse and Lou Pidou. Martha, however, was probably still in the United States winding up her tour with the Marquis Bertrand de Jouvenel. On May 20, another entry: "Mrs. Jouvenel at 2? Will call. Lunch Club." Could this have been another Mme. de Jouvenel, *la vrai* Mme. de Jouvenel, perhaps? Was it Martha returned from the United States? At this point, it isn't clear, but we do recall that Martha said she had visited Lou Pidou during her European amblings. Perhaps HG *was* home and invited her in. The 1934 date book, while clearer, also confounds. For Friday, June 29, HG marked and underlined, "Marty to lunch? 1:15." It would appear from the surrounding information that HG and Martha were in the South of France at the time. She didn't return to the United States until October. The point is that these details conflict with some previous details and challenge our understanding of the nature and the timing of the relationship between HG and Martha. Chief among the conflicts is that they met at the White House in 1935. It may be that they had first met in Europe, perhaps when Martha was running with the young Turks in the South of France.

HG's date book was full of appointments in 1935, when he was in the United States. On March 14, he had lunch at 1:00 P.M. at the White House, and went to a party at 7:30 P.M. at the Park Hotel. On the sixteenth, he was to meet "de Jouvenel" at 8 P.M. On the seventeenth, "M.G."; and the nineteenth, "M., afternoon." These entries also synchronize with the comments in the suppressed pages of his *Postscript*. Upon arrival in the United States in early November 1935, HG was extremely busy. He lunched on the eighteenth with Charles Colebaugh, who, incidentally, became Martha's editor at *Collier's* in 1938, and he made a notation on the twentieth that he would be "c/o F. W. Field, N. Hartford, [Connecticut]." As we have seen, HG spent most of December on the West Coast—staying with Charlie Chaplin and sightseeing in

Southern California. He had engagements with Mary Pickford, Anita Loos, Cecil B. de Mille, and Francis Marion. Back on the East Coast on the twenty-seventh, he noted, "7:15, G," and on the twenty-ninth, he made two entries: "MG lunch and ?," and "MG calls." On the thirtieth, it was "G, black tie." On New Year's Day, 1936, HG entered into his date book, "G, dinner, 7:30," and "cocktail party, BOY MEETS GIRL." Finally, on the first page of his 1936 date book, in the space reserved for memos, HG wrote the intriguing questions: *"Had he changed? Or is it simply that things that had always been there had become more accentuated?"*

Whether Martha and HG met in 1932 or 1934 isn't in the grand scheme of things that important. They certainly met at the White House and the Washington party in March 1935; that evening party, if we can believe HG's account, began their brief interlude. Also, if we can believe HG, they were attracted to each another. He was certainly attracted enough to make a second ocean crossing later in the year, after he had celebrated his sixty-ninth birthday, and she agreed to see him, according to his account.

As mentioned earlier, one of the most intriguing letters floating around the literature on HG—before the arrival of the Closet Correspondence—was the one HG sent Sinclair Lewis in November 1935; this letter stated, among other things, that he hadn't succumbed to the charms of Miss Martha Gellhorn. As it turns out, while visiting Charlie Chaplin in Los Angeles, it occurred to HG that Martha's preface to *Trouble* should be written by Lewis, rather than by himself. HG's full statement to Lewis about the matter was businesslike:

Martha did an undergraduate book about Bryn (Ma? Myar? Mah?) [Mawr] some year or so ago & she went about France & England as Madame Bertrand de Juvenal. She has since been doing work under the Rehabilitation people until she chucked it in anger & despair. She has written a group of short stories which are studies of America in decadence—& I think they are uncommonly good. You might be interested to see them. I wouldn't put anything upon you that I thought wasn't really alive & worthwhile, but I think some interest & advice from you &

possibly a brief preface, might be of very great help to this young woman. Miss Martha Gellhorn, c/o F.V. Field, New Hartford, Connecticut. Write her a note if you care to, or don't—& forget about it. (N.B. She hasn't seduced me & my interest is purely friendly, although she is 27 & quite attractive).

The letter has been used many times to show that while he was attracted to Martha, HG didn't always "capitulate to temptation."[73] This is a puzzle. Either HG lied to Lewis or lied in the suppressed *Postscript* about having had a relationship with Martha. While HG was a lusty man, while he thoroughly enjoyed his trophy women and masterfully deflected responsibility, there is no evidence outside Martha's claims that he lied about his relationships or anything else. Perhaps with this letter, HG not only wished to insinuate his virility but also wanted to save both his and Martha's reputations. After all, Sinclair Lewis not only named his son, Wells Lewis, after HG, but also nominated HG for the Nobel Prize in literature in 1931. In his letter to the Swedish Academy, Lewis wrote that he had been conducting a little survey asking intelligent readers to name the contemporary writer who "most inspired them to a vision of potential greatness in life. Most of them have answered Bernard Shaw or H. G. Wells. Wells' conception of the possibility of Mankind's consciously taking control of our life, instead of leaving it to chance, this combined with his humor, his drama, his portrayal of character, seems to me to make him, more than any other living author who has not yet received the Prize, worthy of your consideration."[74] Lewis wasn't able to persuade the Swedish Academy. It gave the prize for literature in 1931 to a Swede, Erik A. Karlfeldt.

In her April 1983 letter to Gip, in which she told her side of the story regarding her relationship with HG, Martha suggested that if Gip would just read her letters to HG he would see that "they weren't love letters; loving letters maybe, but not more." Gip accepted her invitation to read the letters, then sent them to Martha for her review. After reading her own letters some fifty years after she had written them, Martha packed them up with a note to Gip: "Here are mine—very good too—

not love letters (poor Wells) but loving admiring ones to a man 40 odd years older."[75] Fourteen years later, Martha was singing the same tune. To this author, she wrote: "I give you permission to use [my letters to Wells] if you will make it clear that they are not love letters but simply those of a young woman who felt friendship for a much older man. Wells, I should remind you, was the age of my father; and no beauty."[76] Let us accept Martha's invitation to "just read the letters."

★   ★   ★

"Wells darling, it has been what is technically known as a coon's age since I wrote you, or you wrote me. . . . You may think me a bad mannered bitch," Martha began her February 8, 1938, letter to HG. Irreverent, high-spirited letters were her norm, and they were a blast of fresh air for HG, even when they were critical of him, which was often enough. "Wells darling, You have indeed cut me off without a shilling. It is awful," she mock-complained in January 1944. The flip side was nearly as colorful: "Wells darling, Your little note, written in your usual embroidery, has arrived and cheered me very much."

The Closet Collection contains thirty letters to and from HG, the Wells Family, and Martha Gellhorn. Enclosed in a worn green folder are four cables relating to the publication of Martha's novel, *The Trouble I've Seen*, a fictionalized account of her work as a federal investigator; one letter from HG to Martha; fourteen letters from Martha to HG; and eleven letters between Gip and Martha. In addition, the file contains the galley proof of HG's preface to *The Trouble*, plus a group of letters and contracts between HG and Hamish Hamilton concerning its publication. Except for one letter, nothing is known about HG's correspondence to Martha. The one letter from HG to Martha that survived did so because it was a carbon copy of the original; and good thing, too, since it is a fascinating and enlightening document. Martha made a habit of salting away letters. Responding to the generous offer of Mary Hemingway, Ernest's fourth and last wife, Martha removed her letters to Hemingway from the JFK Library and locked them in her Boston archive.

Martha Gellhorn's letters to HG span nearly a decade, from 1936 to 1945. Like their author, they are many things: girlish and sophisticated, optimistic and pessimistic, silly and wise, but, more than anything else, entertaining. HG, who must have been a connoisseur of letters, having amassed perhaps as many as 100,000 of them throughout his lifetime, thoroughly enjoyed Martha's letters. In suppressed pages of his *Postscript,* he wrote that Martha was continuing to write him "the most interesting letters." In another place, as we have seen, he wrote, "I have never had more amusing love letters." HG typically wrote brief notes of instructions to Marjorie Wells on many of the letters he received. Some of the notes were a single word: "file." Others instructed Marjorie to send Martha a copy of his latest book. Sometimes the notes were more substantial and revealing, such as HG's notation on Martha's letter dated August 23, 1943, agreeing with Martha's critique of the first draft of his *Declaration of the Rights of Man.* HG instructed Marjorie: "Send her the English N. R. of M. [Natural Rights of Man]," and included the following message: "Dear Stooge, Is this better? I agree warmly in all your whimsical criticism of yourself & I will send you some more stuff later. Bless you."

Martha was extremely interested in the march of history and contemporary politics and her letters reflect those interests; indeed, they document the history-making times in which they lived: the machinations of Hitler and Chamberlain, the spirit of the Czech people, the possibility of world war. But Martha also followed contemporary literature and she sent regular book reports about her latest readings. Frequently, HG's works were on her current reading list, just as they had been on Constance's, and when they were, Martha never failed to give her friend her two cents' worth. If she didn't like something, she let him know. She didn't mince words; she never held back. It was one of the traits that endeared her to him.

Martha occasionally delivered praise by way of a letter—not frequently, but genuinely, it would seem. Sometimes she commended HG for a particular work. For example, from Sun Valley just before her marriage to Hemingway, Martha wrote an earnest letter that began with a compliment about HG's latest article on Churchill: "Wells sweetie,

Where are you? I read your piece in *Colliers*. It was good. It was full of faith which is a fine way to be and the only happy way. I wish you'd be somewhere within reach sometime."[77] Two years later, she heaped praise on HG for his last novel, *You Can't Be Too Careful*. "It's a marvellous job of work and made me laugh and also made me furious and I think you are certainly the greatest living authority on the English."[78] Just following a New York City get-together with HG and Hemingway, the latter now her husband, Martha said she loved HG "dearly" and that he was a standout as a "good man." Nineteen days after the bomb was dropped on Hiroshima, she upgraded him: "You are the greatest man in the world."

In her letters, Martha also connected with HG's personal life—where he had been, where he was going, how Moura was, and so on—and she offered the same kind of information about herself in return. For a guarded person, Martha was surprisingly candid with HG. Her extant letters to him do read like letters between very good friends, just as she argued. They exchange books and newspaper clippings. They offer to do errands for each other. They ask for more letters. They inquire about each other's health, each other's plans, each other's friends—Martha about Moura, in particular. They speak about their trade. They make arrangements to see each other, and excuses and apologies when the arrangements don't work out, just as HG and Constance did. They caution each other. They lecture each other. They wish each other well. Their comments can be whimsical: "Why don't you shoot Chamberlain, like a good citizen?" (Martha to HG, June 1938). They can be wise: "No tom cat is happy until the distressful urgency of sex is lifted from it" (HG to Martha, July 1943). For her part, Martha was open and vocal about her feelings for HG:

> I'd love to see you, but maybe you won't be back; and that would be very sad. (1938)

> I didn't call you Friday because I was sure you would be quite as hectic as I was: and no good comes of bursting in and out, with one's breath gone, and one's eyes wild. (1938)

You used to be my great and good friend and I wish you still were. (1938)

I wish you'd be within reach sometime. When and where will I see you, do you suppose? (1940)

I miss you a great deal and there are more things I wish I could talk to you about every day. (1942)

Other letters stretch the "it's-only-friendship" argument:

Do you miss me? (1938)

I again crossed with that odd bird, Freddy Lonsdale. I told him you were off me, so he began to look at me a little queerly (you know, "she no longer knows the right people"—how bitchy I am) but that was okay. . . . Why don't you love me anymore? (1938)[79]

I do not invite myself to stay with you, because I do not think you like me anymore, but perhaps I could come to lunch in all cases, and see what we agree and disagree on. Shall call you up—hope you're in town. (1938)

It was damned disappointing not to see more of you. I love you very much and find you always an enchanting guy. And am your humble servant as you know. (1938)

I am as sad as anything not to have seen you at all since I do dote on you and who knows when I will get back this way again. (1944)

Others stretch it even further:

I miss you very much and send you a big juicy kiss. (1943)

With only one letter in hand from HG to Martha, written some two-and-one-half years after Martha's marriage to Hemingway, it isn't possible to draw many conclusions about HG's perception of his relationship with her, although it is clear that he was familiar with her, and quite comfortable. "B'loved Martha, I've imagined all sorts of careers for you," he wrote on July 1, 1943, "but never one including a vast disorganised household in Cuba surrounded on all sides by (probably now unsaleable) green cigars." And it is clear from that letter that he was so familiar and so comfortable with her that he spoke freely, even on subjects others might have thought taboo: passion, sex, and love. To be sure, small insights can be gleaned from Martha's responses to HG, but some of her comments confound understanding. We will probably never know what triggered this particularly interesting response from Martha on January 19, 1942: "I don't know exactly how to feel about that sentence, 'your technique increases in cunning,' provided cunning is the word you wrote. I always thought cunning was one of the more lowly characteristics of the human race, but [maybe] it is a damn good thing to have."

The first letters in their correspondence were not letters at all, but cables. HG started shopping around for a publisher for Martha soon after boarding the *Majestic* in February 1936 for his return to London. Hamish Hamilton agreed on the spot to advance Martha £30, but HG later proposed several changes in the contract; these irked the publisher, and the relationship between the parties dissolved. HG settled amicably with Putnam after cabling Martha with news of the deal in mid-February.

PUTNAM OFFERS FIFTY POUNDS FIFTEEN PERCENT URGENT TO PUBLISH CABLE ASSENT [Wells][80]

CONTRACT OKAY EXCEPT REFUSE TO GIVE PUTNAMS AMERICAN PUBLICATION RIGHTS CAN GET BETTER TERMS HERE GRATEFUL Stooge

AMERICAN OPTION ON FORTHCOMING NOVELS INCLUDED IN UNEXPIRED STOKES CONTRACTS STOP PUTNAMS CAN

HAVE ENGLISH PUBLICATION RIGHTS ONLY AM PRETTY SICK
FROM OPERATION. MARTY[81] (HG's pencilled note to his secretary:
"Communicate this cable to Putnam at once. Regret I did not know of
the Stokes options.")

WHAT IS THIS OPERATION BEST WISHES PUTNAM WILL SEND
REVISED AGREEMENT BRITISH RIGHTS ONLY LOVE [Wells]

HG's preface to Martha's book opened with a strong gushing
metaphor about the course of human affairs being like the course of a
great vessel without a rudder. Perhaps he started the draft while still
bobbling around at sea. It is "a little less chancy and unpredictable than
the destiny of any other species of swarming animals," the biologist
wrote. He went on to speak of rapids, gorges, places of infinite danger.
All over the world, whole communities have been "swept from sufficiency and contentment and hopefulness into the direst perplexity and
want" over the past few years.

Here, in these carefully grouped stories of Miss Gellhorn, we have a
most vivid rendering of human beings passing from a certain homely
sufficiency of life, the simple kindly life of America in its expanding
phrase, towards a continually contracting existence of need and hopelessness. She is a new writer but her technique has an instinctive direct-
ness and vigour and all she tells is drawn from her own acutely appre-
hended experiences as a worker in the Federal Emergency Relief
Administration. Enlarge this book a million times and you have the
complete American tragedy. Miss Gellhorn seems to me a very considerable writer indeed. She achieves strength of effect without the least sacrifice of veracity, and though her work is saturated with pity never once
do I find her lapsing into sentimentality. . . . I do not think it will be easy
to read it through and not feel a new strength of resolve, to learn, to
work, to persist in learning and working for such a wilful reorganisation
of human life as will make these stories at least seem like an incredible
nightmare of misery in the history of mankind.[82]

As it happened, Martha did not devote much space in her letters to nature's wrath or sweetness. The weather surfaced only once, in March 1936. On a visit with her mother, perhaps a long weekend, she wrote from a historic inn near Independence, Missouri, that she was witnessing "the most lovely dust storm." In the same letter, she said that if he were there with her, she would make him take her to the floods, which were plaguing the Midwest.

Similarly, Martha's health was not much of a topic in her letters, but when she mentioned it, it had by that point become significant. In that fourth telegram to HG, Martha mentioned an operation. Perhaps it was on her foot. Ever since a fall "down the mountain side above Ponte Tresa to Lugano," when she bruised the bone in her right foot, walking was "a slightly dubious pleasure," she told her erstwhile boyfriend, Stan Pennell, from a St. Luke's Hospital in St. Louis in 1931.[83] Receiving hourly treatments for her foot, Martha told Pennell that under a battery of lights, her foot "ripens into red beef."

Another physical trial emerged in the correspondence two years later. By the time Martha limped back to St. Louis in February 1938, after a speaking tour of the Midwest, she was in sorry shape, indeed. In a letter to HG she said that she was exhausted, that she had intestinal flu and "nervous screaming meemies. What a horror it was." On the road across the frozen heartland from January 4 to 30, Martha was spared the second month of the trip when her doctors mercifully cancelled it. She made $100 for her effort—her "beautiful white body," "booming voice," and celebrity—and swore off speaking tours. Coincidentally, HG was also on a speaking tour of the United States, but his experience was altogether different. Martha wrote to him on January 8:

Seems that you were a wow as a lecturer and Mr. Peat's office told me you simply love it, from which I deduce either that you have a screw loose or else you are overflowing with the milk of human kindness, or else you have some kind of weird sense of humor. All the time I was lecturing, leaning against frozen cornstalks, while I spread the word to women in diamonds and false teeth, I thought of you. If you did like it, I would like to know how. Mother heard you in Chicago and said you were the nuts and that you read your speech.

Then Martha returned to her own personal horror: the nights on the Pullman listening to the sounds of "vile strange men" sleeping behind their green curtains; the days spent in awful places shivering from cold; the "kind idiotic lazy cowardly half-baked flabby folk" she had to talk to; and the "awfulness of talking about something you love so much that you ought either to write it in the best words you will ever find, or else shut up (I refer to Spain, and all about it.)" Martha remembered once having seen people swarm HG for an autograph; she remembered that he was calm, collected, and amused by the process. Martha never thought of herself as a celebrity, she said, and God willing, she never again would have to impersonate one.

> And personally I cannot take it, it gives me the shivers just to remember. "What do you think about . . . how did you get your start . . . do you never wear a hat . . . Don't you think women should marry . . . now which ones are the Loyalists, Miss Gellhorn, I just can't keep them all straight.". . . Oh Christ. War and floods and the unemployed never did to me what those audiences did. I got a little queer. I woke in the morning and wept bitterly and hysterically, knowing I'd have to face them again. And I could never learn to take the lecture calmly, but always felt I had to save the damned in one hour. So it was like Billy Sunday and Moses, and now my contract has been cancelled by my doctors, and I am wilting in and out of bed, and leaving for Nassau as soon as my insides permit. In order to forget.

It would be interesting, to say the least, to know how HG interpreted an early letter Martha sent him—the first letter in the Closet Collection. In her letter, dated March 26, 1936, she adopted a little-girl persona; it is almost as if a curly-locked Shirley Temple were speaking, not a sophisticated young woman of the world.

> I shall never write another book which is so sad I could burst into tears. . . . I am a very good girl and my big brothers are coming home to

surprise Mother for the weekend which is vastly exciting (not for you) and as I can't tell anyone else I thought I'd tell you. I now have to go to bed because I have a tummy ache. Do you want to see me in May. Because you don't have to. And I shall not be one of those nuisance-women who collect autographs.

Perhaps part of Martha's demeanor could be attributed to the death of her father two months earlier, on January 25, following surgery. At the time of writing, the Gellhorn children were converging on their mother to provide mental and physical support, no doubt. Whether in his role as friend, lover, surrogate father, or Dutch uncle, HG would get an earful of complaints and disparaging comments from Martha over the course of their decade-long friendship. Her disdain for people, places, and things was a strong thread of conversation, but only slightly stronger than her emerging self-loathing. Martha was often as critical of herself as she was of the imperfect world she reported on, and many of her letters to HG carried disapproval of one kind or another. He, while having a reputation for being thin-skinned and, once crossed, unforgiving, rarely attacked people and places in his letters to his women.

Martha's disgust and loathing often focused on the Midwest and its "flabby folk" and "vile strange men," as we read above. In that same letter, she spoke disparagingly about the Daughters of the American Revolution, who ran the historic inn she and her mother visited. Martha called them "a bunch of reactionary, ill-dressed snobs named Schultz. Pictures of these same witches with high white pompadours hang on the walls." Some thirty years later, she would write to Milt Wolff about her "beloved Mum: She's the best human being I've ever known; I adore her, I only detest St. Louis."[84] Her disdain was not limited to the United States. Martha also grew to despise England and its "ruling class," as she called it. "Gellhorn is renouncing England," she announced to HG on July 7, 1938, just after she had fled it "as one escapes from jail." England had a few good points, to be sure: its plentiful, attentive, bright—but "not imposing"—young men; and its interest in her, which made her "feel like the Queen of the May." But it was the ruling class that she detested: "really thoroughly and seriously."

I despise them as mercenary and without any desires except those concerned with holding on to what they've got. I find them horrifyingly shrewd and horrifyingly empty: and the worst of it is that the People put up with them, tip their hats, grin all over their faces, and are delighted to be ruled, gypped, snubbed and lied to providing the gent who does it is a gentleman. Well, Christ. I prefer lots of other countries: Spain is a paradise of reason and generosity and the finer things of the spirit compared to that green isle. And as for a free press, mother of God. You don't need Goebbels. Anyhow, I'm sick of the country and never want to see it again. I also loathe its comfortableness and its sloth: and reaffirm my dislike of islands and their effect on people's minds.

But earlier, in June, after "inspecting the oncoming war" from Prague, Martha told HG that her enmity had grown considerably. Now she professed, and certainly with good reason, "a marked loathing for the world we live in. Not a good state." In 1942, Martha offered the following about world leaders: "Personally, I am so sick of the phony Biblical eloquence of great men that I can scarcely stand it." By early 1943, she was packing her bags for an extended stay in England; by the beginning of the next year she wrote in a letter to HG from London that it had been a wonderful visit. She had met "marvellous people of such goodness, courage and devotion as to keep my faith in the human race bright for years to come. And I never liked London more than now, though I realize I would have seen it even better in 1940. Still it is something not to have missed it entirely." By the late summer of 1945, Martha Gellhorn was comfortably settled in a house on South Eaton Place. "If London after the war is as wonderful as it was during the war," she told HG, "it seems to me a place where a permanently rootless one might take roots, for a while at least."

Self-doubt and vulnerability, a side of Martha Gellhorn's personality that is rarely shown elsewhere, runs like a strong current through her letters to H. G. Wells. She frequently questioned her critical faculties, her skill as an observer and writer, and her dedication to hard work. We have already seen her perceived failure as a public speaker and celebrity. With regard to her writing skills, Martha told HG that her "slight talent" went to hell in 1938, that she was seriously studying her trade in 1942, and that in 1944, she had become humble about her writing and now didn't know what she once thought she knew. We will explore this doubt about her writing, but it is clear that Martha was haunted by the fear that she was lazy, that her intellect was second-rate, and that perhaps she was not the writer she had once imagined she would become, all of which she communicated to HG. After presenting HG with a laundry list of her activities in 1938, she asked: "You can't really snub me saying I'm a lazy louse can you?" In January 1944 she supposed that HG had cut her out of his life because of the "non-existence" of her mind: "You decided that, what the hell, you had no time to waste on pea-brains.

This is a very gloomy conclusion for me, and I am sad as anything not to have seen you at all since I do dote on you and who knows when I will get back this way again? However, there it is and I must accept being abandoned by you. Perhaps, if I studied very hard, and learned something imposing like chemistry, or geometry, before next I saw you, you would love me again. I will have Charlie Scribner mail you my new novel, which you will no doubt despise, but in any case there is no reason for you to lose touch entirely with the average mind.

★   ★   ★

I take my code out of Hemingway. Unbelievable, isn't it? Do you remember "A Farewell to Arms?" The hero talks to the woman; she is worried about something, and he says: "You're brave. Nothing ever happens to the brave." Which is somehow enough—a whole philosophy—a banner—a song—and a love. And something to fill up time—busily, passionately.

—Martha Gellhorn to Stan Pennell, May 8 or 9, 1931

It is quite possible, indeed quite probable, that part of Martha's self-doubt and/or sense of inadequacy stemmed from her childhood, from a remote, activist mother and an extremely busy, often-absent physician-

father. Her association with Ernest Hemingway didn't diminish her inferiority complex. Who could have survived a relationship such as that
one without lapsing from time to time into self-doubt, especially about
one's trade? After all, her husband was a cultural icon, right up there on
the American altar with Marilyn Monroe and Elvis Presley. Even Martha
had to concede E's great contribution to American literature, as we saw
in the apocryphism piece. Like that of his fellow icons, Hemingway's
legend carries more than its share of darkness. It is clear to anyone with
even a passing knowledge of the man that in addition to his original talent and unique contribution to American literature, as Martha affirmed,
he dragged around more than a few demons. It is widely known, for example, that at the end of his life, Hemingway had drinking as well as
mental and emotional problems; these culminated in his suicide in 1961
when he was only sixty-one. Whether the demons had sprung from his
self-doubt, a carping, hard-edged mother, a distant, largely absentee father, or his ambiguity about his sexuality—things often argued—or
from other things, they often manifested themselves in hard drinking
and indefensible behavior, most notably his urge to control, his grand-
standing, and his womanizing. These demons are a standard part of the
Hemingway legend, and they have been microanalyzed over the forty
years since his death. The women in his life, including Martha, are generally portrayed as the innocent victims of a monstrous evil genius.

At some point, Hemingway certainly became for Martha a despised
evil genius; indeed, he was evil incarnate. It got to a point that she would
not tolerate the mention of his name in her presence, would not allow
anyone to ask her questions about him, and would not permit his name
to appear in articles about her. She even canceled stories at the eleventh
hour when she felt that her terms had been violated. The cause of this
extreme bitterness and behavior can only be surmised. Whether it was
because she was irrevocably paired with Hemingway and his life or
whether he had mortally wounded her—which was entirely possible—is
not clear; perhaps it was something entirely different. Author Victoria
Glendinning offered her own analysis: She felt that by barricading herself from Hemingway, Martha was "fiercely" protecting her personal

life. Hard lines were drawn over this issue. One faction claimed that Martha didn't want to trade on Hemingway's name, while another argued that this was precisely what she did, even to adopting Hemingway's writing style. Despite her measures to separate herself from her former husband once and for all, Martha Gellhorn had to know that she couldn't block the association. She had to know that Hemingway would always figure in her life—and in her death—and he did, in spades.

Martha met her future first husband, and Hemingway his future third wife, in Key West, Florida, during Christmas of 1936, the first Christmas the Gellhorn clan celebrated without its patriarch. It is hard to believe that it was a chance meeting, although that is how it has been explained. Martha, her mother, and her brother Alfred, the latter on vacation from medical school, set out for Miami; but, as the story goes, they hated it, so they immediately jumped on a bus bound for Key West. Once there, Edna supposedly spotted a sign for "Sloppy Joe's," and the rest, as they say, is history.

Several people would claim over the decades that Martha made a play for Hemingway. She knew his work—and his weaknesses. Indeed, Hemingway had been one of Martha's great literary heroes since her college days. She had even borrowed his line from *A Farewell to Arms*— "Nothing ever happens to the brave"—as the epigraph to her first novel. Others, including Orsagh, have argued that the meeting was purely accidental, although she conceded that Martha appeared at the now-famous Sloppy Joe's wearing a slinky black dress and heels; in other words, she was hardly clad in beachwear. At that first meeting, Martha and Hemingway knocked back a run of Papa Dobles, and he was so smitten with her that he forgot the dinner party he and Pauline had scheduled for that evening.[85]

Although it is unlikely that they ticked them off that first night, Martha and Hemingway had a good many things in common—mostly by way of his wives. Wife No. 1, (Elizabeth) Hadley Richardson, was also from St. Louis, was the youngest of four children, and had attended and dropped out of Bryn Mawr. Hadley and Hemingway met soon after her mother died, just as Hemingway and Martha met after her father died. Hadley's father, like Hemingway's, had committed suicide. Hemingway's current wife, Pauline Pfeiffer Hemingway, was born in Piggott, Arkansas, studied journalism at the University of Missouri, and had worked for the Cleveland *Star,* the New York *Daily Telegraph,* and *Vanity Fair*—as its fashion editor. Later, like Martha, she worked in the Paris office of *Vogue.* Hemingway and all four of his wives were Midwesterners. Martha and Hemingway grew up in cities barely six hours apart, and they both reviled their hometowns. He supposedly once quipped that Oak Park, Illinois, was studded with "wide lawns and narrow minds." Both were journalist-writers, both of their fathers were physicians, and both of their mothers were strong, indeed, very strong.

The stories have been told a million times about their romance (instantaneous), their war reporting (on the Spanish Civil War and World War II), their wedding (November 21, 1940), incompatibilities (fierce and too numerous to name), fights (colossal and plentiful), and divorce (December 21, 1945). Stories about how Hemingway urged Martha to come with him to Spain to report on the Spanish Civil War and then left without her and without making any arrangements for her; about how, as soon as she arrived in Spain, he encouraged the ruse that she was a bona fide war correspondent by getting her all the privileges of one; and about how he nagged her into writing. About their four tours of duty in Spain. About how Martha found and refurbished their now-legendary Havana homestead, La Finca Vigia [Lookout Farm]. About their separate parallel lives. About how Martha forced Hemingway to cover China with her in 1941, and to cover World War II with her three years later, and about how Hemingway double-tricked her by stealing her publisher, *Collier's.* About how he supposedly never forgave her for upstaging him at the D-Day invasion. And about their extreme animosity for each other for the rest of their lives. Still, a few stories are worth repeating.

After her family left on or about New Year's Day, 1937, Martha stayed on in Key West for more than a week; she also hung out shamelessly at the Hemingway hacienda ostensibly to get writing pointers from Papa. Martha was heading back to St. Louis when Hemingway caught up with her in Miami, and together they traveled north by train to Jackson,

Mississippi. In all probability, the die was cast, the deal was sealed, well before they parted company at the station. Hemingway went on to New York, where he met with his editor, Max Perkins, and he took the opportunity to plug Martha's short story, "Exile." Within a couple of days, Perkins bought the piece. Martha also suggested that Hemingway pitch Perkins her latest manuscript—echoes of 1935 when H. G. Wells carried Martha's manuscript to two publishers.[86] Hemingway, now making arrangements to go to Spain to cover the Spanish Civil War, signed with a newspaper alliance; according to biographer Kert, Hemingway urged Martha to join him, saying that he could get her in and obtain all the credentials she'd need. When she arrived in New York, however, she found that she had been stood up.

In early March 1937, Martha made a quick clever maneuver, reminiscent of so many others past and future, when she asked for and obtained a letter from *Collier's* editor Kyle Crichton identifying her as a special correspondent for that magazine, which, of course, she wasn't. She later wrote that the letter was intended only to help her "with any authorities who wondered what I was doing in Spain, or why I was trying to get there; otherwise it meant nothing. I had no connection with a newspaper or magazine, and I believed that all one did about a war was go to it, as a gesture of solidarity, and get killed, or survive if lucky until the war was over."[87] Martha would keep her skills well sharpened throughout her long life, through wars and in peacetime, by asking for favors. She certainly did so fifty-three years later, different publisher, different war. In 1990, Martha approached Nicholas Shakespeare, the literary editor of the (London) *Daily Telegraph,* asking for "a letter which will not obligate anyone, you or the *Telegraph* or me, and I may not need it but better to have it. To Whom It May Concern: Martha Gellhorn is a special correspondent for the *Daily Telegraph.* Any courtesies extended to her will be appreciated."[88] Martha planned to go Panama after the troops cleared out. It was "a duty trip," she wrote, adding that "as long as I'm around I have to keep on with the record, how things really are, as near as I can find out." While she frequently endured the discomforts and dangers of covering war, along with everyone else,

Martha had a habit of devising strategies that won her, among other things, "access and transport to battlefronts. When her initiative failed to win her legal means, [she] resorted to sneaking or tricking her way into war zones."[89] In *The Face of War*, Martha claimed that she had launched her career as "an unscathed tourist of wars" with one knapsack and fifty dollars, and that "anything more seemed unnecessary." She hadn't yet celebrated her thirtieth birthday, although she had reinvented herself, yet again. Tough and determined and smart, Martha marched into Hemingway's heart and into history as a war correspondent of considerable mettle and with little, if any, preparation. She was, as we know, a quick study. From the moment she arrived in Spain, "a private battle between dominating male and indomitable female coexisted with and perhaps nurtured the love affair."[90] Meanwhile, Pauline Hemingway, displaced in Hemingway's set of priorities, was left behind in the domestic dust of Key West.

Once in Spain, Martha spun her gears for the first weeks of the first tour, floundering without an assignment. Hemingway suggested that, instead of getting in the way of the working journalists, she write something, *anything*, perhaps a piece about Madrid. Martha took his suggestion, and did her work well. *Collier's* bought her first piece, then a second, and soon thereafter her name appeared on the masthead. "I learned this by accident," she later wrote. "Once on the masthead, I was evidently a war correspondent. It began like that."[91] Edwin Rolfe, a poet and member of the Abraham Lincoln Brigade, later wrote about the journalists who covered the Spanish Civil War—Hemingway, Herbert Matthews, Weldon James, and Robert Capa. In his opinion, the most outstanding American "visitors" were Matthews and Hemingway. Of Hemingway, he later wrote: "The presence of this huge, bull-shouldered man with the questioning eyes and the full-hearted interest in everything that Spain was fighting for instilled in the tired Americans some of his own strength and quiet unostentatious courage . . . the fact that such a man, with so pre-eminent a position in the world, was devoting all of his time and effort to the Loyalist cause did much to inspirit those other Americans who were holding the first-line trenches."

Martha also made an impact, according to Rolfe. She arrived in Spain "in the midst of the April 5th attack, and was forced to spend the day at the brigade's first-aid post, watching the bodies of the wounded and the dead being brought in on stretchers. She afterward memorialized the day in a magazine article, a few copies of which reached Spain and were carefully and gratefully read by the American volunteers."[92]

A little more than a year before she died, Martha wrote in a *London Review of Books* essay, titled "Memory," that she had "believed in the cause of the Spanish Republic as [she] believed in nothing before or since."[93] Earlier, she said that when the war—"our war," she called it—ended, "none of us ever got over it in our hearts. We loved Spain and believed that it was the place where Fascism must be stopped, the last chance." She had said much the same thing in the early 1950s to Rolfe after he sent her a poem about Spain. "It would seem to me that Spain will be, for all of us, the one point of not forgetting, not being disgusted and embittered, in our whole lives." In "Memory," Martha wrote about Madrid, Modesto, and Ernest Hemingway, whom she called "E." throughout. Soon after it was published, she sent it to Milt Wolff with a letter saying, among other things, that it was the first time in more than fifty years that she had used the initial E. She had maintained silence on the subject, she said, "for the simple reason that I never wanted to be associated with him."[94] In a follow-up letter, she told Wolff that she wrote the piece in 1994, when she could still see. "I was not sure whether after more than 50 years of silence I should publish anything that mentioned E. but since it was the last [time I could] ever write properly, I had a sort of commemorative feeling about it, my final real writing." History, she noted, is "a constant disaster. Repeated stupidity drives one half mad."

On January 3, 1991, Martha revealed something else about herself in a letter to her friend Glendinning: that listening to Chopin in her old age brought back powerful and poignant memories of the death of the Spanish Republic and the wasted bravery and suffering that went with it. During artillery bombardments of Madrid, she explained, she and Hemingway "opened the windows against the blasts and played

Chopin on E's wind-up gramophone. Not defiance, I don't think, but a reminder of loveliness in the world."[95] Powerful memories of Spain bubbled up three years later in a letter Martha wrote to her old friend Milton Wolff. Wolff had asked Martha to read the final draft of his manuscript, *Another Hill*, which was in press. She responded on July 15, 1994, and in vintage Gellhorn:

> The imaginary dinner party at the Majestic made me laugh. Dear Joe North would never have delivered speeches in such company and nobody would have sat still for them. It's clear to me that you never slept at the Majestic because you speak glowingly about the sheets. Barcelona was a city without soap, including the hospitals. I think you cannot imagine that. All the linen at the Majestic was rubbed in cold water and ironed. The terrible dark old stains remained on everything and the stink is something I remember still. The city's lack of soap and the general starvation were what made Barcelona hell, not the high flying Italian bombers. As for all the lovely grub and the French wine we supposedly consumed, whatever food we had and by then we had practically none, was tins brought in by anyone who had been to Paris—such as [Robert] Capa who went there to have his films developed.

Despite the slam, Martha said that she loved Wolff's title, that she admired parts of the book "intensely," and that she thought it would be recognized "as a serious and important piece of work. And I do congratulate you on having done it, for writing a book is always like climbing backwards up the Matterhorn." On January 24, 1996, she was thanking Wolff for praising her novella "Till Death Do Us Part," which was to some extent based on another old war buddy, Robert Capa, the brilliant photographer of the Spanish Civil War, and his deceased wife. Martha told Wolff that she often thought about Capa, and that she had two photographs of him, one of which she had received from Ingrid Bergman. "A nice woman. She fell desperately in love with [Capa] when he went to Hollywood after the war and of course wanted to marry him and of course Capa never really wanted to marry anyone and fled.

She told me she had never before met 'a free human being.' I loved him but not that way; he was my blood brother. I think he loved me too though we quarreled incessantly." Martha also noted that Capa stuck by her "entirely" during her break-up with Hemingway, "and in fact made it possible by finding me in tears in Paris after the Liberation and a vile public scene Ernest had made."

> Late at night [Capa] told me to call the Ritz and ask for Mary Welsh's room (I knew nothing of her) and E. would answer and I could then demand a divorce. Capa sat on the floor and coached me, since E. had said he would never give me a divorce, but was caught in the act that night and knew he'd have to. And Capa stuck with me when many quickly dropped me in favor of E., who insisted on a choice: him or me.[96]

Martha was also crazy about Herbert Matthews, the correspondent for the *New York Times,* whom she and Hemingway palled around with during the Spanish Civil War. Matthews had horrendous migraine headaches, and at Teruel, as she later told Wolff, Martha massaged his neck every night to try to help relieve the pain. "I love that man," she wrote Wolff some thirty years later. "H. Matthews could never tell a lie in an age when lying was all but mandatory and highly rewarded. I think he is the most honest journalist of our time."[97] In a farewell letter to Freddie Keller, another friend from the Spanish Civil War, Martha signaled those human qualities that in her opinion constituted "a tremendous success: honesty, loyalty, courage and a beautiful lack of vanity. He was his own man for eighty years. He was one of the best men I ever knew."[98] One year earlier, on January 9, 1992, Martha attacked Wolff for his critique of her newly released collection of novellas. "You madden me by taking fiction as if it were fact. Once, Ernest said to me that I made my stories so real that people believed I was simply reporting fact. But I did not by God. I made up that story about Capa—basing it of course on some of his qualities—but he never spoke of his wife, I never saw her, I knew nothing about an American love and the whole thing is in fact an invention. You must read fiction as fiction and fact as fact; otherwise you insult the writer." Although Martha's enthusiasm for Hemingway was short-lived—arguably only as long as her career as a war correspondent for *Collier's* in Spain—for the rest of her life she would be grateful to E. for at least one thing: the gunfire-recognition lessons he gave her in the early days of the war. Perhaps she also privately savored his epithet for her, according to Kert, as the bravest woman he had ever met,

> braver than most men, including himself. Since courage had come to be the yardstick by which Ernest judged people, Martha's possession of this quality dramatically enhanced his admiration of her. She in turn saw him at his best. "I think it was the only time in his life," she remarked, "when he was not the most important thing there was. He really cared about the Republic and he cared about that war."[99]

Considering the venom they would later release on each other, it seems hard to believe that there was once a time when Martha was Hemingway's chief defender, and vice versa. One such occasion was precipitated over Hemingway's involvement in the making of the film *The Spanish Earth*. Martha became enraged over an article she had read in *Hoy*, reprinted from the *Daily Worker*. Written by the journalist-author Samuel Putnam, a contemporary of Hemingway's, the article claimed that "E saw fit to submit the movie to Franco for approval," Martha told Rolfe in an undated letter from the Finca.

> As you know there has never anywhere been such a suggestion; therefore it was invented by the aforementioned Putnam. I have never been angrier at a piece of libel in my life, and have had just about enough of these guys, with their cheap spirits and their common lies. There is no one anywhere, aside from Putnam and pals, who would for one minute imagine such an accusation to be true. Why do they lie? Who tells them to? I cannot bear much more of that sort of business and I see no reason for unending patience with fools and crooks. That E's absolute goodness and integrity should be rewarded by them with such virulent hating lies

is inadmissible. Are you guys gagged. And if you are not, why the hell don't you say something.

In October 1937, Hemingway's *To Have and Have Not* was published. The war having quieted down and victory appearing to be imminent, he began work on *The Fifth Column,* a thinly veiled story of the complex relationship between himself (a.k.a. Philip Rawlings, a Loyalist secret agent) and Martha (a.k.a. Dorothy Bridges, his beautiful, but lazy, fellow writer-companion). Martha went to Czechoslovakia in the summer of 1938 to survey the country in preparation for a *Collier's* article. Two years later, she published *A Stricken Field,* a novel about the experiences of an American journalist in Prague in the interval between the Munich Pact and the Anschluss. Both Martha and Ernest were criticized for basing their characters on thinly disguised versions of themselves, just as HG had been. Mary Douglas, the heroine of *Stricken Field,* was an American war correspondent in Czechoslovakia, recently back from Spain. Martha wouldn't abandon the autobiographical urge that dominated her work until 1943 and the publication of *Liana.*[100]

Martha returned to the Finca in January 1940, after covering Finland's stand against the Soviet Union in December. She joined Hemingway, who was feeling abandoned. He supposedly bad-mouthed the farm at first, complaining that it was overpriced at $100 a month, and stormed off on a fishing trip. According to the legend, Martha used her own funds to put the place in order, and Hemingway eventually forked over the $12,500 to buy what became a playground-oasis for him and his hunting, fishing, and drinking pals—and an albatross for her.

Edna Gellhorn went out West to visit Martha and Ernest. For whatever reason—perhaps because she adored both of them—she advised against a legal union. "If only I hadn't married E. H.," Martha wrote some fifty years later. "My mother came to Sun Valley, just to urge us NOT to marry. The wise woman. But I never guessed I'd be haunted and hounded by that myth all my life."[101] After Martha and Ernest were married by a justice of the peace in Cheyenne, Wyoming, they went to New York, where they dined with HG. From there, they took off for Cuba, where they celebrated Christmas, and HG sailed for home after two months of lecturing in the United States. It was probably the only time that HG and Hemingway met. Martha, still calling herself Stooge, dashed off a quick note to HG to bid him bon voyage and to assure him that the meeting between the two formidable men in her life had gone well: "Everyone here loves you dearly. Nobody has seen such a good man for a very long time. My husband Mr. Hemingstein thinks you are very good. Myself, I love you as always."[102] In truth, Martha may not have been so pleased with the meeting. She later told Kert that the conversation was "disappointing," largely because Hemingway wouldn't open up.

Even before they met, Hemingway knew something about HG and his work. In one of nearly a hundred recently opened letters from the correspondence of Martha Gellhorn and Ernest Hemingway, the latter gave the former a pep talk about writing—one of dozens from the aficionado to the gringo over the next five years. He told her that she must have patience and not worry about writing, not worry about output. "You see you started in with the wonderful standard of Wells who can write a book and numerless others every year. Only Dumas Pere and Simenon ever wrote more than three good books. Flaubert wrote all his life and only wrote one really good one."[103] In an interview many years later, Martha compared these two men in her life—so different in so many ways, and yet oddly similar. She described HG as self-educated and the most intelligent man she had ever known. Hemingway was "part genius" and also self-educated, and she ranked him "close behind" HG.[104]

The marriage would not be a tie that bound Martha and Ernest. In general and ever thereafter, they went in different directions. In 1942, for example, she took another *Collier's* assignment to the Caribbean. Her novel *Liana* was published in 1944. He, meanwhile, spent many months hunting for Nazis or unspecified insurgents on land; in 1942 and 1943, he was fifteen months at sea on the *Pilar* hunting for German U-boats under the guise of a scientific expedition run by the fictitious "American Museum of Natural History." "But as the months passed and no German sub commander evinced the slightest interest in Hemingway and company—he called this effort the 'Crook Factory'—the cruises of the *Pilar*

turned into fishing trips (courtesy of government-issue gasoline)."[105]
While Hemingway biographers have by and large dismissed the idea that
Hemingway had been involved in true espionage, documents revealed in
mid-2000 argue otherwise. Federal Bureau of Investigation memos indicate that the American embassy and the U.S. Navy paid Hemingway $500
a month to collect information from people he and his pals befriended in
and around Havana and the Caribbean. Michael Reynolds, the late Hemingway biographer, claimed that in so doing, the captain of the *Pilar* was
baiting death: "I think he went out threatening Nazis and shady Cubans
in a bid to get himself killed with honour."[106]

Meanwhile, what there was of married life was anything but smooth
sailing for the Hemingways. He was gregarious and loved having a circle of buddies around him; she was private, a loner. Oddly or not, war
was the environment that worked best for them; it took them outside
themselves, as Martha suggested, and brought them together over a
cause. The domestic scene had the opposite effect, highlighting qualities neither found attractive otherwise.

Some observers saw another source of friction. Hemingway was said
to be controlling and commanding, always putting Martha on the defensive—and on the move. The more he tried to contain her, "the more
she clung to independence," as the story goes.[107] Hemingway told his
biographer, A. E. Hotchner, that the reason for the divorce was simple:
It was a sterile marriage and she was a cold wife. Others, including
Winston Guest, Hemingway's good-spirited millionaire friend and sub-
chasing pal, argued that Martha never loved Hemingway. She once told
Guest that she had picked Hemingway "because of his ability as a
writer and possible remuneration from books. And I thought to myself,
what a tough, mercenary bitch to discuss her husband with me, someone she hardly knew. She didn't imply that she loved him at all. She im-
plied to me that she married him as a practical matter; it might help her
improve her writing."[108] For the record, Martha countered, typically,
with the word "rubbish." She claimed that her career began long before
she met her future husband, and that he did not help advance it one
iota. *Au contraire*, she said:

It should be noted that I never used his name or my association with him, not when I was married to him or ever after. So much for a calculated marriage. But you know, I was regularly blackguarded by Ernest Hemingway in the later years to anyone and everyone. I am used to my curious role as a monster in his life, and it doesn't matter much to me. I loved him as long as I could and when I lost all respect for him as a man—not as a writer—I said so and withdrew and that was that.[109]

In 1984, Arthur Hopcraft, a British television producer, began talking about making a "dramatised biography" about Hemingway and the Spanish Civil War. When Martha found out about it, she was livid and began a writing campaign. One of the people she contacted was the poet Alvah Bessie, a former acquaintance in Spain. In fact, after putting her personal gripe in the hands of her lawyer, she encouraged Bessie to do the same, and also to "alert the chaps." There was no divine right that allowed people to use the names of "real living people," to set them in scenes and give them dialogue. "I left E. H. forty years ago and have kept firmly away from all the ghastly publicity and here I am, a figure of Hopcraft's fancy. . . . I am also infuriated by Hopcraft's version of the Spanish war. I don't know what the law is but am determined not to be present in this or any other Hemingway junk."[110] Still on the warpath about the made-for-television movie, she wrote to Wolff two months later. The television things disgusted her, she said, because

though there are roughly 20 books a year about Hemingway, all propagating the myth and I appear in them (I don't read any but am so told) as the awful ambitious heartless wife, I mind desperately about appearing on TV in the form of an actress called Martha Gellhorn. There is the obligatory sex scene in the Hotel Florida; you can imagine how that charms me. But mainly I have spent 40 years distancing myself from all the Hemingway bilge and hoohah, and I passionately do not want my identity mixed up in it. He was okay in Spain, he was useful and the only time he wasn't a total egomaniac; but he became grotesque and in WW2 he was beyond belief embarrassing. He should be remembered and valued as a writer; as a person he was as awful as geniuses regularly are. Though truth to tell, I don't much like his writing any more because I see, in it, his vainglory.[111]

Although Hemingway has been demonized for his miserable behavior, the recent opening of his correspondence with Martha Gellhorn offers quite a different image, this one of a man who, if not completely sans demons, is only moderately impelled by them, at least for a time. This correspondence reveals a kinder, gentler man; a sympathetic, supportive, and loving, indeed, lovesick, mate, who, as Martha's financial, professional, physical, and emotional helpmate-caretaker, promised her any star in the sky in exchange for her companionship—such as it was. He was certainly miserable when she went away, which was often during their brief marriage. "I am lost without you. Can't sleep, don't want to move; just straight acheing miss you all the time," he wrote his "Dearest Ticklie" from Manila in May 1941, albeit only six months after their wedding. And, from Honolulu some time later, he claimed, "I have been just gnawing sick dumb lonely for you like the animals that just slowly die without their mates."[112]

To be sure, Hemingway was no Boy Scout at this time in his life, but in the recently opened cache of letters to Martha his positive qualities seem to outweigh his faults. His positive qualities also seem to outweigh Martha's. Indeed, in these letters she comes off as an immature, narcissistic, critical, and perennially unhappy woman. He, in great contrast to many if not most representations of him, reads as a conscientious husband and father. It is a great temptation to show this side of Hemingway, which, in turn, reveals another side of Martha. For example,

This Papa, it is clear, is madly in love—at least for a time:

Dearest beloved Chickie, I love you because your feet are so long and because they get cold and because I can take good care of you when you are sick. Also because you are the most beautiful woman I have ever known and the darkest and loneliest and because I never wanted, *nor could stand*, to be married to anybody but my true love. (October 15, 1942)

This Papa is caring:

I love you Bongie and I hope you have good weather and good re-fill-ing of the well of your head and heart. Don't forget to take lime juice in battle for your hair. I can't wait to see you and to sleep with you in big bed with fine cold crackly nights. (September 23, 1941)

This Papa is helpful:

I did all your things: sent pictures and negatives to Colebaugh; cabled your front story press wireless as Chenery requested me; cabled them about it etc. day got in here and got them all off on clipper. Honey, if you want me to I will wait at Wake and help you with your pieces. I hate not being where I can help you. But after this let's not write any more pieces but some decent stories. (May 1941)

This Papa is attentive:

Here is a present for you and also four extremely lucky animals (out of Lapis Lazuli) acquired in my travels to chaperone you across the Pa-cific safely. Also one study in rabbits to show how they should act in-stead of going off away from each other in all directions. (May 1941)

This Papa is understanding:

I would much rather always have you write me gloomy true letters than false happy ones. I understand the gloomy of you and the happy of you and know how they balance up and that you are really happiest when you are gloomy like Goethe and Schiller. (July 7, evening, 1943)

This Papa is devoted:

All I can say is that I will try all my life each day and each night to be good and to help you. I had tried very hard to be a better man and better friend and husband and I think I *was* maybe some better for quite a long time. Now I am starting all over. (Early 1942)

This Papa is proud:

I can't really write at all the way you can well and easily and good. I just nail words together like a bloody carpenter and it is so tough to do.

You are my hero and always will be and I will be good and try to live up to my hero. Thank you very much for haveing come to Key West and for haveing married me. (June 24, 1942)

This Papa is often apologetic and repentant:

Please lets start over and be friends again. 'Ness we be friends there is nothing. It is not such a long way to go. Rilke wrote "Love consists in this, that two solitudes protect and touch and greet each other." I haven't protected you good, and touched you little and have been greeting you scoffingly. But truly I respect and admire you very much and of this date and hour have stopped scoffing. . . . Anyway accept small touch and greeting from the other solitude. (End of May, 1942)

This Papa is endearing:

Dearest Mooky: Am not wakeing you up because you had such a wakefull night with the rain and mugglyness. All cats present and accounted for. Winkie ate everything and full of scamper and purr-purr. Best wouldn't speak to me for some time this morning because Boy was so friendly in the night. But she finally made up when I told her that she brought the rain. (End of May, 1942)

This Papa is funny:

I must really have a good imagination or I couldn't have such detailed and awful dreams. I have dreams as full of detail and as well written and completely rounded as the one I just had at least three times a week. In the dream I took the President to one of the hangings after coasting with him on a bobsled all the way down to Montreux from the top of the bobrun at Les Avants. As you can imagine he never enjoyed anything more and I am probably Minister to Switzerland right now. It's a shame all of these people don't know what they do in my dreams. (October 14, 1942)

This Papa is lonely and vulnerable:

I was away from you so long I only know you well now on a typewriter. We must change that. I am very tired again and sad in my heart.

If you don't like me I don't like me either. I don't mean that fliply. (May 1942)

This Papa is suffering from "chastity":
Think Mr. Scrooby is just going to die off from lack of use. Well he had a hell of a jolly life. So have I had really and read an awful lot of good books and written some too. (September 5, 1942)

This Papa is a one-man pep-band, writing coach, and editor:
Piece on cruise was marvellous. It had some of the finest and loveliest writing you ever did and such a million dollar ear for the back talk. Ni Joyce ni nobody any better ear than my Bong has now. Really wonderful. I love you blessed Mooky. Please come home and let me give you a hugalug. (September 19, 1942)

Get exercise and write whether it is impossible or not. It is nearly always impossible. And don't write shit and stop while you still know what is going to happen. And believe in it. (July 14, 1943)

The only legitimate excuses for a good writer not writing when he or she has a book going are ill health and unsolvable financial difficulties. Everything else is pampering the ego, horse-shit and self luxury. Worry or fear of failure is only cowardice. (March 16, 1943)

This Papa worked hard to create an ideal world for Martha:
. . . please just leave the goddamned house and servants alone and when I come home I will fire who you want fired and hire new ones. Will probably be home quite a long time and will be happiest to do this and to see that no one bothers you and will do nothing but keep bores and bothers away from you and play tennis when you want to and go to the movies and know you write good each day or anyway 3–4 days out of 7 which is tops. . . . please when you hit hard going in book don't then dive into house reform and trouble and then blame all book trouble that every good writer has had since the beginning of writing on the house. (July 14, 1943)

Regardless of his promises to Martha, nearly always kept, and his efforts, often Herculean, regardless of his work at the Finca and his help with Martha's manuscripts, Hemingway was routinely criticized, attacked, and abandoned, his gestures often interpreted as halfhearted or self-serving. As the letters demonstrate, Martha found fault everywhere. She blamed everyone and everything under the sun for her problems, especially with writing, and for her emotional state. She could certainly "ladle out" the blame, as Hemingway said. When she was on vacation with her mother in Florida, Martha complained to Hemingway in Cuba about the shoddy motel and lousy restaurants. He apologized on May 28, 1942, and tried to put a good spin on the situation: "But anyhow you have the sea and the finest beach there is and all sorts of pine country behind. Your cahts send deep purrs and early morning push pushes." A few days later, she complained about her bathing oil; about the weather, which precluded swimming; about his not writing her, which spoiled her vacation. Martha would also grouse that life wasn't intense enough, that she shouldn't have to shoulder the responsibility of running the Finca or caring for his boys while he was out on the boat, and that the Finca was overrun with cats. She complained that E didn't call her often enough when he was away or come in from his boating expeditions to see her mother, who was visiting, and moreover that he was ugly and a lousy dancer. "Now I know how horrible I am because you rightly tell me," he responded in July 1942. "But otherwise I would have been unconscious as the way I liked to dance and thought I could until you told me how I couldn't and never could and never have since. Now I can't dance, (don't ask me) remember the lovely tune."

In September of that year, Martha told her husband something he never wanted to hear: She despised the Finca and everything connected with it. "Was sort of a blow to learn from letter how you hated the Finca but have been trying to understand ever since got letter and probably will get to since get to understand most things haveing been at one time writer." He asked her to remember that one doesn't throw away a lovely place because it needs a coat of paint or because the cook is not performing well.

. . . and everyone needs a place to live and work finally. . . . a piece of good land on a top of a hill with a house on it that I fought hard to get is not something to be thrown away in a whim nor in a humor and you will be old longer than you will be young and you will not like those hotel rooms and they are no place for one's cotsies, nor, when you ever get grown up enough to appreciate them, good childies.[113]

By March 1943, very little good faith or humor was left between them. Hemingway could no longer "stick the atmosphere," as he wrote to Martha. He told her that he knew the house had been a lot of work while he was away and that he greatly appreciated what she had done to keep it going, that he had been working hard himself on two grinding jobs, but he wanted her to believe that everything he did—from running the house to tiptoeing around to keeping pests away—was done to allow her time to write.

Now I come back to an atmosphere as though I were some sort of villain of the piece. Bong I think you have me mixed up with some awful people you have been reading about or seeing in the movies. . . . You are as free as air. Nobody keeps you here. You have always gone away whenever you wanted to. There is no need to destroy me because you feel you have to go out into the world again . . . what you hate is not being as free and as young as we both were when we started for Europe . . . I am really your best and now almost oldest friend as well as your husband who loves you very dearly and you remember through the hatred and the passion and the need to let the fine wild horse run over far open country that I am the one who loves your work most and appreciates it and has tried to help you (as all good writers with good hearts help all good writers) (and so lucky to have such a good one to be with me lucky to have you).

. . . no-one that chased their youth ever caught it and there never was a great race horse that could not be ridden nor that did not have to have a bit in his mouth on race days: and the thing that bridles and bits you and rides you and is your true master is the need to write truly and well.

Your beauty will go.
Your youth will go.

Everything will go except writing well and the only way to write well
is to do it in spite of . . . your surroundings and the sensitiveness of your
soul and the bastard that I am as an excuse for why you can't write. So
maybe why not try writing?

I appreciate greatly what you have done for the house but I would
rather live in it as a hovel and have you writing well than have you skipping writing to bring it to perfection.

. . . there is no land where you can run away from yourself even if
you go to the ends of the earth: which I have been reliably informed are
extremely uncomfortable and almost always infested with fleas.

From your loveing husband who is evidently being kicked out of your
life.

You can get handsomer husbands, and richer, and younger and nobler
and finer. But you won't ever get one who loves you nor appreciates you
nor understands you better. You don't believe this but it is so. I have
given up my life, my children etc without drama or bullshit some
months back. So anything you do to it won't hurt it and you have no
need to worry.

So you are absolutely free now and I wish you a good trip and if it is to
cold countries keep my heart always in your pocket and it will keep your
hands warm. Your Bongie.[114]

Three months later, Martha told HG that his letter had arrived like a
package of food parachuted into the jungle, or passed from a rubber
boat to the survivors of a shipwreck. Hemingway had been away most
of the year on a variety of jobs. "I am so dying for talk," she confessed
to HG on June 9, 1943. "There is a big hollow longing for talk in me:
you would find me a far better listener and learner and giver than I was

that winter where you were like a snowed-in teddy bear with me in Connecticut." Martha explained that the Finca occupied too much of her time. She had loved the place, and put her sweat and tears into refurbishing it. A year earlier, she told HG that she thought his house and hers were the best she'd ever seen; this was certainly a far cry from what she was telling Hemingway. Two years earlier, she wrote that she had been thinking about HG and hoped he was well; she was wondering about his house on the Park—whether it was still standing. She didn't think he would ever be "very impressed by danger and your country is showing up wonderfully now, the best it has in ten years. If they blow up the houses, worse things have happened."[115] Yet, even with the Finca staff, Martha was essentially alone; her ability to speak Spanish extended only to the vocabulary needed to manage the plumbing, tree pruning, upholstery, and marketing. And, while not far from Havana, she rarely left the estate and rarely asked anyone up to it. The more one is alone, she wrote to HG on June 9, 1943, the more "fiercely demanding one becomes, and talk is no longer a careless babbling to make a noise but a rite." She went on:

> One needs to give something true (because one has spent so much time alone trying to think truly) and to hear something definitely better than the varied and revealing talk one makes for oneself. If I said that clearly? So that finally, the more you are alone the more cautious you are about not being alone; and I make plans for talk as hungry people are supposed to imagine meals. But I do nothing about it as I do not want to be disappointed. And now letters, which always seemed to me ideal for talk, are almost finished. It is embarrassing to be overheard, if nothing more.

It is clear from reading Martha's letters that she was a loner—an observer, to be sure, but a loner—and sometimes an excruciatingly lonely one at that. As she confessed to James Fox, a fellow writer, in 1986, "My chosen and protected status is an outsider. I have never seen any place or group I wanted to join."[116] The next year she said much the same thing to Glendinning. She had grown from "a non-gregarious child into a woman who has to be alone most of the time. My problem always used to be that I heard everything people said and most of it drove me up the wall."[117]

Despite her moods, or perhaps because of them, Martha tried to keep on writing, although it was a struggle. It isn't surprising then that work was a major topic of conversation in the correspondence between Martha and HG, just as it was with Moura and Constance. They were both self-defined by their work, and it came perhaps before anything, including relationships. The word hadn't been invented yet, but HG and Martha were workaholics. Work was the glue that held both of their lives together. Throughout her correspondence with HG, Martha would flaunt or demonstrate her dedication to serious work. For example, exhausted for undisclosed reasons, Martha wrote in her first letter to HG that she was "all worn out" in her mind. She had finished *Trouble* and was dealing with her publisher, Putnam, although HG had done most of the work to set up the contract. On a vacation with her mother, Martha wrote from the old Santa Fe trail that "Putnam's are the most divine cherubs and [so] is Huntington. They do everything I ask and there must be a *drefful* snag somewhere."[118] After a long hiatus with no correspondence, Martha wrote to HG in February 1938, again from Missouri and again in a state of nervous exhaustion, this time explained, about that disastrous lecture tour. In the same letter, she asked him why he didn't love her anymore, and then, as if to demonstrate her fine and loveable qualities, argued:

> I haven't changed. And I do work, I've written a hell of a lot, a huge novel that I could not bear to publish though I was offered more than I've ever been for it, but it stank. And masses of articles to make myself a cosy living. And radio broadcasts from Spain for the cause and also the fun and also $100. And now these shitty lectures and then some more articles and then possibly a book. . . . You used to be my great and good friend and I wish you still were. Love, Stooge.

Exhaustion and restoration were common themes in Martha's life and letters. Refreshed and recuperated, she went to Prague in June 1938, but again she was worn down by the experience. "I am very tired and have a bad liver from too much war, and wish everything would become reasonable for once so that honest folk could get a sunburn and cultivate their gardens," she noted in a letter to HG from the Hotel Ambassador the second week of June 1938. She went to England, but didn't see HG, then on to Paris. From France, where she was "whacking out" her *Collier's* piece on England and was "in such a hurry to be free," she wrote on July 7, so that she could swim, get sunburned, and try to write a book. "I won't move or earn money for at least six months, anyhow I hope so. It was damned disappointing not to see more of you, but maybe you'll be coming in my direction sometime and maybe there'll be more leisure."[119] As mentioned, *Collier's Weekly* was a cash cow for HG, and it became Martha's primary employer for several years. Between 1937 and 1945 she would publish more than forty articles for the magazine. As she wrote to HG:

Am coming to London next Sunday, to sweat out my life's blood in behalf of *Collier's* for one week. (June 1938)

I'm finishing a book of short stories (with difficulty) and then going to N.Y. on Nov. 14. After that thank God I shall start working again, rushing off somewhere for Collier's. (October 26, 1940)

This summer, maybe, providing Collier's and everyone else official agrees, I am coming to England. (Spring 1943)

It has been wonderful being here [London]: I have done six articles, none of which are going to change the course of events nor in fact do anything except occupy that unknown and unimaginable thing, a Collier's reader, for a few minutes of his or her spare time. However, I learnt a great deal and if I can instruct no one else I can at least selfishly delight in the fine things I pick up for myself. (January 11, 1944)

Despite her own grueling schedule, Martha always managed to stay up with HG's appearances and his publications as they rolled out. In early 1938, she raved over his latest *Collier's* piece on the "New Americans," calling it "the nuts. Very good about all the big guys, and I wonder if you aren't too hopeful about the young though I hope to heaven you're right. I always find them helpless and frightened and it breaks my heart." In 1941, HG published his last novel, *You Can't Be Too Careful*, which revolves around the life of Edward Albert Tewler, a pitiful little Everyman who refuses to have anything to do with improving the world. Martha later told HG that she had read the saga under amazing conditions, beginning it on a gold train in Dutch Guyana. She called the train a "toy job" that took nine hours to go 110 miles, "and half-naked bush negresses run along the tracks after it waving, and flapping their bosoms, and screaming with laughter. It picks up gold nuggets here and there and puts them in a boxcar without a guard and stops whenever anybody wants to get out and shoot a passing bird or talk with a friend in a thatched hut."[120] Martha continued reading the book in a "hellhole of a town" where the malaria was so bad she had to stay under a net from 6:00 P.M. to 6:00 A.M.; she later passed *You* on to a man she said was the only smart colonel in the entire Caribbean.

Apparently HG wasn't convinced that Martha had actually read his book because she later protested that "of course" she had. This time, she was more specific—and critical: Yes, it was well-written, but she loathed the little man. She told HG that his main character—"that repulsive little man of yours"—

was well-crafted, in fact, marvelous. Such a detailed study in ugliness, like a study of pimples under the microscope. I didn't like the end: it had such a large mocking cheerfulness about it. I wanted the man to be just as conceited for something really small that happened to him: he didn't fit with such a big medal.[121]

And then Martha took the opportunity to critique HG's treatment of women in his fiction. In so doing, she revealed a lot about herself. She said, for example, that HG was "funny" about women. "You do gentle them, you do really believe they are a more real and honest product, don't you? I don't necessarily: neither sex seems to me anything wildly hot: they are only people. But I have observed how you tend towards admiring women. I wonder why?" Martha segued into a discussion about her latest book, *Liana,* which she thought would be finished in a month. She had real doubts about the novel, which was the first of her fictional works not based—loosely or otherwise—on her own life. She also admitted to a "wide cowardice" because she had little confidence and a lot of doubt. "It is difficult always to write with a doubt inside you: and the conviction that no matter what you do, you meant to do something much more." This was a different Martha Gellhorn writing, a vulnerable, even hurting thirty-four-year-old woman. In talking about her latest book, Martha also exposed a great deal about herself and the troubled waters at home.

As for the love part, I do not believe these people are in love: my people that is. Or rather they love other things, but finally not each other. They ought to have two words for love instead of one, and then everyone could think straight. There's friendship and passion: if you mix them in proper quantities you get a very strong brew which is apt to be satisfying for some time. But love?

Anyhow, as my people mooched around and grew, it became clear that they could not be friends because they were not equals: and I have a horrid hooting inability to believe (perhaps because of the times we live in) in the enduring force of passion alone. I think people simply get interested in something else. This is all wrong obviously: we have been raised to believe that people roll on swords and etc. for passion alone, but I think this must be before they have slept together for any length of time, not afterwards.

Oh hell, what do I know? I guess, that's all. But the man is something like me, and I know damn well his job would come before his life (if you can call passion a life): so I think I guessed right in this case. I am very sorry for the girl in the book, but on the whole, I am sorry for women. They are not free: there is no way they can make themselves free. Glands no doubt, and whenever I have time I will have to study biology and find out, if I can. Anyhow, if the book seems any good I will send it to you.

Earlier in the letter Martha reported on the books she had been reading, a standard part of her letters to HG. She said that the fine writers on her side of the pond were "mostly men I am afraid (though I have secretly believed all my life that there was no real sense in competing: the glands a man writes with are stronger, there is a kind of male knowledge that is always broader, there is an endurance to experience that keeps them learning longer)."

Holed up in the lush serenity of the Finca, Martha held the fort, to be sure, but more than anything else, she read and she wrote. One book, Stefan Zweig's autobiography, greatly disturbed her. It was so "unbearable in every line" that she almost couldn't read it. Martha argued in her letter to HG that the pain came from knowing that Zweig killed himself for no personal failure, for no "lonely human reason," except that "the world exhausted him" and he was "driven too far." She wrote so empathetically about displaced people that one must question the source of her emotion and pain. Was she questioning the choices she had made throughout her life about work, home, and homelessness, or was there another source of anguish? Martha's father was born in Germany, and her mother was a Jew.

I do not know exactly why it seems so tragic that a Viennese Jew should kill himself in Brasil but it does: that is too far from home. And finally homelessness is unendurable for others, since that is what torments them. I see it all the time, and keep thinking: my God, it is a small thing, to want only to live on some particular piece of ground. They do not even ask or expect to live well; they do not imagine they can cheat disease, be free of money, look beautiful, work superbly: they only want to suffer and struggle in whatever way they must, on a recognizable soil. It is very little for people to ask: a bare minimum. And I keep wondering if even after the war, all these lost and lonely people will be allowed to come home.[122]

Despite all the emotion Martha unleashed over Zweig, she didn't get much in return from HG; indeed, his response was tepid, although he may not have seen it that way. HG said that he had known Zweig very well, that he was a born collector, was comfortable only among his "cabinets and treasures" in Salzburg, and was thoroughly miserable in England before he was given "some sort of pseudo-job in Brazil." London at that time was in a state of siege, and Zweig was deeply offended "because with many others whose political orientation was a little uncertain, he was restricted to the Bath area."[123]

Martha's melancholy in this letter was triggered by loneliness and Zweig's ordeal, to be sure, but also by an executive decision she had made that continued to haunt her. The overpopulation of cats at the Finca having become unacceptable to her, she arranged to have three of the oldest tomcats neutered. Hemingway, a cat lover of legendary proportions, was on an extended trip on the *Pilar* at the time. As Martha told HG:

I interfered with the lives of three cats, a god-like and repulsive role: considering how this has shaken me, I am baffled that those who rule us do so with such evident satisfaction and lack of insomnia. We have too many cats, and they multiply. It seems to me that cats are really eaten by sex: if one female is not belly-dancing with desire, another is: and the males stalk about, proud, indifferent, but uncontrollably obliging. We now have nine cats and the house will become theirs unless this is stopped. Furthermore I found that their lives were encroaching on mine (there is something very sinister in this) and that I had to think and plan so much for them that I could not do the work I am supposed to do. This may seem nothing to you . . . but I have intervened in the normal lives of living things, who from now onward will only live in part. And it makes me absolutely god-dam sick, and ashamed of myself, and I can't look at the cats who in turn look at me with a silent accusation. It is pretty bad.[124]

Psychologists could have a field day with Martha's act. They might say that she was preoccupied with sex (or lack of it), and repulsed by the cats' open display of it; asserting her power over an absentee husband; wishing to hurt an absentee husband; or subconsciously emasculating her (tomcat of an) absentee husband. Whatever the scenario, Martha was man enough to write to Hemingway about the cat situation. As overseer of the farm, she told him that she was *considering* castrating some of his cats, implying that she hadn't acted on it yet, although she probably already had. His response must have surprised her, for it demonstrated his devotion to her and her needs, however irrational, over his love for his "cotsies."

> About castrateing Dingie I would much prefer to shoot him myself. I love him very much and understand him and if you want him to be castrated please ask the dr. to destroy him instead or I will do it. I suppose Willie's balls can be cut off. But still do not like it. I will shoot them all when I come home if it is necessary. In the meantime I suppose they are all neatly castrated.[125]

That was not the end of the cat affair. In July, Martha decided that it would be best to have four kittens chloroformed, and she told her husband so. Hemingway wrote back suggesting that she pick one and do away with the rest. "Wouldn't that work?" he wrote on the seventh. "If it's necessary to destroy Thruster's kitty I will do it. Poor blind little bastard. Will be glad to do it. Don't mind doing away with any of the things I don't know."

HG was moved by something in Martha's candid letter, for he pencilled in at the bottom: "Reply herewith." His letter in response on July 1, 1943, was as remarkable as Martha's. He told her that he'd love to get together to talk, but then scolded her for "indulging in a lot of vicarious unhappiness"—including the business over Zweig's suicide. He said he thought that her bad conscience over castrating tomcats was "rather excessive." And then he sat her down for a biology lesson that he probably hadn't learned at Huxley's elbow, but, rather, only after years of introspection in the lab of life.

No tom cat is happy until the distressful urgency of sex is lifted from it. Then it becomes a serene and comfortable philosopher. And now listen to a profound truth. There is no "<u>normal</u> life" for any animal. Life on this planet is a continual adjustment of animal types to changing conditions that for any but the very simplest forms change faster than they do. As an exercise, write down what you imagine to be the "normal" life cycle and food of an elephant, a water rat, a horse, a cow and a human being. As a further exercise compare the life cycle of Romeo and Juliet as to age, food, clothing, etc. with your own. In Elizabethan times nobody bathed, a woman was an old woman as soon as she lost her teeth, everybody without exception wore old clothes and stank, and the common preoccupation in sex life was syphilis, recently imported from America. Shakespear was undoubtedly syphilitic, as was Donne. Meditate no more on "normal" lives. The Creation is a scene of "sound and fury signifying nothing" and only now is it entering into the heart of man to take over this lunatics' asylum and put some sense into it.

Having dispensed with sex and passion, HG directed Martha's attention to love. Again, he was on home turf, and again he revealed something of himself in this lesson.

"Love" is a great and complicated affair for which there ought to be a thousand names. "Passion" as the vulgar say with great precision is for the male "all balls." I am so extremely heterosexual that I still cannot understand why so many women seem to want a man, qua man. I can understand their desires for careers and offspring and why old maids like pets. But feminine sexual excitability seems to depend upon slight but important structural differences. Early experiences also establish reaction systems. But this dissertation will have to be cut short for a more convenient season.

HG told Martha that what really occupied his mind, and what should occupy hers and Hemingway's, was the possibility that intelligent people "instead of having these petty orgasms of pity, contempt, indignation and so forth and enjoying our fine sensibilities to the utmost until the ever widening human catastrophe overtakes us," cooperate in some "powerfully unified world movement to stop the rot and take the control of human destiny out of the rule of blind chance." This meant that the Hemingways would have to stop being "fragmentary 'artists'" and subdue themselves in order to take part in a gigantic artistic effort beyond all precedent. "It means you have to exert your two brains a damned lot more than you have ever done." At this point in this letter, HG introduced his draft for an international *Declaration of the Rights of Man.* He asked the Hemingways to scrutinize the "appeal and document" he was sending; to make suggestions and let him know whether they would join the cause. He said he would send the *Rights* statement and challenge to a great many people across the globe. "By the time we have got their adhesions, the evasions or their eloquent silences assembled, we shall for the first time in history know what the world thinks it is up to. We shall have evoked the world idea. So please get to it, Martha."

As promised, HG sent the Hemingways a copy of *The Rights of Man: A Plain Account of the Idea.* It wasn't that plain; the idea came to nearly thirty pages, which included the original set of rights and a 1943 edited version. HG may have hoped that this late-in-life Herculean effort would become his crowning achievement, but the work-in-progress did not hold up well under Martha's scrutiny of August 23, 1945. She savaged the piece, first and foremost for its poor writing. "There are 30 pages of Plan which make dull and difficult and above all completely unmemorable reading. . . . Surely, with all the talent you have between you, you ought to be able to make words that burn, and have light, and can be remembered by themselves. Surely you could make your Bill of Rights, as writing, beautiful, tight, and unforgettable to the ear, the heart and the mind." She also called the piece "fuzzy" and, at least in one place, incomprehensible. Then she lectured HG and gave him a six-point list of suggestions—including "Find a poet to write it, in case you Master Minds have lost the ability to make fine and fierce language"—and then lectured him further and signed off. Still not finished with the business, Martha added a long postscript, which included:

> Upon re-reading [my] letter I find it nonsense; or rather, aside from the point. I send it anyhow. [Mine] is evidently an emotional reaction to an intellectual idea, and you do not want that. Furthermore, we are talking about two different things. You guys are trying to write a guide-book for behavior, and I am asking you why you don't write a call to arms. . . . I find your Bill of Rights unsatisfying and I believed this was because it made no shock of recognition, joy, excitement etc. in my mind. I blamed it on the writing, therefore. But reading it again, I imagine you are not interested at all in the words of your Rights, nor in any emotional reaction; you do want a guide-book. Okay. It's far from bad.

Hemingway, we learn, was otherwise occupied and couldn't add his critique. In her postscript to HG, Martha noted: "Ernest is away which explains his 'eloquent silence.' I'm sorry can't show him the outline." HG's archive buckles under the weight of paper devoted to the various permutations of his *Declaration* and to the replies he received from all over the world. The final version, which like its predecessors contained eleven rights, was published in 1943. According to David Smith, HG was the primary and most important author of the *Declaration,* and with Ritchie Calder, he was the main force in circulating it around the world. In the preface to the *Rights,* however, HG "disclaimed full authorship, although headquarters for the group was still 13 Hanover Terrace [his home], and of course, he saw this copy through the press himself."[126] Whether as a result of Martha's influence or someone else's, the authors tightened and brightened the prose, then had the document translated into dozens of languages, including Swahili, Icelandic, and Olingo. The effort ultimately became the *Universal Declaration of Human Rights,* adopted by the United Nations in 1957.

Regardless of her stinging critique, Martha was delighted to be included in the process. World events, after all, were a major interest of hers, and were at the heart of her letters to HG. In her first letter, she set the tone for her correspondence with the World Brain. "What do you think of Communism?" she asked on March 26, 1936. "When is the war going to start? Do you know what is happening in America; if so, tell me. Will a Charlotte Corday arise to handle Hitler and if so, would it be a good thing; and if so, shall I be she? I haven't much to do now."[127] Two years later, after several tours covering the Spanish Civil War, Martha asked HG how he felt about the war in Spain. "I won't argue it with you at this distance," she said, adding that she was planning to write a book about it, and then return to Spain. "It is a very absorbing war, and I think a very important one, but I guess you don't since you have made no words about it."

From Prague in June 1938, Martha wrote that Czechoslovakia was a very interesting country, and that "If Hitler had stayed a house painter, I think it might have become a model democracy." Anyhow, the Germans seemed to have put the war off for a time, she said, and for that, one must be grateful. Then, sophomorically, she suggested that HG bump off Chamberlain. "What a man. With a face like a nut-cracker and a soul like a weasel. How long are the English going to put up with these bastards who run the country." By 1940, Martha's attitude had matured. After she learned of a U.S. plot to loan Franco $100 million, she fired off an impassioned letter to HG, calling his attention to the woeful situation and hoping it would stir him to action, just as she had so often done with the Roosevelts. It "takes one's breath away," she wrote from Sun Valley on October 26, adding:

> Aside from the evident point, that such a loan to Franco is deadly dangerous to our two countries, there is another moral point, not to be spat on either. If the U.S. wants to pick up where Chamberlain stopped appeasing, how is it going to be possible to raise a thrill of honest passion in the hearts of the people, saying: "defend democracy boys, but kindly overlook the fact that we are financing a dictatorship which is executing an average of thirty people a day, people who believe in democracy." By

God it smells too bad. If there is one hundred million dollars lying around loose why not buy airplanes and send them to England?

Wells, this is really terribly bad: its the path of evil and whoever is behind this loan ought not to be allowed to get away with it. Can you prod a few people in high places, with warning and prophesies? If you're in New York, could you telephone Jay Allen at once, or see Edgar Mowrer if you're in Washington. They'd give you any further dope. But it seems to me now is the time for everyone to ask questions, loudly, saying: what are you boys proving, with this money to Franco, and how many examples of the idiocy of appeasing do you need to have, before you stop being crooked and fools?

Two months later, and from the Lombardy Hotel, Martha, now Mrs. Hemingway, asked HG to take care of himself. "There are going to be so many wars to live through." Two years later, on January 19, 1942, from the Finca, she was still critical of international efforts to ring in peace. It was, she said, probably "an unfortunate thing" to have read some good books and to have a hardworking esteem for words that have meaning and ideas that make sense, especially in times like these. "At the moment I have nothing much else to do except view with alarm. Possibly we will find something more positive and helpful to do as time goes on." Toward the end of that year, Martha threw her hands up in frustration, saying there was no sense in writing to HG about the war. She didn't even know what "the common man like me can do, except pray. Please write me just a little spidery note to say how you are."

Less than three weeks after the United States dropped the atomic bomb on Hiroshima and Nagasaki, Martha wrote to HG from St. Louis. In some ways it is an appropriate final letter in their correspondence. "Wells darling, You are the greatest man in the world. There was probably no reason to doubt this and you will not be surprised by this statement, but the atom bomb has convinced me once and for all. As you are right in everything, I am now looking forward gloomily to living underground in an air-conditioned artificially-lighted tunnel and eating vari-colored pills (instead of Spam and Brussels sprouts as it used to be in the fine old days)." She was, of course, congratulating HG for having predicted this fateful event. In *The World Set Free: A Story of Mankind,* HG forecast nuclear warfare and global destruction. He had studied Frederick Soddy's work on atomic theory and the Curies' work on radium. In his story, atomic degeneration was supposed to produce limitless energy. But after the world had been set free with this energy—"a new world [was] rebuilt in a formal way, proceeding from rural life, to urban life, to a central language, and then to the adoption of metrics, a standard year, and standard money with token coins based on energy . . . and a new education"—the use of atomic energy for evil purposes was on the horizon.[128] In effect, *World Set Free* became the first book about nuclear deterrence.

Martha Gellhorn's pastimes during her youth were travel, swimming, and reading, and she took them with her into her adulthood nearly to the end. Vacation was less an element in Martha's life than travel. If she was traveling—even on assignment—she was more or less on vacation. As she told her friend Stan Pennell at the end of 1931, "Travel is the only thing besides writing which is worth the sweat." Fifty-five years later she would tell another friend, James Fox, that Ponce de Leon was "a nutcase; the fountain of youth is not a little spurt of water but travel. I have only to go to a different country, sky, language, scenery, to feel it worth living."[129] Early on, of course, travel was Martha's ticket out of St. Louis. No reason yet has surfaced to explain her abhorrence of her hometown. From that despised place in March 1936, she confided in HG that she thought she could renew herself physically and spiritually and could "laugh convincingly" if she could only get far enough away from St. Louis.

She got away of course, over and over again. From Paris in June 1938, she wrote: "I was in Prague, inspecting the coming war. Very impressive. Am doing the same in England. Personally, I would like to go swimming in Corsica, and shall as soon as this job is over." After Martha finished her *Collier's* piece, "The Lord Will Provide," she would ship off to "somewhere," she told HG, "to swim and to sunburn." On January 11, 1944, after finishing six articles for *Collier's*, she was heading off to Algiers, "and after mooching about wherever I can get in that area, I shall go home to Cuba." Travel she did, and swim. Between 1937 and 1940, Martha Gellhorn traveled to and throughout at least seven countries, most of them several times: Cuba (three times), Czechoslovakia, England (at least twice), Finland, France (at least three times), Spain (four times), and the United States (at least three times). Her love for swimming—in the nude as often as she could pull it off, so to speak—was well known. Her friend Bill Buford, the fiction editor of *The New Yorker*, said that Martha liked to swim naked at midnight. She also snorkeled well into her last decade, although it isn't known what, in addition to the snorkel, she wore.

Another passion was literary, of course, and Martha shared her literary enthusiasms and anxieties with HG: titles, authors, reviews, and theories about reading and writing, just as Constance had. What did he think of the writing of Kay Boyle, for example?[130] Or how about Henry James? It isn't known how many of Martha's suggestions HG took. In the letter she wrote so passionately about Zweig, she recommended Ira Wolfert's *Tucker's People*, which she thought was a "really fine book . . . and marvelously written." It educated her about "a sort of New York underworld" that she had known nothing about. She went on to say that there are "a few fine guys writing over here":

> There's one strange southern woman named Eudora Welty who writes, when at her best, like nobody and it is quite a something to read: and though perhaps she is a better artist than several of the good men, it somehow does not matter in the end. They will wear better. There's a young poor man in Chicago named Nelson Algren who can write also. I find now, living here in the sunstruck outer darkness, that the people writing are my one last hope for the race: if they go on, something must go on. It so happens writing is the only thing I know a little about, and that is probably why I clutch at it this way.[131]

Henry James was another matter. In the winter of 1942, Martha picked up three of his novels—*The American, Portrait of a Lady,* and *The Euro-*

peans. She told HG the following spring that she had never read James before because the "type" was terrible. However, now as a thirty-four-year-old, she found his novels fascinating, the writer something akin to "a classical Michael Arlen."[132] And then she went into a critique of James. He was classical, she wrote, not because his characters or situations were more moving or realistic, but

> because he writes with such unique care. I think the style is often ridiculous, don't you: and there is an old-lady quality to it that amazes me. Old lady, not fairy. I read the Europeans as if it were a thriller, so anxious to see what became of the people. Nothing becomes of them: you never know them, or else there is nothing to know. James was enchanted with the Baroness and I kept trying to see why, and what there was about her. Like all his characters, she emerges from nothing and to nothing she returns. The man was in love with aristocracy (his word, and his meaning); but I can never see how the aristocrats are so astounding, except that they talk very fancy and spend more money. Am I all wrong? Anyhow, James makes delightful war reading.

Martha also wrote to Edwin Rolfe about Henry James. In her opinion, she said, on December 8, 1942, James had "a perfect dazzling accuracy in detail which I find wonderful and a care and lovingness about the sentences that I admire." In their correspondence, Martha and Hemingway also passed along their critiques on books they had been reading and even passed the books back and forth via the mail. After he finished reading *Tucker's People,* Hemingway told Martha that "It is as good as you say," noting that Wolfert had a tendency "to fall into a sort of *formula* of tenderness that came close to the edge of going sour several times. I don't mean his tenderness going sour but the way everyone was forced into certain forms of it the women especially. Men were cruel but women were all kind. It was a wonderful book though and it is wonderful to have him and to have Algren and Koestler and Aldanov all different and all alone and all good."[133] In June 1942, E. turned the tables. He wrote to his "Dearest Mooky": "Have two wonderful books to send you soon as know where to air-express them. One is a Reggie Fortune novel called Black Land White Land. Other is Beryl Markham's book. God how she can write. Certainly makes me ashamed."

Martha would do quite a bit of thinking aloud about her craft of fiction, how one creates real characters and situation, how one develops plots and writes delightful war reading. She conceded in an August, 1943, letter to HG that while she had no training or taste for abstract thought, she wrote fiction and preferred to read it, "which, translated, means that I see whatever I do see or understand of living through persons, individual detailed moving breathing lives." In the same letter she told HG that for her last novel, she never knew what the characters were going to do, "and I went along like someone managing a Ouija Board a good deal of the time." About her chosen work as a war correspondent, Martha observed that she believed it to be a trade that would outlast many others, and that she was, at last, taking it seriously enough to study it.

> This means long, dreary reading on technical military matters. You can imagine how well I understand what I am reading when I tell you that as far as technical matters go I am unable even to change the ribbon on my own typewriter. Otherwise we are well and following our own trade, which consists of reading and writing. As we are not amateurs at that trade we can do no harm.[134]

Later in the year, Martha announced that she was heading for England "to write some things. Not that it appears there is much relation between what people write and what gets done. That curious hiatus between the written word and the urged deed must depress you sometimes, doesn't it? Depressed the pants off me," she wrote in the spring of 1943. This was a sharp contrast to her state of mind in June 1938, when she told HG that being a journalist was "very lucrative but the slight talent as a writer I once had is now gone to hell, and I don't know what to do about it. Also I have gotten a certain loathing for writing."

Martha's intense interest in her craft undoubtedly reflected her relationship with one of the world's greatest writers. She mentioned her husband several times in her letters to HG. Considering her later moratorium on discussion about her former husband, these few comments carry some weight. She mentioned him in six letters and spoke briefly about their lives together—and apart; her comments were, for the most part, benign. Martha also wrote about her former mate in two letters to Gip Wells, but she spoke only ill in these letters from the 1980s. It isn't clear when HG first learned of Hemingway and vice versa. Martha met HG intimately in 1935; Hemingway intimately eighteen months later. Nor is it known whether Hemingway knew or suspected that HG and Martha had trysted.

Martha mentioned Hemingway in 1942, from the Finca—and indirectly. In an atypically calm mood, she told HG in January that his last letter gave them "great pleasure and makes a beautiful picture in our minds." He had just written to her about a parcel of food—delicacies that Maugham had sent him from the South of France, and which he shared with a group of appreciative friends in war-torn London. In this letter Martha postscripted the message for the censor that her name was Martha Gellhorn Hemingway. It was extremely rare for her to use that name; however, by the fall of 1941, she was typing "Mrs. Ernest Hemingway" above the Finca letterhead.

Early the next year, 1943, after having just finished reading the third James novel, Martha was reminded of a "philosophical" conversation Hemingway and F. Scott Fitzgerald once had—a now famous and oft-repeated conversation—and passed it along to HG. "Scott lived a great deal in Cannes and Antibes and was very much impressed by whatever he considered Society. He once said to Ernest, in an admiring wistful way, 'The rich are not like us, Ernest.' And Ernest said, 'No, they have more money.'"[135] Martha also mentioned that she was writing a novel and was "as absorbed as if I lived in the bottom of a beautiful well with no company except a typewriter." The Hemingways would spend many months of that year apart. When Martha went to England that fall, she spent some time with HG; it would be their last visit with each other. In her next letter, on June 9, 1943, Martha begged HG to find some time for her. She made it clear that she was lonely, and alluded to strains in the marriage. "It so happens that I have been alone most of this year because E. has been away on various jobs." E.'s children had just arrived at the Finca for their annual summer vacation, so Martha had company for a few days before they joined their father for a camping trip. She painted a sweet little vignette for HG:

> The youngest has not started growing, so he seems much younger than Patrick (known as Mouse), the fourteen year old. We have spent the evening reading in different chairs, with slight interruptions like this:
>
> "Mouse, can I just ask you one thing? Where's Cales?" That turns out to be Calais, and Mouse explains.
>
> Then Mouse, reading a rather exhibitionist book about American literature, asks me: "Marty, can I just ask you one thing? What's 'a Catiline.'" And of course I do not know. It's always like that.[136]

In her last letter to H. G. Wells, written from St. Louis on August 25, 1945, a year before his death, Martha talked about her house in London and about putting down roots. She slipped into the last paragraph: "Did you know that E and I were getting divorced? Change and decay in all around I see, in case that is the accurate quotation."

Martha didn't let go without a struggle. In April 1944, and in what appears to have been a last-ditch effort to resurrect the marriage, she talked the old bear into coming out of hibernation and covering the war with her, arguing essentially that he'd lose it if he didn't use it. He did not want to go. He was an old horse, he said, finished with racing, finished with war. As he wrote to Martha on January 31 of that year, "Take not the slightest interest in where am going to go and feel no lilt nor excitement. Just feel like horse, old horse, good, sound, but old, being saddled again to race over the jumps because of unscrupulous owner. Will make same race as always, best that can make, but am neither happy, excited, nor interested." Martha had to know where her husband stood on war. Two years earlier, in September 1942, he had unloaded a few poignant memories. "I thought you couldn't cry ever no matter what they did to you because it was a bad example and that only Italians cried. Used to go off by myself for a walk when I could sometimes and lie down somewhere behind a rock or under a pine tree and cry and cry because things were so bad for everybody. So must have had some finer feelings at one time. It wasn't because it was so bad for me either; really and truly. It was because it was so bad for the gente."

Their reporting of World War II started badly—with a double-trick, as the legend goes. Having first picks on a publisher by virtue of his journalistic seniority, Hemingway signed on with *Collier's,* Martha's magazine since 1937, leaving her without a sponsor. Then, after refusing to arrange a flight for them to go to Europe together, he departed solo—as he had done eight years earlier. Without skipping a beat, Martha found accommodations on a freighter loaded with explosives, and for two weeks, she lived under blackout regulations, the ship zigzagging through murky, freezing, and foggy waters trying to avoid collisions with other vessels. After this long and dangerous trip, she learned that two actresses—Beatrice Lillie and Gertrude Lawrence—accompanied Hemingway on his flight to Europe.[137]

By D-Day the Hemingways were barely speaking. For that large and historic amphibious operation, he put himself on an attack transport the night before; at dawn, he was loaded onto a landing craft that delivered troops ashore. He was then returned to the transport, from where he observed the invasion. It was a good but dangerous viewpoint, and in his writings, Hemingway played it up for all it was worth. Martha once again had to devise her own plan—and it was a beaut, all illegal of course: She hid in the head, or bathroom, of a hospital ship that was scheduled to cross the English Channel on the morning of the invasion. She saw the whole amazing show from the ship, and she also allegedly helped with the wounded; after nightfall on that longest day, Martha sneaked ashore with the stretcher-bearers.

On the Normandy beachhead, [Martha] maneuvered her way around mine fields and barbed wire. Having done everything through official channels, Hemingway found himself confined to watching the action from landing craft. He was angry with [her] for actually getting ashore, and even tried to deny that she did, claiming she could not have done so because she did not have the proper papers. In fact, she had shown more initiative than he had, and he would never forgive her for it.[138]

Martha told Orsagh that she was arrested for her unauthorized actions on D-Day and incarcerated in a nurse's camp. Tolerating the restraints on her freedom for an entire day, Martha "rolled under a barb wire fence and escaped. She persuaded a pilot to take her to Italy, telling him that her fiancé was there and they had to meet immediately."[139] Once again the system was taking a beating.

Of their five less-than-blissful calendar years of marriage, Martha and Hemingway spent perhaps only twelve months under the same roof; the rest of the time they were separated by assignments (mostly Martha's), writing trips, fishing or intelligence tours on the *Pilar* (Ernest's), or by other romances (Ernest's). When their marriage began breaking apart for real and for the last time, Hemingway confided in his son Patrick, then at boarding school: "I hate to lose anyone who can look so lovely and who we taught to shoot and write so well. But have torn up my tickets on her and would be glad to never see her again. . . . Thought I should write you about Marty so you would know what the score is."[140]

Divorce didn't put an end to their disputes. Martha continued to push all Hemingway's hot buttons, and he pushed back. In what apparently was an unsent letter, he let her have it with both barrels. What triggered Papa's wrath was Martha's letter to Mary Hemingway in which she made petty attacks on how they should have shipped her belongings from the Finca and some "nasty cracks" about Hemingway's "ironic and excessive rectitude for having sent them as rapidly as possible."[141] Martha came off sounding like a "journalist playing Dutchess," Hemingway wrote. One of the items she was particularly anxious about was her "good-luck typewriter," as she described it. With that phrase, Martha unwittingly opened herself up to some memorable attacks. Hemingway ranted that she had achieved her success only because she got so much help from him. But he also slammed her exploitive style of war reportage and her many character and physical flaws, as he saw them. It was a cruel letter written by a bitter man who had a fair amount of ammunition and perhaps more than a bit of love left for his former wife. He began with the attention-getting line: "You seem to have a sudden rush of either success or failure to the head and I have never read a more ill-mannered or ungracious letter." He continued:

> It is quite possible that your good-luck typewriter was good-luck because you had someone to go over; correct; suggest changes in; and sometimes even re-write some of its product. Lots of people could hit three hundred in the big leagues if they had a fourth strike instead of the usual three. For instance in titles: A Stricken Field is a good title. So is the quotation it comes from. The Heart of Another is a good title too. They were two of the best that I had, actually. Hope you won't be useing A New Slain Knight this year. Or should I have it registered?[142]

> Marty, do you know something that [I] will always remember and that made me think that maybe everybody shouldn't always do your packing, close up your affairs, do your contract business, read and send in your proofs, read and suggest changes in your Mss., re-write it when necessary in your own style, show you how to re-write it, make [you] rewrite it until from a girl who couldn't write a parse-able sentence you became a stylist; always being careful to eliminate your copyings of me and make you write them in your own way. . . . Do you know when I really thought people shouldn't perhaps do that? When we were chaseing the Kraut and over-running him and keeping him off balance and beating him if the stuff had not been given to the British (We would have had the war over that fall) and you got from the British jeeps to wreck; jeeps to abandon; jeeps to have stolen while we hand-carried the wounded and did the recon on captured German motorcycles.

> I knew then that what all the talk about sacrifice and self-lessness were worth and saw your war; your tax-free, money-making, expense

paid war clear and good. One money makeing ride at night in a Black Widow doesn't clear that. Nor all the other martial ventures that were so lucrative. But believe me you were bankrupt with me when you were running those jeep-loseing expeditions when jeeps were one of the most precious commodities that civilization had. So that's a thought for today after reading your letter again. I'd forgotten how rude, and imperious and preposterous you could be. But you brought it back very clearly.

Now a practical suggestion: Try and find as good or better or much better writer than I am to criticise, correct, suggest plot, changes in plot, remove hystericisms, melodrama, and suggest the necessary re-writing and if necessary outline it and, when necessary do it and then have you put it into your own words again. He will not be able to remove all the melodrama because usually the basic conception of your novels is an extreme melodrama that is not removable but can only be modified and toned down so that it seems like drama instead. This is a very delicate process. What you lack in writing about human beings (grown-ups) generally is a sort of basic good taste and sense of values.

Part of this over-writing comes from your always being your own heroine which, since you are not terribly sound about yourself makes your characters sooner or later quite silly unless someone corrects them. So, for your own sake, get somebody to go over your stuff and help you as above. Otherwise lucky type-writers will not save you.

If you have made up a lot of wonderful lies to yourself about how noble and beautiful and wonderful you are: scrap them; at least for writing. You are not at all noble except in your charities and with your mother; you are, and have been for quite a long time, a product of the beauticians, the medicos etc. . . . and I guess you will always be wonderful to yourself; so keep that. But not for books.

But get somebody who is really good to go over your stuff. Don't get a yes-man or someone you can dominate. (I mean about the typed or printed word) Remember you have written nothing in fiction since The Trouble I've Seen (that had the one wonderful story in) that has not been helped, aided, criticized, helped to be re-written, plot vetted, incident vetted, melodrama cut out, except that thing you were working on at K. W. which was most preposterous, illogical hodgepodge ever was unable to read.

Have decided not to send this. It is too good a letter to waste on some one of your degree of perception. Of you I always remember that you f–ed off whenever the going was tough; that you had a phony accent; much more phony each year; that you had a queer, limited and imitative talent which it was possible to win races with when the imitation was carefully removed by the imitee; that you were always tight and crooked about money; that you always lied (not always; but usually) about anything connected with money; that you had as many unattractive traits as Peggy Guggenheim: but in different places; that you would try to compete with the fireman who was getting you out of a burning building (as a fireman) (this probably admirable) and that you were a career bulldozer. Won't put anything in about your physical make-up, your thousands of rubbers, pots, pans, jars, capsules, grease guns, mud packs, bust lifters, mustache removers, flat foot aids, pessories, or other aids to beauty. I wrote a series of poems about you once in Paris about how even the worms knew you and didn't like the taste when you died. Will see you get them sometime. It was a very good poem; the worm one. Especially when they began to explore the considered, lovely carcass.

Good night, Marty. Sleep well my beloved phony and pretentious bitch.[143]

* * *

In late 1946, after HG died, Martha, like Rebecca West, another former lover of HG's, went to Nuremberg to report on the trials. Six months before, in June, Martha and her friend Virginia Cowles had opened their play, *Love Goes to Press,* which focused on the rivalries and romances of war correspondents, in London.[144] While the two female characters resemble the authors, the lead male sounds like the devil incarnate, Ernest Hemingway. The women are "good-looking, brave, and competent . . . [and] know how to get stories and how to manipulate military officers. The male correspondents, on the other hand, are competitive and covetous of each other's work and quite willing to steal a story or a woman if the opportunity presents itself."[145] In 1993, Martha told her war buddy, Milton Wolff, that it was a silly play that she wrote with a friend "purely to make money." Meanwhile, Hemingway's *Across the River and Through the Trees,* published in 1950, offered more cruel and thinly veiled attacks on Martha. The estranged wife of the story, an aggressive, careerist, and mean-spirited journalist, "had more ambition than Napoleon and about the talent of the average High School Valedictorian."[146]

Like the 1940s, the 1950s were a roller-coaster ride for Martha—and for just about everyone intimately involved with her. In 1950, after she had been divorced for five years, she decided to adopt a baby. With the help of an Italian lawyer and a letter of endorsement from Eleanor Roosevelt, Martha found and adopted Sandor in an orphanage in Florence, Italy. He would be called Sandy, although his legal name was George Alexander Gellhorn. At the time of adoption, Sandy was fifteen months old and his new parent was forty-one and not—by her own admission—a natural mother. Hemingway biographer Jeffrey Meyers claimed that Hemingway wanted a daughter by Martha, but that she was "completely committed to her career as a novelist and war correspondent, was vain about her figure and her looks, may have feared childbirth, probably realized that their marriage would not last, disliked sex with Hemingway and did not want to bear his child."[147] Furthermore, Martha supposedly told a friend that "There's no need to have a child when you can buy one. That's what I did."[148]

Martha made several homes for Sandy, first in Mexico and then in Italy. She had been dating A. David Gurewitsch, a New York pathologist born in Zurich of Russian parents, who was a close friend of Eleanor

Roosevelt's and seemingly a strong object of the first lady's affection. Gurewitsch, a specialist in rehabilitation medicine, was Mrs. Roosevelt's personal physician for sixteen years after she left the White House. Whether that affection was romantic or motherly, requited or un-, is not clear. Mrs. R., however, was ambivalent about sharing Gurewitsch with Gellhorn. She needn't have obsessed over it; the relationship between Martha and Gurewitsch floundered soon enough, although they took two shots at it. Rollyson claimed that Gurewitsch was the love of Martha's life. In 1974, he published *Eleanor Roosevelt: Her Day, A Personal Album*. The book contained a great many candid photographs, most of them taken by Gurewitsch during his travels around the globe with the first lady. It closes with, "She has become a legend of a true spirit of humanity, of selflessness, of the high standards of behavior that are attainable by everyone. She is still the First Lady of the World." Gurewitsch borrowed the last line from Harry Truman. At least Gurewitsch and Martha shared a common love of Eleanor Roosevelt.

In February 1954, Martha and Tom Matthews, the former editor of *Time,* shocked their separate sets of friends and got married. They had known each other back in 1929 and 1930 at the *New Republic*. Matthews began as a proofreader and soon moved up to writing book notes, and then reviews. Educated at Oxford, he, too, was a Midwesterner, a product of Cincinnati, Ohio. "As with Gurewitsch, Gellhorn found the sympathetic, urbane, good-looking man irresistible."[149] It didn't hurt that he was a very wealthy man, although Martha told Milt Wolff in the 1990s that it didn't change anything. Having been married to Matthews, a multimillionaire, "I am here to say there's nothing in it. I didn't use his money for myself, retaining my independence by earning my own expenses but of course he paid for the large grand house which was a nightmare and we crossed the ocean in the grand liners (I have a photo of me in evening dress in the extra expensive upper dining room, looking almost sick with boredom.)"

While marriage and motherhood did not appear to cramp Martha's style or compromise her desires, particularly for travel, reporting, and writing, in fact they did. Her stepson Sandy Matthews remembered

Martha as being attentive and conscientious toward the children. She "did more for us than my father," he said. Sandy Matthews also remembered that Martha's adopted son came home for vacations until he went away to Milton Academy, and then to Columbia University, and that she was always conscientious, though also impatient.[150] Martha and Tom became expats together in London, and Martha settled into a period of virtual domesticity. Still, by all accounts, it was a mismatch. The husband and his wife lived together most of the time for the first four years of their marriage, and they were together "probably half the time after that," according to Sandy Matthews. They would begin to vacation and live apart for long stretches of time, just as Martha and Hemingway had. They also maintained separate friendships. Sandy was sent away for his education to Switzerland, and he vacationed, often *sans mère*, in the United States.[151] One of the things that Martha found particularly unappealing about her son was his propensity to put on weight; indeed, his heaviness repulsed her. Late in her life, on December 5, 1993, she told Milton Wolff that she was taking Sandy to Rome for Christmas. She called her son "a nice chap who threw away his life," which caused him to lose "his place in the queue." Then, too, Martha's nomadic propensities did not much appeal to Matthews. In 1963, they called it quits. Of that union, Martha later told her friend James Fox: "I wasted nine invaluable years on a stupid marriage."[152] She had tried dominant males, and she had tried less dominant males, but neither extreme seemed to hold her attention or affection for long. Sandy Matthews argues that the seeds for the dissolution of the marriage were elsewhere. "Couple the notion that he was a strong character like Martha—but in a different way, with Martha as a writer having to run a large house and look after children which she did conscientiously and you have the seeds of why perhaps the marriage didn't last."[153] Tom Matthews, who dedicated his 1960 autobiography, *Name and Address,* to "Edna Gellhorn, with love," didn't even mention Martha in his book, but he did mention HG once. "I don't remember when it was that doubts about religion first entered my mind," he wrote. "I think it was at boarding school, when I began to read H. G. Wells. By the time I had reached *God The Invisible King* and *Soul of a Bishop* and the one about Job, I was a fledgling Wellsian agnostic and humanist. But never an atheist; my doubts were all of Christianity and the Church."[154]

In better times, Matthews asked one of his staffers at *Time* what she thought about the idea of hiring Martha. According to biographer Rollyson, she said Martha struck her as "a swinging, rather masculine kind of gal." Rollyson also noted that in 1953, Martha described herself to Bernard Berenson as being equal parts male and female. That might not have been an errant thought. Back in 1931, when vacationing with her family, Martha informed Pennell that her "inner man" needed to get healthy fast. Martha told a *Tatler* writer in 1983, "I don't think I was made for marriage." In the 1990s, she turned down Wolff's offer to show her his correspondence with Hemingway. "I honestly don't want to see anything about EH or about TSM, my second husband. I put much futile effort into both marriages and the memory of neither of those men raises my heart [rate] . . . I'd rather forget them and my folly."[155]

Unconnected, or unleashed, Martha traveled a great deal in the 1960s. From 1960 to 1963, she visited ten countries. In 1962, at the age of fifty-three, feeling the need for revival, Martha hatched a plan to escape civilization once and for all: She decided to traverse the African continent, then pitch a tent somewhere on it. This she did, and there she remained for the better part of three years, on the coast above Mombassa and then on the side of a volcano in the Rift Valley. "I had a love affair with the land, the sky, the wild animals," she told the *Tatler.* And then she was off again, this time to the Caribbean, where she wrote *The Lowest Trees Have Tops,* a fantasy novel about a Mexican village where expatriates and exiles find a way to live together.[156] The book, according to Orsagh, helped Martha escape the mental horrors of Vietnam. Martha would report on the Nicaraguan *Contras,* the Arab-Israeli conflict, and the U.S. invasion of Panama. Her loyalty to the United States was all but drained over Vietnam, but the dregs were emptied over Panama. In 1990, announcing to her friend, author James Fox, that she was going to cover Panama, Martha wrote: "We hold shameful passports, you and I; you don't mind and suffer as I do. I can hardly stand the idiocy and mindless cruelty done in my name as a citizen. I wish I were a Dane, Danes never have to be ashamed."[157] Martha called it quits—professionally—with Bosnia, claiming that she was no longer nimble enough to cover war.

In 1983, whatever affection Martha still had for HG went cold. That was the year Gip approached her about publishing the *Postscript,* and the year she read her letters to HG after a fifty-year gap. Martha assumed that once Gip read the letters, he would understand her objection to HG's "imaginary love life" with her. But the fat hit the fire after the *Postscript* was published. Gip, like his father before him, got an earful from Martha; she was livid and accused Gip of having deceived her. Her desire, of course, was to nip in the bud the notion of an affair with HG; she tried to intimidate Gip, by that time an octogenarian, into backing down from his plan to publish his father's book, and, when that didn't work, she threatened him with a lawsuit. We have already read how, in a series of letters to Gip, Martha attempted to set the record straight about what really happened. Her stance on April 26, 1983, was that she was not only innocent but insignificant: that footnote of history, that passing reference.

> . . . and every time it's either factually wrong or pure apocrypha. I'm fairly sick of it and I do not wish to appear as a nut case, in this absurd version—and I wonder if you'll be doing Wells a favor by publishing this book—anyway, absolutely without me included. I won't stand still for it. Anyway, there it is, Gip, and I wish I hadn't seen this because it makes me dislike Wells and I had fond memories and sad memories of him, at the end of his life during the war. I imagine you are a nicer man than he was. I hope you're happy. Do you think he ever was?

After she showed up at an Oxford party in 1986—her first in many years—Martha became a rediscovered star in London's literary constellation, much as Moura had before her. According to Buford, she was "the central figure of something like a literary salon—her own, which met, at her instructions, in her flat on Cadogan Square whenever she made the trip to London."[158] As for London's "top journalists," Sandy Matthews claims that Martha met them one at a time—rarely together. Due to what she described as a "botched" cataract operation, her eyesight was greatly diminished in her later years, but she continued to follow two passions: swimming and snorkeling. On May 10, 1994, Martha told Milt Wolff that she had disabused herself of the notion that "physical vanity never died but I've just about given up. I make an effort in London though I hardly think it worthwhile. My mother, perhaps a few years older than I, used to say, 'Wouldn't it be wonderful to wake up dead?' That's how I feel now, on a grey cold Welsh late afternoon." Occasionally Martha wrote short pieces, as she did in 1996 for that *London Review of Books* piece on "Memory." Cary Nelson, a scholar and authority on the literature of the Spanish Civil War, among other things, described "Memory" as the best short piece of writing he had ever read.[159] Despite her rediscovery, her world acclaim, her book sales, her lifetime as a successful author-journalist, Martha, in the end, felt overlooked and misunderstood. As she related to James Fox, "I'd think maybe my fiction was unknown because too dark, but it isn't, not all of it. I wrote two really funny books—novels. And what about the short stories? I feel lost, all the work ignored as if valueless."[160] Her stepson and literary executor, Sandy Matthews, maintains that Martha felt overlooked partly because when Virago Press republished her books, they did not sell well. "Her journalism, on the other hand, has proved popular and much praised. She regarded herself first and foremost, though, as a writer."

Still, in her seventies she discovered a delightful life—"an unexpected golden plateau, and was all set for a spiffing old age, irresponsible and self-indulgent," but when she hit eighty-four, "that plan was forever spoiled," she told Victoria Glendinning.[161] A chain-smoker and carefree drinker and eater, she had lived a long and essentially ailment-free life— she described herself as "the absurdly unscathed"—until she developed cancer in her last years. Her memory, wit, and tongue remained sharp. On April 1, 1992, she wrote Wolff a little dissertation on old age and her decrepitude. The only reason for objecting to age is that "the body, once so reliable and useful, begins to spring leaks. Mine is [exactly] like my 11 year old Honda, motor runs a treat, body rusts, everything rusts, needs patching." In the fall of that year, she griped to him: "The truth is: I am sick and tired of my body, it is too old for me."

⋆ ⋆ ⋆

With nearly six years of life still ahead, Martha confided in Victoria Glendinning that she had been writing and had finished two pieces, "neither good," she said, noting that she was amazed to find she could still write anything.

> I try to think about my "memoir" but find that almost impossible. Look-ing back is a misery. I don't remember what was fun and funny; I re-member what I wish to forget, the wrong sad hurting things, and I'm so pleased that normally, left to myself, I have a genius faculty for forget-ting, good and bad alike, sign of a mediocre mind, but makes life easier. So now what. I have, for my whole life, ten diaries, those cheap red books with a page a day, and those not filled. One page was too much trouble. But I read two from the seventies and felt suicidal. They are use-less books; they don't tell me where I was or what I was doing, since I knew that; they are only feelings and the feelings are coal black. I stopped because I couldn't bear to look back there and haven't had the nerve to go on with this. I really don't know what to do.[162]

Martha's anger over HG's claim of having had an affair with her, as well as her anger with Gip for having tricked her, had not dissipated by the late 1990s. Her hard edge was evident in a letter to this author: "I did not know that my letters had been included in that embarrassing archive [Closet Correspondence] but I think you will gather that they are hardly love letters," and "There is something strange about Gip Wells wishing to make the other women's letters, which must have been very private, public property."[163]

Still, Martha was willing and able to reminisce about HG until just six months before she died. And, to her credit—and HG's—a few of the stories still made her laugh. She recalled, for example, that when she visited HG at his Hanover Terrace home during the war, she found the seventy-seven-year-old writer in his garage "hanging on some boards, pasting drawings of devils on the walls." HG had assigned each devil a name. Martha remembered seeing a "Stalin" and a "Churchill." Her analysis of the scene was less humorous: By that time, she told this author, HG appeared to be "quite scatty. War drove him mad. He found it all so horrible. He was in despair for the world."[164]

In the year of these recollections, 1997, Martha was still a woman of contradictions. She described herself to this author as "old, weary and occupied—and very busy." When asked about her circle of friends, she replied with the haunting comment: "We are all dead." Martha remembered HG clearly as "a very selfish demanding little man, who thought only about his own convenience." He "rather imposed himself" on her, and "was full of bossiness, a bossy, bossy man," she said several times, echoing what she had written so often before in her letters, "and I got tired of him lecturing me." Still, she had to admit that she, like the world, really hadn't appreciated him. "Wells was an immensely important person in the world, extraordinarily brainy," she said, "but he was enormously frustrated that he wasn't able to get the attention of the world in order to save it from itself."

Martha also recalled HG's bad temper. Once during London's wartime blackouts, she was invited to his home for dinner; she arrived late—understandable under the circumstances. "He was very cross with me," she said. "I got hell for that." And when she left a small piece of bread on her plate, HG jumped all over her. Was she aware that men died so that she could have bread with dinner? "How dare you not finish your bread," he scolded. She also remembered some delightful conversations with HG, especially those that involved making "terrific fun of Henry James."

Martha said she never understood why Moura put up with HG. "She had her own life, loads of friends—doughty and Russian they were, too. Moura guarded her private life, her freedom. She preferred being apart, rather than being permanently attached to Wells." According to Martha,

Moura was a "frightfully funny person, a huge woman, six feet tall, moony and warm-hearted and apt to call you 'Dah-ling.' She was like a large soft bear. Of the two, I think she was much more human." Still, Martha said, HG and Moura "seemed 100 years old to me at the time."

Moura was also a topic in Martha's correspondence. She told this author that Moura was "I suppose [HG's] mistress though it was a very strange combination as both were, to me, very old (this was in 1936) and Wells was notably short and Moura was close to 6 feet tall and very big. I loved Moura who was sublimely Russian, [but] I would not put my hand in the fire about her truthfulness. She was always a delight to be with, unconsciously funny, blissfully vague, used to sponging since she was penniless, and humanly far kinder than Wells."[165] Later, Martha noted:

> I would add that Wells cannot have helped Moura very generously, if at all, because Moura worked constantly to earn her living and a very mediocre living (materially) it was. I am quite sure he left her nothing in his will because she was forced to give up her flat in London finally and move to her son's house in Italy. We all knew that move would kill her as she so depended on her wide social life in London. It did kill her. I was devoted to her.[166]

Thinking about Moura brought back recollections about others, including Rebecca West. "I asked her—a wonderful woman—why she had bothered with Wells," Martha said, never offering Rebecca's answer.[167] Martha never met Marjorie, and she claimed that "Wells never spoke of her as anything except as a super secretary. I saw Gip here at my flat once when he was trying to force me into this ludicrous and disagreeable role as a lover, and [I] disliked him intensely." She said, as she often said and wrote, that she didn't save many letters, and that "anyway, my archive is closed." Why did she go to that extreme? Because she loathed the way biographies were being "written as gossip," she said, "and I would hope to escape the gossip." Any last comments? "HG's son Gip is absolute shit—first-class shit."[168] It was clear that she still believed, more than a decade after her dealings with him, that Gip had double-crossed—or outsmarted—her.

So, finally, what can we say about the relationship between Martha Gellhorn and H. G. Wells? Was the claim of an affair "rubbish," as Martha called it? Was the affair just HG's "illusion," as Gip wondered in his letter to Martha? Was the young Martha innocently looking for a father figure in the months following her father's death? Was she looking for an influential mentor? Was HG an incurable old lech with delusions of grandeur? Did he make up the whole thing? The record he left in the unpublished portions of the *Postscript* and the date books and the trail of calculating deeds that Martha left provide compelling evidence that the two did have a brief affair followed by a long and affectionate friendship; the evidence also suggests that both the relationships were mutually acceptable and beneficial. HG enjoyed the charms of an exciting young woman at a time when he was most vulnerable; the relationship revived and renewed him physically and spiritually. Martha, of course, won his affection and friendship as well as the perks that affection and friendship provided. She seemed to be genuinely fond of HG, indeed, grateful for his role as an emotional backstop; but she also seemed to endear herself to him for favors—just as she had done with so many people. That behavior undoubtedly fell into the category of beating the system—a system that, to be sure, hadn't yet begun serving females very well.

It is an understatement to say that Martha Gellhorn was an actor, not a reactor. She never waited for chance to operate for or against her. She sought people who could help her and then she worked those relationships for all they were worth. She probably planned to meet HG just as she probably planned to meet Hemingway. She used Hemingway to advance her career, just as she had used HG before him. And while Martha may have had a genuine proclivity for privacy, she must have believed that in silence, in self-imposed solitary confinement, she could protect—even control—the past. She must have believed that in her capacity as Keeper of the Truth—or Destructress of Apocryphy—she appeared to be more honest than the next person. In this way, no one would suspect the golden girl of having a darker side, even Machiavellian motives. There is also strong evidence that Martha was haunted and propelled by self-doubt and self-loathing. As we saw in her letters to HG, she often referred to her second-rate intellect, her laziness, and her problems with writing. Those perceived shortcomings haunted her all her life. To Victoria Glendinning fifty years later she wrote:

> I used to worry desperately about wasting time because I saw myself as basically lazy (which I am) and also saw my time wasting as proof of a second-rate brain (which I also have). Perhaps I also felt it was sinful because such a pleasure. I now think it is as necessary as solitude; that's how the compost heap grows in the mind. Anyway I intend to spend the rest of my life wasting time.[169]

And to compound and confound matters, because Martha conspired with silence, we are unlikely to know the whole truth about her. After all is said and done—even with a wealth of information—it is probably impossible to fully know *The Heart of Another*.[170] And in this case, Martha Gellhorn has kept us out of hers.

This examination of Martha Gellhorn hinges on her self-effacing epithet, in which she described herself as "a footnote in history, a passing reference in others' books and letters." For the record, a few years later she told a friend that "the Ostrich is not a fool."[171] But the many people who knew her described her differently: some with praise, some with condemnation. In the 1930s, Eleanor Roosevelt was extremely fond of Martha, indeed, a strong and loyal supporter. In one of her "My Day" columns, the first lady called Martha "a very charming young lady" and "an exciting person with whom to talk."[172] In the 1950s, however, Eleanor was appalled by some of Martha's behavior, especially the remarks she made about her son, Sandor. HG, as we have seen, had many wonderful things to say about Martha; she was vivid, cheery, charming, frank, and fresh. But Colonel Buck Lanham, Hemingway's friend and commanding officer in France during the Battle of the Bulge, offered one of the cruelest and most memorable of all the descriptions ever made about Martha Gellhorn. After having put himself out transporting the Hemingways around the command post during Christmas of 1944, and having given up his own bed for Martha, Lanham got both barrels from Martha. He retaliated, however, by saying that she was "a bitch from start to finish" and "rude, just plain country rude."[173]

Who, then, was the real Martha Gellhorn? She was all of the above: a many-faceted person, gutsy enough to show her various sides. Indeed, one of her distinguishing characteristics was that she seemed to be full of contradictions; her actions and statements were often paradoxical. The trait was not lost on Hemingway. One of the most damning observations anyone ever made about Martha came from him. Reflecting on the difficulty she had in coping with life in China during their 1941 tour, a trip *she* dragged *him* into, Hemingway quipped: "M. loves humanity but can't stand people."[174] Along the same lines, an unnamed source once said that Martha "claimed she loved the poor—actually she loved the rich. She claimed she was a great lover of peace, but wherever there was war she rushed into the fray. She loved her mink coat—and claimed it was her entrée into any office."[175]

There are many examples of paradox in Martha's life. In her professional life, for example, she was a journalist—and a good one by most standards. However, she desperately wanted to be accepted for her novels and short stories, and unfortunately for her, the recognition never came. Martha once was described as a "curiously underrated writer." Quite aware of the epithet, she quipped to Glendinning: "My memorial is going to be a bench in Kew Gardens in London, with my name, the dates of my birth and death, and 'curiously underrated writer' underneath."[176] With Hemingway a standard for good writing, most people are destined to fall short, of course. Living with The Great One—or in his shadow—had to unnerve Martha. But what fueled her unrepentant anger was being enveloped, even entrapped, in Hemingway's myth.[177] Yet, as most of her biographers have recognized, she helped nurture his myth and her place in it.

Regarding her roots, Martha turned her back on St. Louis and the United States when she was twenty-one and lived in one country after another: Cuba, France, Italy, Mexico, Kenya, England, and Wales. The

Midwesterner cultivated a Bryn Mawr "Seven Sisters" accent shortly after enrolling in the school, and she never quite lost it. Later, her speech
reflected her many years of living in Wales and England. She spoke
with a British accent, whether cultivated or assimilated, with all its up-
swings and vocabulary. In her writing, Martha used an odd combination of Briticisms and dated phrases—lines reminiscent of Hemingway,
of all people: "Built in falsehood, children, is bad," she wrote in her
apocryphism piece. She hated the United States, but she wanted to be
read there. As she wrote a friend: "But to be a totem in Britain, as I am
becoming, means nothing much; I wanted to be read in the U.S., where
I hoped my anger would feed other angers."[178]

With regard to romance, and much like the other characters in this
book, Martha seemed to have the urge to marry, and she admitted to
aching loneliness from time to time, but she craved independence and
frequent, long separations. Even on her "honeymoon" tour of China
and the Far East with her new husband Ernest Hemingway, she stayed
on a month by herself. Her marriage to Hemingway lasted five years,
and her open marriage to Tom Matthews, nine; but both couples were
rarely together, and, after divorcing Matthews, Martha never remarried. Then there is the issue of motherhood. Although Martha wrote a
good deal about children, and was seized by the idea of raising a child,
she spent little time with Sandy, and eventually withdrew from him altogether. The other Sandy in her life—Sandy Matthews, her stepson—
is her literary executor.

Martha also had a puzzling relationship with her mother. Although
Edna seemed to be the one person in the world Martha loved uncondi-
tionally, Martha spent very little time with her mother, apart from
short visits. Just before Edna died in St. Louis, Martha, who had been
visiting her, suddenly left town—abandoning her mother and leaving
her sister-in-law to handle the funeral arrangements. Perhaps the
process was too painful for Martha. Or perhaps she didn't want to be in
a position where she would have to grieve in public.[179] When Gip Wells
sent Martha her letters to HG, she returned them with a note, part of
which said: "I have kept my mother's note to Wells. I don't want her involved in Wells' sexual accounts (true and/or false). But can you imag-

ine I'd have let her, whom I adored, thank Wells for taking care of me if there'd been a love-sex affair between us?"[180]

Martha seemed to have a double standard about the purview of biography. On the one hand, she decried the practice of invading people's private lives, including her own; yet on the other, she engaged in it herself; one recalls her *Paris Review* comments about Spender and Hellman. In private, she believed that people deserved what they got. When Milt Wolff turned to Martha for advice on writing a biography, Martha wrote: "If [people] deserve criticism, what is wrong with that?"[181] Moreover, although Martha claimed to be a private person who sought only solitary pursuits, one has to wonder. One must consider the choices she made throughout her life, and the people she pursued: She chose journalism, including war correspondence, which put her in the center of the action, the line of fire; she pursued Bertrand de Jouvenel, the Roosevelts, H. G. Wells, Ernest Hemingway, all of whom had the same effect. This is a fundamental paradox; as Diana, Princess of Wales, and so many other celebrities and darlings of the paparazzi have discovered, you can't have it both ways.

Fundamentally, Martha was a writer. She saw herself as a defender of the downtrodden, but even that had a double edge. "Having written all my life on behalf of the abused," she told Wolff, "I am certain that not one word ever did the slightest good. But I am a writer and know nothing else to do. It is tiring and unrewarding. On the other hand, complete silence is worse, so even if it's only a mouse squeak it is better than nothing."[182]

*   *   *

Martha died on February 15, 1998. The cause—when it was given—was cancer. She wouldn't have been happy with any of her obituary notices. For one thing, like those for Moura, they were filled with errors. Her life, like Moura's and Hemingway's, had become a legend, and legends, like tornadoes, tend to pick up a lot of junk: She was described as a graduate of Bryn Mawr; as having been married to Jouvenel; as having had an eight-year marriage with Hemingway; as having written any number of novels—from eight to thirteen. Also, Martha was, as she feared she would be, identified foremost as Hemingway's wife. The *Washington Post* obit is a good example. Its Web-site story, posted February 17, 1998, and datelined London, began: "Martha Gellhorn, 89, who gained fame as one of the world's first female reporters and as a wife of writer Ernest Hemingway, died at her home here Feb. 15." Her death also provided the opportunity for some good lines. The obit continued: "Like their marriage, their separation was acrimonious. Miss Gellhorn described Hemingway as 'one of the greatest self-created myths in history.'" There were also the glowing, reverential, comments. Buford was quoted as saying that Martha was a travel writer, a journalist, a novelist, "and one of the most eloquent witnesses of the 20th century." One of the great many profiles written in tribute was, in fact, "worshipful." That is how Peter Kurth described Kevin Kerrane's *Salon* magazine piece, titled "Martha's Quest." Kurth's response to Kerrane's profile is one of the most striking pieces that appeared after Martha died. It began:

> Kevin Kerrane's worshipful report on his interviews with journalist Martha Gellhorn reminded me all too vividly of my own encounters with this dreadful woman, this Sacred Cow of combat reporting, whose insistence that no one mention her five-year marriage to Ernest Hemingway might have been merely ludicrous were it not for the mean streak running through it. Kerrane thinks Gellhorn "would have resented" seeing Hemingway's name in her obituaries when she died last month. She'd have done a lot more than that: She'd have screamed, hollered, fussed, fumed, thwarted, threatened, obstructed and, probably, put a hex on the offending reporter.[183]

Kurth went on to say that in 1990, he went to London to interview Martha for *Lear's* magazine, now defunct. She had agreed to the interview on condition that Ernest Hemingway's name not be mentioned "not only anywhere in the story, but anywhere in the magazine." Furthermore, she wanted guarantees in writing, and assurances of no last-minute tricks. When Kurth said he *had* to mention the marriage, she cancelled the story. His counter-obit continued:

Now that Gellhorn's dead, I'm delighted to spread the news: Martha Gellhorn was married to Ernest Hemingway. To be exact, from 1940 to 1945. Her name IS associated with his and it will be for as long as either one of them is remembered. Kerrane has bought the Gellhorn line when he says that, in 1937, she went to Spain on her own, not with Hemingway, in order to report on the Spanish Civil War.

How she got there is immaterial; once she did, she was whisked into the highest echelons of government and reporting thanks to her association with Hemingway and nothing else. Friends of mine who were there with them remembered that Gellhorn was "more Hemingway than he was," constantly talking about "the Front," flopping into a chair at the end of the day, saying, "Jeez, I'm pooped!" and, despite her Bryn Mawr education, dumbing down her speech so her words came out as "dem" and "doze" and "Cripes!" Indeed, to the end of her life Gellhorn liked to surround herself with the toughest of tough-guy journalists, as if she was, in fact, just one of the boys. This was the woman who once savagely attacked Lillian Hellman in the *Paris Review* as a "self-serving apochryphiar." Well, it's out of her control now, wherever she is. The Truth, at last, can breathe.

The *New York Times* headline for Martha was sublimely simple: "Martha Gellhorn, Daring Writer, Dies at 89." Bertrand de Jouvenel appeared (identified as her first husband) in the half-page piece, as did Tom Matthews, and, of course, Ernest Hemingway—mentioned by name ten times, including in the second paragraph, and mentioned indirectly many more times. HG was absent, an *Invisible Man*. Two photographs ran with the story: Martha with—and without—Hemingway. The obituary began:

Martha Ellis Gellhorn, who as one of the first female war correspondents covered a dozen major conflicts in a writing career spanning more than six decades, died on Sunday at her home in London. She was 89.

Ms. Gellhorn was a cocky, raspy-voiced maverick who saw herself as a champion of ordinary people trapped in conflicts created by the rich and powerful. That she was known to many largely because of her marriage to Ernest Hemingway, from 1940 to 1945, caused her unending irritation, especially when critics tried to find parallels between her lean writing style and that of her more celebrated husband. "Why should I be a footnote to somebody else's life?" she bitterly asked in an interview, pointing out that she had written two novels before meeting Hemingway and continued writing for almost a half-century after leaving him.

Martha's phenomenal career was sketched, including the hits she took from critics who saw her writing as "often didactic and sentimental," her journalism too much like fiction, and her fiction too much like journalism. "But her longevity and the compelling pull of her life story overrode such criticisms," the *Times* asserted.

Bill Buford got it right when he noted in *The New Yorker* tribute to Martha, a few months after her death, that one of Martha's many contradictions was that she was "a loner who loved company," and that the contradiction was reconciled through her letters, "the only place where she could have both solitude and intimacy."[184] Eight months before she died, she plunged into that safe intimate realm in a letter to Milt Wolff. Claiming that she had no purpose in life and that she was simply "taking up space," she added that she had just realized that Wolff was "the last person alive whom I know from my long lost real life. I miss Freddy. Not to mention Capa and many others. I do not enjoy the position of sole survivor."[185]

In a way, Martha's life was distilled in the simple, white, preprinted postcard she sent when she didn't have the time or the inclination to answer a query, or when she was too ill to do so. The last sentence is particularly relevant.

I appreciate your writing to me and I thank you. My eyesight has become so feeble, and my energy the same, that I can't any longer manage correspondence. <u>Delighted to receive but unable to give</u>. *With apologies*. Martha Gellhorn.

6

Epilogue: Beyond the Shadow of Love

Christabel I don't like this piece of life that is being left to me. Haven't you a twin sister who would like to nurse a lonely (lonely, not lovely) scrap of cheerfulness through his last ten or twelve years of life?

—HG to Christabel, November 14, 1935

Often, while writing this book, as it filled with lovers and love affairs—former, future, current and concurrent, imagined and unimaginable—I thought about the conversation between Natasha and Sonja in Woody Allen's film *Love and Death,* a farsical parody of Nikolayevich Tolstoy's *War and Peace.* Natasha tries to explain the "complicated situation" of love triangulating over, under, around, and through her circle of friends. "I'm in love with Alexi, he loves Alicia—Alicia is having an affair with Lev—Lev loves Tatiana—Tatiana loves Simkin—Simkin loves me—I love Simkin but in a different way than Alexi," and so on. Cousin Sonja is not entertained by this cavalcade of love stories, but Natasha plows on. "Rifkin is sleeping with Mrs. Pushkin, but Mrs. Pushkin's not sleeping with Rifkin. Kuslov is having adultery with Strogoff's mother. The firm of Mishkin and Mishkin is sleeping with the firm of Raskov and Raskov." Sonja then gets her turn, delivering a vintage Woody

Allen pseudosyllogism on love and suffering and happiness, to which Natasha replies, ending the discussion: "I never want to marry—I just want to get divorced."

The world you are now leaving, like Allen's, also was a tangled web of love relationships. Its cast (of what seemed like thousands) had motivations, needs, and desires just as ridiculous as those that Allen concocted. For example, HG wanted Moura just as she was—only different. Moura wanted HG for "a romantic sexual and personal intimacy," but also, as we now know, for his influence and connections. Martha sought HG's affections for career reasons, at least initially; Constance desired HG primarily for intellectual reasons, although "the game" involved in getting the World Brain surely played a part. HG, as we have seen, coveted Constance and Martha as potential Lover-Shadow wives, but in the end, he couldn't disentangle himself from Moura. In pages that were suppressed from the *Postscript,* HG noted: "I have tried Constance and again Martha—my last flounderings towards the wife idea. Even as I write them down I realize their essential shallowness."[1]

Similarly, their true passions were all over the map. Moura's was Bruce Lockhart. Martha's was travel. Constance's were books and horses. HG's were work, sex, and his Lover-Shadow. "The fundamental love of my life is the Lover-Shadow, and always I have been catching a glimpse of her and losing her in these adventures," HG conceded in the *Postscript.*[2] For decades, he craved having that "dear presence" around him, abroad and at home, a domestic goddess always coming through the garden to meet him and his needs. As we know, Moura would not comply. As HG interpreted it, her "incurable vagrancy" would not hold her in the garden of his desires. She would fail HG and cheat him of his dream of a Lover-Shadow. In the *Postscript* HG predicted his romantic fate: "Friendship perhaps may still be mine, a little fresh love-making perhaps, but not even the delusion of possession. I am sprung. I cared for Moura too much and I cannot begin again in real earnest to create another vital intimacy. . . . My Lover-Shadow has dispersed again and there is no one to whom I can go with the assurance of that envelopment and refuge and comfort for which the distressful heart craves."[3]

His Lover-Shadow, he came to realize, was no longer Moura "but Jane plus Moura plus fantasy—a being made up of a dead woman, a stimulating deception and the last dissolving vestiges of imaginative hope."[4]

What is surprising is that when all was said and done, HG would claim to have loved—*really loved*—very few people throughout his great many mis/adventures with women and romance:

> In all my life I think I have really loved only three women steadfastly; my first wife, my second wife and Moura Budberg. . . . Beyond that, all these women I have kissed, solicited, embraced and lived with, have never entered intimately and deeply into my emotional life. . . . Some at least of these encounters had a loveliness, often a quite accidental loveliness. They could be like flower-shows or walks in springtime or mountain excursions. . . . I cannot make up my mind that I regret any of them.[5]

What then did this procession of ecstatic, regretful, jaded, and hopeful lovers we have watched and listened to throughout these pages get for their trouble, for their liaisons given and taken so freely? Did their "free love" have a price tag after all? For Moura, Constance, and Martha, probably not, or if it did, it was a nominal fee. These women got from HG more or less what they wanted: friendship, affection, sex, advice, information, professional favors, and the glow of celebrity. HG earned their friendships and the rights to their beds, certainly. He also basked in the glow of their beauty, charm, wealth, class, and titles, but he never won their submission. As Odette and Christabel, among others, knew so well, HG craved the excitement of fresh liaisons for the intensity that they brought to his daily life, but ultimately, this road always led to disappointment and loneliness.

His disappointment was greatest with Moura, to be sure, although HG told his readers that he didn't blame Moura for it. His tale was an indictment not of Moura, he claimed, but of life. It was an indictment of the general "misfit" of male and female desires, an indictment of the difference between the way people born of different countries *think*. Moura's was the "thought idiom of an intricate Russian, capable of blackening out anything in her memory she does not like," while HG's was "a mind accustomed to intellectual consistency."[6] Once again, that old chestnut about the incompatibility of brains. In addition, HG acknowledged his unreasonable and "monstrous demands" for a Lover-Shadow, based on the "enormity" of the *persona* he created for himself. "I am, I know, trying to be something too big for my powers. I am an insufficient and often irritable 'great man' with an infantile craving for help."[7]

If we take HG at his word, if we believe what he said in the *Postscript* and in the pages suppressed from it about his conception of the Lover-Shadow, we must conclude that he was totally blind to the obvious: The World Brain didn't understand that, as constructed, his affairs were destined to fail. He didn't understand that he had a fatal attraction to women who, while they enjoyed his company and even adored him, could not satisfy his self-defined monstrous demands for care giving and total submission. These were women who put a premium on *their* independence, after all. In all likelihood, HG never realized or understood that he was asking these women to indenture themselves to him in the same way his mother had indentured him so many times to the drapery trade. He never quite realized that these were not indenturable women. On the other hand, it is quite possible that HG *fully* understood what he was doing, fully understood that his affairs were doomed *because he chose women who could not possibly give him what he wanted*. He may at some level have known all along that his choices allowed him to become frustrated in love, and then to be unfaithful to his lovers, which in turn allowed him to begin the cycle all over again.

While HG understood that his Lover-Shadow was a dream, an ideal of imaginative hope, he also seemed to deceive himself into believing that he could be loyal to one woman, for even when the "ideal woman" did indenture herself to him, as his wife Jane did, HG became just as dissatisfied and just as unfaithful. Christabel Aberconway understood that, and tried to explain it to her good friend. She wrote to HG in April 1935 to comfort him after learning that Moura had refused to marry him:

Quiet happiness, security, safety first—in fact, a charming, cosy, loving and attentive wife, doesn't suit you. It never has, it never will, no matter *how* much you let yourself "go old." Remember, my dear, you've been married twice, and you've always wanted more than marriage can give. Adventure, surprises, that unlooked for visit. That adult "Beep Bo" round the corner. And the sharp fear of losing the person is what <u>keeps</u> you. Any of us could find you a <u>lovely</u> wife. But that is not what you want. Within a year, you'd be lusting after the unattainable.

Odette also understood Pidookaki's propensity to lust after the unattainable and to cut and run from the attained. In a previously suppressed letter to Jane Wells, Odette ably demonstrated her understanding. She told Jane that the self-realization that HG acquired from his work would remain his strongest need. However, his product was "so noble" and "of such universal utility" that the personal claims of others should be subordinated to his work. This was a great and bitter lesson she had to learn, she told HG's wife. Had she not come to feel this so deeply, she could not have stayed with HG, since companionship with him required a good deal of "mortification." Not only was he extraordinarily exacting in his notion of companionship, but also, he

wants irreconcilable things. He feels frustrated and solitary in his mind when a woman has that spiritual submissiveness which to me is the essential characteristic of womanliness, but which makes her a subordinate and he feels thwarted and solitary in his heart when the woman has that sexual detachment and that drive that alone can make her share fully his creative and mental life. He wants a woman to combine an essentially feminine devotion, subtleness and responsiveness with the independence and activities of a man. It seems to me that he's asking for a biological impossibility; the two sets of qualities rule each other out to a great extent.[8]

As Christabel, Odette, Jane, and legions of others knew, the main failure was with HG. He was fundamentally incapable of achieving intimacy with any of the women he chased and loved and hated and married and left. Every time he got close to emotional intimacy, he bolted, blaming it either on his generalized domestic claustrophobia or on the woman. His unfinished business with his mother surely was a shadow over all his affairs, indeed, over all his major relationships. Her Puritan disapproval surely haunted and shamed him, and her cold detachment surely frustrated him. Added to this was his father's emotional remoteness, which virtually assured HG's insatiable desire for nurturing and inability to nurture and be nurtured. No matter how he rationalized them, his monstrous desires were impossible to feed or to shake. Whether he ever understood the true source of his obsessions and frustration is not known. There were hints, however, that HG suspected what he was up against in his own makeup, although even in these words, he may have deceived himself or shortchanged men. In August 1935, he noted in pages that were later suppressed from the *Postscript* that he needed help in his endgame. "I cannot live fully and completely without a woman to love and protect me from myself. It is how I am made, and I suppose it is how most men are made."[9] Perhaps he even startled himself when he told Christabel that his world would be a different place if she weren't in it. She was, after all, "somebody I've never hurt, somebody who's never hurt me." While HG was inherently unable to achieve intimacy with any of his women, he was not alone. Moura, Constance, and Martha were just as unable. As we have seen, each lusted after, pursued, lost, or ran away from a beloved but unattainable mate—Moura from Lockhart, Constance from Crosby, and Martha from Hemingway.

HG came to accept failure, although he continued to deflect the blame, throwing it back on the women and the society. In pages suppressed from the *Postscript,* he wrote that his reader could plainly see not only his urge to live in a generous, free-loving, free-living society but also the defeat of that urge because no such group or culture yet existed. Nevertheless, a "wide and candid life" remained his ideal—forever in the background of his "intenser clutching responses."

I tried to evoke it in my Modern Utopia, and Amber and I set the weakest if not the worst example possible of how it should be done. The other of my main liaisons were free associations that ended in plain defeats inherent in the personalities of my associates, or passed, in the case of Moura, after the heedless relapse into a romantic exclusiveness I have related, after my urgency to marry her and my storm of jealous resentment, into the wary affection, the detached free love, the faintly malicious & yet kindly & always interested intimacy of our later phase. All that I have told—in its satisfactions and inconclusiveness—as plainly as I can.[10]

Although he failed and was condemned by his own standards, HG believed that failure did not prove his standards wrong. In suppressed pages, he wrote: "Plain speech, mental toil to think and tell the truth, and all the courage we can summon to keep and extend human freedom and dignity, is as far as we can get to individual redemption. We must live and die in that struggle, making the most of our imperfections.

"It is hard. Yes. But let me put a colophon to that, and end this balance sheet of a life. At times it has been damned good fun. Exhilaration! The proof of the pudding is in the eating. One does not go on struggling to change a hopeless world or feel as reluctant as I do to leave an entertainment that is altogether evil."[11]

HG's last entries in the *Postscript,* as published, were made April 1942. They were fairly dismal. He wrote that something was bothering Moura "heartbreakingly"; that he was worried about his grandchildren; that, for the time being, he was in a recalcitrant mood. "I have turned my face to the wall," he conceded. HG wrote about Stefan Zweig's suicide, assured his readers that he would never go that way, and briefly discussed his latest projects, *Phoenix* and *You Can't Be Too Careful.* In closing, he noted that he had made two resolutions: to have nothing more to do with bores— "There is no reason now why I should ever be bored again"—and to disregard his critics, especially with regard to *You Can't Be Too Careful.* "Read it again," he suggested, "but don't bother me. You will never get nearer to me now than the waste-paper basket."[12]

HG had written another ending to his Lover-Shadow section in June 1935, but he never used it. Among the suppressed materials are five pages devoted primarily to the Lover-Shadow and his failure to realize her. HG admitted to having "a strong sexual urge and a bias towards a puerile approach to women." These qualities made him concentrate his search on women who would be allies and helpers.

> That I "fell," as people say, for the amorous discipleship of Dusa [Amber], that I had great hopes of a strong alliance with Rebecca, that I believed that Odette's professions of devotion to me could be realised, and that I built up an insubstantial dream of conquering the world at the side of Moura, all these experiences, in spite of their vexations in detail, display the same obstinate recurrence to a personified Lover-Shadow. I have never yet grown sufficiently adult, sufficiently post-sexual, to live alone without the sense of a personal lover. And that lover a woman. That belated lesson I have to sit down to learn now. If ever it can be learnt. And I have to suffer in the process.[13]

Moreover, no woman in what was left of his lifetime would likely accept the aims of his persona, since those aims were "too male and too remote for the feminine imagination." That equal intimate cooperation was beyond dreaming, HG conceded, and besides, his shortcomings— his "infirmities of temper," "moods of inferiority," "many littlenesses and the failing energy of his sex appeal"—would prevent him from holding onto the affection he then seemed to command, or from capturing and dominating the life of a new person. "Intimate personal love is receding from me, and I have to square the conduct of these last years of my life, as well as I can, to that manifest fact."[14]

Even more chilling—disturbing or hopeful, depending on how you view it—are HG's final thoughts, suppressed all these years. While he seemed to have abandoned the notion of finding his Lover-Shadow in his lifetime, he held out hope elsewhere:

Why am I sitting in the night and writing all this down? I am writing to some one—but to whom? A posthumous Lover-Shadow? Who, like that God men invent for the purpose of imaginative refuge, will never have a chance of reacting or not reacting to the Persona I choose to present.

I happen to be most damnably lonely to-night. I cannot sleep and I lack the vitality to turn my mind to other work. So I scribble here on and on and I shall wander about my flat and lie down and get up and scribble a bit more and so worry through the night. And the morning will come in due course and bring a sort of healing distraction with it. Even this night cannot last for ever. I shall shave and bath when the day comes. . . . And it helps me a great deal, posthumous Lover-Shadow, to think that some day you will read what I am writing.[15]

To whom was he speaking? Isabel? Jane? He never said, alas.

*   *   *

Obits Faux and Real

Ten years before he died, H. G. Wells, with considerable wit, and with his wits about him, wrote his own obituary. It was not only faux, it was fabulous—irreverent to the point of outrageous. In fact, of all the obits ever written for the man, his was the only one that got away with murder. Rich with self-deprecating good humor, understatement, deception, and even some unvarnished truth, the imaginative piece was vintage HG. The aging time traveler played devilish games with the genre as he weaved prophecy and fantasy with biographical fact and analysis. He wrapped myth around reality, he intertwined truth and fiction so tightly that the reader was left reeling, wondering what was—and what was not—to be believed. But this was HG's game, and he was at the top of his form.

"The name of Mr. H. G. Wells, who died yesterday afternoon of heart failure at the age of 97, will have few associations for the younger generation," HG began his obit, "But those listeners whose adult memories stretch back to the opening decades of the present century . . . may recall a number of titles of books he wrote and may even find in some odd attic, an actual volume or so of his works." HG produced his obituary for his seventieth birthday at the request of the BBC for a broadcast series; it was then published in *The Listener* on July 15, 1936. Edith Sitwell and Bertrand Russell, among others, also contributed their "last writes" to the series. HG described himself as "one of the most prolific of the 'literary hacks'" of the time. He wrote scientific romances whose original freshness had long since been destroyed by the "general advance of knowledge."

Then, in a streak of bald-faced truth, HG went on to speak of himself as having been an intellectual born of common origins, whose "keenest feeling seems to have been a cold anger at intellectual and moral pretentiousness." He reported that his most interesting quality was his "refusal to accept the social inferiority to which he seemed to be born." Despite his acute ability to foreshadow events—he described his role as "something between a portent and a pioneer"—HG conceded that in life he was ultimately left in the dust of opinion as current events marched past him: "From being a premature, he became a forgotten man," he observed of himself.

Then on he went to more fun and games. HG wrote that his immediate needs were met by a government pension in 1955. He occupied an old tumble-down house upon the border of Regent's park and his bent, shabby, slovenly and latterly somewhat obese figure was frequently to be seen in the adjacent gardens . . . or hobbling painfully about with the aid of a stick, coughing or talking to himself. "Someday," he would be heard to say, "I shall write a book, a *real* book." At the end of the piece, HG turned serious again, reminding his readers that an interesting study had compared him "not inaptly to a reef-soliding coral polyp. Scarcely anything remains of him now and yet without him and his life the reef of common ideas on which our civilization stands could never has arisen."

Newspapers and magazines around the world ran HG's faux obit over the next six months. The *New York Times* published a large part of it in a September 20, 1936, story, which ended with, "Only Mr. Wells's own imagination could envisage him, 19 years hence, reduced in means to a point where he would need a 'small Civil List pension.' He is reputedly worth well over $1,000,000, having earned $100,000 alone on his novel 'Mr. Britling Sees It Through,' while his 'Outline of History' even out-stripped the Bible for a time as a best-seller."

While all this false obituary writing was fun, in a way, nearer to his death HG turned deadly serious. Three years before that day, he asked one last thing of British radio audiences: that they continue to look ahead, to hope, and to carry the torch. The increasingly feeble prophet described himself as "an extreme revolutionary" who considered the doctrines of the Communist Party, as they appeared in the *Daily Worker*, fifty years out of date. And then he said:

> I don't ask you to prepare for a new world, because I realise that a New World is here now. The question is whether our species, we, our children and our children's children, can adapt ourselves and conquer the New World, or whether we are going to spin down this vortex to extinction: extinction which has been the fate of all the mighty races of animals that have lorded it over the world in the past. . . . There is no choice before mankind but a world-wide control of power and production—world-wide, no less—and a world-wide scrapping of our inheritance of hates and aggressions that began less than a thousand generations ago, when wars began. We have to nerve ourselves for that, and there is no other way for us.[16]

*   *   *

As it happened, HG died on August 13, 1946, at the age of seventy-nine, not ninety-seven, after a long battle with diabetes and liver cancer, not the heart attack of his faux obituary. He was a model patient and good humored to the end. His nurse had just checked on him and left the room when he passed away late on that Tuesday afternoon, five weeks before his eightieth birthday. Marjorie wrote to Christabel about the circumstances.

Poor HG had a very unhappy time, I think, during the last two years of his life, although he endured pain and ill health stoically. I am only beginning now to realise how I shall miss him. His last week was very peaceful. We had thought that he was rallying and would any day move off downstairs again. He did parts of the Times crossword every day to the very last. On Tuesday morning he went through the letters with me as usual, making joking comments and then saying, "So everything is in order?" before resting again. At lunch time I left, comparatively happy about him, and soon after four I received a telephone message to say that he was dead. He became very gentle and tired during the last few weeks of his life. His death took us quite by surprise, in spite of our having expected it.[17]

There were many stories about the end of his life, some of them now famous. HG supposedly once snapped at a death-watch visitor who had overstayed: "Can't you see I'm busy dying?" Quite near the end, he is said to have told a friend: "Here I am with one foot in the grave and the other kicking out at everything." Lance Sieveking remembered sitting with HG not long before he died. Apropos of something they had been talking about, HG told Sieveking—with a cheerful smile, no less—that he believed he would die quietly and in bed while eating, just as his father and grandfather had. "It is an hereditary irregularity in our family pulse," he said, noting that his father had died while telling his housekeeper how to make a proper suet pudding. "And [HG] winked at me and smiled and talked of other things."[18]

HG provided nicely for Moura. The *Times* reported that he left his "very dear friend" Maria Baroness Budberg £1,000 and an additional £3,000 with which to purchase an annuity. Moura, however, was perturbed to learn that she would have to pay a £500 legacy tax on some of the money. She told Lockhart that HG had left her the interest on certain shares, which "yielded almost nothing."[19] As Lockhart noted in his diary—and contrary to what has been written—HG had always been generous to Moura. He had given her many presents, including a fine tapestry of Czar Nicholas II and his family, which she displayed in her

London apartment. In July 1935, Lockhart also noted, HG told one of his lady friends that "if [HG] died tomorrow he would not leave £12,000. He has been very generous to his various dependants, legal and otherwise."[20] Before the public auction of HG's estate, Moura purchased several items: a divan bed with mattress, pillows, blankets, and a printed coverlet; nineteen framed drawings and photographs; a badly stained armchair; a Persian rug; a "continental" silver bowl with figures; and an oval wood fruit bowl with carved handles.

The world press responded robustly to the final exit of Herbert George Wells, cranking out long, mostly laudatory, obituaries. Readers from Moscow to Miami were reminded of the writer's incredible output of work. They were told of his guiding beliefs in Utopianism and socialism and of his role as a prophet of progress and crusader for the rational control of world events. The *New York Times* reported HG's many predictions about the A-bomb, the use of tanks and aircraft in warfare, the development of rockets, the 1914 war with Germany, and the way the war would be fought. "He made no claims, however, to being a prophet. Personally a man of great charm, hospitable, cheerful and genial, he never posed as a great man of letters, developed no mannerisms, but remained a typical Englishman of the lower middle classes." *Time* magazine hailed the open and adoring fan of the United States as one of the era's "most devoted, eloquent and honest" voices; *Newsweek* called him a "gigantic intellect"; and the *Times* of London said he was "a genius of faith in knowledge and reason." George Orwell wrote: "No English writer has so deeply influenced his contemporaries as Wells. He was so big a figure, he has played so great a part in forming our picture of the world, that in agreeing or disagreeing with his ideas we are apt to forget his purely literary achievement." In his eloquent eulogy, J. B. Priestley described his friend simply but memorably: HG was "a man whose word was light in a thousand dark places."

Readers also read, however briefly, about HG's personal life, including his early rise to fame and fortune from humble roots in lower-middle-class England. They read about his human qualities: his "untiring physical activity," his ability to "enjoy life in abundant measure," his relentless humanity, his valiant optimism, and his capacity for many deep friendships. In passing, readers learned of his family life—a brief marriage to a cousin, a quick divorce, and another marriage. Jane Wells, HG's second wife, stood steadfastly by HG for thirty-two years, produced two sons, Gip and Frank, and died stoically of cancer in 1927, the papers claimed over and over again. Despite the barrels of ink spent, and the rolls of paper, nothing was said about H. G. Wells's reputation as a Don Juan, about his phenomenal love for life and his equally phenomenal love life, about his extraordinary number of love affairs, short and long, clumsy and smooth, exquisite and not, out of the shadows and in. Readers got what they always get in obituaries: the half-truth. HG, who longed to see "a candid world" emerge in his lifetime, who once said, "Most of us prefer to float half-hidden even from ourselves, in a rich, warm, buoyant, juicy-mass of familiar make-believe," would be relieved to know that the truth is getting out.[21]

Notes

Birth and Death Dates;
Dates of First Meeting H. G. Wells

Moura Budberg (née Maria Zakrevsky), b. March 6, 1892 or 1893, d. Oct. 31, 1974. Met HG in 1920 in Moscow

Constance Coolidge, b. Jan. 4, 1892, d. April 30, 1973. Met HG in December 1934 in Cap Ferrat, France

Martha Gellhorn, b. Nov. 8, 1908, d. Feb. 15, 1998. Met HG in March 1935 in Washington, D.C. (or possibly in June 1934 or in March 1932, both meetings in the South of France)

H. G. Wells, b. Sept. 21, 1866, d. Aug.13, 1946

Jane (Amy Catherine) Wells, b. July 8, 1872, d. Oct. 6, 1927. Met HG in 1893

Marriages

Moura Budberg

Djon von Benckendorff, 1911, Berlin? (He died on April 18, 1919, on his estate in Estonia)

Nikolai Budberg, Nov. 1921, Tallinn, Estonia (divorced in December 1926)

Constance Coolidge

Ray Atherton, Jan. 25, 1910, Paris (divorced April 1924)

Pierre de Jumilhac, Oct. 11, 1924, Paris (divorced May 1929)

Eliot Rogers, Feb. 21, 1930, Santa Barbara (divorced same year)

André Magnus, Oct. 10, 1940, Antibes (Constance died in 1973)

Martha Gellhorn

Bertrand de Jouvenel, summer 1933, Spain; this may have been a common-law marriage
Ernest Hemingway, Nov. 21, 1940, Cheyenne, Wyo. (divorced Dec. 21, 1945)
T. S. Matthews, February 1954 (Divorced 1963)

H. G. Wells

Isabel Wells, Oct. 31, 1891 (separated in 1893, divorced in 1895)
Jane (Amy Catherine Robbins), Oct. 27, 1895 (Jane died in October 1927)

Wells's Trips Abroad

1906 United States
1914 Russia (Petersburg, January)
1916 Italian, French, and German war fronts
1920 Italy, Russia (Petrograd and Moscow, September/October)
1921 United States (October)
1922? United States
1931 United States, Oct. 13–Nov. 14
1934 United States (May); Russia (August)
1935 United States, twice (March, 3 wks; and November 7?–December)
1937 United States (October–November)
1938 Australia (November, via Marseilles, Prague; home via India, Egypt, Athens)
1940 United States

Intelligence and Secret Service Organizations

Great Britain

MI 5, British Security Service, domestic security and intelligence organization
MI 6 British Secret Intelligence Service, foreign intelligence
MI 1c, Directorate of Military Intelligence, later Foreign Intelligence
SOE, Special Operations Executive, paramilitary arm of British Intelligence during World War II.
SIS, Secret Intelligence Service

United States

CIA, Central Intelligence Agency

Russia and the Soviet Union

KGB (Committee for State Security), civilian intelligence organization

NKVD (People's Commissariate for Internal Affairs); predecessor of the KGB (1930s)

Okhrana (Tsarist Secret Police)

Cheka, Vecheka (All Russian Extraordinary Commission for Combating Counterrevolution and Sabotage, formed by Felix Dzerzhinsky), the Bolshevik political police (civilian intelligence) 1917–1922; forerunner of OGPU.

OGPU (United State Political Directorate), the Soviet Political Intelligence Service, 1923–1934; previously the GPU, which replaced the Cheka in 1922.

France

Deuxième Bureau (French Military Intelligence)

Chapter Notes

Preface

1. CM to HGW, April 21, 1930. Christabel McLaren (b. 1890, d. 1974), née Macnaghten, became Lady Aberconway in 1934, after her father-in-law, the 1st baron, died. For the purpose of simplicity, I will call her Christabel Aberconway (CA) throughout.

2. HGW to CA, April 22, 1930.

3. Ibid., April 4, 1932, midnight.

4. Ibid., Nov. 25, 1931.

5. Ibid., March 27, 1935.

6. Ibid., May 20, 1934.

7. Christabel Aberconway, *A Wiser Woman? A Book of Memories* (London: Hutchinson & Co., 1966), 65.

8. The quote was found among the "rejected" manuscript pages (Box 6, Folder 5, WIL-E 2-3, page 240a) for what became *H. G. Wells in Love: Postscript to an Experiment in Autobiography*, ed. G. P. Wells. Hereafter, the manuscript for this work, including its rejected, discarded, suppressed, and unpublished pages, will be cited as the "Postscript."

9. HGW to CA, August, 1935.

10. Her husband, Henry Duncan McLaren, was a businessman, a banker, and a member of the House of Commons. After his father died, he succeeded to the House of Lords. At one time he was Lloyd George's parliamentary personal secretary.

11. CA to HGW, Aug. 15 [1930s].

12. Odette Keun, b. Sept. 10, 1888, d. March 14, 1978.

13. HGW to CA, June 11, 1932.

14. In notes on the manuscript, Gip Wells, HG's eldest son and chief editor, wrote that "most of 'Postscript' was written between the autumn of '34 and summer of '35, but it was extensively revised and extended during 1936 and

1937. A few pages were added and smaller revisions were made during the years up to 1942."

15. Baker was a literature professor at Princeton and a biographer of Ernest Hemingway.

16. H. G. Wells, *H. G. Wells in Love: Postscript to an Experiment in Autobiography,* ed. G. P. Wells (Boston: Little, Brown and Co., 1984), 53.

17. Publication of the *Postscript* coincided with the release of Anthony West's biography of his father. Anthony was born out of wedlock, the son of HG and Rebecca West.

18. The "Closet Correspondence," this author's name for the withheld letters "includes more than 500 letters of a previously suppressed personal correspondence from family and intimate friends. The correspondents include: Christabel Aberconway, Mary Baker, Amber (Reeves) Blanco White, Rosamund Bland, Hedy Gatternigg, Martha Gellhorn, Violet Hunt, Odette Keun, May Nisbet, Margaret Sanger, Brynhild Sharrard, Elizabeth von Arnim ("Little e"), and Rebecca West. Correspondents in the first collection, purchased by the UI Library in 1954, include many of the movers and shakers of the first half of the twentieth century and many of the major literati, "including Winston Churchill, Albert Einstein, Sigmund Freud, James Joyce, Franklin Delano Roosevelt, George Bernard Shaw, and Leon Trotsky. Also, because HG befriended stars from the entertainment world as his interest in filmmaking grew, his archive includes letters from Charlie Chaplin, Walt Disney, Douglas Fairbanks, and Paulette Goddard, among others. Some fifteen hundred additional letters are carbons of letters that HG wrote. The first Wells Collection includes a complete unpublished novel, several unpublished manuscripts, typescripts of stories and articles, personal documents and photographs, address and date books, correspondence, drawings, memorabilia, and HG's personal library.

19. H. G. Wells (1866–1946); Moura Budberg (1892–1974); Constance Coolidge (1892–1973); and Martha Gellhorn (1908–1998). Martha denied the affair to her dying day.

20. David Smith, *H. G. Wells: Desperately Mortal, A Biography* (New Haven and London: Yale University Press, 1986), xi. The historian A.J.P. Taylor once described HG as a "spluttering imaginative little man in a hurry."

21. Grolier, Inc., *New Grolier Multimedia Encyclopedia* (Novato, Calif.: The Software Toolworks, Inc., 1989–1993).

22. A radio adaptation of *War,* narrated by Orson Welles in 1938, sent thousands of people into panic when they thought the Eastern United States had been attacked by Martians.

23. Smith, *Desperately Mortal,* xii.

24. H. G. Wells, *Anticipations of the Reaction of Mechanical and Scientific Progress upon Human Life and Thought* (London: Chapman & Hall, 1902), 252.

25. Wells, *The Anatomy of Frustration* (London: The Cresset Press, 1936), 266, 267.

26. After Leo Szilard, an unusually imaginative nuclear physicist, discovered and patented the nuclear chain reaction, he joined Enrico Fermi at the Manhattan Project, where he was compelled to develop nuclear bombs after having read HG's *World Set Free, A Story of Mankind* (New York: E. P. Dutton & Co., 1914), as Albert Wattenberg, a physics professor emeritus at the University of Illinois, told this author and has said and written many times. Wattenberg was a young University of Chicago graduate student in the early 1940s, when and where he and some seventy other scientists, including Szilard, helped Fermi build and operate the first controlled nuclear chain reaction.

27. From Wells, *World Set Free.*

28. David Smith's phrase.

29. As Smith has suggested. Other similarly influential works were *Love and Mr. Lewisham* (1900), *Marriage* (1912), *Secret Places of the Heart* (1922), and *Apropos of Dolores* (1938).

30. Wells, *Experiment,* 86.

31. Lance Sieveking, *Eye of the Beholder* (London: Hulton Press, 1957), 230.

32. Anatole France's claim.

33. Material for these relationships is drawn from suppressed love letters and other documents, including date books and diaries at Illinois and more than a dozen collections in the United States, England, and France, the latter by way of Russia.

34. This is the extreme case against the man. It is Jeanne and Norman MacKenzie's position as told in *The Life of H. G. Wells: The Time Traveller* (London: The Hogarth Press, 1987). In the epilogue of their revised edition of the book, written after Wells's revelations came out in the *Postscript,* the MacKenzies take a very hard stand against HG, probably the hardest in print to date.

35. Wells, *Anatomy of Frustration,* 215–216.

Chapter 1

1. Petrograd, Russia, is now called St. Petersburg. In August 1914, St. Petersburg's name was changed to Petrograd and remained so for ten years. From 1924 to 1991, it was called Leningrad, and from 1991 to the present it has remained St. Petersburg.

2. H. G. Wells, *H. G. Wells in Love: Postscript to an Experiment in Autobiography,* ed. G. P. Wells (Boston: Little, Brown and Co., 1984), 131.

3. She was an expatriate for her entire adult life, except for a brief time in the 1940s, which she spent in Washington, D.C. Her fondness for the United States was indisputable. In 1932, for example, she told her diary, "Sweet America—the soul of you is beautiful. I am always proud to be of you & one of you, far away tho I am."

4. Charles Francis Adams served as secretary of the navy from 1929 to 1933.

5. In 1932, Constance met a Lady Butterfield when on vacation at St. Moritz. In her diary, Constance later wrote about a conversation they had. Constance told Lady B. that she had "a divine name," and when Lady B. asked Constance her name, she replied: "Oh I have a great many—first one & then another, you know." She would add one more in 1940.

6. It wasn't surprising that she was interested in the writer. Although he typically explored commercialism and its corrupting effects on the middle-class soul, in 1913 he wrote a book about a selfish socialite.

7. Constance Coolidge, "Diary," July 31, 1932.

8. Wells, *Postscript,* 190.

9. Coolidge, "Diary," Feb. 6, 1932.

10. Constance Coolidge to H. G. Wells, Dec. 23, 1945.

11. Coolidge, "Diary," Feb. 6, 1932.

12. Wells, *Postscript,* 191.

13. H. G. Wells, "Postscript," suppressed pages, Box 1, 246.

14. Coolidge, "Diary," Feb. 7, 1932.

15. Wells, "Postscript," suppressed pages, Box 1, 247.

16. HGW to CC, March 16, 1935, and May 25, 1935. He repeated his conversation with Moura to Constance by letter.

17. John Paterson so claimed in *Edwardians: London Life and Letters, 1901–1914* (Chicago: Ivan R. Dee, 1996).

18. David C. Smith, *H. G. Wells: Desperately Mortal, a Biography* (New Haven and London: Yale University Press, 1986), 196 and 364.

19. W. Somerset Maugham, "Some Novelists I Have Known" (from *The Vagrant Mind*), in *Mr. Maugham Himself* (Garden City: Doubleday & Co., 1954), 456.

20. Wells, *Postscript,* 67.

21. Maugham, "Some Novelists," 456.

22. Ibid.

23. Ibid.

24. Ibid.

25. Charles Chaplin, *My Autobiography* (New York: Simon and Schuster, 1964), 360.

26. Norman and Jeanne MacKenzie, *The Life of H. G. Wells: The Time Traveller* (London: The Hogarth Press, 1987), 387.

27. Ibid.

28. OK to MCW, Jan. 3, 1930.

29. Ibid. Odette called HG any number of names derived from Lou Pidou—and some not nearly as charming.

30. Beatrice Potter Webb, *The Diary of Beatrice Webb,* vol. 3, ed. Norman MacKenzie and Jeanne MacKenzie (Cambridge: Harvard University Press, 1984), 124. The Fabian Society was an organization founded in England in 1883 to promote democratic socialism. George Bernard Shaw and Beatrice and Sidney Webb founded the group, which included primarily middle-class intellectuals.

31. Wells, *Postscript,* 68.

32. According to Carl Rollyson in his biography, *Rebecca West: A Life* (New York: Scribner, 1996).

33. Smith, *Desperately Mortal,* 364.

34. As reported by Rollyson.

35. *Sunday Telegraph,* June 17, 1973, as reported by Michael Foot in *H. G.: The History of Mr. Wells* (Washington, D.C.: Counterpoint, 1995), 305.

36. Smith, *Desperately Mortal,* 361.

37. MacKenzies, *Life,* 387, 388.

38. Ibid., 460.

39. Ibid., 459.

40. Wells, *Postscript,* 69, 80, 74, 79.

41. Ibid., 88.

42. Ibid., 95, 96.

43. Ibid., 104. The Frau went back to Austria "very reluctantly," HG wrote, after he rebuffed her, but she returned to his apartment wearing only a raincoat and shoes, and demanded that either he love her or she would kill herself. When his back was turned, as the story goes, she sliced her wrists and armpits with a razorblade. HG sent her to the hospital and arranged with Lord Beaverbrook and Lord Rothermere that there would be a two-week embargo on news dealing with H. G. Wells. HG noted in the *Postscript* that her love for him "evaporated" and that she later married and flourished.

44. Wells, *Postscript,* 125.

45. Ibid., 190.

46. MacKenzies, *Life,* 459.

47. See Ted Morgan, *Maugham* (New York: Simon and Schuster, 1980), 330.

48. Ibid., 331.

49. See Steffen-Fluhr, Nancy. "Paper Tiger: Women and H. G. Wells." *Science Fiction Studies* 12 (1985): 311–329, footnote 21.

50. Patricia Stubbs, *Women and Fiction: Feminism and the Novel,* 1880–1920 (New York: Harper and Row Publishers, 1979), 191. The essay is titled "Mr. Wells's Sexual Utopia."

51. RL to author, Nov. 17, 1997.

52. Maugham, "Some Novelists," 459.

53. Ibid., 457. Smith suggests this is a symptom of diabetes, which HG developed.

54. Foot, *History of Mr. Wells,* 55.

55. Quoted on a BBC interview, date of broadcast unknown.

56. Sieveking, *Eye,* 226.

57. *Evening Standard,* June 17, 1973, as reported by Foot in *History of Mr. Wells,* 306.

58. A comment, like the first one of this paragraph, that was made during a BBC radio interview, date of broadcast unknown.

59. Smith, *Desperately Mortal*, 363.

60. H. G. Wells, *Experiment in Autobiography: Discoveries and Conclusions of a Very Ordinary Brain (Since 1866)*. New York: Macmillan, 1934, 20.

61. The sustaining theme of the book was "the development and consolidation of my *persona*, as a devotee, albeit consciously weak and insufficient, to the evocation of a Socialist World-State" (*Postscript*, 55).

62. Wells, *Experiment*, 348.

63. Ibid., 13.

64. Wells, *Postscript*, 55.

65. Wells, *Anatomy of Frustration*, 227–230.

66. Wells, *Postscript*, 113.

67. Ibid., 56.

68. Steffen-Fluhr, "Paper Tiger," 316.

69. Smith, *Desperately Mortal*, 181.

70. Wells, *Postscript*, 61.

71. Ibid., 17.

72. Wells, "Postscript," suppressed pages, Box 1, 158.

73. As it was published in 1984, the *Postscript* includes a prologue, which is HG's preface to *The Book of Catherine Wells*, and two long chapters. Chapter the First, titled, "On Loves and the Lover-Shadow," has ten parts devoted to the Lover-Shadow, HG's major lovers, and the shadow of age and of suicide; Chapter the Second, "The Last Phase," has a summary chapter of HG's activities from 1935 to 1942, and three short miscellaneous chapters on HG's death, the plan for publication of the *Postscript* and free will.

74. Wells, *Experiment*, 705.

75. Gip Wells, *Postscript*, 16.

76. Ibid.

77. In his 1988 *Slavic Review* review of HG's *Postscript* and Anthony West's biography of H. G. Wells, the Slavic scholar Mikhail Agursky identified HG's guides this way: Andreychin was a former Wobbly (member of the Industrial Workers of the World) of Bulgarian origin who had served as an interpreter during the meeting between Averell Harriman and Trotsky in 1926. "This alone demonstrates Andreychin's GPU affiliation." Constantin Umansky, HG's interpreter, later was Soviet ambassador to the United States.

78. Wells, *Postscript*, 185.

79. Ibid., 185.

80. Ibid., 187, 188.

81. There were other problems for the heirs cum editors. The manuscript papers were heavily edited and there were many versions: Three typescripts—a Top Copy, a "Carbon A" copy, and a "Carbon B" copy—as well as another mass of papers, six boxes in all, including folder upon folder of "discarded" and "rejected" pages. Except for the spans of clean typewritten copy, much of this work in manuscript was sheer hell to read because of HG's sight-defying, loopy, and "spidery" script.

82. MacKenzies, *Life,* 457. They held to the first notion.

83. Foot, *History of Mr. Wells,* 244.

84. Wells, *Postscript,* 235. In a footnote after "*****[the five asterisks stand for M.A.R.T.H.A.] won't mind," Gip added, "She did."

85. Wells, "Postscript," suppressed pages, Box 6, Folder 2, WIL-A-ii, Y. 1; and Box 6, Folder 5, WIL-E, 273.

86. As it was described by the H. G. Wells Society's bibliography.

87. In addition to the love letters, the withheld Wells archive includes photographs and memorabilia, holograph manuscripts, letters to family and friends, and 3,500 letters from publishers, translators, and editors.

88. MG to GPW, April 26, 1983.

89. Odette Keun, "H. G. Wells the Player," *Time and Tide* 15, no. 43 (October 27, 1934): 1346–1348.

Chapter 2

1. H. G. Wells, *Anatomy of Frustration: A Modern Synthesis* (London: The Cresset Press) was published in 1936, and described by the H. G. Wells Society as "the author's interview with himself." The form of the discursive work was borrowed from Robert Burton's *Anatomy of Melancholy,* published in 1621. It was presented as a medical treatise and dealt with the human condition, including various mental states.

2. H. G. Wells, *Experiment in Autobiography: Discoveries and Conclusions of a Very Ordinary Brain (Since 1866)* (New York: Macmillan, 1934), 21, 24.

3. Ibid., 50, 51.

4. Ibid., 27, 28.

5. Ibid., 28.

6. Historian Michael Foot (*H. G.: The History of Mr. Wells* [Washington, D.C.: Counterpoint, 1995]) described HG's ill-matched parents as a wayward father and a repressed mother.

7. Wells, *Experiment,* 50.

8. Ibid., 53

9. Ibid.

10. The Crystal Palace, designed by Sir Joseph Paxton, was built in Hyde Park, London, for the Great Exhibition in 1851. The structure was a significant example of nineteenth-century proto-modern architecture.

11. Ibid., 57.

12. Ibid., 62.

13. Ibid., 159.

14. H. G. Wells, "Thomas Henry Huxley." BBC broadcast, October 4, 1935. Published in the BBC publication *Listener* 15, no. 352 (October 9, 1935): 593–595.

15. Wells, *Experiment,* 267.

16. Foot, *History of Mr. Wells,* 22.

17. Wells, *Experiment*, 352.

18. Ibid., 352, 353.

19. Ibid., 353.

20. Ibid., 353, 354.

21. Ibid., 362.

22. Ibid., 357.

23. Ibid.

24. For an undisclosed reason, HG didn't want the Woolf's to know that he was one of the contributors to the fund for them.

25. As the H. G. Wells Society has described the book.

26. As he said in a BBC interview, date unknown.

27. Wells, *Experiment*, 358.

28. Wells, *Postscript*, 53.

29. Wells, *Experiment*, 389, 390.

30. Ibid., 360. Isabel died well before HG, quite suddenly in September 1931.

31. Ibid., 362, 363.

32. Ibid., 389.

33. Wells, *Postscript*, 25.

34. Jane Wells (Amy Catherine), "The Beautiful House," in *The Book of Catherine Wells* (London: Chatto and Windus, 1928), 69.

35. Wells, *Postscript*, 33.

36. The anecdotes appear in Ralph G. Martin's *Jennie: The Life of Lady Randolph Churchill* (New York: Signet, 1971), 245, and originally in William Pett Ridge's *I Like to Remember* (London: Hodder and Stoughton, n.d.).

37. Cornelia Otis Skinner and Emily Kimbrough, *Our Hearts Were Young and Gay* (New York: Dodd, Mead & Co., 1942), 115, 116.

38. As told during a BBC interview, date unknown.

39. Wells, *Postscript*, 28.

40. Ibid., 35.

41. HGW to CA, Sunday, May 15, 1927.

42. She was born on July 8, 1872.

43. Wells, *Postscript*, 47.

44. Janet Dunbar, *Mrs. G.B.S.: A Portrait* (New York: Harper & Row, 1963), 258, 259.

45. *Times* (London), 8 October 1927.

46. Beatrice Potter Webb, *The Diary of Beatrice Webb*, vol. 3, ed. Norman and Jeanne MacKenzie (Cambridge: Harvard University Press, 1984), 98, 99.

47. Ibid., 98.

48. The children formed their "nursery" in April 1906.

49. Webb, *Diary*, vol. 3, 120, 121. HG's novel to which Beatrice refers, *In the Days of the Comet,* published in 1906, deals with a revolution in men's attitudes brought about by the effects of the gas of a passing comet.

50. According to HG, Rosamund's mother was her governess, Miss Hoatson. Others see her as the daughter of Bland and Edith Nesbit.

51. Webb, *Diary*, vol. 3, 121.

52. Ibid.

53. Ibid., 121, 122.

54. Ibid., 122.

55. Ibid., 122, 123.

56. Ibid., 123, 124.

57. Ibid., 124.

58. Ibid., 132.

59. As reported by Norman and Jeanne MacKenzie, *The Life of H. G. Wells: The Time Traveller* (London: The Hogarth Press, 1987), 256.

60. Webb, *Diary*, vol. 3, 133.

61. Ibid., 138. In 1911, Beatrice Webb told her diary that Amber appeared to be settling down and had made her mind up to "play straight." Meanwhile, in November 1920, Beatrice noted that she and her husband were reconciled to H. G. Wells. "He is fat and prosperous and immensely self-congratulatory; towards us he was affable, but suspicion lurked in his eye and I doubt whether he is really friendly." While she didn't desire to renew the friendship with Wells, she considered herself "too near the end of life to keep up a vendetta with any human being. Also I have never ceased to respect his work, and his History is a gallant achievement. I have still the feeling that in sex relations he is unclean" (November 29, 371).

62. As Priestley said during a BBC radio interview, date unknown.

63. AR to HGW, April 26, 1930.

64. The 921-page work was a comprehensive account of economic life, with chapters on work and leisure, government and commerce, communication, education, and the influence of women. *Work* was conceived as the third part of an educational trilogy, which included *The Outline of History: Being a Plain History of Life and Mankind* (Garden City: Doubleday & Co., 1949) in 1920, and *The Science of Life* (London: Amalgamated Press, 1930), the latter with Julian Huxley and Gip Wells as collaborators.

65. AR to HGW., Feb. 23, 1930.

66. Amber kept her hand in publishing. In 1934, she turned out *The Nationalisation of Banking*, and in 1935, *The New Propaganda*. She told HG that she was working on a piece called *Ethics for Atheists*. In the late 1920s, Amber wrote a letter to HG telling him that she was working on—probably meaning that she was editing—a variety of topics, including trench warfare, ship parts, and "gentlemen trying to persuade a gracious lady to let them make love to her on dunes." She also mentioned that she was helping to "work out a scheme for reorganising what is left of British industry," and was discussing the plan with Philip Snowden. In the 1930s, she wrote to HG that she was trying hard to "get taken for a currency expert" and that the *Daily Herald* printed her articles two months out

of date. In addition, she taught at Cambridge and lectured, including to the Fabian Society.

67. Wells, *Postscript*, 83.

68. Amber also was the model for another strong Wells female character, Isabel Rivers, in *The New Machiavelli*.

69. Wells, *Ann Veronica*, ed. Sylvia Hardy (London, Vermont: Everyman, 1993), 257, 258.

70. Winston and Clementine Churchill, *Winston and Clementine: The Personal Letters of the Churchills*, ed. Mary Soames (Boston, New York: Houghton Mifflin Co., 1998), 32, 33.

71. Ibid., 34.

72. Sieveking, *Eye*, 225.

73. A. J. is often interpreted as A for Amber Reeves, and J for Jane Wells, although it very well could have meant Annajane.

74. Sylvia Hardy, introduction to *Ann Veronica*, by H. G. Wells (London, Vermont: Everyman, 1993), xxxviii. Hardy noted that Victorian and Edwardian novels "abound in heroines who offend against the sexual moral code, but they all come to a bad end."

75. Wells, *Experiment*, 395.

76. Patricia Stubbs, *Women and Fiction: Feminism and the Novel, 1880–1920* (New York: Harper and Row, 1979), xiv.

77. Ibid., 183.

78. Ibid., 184.

79. Hardy, introduction to *Ann Veronica*, xxxiii, xl.

80. As reported in Michael Korda's memoir, *Another Life: A Memoir of Other People* (Random House, 2000), 319.

81. MacKenzies, *Life of H. G. Wells*, 248.

82. AR to HGW, Aug. 24, 1939.

83. In *Black Lamb*, Rebecca West grappled with life and politics in the Balkans. Rollyson also proclaimed her novel, *The Return of the Soldier*, one of the defining works of World War I. "Her biography of St. Augustine is a penetrating study of the religious mind and what she calls the first modern man. Her reports on the Nuremberg trials in *A Train of Powder* and on traitors in *The Meaning of Treason* are modern classics, and she practically invented the form of the nonfiction novel in *Black Lamb and Grey Falcon*. Historian, biographer, novelist, critic, and journalist—Rebecca West's versatility is astonishing." Carl Rollyson, *Rebecca West: A Life* (New York: Scribner, 1996), 11.

84. For his part, Rollyson called H. G. a "sexual magnet" and "the most exciting man of his generation," *Rebecca West*, 39. Rollyson notes that in addition to his piercing blue eyes, short arms, shapeless torso, and tiny feet, HG had "a rather large penis," as reported to biographers Norman and Jeanne MacKenzie by several mistresses. Through interviews with one of Rebecca's physicians, Rollyson also learned about HG's preferences in lovemaking. He apparently was more adventurous than his young companion, Rebecca.

85. Quoted in Gordon Ray, *H. G. Wells & Rebecca West* (New Haven: Yale University Press, 1974), 21, 23.

86. H. G. Wells, "Postscript," suppressed pages, Box 1, 82.

87. Rollyson, *Rebecca West,* 65.

88. As quoted in Rollyson, *Rebecca West,* 57.

89. AW to GPW, undated [1947?]. Some eighty-five previously suppressed letters between the Wests and Wellses are collected in the University of Illinois H. G. Wells Collection's so-called "Closet Correspondence."

90. Wells, *Postscript,* 98.

91. OK to MCW, Jan. 15, 1932.

92. RW to MCW, Jan. 31, 1950.

93. Wells, *Postscript,* 97.

94. Between April 1920 and December 1922, she wrote fifty-five long reviews of 136 novels, by Rollyson's count.

95. Rollyson, *Rebecca West,* 84.

96. Wells, *Postscript,* 102.

97. Ibid., 103.

98. Ibid., 109.

99. Ibid., 110.

100. Wells, "Postscript," suppressed pages, Box 1, 112. At the end of his discourse of Rebecca West, HG gave two harmless examples of West's "queer flashes of a lurid inimitable wit." Suppressed from publication for obvious reasons was a third example of her wit: "In the days just following upon the war, Colonel Wedgwood presided over a conference in a committee room in the House of Commons, with a view to organising liberal opinion in Europe. Israel Zangwill after his fashion swamped the discussion with the peculiar grievances of the Chosen People. 'Mr. Chairman, would it be in order if I moved a Pogrom?' said Rebecca" (112).

101. RW to MCW, Aug. 21, 1946, as reported by Ray, *H. G. Wells & Rebecca West,* 193, 208.

102. DJ to RW, Aug. 29, 1949.

103. Ray's book, *H. G. Wells and Rebecca West,* published in 1974, has been described as a put-up job, whereby the author gained rare access to the subject and her archive in exchange for a highly subjective treatment. Norman and Jeanne MacKenzie described the book as "a curious volume." Patrick Parrinder wrote that every word of Ray's biographical study of West "was vetted by Rebecca West," in David Smith's *Correspondence of H. G. Wells* (London: Pickering & Chatto, 1998). In 1974, Ray sent Gip his typescript so that Gip could correct inaccuracies. On August 7, 1974, Rebecca said in a letter to Gip that while she did not always agree with Ray's interpretations of what she felt, she was "sure he wanted to get the facts dead right." A couple of weeks earlier in a letter to Gip, Rebecca said that Ray's book "would give proof that Heritage was a libel."

104. It is not known why the number of letters from HG fluctuates significantly between six hundred and eight hundred.

105. Anthony West, introduction to *Heritage* (New York: Washington Square Press, 1984).

106. Smith, *H. G. Wells,* 363.

107. MacKenzies, *Life of H. G. Wells,* 331. The person who so described her was D. M. Kennedy in *Birth Control in America.*

108. "The Squire," as she sometimes referred to him, died in June 1943.

109. HG drafted these words on a sheet of paper; the actual telegram has not survived.

110. MS to HGW, Oct. 14, 1941.

111. HG previously attacked the church in Phoenix, suggesting that England return to the Test Acts, which were abolished in 1829 and had prevented Catholics from holding public office. HG also wanted Catholics banned from the foreign and war offices, the diplomatic service, and key positions in education, according to Norman and Jeanne MacKenzie.

112. Leo Lehmann, the editor of the magazine *Converted Catholic* was to distribute *Crux.* Agora Publishing Co. would publish it. Margaret later wrote to Joseph Lewis, who was director of the U.S. Free Thought organization and former president of an international Thomas Paine Society, saying that with the plan she hoped to "at least subject leading publicists and editors in this country to what diabolical plans the Roman Catholic hierarchy are making for the subjugation of our people and the curtailment of freethinking in America. We should unite together on this as a Holy Crusade."

113. MS to HGW, May 23, 1944.

114. Ibid., Sept. 19, 1944.

115. Wells, *Postscript,* 65, 66.

116. MS to HGW, Aug. 14, 1946.

117. Wells, *Postscript,* 116.

118. Ibid., 119.

119. Ibid., 123. The OGPU was the Soviet Union's political intelligence service. *Sous Lenine* was translated into English under the title *My Adventures in Bolshevik Russia.*

120. These facts and the following collected by Monique Reintjes, a Dutch woman who has written a biography of Keun, *Odette Keun* (The Netherlands: Self-Published, 2000).

121. This is Reintje's position.

122. Wells, *Postscript,* 125, 126.

123. Ibid., 129.

124. Ibid., 135.

125. Ibid., 136.

126. Gustav Stresemann was a German politician, chancellor in 1923, and until his death later that year, minister of foreign affairs.

127. Wells, *Postscript,* 141.

128. Ibid., 138.

129. Ibid., 139.

130. HGW to CA, Nov. 18, 1931.

131. Wells, *Postscript,* 132.

132. Wells, *Experiment,* 634.

133. Ibid.

134. Wells, "Postscript," Appendix, suppressed pages, File K–75, W2–2–30b, c and d, 187b/188–187c.

135. OK to HGW, April 10, 1936.

136. Wells, "Postscript," Appendix, suppressed pages, File K–75, W2–2–30d and e, 187c/190, 191.

137. Ibid., W2–2–30e, 191.

138. Ibid.

139. Ibid., W2–2–30a and b, 187a, 187b.

140. Ibid., W2–2–30e and f, 191, 187e/192.

141. David Smith's description.

142. HGW to WH, Aug. 10, 1933.

143. OK to HGW, Dec. 9, 1936.

144. David Smith has suggested that the letters circulating that summer may be the same letters that been offered and withdrawn from sale on several occasions, and which are said to be in Florence, Italy, and "juicy." He says he has never seen said letters and doesn't know anyone who has.

145. Odette Keun, "H. G. Wells the Player," *Time and Tide* 15, nos. 41–43 (October 27, 1934): 1348.

146. Odette Keun, *I Discover the English* (London: John Lane, 1934), 186–201.

147. Wells, "Postscript," Appendix, suppressed pages, File K–75, W2–2–29b, 71.

148. Ibid.

149. Wells, *Postscript,* 160, 161.

Chapter 3

1. H. G. Wells, *Russia in the Shadows* (New York: George H. Doran Co., 1921), 16, 17, 64.

2. H. G. Wells, *H. G. Wells in Love: Postscript to an Experiment in Autobiography,* ed. G. P. Wells (Boston: Little, Brown and Co., 1984), 163, 164.

3. Wells, *Russia,* 174.

4. This according to HG's own report, although others claimed he stayed only a weekend at Gorky's.

5. Wells, *Postscript,* 164.

6. Anthony West, *H. G. Wells: Aspects of a Life* (New York: Random House, 1984), 73.

7. Ultimately, World Literature would bring out some two hundred titles before it shut down in 1924.

8. Antonina Vallentin, *H. G. Wells: Prophet of Our Day* (New York: John Day Co., 1950), 255.

9. Ibid., 255, 256. Perhaps it was not as it seemed. Foot wrote that Harold Nicolson, who attended the talk, later reported to his wife that "one simply could not hear a word. Not a single word. It was rather a disaster" (Michael Foot, *H. G.: The History of Mr. Wells* [Washington, D.C.: Counterpoint, 1995], 221).

10. Wells, *Postscript,* 109, 110.

11. Ibid., 141.

12. Ibid., 167.

13. Ibid., 176.

14. Ibid., 162.

15. *Histoire de la Baronne Boudberg* (Presses Pocket, 1991) by Nina Berberova was published in 1988 and later in 1991, translated by Michel Niquex. The original Russian edition was published in 1981. For *Shadow Lovers,* this author translated Berberova's French into English.

16. Berberova, *Histoire,* 12.

17. It is conceivable that Moura and Peter's father, "Klop" Ustinov, a Russian-German by birth, worked together in covert information-gathering. For several decades Klop served as an informant and an agent runner, recruited by the MI 5. See Stephen Dorril's *MI6: Inside the Covert World of Her Majesty's Secret Intelligence Service* (New York: The Free Press, 2000).

18. Berberova, Histoire., 220.

19. A. West, *Aspects,* 147.

20. Wells, *Postscript,* 227.

21. Tania Alexander, *A Little of All These* (London: Jonathan Cape Ltd., 1987), 146, 148. Alexander's book purports to be "a tribute to the people who lived at Kallijärv, and the spirit which it embodied in the midst of those troubled times" (p. xviii). Oddly enough, Tania Alexander's life would mirror her mother's in several ways. Like her mother, she worked for a publishing firm, translated books, and became involved with the theater—primarily as an advisor. Unlike Moura, she personally raised her three children. At her Oxfordshire home in England, Tania tried to re-create something of the big family, stimulating atmosphere of Kallijärv, she claimed at the end of her book.

22. Alexander, *Little of All,* 146.

23. Interview with author, October 30, 1997. Spence, author of a 1991 biography of Boris Savinkov, has finished a biography of the master spy, indeed, the "Ace of Spies," Sidney Reilly: *Trust No One: The Secret World of Sidney Reilly* (Forthcoming, Feral House).

24. Two BBC documentaries were made: John Mossman's in 1970 and Lovat Dickson's in 1978 or thereabouts.

25. Kathleen Tynan, "The Astonishing History of Moura Budberg—A Flame for Famous Men," *Vogue* (October 1, 1970): 162, 208, 209–211.

26. Her letter was written on April 18. Moura later claimed that Djon, her husband, was murdered on April 19, and her daughter said that he was murdered on April 18.

27. Peters also had concurrent ties with British intelligence, including Scotland Yard.

28. Also called the Vecheka, the All-Russian Extraordinary Commission for Combating Counter-Revolution and Sabotage was set up by the Council of People's Commissars in December 1917, following the Bolshevik's October coup d'état.

29. R. H. Bruce Lockhart, *Retreat from Glory* (New York: G. P. Putnam's Sons, 1934), 222.

30. Several restrictions would be placed on her. Moura was told that a detective would be detailed to her, she would be authorized a stay of only two months, and she could not see any of her acquaintances. She should change her name, get lost in the provinces, or, better yet, marry an Estonian. It was this lawyer who turned matchmaker and brought Moura and Lai Budberg together.

31. Wells, *Postscript*, 164.

32. Alexander, *Little of All*, 148, 153.

33. Ibid., 152.

34. Ibid., 150.

35. Dated November 7, 1918, the memo focused on his activities and the internal situation in Russia. Lockhart concluded that the strength of the Bolshevist movement should not be underestimated. He offered three plans for Allied intervention. His third plan—to intervene immediately, to strengthen their forces in Siberia and in the north, to secure the elimination of Turkey from the war, and to send an expeditionary force through the Black Sea to join General Alexief and march immediately on Moscow to "strike a blow at the very heart of Bolshevism."

36. As Russian historian Gail Owen points out in correspondence with the author, September 12, 2000.

37. In 1929, he started an eight-year hiatus "nailed"—his word—to his desk in London as chief diary writer for the *Evening Standard*. Lockhart devoted the last period of his life to writing books, anonymous gossip columns, and lecturing, and, when possible, fishing. Shortly after the war, Lockhart was posted as commercial secretary to the British legation in Prague. Later, he traveled throughout Central Europe for a subsidiary of the Bank of England, at the same time reporting for the foreign office and contributing stories to London newspapers, including Lord (Max) Beaverbrook's. In September 1939, Lockhart joined the Political Intelligence Department, where he dealt with Central Europe and Balkan issues. He was named director-general of the Political Warfare Executive (PWE), where he gathered intelligence and coordinated British propaganda against the enemy. At the end of his official career in the PWE, he was seen as a weak and ineffective toady, Owen points out.

38. R. H. Bruce Lockhart, *Memoirs of a British Agent* (London: Macmillan, 1985), 243, 244.

39. Alexander, *Little of All*, 148.

40. Lockhart, *Retreat*, 5.

41. R. H. Bruce Lockhart, *The Diaries of Sir Robert Bruce Lockhart,* vol. 1, ed. Kenneth Young (New York: St. Martin's Press, 1973); and *The Diaries of Sir Robert Bruce Lockhart,* vol. 2, ed. Kenneth Young (London: Macmillan, 1980).

42. Lockhart, *Diaries,* 1:156.

43. Robin Lockhart to author, November 17, 1997.

44. Berberova, *Histoire,* 11, 12.

45. Mikhail Agursky, Review of *H. G. Wells in Love: Postscript to an Experiment in Autobiography,* by H. G. Wells, ed. G. P. Wells; and *H. G. Wells: Aspects of a Life,* by Anthony West, *Slavic Review* 47, no. 2 (summer 1988): 329, 330.

46. Buchanan wrote several memoirs of Russia.

47. Meriel Buchanan, *Ambassador's Daughter* (London: Cassell & Co. Ltd, 1958), 170.

48. Meriel Buchanan, *Petrograd: The City of Trouble, 1914–1918* (London: W. Collins Sons, 1919), 239.

49. Miriam's mother, who was American, remarried a Russian named Artsimovich. Miriam's boyfriend at the time was Bobby Yonin, whom Moura described as a rabid Bolshevik.

50. Buchanan, *Ambassador's Daughter,* 143.

51. In *British Agent,* Lockhart claimed that they met at a birthday luncheon Moura threw for Cromie. Robin Lockhart, Bruce Lockhart's son, claimed that it was another acquaintance, Captain George Hill—code name I.K. 8 in Britain's SIS (and British agent Sidney Reilly's good friend)—who introduced his father to Moura. In a letter written in mid-September of that year, Moura told Lockhart that she had given Allen Wardwell, the head of the American Red Cross, part of Garstin's manuscript for safe transport to England. Although she never identified it, the manuscript may have been the one that resulted in the posthumously published book, *The Shilling Soldiers,* a collection of war sketches. Garstin was the author of *Friendly Russia* (1915). H. G. Wells wrote the foreword.

52. Great Britain, Foreign Office, FO 371/3335, file 153174. Thanks to the courageous efforts of the Dutch minister, W. E. Oudendijk, Cromie was carried to the British church, wrapped in the Danish flag, placed in a zinc coffin, and sent back to England. According to Richard H. Ullman, author of *Anglo-Soviet Relations, 1917–1921: Intervention and the War,* vol. 1, (Princeton: Princeton University Press, 1961), 289, Oudendijk rallied the other neutral diplomats still left in Petrograd to give Cromie what effectively was a state funeral.

53. As Gorky told Stefan Zweig. The letter is found in Andrew Barratt and Barry P. Scherr, eds., *Maksim Gorky: Selected Letters* (Oxford: Clarendon Press, 1997), 248.

54. Ibid., 318.

55. Wells, *Postscript,* 186.

56. Ibid., 162.

57. Ibid., 197.

58. In Smith's index under the name Budberg, there are twenty-two page citations for a six-hundred-page book. In West's, sixteen pages for a four-hundred-page book. The MacKenzies discussed Moura on fourteen pages of their nearly

five-hundred-page book (and only eight pages in the earlier 1973 edition). Foot beats them all with thirty-three pages of citations for Moura in his three-hundred-page book.

59. Foot, *History of Mr. Wells,* ix, 187, 261, 262.

60. A. West, *Aspects,* 147.

61. These qualities according to Michael Korda in his *Charmed Lives: A Family Romance* (New York: Random House, 1979).

62. Lockhart, *Diaries,* 2:348.

63. Michael Korda floated the first claim in *Charmed Lives* (p. 215), and Berberova, the second, in *Histoire* (p. 14), which she got from Harold Nicolson's *Journal.* Nicolson was an old and good friend of Lockhart's, parliamentary secretary to the minister of information, and author.

64. Alexander, *Little of All,* 148.

65. Wells, *Postscript,* 165, 166.

66. Alexander, *Little of All,* 151.

67. Alexander claimed that her mother was born in 1893; Berberova said it was 1892. This author accepts the 1892 date.

68. Horrified by France's management of the case, and eager for the jury trial system to appear in Russia—one of his ambitions—Zakrevsky took a fatal step. He wrote an inflammatory letter to the London *Times,* which published it. Alexander wrote that it was considered improper for a Russian senator to interfere openly in French internal politics when relations between France and Russia were so sensitive. Zakrevsky also reportedly attended a secret meeting in Paris at the home of Emile Zola, the purpose of which was to find a way to force a retrial for Dreyfus. Word got around, complaints were made through diplomatic channels, and Zakrevsky was forced to resign. "His career as one of Russia's leading lawyers was shattered," Alexander wrote (*Little of All,* 28).

69. It isn't known when they moved from their Ukraine estate to St. Petersburg.

70. Russian Masonry basically adhered to the "Scottish Rite" branch and was closely linked to French Masonry. Perhaps there was another reason why Moura was educated in this way; or perhaps this explanation of her education was a cover for other arrangements.

71. Djon entered diplomatic service in the Ministry of Foreign Affairs in 1908, and that year was appointed chamberlain to the court of the Czar in St. Petersburg and also a Privy Councilor. Alexander noted that her father was "a brave and fearless man."

72. Several writers, including Berberova and Kenneth Young, claim that Moura and Djon met when Djon was posted to the Russian embassy in London. The Russian Ministry of Foreign Affairs *Yearbook* and the *Almanach de Gotha* place Djon at the Russian embassy in Berlin from 1910 to 1913, not to 1914.

73. Berberova argues that at most, Moura spent a winter at Newnham College in Cambridge, and that Moura and Djon met in London during this time. Alexander says this "is pure fantasy; [she] was never at Cambridge and my father

was at the embassy in Berlin at the time." Michael Foot *(History of Mr. Wells)* agrees with Alexander. "[Moura] had never been educated at Newnham, never been to England." Rache Lovat Dickson claimed that Moura had been at Cambridge for a year before her marriage to Djon, when Djon was posted at the Russian embassy in London. For the record, Newnham has no records showing that a Marie or Moura Zakrevsky ever attended Cambridge on either a short- or long-term basis.

74. David Smith confuses Djon with Count Benckendorff, and in so doing claims that Moura married Djon when he was the Russian ambassador to England. Djon never was an ambassador; his relative, Count Alexander Benckendorff, was the Russian ambassador to London from 1903 until his death in 1917. Lockhart *Diaries* editor Kenneth Young makes much the same mistake. In the first volume, he has Moura marrying Djon Benckendorff in 1911, when he was at the Russian embassy in London. He also claims that Moura divorced Budberg a year after she married him; she probably did that in 1926, not 1922. In a 1998 book about Western secret services, historian Gordon Brook-Shepherd falls into the same trap. He writes in *Iron Maze: The Western Secret Services and the Bolsheviks* (London: Macmillan, 1998) that Marie Zakrveskaia "made a brilliant match in 1922 when she married Count von Benckendorff, then the Tsarist ambassador in London." Dickson's biography seems to be the origin for several of the myths and/or mistakes about Moura, including the story about her Cambridge schooling. It is possible that he heard it directly from Moura.

75. Meriel Buchanan writes in *Ambassador's Daughter* that she and Miriam Artsimovich took first aid courses together and worked in several hospitals side by side, but she never mentioned that Moura did the same. Berberova claimed that Moura took advanced first aid courses and became a "sister of charity" in a military hospital, but no evidence of those activities has been found.

76. Lockhart married his first wife, Jean Haslewood Turner, in 1913. He had several romances during the marriage, Moura being only one of them. His infidelities were the major source of trouble between the Lockharts, who divorced in 1938. Lockhart had a long-term affair with the Countess of Rosslyn, which broke up after they tried living together. His second wife was his wartime secretary, Mollie Beck.

77. Kaplan was officially acquitted of the charge by a Russian court. The case is officially open.

78. For reasons unknown, Moura's letters to Lockhart end in May 1919, and except for one letter in October of that year, they do not begin again until June 1921.

79. Alexander, *Little of All,* 159.

80. Ibid., 67.

81. Aleksander Aleksandrovich Mosolov, a Guards officer at the Imperial Court, and close to the Czar. He was connected to the same circles as the spy Sidney Reilly, and was reputedly corrupt.

82. Before the Revolution, Chukovsky had been a translator at the British embassy—"an interpreter at the Front to Col. Thornhill [British military attaché]," as Moura put it in a letter to Lockhart.

83. MB to BL, Dec. 28, 1918. Perhaps Moura's list was ultimately the basis for the list of titles Gorky intended to publish in his *World Literature* project. Just following her visit, Gorky wrote to Lenin that they would soon finish printing the list of books to be published by World Literature, and that it wouldn't be a bad idea to have these lists translated into all European languages and distributed in Europe and the Scandinavian countries, "so that not only the Western proletariat but also the A. Frances, the Wells's, and the various Scheidemanns can see for themselves not only that the Russian proletariat is not barbaric, but also that it understands internationalism far more extensively than they do, even if they are cultured people, and that even in the vilest conditions one could possibly imagine, our proletariat has been able to achieve in a single year what they should have got done long ago." Barratt and Scherr, *Maksim Gorky,* 205.

84. MB to BL, Feb. 18, 1919. Gabriele D'Annunzio (1863–1938) was an Italian writer and political adventurer.

85. Maxim Gorki, *Fragments from My Diary,* trans. Moura Budberg (New York: Praeger Publishers, 1972), vii, x, xii.

86. Baring dedicated his book, *Mainsprings of Russia*, published in 1914, to HG in the hope that at least one reader would understand it.

87. Foot, *History of Mr. Wells,* 236, 260, respectively.

88. Berberova, *Histoire,* 308.

89. Wells, *Postscript,* 162.

90. Ibid., 168.

91. The Italian's name was Ruffino.

92. Berberova, *Histoire,* 190, 191.

93. Wells, *Postscript,* 168.

94. MB to HGW, Feb. 10, 1923; March 18, 1923; Oct. 11, 1922 or 1923.

95. HGW to MB, Jan. 3, 1938; Oct. 12, 1940; Dec. 5, 1940.

96. Ibid., July 22, 1944. In many of HG's late letters to Moura, one is reminded of John Mortimer's fictional characters Horace Rumpole of the Bailey and his wife, "She Who Must Be Obeyed."

97. Romain Rolland won the Nobel Prize for literature in 1916. He was a good friend and business associate of Gorky's. Hansen is not known.

98. That novel, published in 1924, chronicles Wells's era as it is seen in a dream more than 2,000 years later, the reverse of his *A Modern Utopia* (London: Chapman & Hall, 1905). H. G. Wells Society, *H. G. Wells: A Comprehensive Bibliography* (Edgware, England: Michael Katanka Ltd., 1966) 26.

99. MB to HGW, Oct. 22, 1940. All her references were to HG's works. *Kipps* was released in 1941. *Babes in the Darkling Wood* and *Ararat* were published in 1940. Frederic Warburg and Roger Senhouse owned the publishing house Secker

& Warburg. *All Aboard* was published in 1940. *Kipps,* the film, came out in 1941, *Babes in the Darkling Wood* in 1940.

100. Ibid., May 20, 1927.

101. Ibid., Sept. 27, 1929.

102. Ibid., July 29, 1921.

103. Ibid., May 20, 1927.

104. Ibid., July 28, 1928. The book, subtitled *Blue Prints for a World Revolution,* proposed Wells's matured theory of world revolution through "functional elites" (H. G. Wells Society, 30).

105. Ibid., June 26, 1931.

106. Ibid., July, 1921.

107. HGW to MB., Dec. 5, 1940.

108. Ibid., Jan. 12, 1937.

109. Ibid., March 17, 1942. Later called the "Declaration of Human Rights" and the "Declaration of the Rights of Man." Discussed in Chapter 5.

110. Ibid., Nov. 4, 1932. Copies of the letter were also to be sent to Mrs. B. White, Lady Rhondda, Mrs. Laski, and Miss Voysey. The enclosed papers were "Strategy of Progressive World Effort" and "The Common Objectives of Progressive World Effort," both later incorporated into "There Should Be a Common Creed for Left Parties Throughout All the World."

111. MB to HGW, Feb. 22, 1925.

112. Ibid., April 19, 1928.

113. Ibid., Sept. 14, 1928.

114. Ibid., Oct. 4, 1928?

115. Ibid., Oct. 22, [1925?].

116. Ibid., Oct. 12, 1922.

117. Ibid., June 26, 1931.

118. Wells, *Experiment,* 692.

119. Ibid., 692.

120. Ibid., 692, 693.

121. Ibid., 693.

122. Barratt and Scherr, *Maksim Gorky,* 365. Gorky held a meeting at his apartment in 1932 that Stalin attended. Perhaps that was where and when Stalin and Moura met. It was at that meeting that Stalin supposedly uttered his famous comment about writers being "engineers of human souls." Gorky uses the Russian spelling for Moura's real name, Maria.

123. Ibid., 367, 368.

124. April 28, 1921. Richard Spence, scholar of Russian history, notes that Klishko was connected with the Cheka. Meanwhile, the Russian Trade Delegation, later ARCOS, was regarded by Sir Basil Thomson and others in British intelligence as a hotbed of Bolshevik propaganda and sedition. According to Spence, "It was." It is doubtful that HG knew any of that. Interview with author. October 1, 2001.

125. Barratt and Scherr, *Gorky,* 82.

126. Ivan Rakitsky was an artist living in the Gorky colony. Peter Kriuchkov was Gorky's personal secretary.

127. Alexander, *Little of All*, 12.

128. Ibid., 149.

129. Alexander did give Kira's married name, Clegg.

130. Alexander, *Little of All*, 120.

131. H. G. Wells, "Postscript," suppressed pages, Box 1, 197.

132. Wells, *Postscript*, 143.

133. One also wonders if, assuming she had an abortion, two weeks would have allowed her enough time to "do everything all over again."

134. HGW to CA, April 29, 1934. Sibyl was probably Lady Sibyl Colefax, a friend. She helped HG decorate his flat at Hanover Terrace.

135. HGW to MB, Sept. 26, 1940. The *City of Benares*, with civilians and children aboard, was sunk by the Germans. Halperin is not known, although in her letters to Lockhart, Moura speaks of a Halperin—"a Jew that was conseiller judique to the Embassy, who I saw at the Norwegian Consulate" (Nov. 27, 1919).

136. *Guilty Men* by Frank Owen, about World War II, published in 1940.

137. HG to MB, Oct. 19, 1940. Vanderbilt's winter home, Lou Sueil, was not far from Monaco.

138. Of the 125 letters HG wrote to Moura, Constance, and Martha, only two speak disparagingly of Jews. HG was for restoring Palestine to the Jews as early as 1916.

139. H. G. Wells, *The Anatomy of Frustration* (London: The Cresset Press, 1936), 181.

140. HG to MB, Oct. 12, 1940.

141. The British Museum catalog shows thirty-seven entries identified as works translated by Moura Budberg. Slightly more than half were translated from Russian to English, the others from French to English. Six were translations of Gorky's works. Other Russians Moura translated include Chekov, Turgenev, and Catherine the Great and a book of Russian fairy tales. As for other nationalities, Moura translated DeGaulle's diaries, Simenon's detective novels, and biographies of Franz Liszt and H. G. Wells.

142. Alexander, *Little of All*, 157.

143. MB to HGW, Sept. and Oct. 1940.

144. Interview with author, November 24, 1997.

145. Perhaps this also was the genesis of her alleged covert business with Germany.

146. A. West, *Aspects*, 74.

147. Ibid., 144. West's statement is party confirmed by Aleksei Tolstoy, who in a 1935 letter (recipient unknown) wrote about Moura's visit to Gorky at that time; Agursky, book reviews, 329, 330.

148. NKVD, the People's Commisariate for Internal Affairs, predecessor of the KGB.

149. A. West, *Aspects*, 144.

150. Ibid., 145.

151. West does note in one place that he had verbal communication with Moura and Gip. Gip may very well have been his primary source on this matter.

152. *Little of All*, 154, 155.

153. Ibid., 150.

154. Ibid., 157.

155. Foot, *History of Mr. Wells*, 126.

156. David Smith, interview with author, January 18, 2000.

157. He died prematurely and of unknown causes in January of 1913 in Berlin.

158. General Alexander von Benckendorff (1781–1844) was made the first Count Benckendorff in 1832, and served as chief of police under Czar Nicholas I. Count Alexander Benckendorff (1849–1917) was Russian ambassador to the Court of St. James for fourteen years.

159. Micky (Margaret) Wilson had an affair with Gonne's father. Destitute and unable to raise the illegitimate child that resulted, she signed on to govern the Zakrevsky brood in the Ukraine, mothering two generations over fifty-six years. In 1892, Father Zakrevsky was on an unexplained trip to London when he met up with Maud Gonne and hired Micky. Alexander described it as "semi-official," whatever that meant. In the spring of 1888, when she was twenty-one, Maud Gonne carried secret documents to Czar Alexander III in St. Petersburg that could help forge a Franco-Russian alliance, and thus weaken England. Perhaps this is where she first met Zakrevsky. With Yeats, whom she met in 1889, Gonne worked for nationalist politics, instigating anti-British riots and developing a revolutionary movement.

160. Northcliffe, Alfred Charles William Harmsworth, the first Viscount (1865–1922).

161. As he detailed in his eleven-page letter to Northcliffe on July 17, 1918, HG prepared a memorandum on the Allied claims their "propaganda was to subserve," and conducted several investigations that led to expert reports, a summary of the scientific, technical, and industrial situation in Germany, and an account of the hardships of U-boat crews.

162. HG also befriended some suspicious characters, including Michael Lykiardopoulos, the manager of the Moscow Arts Theatre, whom he met in Moscow in 1914. During World War I, Lyki, a master translator and linguist, also ran the British embassy's propaganda department in Moscow, under Lockhart's supervision. HG also knew the questionable Ivan Maisky, a Menshevik who joined the Bolsheviks in 1921 and then turned to statesmanship, and Maurice Baring, an ubiquitous Russian diplomat, writer, and officer in the Royal Flying Corps.

163. MB to BL, July 1918.

164. Ibid., May 1918.

165. Ibid., Jan. 25, 1919.

166. The caches at the Hoover and the Lilly libraries contain some 185 letters from Moura to Lockhart, and 16 letters from Lockhart to Moura—all unpublished. They run from 1918 to 1959.

167. MB to BL, Dec. 14, 1918.

168. One blunder: A Russian secretary, N. Visanosova, had been assigned to an intelligence officer named Terence Keyes.

169. According to Spence, "Crooked Neck" was Aleksandr Vasilievich Krivoshein, "grand Pooh-Bah of the tsarist regime, senator, finance minister, and arch-reactionary." Krivoshein appears to have led a group that engaged in negotiations with certain Germans in Moscow when he learned that a German military coup d'état against the Bolsheviks was planned for June 21, 1918. A hitch developed over the conditions the Germans placed on the Russians: They were to sever relations with the Allies, but if they could not do that, Germany would "feel obliged to occupy Moscow and the adjacent territory, acting on her own." (Richard Spence, interview with author, February 9, 2000.) In another message, Krivoshein was identified as "Mirbach's man for civil dictator." (Papers of David R. Francis, the U.S. ambassador to Russia, 1916–1918.)

170. The right wing of the Socialist Revolutionaries, the most widely supported of the populist organizations in the twenty years prior to the overthrow of the Czar. Savinkov was a Socialist Revolutionary terrorist, writer, assistant minister of war under Kerensky in 1917, and later a prominent anti-Bolshevik.

171. So, too, has Stephen Koch. In his 1994 book *Double Lives: Spies and Writers in the Secret Soviet War of Ideas Against the West,* Koch devotes several pages to Moura, most of the material based on Berberova's book. Moura was one of two "Ladies of the Kremlin" who was "guided by the Soviet Services. Exactly what the Baroness Budberg's connection to the Soviets may have been remains mysterious, though its importance cannot be doubted," 21.

172. Gail Owen, "Budberg, the Soviets and Reilly," 1988. Primary sources for his work, which is unpublished, include Naval Intelligence and War Office files from the U.S. Archives. Richard B. Spence is the author of *Boris Savinkov: Renegade on the Left* (Boulder: East European Monographs, 1991) and of many articles about intelligence in twentieth-century Russia.

173. Owen, "Budberg," 5, 6. Owen observed that Moura's father "undoubtedly collaborated with the tsarist regime's department of police and probably its political-intelligence arm, the Okhrana," and that her first husband may have been involved with intelligence. Other "likely recipients of Budberg's hospitality," in addition to Cromie, Garstin, and Hicks, were Reilly and Somerset Maugham, both MI 1c, as well as the staff of the British Propaganda Office in Petrograd under Hugh Walpole and Thornhill. Most of these men "veered increasingly toward subversion. Several—notably Hicks, Garstin, Cromie, and Reilly—became active participants in Britain's 1918 undercover efforts to topple Lenin's regime."

174. Ibid., 2.

175. His name is also given as Sigmund Georgievich. In the marriage registration document for Sigmund Georgjevich Rosenblum and Margaret Thomas, dated August 22, 1898, Reilly is described as a twenty-five-year-old consulting chemist from Chancery Lane (making his birthdate in 1873 or 1874). His father, Grigory Jakovlevich Rosenblum, was listed as a landed proprietor. Margaret, twenty-four, was identified as a widow from Paddington; her deceased father, Edward Reilly Callahan, had been a captain in the navy.

176. His arrival was not without difficulty. Apparantly, he was arrested by representatives of the British navy upon entry in Murmansk. The authorities thought his passport dubious, among other things. He was released after he signaled an intelligence officer that he was carrying codes used by MI 6.

177. Lockhart, *British Agent*, 277.

178. Owen, "Budberg," 7. Lockhart was sent home from Russia in 1917 for complaints about his womanizing. He was originally posted as vice-consul to Moscow in 1913.

179. Ibid., 7–8.

180. George Hill was a daring British agent, closely aligned with Reilly. Lockhart called him "Flying Corps Hill." MID, Military Intelligence Department.

181. According to Spence (interview by author, November 3, 1997). Cromie and Reilly were intimately linked in the Lettish Plot and in abortive plans to scuttle the Russian fleet. Cromie was killed shortly after he and Reilly had had a meeting, and just after Reilly had discovered that the security of the plot had been blown. Spence theorizes that Reilly set up Cromie, who had become something of a loose cannon, to be "killed in order to eliminate an unreliable and far too knowledgeable link in the chain. Cromie knew all about Reilly's links to Bolshevik officials."

182. Owen, "Budberg," 9. Owen points out that Alexander's scenario doesn't explain Moura's mysterious layovers in Petrograd, "nor their highly coincidental timing relative to Reilly's countermeasures against the Cheka" (21).

183. As Spence suggested in conversation with the author on October 30, 1997.

184. At some point, Reilly gave Lockhart a silver box to commemorate their work together. The engraving reads: "To R.H. Bruce Lockhart H.B.M.'s Representative in Russia in 1918 (during the Bolshevik Régime) in remembrance of events in Moscow in August & September of that year from his faithful Lieutenant Sidney Reilly."

185. From 1918 to 1922, Owen claims, the Soviet régime "garnered not quite half of all its revenues—admitted and secret—from confiscated property and just over one-third from *valiuta* per se; but they disclosed no more than one ruble in five of such dubious income" (Owen, "Budberg," 14).

186. Owen, "Budberg," 4. Yagoda's real name was Hershel Yaguda.

187. Interview with Owen, November 1997.

188. Robin Lockhart, *The First Man* (New York: Penguin Books, 1987), 58, 59.

189. Robin Lockhart to author, November 17, 1997.

190. Perhaps it was a German journalist, Hans Rudolph Berndorff, who in 1930 wrote a book about the German underworld. In his chapter on Reilly, as Spence notes, Berndorff explored the central question of the spy's death and disappearance, using information from the defector Opperput. Another possible source might have been N. N. Alekseev, a Russian émigré journalist who in 1932 was investigating Reilly, and was firmly convinced that he was alive. Interview with author, October 28, 2000.

191. A Reilly file in the Lockhart papers at the Hoover Institution contains several interesting documents, including a letter from Brigadier General E. L. Spears to Bruce Lockhart. In the letter of January 2, 1967, Spears says that he always thought Reilly returned to Russia in 1925 to search for a valuable collection of coins and Napoleonic relics and because he wanted to get in touch with Boris Savinkov. Reilly's last wife (common-law), Pepita Bobadilla, initiated her own investigation—as best she could—to discover the circumstances of Reilly's death. She unsuccessfully beseeched the *Times* (London) to publish a letter, and she wrote to Winston Churchill. Churchill's response on December 22, 1927, via his secretary, was not much help. He challenged her position as "complete misapprehension. Your husband did not go into Russia at the request of any British official, but he went there on his own private affairs. Mr. Churchill much regrets that he is unable to help you in regard to this matter, because according to the latest reports which have been made public Mr. Reilly met his death in Moscow after his arrest there."

192. There was much fanfare and disappointment over the Public Record Office's 1997–1998 declassification of some MI 5 files. Nothing on operations or part-time "adjunct" government employees was released. Meanwhile, the CIA has refused all the author's requests for information about Moura Budberg; on the basis of national security, it has denied all the author's appeals while steadfastly neither confirming nor denying the existence or nonexistence of such files (CIA to author, June 17, 1997). All the subsequent appeals made on behalf of the author, including efforts by two U.S. senators, were also denied.

193. *Trud* is a daily newspaper published in Moscow and begun in 1921. Articles appear on January 31 and February 7, 1997. They were sent in response to this author's query for information. None of the documents mentioned in the articles was identified.

194. Proponents of this scenario include Orlando Figes, *A People's Tragedy: A History of the Russian Revolution* (New York: Viking Penguin Books, 1997), 822.

195. Barry P. Scherr, interview with author, November 8, 1998.

196. Berberova said she heard the story from Boris Nikolaevsky, a Russian emigré professor and author.

197. Yet it is conceivable that she left the archives with Lockhart in England.

198. Barry P. Scherr, interview with author, November 13, 1998.

199. Agursky, book reviews, 329–330.

200. As Barratt and Scherr have stated in *Maksim Gorky*.

201. HG was in the South of France from mid-March to early April, resting and trying to win back Lou Pidou. He was out of town from May 9 to May 11, spending time with his son Frank, and family, in Digswell. When he arrived back in London, he holed up at the Reform Club until his household had been moved to Hanover Terrace. Moura evidently took these opportunities to go to France, then on to Russia.

202. The malaise occurred at the same time the mysterious messenger supposedly visited Moura.

203. As reported in the summer 1988 issue of *Slavic Review.* Agursky claimed that by the time Aragon reached Gorky, the police had surrounded his house; Gorky died the next day.

204. Wells, *Postscript,* 214. The OGPU was the political intelligence service, previously called the GPU.

205. Alexander, *Little of All,* 127, 128.

206. Oddly, Lockhart apparently didn't see Moura again until March 12, 1937.

207. F.O. 371/3332, file 91788, 155–158.

208. A reference to a related document, "Vidz. 65 parliamentary," has been weeded, buried, or lost.

209. Spence observed that this confirmed what seemed apparent elsewhere: That while Reilly and Hill cultivated—perhaps even diverted—Cromie, "Cromie was not a part of their SIS team." He also noted that Cromie reported his concerns to Admiral Hall, not to Mansfield Cumming, the head of the Secret Service, nor to the DMI. Also, Hall sent his complaint to the foreign office, which nominally oversaw MI 1c/SIS operations at the time. "This certainly adds a bit of color to two episodes: Moura's introduction to Lockhart by SIS operatives, and Cromie's subsequent 'liquidation.'" Owen also noted in correspondence: "That Cromie worked for Naval Intelligence and not the SIS is further confirmed by a good description of his primary objective in 1918—keeping Russian vessels out of German hands—in the semi-official history of the Royal Navy in the period."

210. British Foreign Office, Correspondence with Russia, F.O. 371/3330, file 84714, 313–315. An unnamed Petrograd informant told Cromie that at the Smolny Institute there was a large office of primarily German cipher code experts led by a German professor. All messages, outgoing and incoming, reportedly were first deciphered before being sent or delivered.

211. Interview with author, June 26, 1998.

212. Moura's comments to Lockhart about having been seen walking around Moscow in the company of Germans comes to mind. The branch of the Reich Main Security Office that held the file on Moura was the foreign branch of the Security Service concerned with Russia and the Far East.

213. To date, only one-fourth of the documents have been shipped back to France. They are kept at SHAT, the Historical Service of the French Army, based at the Château de Vincennes. The Deuxième Bureau, which is fed by the Service de Renseignements (the French Secret Service) and counterespionage, gathers

and interprets intelligence for the French High Command. Collectively, they are known as the Special Services (Ronald Seth, *Encyclopedia of Espionage* (Garden City: Doubleday & Co., 1972). In 1940, after the Fall of France, the Germans took the Deuxième Bureau files to Berlin. Five years later, the Russian Red Army carted them off to Moscow, where they remained for fifty years, raked over and weeded. Then in the glow of glasnost, the Russians and the French negotiated a release of the material. But only a few months after the shipments began, they abruptly stopped. Boris Yeltsin's gracious sharing came under criticism, and he caved into it. This author was one of the first Western scholars to use the files.

214. Kusakov was an independent committee of Ukrainian exiles headed by a Colonel S. Kusakov. They were in a loose union with P. A. Boganov's Socialist Revolutionary splinter group in Estonia, the SR Committee of Pskov and Novgorod Provinces, according to Spence. (Interview with author, January 18, 1999).

215. Duff Cooper was a British war hero and statesman, once the First Lord of the Admiralty.

216. Jacob Peters wrote in his 1924 synopsis of the so-called Lockhart case that the Cheka had evidence, including documents, linking Moura to German espionage during the war. It isn't known whether Moura betrayed Peters at some point, provoking him to turn on her in 1924. Spence suggests that Peters's having mentioned Moura's German connection may have been intended to mask her (and his) "British connection."

217. Deuxième Bureau Documents Rapatriés, Dossier on Russian Personalities of Emigration Suspected of Informing the Soviets: Countess Benckendorff, Baron Budberg, Trilby Espenberg, 1921–1936, Carton 608, Dossier 3529.

218. The author may have been Princess Sasha Kropotkin, secretary to Karl Friedrich Nowak, who was Kaiser Wilhelm II's secretary. Sasha was the daughter of Prince Kropotkin, a Russian anarchist. In 1919, Moura wrote to Lockhart saying that she was taking the provisions she had obtained from the Danish Red Cross to the old and ailing prince. She was requested to do so by Sasha Lebedev—quite possibly one and the same Sasha Kropotkin.

219. Lockhart, *Diaries*, 1:302.

220. Leslie Howard, born Leslie Stainer, died in a plane crash on June 1, 1943; the plane was shot down by German aircraft off the coast of Portugal. Howard, a Hungarian by birth, participated in intelligence gathering with at least one British espionage organization, the Z Organization. In August 1933, Lockhart had a meeting, perhaps his first, with Howard. He wrote in his diary that Howard had strong ideas about how he should play the role, and these ideas conformed with Lockhart's. In July 1934, Lockhart again met up with Howard, this time at a luncheon given by Warner Bros. Howard told Lockhart that the first script was so bad that he nearly threw in the towel. "Now, however, the story is very much improved, although there is still one scene to which the Foreign Office may object. I took care to dissociate myself from the picture" (*Diaries*, 1:300).

221. Wells, "Postscript," suppressed pages, Box 1, 228-229.

222. Ibid., 252, 253. Graefenberg wrote *Prelude to the Past.*

223. HG to CA, May 20, 1934, aboard the Olympic.

224. Wells, "Postscript," suppressed pages, Box 6, Folder 5, WIL-E, 245.

225. MB to BL, November 5, 1918.

226. MB to HGW, May 27, 1921.

227. MB to BL, June 24, 1921.

228. Ibid., Jan. 6, 1923.

229. HGW to CA, Aug. 3, 1934.

230. CA to HGW, Aug. 3, 1934.

231. MB to BL, Dec. 19, 1934.

232. Ibid., Dec. 26, 1934.

233. HGW to CA, Jan. 14, 1935.

234. Wells, *Postscript*, 164.

235. Ibid., 111.

236. Ibid., 210.

237. A. West, *Aspects*, 146.

238. Lockhart, *Diaries*, 2:672 (August 26, 1948).

239. See *Colonel Z: The Secret Life of a Master of Spies* by Anthony Read and David Fisher (New York: Viking Penguin, 1985). The Z Organization was a separate autonomous intelligence service for Europe, which ran parallel to Great Britain's Secret Intelligence Service (MI 6). "Without Dansey none of Korda's successful films would have been possible," Read and Fisher write, since Korda and Robert Vansittart funded the studio with money from the SIS (177). In 1942, Korda was knighted for his secret service work for Great Britain. The author thanks Ian Axford for pointing out the Z connection.

Chapter 4

1. H. G. Wells, *H. G. Wells in Love: Postscript to an Experiment in Autobiography*, ed. G. P. Wells (Boston: Little, Brown and Co., 1984), 190.

2. She would own several of them in succession.

3. Pekin, as Beijing then was called.

4. Constance Coolidge, "Diary," April 3 and 4, 1932.

5. As one of very few descendants, Constance was heir to several large estates over her lifetime. CFA was a second father to her.

6. He was the son of John Quincy Adams and Fanny C. Crowninshield. Cousin Charlie was in charge of Harvard's capital funds for thirty years; under his administration, they increased from $15 million to nearly $100 million.

7. *Boston Globe*, week of June 4–10, 1891.

8. Interview with author, November 16, 1995.

9. Coolidge, "Diary," July 16, 1938.

10. H. G. Wells, "Postscript," suppressed pages, Box 1, 228 (240).

11. Daisy was a brilliant socialite much in demand. She was the beautiful and chic daughter of a French duke and an American heiress, the latter of the Singer

sewing machine company. Working as a fashion editor at *Harper's Bazaar,* Daisy reportedly earned $10,000 a year.

12. H. G. Wells, *H. G. Wells in Love: Postscript to an Experiment in Autobiography,* ed. G. P. Wells (Boston: Little, Brown and Co., 1984), 190.

13. David Coolidge to Dobbs, Feb. 18, 1905, written from Canton Avenue in Mattapau, Mass.

14. Constance had decided to keep a series of "private diaries" the year before, in 1904. Her idea was to "write in them all my privat thoughts and in fact write down all that I say and feel." She began writing poetry at this age, and noted in 1905 that "I am going to write a book. I must and shall write a book. I have two plots already." She started that book several times throughout her life, but her contemporaries consistently praised her for her letters. She wrote a story titled "The Moon in the Room," but it hasn't yet surfaced. Constance thought it "rather good, if slightly sweet." She submitted several articles to magazines, but none was accepted.

15. The dates indicate that David Coolidge was in military service when his wife took up with Isaac Norris.

16. Mrs. David Coolidge was born Oct. 25, 1835, and died March 5, 1923.

17. She dated very few of them.

18. Constance had her own health problems—with her menstrual cycle. Her "troubles," as she called them, were so bad that she spent several days a month in bed, even through her late forties. Presumably, she suffered from endometriosis. In her late teens, she underwent some kind of an operation in England, and for most of her adult life she assumed that she was infertile. In her late forties, she apparently became pregnant, but miscarried. In 1930, Constance feared incorrectly that she had contracted syphilis. She rarely discussed babies and children, either in her letters or her diary. Motherhood and child-rearing did not appear to be an issue or interest for her. No longing or regret ever appeared in writing.

19. Atherton would serve brilliantly—with General Leonard Wood in the Philippines, in the State Department at Washington, D.C., and in Athens, before being posted to London in 1924.

20. Nancy Field was the widow of Henry Field, sister-in-law of Marshall Field, and niece of Waldorf Astor. The third woman was Alexandra Emery.

21. CC to Granny, April 1918.

22. Wells, "Postscript," suppressed pages, Box 1, 241. That man would have been a British lad named Eric Brenan, although he preceded her to the United States. It isn't known whether he actually shot himself. There is no record of that in the correspondence.

23. Co-ownership in the stable was the beginning of a long tradition for Constance. Over the course of her life she would co-own a good deal of property— from horses and stables to houses. It became standard operating procedure.

24. Peitaiho, now called Beidaihe, is east of Beijing and on the coast. It was and is a summer resort for government employees, the rich, and the resident foreign population.

25. His close friends and Wallis called him David, not Edward.

26. Atherton's *New York Times* obituary on March 14, 1959, led with his role as the first U.S. ambassador to Canada. For two years, from 1937 to 1939, he was minister to Bulgaria. His next post was minister to Denmark. Following the occupation of Denmark by Germany in 1940, Atherton was named acting chief of the division of European affairs in the State Department. On Aug. 3, 1943, he was appointed minister to Canada, and in November that year, his rank was changed to ambassador. Atherton left the Ottawa post five years later. He next served as an alternate U.S. delegate to the U.N. General Assembly, which met in September 1948.

27. Caresse Crosby, *The Passionate Years* (New York: The Dial Press, 1953), 112.

28. Harry Crosby, *Shadows of the Sun: The Diaries of Harry Crosby,* ed. Edward Germain (Santa Barbara, Ca.: Black Sparrow Press, 1977). Black Sun Press published the first, second, and third series of the diaries in 1928, 1929, and 1930, respectively.

29. C. Crosby, *Passionate Years,* 112. Constance was a Peabody at least by virtue of her aunt's having married one.

30. Polleen Peabody, Caresse's daughter, was less than charmed. She once described Constance as "the most selfish person" she had ever met.

31. C. Crosby, *Passionate Years,* 113.

32. From a poem by Edna St. Vincent Millay.

33. In his writings, Caresse was the Cramoisy Queen; Josephine Bigelow was the Fire Princess; Constance was the Lady of Golden Horse with the Diamond Eyes, the lost lady, the Star of the East, and the Queen of Pekin.

34. H. Crosby, *The Diaries,* 39.

35. Crosby's unpublished letters, poetry, short stories, and notebooks are at Brown University Library.

36. Wells, "Postscript," suppressed pages, Box 1, 229 (241).

37. CC to HC, Nov. 24, [1924?].

38. According to his friend, Malcolm Cowley, author of *Exile's Return.*

39. Wells, "Postscript," suppressed pages, Box 1, 229 (241).

40. Ibid.

41. Ibid., 230 (242).

42. CC to Caresse Crosby, Dec. 12, 1929.

43. Ibid., Dec. 13, 1929. On Jan. 31, 1932, Constance wrote in her diary after seeing Caresse: "Caresse has got much more assurance now & impressed me as being businesslike & efficent—two things I never thought she was. America has done her good. I am glad she is having such success with her printing." Some weeks later, she noted, "She is so sweet. I am very very fond of her, altho it has taken me years to appreciate what she really is, & get underneath all the rather flippant exterior. When Harry was there I never tried."

44. Wells, "Postscript," suppressed pages, Box 1, 228 (240).

45. Perhaps he was referring to the novel *They Shoot Horses Don't They,* by Horace McCoy.

46. His 1971 obituaries described him as a member of a pioneering Santa Barbara newspaper family—the son of Beatrice Fernald Rogers and the grandson of Judge Charles Fernald, a distinguished early California jurist. Like Felix, Eliot was adopted. He was born in Boston three months before Constance. He began with the *Morning Press* in 1926, and continued on with the consolidated *News and Press*. In 1945, he resigned as credit manager of the *News-Press*.

47. André Magnus gave them to a family friend after Constance's death.

48. Coolidge, "Diary," Oct. 21, 1932.

49. CC to HGW, July 1, 1935.

50. Interviews with author, October 1994. Bradlee's grandmother, Helen Suzette Crowninshield deGersdorff, was Constance's godmother.

51. Ben Bradlee, *Ben Bradlee: A Good Life* (New York: Simon & Schuster, 1995), 28.

52. Interview with author, October 1994.

53. Ibid.

54. The Closet Correspondence contains nineteen letters from Constance Coolidge to H. G. Wells, written between 1935 and 1945. Constance kept these and hundreds of other letters that friends, relatives, and lovers wrote to her throughout her long life. Upon his wife's death, André Magnus donated his wife's letters, including those from HG, to the Massachusetts Historical Society. He retained various diaries, albums, photographs, and other papers.

55. The address was 501 Samarkand Drive. The lovely house and its name plaque, affixed to the wall, still stand.

56. Coolidge, "Diary," Nov. 12, 1938.

57. HGW to CC, Oct. 7, 1935.

58. Sir James Hopwood Jeans was a mathematician, physicist, and astronomer.

59. HGW to CC, March 9, 1935.

60. HG published a short story, "The Man Who Could Work Miracles," in 1899, in a collection titled *Tales of Space and Time*. The film was released in 1936.

61. Wells, *Postscript*, 191.

62. HGW to CC, April 21, 1937.

63. Wells, *Postscript*, 190.

64. CC to HGW, March 5, 1935.

65. Wells, *Postscript*, 191.

66. Ibid.

67. As Constance noted in her diary for Nov. 23, 1932, Lymington—the ninth Earl of Portsmouth—"had been eating onions. It was too bad. 'I have loved you my dark lady for 6 years.' He said, 'Darling,' but he had been eating onions & perhaps just for that reason I just smiled. Poor Gerard. He is so nice, but somehow, I don't think I could like anyone with red hair & above all onions, altho I do like onions too when I eat them myself."

68. CC to HGW, March 30, 1936.

69. Aimee Semple McPherson was a controversial evangelist and early radio preacher, who settled in Los Angeles.

70. CC to HGW, [April?] 1936.

71. WSM to CC, Aug. 12, 1936.

72. Ibid., June 18, 1937.

73. Wells, "Postscript," suppressed pages, Box 1, 230 (242).

74. Ibid. Magnus told this author the same story.

75. Ibid. The double murder was in 1929, not 1930.

76. Probably *Miss Barrett's Elopement* by Carola Oman, about Elizabeth Barrett Browning.

77. CC to HGW, Aug. 7 or 8, 1935.

78. HGW to CC, Jan. 22, 1936.

79. CC to HGW, March 30, 1936.

80. He, Jane, and the children lived at Spade House in Sandgate, Kent, from 1900 to 1912. In 1912, they moved to Easton Glebe in Essex, but HG also kept an apartment in London. In 1924, he bought and lived periodically in Lou Bastidon near Grasse in the South of France, and later bought Lou Pidou, where he and Odette shared a roof. He sold Easton Glebe in 1930, three years after Jane died, and lived at 47 Chiltern Court, Clarence Gate, London (N.W. 1) from the summer of 1930 until his move to Hanover Terrace in June 1936.

81. Wells, "Postscript," suppressed pages, Box 6, Folder 5, WIL-E 2 and 3, 240 a.

82. HGW to CA, Aug. 6, 1935.

83. HGW to CC, March 18, 1936.

84. Wells, *Postscript,* 190.

85. Gachet did eventually let his Van Gogh paintings go, of course. He gave many to the Musée du Louvre in 1954, and many others in small groups through the 1950s. Paul Gachet *fils* died in 1962.

86. CC to HGW, July 1, 1935.

87. HGW to CC, Feb. 20, 1935, Aug. 26, 1937, Aug. 6, 1935, Oct. 7, 1935; CC to HGW, April 1935, late August/early Sept., 1935, Dec. 23, 1945.

88. HGW to CC, Jan. 22, 1936.

89. CC to HGW, April 6, 1935.

90. HGW to CC, Oct. 26, 1935.

91. CC to HGW, Feb. 22, 1935; HGW to CC, March 14, 1935, April 8, 1935.

92. CC to Caresse Crosby, July 22, 1936.

93. The article appeared on April 10, 1937, long after the December interview. On December 11, 1936, Edward VIII abdicated his throne "for the woman he loved." On April 27, 1937, the Simpsons were divorced, allowing Wallis and David to marry, which they did on June 3, 1937.

94. Since Constance was the only American quoted in the story, one suspects that she was the source of those comments. One also recalls her comments about Eliot Rogers.

95. Coolidge, "Diary," Jan. 7, 1938.

96. Ibid., Jan. 10, 1938.

97. Among her papers are a few notes from Baron James H. de Rothschild.

98. Perry and Kitty Brownlow, the duke of Windsor's long-term friends.

99. Anne was Anne Strotz, a good friend. Socially prominent, Anne was Mrs. Harold C. Strotz, mother of Jay Gould and well known in Los Angeles society. She died in mid-September, apparently having taken her own life. She was previously married to Jay Gould, grandson of the robber baron. In her diary, Constance wrote, "God bless you Anne dear. You were a beautiful person." Richard Crane became head of the China mission some months after Constance and Ray arrived there. Richard McCreery was an old friend of her father's, a racing enthusiast and close companion in the 1920s and 1930s in Paris.

100. After she finished the book, she wrote the author a long letter congratulating him. "I said I had not believed before that he had the depth or understanding to write such a book. He may not like that, but up to now I have always liked Mary—his wife—better. She seems more of a real person. I think Louis is rather shy by nature, & to cover it he assume a rather flippant manner. He spends a lot of time in the Ritz bar, but of course so did Proust."

101. CC to FF, Jan. 14, 1939.

102. Iles Brody wrote the book. He died in 1953.

103. Wells, "Postscript," suppressed pages, Box 3, 282.

104. CC to Caresse Crosby, Aug. 28, 1954.

105. Magnus was head of publicity for several French enterprises, including Volt Publicité, Télé-Poche, Paris-Jour, and Aigle Azur Press. He also directed various media outlets and projects.

106. The autobiography has not surfaced; nor have any of her writings and translations.

107. Tolstoy's daughter Mary translated the book into English and published it with Holt Rinehart in 1970.

108. Caresse married Bert (Selbert Young), sixteen years her junior, in 1937; they divorced a few years later.

109. Constance once told Caresse that she had borrowed this phrase from "Old Mr. Prince," whom she did not identify. A poem by Sarah Williams, in homage to the astronomer John Brashear, ends, "I have loved the stars too fondly to be fearful of the night." Thanks to astronomer James Kaler of the University of Illinois for the citation of the poem.

Chapter 5

1. MG to author, May 6, 1997.

2. Martha Gellhorn, *View from the Ground* (New York: Atlantic Monthly Press, 1988), 68.

3. Wells worked on the declaration of "fundamental and inalienable rights" from 1939 to 1944.

4. MG to JSP, May 28, 1931.

5. This according to Jacqueline Orsagh, in her "Critical Biography of Martha Gellhorn," a doctoral dissertation.

6. According to John F. Bauman and Thomas H. Coode in *In the Eye of the Great Depression* (DeKalb: Northern Illinois University Press, 1988). The other two pros were Martha Bensley Bruere and Robert Collyer Washburn. About Martha Gellhorn's work for Hopkins, they reported: "Not surprisingly, in her social sleuthing for Hopkins, Gellhorn leaned heavily on social-psychological explanations to interpret the morass of poverty entrapping industrial populations. Peculiarly, in her reports she frequently regarded poverty as symptomatic of a neurotic state characterized by incompetence and emotional lassitude. She dwelled on the chronic poverty which predestined its victims to perpetual indigency. However, in *The Troubles I've Seen* (New York: William Morrow, 1936), based on her FERA experience, she cast the plight of the unemployed in a more sympathetic mold and grappled more with the trauma of families demeaned by the necessity of living on relief. Of all the reporters, Martha Gellhorn most evoked in her reports the pallor and gloom of the Great Depression" (p. 27).

7. John F. Bauman and Thomas H. Coode, *In the Eye of the Great Depression: New Deal Reporters and the Agony of the American People* (DeKalb: Northern Illinois University Press, 1988), 28.

8. MG to MW, April 21, 1990.

9. Ibid., March 9, (1960s).

10. Ibid., Aug. 16, 1991.

11. In *View*, she admitted to having convinced a few "hesitant men," who were being cheated by a crooked contractor, to break the windows of the FERA office at night.

12. Joseph P. Lash, *Love, Eleanor: Eleanor Roosevelt and Her Friends* (New York: Doubleday, 1982), 217.

13. H. G. Wells, *H. G. Wells in Love: Postscript to an Experiment in Autobiography*, ed. G. P. Wells (Boston: Little, Brown and Co., 1984), 193.

14. See David C. Smith, *H. G. Wells: Desperately Mortal* (New Haven and London: Yale University Press, 1986), 309. America was the land of milk and honey for HG. His taxable income in the United States was $21,000 in 1933, $45,000 in 1934, and $29,000 in 1935, "despite the depression" (Norman MacKenzie and Jeanne MacKenzie, *The Life of H. G. Wells: The Time Traveller* [London: The Hogarth Press, 1987], 386).

15. H. G. Wells, "Postscript," suppressed pages, Box 1, 251-252.

16. Ibid., Box 6, Folder 5, WIL-E, 253.

17. Ibid., 269. Frederick Field's house was called Red Hill. In his book, *From Right to Left*, Frederick Vanderbilt Field recalled HG's visit (140).

18. Ibid., Box 1, 269–270.

19. In the suppressed pages of the *Postscript*, HG wrote that he "sketched a film for Paulette Goddard and talked to Charlie Chaplin about a production of *Mr. Polly* with him in the title role." However, left in *Postscript* was an exchange

between HG and Moura in which Moura jokes that she could play the fat woman in Chaplin's version of the film.

20. It ends on page 208.

21. Wells, "Postscript," suppressed pages, Box 3, 257–259. Lewishon was a member of one of New York's first Jewish families and very rich. Martha didn't marry Field, of course, but in 1940 married her first, some say second, husband, Ernest Hemingway. Her father, Dr. Gellhorn, died on January 25.

22. Ibid., Box 6, Folder 5, WIL-E, 264.

23. Ibid., Box 1, 279a.

24. Ibid., 281.

25. Interview with author, May 8, 1997.

26. MG to author, Nov. 12, 1996.

27. Ibid., Jan. 24, 1997.

28. Ibid., Nov. 12, 1996.

29. MG to HGW, Jan. 19, 1942.

30. MG to author, Nov. 12, 1996; MG to GPW, April 26, 1983.

31. Gellhorn, *View*, 68.

32. Ibid.

33. MG to GPW, April 26, 1983.

34. Kevin Kerrane, "Martha's Quest," *Salon* (March 12, 1998). Available: (www.salon.com/media/1998/03/12medias.html).

35. MG to VG, June 8, 1996: "The Correspondent," ed. Bill Buford, *The New Yorker* (June 22 and 29, 1998): 109. A series of letters were published in a long tribute article to Gellhorn after her death. Bill Buford, long-time fiction editor for the magazine, introduced and edited the letters. The article was titled "The Correspondent."

36. EH to MG, Sept. 5, 1942.

37. MG to JSP, Sept. 22, 1931.

38. MG to GPW, April 26, 1983.

39. Rollyson updated *Nothing* in 2001 with publication of *Beautiful Exile: The Life of Martha Gellhorn* (Aurum Press, 2001).

40. Caroline Moorehead's book will be published in 2002 or 2003. Julia Newman's documentary film *Into the Fire: Women in the Spanish Civil War,* was to be released in 2001.

41. Victoria Glendinning, "The Real Thing," *Vogue* (April 1988): 358.

42. Jacqueline Orsagh, "A Critical Biography of Martha Gellhorn" (Ph.D. diss., Michigan State University, 1977), iv. Orsagh traveled to London to meet Martha. Martha cooked her dinner, entrusted her with a personal scrapbook her mother had made for her, and went shopping with her to Harrods, where Martha bought a frying pan. Graduate student Angela Dorman had several interviews, a long correspondence, and apparently a good relationship with Gellhorn for more than a decade. This author also had several interviews and a lively correspondence.

43. John Braun, "Une Fidélité Difficile: The Early Life and Ideas of Bertrand de Jouvenel, 1903–1945" (Ph.D. diss., University of Waterloo, 1985), 8.

44. Pearl K. Bell, "On the Road," *The New Republic* (July 5, 1993): 37.

45. Orsagh, "A Critical Biography," 49.

46. MG to author, Jan. 24, 1997.

47. H. G. Wells, *The Anatomy of Frustration* (London: The Cresset Press, 1936), 262–263.

48. According to Rollyson.

49. Ibid.

50. According to Orsagh.

51. *New Republic* LIX, no. 766 (Aug. 7, 1929): 310–311. Eight months later, on April 30, 1930, she published a second short piece in the same magazine. "Toronto Express" was about the lifelessness of her fellow passengers, as the train was pulling out of New York City and heading for Albany, compared to the vitality of Europeans with whom she traveled by train.

52. Gellhorn, *View*, 66.

53. Ibid.

54. Although Rollyson discusses another "short stay" in 1930, from spring to fall.

55. MG to John Braun, Jan. 2, 1979.

56. MG to MW, May 25, 1991. She also chastised Wolff for giving "that shit Rollyson" an extra royalty. "I sent 4 pages to his publisher, listing simply factual untruths. Nobody worried." Earlier that year, she told Wolff that she was seriously considering writing an autobiography to counter Rollyson's book, which she described as being "full of falsehoods, plain untrue facts, as well as much malice" (Feb. 3, 1991). She had heard that Rollyson was working with Disney moguls to make a movie of her and Ernest's life together during the Spanish Civil War. "The thought makes me feel rising nausea," she told Milt Wolff on Aug. 16, 1991.

57. Braun, "Fidélité," 8.

58. Ibid.

59. Bertrand de Jouvenel, *Un Voyageur dans le Siècle* (Paris: Editions Robert Laffont, 1979), 97.

60. Ibid.

61. *Monde's* letterhead reads: Grand Journal Hebdomadaire International d'Information Littéraire, Artistique, Scientifique et Sociale. In 1928, it was headquartered on rue Montmartre.

62. BJ to HGW, July 3, 1934

63. Wells, *Postscript,* 194.

64. Wells, "Postscript," suppressed pages, Box 4, WIL-D, 233.

65. Ibid., Box 1, 264.

66. Ibid., Box 6, Folder 6, WIL-G, 261.

67. MG to VG, Sept. 22 and 29, 1987: "The Correspondent," 101.

68. Ibid., 102.

69. MG to GPW, Jan. 2, 1985.

70. The second and third letters request meetings with HG; in the sixth letter, Jouvenel spoke about his upcoming trip to America.

71. The main character in HG's novel, *The World of William Clissold.*

72. MG to author, Jan. 24, 1997. He did, to his great regret.

73. Smith, *Desperately Mortal*, 384.

74. Sinclair Lewis to the Swedish Academy, Sept. 8, 1931.

75. MG to GPW, late 1983 or early 1984.

76. MG to author, Jan. 24, 1997.

77. MG to HGW, Oct. 26, 1940.

78. Ibid., Oct. 6, 1942.

79. An American playwright and the son of a seaman, Lonsdale spent much of his life on ocean liners crossing the Atlantic.

80. HG's extant telegrams are handwritten drafts of what he or, more likely, one of his staff sent.

81. Stokes, the New York publisher, released Martha's first book, *What Mad Pursuit*, in 1934.

82. H. G. Wells's preface to *Trouble*.

83. MG to JSP, May 8 or 9, 1931.

84. MG to MW, March 9 [1960s].

85. According to Orsagh.

86. Her own publisher had apparently rejected it. Martha lost faith in the book, and shelved it—the only book manuscript she ever abandoned.

87. Martha Gellhorn, *The Face of War* (New York: Atlantic Monthly Press, 1988), 15.

88. MG to NS, Feb. 15, 1990: "The Correspondent," 105.

89. Orsagh, "A Critical Biography," 170, 171.

90. Ibid., 87.

91. Gellhorn, *The Face of War*, 16. The Madrid piece was titled, "Only the Shells Whine."

92. Edwin Rolfe, *The Lincoln Battalion: The Story of Americans Who Fought in Spain in the International Brigades* (New York: Random House, 1939), 70, 71.

93. Martha Gellhorn, "Memory," *London Review of Books* (December 12, 1996), 3.

94. MG to MW, Jan. 13, 1997.

95. MG to VG, Jan. 3, 1991: "The Correspondent," 105–106.

96. Wolff apparently lost that letter and scenario, and asked for Martha to repeat it in April of 1997. She told the same story, nearly verbatim: "The story you want to remember took place in the Lincoln Hotel, a freezing dump for correspondents in Paris which I reached after the invasion from the south. Capa always had a very cynical eye for EH. I had just been forced by some of the young and increasingly embarrassed soldiers of the US division, which EH rather believed he commanded. He had been abominable at dinner and I was beside myself because I didn't see how I could ever get rid of him. Capa was playing poker,

as usual, in another room and came in to see me around 2 am and found me in tears. He told me to stop crying and call the Ritz Hotel and ask for Mary Walsh and E would answer. 'He is a coward' so catching him in flagrente I could then ask for a divorce. I did that with Capa telling me exactly what to say, E snarling and calling me names. That's how I got a divorce. I knew nothing about Mary. E had refused the very idea of divorce; so Capa saved me. He always stuck with me though many deserted, for E made it a point that nobody could be a friend of mine and his also. Capa always treated E as a joke."

97. MG to MW, March 9, [1960s].

98. Martha Gellhorn, "Letter to a Dead Friend," [1993].

99. Bernice Kert, *The Hemingway Women* (New York: WW Norton & Co., 1983), 299.

100. As Orsagh has pointed out.

101. MG to MW, Aug. 16, 1991.

102. MG to HGW, Sunday, [Dec. 1?], 1940. From her earliest days with him, Martha called Hemingway by this name, his racist, and jabbing name for his mother.

103. EH to MG, June 1, 1942.

104. Orsagh, "A Critical Biography," 406.

105. Kenneth Lynn, *Hemingway* (New York: Fawcett Columbine, 1987), 503.

106. John Harlow, "Hemingway Charged U.S. to Run Spy Ring." *Sunday Times* (London), July 16, 2000.

107. As Orsagh has suggested.

108. Denis Brian, *The True Gen: An Intimate Portrait of Ernest Hemingway by Those Who Knew Him* (New York: Grove Press, 1988), 144.

109. Ibid. It is also quite possible that Martha never invoked Hemingway's name so as to prove her professional independence from him.

110. MG to AB, Oct. 20, 1984.

111. MG to MW, Dec. 6, 1984.

112. Hemingway's Western Union style of letter writing, and his idiosyncratic spelling, grammar, punctuation, and syntax are retained throughout this chapter without notations. In general, he substituted o's for a's (hove for have), added h's after vowels and before consonants (caht for cat), and added e's before gerund endings (haveing for having). He called his children "childies," and his cats "cotsies."

113. EH to MG, Sept. 2, 1942. Hemingway probably didn't send this letter. In his letter of Sept. 2, he wrote: "After got your two letters from Antigua sat up till two a.m. writing sad and bitter letter to you on account of what you wrote about the Finca. But no good send such letter so won't."

114. EH to MG, March 16, 1943.

115. MG to HG, Oct. 26, 1940.

116. MG to JF, July 3, 1986: "The Correspondent," 99.

117. MG to VG, Sept. 30, 1987. "The Correspondent," 101.

118. MG to HGW, March 26, 1936.

119. The article, "The Lord Will Provide for England," was published Sept. 17, 1938.

120. MG to HGW, Oct. 6, 1942.

121. Ibid., June 9, 1943

122. Ibid.

123. HGW to MG, July 1, 1943. *The World of Yesterday* was published in 1943, the year after the Austrian-born poet, playwright, and biographical essayist killed himself.

124. Hemingway would never forgive her for neutering the cats without his knowledge or consent. She publicly maintained that she had decided to have the cats neutered to prevent inbreeding and deformity.

125. EH to MG, June 17, 1943.

126. Smith, *Desperately Mortal*, 433. The Rights were: Right to Life, Protection of Minors, Duty to the Community, Right to Knowledge, Freedom of Thought and Worship, Right to Work, Right in Personal Property, Freedom of Movement, Personal Liberty, Freedom from Violence, and Right of Law Making. See Smith for a more detailed discussion of the history of the original document.

127. Corday assassinated French revolutionary leader Jean Paul Marat.

128. Smith, *Desperately Mortal*, 84. According to Smith, HG's work on atomic energy was not broadcast until after Hiroshima and Nagasaki.

129. MG to JF, July 3, 1986: "The Correspondent," 99.

130. An American who expatriated to France, Boyle published *Death of a Man* in 1936.

131. Welty, a Pulitzer Prize-winning author from Mississippi, was born in 1909, the year before Martha. Algren was raised in the slums of Chicago; he wrote gritty novels that criticized the system and examined poverty.

132. Arlen was a Bulgarian-born novelist of fashionable London life, best known for his best-seller, *The Green Hat*.

133. EH to MG, June 14, 1943.

134. MG to HGW, Jan. 19, 1942.

135. These lines appear in Hemingway's *The Snows of Kilimanjaro*.

136. Hadley Hemingway's son with Ernest, named John (called Jack, and when he was a baby, Bumby), was born in October 1923; Patrick and Gregory, sons of Pauline and Ernest, were born June 1928 and November 1931, respectively.

137. Carl Rollyson, *Nothing Ever Happens to the Brave: The Story of Martha Gellhorn* (New York: St. Martin's Press, 1990), 195.

138. Ibid., 198.

139. Orsagh, "A Critical Biography," 176.

140. EH to Patrick Hemingway, Sept. 15, 1944, *Ernest Hemingway: Selected Letters, 1917–1961*, ed. Carlos Baker (New York, Charles Scribner's Sons, 1981), 571.

141. EH to MG, Aug. 5, 1946. Mary Welsh and Ernest Hemingway married March 14, 1946, in Cuba.

142. These were all titles to Martha's novels.

143. EH to MG, Aug. 5, 1946.

144. Cowles was an American correspondent whose reporting career parallelled Gellhorn's. Cowles's war reminiscences appear in *Looking for Trouble*, published in 1941. The two journalists had a long and cordial friendship.

145. Rollyson, *Nothing*, 218.

146. Hemingway, *Across the River*, 195.

147. Jeffrey Meyers, *Hemingway: A Biography* (New York: Harper & Row Publishers, 1985), 356.

148. Ibid.

149. Rollyson, *Nothing*, 261.

150. SM to author, Sept. 8, 2000. Sandy Matthews's name is William Alexander ("Sandy") P. Matthews.

151. Rollyson claimed that President Kennedy used his influence to obtain U.S. citizenship for Sandy, aged twelve at the time.

152. MG to JF, Sept. 28, 1986: "The Correspondent," 100.

153. SM to author, September 8, 2000.

154. T. S. Matthews, *Name and Address: An Autobiography* (New York: Simon and Schuster, 1960), 302.

155. MG to MW, March 9, [1960s].

156. According to Rollyson, *Nothing*, 288.

157. MG to JF, Jan. 26, 1990: "The Correspondent," 105.

158. Bill Buford, ed., "The Correspondent," 98.

159. Interview with author summer 1998. Nelson is a professor of English at the University of Illinois.

160. MG to JF, Oct. 27, 1989: "The Correspondent," 104.

161. MG to VG, June 8, 1996: "The Correspondent," 109.

162. Ibid., Feb. 2, 1992: "The Correspondent," 107, 108.

163. MG to author, Nov. 12, 1996.

164. Author's interview with Gellhorn, August 7, 1997.

165. MG to author, Jan. 24, 1997.

166. Ibid., May 6, 1997. There is no evidence that Moura was forced to move for financial reasons, nor any proof of Martha's devotion to Moura.

167. Ibid., Jan. 24, 1997.

168. Author's interview with Gellhorn, August 7, 1997.

169. MG to VG, Sept. 30, 1987: "The Correspondent," 101.

170. This is the title of a collection of Gellhorn stories, published in 1941.

171. MG to MW, May 11, 1991.

172. Eleanor Roosevelt, *Eleanor Roosevelt's My Day: Her Acclaimed Columns, 1936–1945*, ed. Rochelle Chadakoff (New York: Pharos Books, 1989), 163.

173. Brian, *True Gen*, 177.

174. Martha Gellhorn, *Travels with Myself and Another* (New York: Dodd, Mead & Co., 1978), 65.

175. Rollyson, *Nothing*, 322.

176. Glendinning, "Real Thing," 359.

177. According to Rollyson.

178. MG to Gary Fisketjon, June 13, 1988: "The Correspondent," 104.

179. As Rollyson suggests.

180. MG to GPW, late 1983 or early 1984.

181. MG to MW, Feb. 3, 1991.

182. Ibid., May 9, 1990.

183. Peter Kurth, Letters to the Editor, *Salon* (March 17, 1998). Available: (www.salon.com/letters/1998/03/17letters.html).

184. Bill Buford, ed., "The Correspondent," *The New Yorker* (June 22–29, 1998), 96–98.

185. MG to MW, June 10, 1997.

Chapter 6

1. H. G. Wells, "Postscript," suppressed pages, Box 1, 263.

2. H. G. Wells, *H. G. Wells in Love: Postscript to an Experiment in Autobiography*, ed. G. P. Wells (Boston: Little, Brown and Co., 1984), 61.

3. Ibid., 200–202.

4. Ibid., 200.

5. Ibid., 60–61.

6. Ibid., 197.

7. Ibid.

8. OK to JW, Jan. 1, probably 1924.

9. Wells, "Postscript," suppressed pages, Box 6, Folder 5, WIL-E, 245.

10. Ibid., Box 6, Folder 6, WIL-G, 261.

11. Ibid., 264.

12. Wells, *Postscript,* 229.

13. Wells, "Postscript," suppressed pages, Box 6, Folder 6, WIL-G, 269, 270.

14. Ibid., 270.

15. Ibid., 270, 271.

16. This was from HG's talk on "Man's Heritage," broadcast Jan. 15, 1943, on the BBC's program *Reshaping Man's Heritage: Biology in the Service of Man;* it was the lead talk in a two-month series. *The Listener* published the talk as the lead story in its Jan. 21, 1943, issue.

17. MCW to CA, Aug. 17, 1946.

18. Sieveking, *Eye,* 227.

19. R. H. Bruce Lockhart, *The Diaries of Sir Robert Bruce Lockhart,* vol. 2, ed. Kenneth Young (New York: St. Martin's Press, 1973), entry for Aug. 26, 1948, 672.

20. Ibid., 324. Most likely Sibyl Colefax.

21. H. G. Wells, *The Anatomy of Frustration* (London: The Cresset Press, 1936), 261.

Sources

Key to Sources, Including Photographs

AG   Archives de la Guerre, Vincennes, France
AM   André Magnus, Paris, France
Au   Author (Andrea Lynn)
BC   Bernard Croza, Mons-en-Laonnois, France
BL   British Library
BN   Bibliotèque Nationale, Paris
Br   Brown University Library
C/P   Counterpoint Press / Perseus Books Group
CTI   Courtauld Institute of Art
D-M   Gareth Davies-Morris, San Diego, California
FCA   Family of Christabel Aberconway
H   Hoover Institution on War, Revolution and Peace, Stanford University
HG   Hulton Getty
HJ   Hugues de Jouvenel, Paris, France
HL   House of Lords Record Office, London
IU   Indiana University Library, Lilly Library
JFK   John Fitzgerald Kennedy Library, Boston, Massachusetts
JM   Jäneda Museum, Estonia
LSE   London School of Economics
LWV   League of Women Voters, St. Louis, Missouri
MHS   Massachusetts Historical Society
PRO   Public Record Office, Kew, England
R   Russian Intelligence Service
RL   Robin Lockhart
S   Sothebys, London
SB   Santa Barbara Historical Museums
SB2   Santa Barbara (Cal.) Historical Society
SB3   Santa Barbara Public Library

SIU   Southern Illinois University Library, Morris Library
Sm   Smith College Library, Sophia Smith Collection
UI   University of Illinois Library, Rare Book and Special Collections Library
UO   University of Oregon, Special Collections and University Archives
Y   Yale University Library, Beinecke Rare Book and Manuscript Library

Archives, Collections

Archives de la Guerre, Vincennes, France, Service Historique de l'Armée de Terre (SHAT), Deuxième Bureau Documents Rapatriés, Carton 608, Dossier 3529

British Library, Additional Mss 52551–52553. Correspondence of H. G. Wells to Christabel Aberconway

Brown University Library, Harry Crosby Ms 88.3, Box 1. Correspondence of Harry Crosby, Caresse Crosby, and Constance Coolidge

Hoover Institution Archives, Sir Robert Hamilton Bruce Lockhart Collection, Box 1. Correspondence of Moura Budberg and R. H. Bruce Lockhart, Reilly File

House of Lords Record Office, Beaverbrook Papers. Diaries and papers of Sir Robert Bruce Lockhart

Indiana University, Lilly Library, the R. Lockhart MSS., Boxes 2 and 5. Correspondence of Moura Budberg and R. H. Bruce Lockhart

Jäneda Museum, Estonia. Photographs from Benckendorff family

John F. Kennedy Library, Ernest Hemingway Papers, Correspondence of Ernest Hemingway (to Martha Gellhorn); photographs of Ernest Hemingway and Martha Gellhorn

Massachusetts Historical Society, Crowninshield-Magnus Papers. Correspondence of Charles Francis Adams, Ray Atherton, Eric Brenan, Lord Brownlow, Charles Antoine Chabannes, Constance Coolidge, David Coolidge, Edward Augustus "Crownie" Crowninshield, Frank Crowninshield, Felix Doubleday, Freddie Foster, Pierre de Jumilhac, Harriet Crowninshield Coolidge Norris, Eliot Rogers. Photograph of Constance Coolidge; image of H. G. Wells picshua

Public Record Office, Great Britain. Foreign Office Correspondence with Russia, F.O. 371/3332, file 91788; 371/3330, file 84714; 371/3335, file 153174

Smith College, Sophia Smith Collection, Margaret Sanger Papers, Box 95. Correspondence of Margaret Sanger (to H. G. Wells)

Southern Illinois University, Special Collections/Morris Library, Caresse Crosby Papers, Collection 140, series 5. Correspondence of Caresse Crosby, Constance Coolidge, and André Magnus

University of Illinois, Rare Book and Special Collections Library, H. G. Wells Collection. Correspondence of Christabel Aberconway, Marie Andreeva, Moura Budberg, Constance Coolidge, Martha Gellhorn, Bertrand de Jouvenel, Maggie Keun, Odette Keun, Sinclair Lewis, Lord Northcliffe (Alfred C. W.

Harmsworth), Amber Reeves, Margaret Sanger, George P. Wells, Marjorie Wells, Anthony West, Rebecca West

University of Illinois, Rare Book and Special Collection Library, Spanish Civil War. Correspondence of Martha Gellhorn (to Edwin Rolfe and Milton Wolff)

University of Oregon, Special Collections and University Archives, Joseph Stanley Pennell Papers, Ax194. Correspondence of Martha Gellhorn

Yale University, Beinecke Library, Collection of American Literature, Sinclair Lewis Papers. Correspondence of Sinclair Lewis (to Swedish Academy); Nina Berberova Papers, Gen. Mss. 182

Interviews

Bradlee, Benjamin
Bradlee, Frederick
Braun, John
Dorman, Angela
Gellhorn, Martha
Grant, Natalie
Hardy, Sylvia
Johannes, Marc
Keun, Michael
McLaren, Anne and Christopher
Magnus, André

Matthews, Sandy
Morange, Patricia
Nelson, Cary
Orsagh, Jacqueline
Owen, Gail
Reintjes, Monique
Scherr, Barry
Smith, David
Spence, Richard
Wattenberg, Albert
Yu, George

Bibliography

Unpublished Correspondence (Major Collections)

Christabel McLaren Aberconway to H. G. Wells, UI
Charles Francis Adams to Constance Coolidge, MHS
Great Britain, Foreign Office with Russia, PRO, UI
Moura Budberg to Bruce Lockhart, H, IU
Moura Budberg to H. G. Wells, UI
Constance Coolidge to David Coolidge, MHS
Constance Coolidge to Isabella Shurtleff Coolidge (Granny), MHS
Constance Coolidge to Caresse Crosby, SIU
Constance Coolidge to Harry Crosby, Br
Constance Coolidge to Freddie Foster, MHS
Constance Coolidge to André Magnus, MHS
Constance Coolidge to H. G. Wells, UI
David Coolidge to Constance Coolidge, MHS
Caresse Crosby to Constance Coolidge, SIU
Harry Crosby to Constance Coolidge, Br
Edward ("Crownie") Crowninshield to Constance Coolidge, MHS
Felix Doubleday to Constance Coolidge, MHS
Freddie Foster to Constance Coolidge, MHS
Martha Gellhorn to Alvah Bessie, UI
Martha Gellhorn to John Braun, private collection
Martha Gellhorn to Stanley Pennell, UO
Martha Gellhorn to Edwin Rolfe, UI
Martha Gellhorn to G. P. Wells, UI
Martha Gellhorn to H. G. Wells, UI
Martha Gellhorn to Milton Wolff, UI
Ernest Hemingway to Martha Gellhorn, JFK
Bertrand de Jouvenel to H. G. Wells, UI
Pierre de Jumilhac to Constance Coolidge, MHS

Bruce Lockhart to Moura Budberg, H
Odette Keun to H. G. Wells, UI
Odette Keun to Marjorie Craig Wells, UI
André Magnus to Constance Coolidge, MHS
André Magnus to Caresse Crosby, SIU
William A. (Sandy) P. Matthews to author.
W. Somerset Maugham to Constance Coolidge, MHS
Amber Reeves to H. G. Wells, UI
Eliot Rogers to Constance Coolidge, MHS
Margaret Sanger to H. G. Wells, UI
Wallis Simpson to Constance Coolidge, MHS
G. P. Wells and Marjorie Craig Wells to Rebecca West, UI
H. G. Wells to Christabel Aberconway, BL
H. G. Wells to Moura Budberg, UI
H. G. Wells to Constance Coolidge, MHS
H. G. Wells to Bertrand de Jouvenel, UI
H. G. Wells to Odette Keun, UI
H. G. Wells to Sarah Wells, UI
Anthony West to G. P. Wells and Marjorie Craig Wells, UI
Rebecca West to G. P. Wells and Marjorie Craig Wells, UI

Unpublished Manuscripts

Braun, John. "Une Fidélité Difficile: The Early Life and Ideas of Bertrand de Jouvenel, 1903–1945." Ph.D. diss., University of Waterloo, 1985.
Coolidge, Constance. "Diaries": 1905, 1932, 1938.
Crosby, Harry. Notebooks, letters, stories, poetry. Mss. 88.3 Brown University Library.
Gellhorn, Martha. "Letter to a Dead Friend [1983?].
Orsagh, Jacqueline. "A Critical Biography of Martha Gellhorn." Ph.D. diss., Michigan State University, 1977.
Owen, Gail. "Budberg, the Soviets, and Reilly." 1988.
Powell, Emmett Dever. "A Textual and Editorial Analysis of the 'Top Copy' in the H. G. Wells Collection of the University of Illinois (Urbana) Library." Master's thesis, University of Illinois, Urbana, Ill., 1996.
Wells, H. G. "Postscript." Suppressed pages. Boxes 1–6. H. G. Wells Collection, University of Illinois Library.
————. Appendix, File K–75.

Published

Aberconway, Christabel. A Wiser Woman? A Book of Memories. London: Hutchinson & Co., 1966.

Agursky, Mikhail. Review of *H. G. Wells in Love: Postscript to an Experiment in Autobiography* and *H. G. Wells, Aspects of a Life. Slavic Review* 47, no. 2 (summer 1988): 329, 330.

Alexander, Tania. *A Little of All These: An Estonian Childhood.* London: Jonathan Cape Ltd., 1987.

Allen, Woody. *Love and Death.* Script, UI Rare Book and Special Collections Library.

Andrew, Christopher. *The Sword and the Shield: The Mitrokhin Archive and the Secret History of the KGB.* New York: Basic Books, 1999.

Baily, Adrian. "Hard Wood." *Tatler* (May, 1983): 124–125.

Baring, Maurice. *The Mainsprings of Russia.* London: Thomas Nelson and Sons, 1914.

Barratt, Andrew, and Barry P. Scherr, eds. *Maksim Gorky: Selected Letters.* Oxford: Clarendon Press, 1997.

Bauman, John F., and Coode, Thomas H. *In the Eye of the Great Depression: New Deal Reporters and the Agony of the American People.* DeKalb: Northern Illinois University Press, 1988.

Bell, Pearl K. "On the Road." *New Republic* (July 5, 1993): 36–39.

Benckendorff, Count Constantine. *Half a Life: The Reminiscences of a Russian Gentleman.* 2d. printing. London: The Richards Press, 1955.

Berberova, Nina. *The Italics Are Mine.* Authorized translation by Philippe Radley. New York: Harcourt, Brace & World, 1969.

———. *Histoire de la Baronne Boudberg.* Presses Pocket, 1991.

Blume, Mary. *Côte d'Azur: Inventing the French Riviera.* New York: Thames and Hudson Ltd., 1992.

———. *Lartigue's Riviera.* Paris: Flammarion, 1997.

Bradlee, Ben. *Ben Bradlee: A Good Life.* New York: Simon & Schuster, 1995.

Brian, Denis. *The True Gen: An Intimate Portrait of Ernest Hemingway by Those Who Knew Them.* New York, Grove Press, 1988.

British Foreign Office: General Correspondence. *Indexes to the "Green" or Secret Papers Among the General Correspondence of the Foreign Office, 1921 to 1938.* Nendeln/Liechtenstein: Kraus-Thomson, 1969.

British Foreign Office. *Russia Correspondence, 1918–1921.* Microfilm Reels, 46–50. The Scholarly Resources microfilm edition of the Public Record Office Collection. F.O. 371, Registers: F.O. 566. Scholarly Resources Inc., Wilmington, Delaware. 1982.

Brook-Shepherd, Gordon. *Iron Maze: The Western Secret Services and the Bolsheviks.* London: Macmillan, 1998.

Bryan, J. III, and Murphy, Charles J. V., *The Windsor Story.* New York: William Morrow & Co., 1979.

Buchanan, Meriel. *Ambassador's Daughter.* London: Cassell & Co. Ltd, 1958.

———. *Petrograd: The City of Trouble, 1914–1918.* London: W. Collins Sons, 1919.

Buford, Bill, Ed. "The Correspondent." *The New Yorker* (June 22–29, 1998): 96–109.

Chaplin, Charles. *My Autobiography.* New York: Simon and Schuster, 1964.

Churchill, Winston and Clementine. *Winston and Clementine: The Personal Letters of the Churchills.* Ed. Mary Soames. Boston, New York: Houghton Mifflin Co., 1998.

Cowley, Malcolm. *Exile's Return.* New York: Penguin Books, 1979.

Crosby, Caresse. *The Passionate Years.* New York: The Dial Press, 1953.

Crosby, Harry. *Shadows of the Sun: The Diaries of Harry Crosby.* Ed. Edward Germain. Santa Barbara, Ca.: Black Sparrow Press, 1977.

Davies, Philip H. J. *The British Secret Services.* Vol. 12 of International Organizations Series. New Brunswick and London: Transaction Publishers, 1996.

Deacon, Richard. *The British Connection: Russia's Manipulation of British Individuals and Institutions.* London: Hamish Hamilton, 1979.

_____. *A History of the British Secret Service.* London: Frederick Muller, 1969.

_____. *A History of the Russian Secret Service.* London: Grafton Books, 1987.

Dickson, Lovat. *H. G. Wells: His Turbulent Life and Times.* New York: Atheneum, 1969.

Documents Rapatriés, Deuxième Bureau, SHAT.

Dorril, Stephen. *MI 6: Inside the Covert World of Her Majesty's Secret Intelligence Service.* New York: The Free Press, 2000.

Dunbar, Janet. *Mrs. G. B. S.: A Portrait.* New York: Harper & Row, 1963.

Field, Frederick. *From Right to Left.* Westport, Conn.: L. Hill, 1983.

Figes, Orlando. *A People's Tragedy: A History of the Russian Revolution.* New York: Viking Penguin Books, 1997.

Flanner, Janet (Genet). *Paris Was Yesterday, 1925–1939.* San Diego: Harvest/HBJ Book, 1988.

Foot, Michael. *H. G.: The History of Mr. Wells.* Washington, D.C.: Counterpoint, 1995.

Francis, David R. *Russia from the American Embassy, April, 1916-November, 1918.* New York: Charles Scribner's Sons, 1921.

Gachet, Paul. *Van Gogh à Auvers: Histoire d'un Tableau.* Paris: Les Beaux-Arts, 1954.

Garstin, Denis. "Denis Garstin and the Russian Revolution." Preface by Sir Hugh Walpole. *Slavonic Review* 17 (1938–1939): 587–605.

Gellhorn, Martha. "The Correspondent." *The New Yorker* (June 22 & 29, 1998): 96–109.

_____. *The Face of War.* New York: Atlantic Monthly Press, 1988.

_____. "Memory." *London Review of Books* (December 12, 1996): 3.

_____. "On Apocryphism." *Paris Review* (Spring 1981): 280–306.

_____. *Point of No Return.* Lincoln: University of Nebraska, 1995.

_____. *Travels with Myself and Another.* New York, Dodd, Mead & Co., 1978.

_____. *The Trouble I've Seen.* New York: William Morrow, 1936.

_____. *View from the Ground.* New York: Atlantic Monthly Press, 1988.

Glendinning, Victoria. "The Real Thing," *Vogue* (April 1988): 359, 398.

_____. *Rebecca West: A Life.* New York: Alfred A. Knopf, 1987.

Gorki, Maxim. *Fragments from My Diary*. Trans. Moura Budberg. New York: Praeger Publishers, 1972.

Grolier, Inc., *New Grolier Multimedia Encyclopedia* (Novato, California: The Software Toolworks, Inc., 1989–1993).

Gurewitsch, A. David. *Eleanor Roosevelt: Her Day*. New York: Quadrangle/The New York Times Book Co., 1974.

Hammond, J. R. *An H. G. Wells Chronology*. New York: St. Martin's Press, 1999.

_____. *An H. G. Wells Companion*. Harper & Row Publishers, 1979.

Hard, William. *Raymond Robins' Own Story*. New York: Harper & Brothers, 1920.

Hardy, Sylvia. Introduction to *Ann Veronica*, by H. G. Wells. London, Vermont: Everyman, 1993, xxxviii.

H. G. Wells Society. *H. G. Wells: A Comprehensive Bibliography*. Edgware, England: Michael Katanka Ltd., 1966.

Hemingway, Ernest. *Across the River and Into the Trees*. New York: Scribner, 1999.

_____. *Selected Letters, 1917–1961*. Ed. Carlos Baker. New York, Charles Scribner's Sons, 1981.

_____. *Snows of Kilimanjaro and other Stories*. New York, Charles Scribner's Sons, 1999.

Hoffman, Frederick J. *The Twenties: American Writing in the Postwar Decade*. New York: The Free Press, 1962.

Hunt, Frazier. *This Bewildered World, and Its Search for a New Rhythm*. New York: Frederick A. Stokes, 1934.

Jouvenel, Bertrand de. *Itinéraire (1928–1976)*. Ed. Eric Roussel. Paris: Plon, 1993.

_____. *Un Voyageur dans le Siècle*. Paris: Editions Robert Laffont, 1979.

Kern, Stephen. *The Culture of Love: Victorians to Moderns*. Cambridge: Harvard University Press, 1994.

Kerrane, Kevin. "Martha's Quest." *Salon* (www.salonmagazine.com/media/1998/03/12medias.html), March 12, 1998.

Kert, Bernice. *The Hemingway Women*. New York: WW Norton & Co., 1983.

Keun, Odette. *I Discover the English*. London: John Lane, 1934.

_____. "H. G. Wells The Player." *Time and Tide* 15, nos. 41–43 (Oct. 13, 20 and 27, 1934): 1249–1251; 1307–1309; 1346–1348.

_____. *My Adventures in Bolshevik Russia*. New York: Dodd, Mead and Co., 1923.

Knight, Marion A., Ed. *Book Review Digest*. New York: H. G. Wilson Co., 1935, 355.

Koch, Stephen. *Double Lives: Spies and Writers in the Secret Soviet War of Ideas Against the West*. New York: The Free Press, 1994.

Kolosov, Leonid. "Moura: She Satisfied the Needs of the Secret Service and the Needs of Famous Authors." *Trud* 7 (Jan. 31 and Feb. 7, 1997): 6, 10.

Korda, Michael. *Charmed Lives: A Family Romance*. New York: Random House, 1979.

_____. *Another Life: A Memoir of Other People*. New York: Random House, 2000.

Kurth, Peter. "Letters to the Editor." *Salon* (www.salonmagazine.com/letters/1998/03/17letters.html), March 17, 1998.

Lash, Joseph P. *Love, Eleanor: Eleanor Roosevelt and Her Friends*. New York: Doubleday & Co., 1982.

Letley, Emma. *Maurice Baring: A Citizen of Europe*. London: Constable, 1991.

Lockhart, R. H. Bruce. *The Diaries of Sir Robert Bruce Lockhart*. Vol. 1. Ed. Kenneth Young. New York: St. Martin's Press, 1973.

_____. *The Diaries of Sir Robert Bruce Lockhart*. Vol. 2. Ed. Kenneth Young. London: Macmillan, 1980.

_____. *Memoirs of a British Agent*. London: Macmillan, 1985.

_____. *Retreat from Glory*. New York: G. P. Putnam's Sons, 1934.

Lockhart, Robin Bruce. *Reilly: Ace of Spies*. New York: Penguin Books, 1967.

_____. *Reilly: The First Man*. New York: Penguin Books, 1987.

Lovat, Laura. *Maurice Baring: A Postscript*. London: Hollis & Carter, 1947.

Lynn, Kenneth. *Hemingway*. New York: Fawcett Columbine, 1987.

McAlmon, Robert, and Kay Boyle. *Being Geniuses Together, 1920–1930*. London: The Hogarth Press, 1984.

MacKenzie, Norman, and Jeanne MacKenzie. *The Fabians*. New York: Simon and Schuster, 1977.

_____. *H. G. Wells: A Biography*. New York: Simon and Schuster, 1973.

_____. *The Life of H. G. Wells: The Time Traveller*. London: The Hogarth Press, 1987.

Mahoney, M. H. *Women in Espionage: A Biographical Dictionary*. Santa Barbara, Ca.: ABC-CLIO, 1993.

Marcosson, Isaac. *Adventures in Interviewing*. New York: Dodd Mead & Co., 1931.

_____. *Turbulent Years*. New York: Dodd, Mead & Co., 1938.

Martin, Ralph G. *Jennie: The Life of Lady Randolph Churchill*. New York: Signet, 1971.

Matthews, T. S. *Name and Address: An Autobiography*. New York. Simon and Schuster, 1960.

Maugham, W. Somerset. "Some Novelists I Have Known" (from *The Vagrant Mind*). In *Mr. Maugham Himself*. Garden City, N.J.: Doubleday & Co., 1954.

Meyers, Jeffrey. *Hemingway: A Biography*. New York: Harper & Row Publishers, 1985.

Morgan, Ted. *Maugham*. New York: Simon and Schuster, 1980.

Mothe, Alain. *Vincent van Gogh à Auvers-sur-Oise*. Paris: Editions du Valhermeil, 1987.

New Yorker. "The Correspondent." Ed. Bill Buford. (June 22–29, 1998): 96–109.

Paterson, John. *Edwardians: London Life and Letters, 1901–1914*. Chicago: Ivan R. Dee, 1996.

Perkin, Joan. *Victorian Women*. New York: New York University Press, 1993.

Ray, Gordon. *H. G. Wells & Rebecca West*. New Haven: Yale University Press, 1974.

Read, Anthony, and David Fisher. *Colonel Z: The Secret Life of a Master of Spies.* New York: Viking Penguin, 1985.

Reintjes, Monique. *Odette Keun.* (The Netherlands: Self-Published, 2000).

Ridge, William Pett. *I Like to Remember.* London: Hodder and Stoughton, n.d.

Rolfe, Edwin. *The Lincoln Battalion: The Story of Americans Who Fought in Spain in the International Brigades.* New York: Random House, 1939, 70, 71.

Rollyson, Carl. *Beautiful Exile: The Life of Martha Gellhorn.* London: Aurum Press, 2001.

_____. *Nothing Ever Happens to the Brave: The Story of Martha Gellhorn.* New York: St. Martin's Press, 1990

_____. *Rebecca West: A Life.* New York: Scribner, 1996.

Roosevelt, Eleanor. *Eleanor Roosevelt's My Day: Her Acclaimed Columns, 1936–1945.* Ed. Rochelle Chadakoff. New York: Pharos Books, 1989.

Russian-American Relations, March, 1917 and March, 1920, Documents and Papers. Comp. and ed. C. K. Cumming and Walter W. Pettit. Westport, Conn.: Hyperion Press, 1977.

Seth, Ronald. *Encyclopedia of Espionage.* Garden City, N.J.: Doubleday & Co., 1972.

Shukman, Harold, Ed. *The Blackwell Encyclopedia of the Russian Revolution.* Revised and updated. Oxford: Blackwell Publishers, 1994.

Sieveking, Lance. *Eye of the Beholder.* London: Hutton Press, 1957.

Skinner, Cornelia Otis, and Emily Kimbrough. *Our Hearts Were Young and Gay.* New York: Dodd, Mead & Co., 1942.

Smith, David C. *Correspondence of H. G. Wells.* London: Pickering & Chatto, 1998.

_____. *H. G. Wells: Desperately Mortal.* New Haven and London: Yale University Press, 1986.

Spence, Richard B. *Boris Savinkov: Renegade on the Left.* Boulder: East European Monographs, 1991.

_____. *Trust No One: The Secret World of Sidney Reilly* (Feral House, 2002).

Steffen-Fluhr, Nancy. "Paper Tiger: Women and H. G. Wells." *Science Fiction Studies* 12 (1985): 311–329, footnote 21.

Stubbs, Patricia, *Women and Fiction: Feminism and the Novel, 1880–1920.* New York: Harper and Row Publishers, 1979.

Symons, Julian, *Makers of the New: The Revolution in Literature, 1912–1939.* New York, Random House, 1987.

Tapert, Annette, and Diana Edkins. *The Power of Style: The Women Who Defined the Art of Living Well.* New York: Crown Publishers, 1994.

Thurman, Judith. *Secrets of the Flesh.* New York: Alfred A. Knopf, 1999.

Tynan, Kathleen. "The Astonishing History of Moura Budberg—A Flame for Famous Men." *Vogue* (October 1, 1970): 162, 208, 209–211.

Ullman, Richard H. *Anglo-Soviet Relations, 1917–1921.* Vol. 1, *Intervention and the War.* Princeton: Princeton University Press, 1961.

Ustinov, Peter. *Dear Me*. Boston: Little, Brown and Co., 1977.

Vallentin, Antonina. *H. G. Wells: Prophet of Our Day*. New York: John Day Co., 1950.

Webb, Beatrice Potter. *The Diary of Beatrice Webb*. Vol. 3. Eds. Norman and Jeanne MacKenzie. Cambridge, Mass.: Harvard University Press, 1984.

Wells, Jane (Amy Catherine). "The Beautiful House." In *The Book of Catherine Wells*. London: Chatto and Windus, 1928.

Wells, H. G. *The Anatomy of Frustration*. London: The Cresset Press, 1936.

_____. *Ann Veronica*. Ed. Sylvia Hardy. London, Vermont: Everyman, 1993.

_____. *Anticipations of the Reaction of Mechanical and Scientific Progress upon Human Life and Thought*. London: Chapman & Hall, 1902.

_____. *Apropos of Dolores*. New York: Charles Scribner's Sons, 1938.

_____. *Experiment in Autobiography: Discoveries and Conclusions of a Very Ordinary Brain (Since 1866)*. New York: Macmillan, 1934.

_____. *H. G. Wells in Love: Postscript to an Experiment in Autobiography*. Ed. G. P. Wells. Boston: Little, Brown and Co., 1984.

_____. *Modern Utopia*. London: Chapman & Hall, 1905.

_____. *The New Machiavelli*. London: John Lane, 1911.

_____. *The Outline of History: Being a Plain History of Life and Mankind*. Garden City, N.J.: Doubleday & Co., 1949.

_____. *Russia in the Shadows*. New York: George H. Doran Co., 1921.

_____. *The Science of Life*. London: Amalgamated Press, 1930.

_____. "Thomas Henry Huxley." BBC broadcast, October 4, 1935, Published in the BBC publication *The Listener* 15, no. 352 (October 9, 1935): 593–595.

_____. "The Time Machine." *H. G. Wells: Selected Short Stories*. Gt. Britain, USA: Penguin Books, 1979.

_____. *Work, Wealth and Happiness of Mankind*. Garden City, N.J.: Doubleday, Doran & Co., 1931.

_____. *World Set Free: A Story of Mankind*. New York: EP Dutton & Co., 1914.

West, Anthony. *H. G. Wells: Aspects of a Life*. New York: Random House, 1984.

_____. *Heritage*. New York: Washington Square Press, 1984.

West, Rebecca. *Selected Letters of Rebecca West*. Ed. Bonnie Kime Scott. New Haven: Yale University Press, 2000.

White, Palmer. *Elsa Schiaparelli: Empress of Paris Fashion*. London: Aurum Press, 1995.

Windsor, Duchess of. *The Heart Has Its Reasons: The Memoirs of the Duchess of Windsor*. New York: David McKay Co., 1956.

Wolff, Geoffrey. *Black Sun: The Brief Transit and Violent Eclipse of Harry Crosby*. New York: Random House, 1976.

Womack, Helen, ed. *Undercover Lies: Soviet Spies in the Cities of the World*. London: Weidenfield & Nicolson, 1998.

Worden, Helen. "Will Mrs. Simpson Go Through with the Marriage?" *Liberty Magazine* (April 10, 1937): 16–17.

Permissions

The author and publishers gratefully acknowledge literary permission from the following:

Tania Alexander, the Associated Press, John Braun, Brown University Library, Counterpoint Press/Perseus Books Group, Dusa McDuff, Literary Executor for Martha Gellhorn, Ernest Hemingway Foreign Rights Trust, Ernest Hemingway Foundation, David Higham Associates, Hoover Institution on War, Revolution and Peace, Indiana University Library (Lilly Library), Hugues de Jouvenel, Annajane Kennard, Literary Executors for Sinclair Lewis, Robin Bruce Lockhart, London School of Economics, McLaren Family, André Magnus, Massachusetts Historical Society, *New York Times*, Richard Ormond, Jacqueline Orsagh, Gail Owen, Alex Sanger, Barry Scherr, Southern Illinois University, Richard Spence, the *Times* (London), University of Illinois Library, University of Oregon Library, the Estate of H. G. Wells, Estate of Anthony West, Estate of Rebecca West.

Picture acknowledgements: Tania Alexander/Jäneda Museum, Brown University Library, Bernard Croza, Gareth Davies-Morris, Literary Executor for Martha Gellhorn, Hoover Institution on War, Revolution and Peace, Hulton Getty Photo Archive, JFK Library, Hugues de Jouvenel, League of Women Voters-St. Louis, Mo., Robin Bruce Lockhart, London School of Economics, McLaren Family, André Magnus, Massachusetts Historical Society, Smith College Library, Sothebys London, Southern Illinois University Library, University of Illinois Library, Yale University Library, the Estate of H. G. Wells, Sharron White.

The author has made every effort to locate the owners of copyrighted materials. If a reader determines that other copyrights are in place, the publisher and the author will undertake to provide acknowledgement in later editions.

Index